AWS for Solutions Architects

Second Edition

The definitive guide to AWS Solutions Architecture for migrating to, building, scaling, and succeeding in the cloud

Saurabh Shrivastava

Neelanjali Srivastav

Alberto Artasanchez

Imtiaz Sayed

BIRMINGHAM—MUMBAI

AWS for Solutions Architects

Second Edition

Senior Publishing Product Manager: Rahul Nair
Acquisition Editor – Peer Reviews: Saby Dsilva
Project Editor: Meenakshi Vijay
Content Development Editor: Georgia Daisy van der Post
Copy Editor: Safis Editing
Technical Editor: Aniket Shetty
Proofreader: Safis Editing
Indexer: Rekha Nair
Presentation Designer: Rajesh Shirsath
Developer Relations Marketing Executive: Priyadarshini Sharma

First published: January 2021
Second edition: April 2023

Production reference: 1210423

Published by Packt Publishing Ltd.
Livery Place
35 Livery Street
Birmingham
B3 2PB, UK.

ISBN 978-1-80323-895-1

`www.packt.com`

To our dear daughter Sanvi, who brings immeasurable happiness and joy to our lives.

– Saurabh and Neelanjali

Foreword

As technology continues to advance at an unprecedented pace, businesses across the globe are constantly seeking new ways to leverage the latest tools and infrastructure to improve their operations. AWS has empowered organizations to achieve more agility, scalability, and cost-efficiency, enabling them to focus on their core business rather than managing infrastructure. The role of a solutions architect requires a special skill set that encompasses a breadth and depth of technological know-how, as well as the potential to link those skills back to business acumen and provide a return on investment. As AWS adoption increases, there is a growing need for professionals who can design and implement solutions on the AWS platform. Based on my 20+ years of teaching experience, "*AWS for Solutions Architects*" is a comprehensive guide to becoming an AWS solutions architect. This book is intended to provide a complete overview of AWS services and their applications.

Cloud computing has grown to be an essential part of contemporary company operations as the globe continues to move toward digital transformation. This book will aid readers in navigating the AWS platform's intricacies and in discovering the platform's enormous potential for development and innovation. The AWS infrastructure, security, storage, computation, networking, databases, and application services are just a few of the many areas it covers. This book has done a commendable job of addressing these topics in sixteen chapters, which offer instructions on how to create and deploy apps using AWS as well as how to enhance the efficiency and performance of AWS infrastructure.

My appreciation extends to the addition of new architectural chapters on the most recent technological environments, such as AWS IoT, ML, blockchain, and big data. The book discusses the DevOps engineer career path so concisely and in such sufficient depth that I use the content of this book in my classroom instruction, followed by exhaustive resources on examination preparation. The book is filled with real-world examples and best practices, such as cloud migration patterns (**The 7 Rs**), which will assist readers in becoming AWS experts.

Recent reunions with a number of my former students have made me aware of their transformation into solutions architects. Whether you are a novice or a seasoned professional, this book will provide you with valuable information about AWS and its services. Having witnessed Saurabh's evolution from a student into the author of this book, I am confident that it will serve as a valuable resource for IT professionals, developers, and business leaders seeking to harness the power of cloud computing with AWS. I strongly recommend this book to anyone interested in learning about AWS and its services, as well as those preparing for the AWS Solutions Architect certification exam. Congratulations to the author for providing the AWS community with such a valuable resource!

Dr. Siddhartha Choubey, Ph.D.

Head of Department, Computer Science & Engineering, SSTC-SSGI Bhilai

Contributors

About the authors

Saurabh Shrivastava is an accomplished technology leader and author with more than two decades of experience in the IT industry. He is currently a Global Solutions Architect Leader at AWS, where he helps enterprise customers and consulting partners on their cloud journeys. Saurabh has also led the global technical partnerships team at AWS and played a key role in launching several strategic initiatives.

In addition to his work at AWS, Saurabh is the co-author of Packt's best-selling book *Solutions Architect's Handbook*, and has authored several blogs and white papers on various topics, such as big data, IoT, machine learning, and cloud computing. He is passionate about the latest innovations and how they can impact our daily lives. Saurabh holds a patent in cloud platform automation and has worked as an enterprise solutions architect, software architect, and software engineering manager in Fortune 50 enterprises, start-ups, and global product and consulting organizations. With his vast experience and expertise, Saurabh is a valuable resource for anyone looking to learn about cloud computing and its various applications.

Neelanjali Srivastav's extensive experience in the software industry as a technology leader, product manager, and agile coach brings a wealth of knowledge to the field. Her passion for helping customers on their data journeys to the cloud is evident in her role as a Senior Product Manager at AWS, where she evangelizes and guides AWS customers and partners in AWS database, analytics, and machine learning services.

Neelanjali is also the co-author of Packt's best-selling book *Solutions Architect's Handbook*, which is a valuable resource for those looking to kick-start their careers as solutions architects. With her experience leading teams of software engineers, solutions architects, and systems analysts to modernize IT systems and develop innovative software solutions for large enterprises, Neelanjali is well equipped to provide insights into the challenges and opportunities in the field.

Neelanjali's expertise in enterprise application management, agile coaching, cloud service management, and orchestration makes her a sought-after speaker and thought leader in the industry. She is dedicated to helping others learn and grow in their careers, and her contributions to the field are sure to make a lasting impact.

Alberto Artasanchez is a solutions architect with expertise in the cloud, data solutions, and machine learning. His career spans over 30 years in various industries. He is an AWS Ambassador and frequently publishes in various cloud and data science publications. Alberto is often tapped as a speaker on topics such as data science, big data, and analytics. He has a strong and extensive track record of designing and building end-to-end machine learning platforms at scale. He also has a long track record of leading data engineering teams. He has a great understanding of how technology drives business value and has a passion for creating elegant solutions to complicated problems.

Imtiaz (Taz) Sayed is a highly experienced technologist with a wealth of expertise in distributed architectures, data analytics, service mesh, databases, and DevOps. As a Principal Specialist Solutions Architect with AWS and the Tech Leader for the Worldwide Data Analytics Solutions Architecture community at AWS, Taz is skilled in developing effective strategies for data architecture, management, and analytics that enable organizations to extract value from their data.

Taz is a passionate advocate for cloud-based architectures and is committed to helping organizations harness modern technologies to achieve their business objectives. He is a well-respected figure in the technology community, having authored blogs, white papers, technical guides, and frequently speaking at industry conferences and events. Taz is known for his ability to translate complex technical concepts into easily understood language that can be comprehended by a wider audience.

About the reviewers

Guillaume Marchand has been a Principal Solutions Architect at AWS France for over 6 years, working in media and entertainment. He holds all of the associate and professional AWS certifications, and the Kubernetes Administrator certification. He is often a speaker for cloud events like AWS Summits and AWS re:Invent. He has nearly 20 years of experience in enterprise IT; he started his career as developer and project manager for several system integrators, especially working on digital projects, before working for a TV broadcaster as a lead architect for their streaming platform.

Trevor Spires is a Solutions Architecture leader with over 10 years of experience in the cloud, data centers, networking and security, and community-building spaces. He is currently the Head of Solutions Architecture at Common Room. Trevor has a passion for building online communities and mentoring people through their tech careers, which is why he contributed to this book. He has an active LinkedIn and YouTube following, and he encourages readers to follow him online to stay connected with his work.

I would like to thank my partner, Marita, for her endless love and support. A special thanks to my parents, Ann and Lee, for teaching me the principles of integrity, hard work, and a positive attitude. Finally, I'd like to thank my sister Jill and best friend Nate for helping me through some of life's most challenging decisions. I would not be the man I am today without the love of my family, my friends, and my partner.

Werner Dijkerman is a freelance cloud, Kubernetes (certified), and DevOps engineer. He's currently focused on, and working with, cloud-native solutions and tools including AWS, Ansible, Kubernetes, and Terraform. He is also focused on Infrastructure as Code and monitoring the correct "thing" with tools such as Zabbix, Prometheus, and the ELK Stack, with a passion for automating everything and avoiding doing anything that resembles manual work.

Big thanks, hugs, and shoutout to everyone at Packt! You have helped me to grow as a person and I also enjoyed working with you very much!

Table of Contents

Chapter 6: Harnessing the Power of Cloud Computing 179

Chapter 7: Selecting the Right Database Service 221

Chapter 11: Data Warehouses, Data Queries, and Visualization in AWS 393

Chapter 12: Machine Learning, IoT, and Blockchain in AWS 427

Chapter 13: Containers in AWS 463

Chapter 14: Microservice Architectures in AWS 505

Preface

The adoption rate of cloud technologies keeps accelerating, and the question is no longer if cloud computing will be the dominant paradigm, but how fast companies of all sizes will adopt it.

Amazon Web Services (AWS) is one of the leading cloud computing providers that offers a wide range of services to build, deploy, and manage scalable, cost-effective, and reliable cloud applications. AWS is used by millions of customers worldwide, ranging from startups to enterprises. It continues to innovate and expand its offerings to meet the growing demand for cloud-based solutions.

This book is designed to help AWS Solutions Architects understand and leverage the full range of AWS services to build effective cloud solutions that meet the needs of their organizations. It covers a comprehensive set of AWS services, including core services, data services, analytics, security, compute, networking, storage, machine learning, and the Well-Architected Framework.

Each chapter provides a detailed explanation of AWS services and features, along with use cases and examples to demonstrate how these services can be used to solve real-world business problems. The book also includes best practices and recommendations for designing, deploying, and managing AWS solutions.

In this book, readers will learn about the core AWS services, such as **Amazon Elastic Compute Cloud (EC2)**, **Amazon Simple Storage Service (S3)**, and **Amazon Relational Database Service (RDS)**, and how to use them to build and deploy scalable and secure applications. They will also explore AWS data services, including Amazon DynamoDB, Amazon Redshift, and **Amazon Elastic MapReduce (EMR)**, and how they can be used to manage and analyze large amounts of data.

Additionally, the book covers AWS security services, such as **Amazon Identity and Access Management (IAM)**, Amazon CloudTrail, and Amazon GuardDuty, and how they can enhance the security and compliance of AWS environments.

Readers will also learn about AWS networking services, including **Amazon Virtual Private Cloud (VPC)** and Amazon Route 53, and how they can be used to build and manage network infrastructure in the cloud.

Moreover, the book discusses AWS compute services, including AWS Lambda, **Amazon Elastic Container Service** (**ECS**), and **Amazon Elastic Kubernetes Service** (**EKS**), and how they can be used to run and manage applications in the cloud. It also covers AWS storage services, including **Amazon Elastic Block Store** (**EBS**), **Amazon Elastic File System** (**EFS**), and **Amazon Simple Storage Service** (**S3**), and how they can be used to store and manage data in the cloud.

Furthermore, the book explores AWS machine learning services, including Amazon SageMaker, Amazon Rekognition, and Amazon Comprehend, and how they can be used to build intelligent and predictive applications in the cloud. It discusses the AWS Well-Architected Framework and its five pillars: operational excellence, security, reliability, performance efficiency, and cost optimization, and how to use it to design and build well-architected solutions on AWS.

This book is a valuable resource for AWS Solutions Architects who want to learn about the full range of AWS services and how to use them to build effective cloud solutions. It is also suitable for IT professionals and developers who want to expand their knowledge of AWS and build scalable, reliable, and cost-effective cloud applications.

Who is this book for

This book is intended for a wide range of readers, including:

Solutions Architects: This book is ideal for AWS Solutions Architects who want to deepen their knowledge of AWS services and best practices. It covers all the essential AWS services and the Well-Architected Framework, making it a valuable resource for Solutions Architects preparing for the AWS Solutions Architect certification exam.

IT Professionals and Developers: This book is also suitable for IT professionals and developers who want to learn how to build, deploy, and manage scalable, cost-effective, and reliable cloud solutions on AWS. It covers a comprehensive set of AWS services, including data services, analytics, security, compute, networking, storage, machine learning, and the Well-Architected Framework, making it a valuable resource for professionals who want to expand their knowledge of AWS.

Business Executives and Managers: This book is also relevant for business executives and managers who want to understand the benefits and potential of cloud computing and AWS. It covers a range of AWS services and use cases, making it a valuable resource for executives who want to make informed decisions about cloud adoption strategies.

Overall, this book is suitable for anyone who wants to learn how to leverage AWS services to build scalable, cost-effective, and reliable cloud solutions, regardless of their level of experience with AWS or cloud computing.

What this book covers

Chapter 1, Understanding AWS Principles and Key Characteristics, describes the ubiquity of cloud computing, AWS' market share, its revenue, and its adoption across industries. In this chapter, we provide an overview of cloud computing and AWS, including the key principles and characteristics of the AWS cloud. We will discuss the benefits of cloud computing and how AWS provides scalable, flexible, and cost-effective cloud solutions to meet the needs of businesses and organizations of all sizes.

Chapter 2, Understanding the AWS Well-Architected Framework and Getting Certified, we will dive into the AWS Well-Architected Framework, which provides a set of best practices for designing and operating reliable, secure, efficient, and cost-effective systems on AWS. We will explore the six pillars of the Well-Architected Framework: operational excellence, security, reliability, performance efficiency, cost optimization, and sustainability. Additionally, we will discuss the AWS Certification program, which includes the AWS Certified Solutions Architect certification. We will provide guidance and tips for preparing for the AWS Certified Solutions Architect exam, including recommended resources, study materials, and practice exams.

Chapter 3, Leveraging the Cloud for Digital Transformation, begins to describe the AWS infrastructure and its services and how it can be used to achieve digital transformation across your enterprise. This chapter discusses how organizations can leverage the cloud to drive digital transformation initiatives and explores the benefits of cloud-based digital transformation, including increased agility, innovation, and cost savings. We will also discuss the challenges and considerations that organizations must address when embarking on a digital transformation journey.

Chapter 4, Networking in AWS, dives into the networking and content delivery services offered by AWS. We will explore how AWS provides a highly available and scalable network infrastructure that can support a wide range of workloads and applications. This chapter provides a solid understanding of the networking and content delivery services offered by AWS and how to configure and use these services to support various workloads and applications.

Chapter 5, Storage in AWS – Choosing the Right Tool for the Job, explores the various storage options available in AWS and how to choose the right tools for different scenarios. We will discuss the importance of data storage and management in modern applications, as well as the benefits and trade-offs of various storage options in AWS.

Chapter 6, *Harnessing the Power of Cloud Computing*, looks at the various compute services offered by AWS and how to leverage them to harness the power of cloud computing. We will discuss the benefits of cloud computing, including scalability, cost-effectiveness, and flexibility, as well as the trade-offs and considerations for various compute options in AWS.

Chapter 7, *Selecting the Right Database Service*, goes through the various database services offered by AWS and how to choose the right service for your application needs. We will discuss the importance of database selection in modern applications and the benefits and trade-offs of various database options in AWS.

Chapter 8, *Best Practices for Application Security, Identity, and Compliance*, discusses best practices for ensuring application security and compliance in AWS. We will explore the various security services and features provided by AWS and look at how to design and implement a security strategy that meets industry standards and regulations.

Chapter 9, *Driving Efficiency with CloudOps*, explores how to optimize efficiency in AWS through cloud operation automation. We will discuss the benefits of automation and DevOps and the trade-offs and considerations for implementing these practices in AWS.

Chapter 10, *Big Data and Streaming Data Processing in AWS*, looks at how AWS supports big data and streaming data processing. We will start by discussing the core concepts of big data and streaming data and how they differ from traditional data processing approaches. We will also discuss the challenges of processing big data and streaming data at scale and how AWS provides solutions to these challenges.

Chapter 11, *Data Warehouses, Data Queries, and Visualization in AWS*, delves into how AWS supports data warehousing, data querying, and data visualization. We will start by discussing the core concepts of data warehousing, including data modeling, data integration, and data storage. We will also discuss the challenges of implementing a data warehouse and how AWS provides solutions to these challenges.

Chapter 12, *Machine Learning, IoT, and Blockchain in AWS*, examines how AWS supports machine learning, IoT, and blockchain. We will start by discussing the core concepts of these technologies, including their applications and benefits. We will also discuss the challenges of implementing these technologies and how AWS provides solutions to these challenges.

Chapter 13, Containers in AWS, discusses how AWS supports containerization, container orchestration, and container management. We will start by discussing the core concepts of containers, including their benefits and limitations. We will also discuss the challenges of implementing containers and how AWS provides solutions.

Chapter 14, Microservice Architectures in AWS, looks into how AWS supports microservice architectures. We will start by discussing the core concepts of microservices, event-driven architectures, and domain-driven designs, including their benefits and limitations. We will also discuss the challenges of implementing these architectures and how AWS provides solutions.

Chapter 15, Data Lake Patterns – Integrating Your Data across the Enterprise, explores how AWS supports data lake patterns for integrating data across the enterprise. We will start by discussing the core concepts of data lakes, including their benefits and limitations. We will also discuss the challenges of implementing data lakes and how AWS provides solutions to these challenges.

Chapter 16, Hands-On Guide to Building an App in AWS, provides a hands-on guide to building an application in AWS. We will start by discussing the key considerations for designing an application in the cloud, including scalability, availability, security, and cost optimization. We will provide a solid understanding of how to design, build, and deploy applications in AWS and how to optimize their use of AWS services for application development. This knowledge will be essential for developing scalable and reliable applications in the cloud.

If you enjoyed this book, you may also enjoy *Solutions Architect's Handbook: Kick-start your career as a solutions architect by learning architecture design principles and strategies, 2nd Edition, also from Packt.* You can find this book on Amazon at `https://www.amazon.com/Solutions-Architects-Handbook-Kick-start-architecture/dp/1801816611`. This book provides a comprehensive guide to the role of a solutions architect, covering everything from design principles and strategies to best practices for implementing and maintaining architectures in the cloud. With practical examples and real-world scenarios, this book is a valuable resource for anyone interested in becoming a solutions architect or improving their skills in this field.

To get the most out of this book

To get the most out of this book, readers should have a basic understanding of cloud computing. A general grasp of IT terminology would also be helpful. Readers are encouraged to have an AWS account and access to the AWS Management Console, as this will allow them to follow along with the examples and exercises in the book.

It is recommended that readers go through the book sequentially and dive deep into the examples provided. This will ensure a comprehensive understanding of the material and help readers to apply the concepts to real-world scenarios.

In addition, readers should take advantage of the many resources available from AWS, including documentation, whitepapers, and online training courses. These resources can provide additional context and depth to the topics covered in the book.

Finally, readers are encouraged to engage with the AWS community, including online forums, user groups, and social media channels. This will provide opportunities to network with other AWS professionals, share knowledge and best practices, and stay updated with the latest AWS developments.

Download the color images

We also provide a PDF file that has color images of the screenshots/diagrams used in this book. You can download it here: `https://packt.link/VWYwG`.

Conventions used

There are a number of text conventions used throughout this book.

`CodeInText`: Indicates code words in text, database table names, folder names, filenames, file extensions, pathnames, dummy URLs, user input, and Twitter handles. For example: "The `groupFiles` and `groupSize` parameters need to be configured to enable file grouping."

A block of code is set as follows:

```
dyf = glueContext.create_dynamic_frame_from_options("s3",
    {'paths': ["s3://path-to-files/"],
    'recurse':True,
    'groupFiles': 'inPartition',
    'groupSize': '2084236'},
    format="json")
```

Any command-line input or output is written as follows:

```
aws emr add-steps --cluster-id j-123456789EXAMPLE --steps Type=CUSTOM_
JAR,Name=SABookCustomJar,ActionOnFailure=CONTINUE,Jar=s3://sa-book-bucket/
book-jar.jar,Args=["s3://sa-book-bucket/input-data","s3://sa-book-bucket/
output-data"]
```

Bold: Indicates a new term, an important word, or words that you see on the screen. For instance, words in menus or dialog boxes appear in the text like this. For example: "AWS allows you to quickly provision hardware through the AWS console using the **Command-Line Interface** (**CLI**) or an API, among other methods."

Warnings or important notes appear like this.

Tips and tricks appear like this.

Get in touch

Feedback from our readers is always welcome.

General feedback: Email `feedback@packtpub.com` and mention the book's title in the subject of your message. If you have questions about any aspect of this book, please email us at `questions@packtpub.com`.

Errata: Although we have taken every care to ensure the accuracy of our content, mistakes do happen. If you have found a mistake in this book, we would be grateful if you reported this to us. Please visit `http://www.packtpub.com/submit-errata`, click **Submit Errata**, and fill in the form.

Piracy: If you come across any illegal copies of our works in any form on the internet, we would be grateful if you would provide us with the location address or website name. Please contact us at `copyright@packtpub.com` with a link to the material.

If you are interested in becoming an author: If there is a topic that you have expertise in and you are interested in either writing or contributing to a book, please visit `http://authors.packtpub.com`.

Share your thoughts

Once you've read *AWS for Solutions Architects, Second Edition*, we'd love to hear your thoughts! Scan the QR code below to go straight to the Amazon review page for this book and share your feedback.

`https://packt.link/r/180323895X`

Your review is important to us and the tech community and will help us make sure we're delivering excellent quality content.

Join us on Discord!

Read this book alongside other users, cloud experts, authors, and like-minded professionals.

Ask questions, provide solutions to other readers, chat with the authors via. Ask Me Anything sessions and much more.

Scan the QR code or visit the link to join the community now.

`https://packt.link/cloudanddevops`

Download a free PDF copy of this book

Thanks for purchasing this book!

Do you like to read on the go but are unable to carry your print books everywhere? Is your eBook purchase not compatible with the device of your choice?

Don't worry, now with every Packt book you get a DRM-free PDF version of that book at no cost.

Read anywhere, any place, on any device. Search, copy, and paste code from your favorite technical books directly into your application.

The perks don't stop there, you can get exclusive access to discounts, newsletters, and great free content in your inbox daily

Follow these simple steps to get the benefits:

1. Scan the QR code or visit the link below

https://packt.link/free-ebook/9781803238951

2. Submit your proof of purchase
3. That's it! We'll send your free PDF and other benefits to your email directly

1

Understanding AWS Principles and Key Characteristics

The last decade has revolutionized the IT infrastructure industry; cloud computing was introduced and now it is everywhere, from small start-ups to large enterprises. Nowadays, the cloud is the new normal. It all started with Amazon launching a cloud service called **Amazon Web Services** (**AWS**) in 2006 with a couple of services.

Netflix migrated to AWS in 2008 and became a market disrupter. After that, there was no looking back and there were many industry revolutions led by cloud-born start-ups like Airbnb in hospitality, Robinhood in finance, Lyft in transportation, and many more. The cloud rapidly gained the market share, and now big names like Capital One, JP Morgan Chase, Nasdaq, the NFL, and General Electric are all accelerating their digital journey with cloud adoption.

Even though the term 'cloud' is pervasive today, not everyone understands what the cloud is as it can be different things for different people, and it is continuously evolving. In this chapter, you will learn what the cloud is, and then what AWS is more specifically. You will learn about the vast and ever-growing influence and adoption of the cloud in general and of AWS in particular. After that, you will start getting introduced to some elementary cloud and AWS terms to get your feet wet with the lingo while gaining an understanding of why cloud computing is so popular. In this chapter, we will cover the following topics:

- What is cloud computing?
- What is **Amazon Web Services** (**AWS**)?
- The market share, influence, and adoption of AWS

- Basic cloud and AWS terminology
- Why is AWS so popular?

Let's get started, shall we?

What is cloud computing?

What exactly is cloud computing? It is a term often thrown around by many people who don't understand it and wonder what it means. Having your infrastructure in the cloud does not mean you have your servers up in the sky. Let's try to define it plainly.

Essentially, **cloud computing** is outsourcing a company's hardware and software infrastructure to a third party. At a high level, it is the on-demand availability of IT resources such as servers, storage, databases, and so on over the web, without the hassle of managing physical infrastructure. Instead of having their own data center, enterprises borrow someone else's data center. Cloud computing has many advantages:

- Economies of scale are associated with buying in bulk.
- You only pay for the time you use the equipment in increments of minutes or seconds.
- Arguably one of the most important benefits is the ability to scale up, out, down, and in.

When using cloud computing, you are not buying the equipment; you are leasing it. Equipment leasing has been around for a long time, but not at the speeds that cloud computing provides. Cloud computing makes it possible to start a resource within minutes, use it for a few hours, minutes, or even seconds, and then shut it down. You will only pay for the time you use it. Furthermore, with the advent of *serverless* computing, such as AWS Lambda services, we don't even need to provision servers, and we can call a Lambda function and pay by the function call. The idea of being able to *scale out* and *scale in* is often referred to as **elasticity** or **elastic computing**. This concept allows companies to treat their computing resources as just another utility bill and only pay for what they need at any given moment in time.

The best way to understand the cloud is to take the electricity supply analogy. To get light in your house, you just flip a switch on, and electric bulbs light up your home. In this case, you only pay for your electricity use when you need it; when you switch off electric appliances, you do not pay anything. Now, imagine if you needed to power a couple of appliances, and for that, you had to set up an entire powerhouse. It would be costly, right? It would involve the costs of maintaining the turbine and generator and building the whole infrastructure. Utility companies make your job easier by supplying electricity in the quantity you need.

They maintain the entire infrastructure to generate electricity and they can keep costs down by distributing electricity to millions of houses, which helps them benefit from mass utilization. Here, the utility companies represent cloud providers such as AWS, and the electricity represents the IT infrastructure available in the cloud.

While consuming cloud resources, you pay for IT infrastructure such as computing, storage, databases, networking, software, machine learning, and analytics in a pay-as-you-go model. Here, public clouds like AWS do the heavy lifting to maintain IT infrastructure and provide you with on-demand access over the internet. As you generally only pay for the time and services you use, most cloud providers can provide massive scalability, making it easy to scale services up and down. Where, traditionally, you would have to maintain your servers all by yourself on-premise to run your organization, now you can offload that to the public cloud and focus on your core business. For example, Capital One's core business is banking and it does not run a large data center.

As much as we tried to nail it down, this is still a pretty broad definition. For example, we specified that the cloud can offer software, that's a pretty general term. Does the term software in our definition include the following?

- Video conferencing
- Virtual desktops
- Email services
- Contact center
- Document management

These are just a few examples of what may or may not be included as available services in a cloud environment. When AWS started, it only offered a few core services, such as compute (Amazon EC2) and basic storage (Amazon S3). AWS has continually expanded its services to support virtually any cloud workload. As of 2022, it has more than 200 fully featured services for computing, storage, databases, networking, analytics, machine learning, artificial intelligence, Internet of Things, mobile, security, hybrid, virtual and augmented reality, media, application development, and deployment. As a fun fact, as of 2023, Amazon **Elastic Compute Cloud (EC2)** alone offers over 500 types of compute instances.

For the individual examples given here, AWS offers the following:

- Video conferencing – Amazon Chime
- Virtual desktops – AWS WorkSpaces

- Email services – Amazon WorkMail
- Contact Center – Amazon Connect
- Document Management – Amazon WorkDocs

Not all cloud services are highly intertwined with their cloud ecosystems. Take these scenarios, for example:

- Your firm may be using AWS services for many purposes, but they may be using WebEx, Microsoft Teams, Zoom, or Slack for their video conference needs instead of Amazon Chime. These services have little dependency on other underlying core infrastructure cloud services.
- You may be using Amazon SageMaker for artificial intelligence and machine learning projects, but you may be using the TensorFlow package in SageMaker as your development kernel, even though Google maintains TensorFlow.

If you are using Amazon RDS and choose MySQL as your database engine, you should not have too much trouble porting your data and schemas over to another cloud provider that supports MySQL if you decide to switch over. However, it will be a lot more difficult to switch to some other services. Here are some examples:

- Amazon DynamoDB is a NoSQL proprietary database only offered by AWS. If you want to switch to another NoSQL database, porting it may not be a simple exercise.
- Suppose you are using CloudFormation to define and create your infrastructure. In that case, it will be difficult, if not impossible, to use your CloudFormation templates to create infrastructure in other cloud provider environments. Suppose the portability of your infrastructure scripts is important to you, and you are planning on switching cloud providers. In that case, using Ansible, Chef, or Puppet may be a better alternative.
- Suppose you have a streaming data requirement and use Amazon Kinesis Data Streams. You may have difficulty porting out of Amazon Kinesis since the configuration and storing mechanism are quite dissimilar if you decide to use another streaming data service like Kafka.

As far as we have come in the last 15 years with cloud technologies, I think vendors realize that these are the beginning innings, and locking customers in right now while they are still deciding who their vendor should be will be a lot easier than trying to do so after they pick a competitor.

However, looking at a cloud-agnostic strategy has its pros and cons. You want to distribute your workload between cloud providers to have competitive pricing and keep your options open like in the old days. But each cloud has different networking needs, and connecting distributed workloads between clouds to communicate with each other is a complex task. Also, each major cloud provider, like AWS, Azure, and GCP, has a breadth of services, and building a workforce with all three skill sets is another challenge.

Finally, clouds like AWS provide economy of scale, which means the more you use, the more the price goes down, which may not benefit you if you choose multi-cloud. Again, it doesn't mean you cannot choose a multi-cloud strategy, but you have to think about logical workload isolation. It would not be wise to run the application layer in one cloud and the database layer in other, but you can think about logical isolation like running the analytics workload and application workload in a separate cloud.

In this section, you learned about cloud computing at a very high level. Let's learn about the difference between the public and private clouds.

Private versus public clouds

A private cloud is a service dedicated to a single customer—it is like your on-premise data center, which is accessible to one large enterprise. A private cloud is a fancy name for a data center managed by a trusted third party. This concept gained momentum to ensure security as, initially, enterprises were skeptical about public cloud security, which is multi-tenant. However, having your own infrastructure in this manner diminishes the value of the cloud as you have to pay for resources even if you are not running them.

Let's use an analogy to understand the difference between private and public clouds further. The gig economy has great momentum. Everywhere you look, people are finding employment as contract workers. One of the reasons contract work is getting more popular is because it enables consumers to contract services that they may otherwise not be able to afford. Could you imagine how expensive it would be to have a private chauffeur? But with Uber or Lyft, you almost have a private chauffeur who can be at your beck and call within a few minutes of you summoning them.

A similar economy of scale happens with a public cloud. You can have access to infrastructure and services that would cost millions of dollars if you bought them on your own. Instead, you can access the same resources for a small fraction of the cost.

In general, private clouds are expensive to run and maintain in comparison to public clouds. For that reason, many of the resources and services offered by the major cloud providers are hosted in a shared tenancy model. In addition to that, you can run your workloads and applications on a public cloud securely: you can use security best practices and sleep well at night knowing that you use AWS's state-of-the-art technologies to secure your sensitive data.

Additionally, most major cloud providers' clients use public cloud configurations. That said, there are a few exceptions even in this case. For example, the United States government intelligence agencies are a big AWS customer. As you can imagine, they have deep pockets and are not afraid to spend. In many cases with these government agencies, AWS will set up the AWS infrastructure and dedicate it to the government workload. For example, AWS launched a Top Secret Region–AWS Top Secret-West–which is accredited to operate workloads at the Top-Secret U.S. security classification level. The other AWS GovCloud regions are:

- GovCloud (US-West) Region - Launched in 2011

  Availability Zones: 3
- GovCloud (US-East) Region - Launched in 2018

  Availability Zones: 3

AWS GovCloud (US) is a set of AWS Regions that have been purposely isolated to enable U.S. government entities and clients to transfer sensitive workloads to AWS. This platform caters to particular regulatory and compliance standards such as Department of Defense Security Requirements Guide (DoD SRG) Impact Levels 4 and 5, Federal Risk and Authorization Management Program (FedRAMP) High, and Criminal Justice Information Services (CJIS), among others.

Public cloud providers such as AWS provide you choices to adhere to compliance needs as required by government or industry regulations. For example, AWS offers Amazon EC2 dedicated instances, which are EC2 instances that ensure that you will be the only user for a given physical server. Further, AWS offers AWS Outpost, where you can order server racks and host workloads on-premise using the AWS control plane.

Dedicated instance and outpost costs are significantly higher than on-demand EC2 instances. On-demand instances are multi-tenant, which means the physical server is not dedicated to you and may be shared with other AWS users. However, just because the physical servers are multi-tenant doesn't mean that anyone else can access your server as those will be dedicated virtual EC2 instances accessible to you only.

As we will discuss later in this chapter, you will never know the difference when using EC2 instances if they are hosted on a dedicated physical server compared to a multi-tenant server because of virtualization and hypervisor technology. One common use case for choosing dedicated instances is government regulations and compliance policies that require certain sensitive data to not be in the same physical server with other cloud users.

Now that we have gained a better understanding of cloud computing in general, let's get more granular and learn about how AWS does cloud computing.

What is AWS (Amazon Web Services)?

With over 200 fully-featured services available across the world, **Amazon Web Services** (**AWS**) is the most widely used cloud platform globally. Even though there are a few worthy competitors, it doesn't seem like anyone will push them off the podium for a while.

For example, keeping up with AWS' pace of innovation can be challenging. The growth of AWS services and features has been tremendous each year, as demonstrated in the graph below. In 2011, AWS introduced over 80 significant services and features, followed by nearly 160 in 2012, 280 in 2013, 516 in 2014, 722 in 2015, 1,017 in 2016, 1,430 in 2017, 1,957 in 2018, 2,345 in 2019, 2,757 in 2020, and 3,084 in 2021.

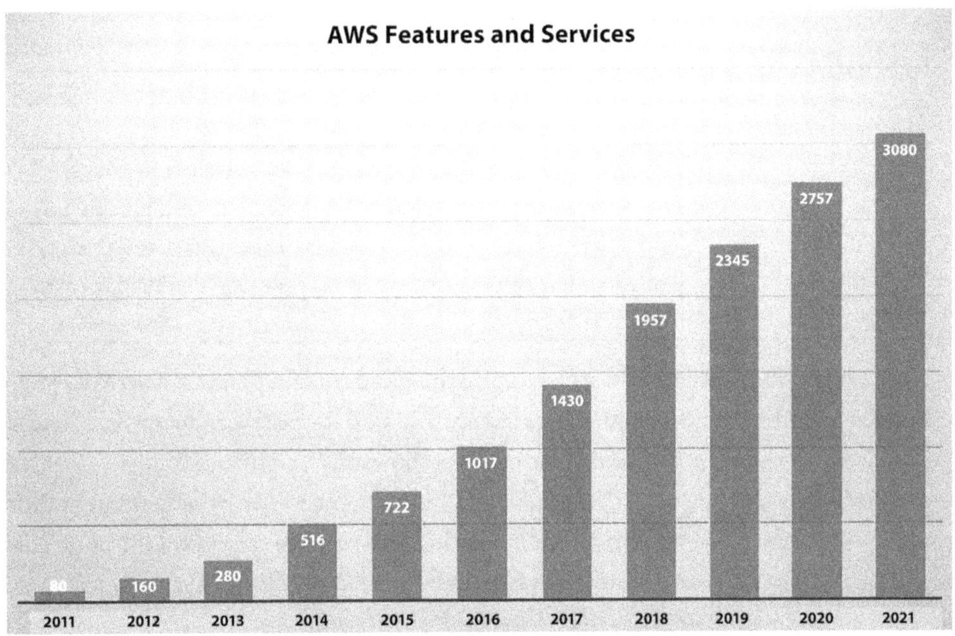

Figure 1.1: AWS – number of features released per year

There is no doubt that the number of offerings will continue to grow at a similar rate for the foreseeable future. Gartner named AWS as a leader for the 12th year in a row in the 2022 Gartner Magic Quadrant for Cloud Infrastructure & Platform Services. AWS is innovating fast, especially in new areas such as machine learning and artificial intelligence, the **Internet of Things (IoT)**, serverless computing, blockchain, and even quantum computing.

The following are some of the key differentiators for AWS in a nutshell:

Oldest and most experienced cloud provider	AWS was the first major public cloud provider (started in 2006) and since then it has gained millions of customers across the globe.
Fast pace of innovation	AWS has 200+ fully featured services to support any cloud workload. They released 3000+ features in 2021 to meet customer demand.
Continuous price reduction	AWS has reduced its prices across various services 111 times since its inception in 2006 to improve the **Total Cost of Ownership (TCO)**.
Community of partners to help accelerate the cloud journey	AWS has a large Partner Network of 100,000+ partners across 150+ countries. These partners include large consulting partners and software vendors.
Security and compliance	AWS provides security standards and compliance certifications to fulfill your local government and industry compliance needs.
Global infrastructure	As of January 2023, AWS has 99 Availability Zones within 31 geographic Regions, 32 Local Zones, 29 Wavelength Zones, 410+ Points of Presence (400+ Edge locations and 13 regional mid-tier caches) in 90+ cities across 47 countries. For the latest information, refer to `https://aws.amazon.com/about-aws/global-infrastructure/`.

It's not always possible to move all workloads into the cloud, and for that purpose, AWS provides a broad set of hybrid capabilities in the areas of networking, data, access, management, and application services. For example, VMware Cloud on AWS allows customers to seamlessly run existing VMware workloads on AWS with the skills and toolsets they already have without additional hardware investment. If you want to run your workload on-premise, then AWS Outposts enables you to utilize native AWS services, infrastructure, and operating models in almost any data center, co-location space, or on-premises facility if you prefer to run your workload on-premise. You will learn more details about hybrid cloud services later in this book.

This is just a small sample of the many AWS services that you will see throughout this book. Let's delve a little deeper into how influential AWS currently is and how influential it has the potential to become.

The market share, influence, and adoption of AWS

For the first nine years of AWS's existence, Amazon did not break down its AWS sales, and since 2015 Amazon started reporting AWS sales separately. As of April 2022, Microsoft does not fully break down its Azure revenue and profit in its quarterly reports. They disclosed their Azure revenue growth rate without reporting the actual revenue number, instead burying Azure revenues in a bucket called Commercial Cloud, which also includes items such as Office 365 revenue. Google has been cagey about breaking down its **Google Cloud Platform** (**GCP**) revenue for a long time. Google finally broke down its GCP revenue in February 2019, but GCP also combines its cloud and workplace (G-suite) tools in the same bucket.

AWS has a large market share with a $80.1 B run rate in 2022 and a 29% year-over-year growth. It is predicted to hit $100 B business by end of 2023, which is phenomenal for a business of its size. As of 2022, AWS is leading cloud IaaS with 34% of the market share as per TechRadar's global cloud market report. AWS has done a great job of protecting its market share by adding more and more services, adding features to existing services, building higher-level functionality on top of the core services it already offers, and educating the masses on how to best use these services.

We are in an exciting period when it comes to cloud adoption. Until a few years ago, many C-suite executives were leery of adopting cloud technologies to run their mission-critical and core services. A common concern was that they felt having on-premises implementations was more secure than running their workloads on the cloud.

It has become apparent to most of them that running workloads on the cloud can be just as secure as running them on-premises. There is no perfectly secure environment, and it seems that almost every other day, we hear about sensitive information being left exposed on the internet by yet another company. But having an army of security experts on your side, as is the case with the major cloud providers, will often beat any security team that most companies can procure on their own.

The current state of the cloud market for most enterprises is a state of **Fear Of Missing Out** (**FOMO**). Chief executives are watching their competitors jump in on cloud technology, and they are concerned that they will be left behind if they don't leap.

Additionally, we see an unprecedented level of disruption in many industries propelled by the power of the cloud. Let's take the example of Lyft and Uber. Both companies rely heavily on cloud services to power their infrastructure, and old-guard companies in the space, such as Hertz and Avis, that depend on older on-premises technology are getting left behind. Part of the problem is the convenience that Uber and Lyft offer by being able to summon a car on demand. But the inability to upgrade their systems to leverage cloud technologies undoubtedly played a role in their diminishing share of the car rental market.

Let's continue learning some of the basic cloud terminologies and AWS terminology.

Basic cloud and AWS terminology

There is a constant effort by technology companies to offer common standards for certain technologies while providing exclusive and proprietary technology that no one else offers. An example of this can be seen in the database market. The **Standard Query Language** (**SQL**) and the ANSI-SQL standard have been around for a long time. The **American National Standards Institute** (**ANSI**) adopted SQL as the SQL-86 standard in 1986. Since then, database vendors have continuously supported this standard while offering various extensions to make their products stand out and lock in customers to their technology.

Cloud providers provide the same core functionality for a wide variety of customer needs, but they all feel compelled to name these services differently, no doubt in part to try to separate themselves from the rest of the pack. As an example, every major cloud provider offers compute services. In other words, it is simple to spin up a server with any provider, but they all refer to this compute service differently:

- AWS uses **Elastic Compute Cloud** (**EC2**) instances.
- Azure uses **Azure Virtual Machines**.
- GCP uses **Google Compute Engine**.

The following tables give a non-comprehensive list of the different core services offered by AWS, Azure, and GCP and the names used by each of them. However, if you are confused by all the terms in the tables, don't fret. We will learn about many of these services throughout the book and when to use them.

Service	AWS	Azure	GCP
Compute	• Amazon EC2 • Lightsail	• Azure Virtual Machines • Virtual Machine Scale Sets	• Google Compute Engine • Graphics Processing Unit (GPU)
Containers	• Amazon Elastic Container Service (ECS) • Amazon Fargate • Elastic Container Service for Kubernetes • Elastic Container Registry • Batch • Amazon EMR	• Azure Kubernetes Service (AKS) • Container Instances • Batch • Service Fabric • Cloud Services	• Google Kubernetes Engine • Knative • Container Security

Figure 1.2: Cloud provider terminology and comparison (part 1)

These are some of the other services, including serverless technology services and database services:

Service	AWS	Azure	GCP
Serverless Technologies	• AWS Lambda	• Azure Functions	• Google Cloud Functions
Relational Databases	• Amazon **Relational Database Service (RDS)** • Aurora • Redshift	• Azure SQL Database • Data Warehouse • Server Stretch Database • Table Storage • Redis Cache • Data Factory	• Google Cloud SQL • Cloud Spanner
NoSQL Databases (Key Value)	• Amazon DynamoDB	• Azure Table Storage	• Google Cloud Datastore • Google Cloud Bigtable
NoSQL Databases (Indexed)	• Amazon SimpleDB	• Azure Cosmos DB	• Google Cloud Datastore
Object Storage	• Amazon **Simple Storage Service (S3)**	• Azure Blob Storage	• Google Cloud Storage
File Storage	• Amazon **Elastic Block Store (EBS)** • Snowball • Snowball Edge • Snowmobile • Amazon **Elastic File System (EFS)**	• Azure Managed Disks • Azure File Storage	• Google Compute Engine Persistent Disks • Persistent Disk • ZFS/Avere • Transfer Appliance • Transfer Service
Archival Storage	• Amazon Glacier	• Azure Archive Storage	• Google Cloud Storage Nearline and Coldline

Figure 1.3: Cloud provider terminology and comparison (part 2)

These are additional services:

Service	AWS	Azure	GCP
Domain Name Service (DNS)	• Amazon Route 53	• Azure DNS	• Google Cloud DNS
Peering	• Amazon DirectConnect	• Azure ExpressRoute	• Google Cloud Interconnect
Virtual Networking	• Amazon **Virutual Private Cloud (VPC)**	• Azure **Virutual Networks (VNets)**	• Google Virtual Private Cloud
Elastic Load Balancing	• Amazon Elastic Load Balancer	• Azure Load Balancer	• Google Cloud Load Balancing
PaaS services	• AWS Elastic Beanstalk • VMware Cloud on AWS	• App Service and Cloud Services	• Google App Engine
Machine Learning	• SageMaker • Machine Learning • Rekognition • Lex • Polly • Comprehend • Translate • Transcribe • DeepLens • Deep Learning AMIs	• Machine Learning • Azure Bot Service • Cognitive Services	• Google Cloud Machine Learning Engine • Dialogflow • Google Cloud Natural Language • Google Cloud Speech API • Google Cloud Translation API • Google Cloud Video Intelligence • Google Cloud Job Discovery

Figure 1.4: Cloud provider terminology and comparison (part 3)

The next section will explain why cloud services are becoming popular and why AWS adoption is prevalent.

Why is AWS so popular?

Depending on who you ask, some estimates peg the global cloud computing market at around 545.8 billion USD in 2022, growing to about 1.24 trillion USD by 2027. This implies a **Compound Annual Growth Rate** (**CAGR**) of around 17.9% for the period.

There are multiple reasons why the cloud market is growing so fast. Some of them are listed here:

- Elasticity and scalability
- Security
- Availability
- Faster hardware cycles
- System administration staff

In addition to the above, AWS provides access to emerging technologies and faster time to market. Let's look at the most important reason behind the popularity of cloud computing (and, in particular, AWS) first.

Elasticity and scalability

The concepts of *elasticity* and *scalability* are closely tied. Let's start by understanding scalability. In the context of computer science, *scalability* can be used in two ways:

- An application can continue to function correctly when the volume of users and/or transactions it handles increases. The increased volume is typically handled by using bigger and more powerful resources (scaling up) or adding more similar resources (scaling out).
- A system can function well when it rescales and can take full advantage of the new scale. For example, a program is scalable if it can be reinstalled on an operating system with a bigger footprint. It can take full advantage of the more robust operating system, achieving greater performance, processing transactions faster, and handling more users.

Scalability can be tracked over multiple dimensions, for example:

- **Administrative scalability** – Increasing the number of users of the system
- **Functional scalability** – Adding new functionality without altering or disrupting existing functionality
- **Heterogeneous scalability** – Adding disparate components and services from a variety of vendors
- **Load scalability** – Expanding capacity to accommodate more traffic and/or transactions
- **Generation scalability** – Scaling by installing new versions of software and hardware
- **Geographic scalability** – Maintaining existing functionality and SLAs while expanding the user base to a larger geographic region.

Scalability challenges are encountered by IT organizations all over daily. It is difficult to predict demand and traffic for many applications, especially internet-facing applications. Therefore, it is difficult to predict how much storage capacity, compute power, and bandwidth will be needed.

Say you finally launch a site you've been working on for months and within a few days you begin to realize that too many people are signing up and using your service. While this is an excellent problem, you better act fast, or the site will start throttling, and the user experience will go down or be non-existent. But the question now is, how do you scale? When you reach the limits of your deployment, how do you increase capacity? If the environment is on-premises, the answer is *very painful*. You will need approval from the company leadership. New hardware will need to be ordered. Delays will be inevitable. In the meantime, the opportunity in the marketplace will likely disappear because your potential customers will bail to competitors that can meet their needs. Being able to deliver quickly may not just mean getting there first. It may be the difference between getting there first and not getting there in time.

If your environment is on the cloud, things become much simpler. You can simply spin up an instance that can handle the new workload (correcting the size of a server can even be as simple as shutting down the server for a few minutes, changing a drop-down box value, and restarting the server again). You can *scale* your resources to meet increasing user demand.

The scalability that the cloud provides exponentially improves the time to market by accelerating the time it takes for resources to be provisioned.

NOTE

There are two different methods for scaling resources: scaling up (vertical scaling) and scaling out (horizontal scaling).

Scaling up is achieved by getting a bigger boat. For example, AWS offers a range of different-sized instances, including; nano; micro; small; medium; large; xlarge; 2x, 4x, 8x, 16x, and 32x large. So, if you are running a job on a medium instance and the job starts hitting the performance ceiling for that size, you could swap your work to a large or xlarge instance. This could happen because a database needs additional capacity to perform at a prescribed level. The new instance would have a better CPU, more memory, more storage, and faster network throughput. Scaling up can also be achieved using software – for example, allocating more memory or overclocking the CPU.

While scaling up is achieved by using more powerful nodes, scaling out is achieved by adding more nodes. Scaling out can be achieved in the following ways:

- Adding infrastructure capacity by adding new instances or nodes on an application-by-application basis
- Adding additional instances independently of the applications
- Adding more processes, connections, or shards with software

Scaling out is particularly valuable for multi-tiered architectures where each tier has a well-defined responsibility as it allows you to modify just one resource where a bottleneck exists and leave the other resources alone. For example, if you are running a multi-tiered architecture and discover that an application server is running at 95% CPU, you can add additional application servers to help balance the load without having to modify your web server or database server.

These scaling options can also be used simultaneously to improve an application. For example, in addition to adding more instances to handle traffic, more significant and capable instances can be added to the cluster.

As well as making it easy to scale resources, AWS and other cloud operators allow you to quickly adapt to shifting workloads due to their elasticity. Elasticity is defined as the ability of a computing environment to adapt to changes in workload by *automatically* provisioning or shutting down computing resources to match the capacity needed by the current workload.

These resources could be a single instance of a database or a thousand copies of the application and web servers used to handle your web traffic. These servers can be provisioned within minutes. In AWS and the other main cloud providers, resources can be shut down without having to terminate them completely, and the billing for resources will stop if the resources are shut down.

The ability to quickly shut down resources and, significantly, not be charged for that resource while it is down is a very powerful characteristic of cloud environments. If your system is on-premises, once a server is purchased, it is a sunk cost for the duration of the server's useful life. In contrast, whenever we shut down a server in a cloud environment. The cloud provider can quickly detect that and put that server back into the pool of available servers for other cloud customers to use that newly unused capacity.

This distinction cannot be emphasized enough. The only time absolute on-premises costs may be lower than cloud costs is when workloads are extremely predictable and consistent. Computing costs in a cloud environment on a per-unit basis may be higher than on-premises prices, but the ability to shut resources down and stop getting charged for them makes cloud architectures cheaper in the long run, often in a quite significant way.

The following examples highlight how useful elasticity can be in different scenarios:

- **Web storefront** – A famous use case for cloud services is to use them to run an online storefront. Website traffic in this scenario will be highly variable depending on the day of the week, whether it's a holiday, the time of day, and other factors—almost every retail store in the USA experiences more than a 10x user workload during Thanksgiving week. The same goes for Boxing Day in the UK, Diwali in India, Singles' Day in China, and almost every country has a shopping festival. This kind of scenario is ideally suited for a cloud deployment. In this case, we can set up resource auto-scaling that automatically scales up and down compute resources as needed. Additionally, we can set up policies that allow database storage to grow as needed.
- **Big data workloads** – As data volumes are increasing exponentially, the popularity of Apache Spark and Hadoop continues to increase to analyze GBs and TBs of data. Many Spark clusters don't necessarily need to run consistently. They perform heavy batch computing for a period and then can be idle until the next batch of input data comes in. A specific example would be a cluster that runs every night for 3 or 4 hours and only during the working week. In this instance, you need decoupled compute and data storage where you can shut down resources that may be best managed on a schedule rather than by using demand thresholds.

Or, we could set up triggers that automatically shut down resources once the batch jobs are completed. AWS provides that flexibility where you can store your data in Amazon Simple Storage Service (S3) and spin up an Amazon Elastic MapReduce (EMR) cluster to run Spark jobs and shut them down after storing results back in decoupled Amazon S3.

- **Employee workspace** – In an on-premise setting, you provide a high configuration desktop/laptop to your development team and pay for it for 24 hours a day, including weekends. However, they are using one-fourth of the capacity considering an eight-hour workday. AWS provides workspaces accessible by low configuration laptops, and you can schedule them to stop during off-hours and weekends, saving almost 70% of the cost.

Another common use case in technology is file and object storage. Some storage services may grow organically and consistently. The traffic patterns can also be consistent. This may be one example where using an on-premises architecture may make sense economically. In this case, the usage pattern is consistent and predictable.

Elasticity is by no means the only reason that the cloud is growing in leaps and bounds. The ability to easily enable world-class security for even the simplest applications is another reason why the cloud is becoming pervasive.

Security

The perception of *on-premises* environments being more secure than cloud environments was a common reason companies big and small would not migrate to the cloud. More and more enterprises now realize that it is tough and expensive to replicate the security features provided by cloud providers such as AWS. Let's look at a few of the measures that AWS takes to ensure the security of its systems.

Physical security

AWS data centers are highly secured and continuously upgraded with the latest surveillance technology. Amazon has had decades to perfect its data centers' design, construction, and operation.

AWS has been providing cloud services for over 15 years, and they have an army of technologists, solution architects, and some of the brightest minds in the business. They are leveraging this experience and expertise to create *state-of-the-art* data centers. These centers are in nondescript facilities. You could drive by one and never know what it is. It will be extremely difficult to get in if you find out where one is. Perimeter access is heavily guarded. Visitor access is strictly limited, and they always must be accompanied by an Amazon employee.

Every corner of the facility is monitored by video surveillance, motion detectors, intrusion detection systems, and other electronic equipment. Amazon employees with access to the building must authenticate themselves four times to step on the data center floor.

Only Amazon employees and contractors that have a legitimate right to be in a data center can enter. Any other employee is restricted. Whenever an employee does not have a business need to enter a data center, their access is immediately revoked, even if they are only moved to another Amazon department and stay with the company. Lastly, audits are routinely performed and are part of the normal business process.

Encryption

AWS makes it extremely simple to encrypt data at rest and data in transit. It also offers a variety of options for encryption. For example, for encryption at rest, data can be encrypted on the server side, or it can be encrypted on the client side. Additionally, the encryption keys can be managed by AWS, or you can use keys that are managed by you using tamper-proof appliances like a **Hardware Security Module** (**HSM**). AWS provides you with a dedicated cloud HSM to secure your encryption key if you want one. You will learn more about AWS security in *Chapter 8, Best Practices for Application Security, Identity, and Compliance.*

AWS supports compliance standards

AWS has robust controls to allow users to maintain security and data protection. We'll discuss how AWS shares security responsibilities with its customers, but the same is true of how AWS supports compliance. AWS provides many attributes and features that enable compliance with many standards established in different countries and organizations. By providing these features, AWS simplifies compliance audits. AWS enables the implementation of security best practices and many security standards, such as these:

- STAR
- SOC 1/SSAE 16/ISAE 3402 (formerly SAS 70)
- SOC 2
- SOC 3
- FISMA, DIACAP, and FedRAMP
- PCI DSS Level 1
- DOD CSM Levels 1-5
- ISO 9001 / ISO 27001 / ISO 27017 / ISO 27018

- MTCS Level 3
- FIPS 140-2
- I TRUST

In addition, AWS enables the implementation of solutions that can meet many industry-specific standards, such as these:

- **Criminal Justice Information Services (CJIS)**
- **Family Educational Rights and Privacy Act (FERPA)**
- **Cloud Security Alliance (CSA)**
- **Motion Picture Association of America (MPAA)**
- **Health Insurance Portability and Accountability Act (HIPAA)**

The above is not a full list of compliance standards; there are many more compliance standards met by AWS according to industries and local authorities across the world.

Another important thing that can explain the meteoric rise of the cloud is how you can stand up high-availability applications without paying for the additional infrastructure needed to provide these applications. Architectures can be crafted to start additional resources when other resources fail. This ensures that we only bring additional resources when necessary, keeping costs down. Let's analyze this important property of the cloud in a deeper fashion.

Availability

Intuitively and generically, the word *"availability"* conveys that something is available or can be used. In order to be used, it needs to be up and running and in a functional condition. For example, if your car is in the driveway, it is working, and is ready to be used then it meets some of the conditions of availability. However, to meet the technical definition of *"availability,"* it must be turned on. A server that is otherwise working correctly but is shut down will not help run your website.

NOTE

Often high availability is confused with fault tolerance. A system can be 100% available but 50% fault tolerant. For example, suppose you need four servers to handle your application load and provide the required performance. You have built redundancy by putting two servers in two different data centers. In that case, your system is 100% available and 100% fault tolerant. But for some reason, one of the data centers has gone down. Your system is still 100% available but running at half capacity, which may impact system performance and user experience, which means fault tolerance is reduced to 50%. To achieve 100% fault tolerance, you must put eight servers, positioning four in each data center.

In mathematical terms, the formula for availability is simple:

$$\text{Availability} = \frac{\text{Uptime}}{(\text{Uptime} + \text{Downtime})}$$

For example, let's say you're trying to calculate the availability of a production system in your company. That asset ran for 732 hours in a single month. The system had 4 hours of unplanned downtime because of a disk failure and 8 hours of downtime for weekly maintenance. So, a total of 12 hours of downtime.

Using the preceding formula, we can calculate the following:

Availability = 732 / (732 + 12)

Availability = 732 / 744

Availability = 0.9838

Availability = 98.38%

It does not matter if your computing environment is on your premises or using the cloud – availability is paramount and critical to your business.

When we deploy infrastructure in an on-premises environment, we have two choices. We can purchase just enough hardware to service the current workload or ensure that there is enough excess capacity to account for any failures. This extra capacity and eliminating single points of failure is not as simple as it may seem. There are many places where single points of failure may exist and need to be eliminated:

- Compute instances can go down, so we need a few on standby.
- Databases can get corrupted.
- Network connections can be broken.
- Data centers can flood or be hit by earthquakes.

In addition to eliminating single points of failure, you want your system to be resilient enough to automatically identify when any resource in the system fails and automatically replace it with an equivalent resource. Say, for example, you are running a Hadoop cluster with 20 nodes, and one of the nodes fails. In that case, a recommended setup is immediately and automatically replacing the failed node with another well-functioning node. The only way this can be achieved on a pure *"on-prem"* solution is to have excess capacity servers sitting ready to replace any failing server nodes.

In most cases, the only way this can be achieved is by purchasing additional servers that may never be used. As the saying goes, *it's better to have and not need than to need and not have*. The price that could be paid if we don't have these resources when needed could be orders of magnitude greater than the hardware price, depending on how critical the system is to your business operations.

Using the cloud simplifies the *"single point of failure"* problem and makes it easy to provision resources. We have already determined that provisioning software in an on-premises data center can be long and arduous. However, cloud services like AWS allow you to start up resources and services automatically and immediately when you need them and you only get charged when you start using these newly launched resources. So, we can configure minimal environments knowing that additional resources are a click away.

AWS data centers are built in different regions across the world. All data centers are *always-on* and deliver services to customers. AWS does not have *"cold"* data centers. Their systems are extremely sophisticated and automatically route traffic to other resources if a failure occurs. Core services are always installed in an `N+1` configuration. In the case of a complete data center failure, there should be the capacity to handle traffic using the remaining available data centers without disruption.

AWS enables customers to deploy instances and persist data in more than one geographic region and across various data centers within a region. Data centers are deployed in fully independent zones. Data centers are constructed with enough separation between them such that the likelihood of a natural disaster affecting two of them simultaneously is very low. Additionally, data centers are not built in flood zones.

Data centers have discrete **Uninterruptable Power Supplies** (**UPSes**) and onsite backup generators to increase resilience. They are also connected to multiple electric grids from multiple independent utility providers. Data centers are connected redundantly to multiple tier-1 transit providers. Doing all this minimizes single points of failure, and improves availability. You will learn more details about AWS global infrastructure in *Chapter 4, Networking in AWS.*

Faster hardware cycles

When hardware is provisioned on-premises, it starts becoming obsolete from the instant that it is purchased. Hardware prices have been on an exponential downtrend since the first computer was invented, so the server you bought a few months ago may now be cheaper, or a new version of the server may be out that's faster and still costs the same. However, waiting until hardware improves or becomes cheaper is not an option. A decision needs to be made at some point to purchase it.

Using a cloud provider instead eliminates all these problems. For example, whenever AWS offers new and more powerful processor types, using them is as simple as stopping an instance, changing the processor type, and starting the instance again. In many cases, AWS may keep the price the same or even cheaper when better and faster processors and technology become available, especially with their own proprietary technology like the Graviton chip.

The cloud optimizes costs by building virtualization at scale. **Virtualization** is running multiple virtual instances on top of a physical computer system using an abstract layer sitting on top of actual hardware. More commonly, virtualization refers to the practice of running multiple operating systems on a single computer at the same time. Applications running on virtual machines are unaware that they are not running on a dedicated machine and share resources with other applications on the same physical machine.

A **hypervisor** is a computing layer that enables multiple operating systems to execute in the same physical compute resource. The operating systems running on top of these hypervisors are **Virtual Machines** (**VMs**) – a component that can emulate a complete computing environment using only software but as if it was running on bare metal. Hypervisors, also known as **Virtual Machine Monitors** (**VMMs**), manage these VMs while running side by side. A hypervisor creates a logical separation between VMs.

It provides each of them with a slice of the available compute, memory, and storage resources. It allows VMs not to clash and interfere with each other. If one VM crashes and goes down, it will not make other VMs go down with it. Also, if there is an intrusion in one VM, it is fully isolated from the rest.

AWS uses its own proprietary Nitro hypervisor. AWS's next-generation EC2 instances are built on the AWS Nitro System, a foundational platform that improves performance and reduces costs. Typically, hypervisors secure the physical hardware, while the BIOS virtualizes the CPU, storage, and networking, providing advanced management features. The AWS Nitro System enables the segregation of these functions, transferring them to dedicated hardware and software, and delivering almost all server resources to EC2 instances.

System administration staff

An on-premises implementation may require a full-time system administration staff and a process to ensure that the team remains fully staffed. Cloud providers can handle many of these tasks by using cloud services, allowing you to focus on core application maintenance and functionality and not have to worry about infrastructure upgrades, patches, and maintenance.

By offloading this task to the cloud provider, costs can come down because the administrative duties can be shared with other cloud customers instead of having a dedicated staff. You will learn more details about system administration in *Chapter 9, Driving Efficiency with CloudOps*.

This ends the first chapter of the book, which provided a foundation on the cloud and AWS. As you move forward with your learning journey, in subsequent chapters, you will dive deeper and deeper into AWS services, architecture, and best practices.

Summary

This chapter pieced together many of the technologies, best practices, and AWS services we cover in the book. As fully featured as AWS has become, it will certainly continue to provide more and more services to help enterprises, large and small, simplify the information technology infrastructure.

In this chapter, you learned about cloud computing and the key differences between the public and private cloud. This lead into learning more about the largest public cloud provider, AWS, and about its market share and adoption.

We also covered some reasons that the cloud in general and AWS, in particular, are so popular. As we learned, one of the main reasons for the cloud's popularity is the concept of elasticity, which we explored in detail. You learned about AWS services growth over the year along with it's key differentiators from other cloud providers. Further, you explored AWS terminology compared to other key players like Azure and GCP. Finally, you learned about the benefits of AWS and the reasons behind its popularity.

AWS provides some of the industry's best architecture practices under their Well-Architected Framework. Let's learn more about it. In the next chapter, you will learn about AWS's Well-Architected Tool and how you can build credibility by getting AWS certified.

Join us on Discord!

Read this book alongside other users, cloud experts, authors, and like-minded professionals.

Ask questions, provide solutions to other readers, chat with the authors via. Ask Me Anything sessions and much more.

Scan the QR code or visit the link to join the community now.

`https://packt.link/cloudanddevops`

2

Understanding the AWS Well-Architected Framework and Getting Certified

In the previous chapter, you got a glimpse of AWS's innovation pace and broad service offerings. As a solutions architect, you might wonder how these services come together to address various parameters of your IT workload needs. You may also wonder how you can ensure your architecture is following best practices while achieving your business needs. For that purpose, AWS provides architecture guidance in a cloud-native way using its Well-Architected Framework.

In this chapter, you will learn details about the Well-Architected Framework and how to apply best practices for every component of your cloud application. You will go through the six pillars of the Well-Architected Framework and the AWS Well-Architected Lenses for specific workloads such as serverless, analytics, IoT, etc. You will learn about using the AWS Well-Architected tool to validate your architecture against AWS-recommended best practices by conducting a **Well-Architected Review (WAR)**.

Further, you will then learn how we can take a slice of the cloud pie and build your credibility by becoming certified. Finally, toward the end of the chapter, we will look at some tips and tricks you can use to simplify your journey to obtain AWS certifications. We will also look at some frequently asked questions about the AWS certifications.

In this chapter, we will cover the following topics:

- The AWS Well-Architected Framework

- The six pillars of the Well-Architected Framework
- AWS Well-Architected Lenses
- Building credibility and getting certified
- Learning tips and tricks for obtaining AWS certifications
- Some frequently asked questions about AWS certifications

Let's get started by looking at a holistic architecture approach in AWS.

The AWS Well-Architected Framework

As a solutions architect, you may have questions about architecture optimization for reliability, scaling, high availability, performance, and security even before getting started with various AWS services. You may ask how the AWS cloud will accommodate those needs and compare it with your existing on-premise architecture practice.

AWS built the Well-Architected Framework to address those needs. The Well-Architected Framework provides customers with access to AWS's Well-Architected content. This content is based on extensive architectural reviews with clients, helping to identify and mitigate potential architectural risks while promoting best practices.

AWS also created the **WAR** to help customers have better outcomes when building architectures on AWS. You can understand the areas of your architecture that could be improved, which in turn helps you address areas you have been firefighting and that distract from adding value. As you go through the review process, you can learn about new capabilities to add value to your application and drive better outcomes to build and operate workloads on the cloud. With this, you can get the following benefits:

- Learn strategies and best practices for architecting in the cloud
- Measure your architecture against best practices
- Improve your architecture by addressing any issues

AWS has six Well-Architected pillars covering the breadth and depth of architecture along with the WAR to validate them. Let's learn more about it.

The six pillars of the Well-Architected Framework

The cloud in general, and AWS in particular, is so popular because it simplifies the development of Well-Architected Frameworks. If there is one *must-read* AWS document, it is *AWS Well-Architected Framework*, which spells out the six pillars of the Well-Architected Framework.

The full document can be found here: `https://docs.aws.amazon.com/wellarchitected/latest/framework/welcome.html`.

AWS provides the Well-Architected tool, which provides prescriptive guidance about each pillar to validate your workload against architecture best practices and generate a comprehensive report. Please find a glimpse of the tool below:

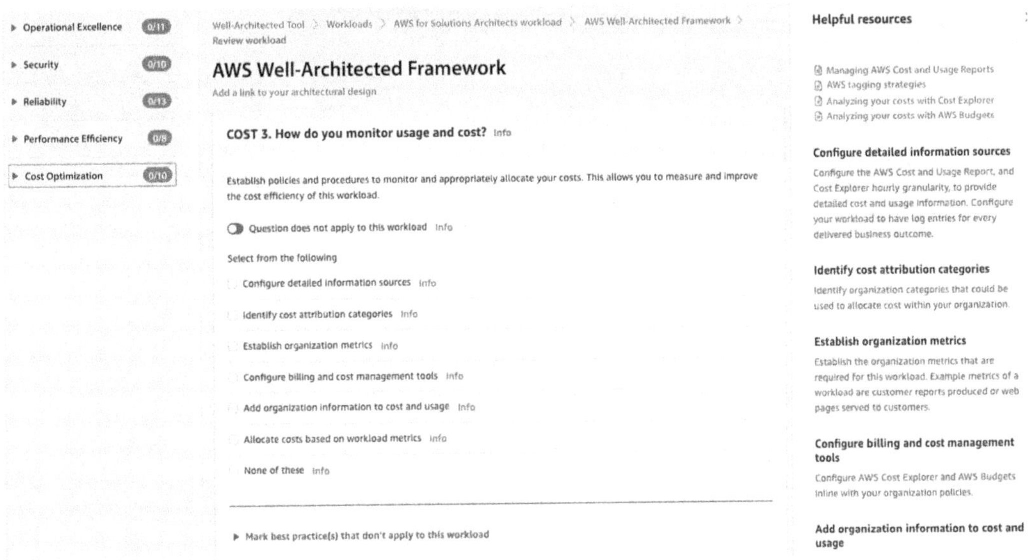

Figure 2.1: AWS Well-Architected tool

To kick off a WAR for your workload, you first need to create an AWS account and open the Well-Architected tool. To start an architecture review per the gold standard defined by AWS, you need to provide workload information such as the name, environment type (production or pre-production), AWS workload hosting regions, industry, reviewer name, etc. After submitting the information, you will see (as in the above screenshot) a set of questions about each Well-Architected pillar, with the option to select what is most relevant to your workload. AWS provides prescriptive guidance and various resources for applying architecture best practices to questions within the right-hand navigation.

As AWS has provided detailed guidance for each Well-Architected pillar in their document, let's look at the main points about the six pillars of the Well-Architected Framework.

The first pillar – security

Security should always be a top priority in both on-premises and cloud architectures. All security aspects should be considered, including data encryption and protection, access management, infrastructure security, network security, monitoring, and breach detection and inspection.

To enable system security and to guard against nefarious actors and vulnerabilities, AWS recommends these architectural principles:

- Implement a strong identity foundation
- Enable traceability
- Apply security at all levels
- Automate security best practices
- Protect data in transit and at rest
- Keep people away from data
- Prepare for security events

You can find the security pillar checklist from the Well-Architected tool below, which has ten questions with one or more options relevant to your workload:

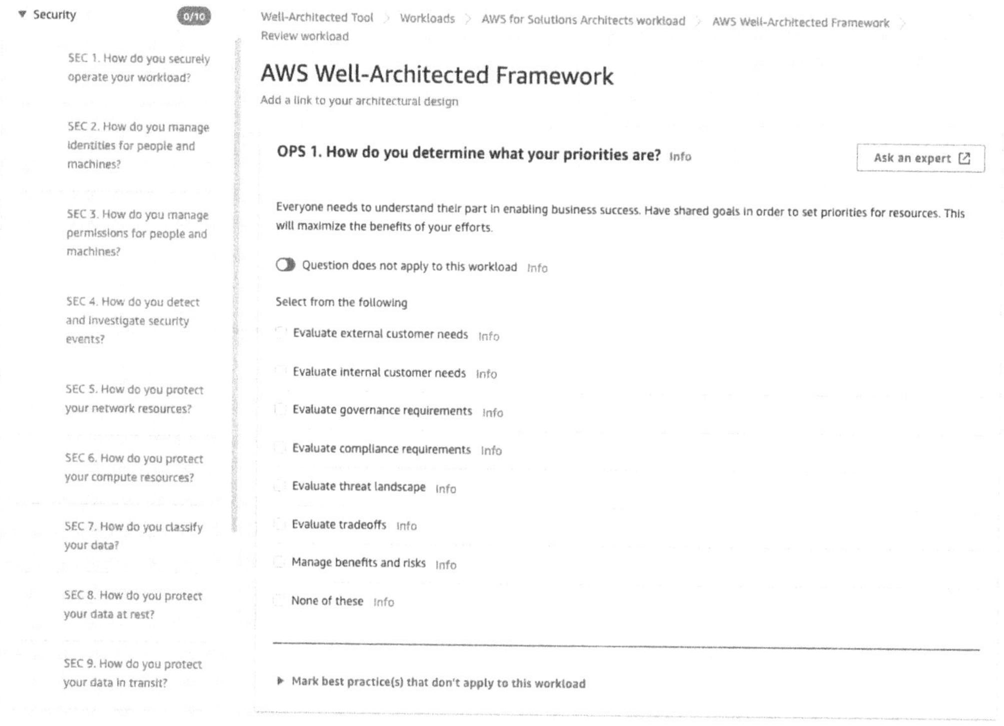

Figure 2.2: AWS Well-Architected Security pillar

In the preceding screenshot, in the left-hand navigation, you can see questions related to security best practices, and for each question, there will be multiple options to choose from per your workload. Answering these questions will help you to determine the current state of your workload security and highlight if there are any gaps in the WAR report such as **High-Risk Issues (HRIs)**. You can find more details on the security pillar by referring to the AWS Well-Architected Framework user document: `https://docs.aws.amazon.com/wellarchitected/latest/security-pillar/welcome.html`.

To gain practical experience in implementing optimal security practices, it is advisable to complete the well-architected security labs. You can find details on the labs here: `https://www.wellarchitectedlabs.com/security/`.

The next pillar, reliability, is almost as important as security, as you want your workload to perform its business functions consistently and reliably.

The second pillar – reliability

Before discussing reliability in the context of the Well-Architected Framework, let's first get a better understanding of reliability as a concept. Intuitively, a resource is said to have *"reliability"* if it often works when we try to use it. You will be hard-pressed to find an example of anything that is perfectly reliable. Even the most well-manufactured computer components have a degree of *"unreliability."* To use a car analogy, if you go to your garage and you can usually start your car and drive it away, then it is said to have high *"reliability."* Conversely, if you can't trust your car to start (maybe because it has an old battery), it is said to have low *"reliability."*

Reliability is the probability of a resource or application meeting a certain performance standard and continuing to perform for a certain period of time. Reliability is leveraged to gain an understanding of how long the service will be up and running in the context of various real-life conditions.

Note

Reliability and availability are sometimes erroneously used interchangeably. To continue with the car analogy, for your car to be available, it must be functional, ready for use, turned on, and ready to go. These conditions make it have high *availability*. For your car to have high *reliability*, it must start most of the time – you can depend on it being able to function.

Reliability is the measurement of how long a resource performs its intended function, whereas availability is the measurement of how long a resource is in operation as a percentage of the total time it was in operation and not in operation (see the *Availability* section of the previous chapter for more information). For example, a machine may be available 90% of the time but have a reliability of 75%. The two terms are related but different and have different meanings. They have different objectives and can have different costs to maintain certain service levels.

The reliability of an application can be difficult to measure. There are a couple of methods to measure reliability. One of them is to measure the probability of failure of the application components that may affect the availability of the whole application.

More formally, we can calculate the **Mean Time Between Failures** (**MTBF**):

$$\text{MTBF} = \frac{(\text{total elapsed time} - \text{sum of downtime})}{\text{number of failures}}$$

MTBF represents the time elapsed between component failures in a system. The metric used to measure time in MTBF is typically hours, but it can also be measured in other units of time such as days, weeks, or years depending on the specific system, component, or product being evaluated.

Similarly, **Mean Time To Repair** (**MTTR**) may be measured as a metric representing the time it takes to repair a failed system component. Ensuring the application is repaired on time is essential to meet service-level agreements. Other metrics can be used to track reliability, such as the fault tolerance levels of the application. The greater the fault tolerance of a given component, the lower the susceptibility of the whole application to being disrupted in a real-world scenario.

As you can see, reliability is a vital metric for assessing your architecture. The reliability of your architecture should be as high as possible, and the Well-Architected Framework recognizes the importance of this with its second pillar, Reliability. A key characteristic of the Reliability pillar is minimizing or eliminating single points of failure. Ideally, every component should have a backup. The backup should be able to come online as quickly as possible and in an automated manner, without human intervention.

Self-healing is another important concept to attain reliability. An example of this is how Amazon S3 handles data replication. Before returning a `SUCCESS` message, S3 saves your objects redundantly on multiple devices across a minimum of three **Availability Zones** (**AZs**) in an AWS Region. This design ensures that the system can withstand multiple device failures by rapidly identifying and rectifying any lost redundancy. Additionally, the service conducts regular checksum-based data integrity checks.

The Well-Architected Framework paper recommends these design principles to enhance reliability:

- Automatically recover from failure
- Test recovery procedures
- Scale horizontally to increase aggregate workload availability
- Stop guessing capacity
- Manage changes in automation

You can find the reliability pillar checklist from the Well-Architected tool below:

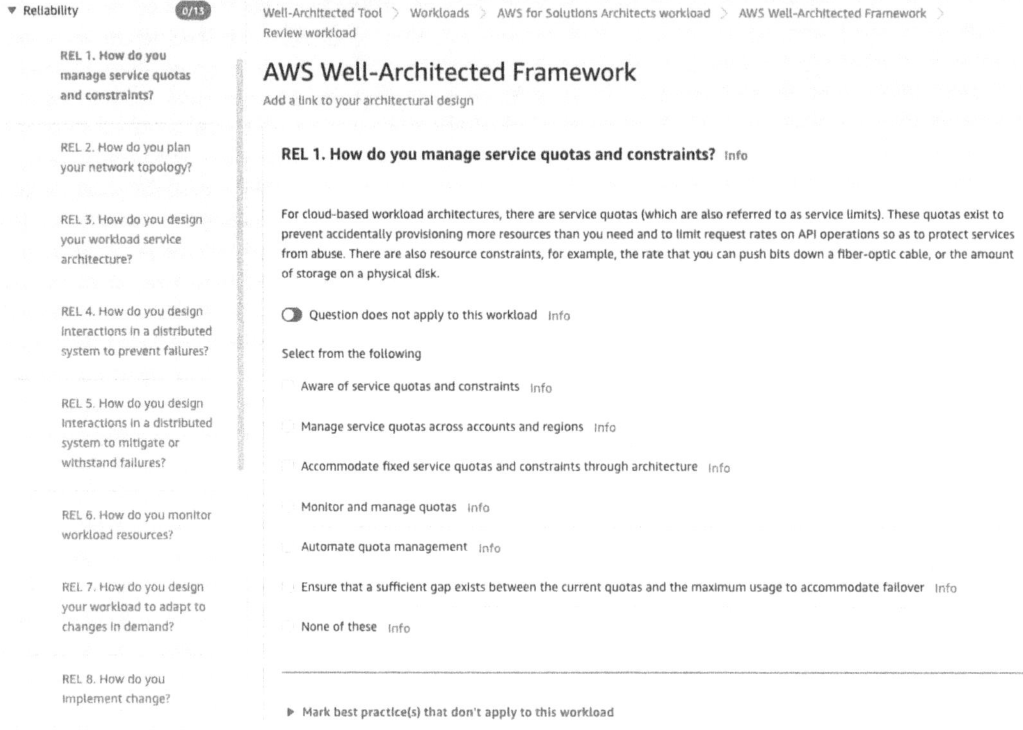

Figure 2.3: AWS Well-Architected reliability pillar

In the preceding screenshot, you can see questions related to achieving reliability best practices in the left-hand navigation. Answering these questions will help you determine the current state of your workload reliability and highlight HRIs, which you must fix. You can find more details on the reliability pillar by referring to the AWS Well-Architected Framework user doc: `https://docs.aws.amazon.com/wellarchitected/latest/reliability-pillar/welcome.html`.

Reliability is a complex topic that requires significant effort to ensure that all data and applications are backed up appropriately. To implement the best reliability practices, the well-architected labs can be utilized, providing hands-on experience in applying optimal reliability strategies. You can find details on the labs here: `https://www.wellarchitectedlabs.com/reliability/`.

To retain users, you need your application to be highly performant and to respond within seconds or milliseconds as per the nature of your workload. This makes performance a key pillar when building your application. Let's look at more details on performance efficiency.

The third pillar – performance efficiency

In some respects, over-provisioning resources is just as bad as not having enough capacity to handle your workloads. Launching a constantly idle or almost idle instance is a sign of bad design. Resources should not be at full capacity and should be utilized efficiently. AWS provides various features and services to assist in creating architectures with high efficiency. However, we are still responsible for ensuring that the architectures we design are suitable and correctly sized for our applications.

When it comes to performance efficiency, the recommended design best practices are as follows:

- Democratize advanced technologies
- Go global in minutes
- Use serverless architectures
- Experiment more often
- Consider mechanical sympathy

You can find the Performance efficiency pillar checklist from the Well-Architected tool below with eight questions covering multiple aspects to make sure your architecture is optimized for performance:

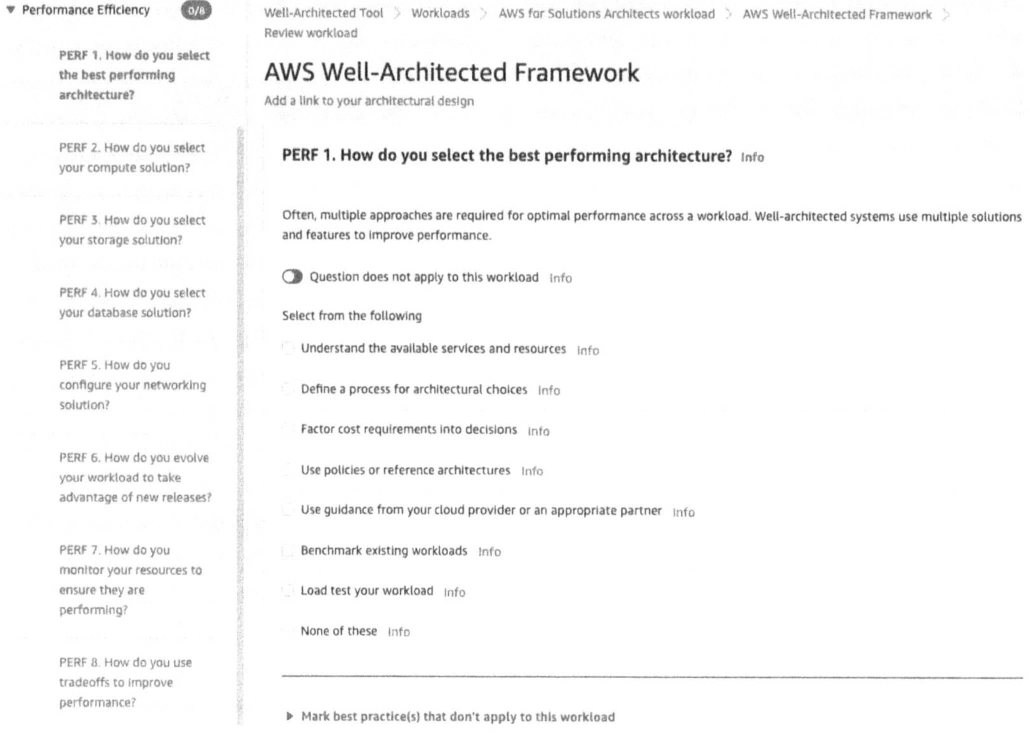

Figure 2.4: AWS Well-Architected performance pillar

In the preceding screenshot, you can see questions related to building performant applications, and answering these questions will help you identify and improve your workload performance. You can find more details on the performance efficiency pillar by referring to the AWS Well-Architected Framework user doc: `https://docs.aws.amazon.com/wellarchitected/latest/performance-efficiency-pillar/welcome.html`.

Monitoring is critical to performance, as it helps identify potential issues within a system and optimize it for optimal operation. To effectively monitor your workload for performance, hands-on labs are available that provide practical experience and help to implement appropriate monitoring techniques. You can find details on the labs here: `https://www.wellarchitectedlabs.com/performance-efficiency/`.

Cost optimization is one of the primary motivators for businesses to move to the cloud as per Gartner's *6 Steps for Planning a Cloud Strategy*. However, the cloud can become expensive if you don't apply best practices and run the cloud workload the same way you run an on-premises workload. The cloud can save you tons of money with proper cost optimization techniques. Let's look into the next pillar, cost optimization.

The fourth pillar – cost optimization

This pillar is related to the third pillar. Suppose your architecture is efficient and can accurately handle varying application loads and adjust as traffic changes.

Additionally, your architecture should identify when resources are not being used and allow you to stop them or, even better, stop those unused compute resources for you. In this department, AWS provides autoscaling, which allows you to turn on monitoring tools that will automatically shut down resources if they are not being utilized. We strongly encourage you to adopt a mechanism to stop resources once they are identified as idle. This is especially useful in development and test environments.

To enhance cost optimization, these principles are suggested:

- Implement cloud financial management
- Adopt a consumption model
- Measure overall efficiency
- Stop spending money on undifferentiated heavy lifting
- Analyze and attribute expenditure

Whenever possible, use AWS-managed services instead of services you need to manage yourself. Managed cloud-native services should lower your administration expenses. You can find the cost optimization pillar checklist from the Well-Architected tool below with ten questions covering multiple aspects to make sure your architecture is optimized for cost:

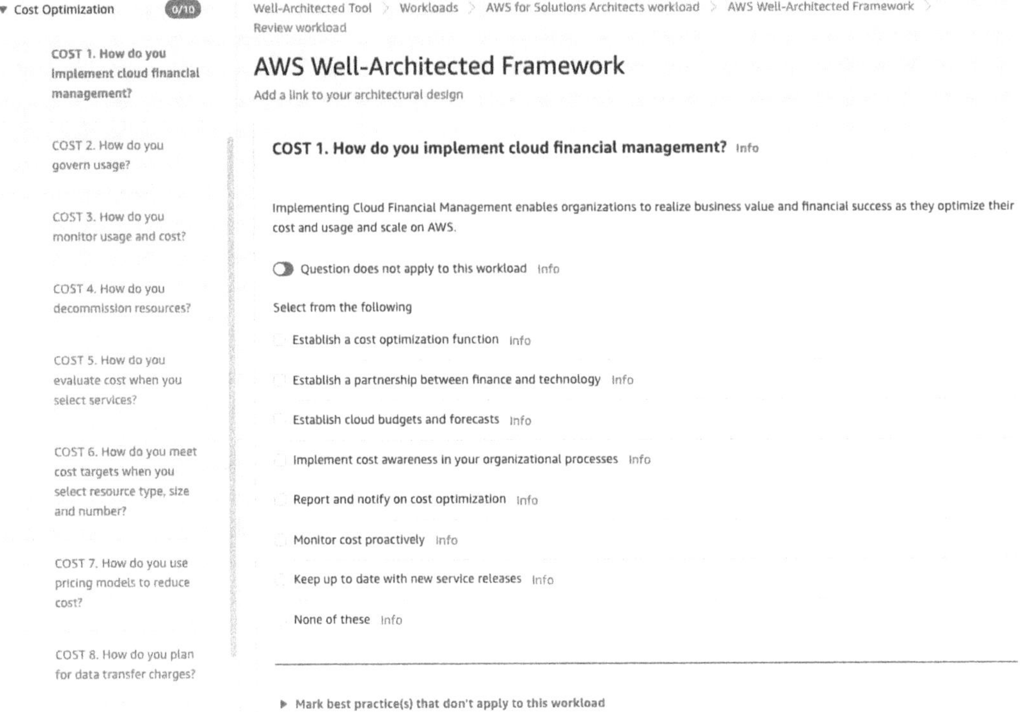

Figure 2.5: AWS Well-Architected cost optimization pillar

In the preceding screenshot, you can see questions about cost optimization best practices, and answering these questions will help you save costs by optimizing your workload for the cloud. You can find more details on the cost optimization pillar by referring to the AWS Well-Architected Framework user doc: `https://docs.aws.amazon.com/wellarchitected/latest/cost-optimization-pillar/welcome.html`.

One of the primary motivations for businesses to move to the cloud is cost savings. It is essential to optimize costs to realize a return on investment after migrating to the cloud. To learn about the best practices for cost monitoring and optimization, hands-on labs are available that provide practical experience and help to implement effective cost management strategies. You can find details on the labs here: `https://www.wellarchitectedlabs.com/cost/`.

Significant work starts after deploying your production workload, making operational excellence a critical factor. You need to make sure your application maintains the expected performance in production and improves efficacy by applying as much automation as possible. Let's look at more details of the operational excellence pillar.

The fifth pillar – operational excellence

The operational excellence of a workload should be measured across these dimensions:

- Agility
- Reliability
- Performance

The ideal way to optimize these key performance indicators is to standardize and automate the management of these workloads. To achieve operational excellence, AWS recommends these principles:

- Perform operations as code
- Make frequent, small, reversible changes
- Refine operation procedures frequently
- Anticipate failure
- Learn from all operational failures

You can find the operational excellence pillar checklist from the Well-Architected tool below with eleven questions covering multiple aspects to make sure your architecture is optimized for running in production:

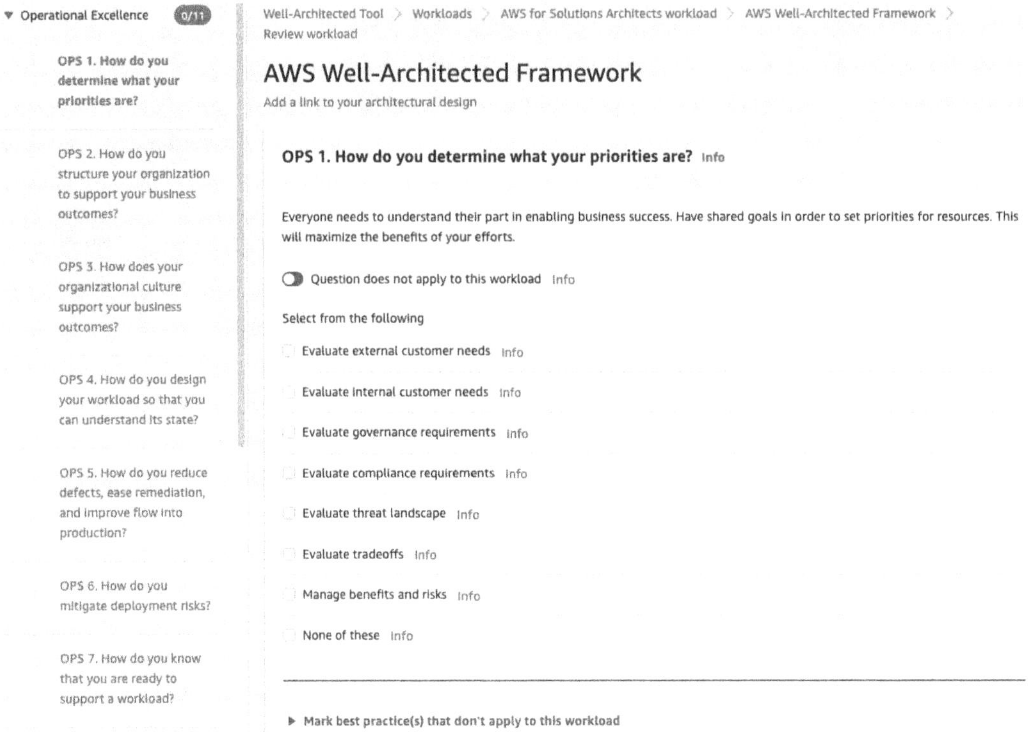

Figure 2.6: AWS Well-Architected operational excellence pillar

In the preceding screenshot, you can see questions about driving operational excellence best practices. Answering these questions will help you achieve efficiency and agility by automating your workload infrastructure, application deployment, monitoring, and alerts. You can find more details on the operational excellence pillar by referring to the AWS Well-Architected Framework user doc: `https://docs.aws.amazon.com/wellarchitected/latest/operational-excellence-pillar/welcome.html`.

Operational excellence is the true value of the cloud, as it enables the automation of production workloads and facilitates self-scaling. Hands-on guidance for implementing best practices in operational excellence is available through the well-architected labs, providing practical experience to optimize the operational efficiency of a system. You can find details on the labs here: `https://www.wellarchitectedlabs.com/operational-excellence/`.

Sustainability is now the talk of the town, with organizations worldwide recognizing their social responsibilities and taking the pledge to make business more sustainable. As a leader, AWS was the first cloud provider to launch suitability as an architecture practice at re:Invent 2021. Let's look into more details of the sustainability pillar of the Well-Architected Framework.

The sixth pillar – sustainability

As more and more organizations adopt the cloud, cloud providers can lead the charge to make the world more sustainable in improving the environment, economics, society, and human life. *The United Nations World Commission on Environment and Development* defines sustainable development as *"development that meets the needs of the present without compromising the ability of future generations to meet their own needs"*. Your organization can have direct or indirect negative impacts on the Earth's environment through carbon emissions or by damaging natural resources like clean water or farming land. To reduce environmental impact, it's important to talk about sustainability and adopt it in practice wherever possible. AWS is achieving that by adding the sixth pillar to its Well-Architected Framework, with the following design principles:

- Understand your impact
- Establish sustainability goals
- Maximize utilization
- Anticipate and adopt new, more efficient hardware and software offerings
- Use managed services
- Reduce the downstream impact of your cloud workloads

You can find the sustainability pillar checklist from the Well-Architected tool below with six well-thought-out questions covering multiple aspects to make sure your architecture is sustainable:

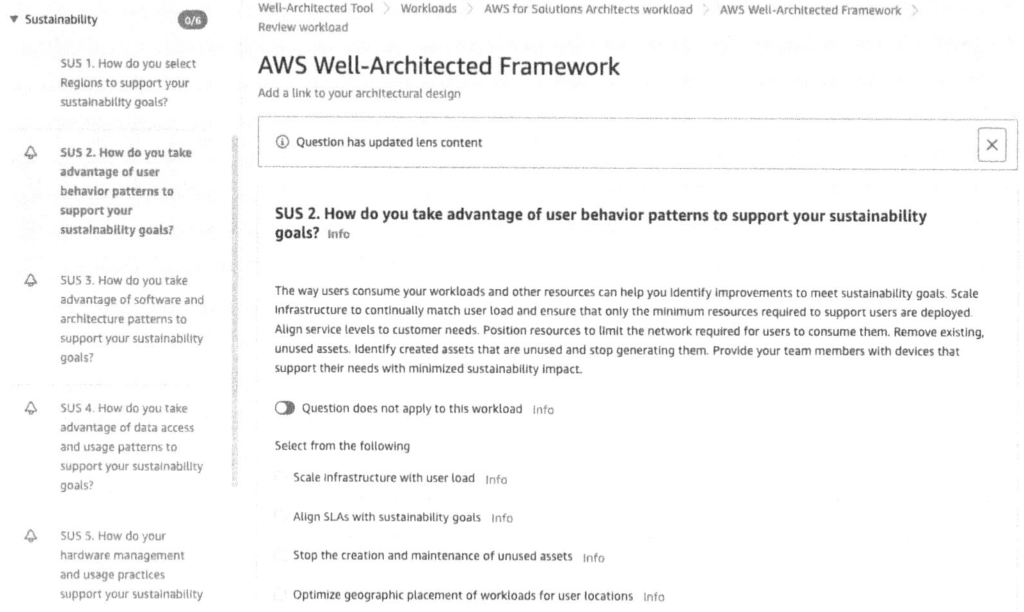

Figure 2.7: AWS Well-Architected sustainability pillar

In the preceding screenshot, you can see questions related to understanding if your workload is helping you to achieve your sustainability goals and how AWS can help you meet these goals. You can find more details on the sustainability pillar by referring to the AWS Well-Architected Framework user doc: `https://docs.aws.amazon.com/wellarchitected/latest/sustainability-pillar/sustainability-pillar.html`.

Making conscious choices and having an awareness of your carbon footprint is essential to drive sustainability. AWS provides ways to save energy through their services, and with the help of the well-architected labs, workloads can be made sustainable and environmentally aware. You can find details on the labs here: `https://www.wellarchitectedlabs.com/sustainability/`.

While the Well-Architected Framework provides more generic guidance for optimizing your architecture, which is applicable across workloads, there is a need for more specific architectural practice for specialized workloads. That's why AWS published Well-Architected Lenses to address workload and domain-specific needs. Let's take an overarching view of AWS's Well-Architected Lenses.

AWS Well-Architected Lenses

As of April 2022, AWS has launched 13 Well-Architected Lenses addressing architecting needs specific to technology workloads and industry domains. The following are the important available lenses for AWS's Well-Architected Framework:

- **Serverless Applications Lens** – Building a serverless workload saves costs and offloads infrastructure maintenance to the cloud. The Serverless Applications Lens provides details on best practices to architect serverless application workloads in the AWS cloud. More information on the design principles is available on the AWS website: `https://docs.aws.amazon.com/wellarchitected/latest/serverless-applications-lens`.
- **Internet of Things (IoT) Lens** – To design an IoT workload, you must know how to manage and secure it on millions of devices that need to connect over the internet. The IoT Lens provides details on designing an IoT workload. More details on design principles are available on the AWS website: `https://docs.aws.amazon.com/wellarchitected/latest/iot-lens`.
- **Data Analytics Lens** – Data is the new gold. Every organization is trying to put its data to the best use to get insights for its customers and improve its business. The Data Analytics Lens provides best practices for building a data pipeline. More details on the design principles are available on the AWS website: `https://docs.aws.amazon.com/wellarchitected/latest/analytics-lens`.
- **Machine Learning (ML) Lens** – ML applies to almost any workload, especially getting future insights from historical data. With the ever-increasing adoption of ML workloads, it is essential to have the ability to put an ML model into production and use it at scale. The ML Lens provides best practices for training, tuning, and deploying your ML model. More details on the design principles are available on the AWS website: `https://docs.aws.amazon.com/wellarchitected/latest/machine-learning-lens`.
- **Hybrid Networking Lens** – Networking is the backbone of any application workload, whether on-premises or in the cloud. As enterprises are adopting the cloud, the need for a hybrid cloud setup is increasing every day, to establish communication between on-premises and cloud workloads. The AWS Hybrid Networking Lens introduces best practices for designing networks for the hybrid cloud. More details on the design principles are available on the AWS website: `https://docs.aws.amazon.com/wellarchitected/latest/hybrid-networking-lens`.

Above, we have covered some of the important lenses, but I encourage you to explore other industry-focused Well-Architected Lenses such as gaming, streaming media, finance, and workload-specific lenses, including SAP, SaaS, **HPC** (**High-Performance Computing**), and **FTR** (**Functional Technical Review**) to validate your cloud platforms. You can apply various lenses when defining your workload in AWS's Well-Architected tool, as shown below:

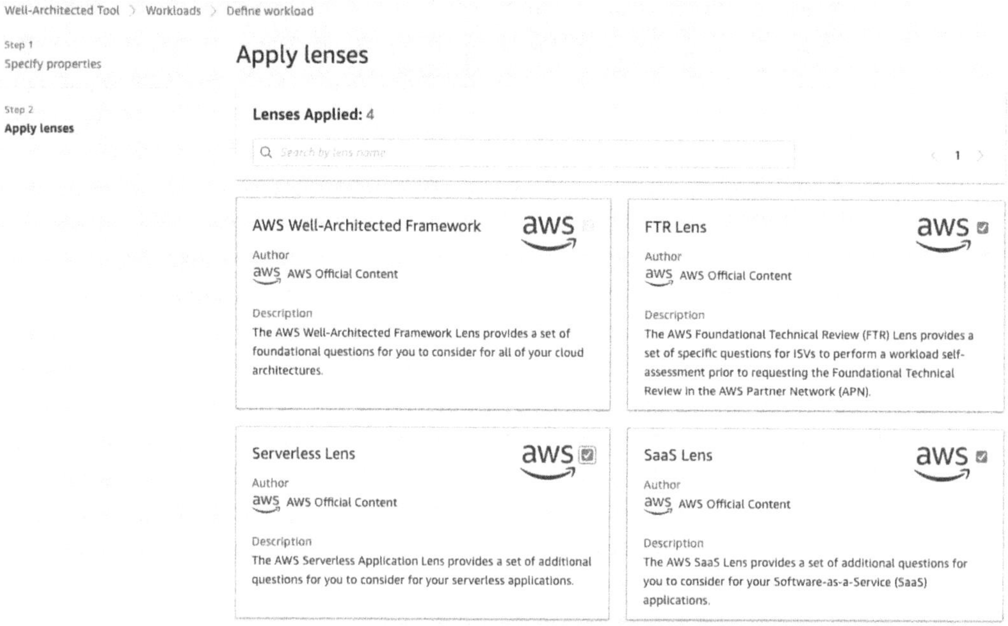

Figure 2.8: AWS Well-Architected Lenses

After applying a lens to your workload, you will get a best practice checklist specific to the domain; for example, the screenshot below shows a Well-Architected checklist for the Serverless Lens:

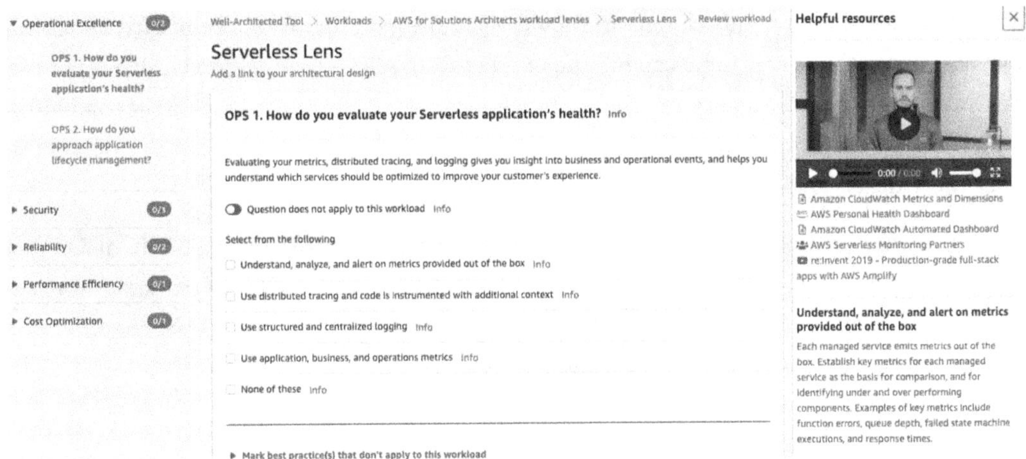

Figure 2.9: AWS Well-Architected Serverless Lens

As shown in the preceding screenshot, much like AWS's WAR tool where you saw six pillars in the previous section, each lens has questions related to 5 key pillars to validate workloads and identify HRIs.

AWS users must constantly evaluate their systems to ensure that they follow the recommended principles of the AWS Well-Architected Framework and AWS Well-Architected Lenses and that they comply with and follow architecture best practices. As you must be getting more curious about AWS by now, let's learn how to build your knowledge of the AWS cloud and establish yourself as a subject matter expert.

Building credibility and getting certified

It is hard to argue that the cloud is not an important technology shift. We have established that AWS is the clear market and thought leader in the cloud space.

Now, enterprises are eager to adopt cloud technologies because they do not want to fall behind their competition and become obsolete. Hopefully, by now, you are excited to learn more about AWS and other cloud providers, or at the very least, you're getting a little nervous and have a little FOMO yourself.

We will devote the rest of this chapter to showing you the path of least resistance for becoming an AWS guru and someone who can bill themselves as an AWS expert. As with other technologies, it is hard to become an expert without hands-on experience, and it's hard to get hands-on experience if you can't demonstrate that you're an expert. The best method, in my opinion, to crack this chicken-and-egg problem is to get certified.

Fortunately, AWS offers a wide array of certifications to demonstrate deep AWS knowledge and expertise to potential clients and employers. As AWS creates more and more services, they continue to offer new certificates aligned with these new services. The following are the available AWS certification listed on the AWS website as of April 2022.

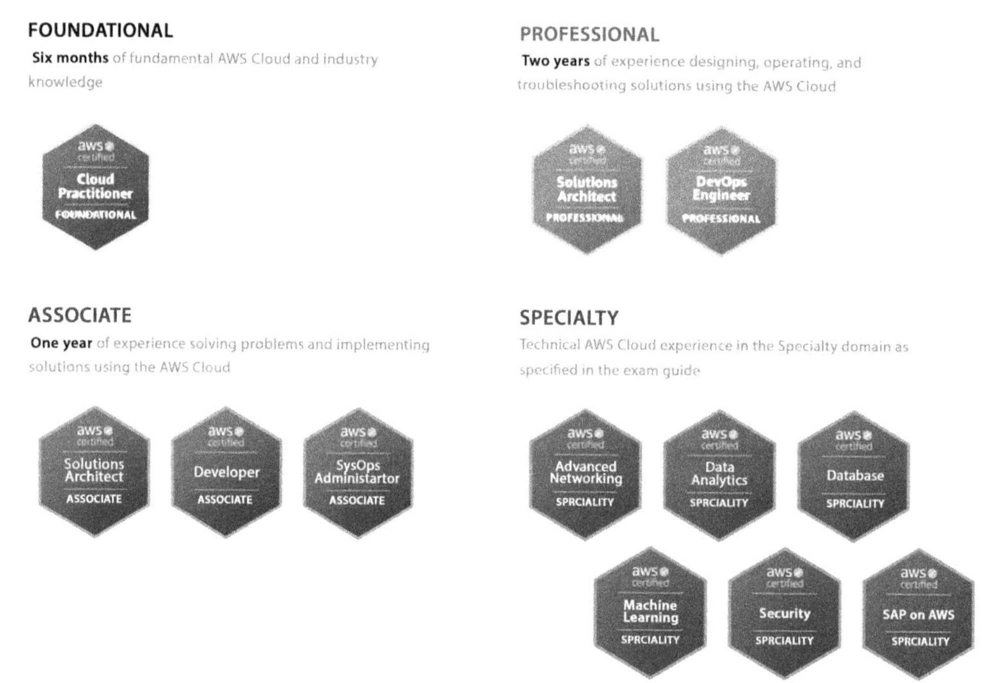

Figure 2.10: AWS certifications

In the screenshot above, you can see that AWS has certifications for everyone. If you are starting out or working in a non-tech domain, it's better to go for foundational certifications. To gain further knowledge, you can choose associated certifications and become an expert by gaining specialist and professional certifications.

AWS continuously updates existing certification exams to accommodate all new services and feature launches. Let's review the available certifications and how they fit into your career aspirations to enhance your current skills in the cloud.

Building a non-tech AWS cloud career

You may see working with the cloud as a very tech-savvy job. However, that is not always the case. Several cloud roles don't require deep technical knowledge; just a basic understanding will get your foot in the door to start a cloud career. For example, anyone from a sales and marketing background can thrive in cloud marketing, cloud business development, or a cloud sales role without deep technical knowledge. Similarly, program managers are required in any industry where basic cloud knowledge will help you get started in the role. However, it's recommended to build cloud foundation knowledge to prepare yourself better, which you can gain from an AWS Certified Cloud Practitioner certification. Let's look into more details.

AWS Certified Cloud Practitioner – Foundational

This is the most basic certification offered by AWS. It is meant to demonstrate a broad-stroke understanding of the core services and foundational knowledge of AWS. It is also a good certification for non-technical people that need to be able to communicate using the AWS lingo but are not necessarily going to be configuring or developing in AWS. This certification is ideal for demonstrating a basic understanding of AWS technologies for people such as salespeople, business analysts, marketing associates, executives, and project managers.

The AWS Solutions Architect path

Solutions architect is one of the most sought-after roles in the cloud industry. Often, solutions architects carry the responsibilities of designing a workload in the cloud and applying architecture best practices using the AWS Well-Architected Framework. The following AWS certifications can help you kick-start your career as an AWS cloud solutions architect.

AWS Certified Solutions Architect – Associate

IMPORTANT NOTE: On August 31st, 2022, a new version of the AWS Certified Solutions Architect - Associate exam became available.

This is the most popular certification offered by AWS. Many technically minded developers, architects, and administrators skip taking the Cloud Practitioner certification and start by taking this certification instead. If you are looking to demonstrate technical expertise in AWS, obtaining this certification is a good start and the bare minimum to demonstrate AWS proficiency. However, to demonstrate proficiency in architecting IT workloads in the AWS cloud, you should pursue the Solutions Architect – Professional certification as mentioned below.

AWS Certified Solutions Architect – Professional

This certification is one of the toughest to get and at least five to six times harder than the Associate-level certification. Earning this certification will demonstrate to employers that you have a deep and thorough understanding of AWS services, best practices, and optimal architectures based on the particular business requirements for a given project. Obtaining this certification shows potential employers that you are an expert in designing and creating distributed systems and applications on the AWS platform. It used to be that having at least one of the Associate-level certifications was a prerequisite to sitting for the Professional-level certifications, but AWS has eliminated that requirement.

You can refer to *Solution Architect's Handbook 2nd Edition* available on Amazon (`https://www.amazon.com/gp/product/1801816611`), for more details on the AWS solutions architect role and to gain in-depth knowledge of building use-case-focused architecture on the AWS platform.

DevOps is one of the key components for operationalizing any workload. Let's learn more about the DevOps path in AWS.

The AWS Cloud DevOps Engineer path

DevOps is a critical engineering function that makes a development team more agile by automating the deployment pipeline. Automation is key to adopting the cloud and using its full potential, where a DevOps engineer plays an essential role. Gaining the AWS certification can help you navigate the DevOps path with AWS.

AWS Certified SysOps Administrator – Associate

This certification will demonstrate to potential employers and clients that you have experience deploying, configuring, scaling up, managing, and migrating applications using AWS services. You should expect the difficulty level of this certification to be a little bit higher than the other Associate-level certifications, but also expect quite a bit of overlap in the type of questions that will be asked with this certification and the other Associate-level certifications.

AWS Certified DevOps Engineer – Professional

This advanced AWS certification validates knowledge on how to provision, manage, scale, and secure AWS resources and services. This certification will demonstrate to potential employers that you can run their DevOps operations and proficiently develop solutions and applications in AWS. This certification is more challenging than any Associate certification but easier than the AWS Solutions Architect Professional certification.

The AWS Cloud Developer path

Developers are central to any IT application. They are builders who bring life to ideas, making developers vital in the cloud. However, software developers are more focused on programming languages and algorithms but build software in the cloud; they need to be aware of various development tools that cloud providers facilitate. The following is the certification to gain the required cloud knowledge for building software in AWS.

AWS Certified Developer – Associate

Obtaining this certification will demonstrate your ability to design, develop, and deploy applications in AWS. Even though this is a developer certification, do not expect coding in any questions during the exam. However, knowing at least one programming language supported by AWS will help you achieve this certification. Expect to see many of the same concepts and similar questions to what you would see in the Solutions Architect certification. AWS doesn't have any professional certification for developers, but it is recommended to pursue AWS DevOps Engineer certifications to scale and operationalize your software application in the cloud.

While we have talked about the generalist career path in the cloud, several specialty paths are available where AWS has certifications to validate your knowledge. Let's look into the AWS certifications overview if you have expertise in a specific area.

The AWS Specialty Solutions Architect path

While generalist solutions architects design overall workloads, they need to dive deep into certain areas where more in-depth knowledge is required. In that case, specialist solutions architects come to the rescue; they provide their expertise to apply best practices for a specific domain such as security, networking, analytics, ML, etc. You have seen in the Well-Architected tool sections that AWS has domain-specific lenses to optimize specialty workloads and engage specialist solutions architects. The following are AWS certifications to validate your specialty knowledge in the AWS cloud.

AWS Certified Advanced Networking – Specialty

This AWS specialty certification demonstrates that you possess the skills to design and deploy AWS services as part of a comprehensive network architecture and the know-how to scale using best practices. This is one of the hardest certifications to obtain, like AWS Certified Solutions Architect – Professional. To pass the networking specialty exam, you have to put in additional effort.

For most exams, you go through online courses on famous learning platforms such as A Cloud Guru/Udemy and take practice exams before attending the actual exam. But for the networking specialty certification, that will not be enough. You need to go through other resources such as AWS whitepapers, blogs, and AWS re:Invent videos and take notes. You must review multiple resources until you are clear about concepts and keep revising your notes. We will discuss learning resources in more detail later in this chapter, under the *Learning tips and tricks for obtaining AWS certifications* section.

AWS Certified Security – Specialty

Possessing the AWS Certified Security – Specialty certification demonstrates to potential employers that you are well versed in AWS and the ins and outs of AWS security. It shows that you know security best practices for encryption at rest, encryption in transit, user authentication and authorization, and penetration testing, and are generally able to deploy AWS services and applications in a secure manner that aligns with your business requirements.

AWS Certified Machine Learning – Specialty

This is an excellent certification to have in your pocket if you are a data scientist or a data analyst. It shows potential employers that you are familiar with many of the core ML concepts and the AWS services that can be used to deliver ML and artificial intelligence projects.

AWS Certified Database – Specialty

Having this certification under your belt demonstrates to potential employers your mastery of the persistence services in AWS and your deep knowledge of the best practices needed to manage them. Some of the services tested are these:

- Amazon RDS
- Amazon Aurora
- Amazon Neptune
- Amazon DynamoDB
- Amazon QLDB
- Amazon DocumentDB

AWS Certified Data Analytics – Specialty

Completing this certification demonstrates to employers that you have a good understanding of the concepts needed to perform data analysis on petabyte-scale datasets. This certification shows your ability to design, implement, and deploy analytics solutions that deliver insights by enabling data visualization and implementing the appropriate security measures.

AWS Certified SAP – Specialty

SAP specialty is a new certification exam that became available starting in April 2022. The AWS SAP specialty certification is for SAP professionals to demonstrate their knowledge of the AWS cloud. It shows your ability to implement, migrate, and support SAP workloads in AWS using AWS's Well-Architected Framework.

While AWS continues to add new certifications to validate your cloud skills, they also retire old certifications that are not relevant over time; for example, AWS had a Big Data Specialty certification, which checked your knowledge of databases, ML, and analytics. Over time, as the use of databases and AI/ML increased, AWS launched separate certifications called AWS Database – Specialty and AWS Machine Learning – Specialty. In April 2020, AWS deprecated the Big Data – Specialty certification and renamed it the AWS Analytics – Specialty certification to focus just on data analytics services. Similarly, AWS retired the AWS Certified Alexa Skill Builder – Specialty exam on March 23, 2021.

Let's learn some tips and tricks for obtaining AWS certifications.

Learning tips and tricks for obtaining AWS certifications

Now that we have learned about the various certifications offered by AWS, let's learn about some of the strategies we can use to get these certifications with the least amount of work possible, and what we can expect as we prepare for these certifications.

Focus on one cloud provider

Some enterprises are trying to adopt a cloud-agnostic or multi-cloud strategy. The idea behind this strategy is not to depend on only one cloud provider. In theory, this seems like a good idea, and some companies such as Databricks, Snowflake, and Cloudera offer their wares to be run using the most popular cloud providers.

However, this agnosticism comes with some difficult choices. One way to implement this strategy is to choose the least common denominator, for example, only using compute instances so that workloads can be deployed on various cloud platforms. Implementing this approach means that you cannot use the more advanced services offered by cloud providers. For example, using AWS Lambda in a cloud-agnostic fashion is quite tricky.

Another way that a multi-cloud strategy can be implemented is by using more advanced services, but this means that your staff will have to know how to use these services for all the cloud providers you decide to use. You will be a *jack of all trades and a master of none*, to use the common refrain.

Similarly, it isn't easy to be a cloud expert across vendors individually. It is recommended to pick one cloud provider and try to become an expert on that one stack. AWS, Azure, and GCP, to name the most popular options, offer an immense amount of services that continuously change and get enhanced, and they keep adding more services. Keeping up with one of these providers is not an easy task. Keeping up with all three, in my opinion, is close to impossible. Pick one and dominate it.

Focus on the Associate-level certifications

As we mentioned before, there's quite a bit of overlap between the Associate-level certifications. In addition, the jump in difficulty between the Associate-level certificates and the Professional-level ones is quite steep.

It's highly recommended to sit for at least two, if not all three, of the Associate-level certifications before attempting the Professional-level certifications. Not only will this method prepare you for the Professional certifications but having multiple Associate certifications will also make you stand out against others that only have one Associate-level certificate.

Get experience wherever you can

AWS recommends having one year of experience before taking the Associate-level certifications and two years of experience before sitting for the Professional-level certifications. This may seem like a *catch-22* situation. How can you get experience if you are not certified? However, it's a recommendation and not a mandatory requirement. This means that you can gain experience in training and study for the exam. You can do your project using an AWS Free Tier account with a pretty decent number of services available in the first year, and you can gain good hands-on experience.

The best way to get certified

Before we get to the best way to get certified, let's look at the worst way. Amazon offers extremely comprehensive documentation. You can find this documentation here: `https://docs.aws.amazon.com/`.

AWS docs are a great place to help you troubleshoot issues you may encounter when you are directly working with AWS services or perhaps to size the services you will be using correctly. However, they are not a good place to study for exams. It will get overwhelming quickly, and much of the material you will learn about will not be covered in the exams.

The better way to get certified is to use the training materials that AWS specifically provides for certification, starting with the roadmaps of what will be covered in each certification. These roadmaps are a good first step toward understanding the scope of each exam.

You can begin to learn about all these roadmaps, or learning paths, as AWS likes to call them, here: `https://aws.amazon.com/training/learning-paths/`.

You will find free online courses and paid intensive training sessions for these learning paths. While the paid classes may be helpful, they are not mandatory for you to pass the exam.

Before you look at the learning paths, the first place to find out the scope of each certification is the study guides available for each certification. In these study guides, you will learn at a high level what will and what won't be covered for each exam. For example, the study guide for the AWS Cloud Practitioner Certification can be found here: `https://d1.awsstatic.com/training-and-certification/docs-cloud-practitioner/AWS-Certified-Cloud-Practitioner_Exam-Guide.pdf`.

Now, while the training provided by AWS may be sufficient to pass the exams, and I know plenty of folks that have passed the certifications using only those resources, there are plenty of third-party companies that specialize in training people with a special focus on the certifications. The choices are almost endless. Let's look at a few more resources here.

Getting started in AWS

AWS launched the Skill Builder portal (`https://explore.skillbuilder.aws/`), which enhances AWS's training portal.

AWS Skill Builder has thousands of self-paced digital training sessions and learning paths, as shown below.

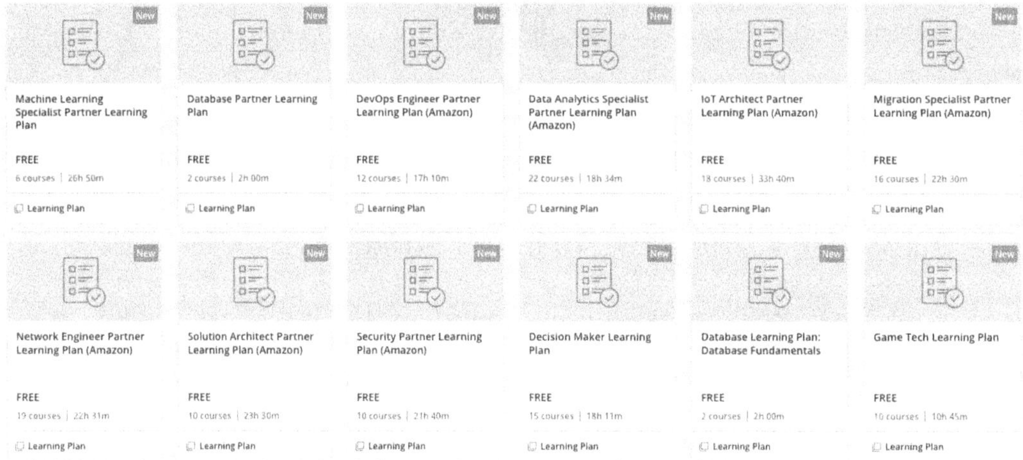

Figure 2.11: AWS Skill Builder learning paths

You can pick any learning path you need and explore related digital courses. If you want classroom training, that is available in the AWS training portal; however, it may come with a price. AWS provides free cloud practitioner training in its Skills Center, where you can register and get instructor-led training for free. AWS has also opened its first free training center located in Seattle and is planning to expand in the coming months. If you have Skills Centers where you are, you can benefit by registering on the AWS website directly: `https://aws.amazon.com/training/skills-centers/`.

Online courses

In addition to the courses provided by AWS, other training organizations and independent content creators provide excellent courses for obtaining AWS certifications.

A Cloud Guru

A Cloud Guru has been around since 2015, which is a long time in cloud years. A Cloud Guru has courses for most of the AWS certifications. They have a few other courses unrelated to certifications that are also quite good. Linux Academy used to be another good resource to use to prepare for a certification exam, but that got acquired by A Cloud Guru, which means now you can access the best of these in one place.

They used to charge by the course, but a few years back, they changed their model to a monthly subscription, and signing up for it gives you access to the whole site. The training can be accessed here: `https://acloud.guru/`.

Udemy courses

Several independent content creators on Udemy, such as Stephane Maarek and Jon Bonso, have excellent content and are passionate about AWS, with a growing following. For example, as of April 2022, Stephane Maarek's Solution Architect Associate course has over half a million students with over 120,000 ratings and a satisfaction rating of 4.7 stars out of 5.

The pricing model used is also similar to Whizlabs. The practice exams are sold separately from the online courses. You can choose the pricing, from a monthly subscription to a course fee, depending on your strategy, such as if you want to get an individual certification or target multiple/all AWS certifications.

You can also explore other training providers such as Cloud Academy and Coursera. However, you don't need to sign up for multiple course providers.

YouTube videos

As always, YouTube is an excellent source of free learning. AWS has its own YouTube channel with nearly 600,000 subscribers and 14,000 videos. These videos cover AWS services by AWS product managers and solutions architects. AWS uploads all re:Invent and summit videos on the YouTube channel, the best resources to dive deep into any services. You can find several playlists people have created to prepare for certifications.

Books

If you are a book reader, there are multiple AWS certification-related books available on Amazon, which you can refer to prepare for the exam. If you are preparing for the AWS Solutions Architect – Professional exam and are solidifying concepts, refer to *Solution Architect's Handbook* (`https://www.amazon.com/gp/product/1801816611`). It explains multiple architectural patterns using the AWS platform and goes deep into using each of the Well-Architected pillars to apply architectural best practices.

Practice exam websites

It doesn't matter how much you are reading or how many courses you watch, there are always knowledge gaps, and practice exams are the best sources to identify and focus on weak areas. Let's look at some practice exam resources.

AWS practice question sets

AWS recently launched practice question sets for all the certifications in their Skill Builder portal. These are the AWS certification official practice question sets featuring 20 questions developed by AWS to demonstrate the style of AWS certification exams. These exam-style questions include detailed feedback and recommended resources to help you prepare for your exam. It is an excellent source to understand exam patterns and difficulty levels.

The following is a sample list, which you can access using the link `https://explore.skillbuilder.aws/learn` and select the filter **Exam Preparation** under **Training Category**.

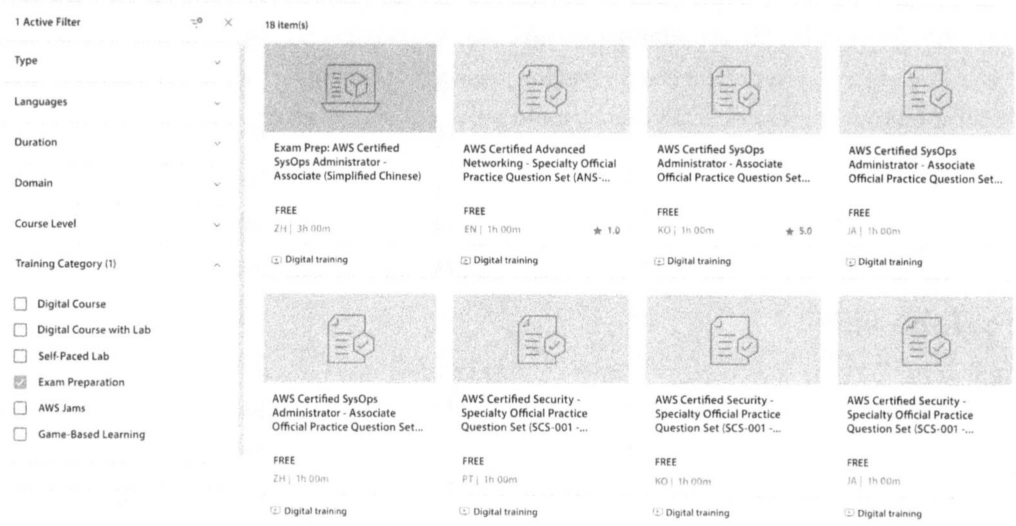

Figure 2.12: AWS certification practice question sets

There are free practice exams available for almost all available certifications. Let's look at more third-party resources for more practice exam choices.

Whizlabs

Whizlabs (`https://www.whizlabs.com/`) is suitable for Associate-level certification and testing your knowledge in multiple areas to find weak points. Whizlabs also provides answers with detailed explanations and associated resources that can help you fill any knowledge gaps by exploring related content against questions you got wrong.

Whizlabs divides the charges for their training between their online courses and their practice tests. One disadvantage of Whizlabs is that, unlike the exam simulator with A Cloud Guru, where they have a bank of questions and randomly combine them, the Whizlabs exam questions are fixed and cannot be shuffled to create a different exam.

They also have a free version of their practice exams for most certifications, with 20 free questions.

BrainCert

Like Whizlabs, you can use BrainCert for AWS Professional and Specialty level certification (`https://www.braincert.com`). They have a perfect set of questions that are similar to the exam's difficulty level with detailed explanations for each answer. While Whizlabs practice exams have lifetime validity, BrainCert provides only one-year validity.

Tutorials Dojo

Tutorials Dojo is another good practice exam website you can access by visiting `https://tutorialsdojo.com/`. It has recently received great reviews from the cert community and has good-quality questions for AWS Specialty certification exams.

The same strategy as mentioned before can be used with Whizlabs or BrainCert. You don't need to sign up for multiple vendors for the more straightforward exams, but you can combine a couple for the harder exams.

Certification preparation approach

Video courses such as Udemy and A Cloud Guru are used the most to prepare for certifications. The following is the recommendation for tackling the training:

- Unless you have previous experience with the covered topics, watch all the training videos at least once. If it's a topic you feel comfortable with, you can play the videos at a higher speed, and then you will be able to watch the full video faster.
- For video lessons that you find difficult, watch them again. You don't have to watch all the videos again – only the ones that you found difficult.
- Make notes of topics that seem to be pretty new to you. Writing notes always clears your thoughts.
- Make sure to take any end-of-section quizzes, wherever available.
- Once you finish watching the videos, the next step is to attempt some practice exams.

The above recommendation remains true if you are choosing books for your exam preparation, where you want to take notes and re-visit chapters where the topic is new to you.

Finally, keep taking practice exams until you feel confident and consistently correctly answer a high percentage of the questions (anywhere between 80% and 85%, depending on the certification).

The questions provided in the exam simulator will not be the same as the ones from the exam, but they will be of a similar difficulty level, and they will all be in the same domains and often about similar concepts and topics.

By using the exam simulator, you will achieve a couple of things. First, you will be able to gauge your progress and determine whether you are ready for the exam. I suggest you keep taking the exam simulator tests until you consistently score at least 85% or above. Most real certifications require you to answer 75% of the questions correctly, so consistently scoring a little higher should ensure that you pass the exam.

Some of the exams, such as the Security – Specialty exam, require a higher percentage of correct answers, so you should adjust accordingly. Using the exam simulator will also enable you to figure out which domains you are weak in. After taking a whole exam in the simulator, you will get a list detailing exactly which questions you got right and which were wrong, and they will all be classified by domain.

So, if you get a low score in a certain domain, you know that's the domain that you need to focus on when you go back and review the videos again. Lastly, you will be able to learn new concepts by simply taking the tests in the exam simulator.

Now, let's address some of the questions that frequently arise while preparing to take these certifications.

Some frequently asked questions about the AWS certifications

While preparing for certifications, you may have several questions, like where to start and how to finish. The following sections will list frequently asked questions that often come to mind.

How long will it take to get certified?

A question frequently asked is how many months you should study for before sitting down for the exam. Look at that in terms of hours instead of months.

As you can imagine, you will be able to take the exam a lot sooner if you study for 2 hours every day instead of only studying for 1 hour a week. If you decide to take some AWS-sponsored intensive full-day or multi-day training, that may go a long way toward shortening the cycle.

One way to optimize your time is instead of watching videos, you can listen to them in the car or while on the train going into the city. Even though watching them is much more beneficial, you can still embed key concepts while listening to them, and that time would have been dead time anyway.

You don't want to space out the time between study sessions too much. If you do that, you may find yourself in a situation where you start forgetting what you have learned. The number of hours it will take you will also depend on your previous experience. If you are working with AWS for your day job, that will shorten the number of hours needed to complete your studies.

The following subsections will give you an idea of the amount of time you should spend preparing for each exam.

The Cloud Practitioner certification

Preparing for this certification typically takes between 15 and 25 hours. Achieving this credential will help you develop skills and acquire critical knowledge related to implementing cloud initiatives. By earning the AWS Certified Cloud Practitioner certification, you can demonstrate your fluency with the cloud and validate your foundational knowledge of AWS.

Associate-level certifications

If you don't have previous AWS experience, plan to spend between 70 and 100 hours preparing. Also, keep in mind that there is considerable overlap between the other certifications once you pass one of the Associate certifications. It will not take another 70 to 100 hours to obtain the second and third certifications. As mentioned in this chapter, it is highly recommended to take the two other Associate-level certifications soon after passing the first one.

Expect to spend another 20 to 40 hours studying for the two remaining certifications if you don't wait too long to take them after passing the first one.

Professional-level certifications

There is quite a leap between the Associate-level certifications and the Professional-level certifications. The domain coverage will be similar, but you will need to know how to use the AWS services covered in much more depth, and the questions will certainly be harder. Assuming you took at least one of the Associate-level certifications, expect to spend another 70 to 100 hours watching videos, reading, and taking practice tests to pass this exam.

AWS removed the requirement of having to take the Associate-level certifications before being able to sit for the Professional-level certifications. However, it is still probably a good idea to take at least some Associate exams before taking the Professional-level exams.

As is the case with the Associate-level exams, once you pass one of the Professional-level exams, it should take much less study time to prepare for another Professional exam as long as you don't wait too long to take the second exam and forget everything.

Specialty certifications

I am lumping all the Specialty certifications under one subheading, but there is significant variability in the difficulty level between all the Specialty certifications. If you have a background in networking, you will be more comfortable with the Advanced Networking certification than with the Data Science certification.

When it comes to these certifications, you may be better off focusing on your area of expertise unless you are collecting all certifications. For example, if you are a data scientist, the Machine Learning – Specialty certification and Analytics certification may be your best bet.

Depending on your experience, expect to spend about these amounts of time:

- Security – Specialty – 40 to 60 hours
- SAP – Specialty – 40 to 60 hours
- Machine Learning – Specialty – 50 to 70 hours
- Data Analytics – Specialty– 40 to 60 hours
- Database – Specialty – 30 to 50 hours
- Advanced Networking – Specialty – 50 to 70 hours

How to request additional exam time

An additional 30 minutes can make a lot of difference between passing and failing exams, especially when sitting for more challenging exams such as AWS Professional and Specialty certifications. An essential tip for **non-native English speakers** is that you can request an extra 30 minutes to complete the exam. Take the following steps to get an additional 30 minutes:

1. Click on the home page of your CertMetrics account: `https://www.certmetrics.com/amazon/`
2. On the right, click the **Request Exam Accommodations** button

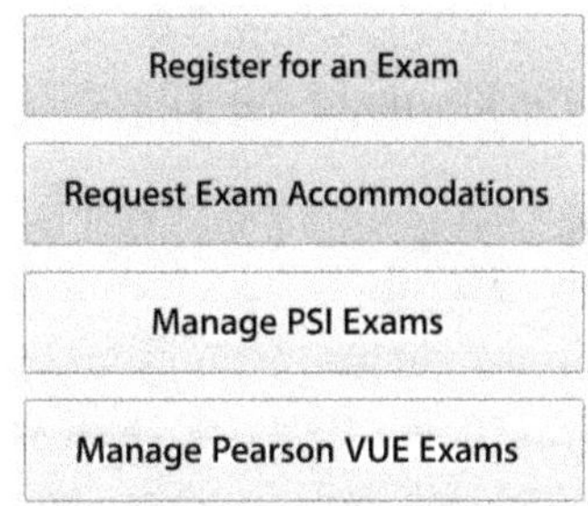

Figure 2.13: Request Exam Accommodations button

3. Click the **Request Accommodation** button
4. Select **ESL +30 Minutes** from the accommodation dropdown
5. Click **Create** and you will see the following approval request available under the **Exam Registration** tab

Accommodation	Status	Expires	Download Documentation	
ESL +30 MINUTES	Approved			Edit

Figure 2.14: Exam Registration tab

Make sure to apply for the accommodation before scheduling your exam as it won't be applicable to already scheduled exams. It's a one-time activity and applies to all future exam registrations after getting approval.

What are some last-minute tips for the day of the exam?

AWS offers two exam modes: remote and on-site at an AWS authorized exam center. When taking an AWS certification exam at a testing center, the on-site staff will help with check-in, exam access on test center computers, and will answer any questions. On the other hand, with online exam proctoring, you can take the same exam with the same allotted time as you would in a testing center, but on your own computer. During the exam, a proctor will remotely monitor your progress.

A decent half marathon time is about 90 minutes, which is how long you get to take the Associate-level exams, and a good marathon time is about 3 hours, which is how long you get to take the Professional-level exams.

Keeping focus for that amount of time is not easy. For that reason, you should be well rested when you take the exam. It is highly recommended to take the exam on a day when you don't have too many other responsibilities; I would not take it after working a full day. You will be too burned out.

Make sure you have a light meal before the exam – enough so that you are not hungry during the test and feel energetic, but not so much that you feel sleepy from digesting all that food.

Just as you wouldn't want to get out of the gate too fast or too slow in a race, keep pace yourself during the exam. You also don't want to be beholden to the clock, checking it constantly. The clock will always appear in the top-right part of the exam, but you want to avoid looking at it most of the time. I recommend writing down on the three sheets you will receive where you should be after every 20 questions and checking the clock against these numbers only when you have answered 20 questions. This way, you will be able to adjust if you are going too fast or too slow, but you will not spend excessive time watching the clock.

The above is just a recommendation, however; everyone has their own strategy which you can build when practicing the exam. Apply whatever strategy best fits your style. Let's now summarize what we have learned in this chapter.

Summary

This chapter pieced together many of the technologies, best practices, and AWS services covered in the book. We weaved it all together into AWS's Well-Architected Framework, which you should be able to leverage and use for your projects.

You learned about AWS's Well-Architected Framework and how to use the AWS Well-Architected tool to validate your architecture against AWS-provided best practices. All workloads are not the same, and you learned about AWS's Well-Architected Lenses focusing on specific workloads.

After reviewing the architecture best practices, you have hopefully convinced yourself to hop aboard the cloud train. One of the easiest ways to build credibility is to get certified. We learned that AWS offers 12 certifications. We learned that the most basic one is AWS Cloud Practitioner and that the most advanced certifications are the Professional-level certifications. In addition, as of 2022, we learned that there are six Specialty certifications for various domains. We also covered some of the best and worst ways to obtain these certifications.

Finally, we hope you are now curious enough to potentially get at least some of AWS's certifications. I hope you are excited about the possibilities that AWS can bring.

The next chapter will cover how the AWS infrastructure is organized and how you can leverage the cloud to drive digital transformation initiatives.

3

Leveraging the Cloud for Digital Transformation

AWS has come a long way since Amazon started in 2006 when it offered just two primary services. In this chapter, you will begin by understanding cloud computing models. Further, you will learn the differences between **Software as a Service** (**SaaS**), **Platform as a Service** (**PaaS**), and **Infrastructure as a Service** (**IaaS**) and how AWS complements each model with its services and infrastructure. You will also learn how today's businesses use AWS to transform their technology infrastructure, operations, and business practices completely.

In this chapter, we will cover the following topics:

- Cloud computing models: PaaS, IaaS, and SaaS
- Cloud migration strategy
- Implementing a digital transformation program
- The **AWS Cloud Adoption Framework** (**AWS CAF**)
- Architectures to provide high availability, reliability, and scalability

Without further ado, let's get down to business and learn about terms commonly used to specify how much of your infrastructure will live in the cloud versus how much will stay on-premises.

Cloud computing models

Cloud computing allows organizations to focus on their core business and leave unwanted work like IT infrastructure capacity planning, procurement, and maintenance to cloud providers.

As cloud computing has grown exponentially in recent years, different models and strategies have surfaced to help meet the specific needs of organizations as per their user base. Each type of cloud computing model provides you with additional flexibility and management.

There are many ways to classify cloud services, and understanding the differences between them helps you decide what set of services is suitable for your application workload. In this section, we will cover a common classification. Cloud services can be categorized as follows:

- **Infrastructure as a Service** (**IaaS**)
- **Platform as a Service** (**PaaS**)
- **Software as a Service** (**SaaS**)

As the names indicate, each model provides a service at a different stack level.

Each of these solutions has its advantages and disadvantages. It is essential to fully understand these tradeoffs to select the best option for your organization:

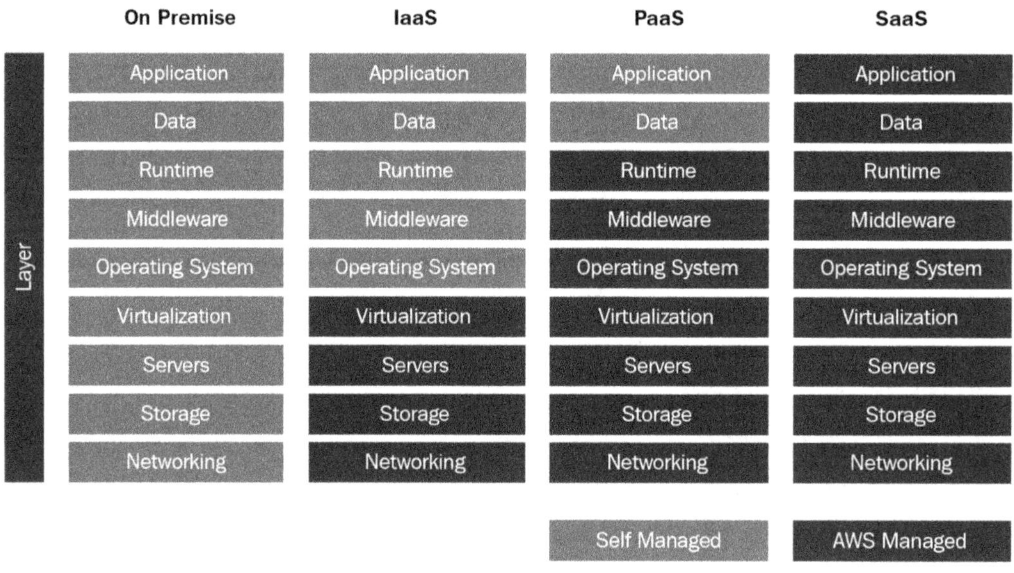

Figure 3.1: Cloud service classification

As you can see in the preceding figure, the amount of services managed by yourself or AWS determines how the stack will be classified. On one extreme, we have an on-premises environment, where all the infrastructure is located in your own data center. On the other extreme, we have a SaaS architecture, where all the infrastructure is located on the cloud.

The following sections will explore the advantages and disadvantages of using each and examples of services under each classification.

Understanding IaaS

Cloud infrastructure services, also known as **IaaS**, comprise highly flexible, fault-tolerant compute and storage resources. IaaS provides access, complete management, and monitoring of compute, storage, networking, and other miscellaneous services. IaaS enables enterprises to use resources on an *as-needed* basis, so they don't need to purchase equipment.

IaaS leverages virtualization technology. AWS allows you to quickly provision hardware through the AWS console using the **Command-Line Interface** (**CLI**) or an API, among other methods. By using an IaaS platform, a business can provide a whole host of resources and functionality with its current infrastructure without the headache of physically maintaining it. From a user perspective, they need to be aware that the backend services are being provided by an IaaS platform instead of a company-owned data center.

As you saw in *Figure 3.1*, when using the IaaS solution, you are responsible for managing more aspects of the stack, such as applications, runtime, operating systems, middleware, and data. However, in these cases, AWS will manage servers, hard drives, networking, virtualization, databases, and file storage.

You will now learn the advantages and disadvantages of IaaS services and look at some IaaS use cases; finally, you will see some examples of IaaS offerings.

Advantages of IaaS

In the IaaS model, you have maximum control, which means you can achieve the required flexibility as per your application's needs. These are the advantages of using the IaaS model:

- It offers the most flexibility of all the cloud models.
- Provisioning of compute, storage, and networking resources can be done quickly.
- Resources can be used for a few minutes, hours, or days.
- Complete control of the infrastructure.
- Highly scalable and fault-tolerant.

Disadvantages of IaaS

In the IaaS model, having more control means putting additional effort into maintaining, monitoring, and scaling infrastructure. However, there are disadvantages to the IaaS model, some of which, such as data encryption and security issues, vendor lock-in, potential cost overruns, and configuration issues, are also applicable to SaaS and PaaS solutions. More specifically, the disadvantages of IaaS include the following:

- **Security**: In this case, customers have much more control over the stack, and for this reason, it is highly critical that they have a comprehensive plan in place for security. Since customers manage applications, data, middleware, and the operating system, there are possible security threats, such as if certain ports are left open, and intruders guess which ports are open. Attacks from insiders with unauthorized access and system vulnerabilities can expose data between the backend servers and VMs from nefarious sources.
- **Legacy systems**: While customers can migrate legacy applications into AWS, the older hardware may need help to provide the needed functionality to secure the legacy applications. Modifications to older applications may be required, potentially creating new security issues unless the application is thoroughly tested for new security vulnerabilities.
- **Training costs**: As with any new technology, training may be needed for the customer's staff to get familiar with the new infrastructure. The customer is ultimately responsible for securing their data and resources, computer backups, and business continuity. With this training, it may be easier to secure the necessary staff to support and maintain the new infrastructure.

Let's look at some use cases where you may want to use the IaaS model.

Use cases for IaaS

IaaS is best suited to certain scenarios. This is also true for SaaS and PaaS, as we will see in upcoming sections. IaaS is most suitable when enterprises want more control over their infrastructure. Some of the most common instances when IaaS is used are as follows:

- Backups and snapshots
- Disaster recovery
- Web hosting
- Software development environments
- Data analytics

IaaS provides more flexibility to organizations with granular control; however, that comes with the price of resource management overhead, and you may need help to realize the actual value of the cloud. Let's look at some examples of IaaS services provided by AWS.

Examples of AWS IaaS services

These are a few of the IaaS services offered by AWS:

- **Elastic Compute Cloud (EC2)**: One of the most popular services in AWS. EC2 is essentially a server on the cloud.
- **Elastic Block Storage (EBS)**: Amazon EBS is block-level storage. You can think of it as a **SAN (Storage Area Network)** drive on the cloud.
- **Elastic File Storage (EFS)**: Amazon EFS is file-level storage. You can think of it as a **NAS (Network Attached Storage)** drive on the cloud.

There are many other AWS IaaS services that you will learn about through this book. Now, let's learn about **Software as a Service (SaaS)**.

Understanding SaaS

SaaS, or *cloud application services*, are services where the cloud provider does most of the heavy lifting (in this case, AWS). As you saw in *Figure 3.1*, you will not have to install software or worry about the operating system or software patches for SaaS. Your focus will be on customizing the application's business logic and supporting your users. Most SaaS systems will only need browser access as most of the computation will be done on the cloud side.

SaaS eliminates the need for your staff to visit individuals' devices regarding software installation. Cloud providers such as AWS are fully responsible for any issues on the server, middleware, operating system, and storage levels. Let's now analyze the characteristics that make up SaaS, the advantages and disadvantages of using a SaaS deployment, and some examples.

Characteristics of SaaS

These are the clues that will help determine if a service is SaaS:

- It is managed by the vendor (such as AWS).
- It is hosted on a third-party server.
- It can be accessed over the internet.
- AWS manages applications, infrastructure, operating systems, software patches, and updates.

These characteristics make SaaS unique compared to other models and help organizations offload the burden of infrastructure management to cloud providers such as AWS. Let's look at some more advantages of the SaaS model.

Advantages of SaaS

SaaS has several advantages:

- Reducing the time, money, and effort spent on repetitive tasks
- Shifting the responsibility for installing, patching, configuring, and upgrading software across the service to a third party
- Allowing you to focus on the tasks that require more personalized attention, such as providing customer service to your user base

A SaaS solution allows you to get up and running efficiently. This option, versus the other two solutions, requires the least effort. This option enables companies big and small to launch services quickly and finish a project on time.

Disadvantages of SaaS

SaaS solutions have some limitations as well:

- **Interoperability**: Interoperability with other services may be complex. For example, if you need integration with an on-premises application, it may be more complicated to perform this integration. Most likely, your on-premises installation uses a different interface, complicating the integration. Your on-premises environment is an assortment of technology from different vendors, making it challenging to integrate. In contrast, before you spin up your first service, AWS goes to great lengths and performs rigorous testing to ensure that services interoperate and integrate smoothly.
- **Customization**: The convenience of having a vendor such as AWS manage many things for you comes at a price. Opportunities for customization in a SaaS solution will not be as great as with other services that are further down in the stack. For example, an on-premises solution that offers complete control of all levels in the stack will allow full customization. In your on-premises environment, you install the patch if there is a requirement to use a particular version of Linux with a specific security patch. In contrast, installing a particular version of Linux is impossible if you use AWS Lambda as your deployment environment. In fact, with AWS Lambda, the operating system being used under the covers is transparent to you.

- **Lack of control:** If your organization requires that you only use a particular approved version of an operating system, this may not be appropriate. For example, there might be a regulatory requirement requiring detailed testing approval of the underlying operating systems, and if the version is changed, a retest and approval are required. In this case, SaaS will most likely not be an acceptable solution. In a SaaS environment, you have non-deterministic latency issues. In other words, controlling how long your processes will take requires a lot of work.
- **Limited features:** If the SaaS solution you are using does not offer a feature you require, you might only be able to use that feature if the SaaS vendor provides that feature in the future.

Use cases for SaaS

SaaS is best suited for scenarios when you want to use out-of-the-box applications without managing application code or IT infrastructure. You may choose a SaaS solution when you don't see a return on investment for building the platform due to a small number of users, or when you need in-house expertise. Some of the most common instances when SaaS is used are as follows:

- Payroll applications such as ADP
- **Customer Relationship Management (CRM)** solutions such as Salesforce
- Workplace collaboration solutions, including Zoom, Cisco Webex, Amazon Chime, Microsoft Teams, Slack, etc.
- Office management solutions such as Microsoft Office 365
- Workspace solutions, including Amazon WorkSpaces, Google Workspace, Microsoft Workspace, etc.

SaaS reduces the risk for organizations as all the application development and maintenance work is offloaded to vendors. Let's look at some examples of SaaS services provided by AWS.

Examples of AWS SaaS solutions

Some of the services that AWS offers that could be classified as SaaS solutions are as follows:

- **Amazon Connect:** Amazon Connect is a cloud-based contact center that offers businesses a cost-effective solution to deliver exceptional customer service across various communication channels with ease. It leverages Amazon's innovative AI & ML technologies directly in Amazon Connect without having to manage complex integrations. By utilizing Amazon Lex, you can create voice and text chatbots that enhance contact center efficiency. Similarly, Contact Lens for Amazon Connect can aid in comprehending the tone and patterns of customer interactions, while Amazon Connect Wisdom can minimize the amount of time agents spend searching for solutions.

- **Amazon WorkSpaces**: This allows system administrators to provide virtual Microsoft Windows or Linux **Virtual Desktop Infrastructure** (**VDI**) for their users. It obviates the need to purchase, procure, and deploy hardware and eliminates the need to install the software. Administrators can add or remove users as the organization changes. Users can access their VDIs from various supported devices and web browsers. With Amazon WorkSpaces, you no longer have to visit every machine to install commonly used software such as Microsoft Office and other security software. Amazon WorkSpaces enables virtual environments for your users where this software is already installed, and all they need is access to a browser.
- **Amazon QuickSight**: This business intelligence and analytics service creates charts and visualizations, performs ad hoc analysis, and obtains business insights. It seamlessly integrates with other AWS services to automatically discover AWS data sources.
- **Amazon Chime**: Similar to Slack and Zoom, Amazon Chime can be used for online meetings, video conferencing and calls, online chat, and sharing content.

Above are a few examples of SaaS solutions provided by AWS; however, AWS relies on its partner network to build SaaS solutions using AWS-provided services and published in AWS Marketplace for customers to purchase. Let's look at some third-party SaaS solutions.

Examples of third-party SaaS solutions

Many third-party vendors, including some that offer their services on AWS Marketplace, are SaaS solutions. There are multiple examples, but here are a few that decided to build their SaaS offerings on AWS:

- **Splunk**: A software platform that enables search, aggregation, analysis, and visualizations of machine-generated data collected from disparate sources such as websites, mobile apps, sensors, and IoT devices.
- **Sendbird**: A chat solution specializing in real-time chat and messaging development for mobile apps and websites. It provides client-side SDKs in various languages, a user-friendly dashboard, and moderation tools.
- **Twilio**: A company that offers various ways to securely communicate with customers, including email, SMS, fax, voice, chat, and video. Whenever you get an SMS to prove your identity when you log into your bank account, there is a decent chance that Twilio was involved in the process.

This concludes the SaaS section. The following section will cover PaaS, another common paradigm in cloud deployments.

Understanding PaaS

Defining a SaaS service is easy. If AWS manages everything, it's a SaaS service. The same applies to a definition of an on-premises service. If you manage everything on your infrastructure, it's clear you have an on-premises service. As you begin going up and down the stack and start taking over some of the components' management or offloading some of the management, the line starts getting fuzzy. We'll still try to provide you with a definition for PaaS.

An initial definition could be this: any application where you are responsible for the maintenance of some of the software and some of the configuration data. More formally, **Platform as a Service (PaaS)** is a cloud computing service that supplies an environment to enable its users to develop, run, and manage data and applications without worrying about the complexity associated with provisioning, configuring, and maintaining the infrastructure. These complexities come in the IaaS model, where you are responsible for creating applications, including the servers, storage, and networking equipment.

As you saw in *Figure 3.1*, PaaS is like SaaS in some ways. Still, instead of providing services to end-users that do not need to be technically savvy to use the software, PaaS delivers a platform for developers to potentially use the PaaS service to develop SaaS solutions.

PaaS enables developers to design and create applications while operating at a very high level of abstraction and focusing primarily on business rules and user requirements. These applications, sometimes called middleware, can be highly scalable and available if developed appropriately. Let's take an example of a PaaS service called Amazon **Relational Database Service (RDS)**, where AWS provides managed relational databases such as Oracle, MS SQL, PostgreSQL, and MariaDB in the cloud. AWS handles database engine installation, patching, backup, recovery, repair, etc. You need to build a schema and store your data as per business needs.

Like SaaS, PaaS takes advantage of virtualization technology. Resources can be started or shut down depending on demand. Additionally, AWS offers a wide selection of services to support PaaS applications' design, development, testing, and deployment, such as AWS Amplify to develop web and mobile apps.

Let's now look into the advantages and disadvantages of PaaS, some use cases for PaaS, and some examples of services that are considered PaaS services.

Advantages of PaaS

It doesn't matter if you are a three-person start-up or a well-established multinational; using PaaS provides many benefits, such as:

- Cost-effective and continuous development, testing, and deployment of applications, as you don't need to manage the underlying infrastructure
- High availability and scalability
- Straightforward customization and configuration of an application
- Reduction in development effort and maintenance
- Security policy simplification and automation

Now that you've learned about the PaaS model's pros, let's consider some cons.

Disadvantages of PaaS

PaaS solutions have some limitations as well:

- **Integrations**: Having multiple parties responsible for the technology stack creates complexity in how integrations must be performed when developing applications. That becomes particularly problematic when legacy services are on-premises and are not scheduled to be moved to the cloud soon. One of the reasons enterprises like to minimize the number of technology vendors is not to allow these vendors to be able to point fingers at each other when something goes wrong. When something invariably goes wrong, enterprises know precisely who they must contact to fix the problem.
- **Data security**: The data will reside in a third-party environment when running applications using a PaaS solution. This poses concerns and risks. There might also be regulatory requirements to be met to store data in a third-party environment. Customers might have policies that limit or prohibit the storage of data *off-site*. For example, China recently passed regulations that require **Personally Identifiable Information** (**PII**) generated in China not to leave China. More specifically, if you capture your customer's email on your site and your site is available in China, the servers that store the email must reside in China, and that email cannot leave the country. Using a PaaS approach to comply with this regulation requires standing up full-fledged infrastructure mimicking your existing infrastructure in other locations.
- **Runtime issues**: PaaS solutions may not support the language and framework that your application may require. For example, if you need an old version of a Java runtime, you might not be able to use it because it may no longer be supported.

- **Legacy system customization**: Existing legacy applications and services might require more integration work. Instead, complex customization and configuration needs to be done for legacy applications to integrate with the PaaS service properly. The result might yield a non-trivial implementation that may minimize the value provided by your PaaS solution. For example, many corporations rely on mainframes for at least some of their needs. If they wanted to move these mainframe applications to the cloud, they would have to rewrite the applications that do not require a mainframe since mainframes are not one of the types of hardware that most typical cloud providers support.
- **Operational limitations**: Even though you have control of some of the layers in the PaaS stack, other layers are controlled and maintained by AWS. If the AWS layers need to be customized, you have little or no control over these optimizations. For example, if you are required to use a particular operating system but your PaaS provider does not support it, you are stuck with choosing one from the list of available operating systems.

Let's look at when it makes sense to use the PaaS model in more detail.

PaaS use cases

PaaS can be beneficial and critical to today's enterprises' success. Here are some examples of PaaS use cases:

- **Business Process Management** (**BPM**): Many enterprises use PaaS to enable BPM platforms with other cloud services. BPM software can interoperate with other IT services. These combinations of services enable process management, implementation of business rules, and high-level business functionality.
- **Business Analytics/Intelligence** (**BI**): BI tools delivered via PaaS enable enterprises to visualize and analyze their data, allowing them to find customer patterns and business insights. This enables them to make better business decisions and more accurately predict customer demand, optimize pricing, and determine which products are their best sellers.
- **Internet of Things** (**IoT**): IoT is a key driver for PaaS solution adoption and will likely be even more critical in the coming years. You have only scratched the surface of IoT applications enabled by a PaaS layer.
- **Databases**: A PaaS layer can deliver persistence services. A PaaS database layer can reduce the need for system administrators by providing a fully managed, scalable, and secure environment. You will visit the topic more deeply in a later chapter, but AWS offers a variety of traditional and NoSQL database offerings.

- **API management and development**: An everyday use case for PaaS is to develop, test, manage, and secure APIs and microservices.
- **Master Data Management (MDM)**: MDM came about from the need of businesses to improve the quality, homogeneity, and consistency of their critical data assets. This critical data includes the customer, product, asset, and vendor data. MDM is used to define and manage this critical data. Additionally, it provides a single point of reference or a *single source of truth* for this data. MDM enables methods for ingesting, consolidating, comparing, aggregating, verifying, storing, and routing essential data across the enterprise while ensuring a common understanding, consistency, accuracy, and quality control. PaaS platforms have proven to be a boon for developing MDM applications, enabling them to process data quickly and efficiently.

Using PaaS is beneficial, sometimes even critical, in many applications. PaaS can streamline a workflow when several parties simultaneously work on the same task. PaaS is functional when customized applications need to be created. PaaS can reduce development and administration costs. Let's look at some examples of AWS PaaS services.

Examples of AWS PaaS services

Here are some examples of the most popular PaaS offerings in the AWS ecosystem:

- **AWS Elastic Beanstalk**: Beanstalk is a simple service that enables the deployment of web applications in various programming languages and can scale up and down automatically.
- **Amazon RDS**: Amazon RDS is another excellent example of a PaaS. Amazon offers a variety of databases, such as MySQL, Postgres, and Oracle. When using Amazon RDS to use these databases, You can focus on writing your applications against them and let Amazon handle the underlying management of the database engine.
- **AWS Lambda**: Lambda is another relatively simple and fully managed service that can quickly scale to handle thousands of requests per second. It requires almost no configuration and removes the worry of providing your hardware. AWS Lambda is called a **Function as a Service** (**FaaS**).
- **Amazon Elastic Kubernetes Service** (**Amazon EKS**): Amazon EKS is a fully managed service that enables running Kubernetes on the cloud without installing Kubernetes or deploying your servers.

Now that we have explored SaaS, PaaS, and IaaS in detail, let's see when it's appropriate to use each of them.

Choosing between SaaS, PaaS, and IaaS

Each model you learned, including the on-premises model, has advantages and disadvantages. The one you choose depends on your specific business requirements, the features needed, and the developers and testers that comprise your team. You might need an entirely *out-of-the-box* solution, and *time to market* might be a more important consideration than price. Or perhaps you have regulatory constraints that force you to control the environment completely. AWS offers a lot of assurances regarding their **Service Level Agreements** (**SLAs**) and compliance certifications. The more levels in the stack you decide to manage, the more effort you will exert to verify that your systems comply with the different regulations.

In general, one good rule of thumb is to let AWS take over the management of your resources whenever possible. You only take over the responsibility when necessary. For example, imagine trying to implement the functionality that Amazon Elastic Load Balancing or Elastic Kubernetes Service provides.

There are two main reasons why you should use IaaS or PaaS instead of SaaS:

- The use case requires a specific type of database or software not supported by the AWS SaaS solutions. For example, you may already have purchased Tableau licenses for your organization and built reports. So instead of using Amazon QuickSight as a SaaS BI platform, you can install Tableau in EC2 instances as an IaaS model.
- The total cost of ownership of running an application using PaaS or IaaS is significantly lower than the SaaS model. A specific example may be AWS Athena versus using Apache Presto directly. If you plan to run thousands of queries per day, with the current cost structure, some cloud users have found deploying Presto more cost-effective than using AWS Athena. Another option is to use Amazon Redshift as a PaaS model rather than Athena as a SaaS model cost-efficiently. It's important to note that these cost calculations should be carried out using all relevant costs, including staffing and support costs, not just software costs.

As you've learned about different cloud computing models and understand how to make the right choices, let's learn about cloud migration strategies.

Cloud migration strategy

The proportion of IT spending shifting to the cloud is accelerating, with predictions that over 45% of system infrastructure, infrastructure software, application software, and more will move from traditional solutions to the cloud by 2024.

Migrating to the AWS cloud makes your organization more innovative by enabling it to experiment and be agile. The ability to move quickly and achieve business values for your users truly matters for your company's cloud migration.

By migrating your digital assets to the cloud, you can gain insights from your data, innovate faster, modernize aging infrastructure, scale globally, and restructure organizational models to create better customer experiences. Often, cost reduction is one of the primary drivers of migrating workloads to the cloud. In practice, organizations regularly see the value of migration going well beyond the cost savings from retiring legacy infrastructure.

As you have started to discover, there are additional tasks you can perform in addition to migrating workflows to the cloud. What tasks should be performed and when they should be done will depend on the available budget, staff technical expertise, and leadership buy-in.

It is hard to create discrete cohorts to classify these tasks since they are more of a continuum. Having said this, and without further ado, let's attempt to create a classification. Keep in mind that this classification is not meant to be dogmatic. You may run into other ways to classify this migration. Additionally, you can mix and match the approaches, depending on your needs. For example, your CRM application may be moved without changing it. But perhaps your accounting software was built in-house, and now you want to use a vendor-enabled solution such as QuickBooks Online.

AWS use a three-phase approach that integrates modernization into the migration transition. AWS's three-phase process and the seven migration patterns help provide the guiding principles for structuring the cloud migration journey so you can quickly realize continuous, quantifiable business value. Let's look at this pattern in the three-phase migration process.

The three-phase migration process

The AWS cloud migration project typically executes in three phases, from discovery to building cloud readiness and finally migrating to the cloud. The following are three phases of cloud migration:

1. **Assessment phase** – Assessment is the first phase of cloud migration, where you need to conduct a feasibility study of your existing on-premise workload to build cloud readiness. In this phase, you can build cost projections and size your workload to run it in the cloud. The assessment phase helps you to build a business case for cloud migration. AWS acquired TSO logic in 2019 and launched it as the AWS Migration Evaluator, which can gather data from your on-premise workload and provide estimated cost savings in AWS.

You can learn more about migration evaluators by visiting the AWS page here: `https://aws.amazon.com/migration-evaluator/`. It helps you to define a roadmap for AWS migration, look at licensing and server dependencies and generate a **Migration Readiness Assessment (MRA)** report. Further, You can use the AWS **Cloud Adoption Framework (CAF)** to build cloud readiness and plan your migration strategy. You will learn more details about CAF later in this chapter.

2. **Mobilize phase** – The mobilize phase comes after the assessment phase to address gaps in cloud readiness. In this phase, based on the assessment conducted in the previous phase, you want to build cloud skills in your organization to handle cloud operations. It would be best to build a baseline environment, such as account and user setup, using AWS Landing Zone in order to move your workload. AWS provides the **Cloud Adoption Readiness Tool**, also known as **CART**, which helps you plan for cloud adoption based on your migration readiness. You can learn more about CART from the AWS page: `https://cloudreadiness.amazonaws.com/#/cart`. Further, AWS provides Migration Hub, which facilitates a centralized place for application tracking and migration automation across multiple AWS tools. You can learn more about the AWS migration hub by visiting the AWS page: `https://aws.amazon.com/migration-hub/`.
3. **Migrate and modernize phase** – After building a solid foundation in the mobilize phase, it is time to migrate and modernize. In this phase, you will design, migrate, and validate your workload in the cloud. You can start with creating workstreams such as foundation, governance, and migration to ensure your cloud migration project is operation ready. Further, you can subdivide the migrate phase into two parts, where in the initial phase, you build a runbook for migration and in the implementation phase, you perform the actual migration. Cloud migration allows you to modernize your business by refactoring legacy workloads. However, it may not be necessary to migrate and modernize in one go. Often, the best approach is to move rapidly to the cloud by performing lift and shift; after that, you can modernize by re-architecting the application in AWS and making it more cloud-native.

You can refer to AWS's prescriptive guidance to learn about the above three-phase cloud migration approach in detail – `https://docs.aws.amazon.com/prescriptive-guidance/latest/large-migration-guide/phases.html`. These phases are standard guidelines for successful cloud migration; however, each organization may have varying needs, and these guidelines are not set in stone.

Let's review the migration patterns, also known as "The 7 Rs," for migrating to the cloud and learn when to pick one over the others.

Cloud migration patterns – The 7 Rs

There is more than one way to handle migration. The following are the 7 Rs of cloud migration patterns defined by AWS:

1. Rehost
2. Re-platform
3. Refactor
4. Relocate
5. Repurchase
6. Retain
7. Retire

Creating a detailed strategy that identifies your workloads' best patterns is essential to accelerating your cloud journey and achieving your desired business objectives. The following diagram shows the 7 Rs cloud migration model.

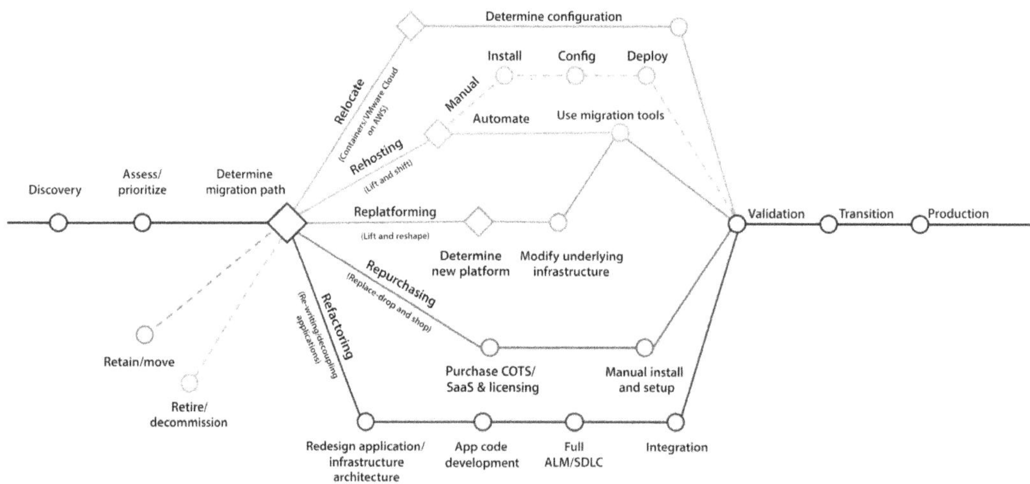

Figure 3.2: 7 Rs of AWS cloud migration

The diagram above is taken from the AWS blog: `https://aws.amazon.com/blogs/enterprise-strategy/new-possibilities-seven-strategies-to-accelerate-your-application-migration-to-aws/`.

Let's fully summarize the 7 Rs and what each migration pattern brings to the table.

Rehost in the cloud

This method is also commonly known as *lift and shift*. With this method, you perform the least work to move your workloads to the cloud by rehosting your application in the cloud. Applications are rehosted as they are in a different environment. Services are simply migrated. Let's say, for example, that you are hosting a simple three-tier application on your on-premises environment that is using the following:

- A web server
- An app server
- A database server

Using the *lift and shift* strategy, you would set up three similar servers on the cloud, install the applicable software on each server, and migrate the necessary data. Therefore, this approach will have the lowest migration costs. However, this simplicity comes at a price. Any problems in the existing applications will come along during the migration. If the current applications are obsolete and suboptimal, they will remain obsolete and suboptimal.

Have you ever had to move from one house to another? It's a painful process. In broad strokes, there are two ways that you can pack for the move:

- You can just put everything in a box and move it to the new house.
- You can be judicious and sort through what you have, item by item, and decide whether you will toss, sell, recycle, or take the thing with you.

Packing everything and going is quick because you avoid sorting through everything, but as you know, it can be more expensive because you will be moving more things, and it is painful because you may realize later that you should not have moved some items.

The move to the cloud is similar. Using the *lift and shift* strategy is good if you are already confident that your processes and workflows are solid and do not need to be changed, but this is rarely the case. This approach takes everything from the on-premise data center and moves it to the cloud. However, additional work is still required, such as preparing servers, creating VPCs, managing user access, and other tasks. You can automate most rehosting with AWS-provided tools such as CloudEndure and Migration Evaluator. AWS Server Migration Service offers agentless capabilities when you cannot install an agent on the server—making it faster and easier for you to migrate large workloads from on-premises to AWS using a snapshot of the existing servers.

The lift and shift approach may not always allow us to optimize the desired cost. However, it is the first step toward the cloud and is still a highly cost-effective option for many organizations. This approach is often the best choice if you want to start the migration process while getting a feel for cloud benefits. Let's look into other approaches.

Re-platform in the cloud

Re-platforming your services to run in the cloud entails migrating the applications and changing the underlying infrastructure architecture. However, the code of the higher-level services will not be changed. This way, you can leverage the existing code base, languages, and frameworks that you are currently using. It may be a good balance between taking advantage of some of the properties of the cloud, such as elasticity and scalability, without making wholesale changes to your existing applications. For example, while migrating to the cloud, you can upgrade Windows-based applications running on an older version, such as *Windows Server 2008, to the latest version, such as *Windows Server 2022.

It is advisable to use this method when you are comfortable with your current set of applications but want to take advantage of certain cloud advantages and functionality. For example, you can add failover to your databases without buying the software to run this setup reliably. If you were implementing this functionality *on-premises*, you would have to own all the infrastructure. A specific example is Oracle Data Guard, which allows you to implement this failover but not without having to install the product, and you need enough expertise to ensure that the product is configured correctly. Instead, when you are in a cloud environment, you can leverage the virtualization nature of the cloud, and costs can be shared with other cloud customers.

Refactor in the cloud

Refactoring gives you the opportunity to re-architecture your applications. For example, changing your monolithic apps to a more modular microservice-based architecture and making them a cloud-native serverless application. Refactoring is an advanced approach that adds agility and innovation to your business to meet user demand.

The refactoring approach will enable you to use all the cloud features and fully take advantage of them. This will allow you to use state-of-the-art technologies to create new services and reinvent your existing business workflows. There will be considerable work to accomplish this rewrite. In many cases, especially for established enterprises that new start-ups disrupt, they will soon find themselves relegated to a footnote in history if they don't reinvent themselves.

This approach allows you to make wholesale changes and start from scratch to create your new applications and workflows. It is essential to have subject matter experts and business experts involved in the design process because you may want to change how you do business and suspend all your current beliefs about how things should be done. Overall, migration is a long process and requires the involvement of application developers, business stakeholders, infrastructure engineers, security experts, etc. Collaboration between different teams in organizations is necessary because significant changes to apps and infrastructure are critical for success.

Revise before migrating to the cloud

Another potential strategy is to modify, optimize, and enhance the existing applications and code base before migrating to the cloud in preparation for doing so. Only then do you rehost or refactor the applications to the cloud. This may be a good strategy and provide business continuity and enhancement in the long run. The downside of this approach is the cost associated with changing and testing the code upfront. In addition, changing the code in the on-premises environment may only allow you to take advantage of some of the features that creating the code in the cloud would offer. For example, creating reports using AWS QuickSight. AWS QuickSight is an excellent tool for creating dashboards and reports. However, AWS QuickSight can only be used in a cloud environment, not in your on-premises environment, because QuickSight is only supported within AWS.

This method suits you when you know that your applications are suboptimal and need to be revised. You take cloud migration as an opportunity to enhance and fix your applications. Using this approach, you will only need to test your application once. The drawback is that if things go south, it may be challenging to ascertain if the problems that cropped up are because of new bugs in the code or because you migrated to the cloud.

Repurchase in the cloud

Repurchase replaces your existing environment and is known as "drop and shop"; you drop legacy applications and purchase more cloud-native software in the repurchase. So with this method, instead of rebuilding your applications, you get rid of them and replace them with commercially available SaaS alternatives such as Salesforce, Workday, ServiceNow, Datadog for Observability, or SAP. Depending on how deep and skilled your talent pool is and their areas of expertise, this option may or may not be more expensive than rebuilding your application.

Using this option, your software costs will likely be higher, but lower development and maintenance costs will be offset. If you decide to rebuild, you will not have to pay for CRM and commercial software licenses, but development cycles will likely be longer. You will have fewer defects, and higher maintenance may apply.

The previous methods of migration implied that all development was done in-house. One difference with the repurchase approach is migrating from in-house systems to software built by professional vendors. As with the other approaches, this approach has advantages and disadvantages. One of the advantages is that the learning curve and the development life cycle will be shortened, where more development will be needed. However, a disadvantage is that the software will require additional licenses and drive the adoption of new solutions that the company may not have used earlier.

Relocate to the cloud

The relocation method allows you to move your applications to the cloud without any changes. For example, you can relocate VMware-based on-prem applications to AWS without any changes. It will also help maintain consistent operations between VMware and the AWS cloud.

Overall, the cloud approach, where you focus on a pay-as-you-go model and reduce CapEx cost, will help you to reduce the **Total Cost of Ownership** (**TCO**) as you move to operational costs from upfront capital investment. After moving to the cloud, you can optimize or re-architect to take advantage of the various AWS services. You can add advanced features such as data engineering, machine learning, containerization, and mobility capabilities backed by the power of AWS.

Retain on-premises

The retain method means doing nothing for now and leaving your on-premises workload as-is. You may decide to keep your application on-premises due to it being near the end of its life, or because it's too complex to move now. For example, organizations often decide to retain mainframe application as it has decades of tech debt that no one knows how to migrate, and they need more planning.

Another example is enterprises that want to keep their applications on-premises and near to users due to the need for ultra-low latency or because of compliance regions, especially in the finance industry. In those cases, retaining your application on-premises and working with a hybrid cloud may be the best solution.

Retire

Finally, while analyzing your workload for cloud migration, you may realize that many servers are running unutilized, or you have decided to replace the existing application with cloud-native software.

The retire method is to decommission unwanted portions of your IT workload. During the discovery phase of your migration, you may encounter applications no longer being used. By rationalizing your IT portfolio, you can identify assets that are no longer valuable and can be turned off. It will strengthen your business case and direct your team toward maintaining the more widely used resources.

AWS provides prescriptive guidance to plan and decide which migration strategy will fit your workload. You can refer to the AWS guide at `https://docs.aws.amazon.com/prescriptive-guidance/latest/application-portfolio-assessment-guide/prioritization-and-migration-strategy.html` to customize the flow for your enterprise on-premise workload while working on migration planning. Let's look into some of the tools provided by AWS to help you with cloud migration.

Migration assessment tools

You don't have to reinvent the wheel as you migrate your workloads and projects from your current environment to the cloud. As you can imagine, many others have already started this journey. AWS and third-party vendors offer various tools to facilitate this process. A few examples of services and tools that are worth exploring are as follows:

- **AWS Migration Hub**: AWS Migration Hub is a central repository that can be used to keep track of a migration project.
- **AWS Application Discovery Service**: AWS Application Discovery Service automates the discovery and inventory tracking of different infrastructure resources, such as servers and dependencies.
- **AWS Migration Pattern Library**: This is a collection of migration templates and design patterns that can assist in comparing migration options and alternatives.
- **Cloud Endure Migration**: Cloud Endure Migration is a product offered by AWS that simplifies cloud migration by automating many steps that are necessary to migrate to the cloud.
- **AWS Data Migration Service**: This service can facilitate data migration from your on-premises databases to the cloud, for example, into Amazon RDS.

This is a partial list. Many other AWS and third-party services can assist in your migration. You can find the complete list by visiting the AWS migration page: `https://aws.amazon.com/free/migration/`.

Now that you have reviewed the different ways to migrate to the cloud, let's understand why you might want to migrate to the cloud to begin with. You will gain this understanding by learning about the concept of digital transformation. Let's now dive deeper into how organizations leverage digital transformation using the cloud model.

Implementing a digital transformation program

You spent some time understanding AWS cloud migration strategies in the previous section. In this section, you will learn how to transform legacy on-premises technologies into the cloud.

As you can imagine, this can be a challenging exercise, especially for large enterprises that have a long history of using old technologies and making significant investments in them. Deciding to start migrating applications and on-premises services to the cloud is a decision that takes time to make. A complete migration will likely take years and potentially cost millions of dollars in migration, transformation, and testing costs.

For this reason, important decisions need to be made along the way. Some of the most critical decisions that need to be made are as follows:

- Should you perform the bare minimum amount of tasks to achieve the migration, or do you want to use this change as an opportunity to refactor, enhance, and optimize our services? Doing the bare minimum (only migrating your workloads to the cloud) will mean that any problems and deficiencies in the current environment will be brought over to the new environment.
- Should the migration be purely technological, or should you use this opportunity to transform current business processes? You could thoroughly assess how your organization does business today and determine how to improve it. This will create efficiencies, cut costs, and increase customer satisfaction. However, this option will inherently have a higher upfront cost and may or may not work.

In this section, you will start learning the primary strategies for migration to the cloud and weigh up some of the options. It explains why and how you may want to undertake a digital transformation and the benefits and pitfalls that can come with this.

What exactly is a digital transformation?

The term "digital transformation" is more complex and harder to define because it is overloaded to the point that it has become a nebulous concept. Like many fantastic technology trends, it is over-hyped and over-used.

According to **International Data Corporation (IDC)**, some studies report that up to 40% of tech spending will be on digital transformation, while enterprises plan to spend over $2.8 trillion by 2025. The source of these details is the following website: `https://www.idc.com/`.

The term "digital transformation" has become something that simply means platform modernization, including migrating on-premises infrastructure to the cloud. You can blame CIOs, consultants, and third-party vendors for this confusion. They are all trying to convince the C-Suite that their solution can cover today's enterprise infrastructure and business requirements.

But savvy high-level executives understand that there is no magic bullet, and a digital transformation will require planning, strategizing testing, and a great deal of effort to accomplish.

Let's nail it down and define it.

DIGITAL TRANSFORMATION DEFINITION:

Digital transformation involves using the cloud and other advanced technology to create new or change existing business flows. It often involves changing the company culture to adapt to this new business type. The end goal of digital transformation is to enhance the customer experience and to meet ever-changing business and market demand. Now, cloud migration is an essential part of digital transformation.

A digital transformation is an opportunity to reconsider everything, including the following:

- The current structure of teams and departments
- Current business flows
- The way new functionality is developed

For a digital transformation to succeed, it should be broader than one aspect of the business, such as marketing, operations, or finance. It should eventually be all-encompassing and cover the whole gamut of how you engage with your customers. It should be an opportunity to completely transform how you interact with your potential and existing customers. It should go beyond simply swapping one server in one location for another more powerful or cheaper one in the cloud.

In some regards, start-ups have a big advantage over their more significant, established rivals because they don't have to unlearn and reimagine their processes. Start-ups have a clean slate that can be filled with anything in the AWS service catalog and other technologies. Existing players must wipe the slate clean while keeping their existing client base and finding a way to keep the trains running while performing their digital transformations.

Digital transformation goes well beyond changing an enterprise's technology infrastructure. For a digital transformation to be successful, it must also involve rethinking processes, using your staff in new ways, and fundamentally changing how business is done.

Disruptive technological change is usually undertaken to pursue new revenue sources or increase profits by creating efficiencies. Today's customers continue to raise the bar of expectations driven by so many successful businesses that have delivered on the execution of their digital transformations.

In the next section, you will learn about some of the forces that push companies into embarking on digital transformation. The status quo is a powerful state. Most companies will find it challenging to move from what's already working, even though they may realize that the current approach could be better. It usually takes significant pressure to bite the bullet and migrate to the cloud finally.

Digital transformation drivers

One of the most important reasons companies are finally beginning to migrate their workloads to the cloud and transform their business is because they realize if they don't disrupt themselves, someone else will do it for them. They see competition from start-ups that can start with a clean slate and without legacy baggage, and they also see incumbent competitors embarking on digital transformation initiatives.

Another obvious example is none other than Amazon's e-commerce operations. In this case, many of its competitors failed to adapt and have been forced to declare bankruptcy. A partial list of famous retailers that had to file for bankruptcy is as follows:

- Tailored Brands
- Lord & Taylor
- Brook Brothers
- Lucky Brand
- GNC
- J.C. Penney
- Neiman Marcus
- J. Crew
- Modell's Sporting Goods
- Pier 1

Let's take examples of companies that have survived and thrived by migrating to the cloud or creating their applications in the cloud.

Digital transformation examples

Digital transformation without tangible positive business outcomes will inevitably result in a short stay with your employer or the marketplace. Innovation might be refined in academia and research institutions. Still, in the business world, innovation must always be tied to improvement in business metrics such as increased sales or higher profits.

Remember that digital transformation could mean more than just moving your operations to the cloud. As you saw in the previous section, it may involve refactoring and replacing existing processes. Furthermore, it could also mean utilizing other previously unused technologies, such as robotics, the **Internet of Things** (**IoT**), blockchain, and machine learning.

For example, how many restaurants offer advanced booking through the web or via a mobile app?

A few more concrete examples are as follows:

- TGI Fridays use virtual assistants to enable mobile ordering.
- McDonald's uses voice recognition technology in their drive-throughs, and they have almost replaced their point-of-sale system with a self-ordering kiosk.
- Chipotle restaurants in the US have entirely changed their ordering model during the Covid-19 pandemic. Instead of allowing customers to enter the restaurant and order, customers had to place their orders via the Chipotle mobile app. Customers would get a time when they could come up and pick up their order or, if they ordered far enough in advance, they could choose when to pick it up.
- Rocket Mortgage (previously Quicken Loans) has upended the mortgage industry by enabling consumers to apply for a mortgage in a streamlined manner and without needing to speak to a human. To achieve this, they heavily relied on technology, as you can imagine.

What are some best practices when implementing a digital transformation? In the next section, we will help you navigate so that your digital transformation project is successful, regardless of how complicated it may be.

Digital transformation tips

There are many ways to implement a digital transformation. Some methods are better than others. This section will cover some of our suggestions to shorten the implementation time and minimize disruption to your existing customer base. Let's look at those tips.

Tip #1 – Ask the right questions

You should not just be asking this:

- How can we do what we are doing faster and better?

You should also be asking the following:

- How do we change what we are doing to serve our customers better?
- Can we eliminate certain lines of business, departments, or processes?
- What business outcomes do we want to achieve when interfacing with our customers?
- What happens if we do not do anything?
- What are our competitors doing?

Having a precise understanding of your customer's journey and experience is critical.

Tip #2 – Get leadership buy-in

Digital transformations have a much better chance of success when performed from the top down. If there is no buy-in from the CEO and the rest of the C-Suite, cloud adoption is destined to be relegated to a few corners of the enterprise but has no chance of full adoption. This does not mean that a **Proof of Concept (POC)** cannot be performed in one department to work out the kinks. Once the technology is adopted in that department, the bugs are worked out, and tangible business results are delivered, we can roll out this solution to all other departments.

Tip #3 – Delineate objectives

In this day and age, where Agile development is so prevalent, it is not uncommon to pivot and change direction as new requirements are discovered. However, the overall objective of the digital transformation should be crystal clear. Is the objective to merely lift and shift the current workflows into the cloud? Then keep your eye on the prize and ruthlessly concentrate on that goal. Is the digital transformation supporting a merger between two companies? In that case, completing the union of both companies' backend systems and operations should take precedence over everything else. Whatever the goal is, you need to focus on completing that objective before taking on other initiatives and transformations.

Tip #4 – Apply an agile methodology to your digital transformation

Embrace adaptive and agile design. The days of waiting for a couple of years to start seeing results, only to discover that you were climbing the wrong mountain, are over.

Many corporations now run with lean budgets and only provide additional resources once milestones have been reached and functionality has been delivered. Embracing an adaptive design enables transformation advocates to quickly tweak the transformation strategy and deploy staffing and resources where they can have the highest impact.

There needs to be a healthy push and pull between accomplishing the objectives for the digital transformation and the inevitable changes in how the goals will be met. If some of the objectives change midstream, these changes need to be clearly defined again. Make sure to precisely spell out what is changing, what is new, and what is no longer applicable.

Agile increases ROI by taking advantage of features as soon as they are available instead of waiting for all functionality to be delivered. Adaptability must be deeply ingrained in the ethos and culture of your digital transformation team members.

Look for singles rather than home runs. Home run hitters typically also have a lot of strikeouts. Players that specialize in hitting singles get on base much more often. You should take the same approach in your digital transformation. Instead of attempting a moon shot, taking smaller steps that produce results is highly recommended. If you can demonstrate value early in your transformation, this will validate your approach and show leadership that your approach is working. How much job security do you think you will have if your transformation takes three years and the project falls behind with no tangible results?

Pick the low-hanging fruit and migrate those workloads first. You will be able to provide quick results with this approach and learn from the mistakes you make in the process, which will help you when you need to accomplish other, more difficult migrations.

Tip #5 – Encourage risk-taking

In other words, fail fast. There are only so many times you can fail to deliver results. But if failing only takes one week and you have a month to deliver results, that affords us the luxury of failing three times before we get it right the fourth time. Therefore, in the first couple of attempts, you can attempt to shoot further and achieve more. Ideally, you don't have to completely throw out the work performed in the first few attempts, and you can reuse what was created in the first phases. But at the very least, you can use the lessons learned from those mistakes.

It's better to disrupt yourself than to have someone do it for you.

Tip #6 – One-way door vs. two-way door decisions

One way to define risk strategy is to understand if investing in digital transformation for a project or department is a one-way door or two-way door decision.

A one-way door decision is where once you start, there is no way to go back due to the amount of investment, and a two-way door decision is where you can easily roll back steps and reduce the risk. Try to have more two-way door decisions where you can retract if things go wrong and have fewer one-day door decisions where you have to move forward once started, and there is no looking back.

You can be more agile and fast in two-way door decisions where you define the existing strategy and timeline; however, you need to be extra careful and analyze more data for one-way door decisions. For example, in a two-way door decision, you can move your HR payroll application to migrate to the cloud and keep an exit strategy to purchase SaaS solutions like Workday or ADP if migration is incomplete in two months or after specific budgets. However, if you decide to move your e-commerce application to the cloud, it will impact your end-user experience. Hence, you must carefully analyze data as it will be a one-way door decision, and there is no going back without a significant impact.

Tip #7 – Clear delineation of roles and responsibilities

Fully delineate roles and responsibilities. Make sure that all team members are aligned on their responsibilities and check that there are no gaps in your team. Ideally, you will have a good mix of people with vast experience in cloud migration, digital transformation, and process optimization. Couple that with engineers and analysts that are not billing at an expert rate but can execute the plan laid out by these expert resources.

Current technology in general, and AWS in particular, is changing at an ever-increasing pace. Therefore, attracting talent with the right skills is an essential yet difficult step in digital transformation.

Some of the positions that will most likely need to be filled in your journey are as follows:

- Software engineers
- Infrastructure architects
- Cloud computing specialists
- Data analysts and data scientists
- Solution architects
- Security specialists
- Project managers
- Quality assurance testers
- DevOps administrators

- UX designers
- Trainers and documentation specialists
- Business analysts

The above is a partial list of positions, and your project may require more or fewer people to fill these roles. Not all roles will be required. And in your case, you may need additional roles to those included in this list.

This section taught us best practices and what to do in your cloud migration project. In the next section, you will learn what you should not do and how to avoid making mistakes.

Digital transformation pitfalls

There are many more ways to fail and not as many ways to succeed. There are, however, common patterns to how digital transformations typically fail. Let's review some of them.

Lack of commitment from the C-suite

Even when the CEO says they are committed to completely transforming their business, they may still clearly delineate a vision and the path to success or fail to provide the necessary resources for the transformation to succeed.

Not having the right team in place

It isn't easy to know what you don't know because you don't know it. It may take reading this sentence a couple of times before it can be understood. Still, the important takeaway is that you should engage people that have performed similar digital transformations to the one you are trying to attempt. Why reinvent the wheel if someone else has already invented it?

Many reputable consulting companies specialize in cloud migration and digital transformation. Your chance of success increases exponentially if you engage them to assist you with your initiative. They understand the challenges, and they can help you avoid the pitfalls. AWS has an extensive Partner Network that can help you migrate to the cloud.

These resources may come with a hefty price tag, and engaging them may take work. Many digital transformation initiatives fail because of a failure to engage the people with the right expertise to perform them.

Internal resistance from the ranks

With many of these transformations, there may be an adjustment in personnel. Some new people may join the team, in some cases permanently. Some consulting staff may be brought in temporarily, and some staff may become obsolete and need to be phased out. It is essential to consider the friction these changes will create and deal with them accordingly. When moving workloads to the cloud, some of the on-premises administrators may no longer be required, and you can fully expect that they may be a roadblock to the completion of the migration of these workflows.

Specifically, it is common for infrastructure and system administrators to resist cloud adoption. They often sense that some of their responsibilities may disappear or change; in many instances, they are right. Properly communicating the objective with a focus on training, how the migration will occur, and delineating new responsibilities is key to a successful migration.

Going too fast

To succeed, you must crawl before you walk and walk before you run. It is essential to prove concepts at a smaller scale before scaling them up across the enterprise and before you spend millions of dollars. Taking this route will allow you to make small mistakes and refine the transformation process before implementing it enterprise-wide. Remember one-way vs. two-way door decisions while investing in cloud migration projects.

A highly recommended method is to perform PoC projects before going all in, not just for cloud migration but for any project in general. For example, if you have 100 databases in your organization, it is okay to migrate only one or a few to the cloud instead of doing all of them simultaneously.

Going too slow

Once you prove the process in a couple of guinea pig departments, it is also essential to refrain from implementing the lessons learned one department at a time. Once you have the suitable template, it is recommended to roll out the new technology across the board. Taking a step-by-step approach may need to be faster to enable you to keep up with more nimble competitors.

Once you get familiar with the migration process and absorb the lessons learned from the first migration, you can accelerate your migration and migrate more applications.

Outdated rules and regulations

In some cases, the reason for failure may be outside the hands of the company's leadership. Current regulations may be a stumbling block to success. In this case, business leaders may have made the mistake of thinking they would be able to change the rules and failed, or the rules may have changed in the middle of the game.

Take, for example, the real estate industry in the US. Proving that someone owns a property and recording such ownership requires recording physical documents in the courthouse, in many cases requiring wet signatures. With the advent of blockchain and other enabling concepts, the technology already exists to transform local governments' archaic and heterogeneous methods. However, a patchwork of laws at the state level and a wide array of methods used to record these documents at the county level are disrupting this industry and preventing this technology from being implemented.

Another example was at an online pharmacy. They wanted a pill-dispensing robot to fill thousands of prescriptions per minute. As you can imagine, this was an expensive machine costing millions of dollars. However, the company had a restriction: they had to be faxed for medicine prescriptions to be filled, and many customers had trouble faxing in their prescriptions. Hence, the robot pill dispenser ended up being heavily underutilized. Other reasons contributed to its demise, but unfortunately, this enterprise eventually went under.

AWS provides the **Cloud Adoption Framework** (**CAF**) to help you start with digital transformation. Let's learn more details about it.

The AWS Cloud Adoption Framework (AWS CAF)

As discussed in the previous section, cloud adoption has some critical pitfalls. The organization may have started well with the pilot but could not move it further, or tech leadership may need to be aligned to focus on cloud modernization. In some cases, even if an organization migrates to the cloud, it cannot realize its full value, as replicating the on-premise model to the cloud can fail to reduce cost or increase flexibility. To help customers overcome these pitfalls, AWS designed the Cloud Adoption Framework by applying their learning across thousands of customers who completed their cloud migration to AWS.

The AWS Cloud Adoption Framework is a mechanism for establishing a shared mental model for cloud transformation. It utilizes AWS's experience and best practices to enable customers to build business transformation in the cloud. It further helps validate and improve cloud readiness while evolving your cloud adoption roadmaps.

The CAF helps to identify business outcomes such as risk, performance, revenue, and operational productivity. The following diagram provides a full view of the AWS CAF:

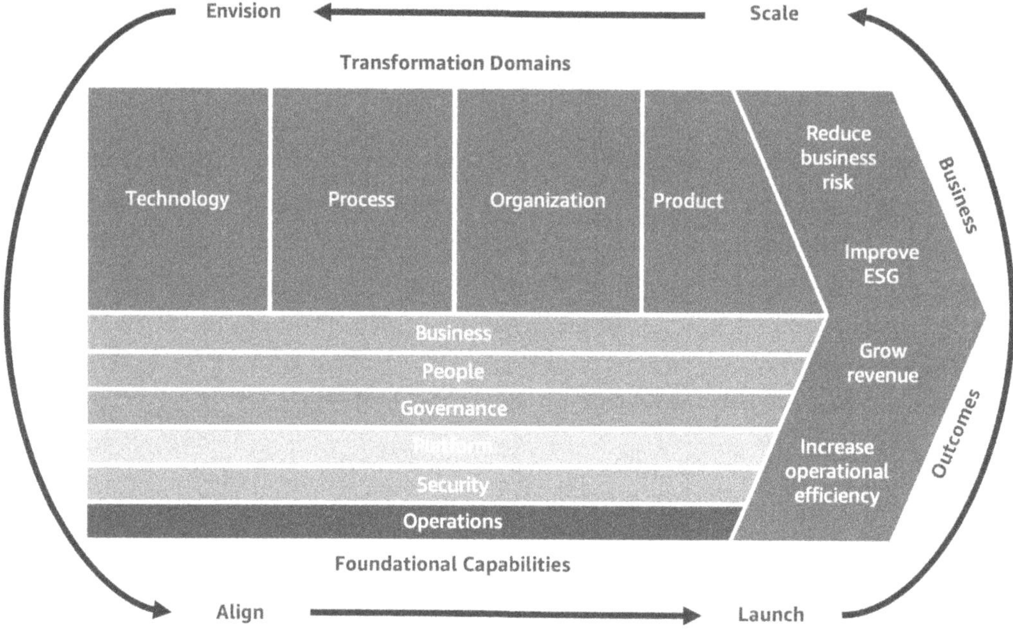

Figure 3.3: AWS Cloud Adoption Framework (CAF)

As shown in the preceding diagram, the AWS CAF proposes four incremental and iterative phases for organizations to succeed in their digital transformation journey:

- **Envision** – Understand business transformation opportunities with your strategic goals, and take buy-ins from senior executives to drive change. Define quantified business outcomes to drive value.
- **Align** – Identify gaps and dependencies across the organization to create a plan for cloud readiness and drive stakeholder alignment at all organizational levels.
- **Launch** – Build proof of concept and deliver impactful, successful pilots who can define future directions. Adjust your approach from pilot projects to build a production plan.
- **Scale** – Scale pilots to take it to production and realize continuous business value.

You can learn more about the AWS CAF by visiting their page: `https://aws.amazon.com/professional-services/CAF/`.

Further, the AWS CAF identifies four transformation domains that help customers accelerate their business outcomes. The following are the digital transformation opportunities:

- **Technology transformation** using cloud migration and modernization approach in the cloud.
- **Process transformation** using a data and analytics approach with cloud technology.
- **Organizational transformation** by building an efficient operating model in the cloud.
- **Product transformation** by building cloud-focused business and revenue models.

Transformation domains are enabled by a set of foundational capabilities that offer expert advice on optimizing digital transformation by harnessing the power of cloud services. The AWS CAF organizes these capabilities into six perspectives: business, people, governance, platform, security, and operations, with each perspective encompassing a distinct set of capabilities that are managed by various stakeholders involved in the cloud transformation process. By leveraging these capabilities, customers can improve their cloud readiness and transform their operations effectively.

Every organization's cloud journey is unique. To succeed in their transformations, organizations must define their desired cloud transformation state, understand cloud readiness, and close the gaps. However, driving digital transformation through cloud adoption is not new, and many organizations have already implemented it. So, you don't need to reinvent the wheel and can take advantage of the learning offered by AWS.

Now that we have examined computing models (IaaS, PaaS, and SaaS) and migration strategies, the question remains: what architecture should you use in the cloud?

Architectures to provide high availability, reliability, and scalability

We have come a long way in making our systems more reliable, scalable, and available. It wasn't that long ago that we didn't think of saving precious photographs and documents on our PC hard drives, assuming disk drives would be able to store this data indefinitely. Even though PC components have decent reliability, they will eventually fail. It's the nature of hardware with moving parts such as disk drives.

Since then, significant advances have been made to increase the reliability of individual components; however, the real increase in reliability comes from redundantly storing information on multiple devices and in different locations. Doing so increases reliability exponentially.

For example, the S3 Standard service stores file redundantly with at least six copies and in at least three data centers. If a copy is corrupted, the S3 storage system automatically detects the failure and replicates the file using one of the remaining uncorrupted copies. Just like that, the number of copies for a file remains constant. So, for S3 to lose a file, all six replicas must fail simultaneously. The likelihood of this happening naturally is extremely rare. We will learn more about S3 and AWS's other storage options in *Chapter 5, Storage in AWS – Choosing the Right Tool for the Job*, but for now it is enough to know that AWS offers many different ways to redundantly store data.

NOTE

The concept of copying data across resources to increase reliability and availability is known as **redundancy**. Redundancy is easy to implement with copies of files and objects. It is a much more difficult problem to implement with databases. The reason it's hard is that replicating the state across machines is challenging.

It is also important to note that in the database context, redundancy has two meanings. One being *"bad"* redundancy and the other being *"good"* redundancy. Many of the database services that AWS offers provide *"good"* redundancy out of the box. Some of these services can easily and automatically replicate data for you. For example, Amazon DynamoDB automatically replicates data as it is inserted or updated. Another example is the Amazon RDS system's capability to create read replicas easily. These processes are completely transparent to the user of the service and the administrators and are guaranteed to be eventually consistent.

Examples of *"bad"* redundancy are unnecessarily denormalized database tables or manual copies of files. Using these methods to create redundancy will most likely lead to inconsistent data, inaccuracies, and erroneous analysis of your data.

In the following three subsections, we will learn about four different types of application architectures:

- Active architecture
- Active/passive architecture
- Active/active architecture
- Sharding architecture

Each one has different advantages and disadvantages. Let's learn about each one of them in more detail.

Active architecture

In this architecture, there is only one storage resource with a single point of failure. An architecture like this can be described as functional architecture. If your hard drive fails, you are out of luck. This name might not seem entirely intuitive. You can imagine this architecture as a circus performer working without a net. If something fails, there is no backup recovery plan.

The following diagram illustrates the architecture. We have only one **Active Node**, and if any hardware failure occurs with the node, the whole system fails:

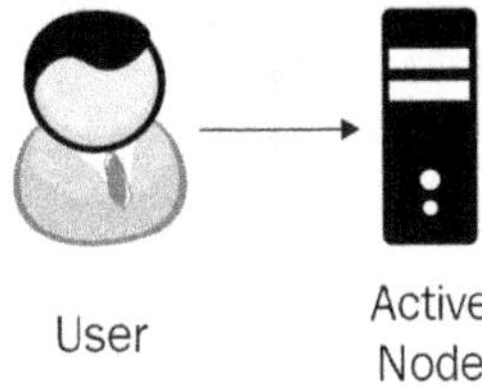

Figure 3.4: Active architecture

In the next section, let's look at the active/passive architecture.

Active/passive architecture

The next logical evolution to implement a more available architecture is to have a simple backup. Instead of having just one resource, a simple solution is to let a primary server (the active node) handle reads and writes and synchronize its state on a secondary server (the passive node). This is known as active/passive architecture.

As we can see in the following diagram, the system is composed of two resources. During regular operation, users communicate with the **Active Node**, and any changes to the **Active Node** get replicated to the **Passive Node**:

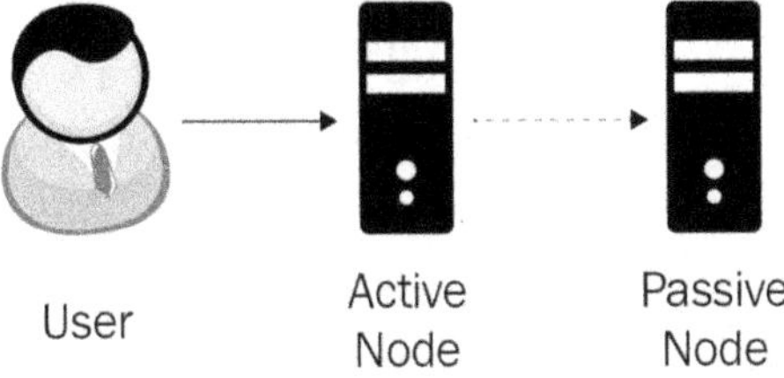

Figure 3.5: Active/passive architecture

An active/passive architecture improves availability by having a fresh copy of all your critical data. As we see in the following diagram, if the active node fails, you can manually or automatically redirect the traffic to the passive node. In this case, the passive node becomes the active node, and then you can take the necessary steps to fix or replace the failed node. There will be a period of time when you are replacing the failed node, and the whole system can fail if the new active node fails before you can replace the failed node. The following diagram illustrates this process:

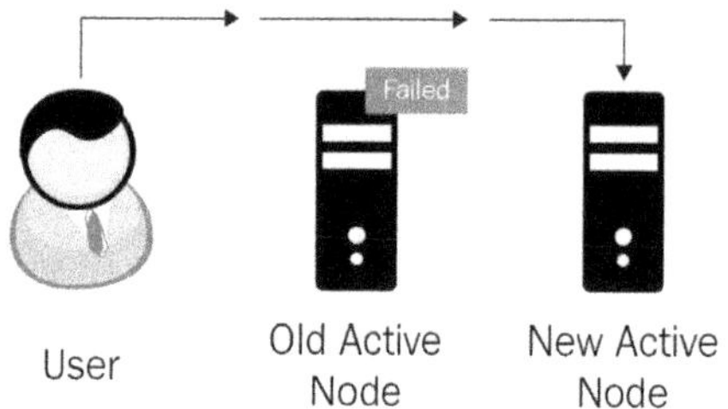

Figure 3.6: Active/passive architecture with an active down node

The first generations of active/passive architectures used a synchronous transaction process. Transactions were not committed until the passive node acknowledged that it had processed the writes. This was not a suitable solution. If the passive node went down, it became a bottleneck in the architecture. This architecture can actually decrease the system's reliability because now, two components can fail, bringing the whole system down.

To improve availability, later generations of this architecture used asynchronous replication.

Asynchronous replication is a store-and-forward method to back up data. Asynchronous replication stores data in primary storage first (synchronously). After this, it sends a request to write the data in a secondary storage location without waiting for this second write to finish. This approach speeds up the storage process. If the write to the second location fails, the process will keep trying multiple times until it succeeds. It doesn't matter if it takes a couple of tries because the requester is not waiting for the process to finish.

While the high-level architecture looks quite similar, it can now handle failures in the active or passive nodes while continuing to process transactions.

The drawbacks of this architecture are as follows:

- The system will still fail if both nodes fail during similar timeframes.
- Any data not replicated to the passive node when the active node goes down will be lost.

- Since the passive node is used just for backup purposes, the performance and throughput of the system are limited by the capacity of the active node, and the capacity of the passive node is wasted because it is not handling any user traffic.

As applications became more complex and started handling worldwide internet traffic, and user expectations grew to have *"always on"* availability, the active/passive architecture could not scale to handle these new demands, and new architecture was needed.

The following architecture we will learn about avoids some of the shortcomings of the active/passive architecture at the expense of added complexity and additional hardware.

Active/active architecture

In active-active architecture, you replicate your workload to another set of nodes. When a user sends the request, you can distribute the traffic between these two nodes. If one node goes down, you always have other nodes up and running to serve user traffic. To achieve reliability, you need to ensure workload replication happens in the physically separated region, so if something happens to one data center, it should not impact others.

AWS provides the ability to easily configure active-active architecture across its globally distributed infrastructure and route traffic between them using its DNS service Amazon Route 53 and content distribution service AWS CloudFront. Full active-active architecture may come with a cost if you replicate the entire workload to achieve 100% fault tolerance and high availability. However, if your system doesn't need to be fully fault-tolerant, you can use less costly options such as warm stand-by, where you can keep low-capacity servers in a secondary site and divert a small amount of traffic, like 5%. If the primary site goes down, you can quickly scale the secondary site to full capacity and make it primary.

Let's look at another way to achieve high availability.

Sharding architecture

Building on the active/passive architecture, engineers developed a new architecture where there are multiple nodes, and all nodes participate in handling traffic. This architecture divides the work using a scheme to parcel out the work. One method is to divide the work using a primary key. A primary key is a number, and you have ten shards. We could set up the process so requests with a primary key starting with 1 would be sent to the first shard. If it begins with a 2, it goes to the second shard, and so on.

The following figure shows an example of sharding architecture:

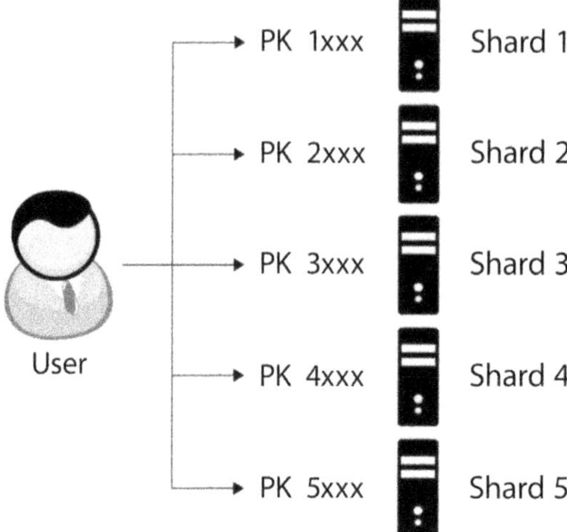

Figure 3.7: Sharding architecture

As you may have already guessed, if you use this scheme, you should ensure that your keys are balanced and that there is a relatively even distribution of transactions across all the numbers. An example of a potentially unbalanced key would be if you have a polling application, your table stores the votes, and your key is the candidates in the election. It is possible that only a few of the candidates will get the majority of the votes.

Also, as you can imagine, **sharding architecture** increases throughput, increases availability, and reduces the number of system failures. One drawback is that a sharding system can be complex to implement. However, there are more services such as DynamoDB that implement sharding managed by AWS, so you do not need to worry about the sharding implementation details and can focus purely on the business logic of your application.

As we saw in this section and learned about these three common architectures, each has different advantages and disadvantages. Whenever possible, an active architecture should be avoided except for simple projects that are not mission-critical and for development work. When using an active architecture, we are risking the loss of data. Active architectures are inherently *"single-point-of-failure"* architectures. However, as expected, architectures that offer higher availability are more expensive solutions that require more resources.

The architectures discussed in this section are simple, but powerful, and these basics are worth keeping in the back of your mind as we discuss different ways to use AWS throughout coming chapters. However, regardless of how you choose to shape your system, it is worth making sure that it is as resilient as possible. With this in mind, let's finish our discussion with a quick look at chaos engineering.

Chaos engineering

Chaos engineering is a methodology devoted to building resilient systems by purposely trying to break them and expose their weaknesses. It is much better to deal with a problem when we expect it to happen. A well-thought-out plan needs to be in place to manage failure that can occur in any system. This plan should allow the system's recovery in a timely manner so that our customers and our leadership can continue to have confidence in our production systems.

One element of this plan could be having a clearly established **Recovery Point Objective** (**RPO**) and **Recovery Time Objective** (**RTO**). The concepts of RPO and RTO, in addition to an analysis of the business impact, will provide the foundation to nail down an optimal recommendation for a business continuity plan. The strategy should ensure that normal business operations resume within an acceptable time frame that meets or exceeds the RPO and RTO for the agreed-upon **Service Level Agreement** (**SLA**).

RTO is the targeted time that can elapse after a problem occurs with a resource and before it again becomes accessible. In other words, it is the amount of time needed to recover and make a service available to maintain business continuity. The time elapsed should not exceed that which is specified in an SLA. This time interval is called **tolerance**. For example, if your SLA specifies that the accounting database cannot be unavailable for more than 60 minutes, there is an outage, and the database is back up and running within 40 minutes, then that outage has met the RTO.

RPO refers to how old the data that is restored can be. In other words, it is the time between a data corruption incident and the last backup taken. This will be closely tied to the architecture used and how often data is replicated. Any data that is lost that was not saved during this period will be lost and will have to be manually re-entered. For example, say a database is automatically backed up every five minutes and a component fails causing the database to go down. After this, if it is determined that 3 minutes worth of updates are lost because they weren't written to the backup, and the SLA specifies an RPO of 10 minutes then the 3 minutes of lost data are within an acceptable range as dictated by the SLA.

However, RTO and RPO are only objectives – meaning they is what we expect will happen. They need to be compared with the **Recovery Point Actual (RPA)** and **Recovery Time Actual (RTA)** which describe what actually happened. In other words, RTO and RPO are estimates of what will happen. RPA and RTA are measurements of what actually occurred. If the actual time (RTA) it takes to recover is longer than the objective (RTO), it means that your SLA was not met, and you need to do better. To ensure you are ready, a plan must be put in place to test your recovery steps and ensure you meet the objectives.

Establishing an RTO and RPO is one example of what could be included in your plan to manage failure. No matter what steps are taken in your plan, it is highly recommended to schedule planned outages to test it. This is where chaos engineering comes into play.

A common refrain is that *"we learn more from failure than we learn from success"*. Chaos engineering takes this refrain and applies it to computing infrastructure. However, instead of waiting for failure to occur, chaos engineering creates these failure conditions in a controlled manner to test the resiliency of our systems.

Systemic weaknesses can take many forms. Here are some examples:

- Insufficient or non-existent fallback mechanisms any time a service fails.
- Retry storms result from an outage and timeout intervals that are not correctly tuned.
- Outages from downstream dependencies.
- A single-point-of-failure crash in upstream systems causes cascading failures.

Retry storms can occur when timeout intervals and outage handling are not appropriately configured, leading to a high volume of repeated requests to a service that is experiencing issues. When a service outage occurs, the client may attempt to retry the failed request, which can lead to an overwhelming number of requests being sent to the service when it is already experiencing high traffic or is not available. This increased traffic can further worsen the outage, leading to a vicious cycle of repeated retries and degraded service performance. Therefore, it is crucial to properly configure timeout intervals and retry policies to prevent retry storms and minimize the impact of outages.

Chaos engineering is a series of experiments to continuously test fragility and find weaknesses in our systems to harden and reinforce them. The steps that can be taken to implement each one of these experiments are the following:

1. Define the *"steady state"* of the system. This is a set of metrics for the system that signals what expected behavior should be.

2. Make an assumption (the hypothesis) that this steady state will continue to prevail under *"normal conditions"* (the control group) as well as under *"abnormal conditions"* (the experimental group).
3. Introduce *"chaos"*. Change conditions that mimic real-world events such as a server crash, a hard drive malfunction, severed network connections, system latency, etc.
4. Attempt to disprove the hypothesis by observing the differences between the steady state (the control group) and the altered state (the experimental group).
5. Make improvements to the system based on the results observed from running the experiment.

The following diagram illustrates this cycle of steps:

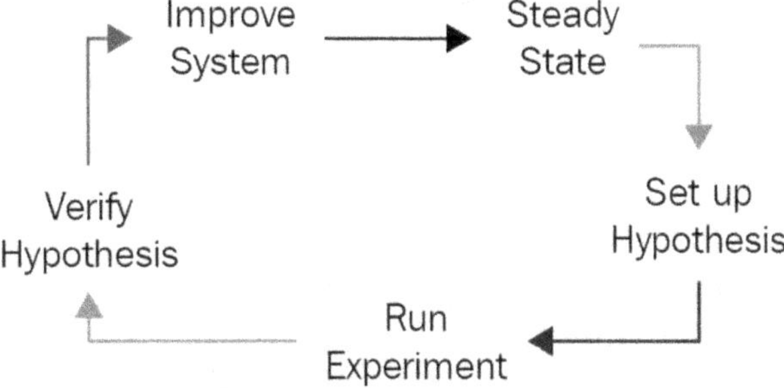

Figure 3.8: Chaos engineering cycle

If we cannot disrupt the steady state after introducing chaos (traffic still flows and users are still serviced), this will increase our confidence in the system. Whenever a weakness is found, appropriate measures can be taken to close the gap and eliminate the weakness. But it happens under controlled conditions, on our terms rather than in the form of a phone call or a text at 3 A.M. This is the perfect application of the adage. *You learn more from failure than success.*

When you introduce a form of chaos that cannot break the system, it's proof that your system can handle that chaotic scenario. Only when an experiment makes the system fail do you realize you have a weakness or vulnerability that needs to be addressed. As such, chaos engineering is a valuable method for testing the strength of your cloud environment and improving it.

Summary

This chapter taught you about cloud computing models, such as IaaS, PaaS, and SaaS. You dove deep into each model to understand its value proposition and how it can fit your IT workload needs.

You then pivoted to understand how to implement a digital transformation program and migrate to the cloud. You learned that not all cloud migration programs are created equal and that some companies use their migration to the cloud to implement further change in their organization. You also learned about cloud migration strategy and how the AWS 7 Rs migration strategy could help you build a migration and modernization plan.

Since processes will have to be retested anyway, why not take advantage of this and implement ways to improve the company's processes and business workflows?

You also covered the drivers for digital transformation and visited some examples of successful digital transformation. You saw some valuable tips to ensure the success of your digital transformation and some pitfalls that should be avoided so that your transformation runs smoothly. You further learned how the AWS **Cloud Adoption Framework** (**CAF**) could help you to accelerate a successful digital transformation journey.

Finally, you examined a few simple architectures that can be utilized in the cloud to improve availability, reliability, and scalability. These included the active architecture, active/passive architecture, active/active architecture, and sharding architecture. You then finished the chapter with a brief look at a method to improve your architecture called chaos engineering.

In the next chapter, you will learn how to use AWS global infrastructure to create business solutions that can help you with your digital transformation initiatives. You will explore technology and learn about networking in AWS, a foundational pillar of starting your AWS technical journey.

Join us on Discord!

Read this book alongside other users, cloud experts, authors, and like-minded professionals.

Ask questions, provide solutions to other readers, chat with the authors via. Ask Me Anything sessions and much more.

Scan the QR code or visit the link to join the community now.

https://packt.link/cloudanddevops

4

Networking in AWS

Enterprises today have become exponentially more agile by leveraging the power of the cloud. In this chapter, we will highlight the scale of AWS Global Infrastructure and teach you about AWS networking foundations.

Networking is the first step for any organization to set up its landing zone and the entire IT workload built on top of it. You could say that networking is the backbone of the IT application and infrastructure workload. AWS provides various networking services for building your IT landscape in the cloud and in this chapter, you will dive deep into AWS networking services.

Every business is now running at a global scale and organizations need to target global populations with their product. With a traditional on-premise IT workload, it becomes challenging to scale globally and provide the same user experience across the globe. AWS helps solve these problems through edge networking, and you will learn more about deploying your application for global users without compromising their experience. Furthermore, you will learn about network security and building a hybrid cloud.

In this chapter, you will learn about the following topics:

- Learning about the AWS Global Infrastructure
- AWS networking foundations
- Edge networking
- Building hybrid cloud connectivity in AWS
- AWS cloud network security

Without further ado, let's get down to business.

Learning about the AWS Global Infrastructure

The infrastructure offered by AWS is highly secure and reliable. It offers over 200 services. Most are available in all AWS Regions worldwide, spread across 245 countries. Regardless of the type of technology application you are planning to build and deploy, AWS is sure to provide a service that will facilitate its deployment.

AWS has millions of customers and thousands of consulting and technology partners worldwide. Businesses large and small across all industries rely on AWS to handle their workloads. Here are some statistics to give you an idea of the breadth of AWS's scale. AWS provides the following as its global infrastructure:

- 26 launched Regions and 8 announced Regions
- 84 Availability Zones
- Over 110 Direct Connect locations
- Over 310 Points of Presence
- 17 Local Zones and 32 announced LZs
- 24 Wavelength Zones

IMPORTANT NOTE

These numbers are accurate at the time of writing this book. By the time you read this, it would not be surprising for the numbers to have changed.

Now that we have covered how the AWS infrastructure is organized at a high level, let's learn about the elements of the AWS Global Infrastructure in detail.

Regions, Availability Zones, and Local zones

How can Amazon provide such a reliable service across the globe? How can they offer reliability and durability guarantees for some of their services? The answer reveals why they are the cloud leaders and why it's difficult to replicate what they offer. AWS has billions of dollars worth of infrastructure deployed across the world. These locations are organized into different Regions and Zones. More formally, AWS calls them the following:

- AWS Regions
- **Availability Zones** (**AZs**)
- **Local Zones** (**LZs**)

As shown in the following diagram, an AZ is comprised of multiple distinct data centers, each equipped with redundant power, networking, and connectivity, and located in separate facilities.

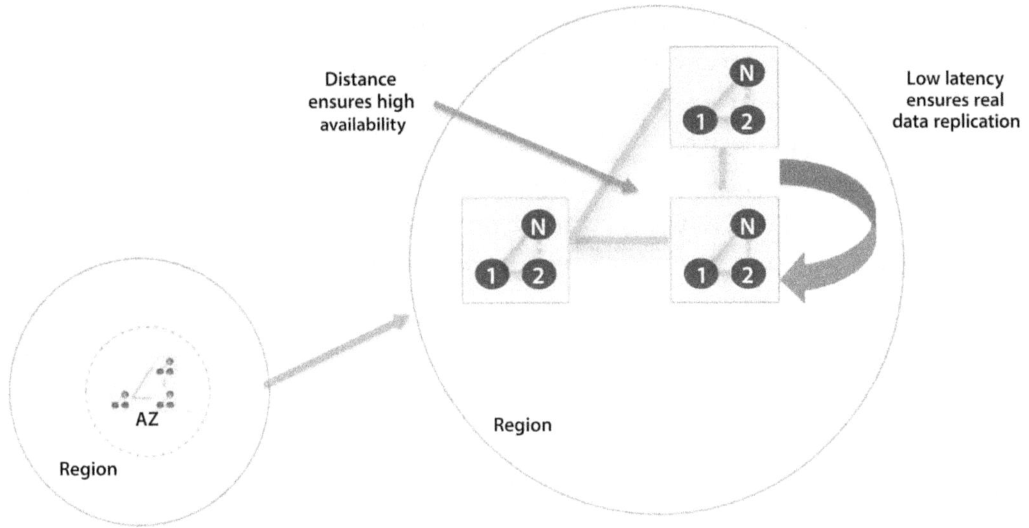

Figure 4.1: AWS Regions and AZs

AWS Regions exist in separate geographic areas. Each AWS Region comprises several independent and isolated data centers (AZs) that provide a full array of AWS services.

AWS is continuously enhancing its data centers to provide the latest technology. AWS's data centers have a high degree of redundancy. AWS uses highly reliable hardware, but the hardware is not foolproof. Occasionally, a failure can happen that interferes with the availability of resources in each data center. Suppose all instances were hosted in only one data center. If a failure occurred with the whole data center, then none of your resources would be available. AWS mitigates this issue by having multiple data centers in each Region.

By default, users will always be assigned a default Region. You can obtain more information about how to change and maintain AWS environment variables using the AWS CLI by visiting this link: `https://docs.aws.amazon.com/cli/latest/userguide/cli-configure-envvars.html`.

In the following subsection, we will look at AWS Regions in greater detail and see why they are essential.

AWS Regions

AWS Regions are groups of data centers in one geographic location that are specially designed to be independent and isolated from each other. A single Region consists of a collection of data centers spread within that Region's geographic boundary. This independence promotes availability and enhances fault tolerance and stability. While working on the console, you will see AWS services available in that Region. There is a possibility that a particular service is not available in your Region. Eventually, all services become **generally available** (**GA**) after their launch; however, the timing of availability may differ between different Regions. Some services are global – for example, **Direct Connect Gateway** (**DXGW**), **Identity and Access Management** (**IAM**), CloudFront, and Route53.

Other services are not global but allow you to create inter-Region fault tolerance and availability. For example, Amazon **Relational Database Service** (**RDS**) allows you to create read replicas in multiple Regions. To find out more about this, visit `https://aws.amazon.com/blogs/aws/cross-region-read-replicas-for-amazon-rds-for-mysql/`.

One of the advantages of using such an architecture is that resources will be closer to users, increasing access speed and reducing latency.

Another obvious advantage is that you can serve your clients without disruption even if a whole Region becomes unavailable by planning your disaster recovery workload to be in another Region. You will be able to recover faster if something goes wrong, as these read replicas can be automatically converted to the primary database if the need arises.

As of May 2022, there are 26 AWS Regions and 8 announced Regions. The naming convention that is usually followed is to list the country code, followed by the geographic region, and the number. For example, the US East Region in Ohio is named as follows:

- Location: US East (Ohio)
- Name: us-east-2

AWS has a global cloud infrastructure, so you can likely find a Region near your user base, with a few exceptions, such as Russia. If you live in Greenland, it may be a little further away from you – however, you will still be able to connect as long as you have an internet connection.

In addition, AWS has dedicated Regions specifically and exclusively for the US government called AWS GovCloud. This allows US government agencies and customers to run highly sensitive applications in this environment. AWS GovCloud offers the same services as other Regions, but it complies explicitly with requirements and regulations specific to the needs of the US government.

The full list of available Regions can be found here: `https://docs.aws.amazon.com/AWSEC2/latest/UserGuide/using-regions-availability-zones.html#concepts-available-regions`.

As AWS continues to grow, do not be surprised if it offers similar Regions to other governments worldwide, depending on their importance and the demand they can generate.

AWS AZs

As we discussed earlier, AZs are components of AWS Regions. The clusters of data centers within a Region are called AZs. A single AZ consists of multiple data centers. These data centers are connected to each other using AWS-owned dedicated fiber optic cables and located within a 60-mile radius, which is far enough to avoid localized failures, yet achieves a faster data transfer between the data centers. AZs have multiple power sources, redundant connectivity, and redundant resources. All this translates into unparalleled customer service, allowing them to deliver highly available, fault-tolerant, and scalable applications.

The AZs within an AWS Region are interconnected. These connections have the following properties:

- Fully redundant
- High-bandwidth
- Low-latency
- Scalable
- Encrypted
- Dedicated

Depending on the service you are using, if you decide to perform a multi-AZ deployment, an AZ will automatically be assigned to the service, but for some services, you may be able to designate which AZ is to be used.

Every AZ forms a completely segregated section of the AWS Global Infrastructure, physically detached from other AZs by a substantial distance, often spanning several miles. Each AZ operates on a dedicated power infrastructure, providing customers with the ability to run production applications and databases that are more resilient, fault-tolerant, and scalable compared to relying on a single data center.

High-bandwidth, low-latency networking interconnects all the AZs – but what about fulfilling the need for low-latency bandwidth within a highly populated city? For that, AWS launched LZs. Let's learn more about them.

AWS LZs

While AZs focus on covering larger areas throughout regions, such as US-West and US-East, AWS fulfills the needs of highly populated cities through LZs. AWS LZs are newer components in the AWS infrastructure family. LZs place select services close to end users, allowing them to create AWS applications that deliver single-digit, millisecond responses. An LZ is the compute and storage infrastructure located close to high-population areas and industrial centers, and offers high-bandwidth, low-latency connectivity to the broader AWS infrastructure. Due to their proximity to the customer, LZs facilitate the delivery of applications that necessitate latency in single-digit milliseconds to end-users. As of March 2023, AWS had has 32 LZs.

AWS LZs can run various AWS services, such as Amazon Elastic Compute Cloud, Amazon Virtual Private Cloud, Amazon Elastic Block Store, Amazon Elastic Load Balancing, Amazon FSx, Amazon EMR, Amazon ElastiCache, and Amazon RDS in geographic proximity to your end users.

The naming convention for LZs is to use the AWS Region followed by a location identifier, for example, **us-west-2-lax-2a**. Please refer to this link for the latest supported services in LZs – `https://aws.amazon.com/about-aws/global-infrastructure/localzones/features/?nc=sn&loc=2`.

Now you have learned about the different components of the AWS Global Infrastructure, let's look at the benefits of using AWS infrastructure.

Benefits of the AWS Global Infrastructure

The following are the key benefits of using AWS's cloud infrastructure:

- **Security** – One of the most complex and risky tasks is to maintain security, especially when it comes to the data center's physical security. With AWS's shared security responsibility model, you offload infrastructure security to AWS and focus on the application security that matters for your business.
- **Availability** – One of the most important factors for the user's experience is to make sure your application is highly available, which means you need to have your workload deployed in a physically separated geographic location to reduce the impact of natural disasters. AWS Regions are fully isolated, and within each Region, the AZs are further isolated partitions of AWS infrastructure. You can use AWS infrastructure with an on-demand model to deploy your applications across multiple AZs in the same Region or any Region globally.

- **Performance** – Performance is another critical factor in retaining and increasing the user base. AWS provides low-latency network infrastructure by using redundant 100 GbE fiber, which leads to terabits of capacity between regions. Also, you can use AWS Edge AZs for applications that require low millisecond latency, such as 5G, gaming, AR/VR, and IoT.
- **Scalability** – When user demands increase, you must have the required capacity to scale your application. With AWS, you can quickly spin up resources, deploying thousands of servers in minutes to handle any user demand. You can also scale down when demand goes down and don't need to pay for any overprovisioned resources.
- **Flexibility** – With AWS, you can choose how and where to run your workloads; for example, you can run applications globally by deploying into any of the AWS Regions and AZs worldwide. You can run your applications with single-digit millisecond latencies by choosing AWS LZs or AWS Wavelength. You can choose AWS Outposts to run applications on-premises.

Now that you have learned about the AWS Global Infrastructure and its benefits, the next question that comes to mind is how am I going to use this infrastructure? Don't worry – AWS has you covered by providing network services that allow you to create your own secure logical data center in the cloud and completely control your IT workload and applications. Furthermore, these network services help you to establish connectivity to your users, employees, on-premises data centers, and content distributions. Let's learn more about AWS's networking services and how they can help you to build your cloud data center.

AWS networking foundations

When you set up your IT infrastructure, what comes to mind first? I have the servers now – how can I connect them to the internet and each other so that they can communicate? This connectivity is achieved by networking, without which you cannot do anything.

Networking concepts are the same when it comes to the cloud. In this chapter, you will not learn what networking is, but instead how to set up your private network in the AWS cloud and establish connectivity between the different servers in the cloud and from on-premises to an AWS cloud. First, let's start with the foundation; the first step to building your networking backbone in AWS is using Amazon VPC.

Amazon Virtual Private Cloud (VPC)

VPC is one of the core services AWS provides. Simply speaking, a VPC is your version of the AWS cloud, and as the name suggests, it is "private," which means that by default, your VPC is a logically isolated and private network inside AWS. You can imagine a VPC as being the same as your own logical data center in a virtual setting inside the AWS cloud, where you have complete control over the resources inside your VPC. AWS resources like AWS servers, and Amazon EC2 and Amazon RDS instances are placed inside the VPC, including all the required networking components to control the data traffic as per your needs.

Creating a VPC could be a very complex task, but AWS has made it easy by providing **Launch VPC Wizard**. You can visualize your network configuration when creating the VPC. The following screenshot shows the VPC network configuration across two AZs, **us-east-1a** and **us-east-1b**:

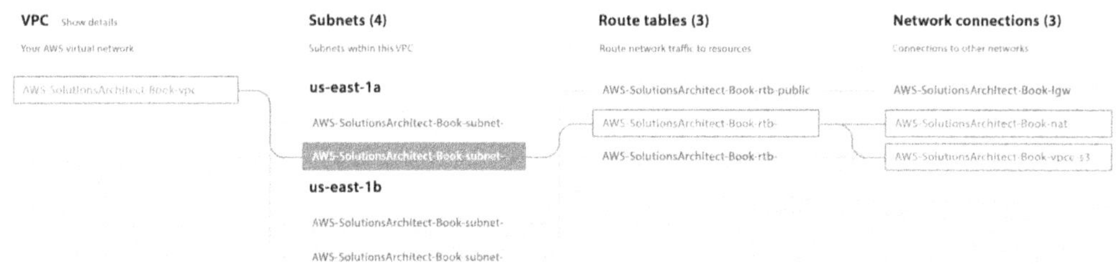

Figure 4.2: AWS VPC configuration with a private subnet flow

In the preceding diagram, you can see VPCs spread across two AZs, where each AZ has two subnets – one public and one private. The highlighted flow shows the data flow of a server deployed into a private subnet of the **us-east-1** AZ. Before going into further details, let's look at key VPC concepts to understand them better:

- **Classless Inter-Domain Routing (CIDR) blocks**: CIDR is the IP address range allocated to your VPC. When you create a VPC, you specify its set of IP addresses with CIDR notation. CIDR notation is a simplified way of showing a specific range of IP addresses. For example, `10.0.0.0/16` covers all IPs from `10.0.0.0` to `10.0.255.255`, providing 65,535 IP addresses to use. All resources in your VPC must fall within the CIDR range.
- **Subnets**: As the name suggests, the subnet is the VPC CIDR block subset. Partitions of the network are divided by the CIDR range within the range of IP addresses in your VPC. A VPC can have multiple subnets for different kinds of services or functions, like a frontend subnet (for internet access to a web page), a backend subnet (for business logic processing), and a database subnet (for database services).

Subnets create trusted boundaries between private and public resources. You should organize your subnets based on internet accessibility. A subnet allows you to define clear isolation between public and private resources. The majority of resources on AWS can be hosted in private subnets. You should use public subnets under controlled access and use them only when it is necessary. As you will keep most of your resources under restricted access, you should plan your subnets so that your private subnets have substantially more IPs available than your public subnets.

- **Route tables:** A routing table contains a set of rules called routes. Routes determine where the traffic will flow. By default, every subnet has a routing table. You can manually create a new route table and assign subnets to it. For better security, use the custom route table for each subnet.
- An **Internet Gateway (IGW)**: The IGW sits at the edge of the VPC and provides connectivity between your VPC resources and the public network (the internet). By default, internet accessibility is denied for internet traffic in your environment. An IGW needs to be attached to your public subnet through the subnet's route table, defining the rules to the IGW. All of your resources that require direct access to the internet (public-facing load balancers, NAT instances, bastion hosts, and so on) would go into the public subnet.
- **Network Address Translation (NAT) gateways:** A NAT gateway provides outbound internet access to the private subnet and prevents connections from being initiated from outside to your VPC resources. A private subnet blocks all incoming and outgoing internet traffic, but servers may need outgoing internet traffic for software and security patch installation. A NAT gateway enables instances in a private subnet to initiate outbound traffic to the internet and protects resources from incoming internet traffic. All restricted servers (such as database and application resources) should deploy inside your private subnet.
- **Security Groups (SGs)**: SGs are the virtual firewalls for your instances to control inbound and outbound packets. You can only use allow statements in the SG, and everything else is denied implicitly. SGs control inbound and outbound traffic as designated resources for one or more instances from the CIDR block range or another SG. As per the principle of least privilege, deny all incoming traffic by default and create rules that can filter traffic based on TCP, UDP, and **Internet Control Message Protocol (ICMP)**.
- **Network Access Control List (NACL)**: A NACL is another firewall that sits at the subnet boundary and allows or denies incoming and outgoing packets. The main difference between a NACL and an SG is that the NACL is stateless – therefore, you need to have rules for incoming and outgoing traffic. With an SG, you need to allow traffic in one direction, and return traffic is, by default, allowed.

You should use an SG in most places as it is a firewall at the EC2 instance level, while a NACL is a firewall at the subnet level. You should use a NACL where you want to put control at the VPC level and also deny specific IPs, as an SG cannot have a deny rule for network traffic coming for a particular IP or IP range.

- **Egress-only IGWs**: These provide outbound communication from **Internet Protocol version 6 (IPv6)** instances in your VPC to the internet and prevent the inbound connection from the internet to your instances on IPv6. IPv6, the sixth iteration of the Internet Protocol, succeeds IPv4 and employs a 128-bit IP address. Like IPv4, it facilitates the provision of unique IP addresses required for internet-connected devices to communicate.
- **DHCP option sets**: This is a group of network information, such as DNS name server and domain name used by EC2 instances when they launch.
- **VPC Flow Logs**: These enable you to monitor traffic flow to your system VPC, such as accepted and rejected traffic information for the designated resource to understand traffic patterns. Flow Logs can also be used as a security tool for monitoring traffic reaching your instance. You can create alarms to notify you if certain types of traffic are detected. You can also create metrics to help you identify trends and patterns.

To access servers in a private subnet, you can create a bastion host, which acts like a jump server. It needs to be hardened with tighter security so that only appropriate people can access it. To log in to the server, always use public-key cryptography for authentication rather than a regular user ID and password method.

A VPC resides only within an AWS Region where it can span across one or more AZs within the Region. In the following diagram, two AZs are being utilized within a Region. Furthermore, you can create one or more subnets inside each AZ, and resources like EC2 and RDS are placed inside the VPC in specific subnets. This architecture diagram shows a VPC configuration with a private and public subnet:

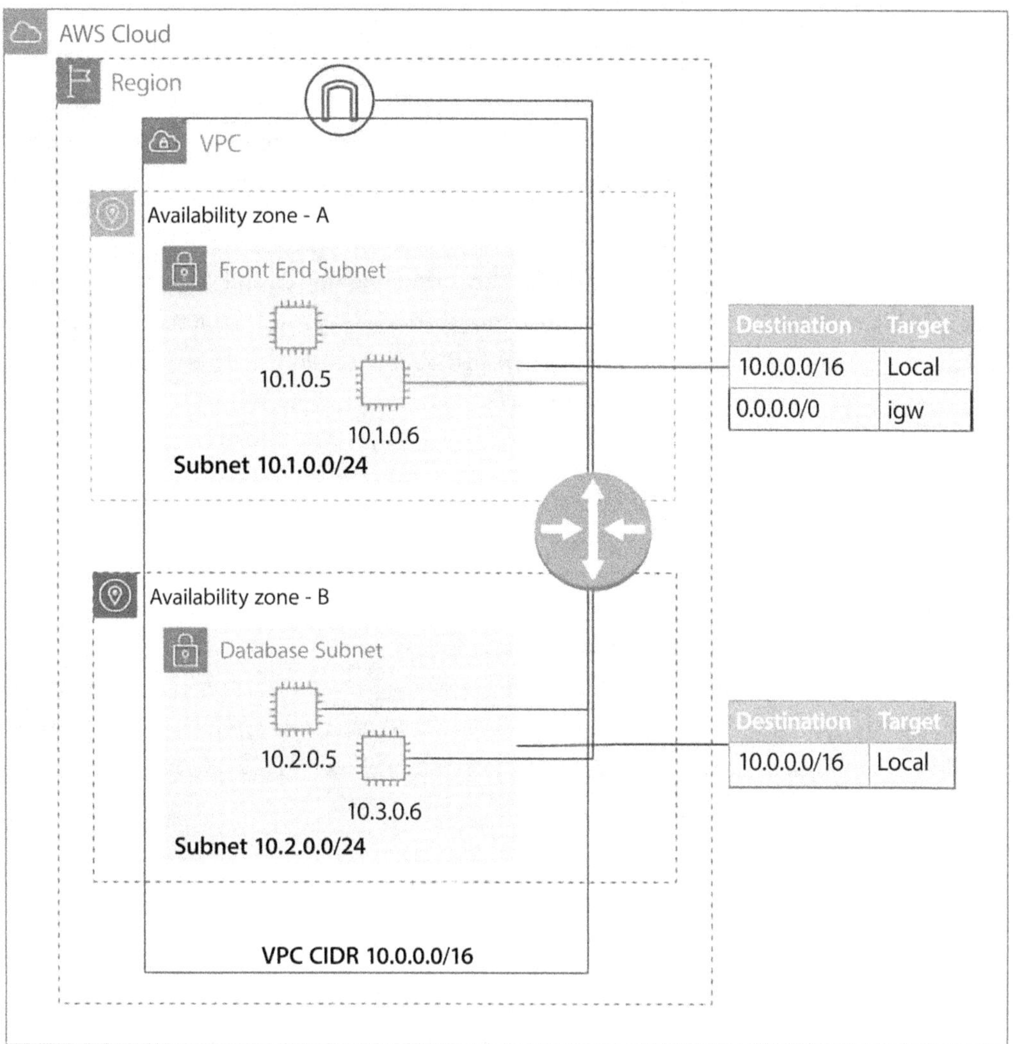

Figure 4.3: AWS VPC network architecture

As shown in this diagram, VPC subnets can be either private or public. As the name suggests, a private subnet doesn't have access to and from the internet, and a public subnet does. By default, any subnet you create is private; what makes it public is the default route – as in, `0.0.0.0/0`, via the IGW.

The VPC's route tables comprise directives for packet routing, and a default route table exists. However, unique route tables can be assigned to individual subnets. By default, all VPC subnets possess interconnectivity. This default behavior can be modified with VPC enhancements for more precise subnet routing, which enables configuration of subnet route tables that direct traffic between two subnets in a VPC through virtual appliances like intrusion detection systems, network firewalls, and protection systems.

As you can see, AWS provides multiple layers for network configuration and security at each layer that can help to build and protect your infrastructure. If attackers can access one component, they must restrict to limited resources by keeping them in their isolated subnet. Due to the ease of VPC creation and building tighter security, organizations tend to create multiple VPCs, which makes things more complicated when these VPCs need to communicate with each other. To simplify this, AWS provides **Transit Gateway (TGW)**. Let's learn more about it.

AWS TGW

As customers are spinning more and more VPCs in AWS, there is an ever-increasing need to connect various VPCs. Before TGW, you could connect VPCs using VPC peering, but VPC peering is a one-to-one connection, which means that resources within peered VPCs only can communicate with each other. If multiple VPCs need to communicate with each other, which is often the case, it results in a complex mesh of VPC peering. For example, a shown in the diagram below, if you have 5 VPCs, you need 10 peering connections.

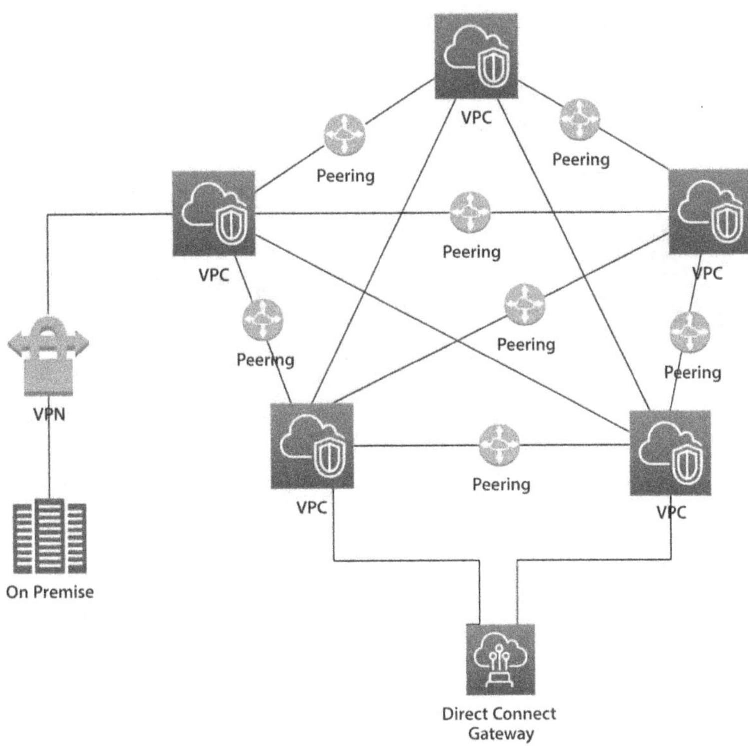

Figure 4.4: VPC connectivity using VPC peering without TGW

As you can see in the preceding diagram, managing so many VPC peering connections will become challenging, and there is also a limit on the number of peering connections per account. To overcome this challenge, AWS released TGW. TGW needs one connection called an attachment to a VPC, and you can establish full- or part-mesh connectivity easily without maintaining so many peering connections.

The following diagram shows simplified communication between five VPCs using TGW.

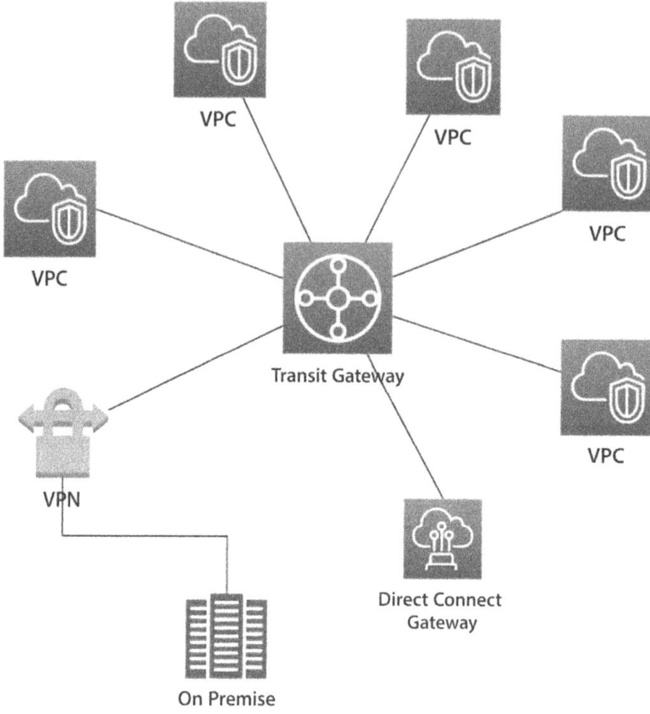

Figure 4.5: VPC connectivity with TGW

AWS TGW is a central aggregation service spanned within a Region, which can be used to connect your VPCs and on-premises networks. TGW is a managed service that takes care of your availability and scalability and eliminates complex VPN or peering connection scenarios when connecting with multiple VPCs and on-premises infrastructure. You can connect TGWs in different Regions by using TGW peering.

TGW is a Regional entity, meaning you can only attach VPCs to the TGW within the same Region, and per VPC, the bandwidth reserved is 50 Gbps. However, one TGW can have up to 5,000 VPC attachments.

In this section, you have learned how to establish network communication between VPCs, but what about securely connecting to resources such as Amazon S3 that live outside of a VPC or other AWS accounts? AWS provides PrivateLink to establish a private connection between VPCs and other AWS services. Let's learn more about AWS PrivateLink.

AWS PrivateLink

AWS PrivateLink establishes secure connectivity between VPCs and AWS services, preventing exposure of traffic to the internet. PrivateLink allows for the private connection of a VPC with supported AWS services hosted by different AWS accounts.

You can access AWS services from a VPC using the Gateway VPC endpoint and Interface VPC endpoint. Gateway endpoints do not support PrivateLink but allow for connection to Amazon S3 and DynamoDB without the need for an IGW or NAT device in your VPC. For other AWS services, an interface VPC endpoint can be created to establish a connection to services through AWS PrivateLink.

Enabling PrivateLink in AWS requires the creation of an endpoint network interface within the desired subnet, and assignment of a private IP address from the subnet address range for each specified subnet in the VPC. You can view the endpoint network interface in your AWS account, but you can't manage it yourself.

PrivateLink essentially provides access to the resources hosted in other VPC or other AWS accounts within the same subnet as the requester. This eliminates the need to use any NAT gateway, IGW, public IP address, or VPN. Therefore, it provides better control over your services, which are reachable via a client VPC.

As shown in the following diagram, AWS PrivateLink enables private connectivity between the **Service Provider** and **Service Consumer** using AWS infrastructure to exchange data without going over the public internet. To achieve this, the **Service Provider** creates an **Endpoint Service** in a private subnet.

In contrast, the **Service Consumer** creates an endpoint in a private subnet with the **Service Provider**'s service API as the target.

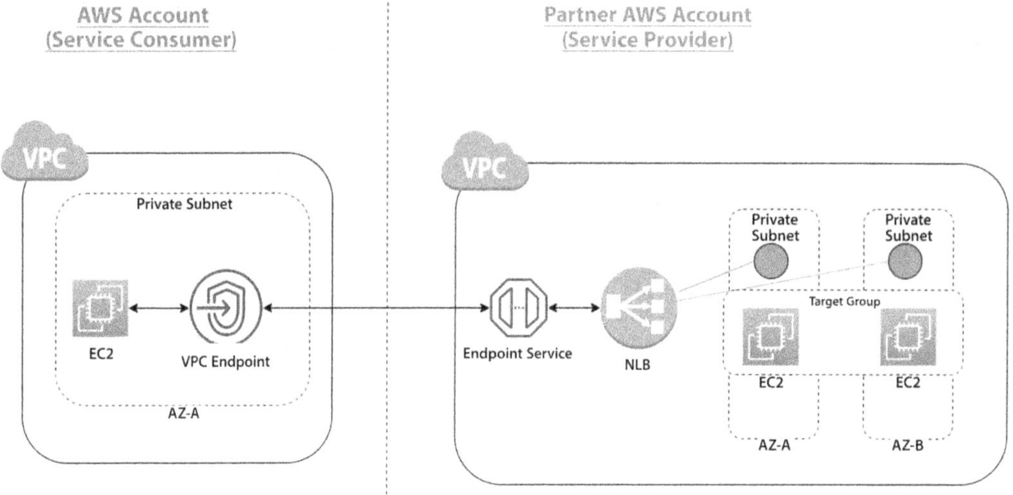

Figure 4.6: PrivateLink between partner Service Provider and Service Consumer accounts

As shown in the preceding architecture diagram, the partner sets up an **Endpoint Service** to expose the service running behind the load balancer (**NLB**). An **NLB** is created in each **Private Subnet**. These services are running on **EC2** instances hosted inside a **Private Subnet**. The client can then create a **VPC Endpoint** with the target as the **Endpoint Service** and use it to consume the service.

Let's look at another pattern shown in the following diagram, which depicts the use of PrivateLink between a **Service Consumer** on an AWS account and an on-premises **Service Provider**.

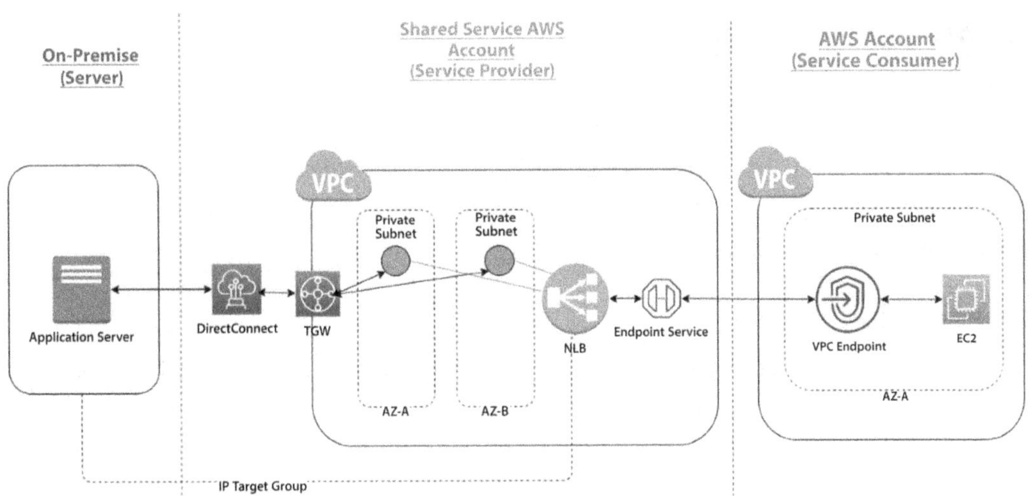

Figure 4.7: PrivateLink between a shared Service Provider, on-premise server, and a Service Consumer account

In this setup, the on-premise servers are the service providers. The **NLB** in the **Shared Service** account is configured with an auto-scaling group with targets referencing the IP addresses of the on-premise servers. The **NLB** is then exposed as an **Endpoint Service**. The **Service Consumer** account can consume this **Endpoint Service** by creating a **VPC Endpoint**. Here, **DirectConnect** provides a dedicated high-speed fiber optics line between the on-premises server and AWS Regions. You will learn more about DirectConnect in this chapter in the *Building Hybrid Cloud Connectivity in AWS* section.

Now, many applications run globally and target to harness users in every corner of the world to accelerate their business. In such a situation, it becomes essential that your users have the same experience while accessing your application regardless of their physical location. AWS provides various edge networking services to handle global traffic. Let's learn more about this.

Edge networking

Edge networking is like last-mile delivery in the supply chain world. When you have users across the world, from the USA to Australia and India to Brazil, you want each user to have the same experience regardless of the physical location of your server where the application is hosted. There are serval components that play their role in building last mile networking. Let's explore them in detail.

Route 53

Amazon Route 53 is a fully managed, simple, fast, secure, highly available, and scalable DNS service. It provides a reliable and cost-effective means for systems and users to translate names like `www.example.com` into IP addresses like `1.2.3.4`. Route 53 is a domain register where you can register a new domain. You can choose an available domain and add it to the cart from the AWS Console and define contacts for the domain. AWS allows you to transfer your domains to AWS and between accounts.

In Route 53, AWS assigns four name servers for all domains, as shown in the screenshot: one for **.com**, one for **.net**, one for **.co.uk**, and one for **.org**. Why? For higher availability! If there is an issue with the **.net** DNS services, the other three continue to provide high availability for your domains.

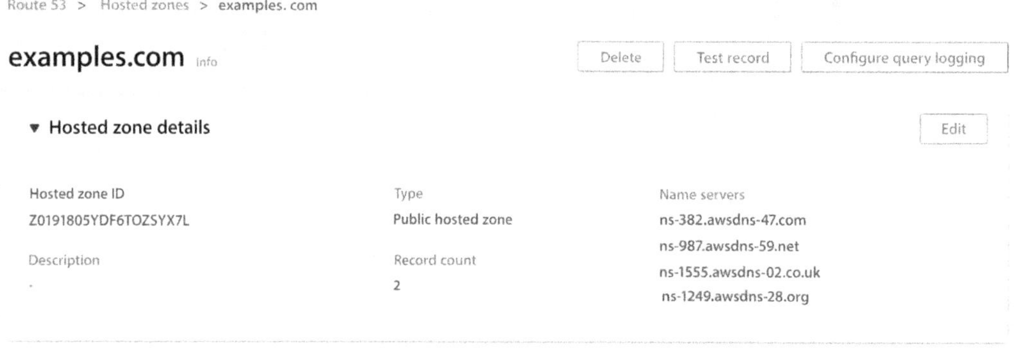

Figure 4.8: Route 53 name server configuration

Route 53 supports both public and private hosted zones. Public hosted zones have a route to internet-facing resources and resolve from the internet using global routing policies. Meanwhile, private hosted zones have a route to VPC resources and resolve from inside the VPC. It helps to integrate with on-premises private zones using forwarding rules and endpoints.

Route 53 provides IPV6 support with end-to-end DNS resolution and support for IPv6 forward (AAAA) and reverse (PTR) DNS records, along with health check monitoring for IPv6 endpoints. For PrivateLink support, when configuring, you can specify a private DNS name, and the Route 53 resolver will resolve it to the PrivateLink endpoint.

Route 53 provides the following seven types of routing policies for traffic:

- **Simple routing policy** – This is used for a single resource (for example, a web server created for the `www.example.com` website).
- **Failover routing policy** – This is used to configure active-passive failover.
- **Geolocation routing policy** – This routes traffic based on the user's location.
- **Geoproximity routing policy** – This is used for geolocation when users are shifting from one location to another.
- **Latency routing policy** – This optimizes the best latency for the resources deployed in multiple AWS Regions.
- **Multivalue answer routing policy** – This is used to respond to DNS queries with up to eight healthy, randomly selected records.
- **Weighted routing policy** – This is used to route traffic to multiple resource properties as defined by you (for example, you want to say 80% traffic to site A and 20% to site B).

You can build advanced routing policies by nesting these primary routing policies into traffic policies; the following diagram shows a nested policy architecture.

Figure 4.9: Route 53 nested routing policy

In the preceding diagram, you can see the policy is **Geolocation**-based, which routes traffic based on the user's location and its proximity to the nearest Region. In the second level, you have a nested policy defined as a **Weighted** policy within the region that routes traffic to servers based on the weight you have defined to route traffic to individual application servers. Advanced routing policies can be built by nesting the seven primary routing policies into traffic policies. You can find more details on this routing policy in the AWS user document here – `https://docs.aws.amazon.com/Route53/latest/DeveloperGuide/routing-policy.html`.

Route 53 Resolver rules tell Route 53 to query a domain. For DNS zones that should resolve on-premises, add a forward rule and point toward the appropriate outbound resolver. Public hosted zones route traffic to internet-facing resources and resolve from the internet using global routing policies. Private hosted zones route traffic to VPC resources and resolve from inside the VPC. Private hosted zones integrate with on-premises private zones using forwarding rules and endpoints.

Route 53 is the only service in which AWS offers 100% SLA, which means AWS makes its best effort to ensure it is 100% available. If Route 53 does not meet the availability commitment, you will be eligible to receive a Service Credit.

While Route 53 helps to direct global traffic to your server, there could be latency if you wanted to deliver significant static assets, such as images and videos, to users far from your servers' deployment Region. AWS provides CloudFront as a content distribution network to solve these latency problems. Let's learn more about it.

Amazon CloudFront

Amazon CloudFront is a content delivery service that accelerates the distribution of both static and dynamic content like image files, video files, and JavaScript, CSS, or HTML files, through a network of data centers spread across the globe. These data centers are referred to as **edge locations**. When you use CloudFront to distribute your content, users requesting content get served by the nearest edge location, providing lower latency and better performance.

As of 2022, AWS has over 300 high-density edge locations spread across over 90 cities in 47 countries. All edge locations are equipped with ample cache storage space and intelligent routing mechanisms to increase the edge cache hit ratio. AWS content distribution edge locations are connected with high-performance 100 GbE network devices and are fully redundant, with parallel global networks with default physical layer encryption.

Suppose you have an image distribution website, `www.example.com`, hosted in the US, which serves art images. Users can access the URL `www.example.com/art.png`, and the image is loaded. If your server is close to the user, then the image load time will be faster, but if users from other locations like Australia or South Africa want to access the same URL, the request has to cross multiple networks before delivering the content to the user's browser. The following diagram shows the HTTP request flow with Amazon CloudFront.

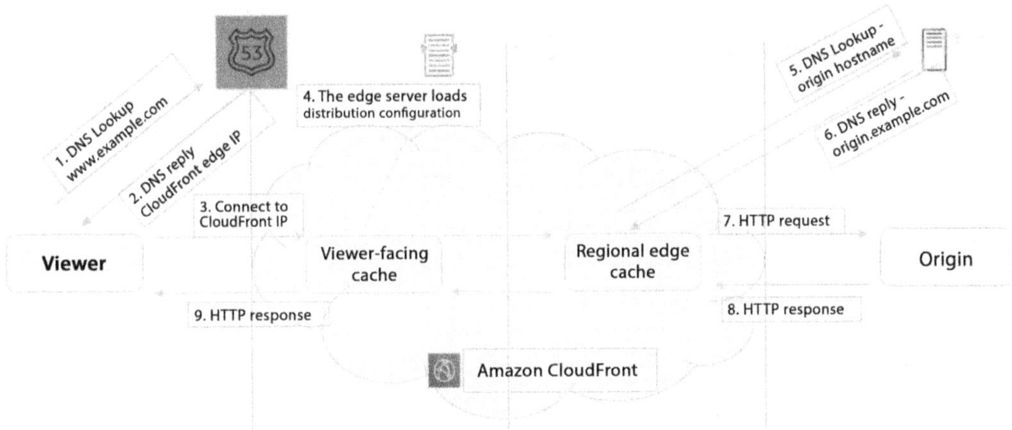

Figure 4.10: HTTP request flow with Amazon CloudFront

As shown in the preceding diagram, when a viewer requests access to page content from the origin server – in this case, `www.example.com` – Route 53 replies with the CloudFront edge IP and redirects the user to the CloudFront location. CloudFront uses the following rules for content distribution:

- If the requested content is already in the edge data center, which means it is a "cache hit," it will be served immediately.
- If the content is not at the edge location (a "cache miss"), CloudFront will request the content from the original location (the web server or S3). The request flows through the AWS backbone, is delivered to the customer, and a copy is kept for future requests.
- If you are using CloudFront, it also provides an extra layer of security since your origin server is not directly exposed to the public network.

CloudFront eliminates the need to go to the origin server for user requests, and content is served from the nearest location. CloudFront provides security by safeguarding the connection between end-users and the content edge, as well as between the edge network and the origin. By offloading SSL termination to CloudFront, the performance of applications is improved since the burden of processing the required negotiation and SSL handshakes is removed from the origins.

CloudFront is a vast topic, and you can learn more about it here – `https://aws.amazon.com/cloudfront/features/`.

In this section, you learned how CloudFront improves performance for both cacheable content and a wide range of applications over TCP, UDP, and MQTT. To address this traffic, AWS provides **AWS Global Accelerator** (**AGA**), which improves the availability and performance of your applications with local or global users. Let's learn more about it.

AWS Global Accelerator (AGA)

AGA enhances application availability and performance by offering fixed static IP addresses as a single entry points, or multiple entry points, to AWS Regions, including ALBs, NLBs, and EC2 instances. AGA utilizes the AWS global network to optimize the path from users to applications, thereby improving the performance of TCP and UDP traffic. AGA continuously monitors the health of application endpoints and promptly redirects traffic to healthy endpoints within 1 minute, in the event of an unhealthy endpoint detection.

AGA and CloudFront are distinct services offered by AWS that employ the AWS global network and its edge locations. While CloudFront accelerates the performance of both cacheable (e.g., videos and images) and dynamic (e.g., dynamic site delivery and API acceleration) content, AGA enhances the performance of various applications over TCP or UDP. Both services are compatible with AWS Shield, providing protection against DDoS attacks. You will learn more about AWS Shield in *Chapter 8, Best Practices for Application Security, Identity, and Compliance.*

AGA automatically reroutes your traffic to the nearest healthy endpoint to avoid failure. AGA health checks will react to customer backend failure within 30 seconds, which is in line with other AWS load-balancing solutions (such as NLB) and Route 53. Where AGA raises the bar is with its ability to shift traffic to healthy backends in as short a timeframe as 30 seconds, whereas DNS-based solutions can take minutes to hours to shift the traffic load. Some key reasons to use AGA are:

- **Accelerate your global applications** – AGA intelligently directs TCP or UDP traffic from users to the AWS-based application endpoint, providing consistent performance regardless of their geographic location.
- **Improve global application availability** – AGA constantly monitors your application endpoints, including but not limited to ALBs, NLBs, and EC2 instances. It instantly reacts to changes in their health or configuration, redirecting traffic to the next closest available endpoint when problems arise. As a result, your users experience higher availability. AGA delivers inter-Region load balancing, while ELB provides intra-Region load balancing.

ELB in a Region is a suitable candidate for AGA as it evenly distributes incoming application traffic across backends, such as Amazon EC2 instances or ECS tasks, within the Region. AGA complements ELB by expanding these capabilities beyond any single Region, enabling you to create a global interface for applications with application stacks located in a single Region or multiple Regions.

- **Fixed entry point** – AGA provides a set of static IP addresses for use as a fixed entry point to your AWS application. Announced via anycast and delivered from AWS edge locations worldwide, these eliminate the complexity of managing the IP addresses of multiple endpoints and allow you to scale your application and maintain DDoS resiliency with AWS Shield.
- **Protect your applications** – AGA allows you to serve internet users while keeping your ALBs and EC2 instances private.

AGA allows customers to run global applications in multiple AWS Regions. Traffic destined to static IPs is globally distributed, and end user requests are ingested through AWS's closest edge location and routed to the correct regional resource for better availability and latency. This global endpoint supports TCP and UDP and does not change even as customers move resources between Regions for failover or other reasons (i.e., client applications are no longer tightly coupled to the specific AWS Region an application runs in). Customers will like the simplicity of this managed service.

As technology becomes more accessible with the high-speed networks provided by 5G, there is a need to run applications such as connected cars, autonomous vehicles, and live video recognition with ultra-low latency. AWS provides a service called AWS Wavelength, which delivers AWS services to the edge of the 5G network. Let's learn more about it.

AWS Wavelength

AWS Wavelength is designed to reduce network latency when connecting to applications from 5G-connected devices by providing infrastructure deployments within the Telco 5G network service providers' data centers. It allows application traffic to reach application servers running in Wavelength Zones, as well as AWS compute and storage services. This eliminates the need for traffic to go through the internet, which can introduce latency of up to 10s of milliseconds and limit the full potential of the bandwidth and latency advancements of 5G.

AWS Wavelength allows for the creation and implementation of real-time, low-latency applications, such as edge inference, smart factories, IoT devices, and live streaming. This service enables the deployment of emerging, interactive applications that require ultra-low latency to function effectively.

Some key benefits of AWS Wavelength are:

- **Ultra-low latency for 5G** – Wavelength combines the AWS core services, such as compute and storage, with low-latency 5G networks. It helps you to build applications with ultra-low latencies using the 5G network.
- **Consistent AWS experience** – You can use the same AWS services you use daily on the AWS platform.
- **Global 5G network** – Wavelength is available in popular Telco networks such as Verizon, Vodafone, and SK Telecom across the globe, including the US, Europe, Korea, and Japan, which enables ultra-low latency applications for a global user base.

Wavelength Zones are connected to a Region and provide access to AWS services. Architecting edge applications using a hub-and-spoke model with the Region is recommended for scalable and cost-effective options for less latency-sensitive applications.

As enterprises adopt the cloud, it will not be possible to instantly move all IT workloads to the cloud. Some applications need to run on-premises and still communicate with the cloud. Let's learn about AWS services for setting up a hybrid cloud.

Building hybrid cloud connectivity in AWS

A hybrid cloud comes into the picture when you need to keep some of your IT workload on-premises while creating your cloud migration strategy. You may have decided to keep them out of the cloud for various reasons, such as compliance and the unavailability of out-of-the-box cloud services such as a mainframe, when you need more time to re-architect them, or when you are waiting to complete your license term with an existing vendor. In such cases, you need highly reliable connectivity between your on-premises and cloud infrastructure. Let's learn about the various options available from AWS to set up hybrid cloud connectivity.

AWS Virtual Private Network (VPN)

AWS VPN is a networking service to establish a secure connection between AWS, on-premises networks, and remote client devices. There are two variants of AWS VPN: Site-to-Site VPN and AWS Client VPN. AWS Site-To-Site VPN establishes a secure tunnel between on-premises and AWS Virtual Private Gateways or AWS TGWs.

It offers fully managed and highly available VPN termination endpoints at AWS Regions. You can add two VPN tunnels per VPN connection, which is secured with an IPsec Site-to-Site tunnel with AES-256, SHA-2, and the latest DH groups. The following diagram shows the AWS Site-to-Site VPN connection.

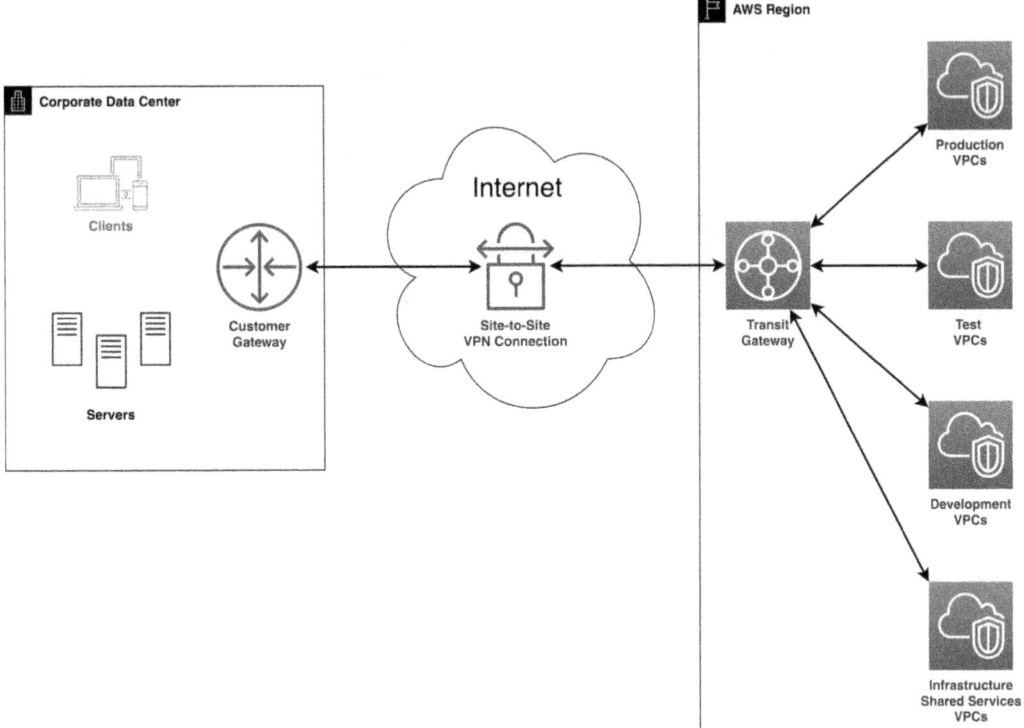

Figure 4.11: AWS Site-to-Site VPN with TGW

As depicted in the preceding diagram, a connection has been established from the customer gateway to the AWS TGW using Site-To-Site VPN, which is further connected to multiple VPCs.

AWS Client VPN can be used with OpenVPN-based VPN client software to access your AWS resources and on-premises resources from any location across the globe.

AWS Client VPN also supports a split tunneling feature, which can be used if you only want to send traffic destined to AWS via Client VPN and the rest of the traffic via a local internet breakout.

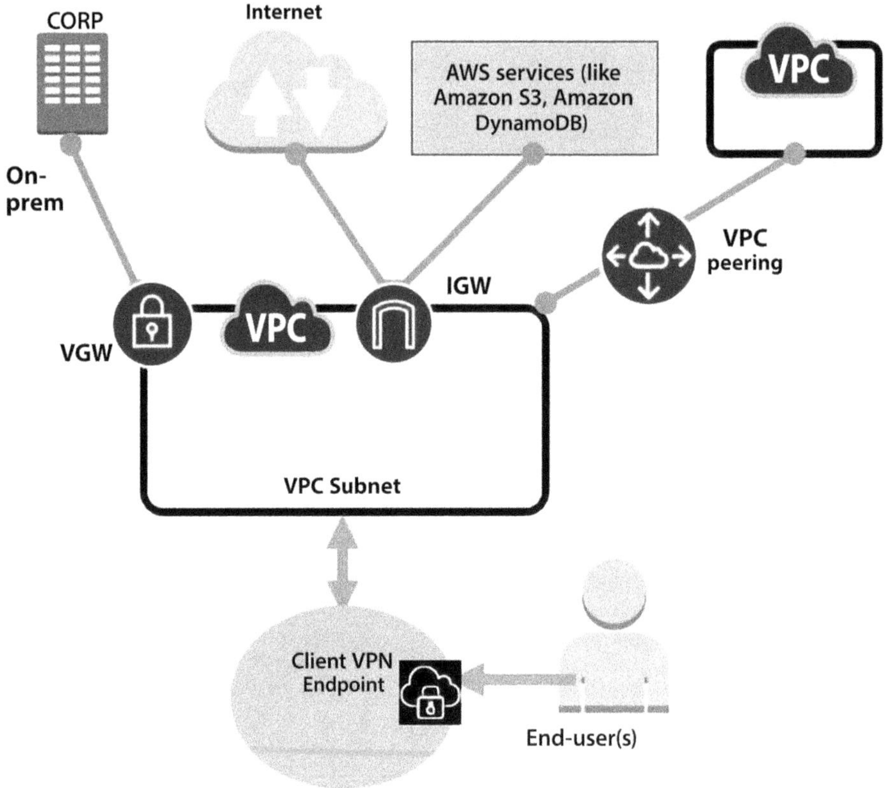

Figure 4.12: AWS Client VPN

AWS Client VPN provides secure access to any resource in AWS and on-premises from anywhere using OpenVPN clients. It seamlessly integrates with existing infrastructure, like Amazon VPC, AWS Directory Service, and so on.

AWS Direct Connect

AWS Direct Connect is a low-level infrastructure service that enables AWS customers to set up a dedicated network connection between their on-premises facilities and AWS. You can bypass any public internet connection using AWS Direct Connect and establish a private connection linking your data centers with AWS. This solution provides higher network throughput, increases the consistency of connections, and, counterintuitively, can often reduce network costs.

There are two variants of Direct Connect, dedicated and hosted. A dedicated connection is made through a 1 Gbps, 10 Gbps, or 100 Gbps dedicated Ethernet connection for a single customer. Hosted connections are obtained via an AWS Direct Connect Delivery Partner, who provides the connectivity between your data center and AWS via the partner's infrastructure.

However, it is essential to note that AWS Direct Connect does not provide encryption in transit by default. Suppose you want to have encryption in transit. In that case, you have two choices – you can either use AWS Site-To-Site VPN to provide IPsec encryption for your packets, or you can combine AWS Direct Connect with AWS Site-to-Site VPN to deliver an IPsec-encrypted private connection while, at the same time, lowering network costs and increasing network bandwidth throughput.

The other option is to activate the MACsec feature, which provides line-rate, bi-directional encryption for 10 Gpbs and 100 Gpbs dedicated connections between your data centers and AWS Direct Connect locations. MACsec is done at the hardware; hence, it provides better performance. To encrypt the traffic, you can also use an AWS technology partner as an alternative solution to encrypt this network traffic.

AWS Direct Connect uses the 802.1q industry standard to create VLANs. These connections can be split into several **virtual interfaces (VIFs)**. This enables us to leverage the same connection to reach publicly accessible services such as Amazon S3 by using an IP address space and private services such as EC2 instances running in a VPC within AWS. The following are AWS Direct Connect interface types:

- **Public virtual interface:** This is the interface you can use to access any AWS public services globally, which are accessible via public IP addresses such as Amazon S3. A public VIF can access all AWS public services using public IP addresses.
- **Private virtual interface**: You can connect to your VPCs using private VIFs using private IP addresses. You can connect to the AWS Direct Connect gateway using a private VIF, allowing you to connect to up to 10 VPCs globally with a single VIF, unlike connecting a private VIF to a Virtual Private Gateway associated with a single VPC.
- **Transit virtual interface**: A transit VIF is connected to your TGW via a Direct Connect gateway. A transit VIF is supported for a bandwidth of 1 Gbps or higher.

The following diagram has put together various AWS Direct Connect interfaces, showing the use of various interfaces while designing your hybrid cloud connectivity.

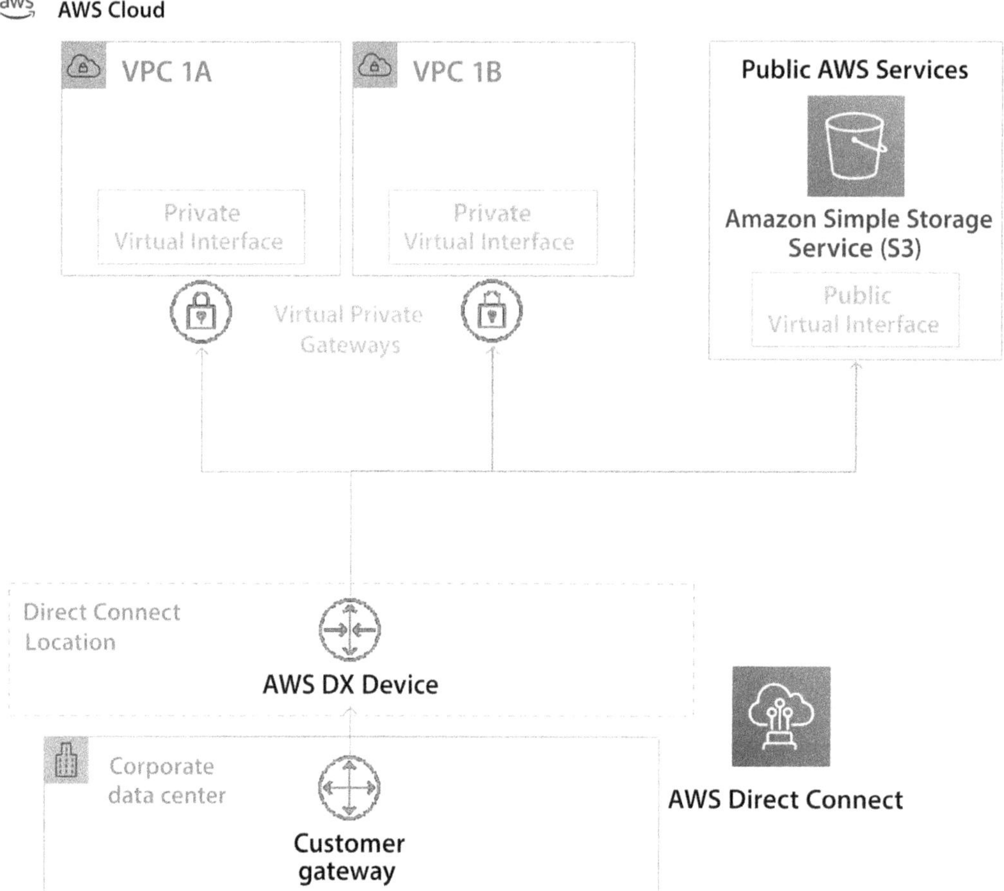

Figure 4.13: AWS Direct Connect interface types

The preceding diagram shows the corporate data center connected to the AWS cloud using the Direct Connect location. Most of your application workloads, such as the web server, app server, and database server, run inside the VPC under a private restricted network, so a private VIF connects to VPCs across different AZs. Conversely, Amazon S3 is in the public domain, where you might host static pages, images, and videos for your applications connected through a public VIF.

AWS Direct Connect can reduce costs when workloads require high bandwidth. It can reduce these costs in two ways:

- It transfers data from on-premises environments to the cloud, directly reducing cost commitments to **Internet Service Providers (ISPs)**.
- The costs of transferring the data using a dedicated connection are billed using the AWS Direct Connect data transfer rates and not the internet data transfer rates, which are lower.

Network latency and responses to requests can be highly variable. Workloads that use AWS Direct Connect have a much more homogenous latency and consistent user experience. Direct connection comes with a cost; you may only sometimes need such high bandwidth and want to optimize costs better. For such cases, you may want to use AWS VPN, as discussed in the *AWS Virtual Private Network (VPN)* section.

You have learned about different patterns of setting up network connectivity within an AWS cloud and to or from an AWS cloud, but for a large enterprise with branch offices or chain stores, connecting multiple data centers, office locations, and cloud resources can be a very tedious task. AWS provides Cloud WAN to simplify this issue. Let's learn more about it.

AWS Cloud WAN

How many of you would be paged if your entire network suddenly went down? Let's take an example, Petco, which has over 1,500 locations. Imagine what happens on a network like that on any given day. One way to connect your data centers and branch offices is to use fixed, physical network connections. These connections are long-lived and not easy to change quickly.

Many use AWS Site-to-Site VPN connections for connectivity between their locations and AWS. Alternatively, you bypass the internet altogether and use AWS Direct Connect to create a dedicated network link to AWS. And some use broadband internet with SD-WAN hardware to create virtual overlay networks between locations. Inside AWS, you build networks within VPCs and route traffic between them with TGW. The problem is that these networks all take different approaches to connectivity, security, and monitoring. As a result, you are faced with a patchwork of tools and networks to manage and maintain.

For example, to keep your network secure, you must configure firewalls at every location, but you are faced with many different firewalls from many different vendors, and each is configured slightly differently than the others. Ensuring your access policies are synced across the entire network quickly becomes daunting. Likewise, managing and troubleshooting your network is difficult when the information you need is kept in many different systems.

Every new location, network appliance, and security requirement makes things more and more complicated. We see many customers struggle to keep up. To solve these problems, network architects need a way to unify their networks so that there is one central place to build, manage, and secure their network. They need easy ways to make and change connections between their data centers, branch offices, and cloud applications, regardless of what they're running on today. And they need a backbone network that can smoothly adapt to these changes.

AWS Cloud WAN is a global network service enabling you to create and manage your infrastructure globally in any AWS Region or on-premises. Consider it a global router that you can use to connect your on-premises networks and AWS infrastructure. AWS Cloud WAN provides network segmentation to group your network or workloads, which can be located across any AWS Region. It takes care of the route propagation to connect your infrastructure without manually maintaining the routing.

AWS Cloud WAN provides network segmentation, which means you can divide your global network into separate and isolated networks. This helps you to control the traffic flow and cross-network access tightly. For example, a corporate firm can have a network segment for invoicing and order processing, another for web traffic, and another for logging and monitoring traffic.

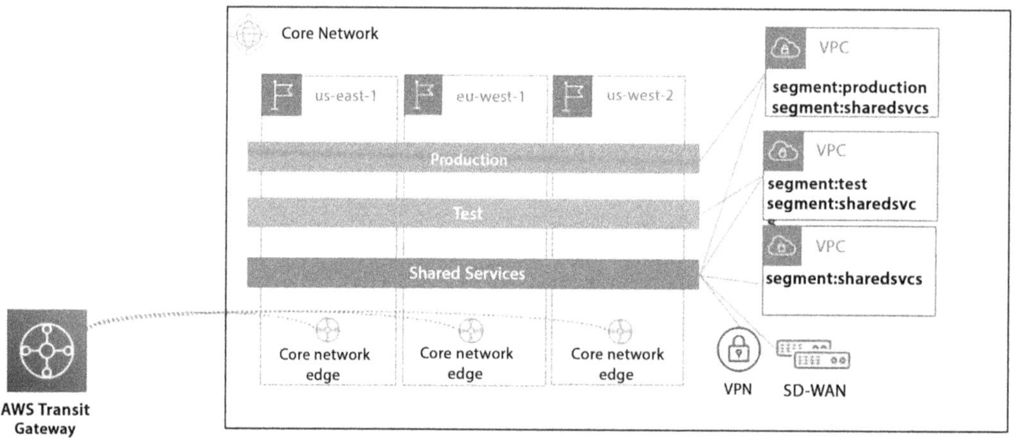

Figure 4.14: AWS Cloud WAN architecture

When using Cloud WAN, you can see your entire network on one dashboard, giving you one place to monitor and track metrics for your entire network. Cloud WAN lets you spot problems early and respond quickly, which minimizes downtime and bottlenecks while helping you troubleshoot problems, even when data comes from separate systems. Security is the top priority, and throughout this chapter, you have learned about the security aspect of network design.

Let's go into more detail to learn about network security best practices.

AWS cloud network security

Security is always a top priority for any organization. As a general rule, you need to protect every infrastructure element individually and as a group – like the saying, "Dance as if nobody is watching and secure as if everybody is." AWS provides various managed security services and a well-architected pillar to help you design a secure solution.

You can implement secure network infrastructure by creating an allow-list of permitted protocols, ports, CIDR networks, and SG sources, and enforcing several policies on the AWS cloud. A NACL is used to explicitly block malicious traffic and segment the edge connectivity to the internet, as shown in the following diagram.

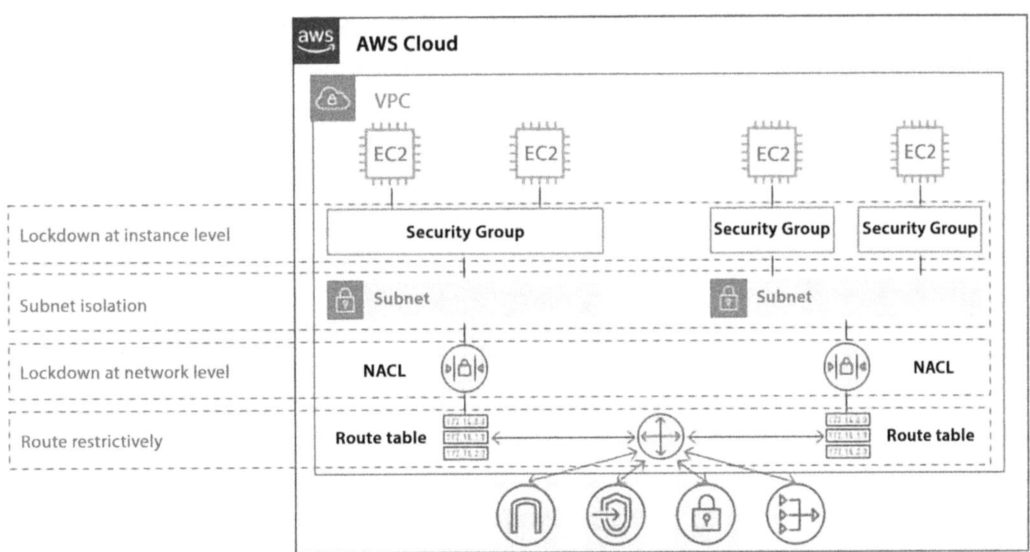

Figure 4.15: SGs and NACLs in network defense

As shown in the preceding diagram, SGs are the host-level virtual firewalls that protect your EC2 instance from the traffic coming to or leaving from a particular instance. An SG is a stateful firewall, which means that you need to create a rule in one direction only, and the return traffic will automatically be allowed. A NACL is also a virtual firewall that sits at the subnet boundary, regulating traffic in and out of one or more subnets. Unlike an SG, a NACL is stateless, which means you need both inbound and outbound rules to allow specific traffic.

The following table outlines the difference between SGs and NACLs.

SG	NACL
The SG is the first layer of defense, which operates at the instance level.	A NACL works at the subnet level inside an AWS VPC.
You can only add "allow" security rules.	You can explicitly add a "deny" rule in addition to allow rules. For example, you can deny access to a specific IP address.
The SG is stateful, which means once you add an inbound allow rule, it automatically adds an outbound allow rule. For example, for a CRM server to respond, you have only to allow a rule to accept traffic from the IP range.	A NACL is stateless, meaning if you add an inbound allow rule, you must add an explicit allow rule. For a CRM server to respond, you must add both allow and deny rules to accept traffic from the IP range.
If you have added multiple rules in the instance, the SG will validate all rules before deciding whether to allow traffic.	In a NACL, you define rule priority by assigning values, such as 100 or 200. The NACL processes the rules in numerical order.
As an SG is at the instance level, it applies to an instance only.	As a NACL is at the subnet level, it automatically applies to all instances in the subnets it's linked to.

Table 4.1: Comparison between security groups and network access control lists

While the SG and NACL provide security inside the VPC, let's learn more about overall AWS network security best practices.

AWS Network Firewall (ANFW)

ANFW is a highly available, fully redundant, and easy-to-deploy managed network firewall service for your Amazon VPC, which offers a service-level agreement with an uptime commitment of 99.99%. ANFW scales automatically based on your network traffic, eliminating the need for the capacity planning, deployment, and management of the firewall infrastructure.

ANFW supports open source Suricata-compatible rules for stateful inspection. It provides fine controls for your network traffic, such as allowing or blocking specific protocol traffic from specific prefixes. ANFW also supports third-party integration to source-managed intelligent feeds.

ANFW also provides alert logs that detail a particular rule that has been triggered. There is native integration with Amazon S3, Amazon Kinesis, and Amazon CloudWatch, which can act as the destination for these logs.

You can learn about various ANFW deployment models by referring to the detailed AWS blog here – `https://aws.amazon.com/blogs/networking-and-content-delivery/deployment-models-for-aws-network-firewall/`.

Let's learn more about network security patterns and anti-patterns, keeping SGs and NACL in mind.

AWS network security patterns – best practices

Several patterns can be used when creating an SG and NACL strategy for your organization, such as:

- **Create the SG before launching the instance(s), resource(s), or cluster(s)** – This will force you to determine if a new SG is necessary or if an existing SG should be used. This enables you to pre-define all the rules and reference the SG at creation time, especially when creating these programmatically or via a CloudFormation/Landing Zone pipeline. Additionally, you should not use the default SG for your applications.
- **Logically construct SGs into functional categories based on their application tier or role they perform** – Consider the number of distinct tiers your application has and then logically construct the SGs to match those functional components. For a typical three-tier architecture, a minimum of three SGs should be used (e.g., a web tier, an app tier, and a DB tier).
- **Configure rules to chain SGs to each other** – In an SG rule, you can authorize network access from a specific CIDR address range or another SG in your VPC. Either option could be appropriate, depending on your environment. Generally speaking, organizations can "chain" the SGs together between application tiers, thus building a logical flow of allowed traffic from one SG to another. However, an exception to this pattern is described in the following pattern.
- **Restrict privileged administrative ports (e.g., SSH or RDP) to internal systems (e.g., bastion hosts)** – As a best practice, administrative access to instances should be blocked or restricted to a small number of protected and monitored instances – sometimes referred to as bastion hosts or jump boxes.
- **Create NACL rule numbers with the future in mind** – NACLs rules are evaluated in numerical order based on the rule number, and the first rule that matches the traffic will be used. For example, if there are 10 rules in an NACL and rule number 2 matches `DENY SSH traffic` on port 22, the other 8 rules never get evaluated, regardless of their content. Therefore, when creating NACL rules, it is best practice to leave gaps between the rule numbers – 100 is typically used. So, the first rule has a rule number of 100, and the second rule has a rule number of 200.

If you have to add a rule between these rules in the future, you can add a new rule with rule number 150, which still leaves space for future planning.

- **In well-architected, high-availability VPCs, share NACLs based on subnet tiers** – The subnet tiers in a well-architected, high-availability VPC should have the same resources and applications deployed in the same subnet tiers (e.g., the web and app tiers). These tiers should have the same inbound and outbound rule requirements. In this case, it is recommended to use the same NACL to avoid making administrative changes in multiple places.
- **Limit inbound rules to the minimum required ports and restrict access to commonly vulnerable ports** – As with hardware firewalls, it is important to carefully determine the minimum baseline for inbound rules required for an application tier to function. Reducing the ports allowed greatly reduces the overall attack surface and simplifies the management of the NACLs.
- **Finally, audit and eliminate unnecessary, unused, or redundant NACL rules and SGs** – As your environment scales, you may find that unnecessary SGs and NACL rules were created or mistakenly left behind from previous changes.

AWS network security anti-patterns

While the previous section described patterns for using VPC SGs and NACLs, there are a number of ways you might attempt to configure or utilize your SGs and NACL in non-recommended ways. These are referred to as "anti-patterns" and should be avoided.

- The default SG is included automatically with your VPC. Whenever you launch an EC2 instance or any other AWS resource in your VPC, it is linked to the default SG. Using the default SG does not provide granular control. You can create custom SGs and add them to instances or resources. You can create multiple SGs as per your applications' needs, such as a web server EC2 instance or an Aurora database server.
- If you already have SGs applied to all instances, **do not** create a rule that references these in other SGs. By referencing an SG applied to all instances, you are defining a source or destination of all instances. This is a wide-open pointer to or from everything in your environment. There are better ways to apply least-privileged access.
- Multiple SGs can be applied to an instance. Within a specific application tier, all instances should have the same set of SGs applied to them. However, ensure a tier's instances have a uniform consistency. Suppose web servers, application servers, and database servers co-mingle in the same tier. In this case, they should be separated into distinct tiers and have tier-specific SGs applied to them. **Do not** create unique SGs for related instances (one-off configurations or permutations).

- Refrain from sharing or reusing NACLs in subnets with different resources – although the NACL rules may be the same now, there is no way to determine future rules required for the resources. Since the resources in the subnet differ (e.g., between different applications), resources in one subnet may need a new rule that isn't needed for the resources in the other subnet. However, since the NACL is shared, opening up the rule applies resources in both subnets. This approach does not follow the principle of least privilege.
- NACLs are stateless, so rules are evaluated when traffic enters and leaves the subnet. You will need an inbound and outbound rule for each two-way communication. This anti-pattern shouldn't be encountered because you are only using NACLs as guardrails. Evaluating large complex rule sets on traffic coming in and out of the subnet will eventually lead to performance degradation.

It is recommended to periodically audit for SGs and NACLs rules that are unnecessary or redundant and delete them. This will reduce complexity and help prevent reaching the service limit accidentally.

AWS network security with third-party solutions

You may not always want to get into all the nitty-gritty details of AWS security configuration and look for more managed solutions. AWS's extensive partner network builds managed AWS solutions to fulfill your network security needs. Some of the most popular network security solutions provided by the following **integrated software vendor** (**ISV**) partners in AWS Marketplace are below:

- **Palo Alto Networks** – Palo Alto Networks has introduced a Next-Generation Firewall service that simplifies securing AWS deployments. This service enables developers and cloud security architects to incorporate inline threat and data loss prevention into their application development workflows.
- **Aviatrix** – The Aviatrix Secure Networking Platform is made up of two components: the Aviatrix controller (which manages the gateways and orchestrates all connectivity) and the Aviatrix Gateways that are deployed in VPCs using AWS IAM roles.
- **Check Point** – Check Point CloudGuard Network Security is a comprehensive security solution designed to protect your AWS cloud environment and assets. It provides advanced, multi-layered network security features such as a firewall, IPS, application control, IPsec VPN, antivirus, and anti-bot functionality.
- **Fortinet** – This provides firewall technology to deliver complete content and network protection, including application control, IPS, VPN, and web filtering. It also provides more advanced features like vulnerability management and flow-based inspection work.

- **Cohesive Networks** – Cohesive's VNS3 is a software-only virtual appliance for connectivity, federation, and security in AWS.

In addition to these, many more AWS-managed solutions are available through partners like Netskope, Valtix, IBM, and Cisco. You can find the complete list of network security solutions available in the AWS Marketplace using this link – `https://aws.amazon.com/marketplace/search/results?searchTerms=network+security`.

AWS cloud security has multiple components, starting with networking as a top job. You can learn more about AWS security by visiting their security page at `https://aws.amazon.com/security/`.

Summary

In this chapter, you started with learning about the AWS Global Infrastructure and understanding the details of AWS Regions, AZs, and LZs. You also learned about the various benefits of using the AWS Global Infrastructure.

Networking is the backbone of any IT workload, whether in the cloud or in an on-premises network. To start your cloud journey in AWS, you must have good knowledge of AWS networking. When you start with AWS, you create your VPC within AWS. You learned about using an AWS VPC with various components such as an SG, a NACL, a route table, an IGW, and a NAT gateway. You learned how to segregate and secure your IT resources by putting them into private and public subnets.

With the ease of creating VPC in AWS organizations, multiple VPCs tend to be created, whether it is intentional to give each team their own VPC, or unintentional when the dev team creates multiple test workloads. Often, these VPCs need to communicate with each other; for example, the finance department needs to get information from accounting. You learned about setting up communication between multiple VPCs using VPC peering and TGW. You learned to establish secure connections with services on the public internet or other accounts using AWS PrivateLink.

Further, you learned about AWS edge networking to address the global nature of user traffic. These services include Route 53, CloudFront, AGA, and AWS Wavelength. You then learned about connecting an on-premises server and an AWS cloud. Finally, you closed the chapter with the network security best practices, patterns and anti-patterns, and third-party managed network security solutions available via the AWS partner network.

As you start your journey of learning about the AWS core services, the next topic is storage. AWS provides various types of storage to match your workload needs. In the next chapter, you will learn about storage in AWS and how to choose the right storage for your IT workload needs.

5

Storage in AWS – Choosing the Right Tool for the Job

Storage is a critical and foundational service for any cloud provider. If this service is not implemented in a durable, available, efficient, low-latency manner, it doesn't matter how many other excellent services are offered.

File, block, and object storage are at the core of many applications. In *Chapter 7, Selecting the Right Database Service,* we will learn about other storage services focused on databases. However in this chapter, we will focus on basic file and object storage.

In this chapter, we will first look at Amazon EBS, EFS, and S3. We will then look at the difference between block storage and object storage. We will also look at versioning in Amazon S3 and explore Amazon S3 best practices.

In this chapter, we will cover the following topics:

- Understanding local storage with Amazon **Elastic Block Store** (**EBS**)
- Investigating file storage with Amazon **Elastic File System** (**EFS**)
- Using Amazon FSx to manage file systems
- Versioning in Amazon S3
- Choosing the right cloud storage type
- Exploring Amazon S3 best practices
- Building hybrid storage with AWS Storage Gateway and AWS Backup

Moving storage workloads to the cloud has been one of the main ways to address strategic priorities, such as increasing an organization's agility, accelerating its ability to innovate, strengthening security, and reducing cost. Let's learn how all of this can be achieved in AWS.

Understanding Amazon Elastic Block Store

Block storage is a foundational storage technology that has been around since the early days of computing. The hard drive in your laptop, the memory in your mobile phone, and all other forms of data storage, from USB thumb drives to storage arrays that organizations place in their data centers, are all based on block storage.

Persistent block storage that can be used with Amazon EC2 instances is provided by **Amazon Elastic Block Store** (**EBS**). When using EC2, you have the option to use local instance storage or EBS for block storage:

- **Instance storage** is great for high-performance (over 80K IOPS and over 1,750 MB/s throughput) and low-latency (under 1 ms) applications. However, instance storage is ephemeral, which means when you stop, hibernate, or terminate an EC2 instance, every block of storage in the instance store is reset. Therefore, do not rely on instance storage for valuable, long-term data.
- **EBS volumes** provide excellent performance and persistent storage. EBS allows your customer to correctly size their instance for the memory and CPU they need, relying on EBS for their storage, which they can independently size on capacity, IOPS, or throughput.
- **SAN** (**Storage Area Network**) in the cloud – With io2 Block Express, you can now achieve SAN-like performance in the cloud.

In simple terms, Amazon EBS is a hard drive for a server in AWS. One advantage of Amazon EBS over many typical hard drives is that you can easily detach it from one server and attach it to another server using software commands. Usually, with other servers outside of AWS, this would require physically detaching the hard drive and physically attaching it to another server.

When using Amazon EBS, data is persisted. This means that data lives even after the server is shut down. Like other services, Amazon EBS provides high availability and durability.

Amazon EBS should not be confused with the instance store available in EC2 instances. EC2 instance stores deliver ephemeral storage for EC2 instances. One of the use cases for EC2 instance stores would be any data that does not need to be persisted, such as the following:

- Caches

- Buffers
- Temporary files
- Temporary variables

If data needs to be stored permanently, the following Amazon EBS options are available.

General-purpose Solid-State Devices (SSDs)

General-purpose **Solid-State Device** (**SSD**) storage provides a solid balance of cost and performance. It can be applied to a wide array of use cases, such as the following:

- Virtual desktops
- Development and staging environments
- Application development

There are two types of general-purpose SSD volume available, gp2 and gp3. They come in a volume size of 1 TB to 16 TB with **input/output operations per second** (**IOPS**) up to 16,000. IOPS is a useful way to measure disk performance. The gp3 is the latest generation of SSD volume, which costs 20% less than the gp2 volume and provides four times more throughput up to 1,000 MiB/s. A gp3 volume provides 128MiB/s throughput and 3,000 IOPS performance which can scale up to 16,000 IOPS and 1,000 MiB/s if needed with nominal charges.

Provisioned IOPS SSD

Amazon EBS storage volumes with Provisioned IOPS SSD are intended for low-latency workloads that require high IOPS and throughput. They are designed to provide the highest performance and are ideal for critical and IOPS-intensive applications. This type of storage is ideally suited for mission-critical applications that require a high IOPS performance, such as the following:

- Business applications
- Production databases, including SAP HANA, MS SQL Server, and IBM DB2

There are two types of provisioned IOPS SSDs available, io1 and io2. They come in a volume size of 4 TB to 16 TB with IOPS up to 64,000. The io2 is a next-generation volume and offers a consistent baseline performance of up to 500 IOPS/GB compared to io1, which offers 50 IOPS/GB performance. Improving further on performance, AWS launched the "io2 Block Express" volume, which comes in volume sizes of 4 TB to 64 TB with IOPS up to 256,000.

Throughput Optimized HDD

Throughput Optimized **HDDs** (**Hard Disk Drives**) offer excellent value, providing a reasonable cost for workloads that call for high performance and have high throughput requirements. Typical use cases include:

- Big data applications
- Log processing
- Streaming applications
- Data warehouse applications

Throughput Optimized HDDs, also known as st1, come in volume sizes of 125 GB to 16TB with 500 IOPS per volume. An st1 volume baseline performance scales with the size of the volume. Here, instead of measuring in IOPS, we're talking throughput in MB/second. The baseline is 40MB/second per TB provisioned, up to 500MB/second. These are not designed for boot volumes and you have a minimum capacity of 125 GiB. But you can go up to 16 TiB.

Cold HDD

This type of storage is normally used for applications that require optimizing costs with large volumes of data—typically, data that needs to be accessed infrequently. Cold HDD also goes by sc1 and comes in volume sizes 125 GB to 16TB with 250 IOPS per volume.

IMPORTANT NOTE

This would be a good time to note the following. EC2 instances are virtualized, and there isn't a one-to-one relationship between servers and EC2 instances. Similarly, when you use EBS storage, a single physical storage device is not assigned to you by AWS; instead, you get a slice of several devices that store the data in a distributed fashion across data centers to increase reliability and availability. You can attach an EBS volume to an EC2 instance in the same AZ only; however, you can use a snapshot to create multiple volumes and move across AZs.

In addition, Amazon **Elastic Block Store** (**EBS**) volumes are replicated transparently by design. Therefore, it is unnecessary to provide extra redundancy by setting up RAID or other redundancy strategies.

Amazon EBS volumes are by default highly available, durable, and reliable. This redundancy strategy and multiple server replication are built into the base price of Amazon EBS volumes. Amazon EBS volume files are mirrored across more than one server within an **Availability Zone** (**AZ**). This will minimize data loss. More than one device will have to fail simultaneously for data loss to occur. Amazon EBS volumes will also self-heal and bring in additional healthy resources if a disk fails.

Amazon EBS volumes offer at least twenty times more reliability than traditional commodity devices. Let's learn about EBS Snapshots.

Amazon EBS Snapshots

Amazon EBS also provides a feature to quickly and automatically create snapshots. The backups of data volumes can be performed incrementally. For example, if you have a device with 100 GB of data, the first day the snapshot is created, the snapshot will have to reflect all 100 GB. If, the next day, 5 GB of additional data is added, when the next snapshot is taken, EBS is smart enough to realize that it only needs to account for the new data. It can use the previous snapshot with the latest backup to recreate the full picture. This incremental snapshot strategy will translate into lower storage costs.

Snapshots can be compressed, mirrored, transferred, replicated, and managed across multiple AWS AZs using the Amazon Data Lifecycle Manager.

Amazon EBS Snapshots are stored as Amazon S3 objects. Amazon EBS Snapshots are accessed using the Amazon EBS API, and they cannot be accessed directly by users. Snapshots are stored as **Amazon Machine Images** (**AMIs**), and therefore, they can be leveraged to launch an EC2 instance.

While optimizing the cost, the first place to look is into unused EBS Snapshots. People often take EBS Snapshots even for the dev/test environment and never access them, causing additional costs. You should always use lifecycle management to delete unused EBS Snapshots as needed. For example, you can set up a policy to delete any EBS Snapshots which are tagged as dev/test and are older than six months.

We have learned about many EBS volumes; now let's understand how to choose the right EBS volume.

Choosing the right EBS volume

As you learned in the previous section, EBS offers 4 volume types in two different buckets: SSD and HDD. The first step in helping you size your storage is to understand whether your workload is sequential or random I/O:

- **SSD** (gp2, gp3, io1, io2, and io2 Block Express) is great for random I/O applications such as boot volumes and databases (MySQL, SQL, PostgreSQL, Oracle, Cassandra, MongoDB, SAP, etc.). Performance is measured on disk I/O (IOPS).
- **HDD** (st1 and sc1) is great for sequential I/O applications like EMR/Hadoop, Kafka, Splunk, media streaming, and logs, as well as any colder data that is infrequently accessed. Performance is measured on throughput (MB/s).

From there, you can use AWS documentation (`https://aws.amazon.com/ebs/volume-types/`) to help decide which specific volume will best suit your needs and give the best price for performance. Here is a decision tree to help in the process:

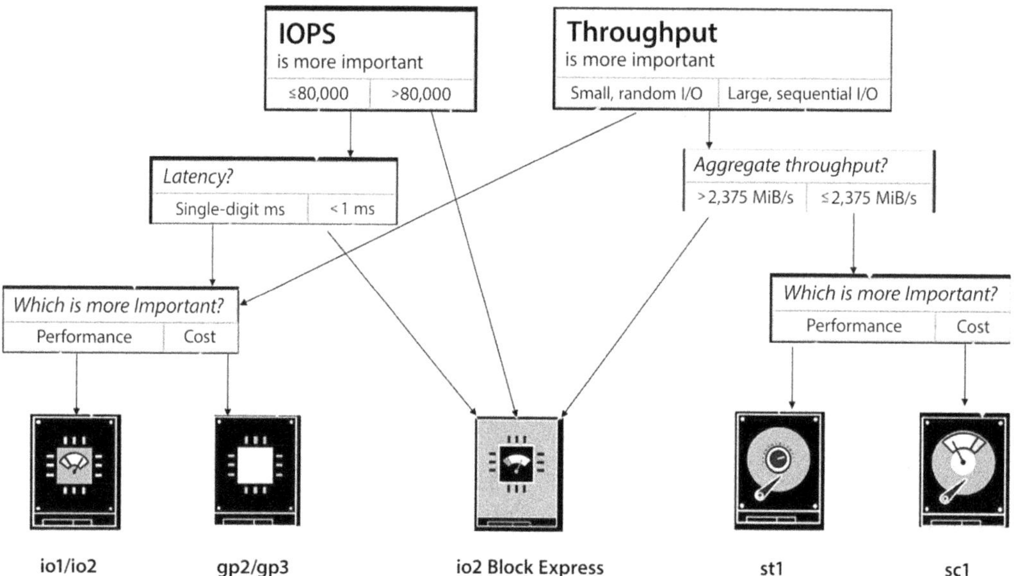

Figure 5.1: Decision tree to select the EBS volume

To understand the approach for choosing the right EBS volume, let's dive a little more into the two SSD-backed products, gp3 and io2. Starting with the **gp3 volume**, it is a volume type you can spend a lot of time with analyzing data, analyzing workloads, and developing it to achieve the performance sweet spot for 70 to 80% of the workloads. gp3 satisfies nearly all workloads and is designed to be a truly general-purpose volume. That's why it has the name general purpose, so if you don't know which volume type to use, it is highly recommended that you start with gp3. Additionally, with gp3, you have the ability to provision more IOPS and more throughput when you need it without being dependent on storage size.

The low latency of gp3, which is measured in single-digit milliseconds, makes it well suited for applications that are sensitive to latency, such as interactive applications, boot volumes, development and testing environments, burst databases, and various other use cases. But what about sub-millisecond latency? Now, if you are looking for very high performance and low latency, use **io2 Block Express volumes,** which offer 4 times the performance of io1, up to 256,000 IOPS, 4,000 MB/s throughput, and you can provision up to 4x more storage – up to 64 TB.

Now, we move on to the media workload, which is for your rendering farms, transcoding, encoding, and any sort of streaming product. Here, you typically have a higher throughput requirement, mostly sequential and fairly sustained, especially when you have a pretty substantial render job. For these kinds of workloads, **Throughput Optimized HDDs** (also known as **st1s**) might be a good fit. These are good for large blocks, high throughput, and sequential workloads.

SC1 is a low-cost storage option that is ideal for storing infrequently accessed data, such as data that is accessed once a month or less. It is a good choice for cold storage or for storing data that is not accessed very often. ST1, on the other hand, is a low-cost storage option that is designed for storing frequently accessed data, such as data that is accessed on a daily or weekly basis. It is a good choice for data that is accessed frequently, but not in real time.

In summary, the main difference between SC1 and ST1 is their intended use cases. SC1 is designed for infrequently accessed data, while ST1 is designed for frequently accessed data.

In a nutshell, with EBS, you get persistent storage, which enables you to stop and start your instances without losing your storage and you can build cost-effective point-in-time snapshots of the volumes that you are storing in S3. For security, EBS provides built-in encryption so you don't need to manage your own. For monitoring, EBS has better volume monitoring with EBS CloudWatch metrics. It is designed for 99.999% availability and is highly durable with an annual failure rate of between 0.1% and 0.2%.

This wraps up what we wanted to say about the Amazon EBS service. Now, let's move on to another important service—Amazon Elastic File System.

Investigating Amazon Elastic File System (EFS)

Amazon EFS implements an elastic, fully-managed **Network File System** (**NFS**) that can be leveraged by other AWS Cloud services and on-premises infrastructure. Amazon EFS natively integrates with the complete family of AWS compute models, and can scale as needed to provide parallel, shared access to thousands of Amazons EC2 instances as well as AWS container and serverless compute models from AWS Lambda, AWS Fargate, Amazon **Elastic Container Service** (**ECS**), and Amazon **Elastic Kubernetes Service** (**EKS**).

The main difference between EBS and EFS is that several EC2 instances can be mounted to an EFS volume simultaneously, while an EBS volume can be attached to only one EC2 instance. Amazon EFS provides shared file storage that can elastically adjust on demand to expand or shrink depending on how much space your workloads require. It can grow and shrink as you add and remove files. Other than that, the structure will be like it is with Amazon EBS. Amazon EFS provides a typical file storage system where files can be organized into directories and subdirectories.

Common use cases for EFS volumes include:

- Web serving and content management systems for WordPress, Drupal, Moodle, Confluence, and OpenText.
- Data science and analytics for TensorFlow, Qubole, and Alteryx.
- Media processing, including video editing, sound design, broadcast processing, studio production, and rendering. This often depends on shared storage to manipulate large files.
- Database backups for Oracle, Postgres, Cassandra, MongoDB, CouchDB, and SAP HANA.
- Hosting CRM applications that require hosting within the AWS data center but need to be managed by the AWS customer.

The following are the key benefits of using EFS:

- EFS is **elastic**, automatically scaling up or down as you add or remove files, and you pay only for what you use. Your performance automatically scales with your capacity. By the way, EFS file systems scale to petabytes in size.
- EFS is also highly available and designed to be highly durable. AWS offers a 4 9s availability SLA (99.99% availability) and is designed for 11 9s of data durability (which means it delivers 99.999999999% durability across multiple AZs).

To achieve these levels of availability and durability, all files and directories are redundantly stored within and across multiple AZs. EFS file systems can withstand the full loss of a single AZ, while still providing the same quality of service in the other AZs.

- EFS is serverless; you don't need to provision or manage any infrastructure or capacity. And as your workload scales up, so does your file system, automatically accommodating any additional storage or connection capacity that you need.
- EFS file systems support up to tens of thousands of concurrent clients, no matter the type. These could be traditional EC2 instances, containers running in one of your self-managed clusters or in one of the AWS container services, Elastic Container Service, Elastic Kubernetes Service, and Fargate – or in a serverless function running in AWS Lambda. You can also access your EFS file systems from on-premises through AWS Direct Connect and AWS VPN.
- In terms of performance, EFS file systems provide low, consistent latencies (in the single digit millisecond range for active file system workloads), and can scale to tens of GB/s of throughput and support over 500,000 IOPS.
- Finally, EFS storage classes provide you with automatic cost-optimization and help you achieve an optimal price/performance blend for your workloads. Files that you aren't using frequently will be automatically moved from the Standard storage class to the lower-cost EFS **Infrequent Access** (**IA**) storage class, completely transparently to users and applications. IA costs 92% less than Standard.

You can learn more about EFS by visiting the AWS website: `https://aws.amazon.com/efs/`.

While EFS provides generic file system storage, there is a need for file system-specific storage to handle the workload optimized for a particular file system. For that, AWS provides Amazon FSx.

Using Amazon FSx to manage file systems

Amazon FSx is a managed file storage service offered by AWS. It is a fully managed service that allows users to store and access files over the internet using the industry-standard **network file system** (**NFS**) and **server message block** (**SMB**) protocols.

FSx is designed to provide high performance and high availability for file storage, making it a good choice for applications that require fast access to files or data. It supports a wide range of workloads, including big data analytics, content management, and video editing.

FSx offers two main types of file storage: FSx for Lustre and FSx for Windows File Server. FSx for Lustre is a high-performance file system that is optimized for workloads that require low-latency access to data, such as high-performance computing and machine learning.

FSx for Windows File Server is a fully managed native Microsoft Windows file system that is compatible with the SMB protocol and is ideal for applications that require seamless integration with Microsoft Windows.

Overall, Amazon FSx is a fully managed file storage service that provides high performance and high availability for file storage, making it a good choice for applications that require fast access to files or data.

You may want to use Amazon FSx for the following use cases:

- Migrating file system-specific workloads to the cloud.
- Running ML and analytics applications using **high-performance computing** (**HPC**) with FSx Lustre.
- Hosting and editing media and entertainment workloads where high performance is needed.
- Creating a backup of file system-specific storage in the cloud for business continuity strategy.

In this section, you learned about Amazon EFS/FSx file storage, which can be compared to **NAS** (**Network Attached Storage**) in the on-premises data center. Further, you went into details about Amazon EBS, which is block storage and can be compared with **SAN** (**Storage Area Network**) in an on-premise environment. Let's now learn about the object storage system in AWS called Amazon **Simple Storage Service** (**S3**).

Learning about Amazon Simple Storage Service (S3)

Amazon S3 was the first AWS service launched 16 years ago on Pi Day, March 14, 2006. After the launch of S3, AWS also launched many other services to complement S3. S3 is durable, highly available, and very scalable online storage. S3 comes in various tiers including:

- S3 Standard
- Amazon S3 Intelligent-Tiering
- Amazon S3 Standard-IA
- Amazon S3 One Zone-IA
- Amazon S3 Glacier
- Amazon S3 Glacier Deep Archive

While we will explore each of the above tiers in detail in the subsections below, let's briefly explore some of the more common attributes that apply to multiple S3 service tiers:

- **Durability**: Data is stored durably, with 11 9s across a minimum of 3 AZs to provide resiliency against an AZ failure for S3 Standard, S3 Intelligent-Tiering, and S3 Standard-IA. S3 One Zone-IA has11 9s across 1 Availability Zone. This means that if you stored 10K objects, on average, you would lose 1 object every 10M years with S3.
- **Availability**: S3 Standard is designed for 99.99% availability, with monetary penalties introduced at 99.9% per the S3 SLA. S3 Intelligent-Tiering and S3 Standard-IA are built to be 99.9% available, while S3 One Zone-IA is built to be 99.5% available. These three classes are backed by a 99% availability SLA. There are no scheduled maintenance windows – the service is maintained, upgraded, and scaled as it operates. 99.99% availability means that the service is down for less than 52 minutes a year.
- **Utility pricing**: There is no upfront capital expenditure, and pay for what you use pricing (100% utilization). Volume discounts as usage scales.
- **Scalability**: Instant scalability for storage and delivery.

Let's analyze the various S3 tiers in detail.

S3 Standard

When Amazon launched the S3 service, it was simply called Amazon S3. Amazon now offers various object storage services, and they all use the S3 moniker, so Amazon has renamed Amazon S3 as Amazon S3 Standard.

S3 Standard delivers highly performant, available, and durable storage for data that will be accessed frequently. S3 Standard has low latency, high performance, and high scalability. S3 Standard is suited for a long list of use cases, including the following:

- Websites with dynamic content – You can host website HTML pages in S3 and directly attach them to your domain which will be very low cost as you don't need any server to host your website. Further, you can supplement your website with dynamic content like videos and images by putting them into S3.
- Distribution of content – To make your website fast for a global audience, you can host your content in S3, which will be cached in an edge location by AWS's content distribution network service called AWS CloudFront.
- Data analytics and processing – You can host a large amount of data and scale it on demand for your analytics and machine learning needs.

- Mobile and gaming applications – You can supplement your application by storing all application heavy data like images and videos in S3 and load them on-demand to improve application performance.

S3 Standard can be used to persist many types of objects, such as Plaintext, HTML, JSON, XML, AVRO, Parquet, and ORC files. S3 Standard is one of the most popular services, addressing a wide range of use cases. You can learn more about S3 by visiting the AWS page here - `https://aws.amazon.com/s3/`.

Let's now look at another service in the S3 family, Amazon S3 Intelligent-Tiering, and let's learn what makes it intelligent.

Amazon S3 Intelligent-Tiering

The S3 Intelligent-Tiering storage service can reduce expenses by systematically moving files to use the most cost-effective way to store data while having no impact on operations or performance. It can do this by keeping the files in two tiers:

- An optimized tier for frequent access
- An optimized tier for infrequent access that has a lower cost

Amazon S3 constantly scans access patterns of files and transfers files that have not been accessed. If a file has not been accessed for 30 days straight, it is moved to the infrequent access tier. If a file in the infrequent access tier is retrieved, it is again transferred to the frequent access tier.

With the S3 Intelligent-Tiering storage class, the additional cost comes from the monitoring charge. There are no fees for retrieval, and there are no additional file transfer fees when objects are transferred between the tiers. S3 Intelligent-Tiering is a good solution when we know that data will be needed for a long time but we are uncertain about how often this data will be accessed.

S3 services can be enabled granularly up to the object level. For example, a given bucket can have one object that uses S3 Standard, another using S3 Intelligent-Tiering, one more with S3 Standard-IA, and one with S3 One Zone-IA (we are going to cover these two other services in the next few sections).

Note: To take advantage of auto-tiering capability, it is recommended to aggregate objects smaller than 128KB to meet the minimum size requirement. This enables the objects to be automatically tiered and reduces storage costs. Smaller objects, which are not monitored, are always charged at the rates of the Frequent Access tier, without any additional monitoring or automation charges.

So, what if we know that the data we create and store will be infrequently accessed? Amazon offers a service ideally suited for that, which will also be cheaper than Amazon S3 Standard.

Amazon S3 Standard-IA (Infrequent Access)

Depending on the use case for your data, this storage class might be the ideal solution for your data storage needs. The data can be accessed at the same speed as S3 Standard, with some tradeoffs on the resiliency of the data. For example, if you are storing monthly payroll data, it is going to be accessed most in the last week of each month, so it's better to use S3 Standard-IA (**Infrequent Access**) to save cost.

S3 Standard-IA offers a similar profile to the Standard service but with a lower cost for storage and with a retrieval fee billed per GB. Combining low cost with high performance makes S3 Standard-IA a well-suited option for use cases such as backups, snapshots, long-term storage, and a file repository for disaster recovery. S3 Lifecycle policies could be used to move files between storage classes without any coding needed automatically.

It is recommended that you configure your Amazon S3 to manage your items and keep them cost-effectively stored throughout their lifecycle. An S3 Lifecycle configuration is a set of rules that specify how Amazon S3 handles a collection of objects. By using S3 Lifecycle configuration rules, you can instruct Amazon S3 to transition objects to more cost-effective storage classes, or to archive or delete them automatically after a specified period of time.

You can learn more details on setting up the S3 Lifecycle by visiting the AWS user document here - `https://docs.aws.amazon.com/AmazonS3/latest/userguide/how-to-set-lifecycle-configuration-intro.html`.

So, what if your data is not that critically important and you are willing to give up some durability in exchange for a cheaper alternative? Amazon has a service that fits that criteria. We'll learn about it in the next section.

Amazon S3 One Zone-IA

A better name for S3 Standard-IA might be *S3 Standard-IA; that is not critical.* Like the previous service, S3 Standard-IA, S3 One Zone-IA can be used for files that need to be retrieved with less frequency but need rapid access. This service is cheaper than S3 Standard because instead of storing data in three AZs, S3 One Zone-IA persists data in only one AZ with the same durability.

S3 One Zone-IA is a good solution for use cases that don't need the reliability of S3 Standard or S3 Standard-IA and therefore get a lower price. The reliability is still high, and it still has duplication, but this duplication is not done across AZs. It's a suitable option for storing files such as backup files and data that can be quickly and easily recreated. It can also be a cost-effective way to store data that has been copied from another AWS Region with S3 Cross-Region Replication.

IMPORTANT NOTE

Keep in mind that these files will be unavailable and potentially destroyed if an AZ goes down or is destroyed. So, it should only be used with files that are not mission-critical.

S3 One Zone-IA delivers similar high throughput, durability, and speed to S3 Standard, coupled with an inexpensive retrieval cost.

So far, we have looked at services that allow us to access the data immediately. What if we are willing to give up that immediate accessibility in exchange for an even cheaper service? Amazon S3 Glacier fits that bill. We'll learn about it in the next section.

Amazon S3 Glacier

When it's known that a file will not be needed immediately, S3 Glacier is a good option. S3 Glacier is a secure, durable class for data archiving. It is significantly cheaper than S3 Standard, but it will take longer to retrieve an S3 Glacier file. Data can be stored on S3 Glacier at a cost that would be competitive with an on-premises solution. Within S3 Glacier, the options and pricing are flexible.

Amazon S3 Glacier storage classes are designed specifically for archiving data, offering superior performance, retrieval flexibility, and cost-effective storage options in the cloud. These storage classes provide virtually unlimited scalability, as well as 11 nines of data durability, ensuring the safety and reliability of your data over the long term.

S3 Glacier provides three different storage classes: S3 Glacier Instant Retrieval, S3 Glacier Flexible Retrieval, and S3 Glacier Deep Archive. **S3 Glacier Flexible Retrieval** is the base storage class of S3 Glacier and is designed for long-term storage of data that is accessed infrequently. It is a low-cost storage option that is ideal for storing data that is accessed once a year or less. You can use this option if you need to retrieve data in minutes to 12 hours time. **S3 Glacier Deep Archive** is the lowest-cost storage class of S3 Glacier and is designed for long-term storage of data that is accessed once a year or less.

It is the lowest-cost storage option provided by AWS and is ideal for storing data that is rarely accessed and does not need to be retrieved quickly. You can use this option if you can wait for data for 12 hours to 24 hours time to retrieve data. **S3 Glacier Instant Retrieval** is a storage class that allows you to query and analyze data stored in S3 Glacier without having to retrieve the entire data set. It allows you to run SQL queries on your data in S3 Glacier and only retrieves the data that is needed for the query, providing faster and more cost-effective access to your data. You should use this option if you need to retrieve data immediately in milliseconds, however, the faster data retrieval time comes with higher cost. These storage classes are designed for different use cases and provide low-cost options for storing data that is infrequently accessed. You can choose them as per your workload requirements.

S3 Glacier Deep Archive is Amazon S3's cheapest option for object storage. It enables long-term storage. It is suited for files that are only going to be retrieved occasionally. It is designed for customers that are required to keep data for seven years or longer to meet regulatory compliance regulations such as in the financial industry, healthcare industry, and government agencies.

In many cases, heavy penalties can accrue if these rules are not adequately followed. Other good use cases are backup and disaster recovery. Many customers are using this service instead of magnetic tape systems. S3 Glacier Deep Archive can be used in conjunction with Amazon S3 Glacier, allowing data to be retrieved faster than the Deep Archive service.

In the following figure, we have a summary of the profile of storage classes and how they compare to each other:

	S3 Standard	S3 Intelligent-Tiering*	S3 Standard-IA	S3 One Zone-IA†	S3 Glacier Instant Retrieval	S3 Glacier Flexible Retrieval	S3 Glacier Deep Archive
Designed for durability	99.999999999% (11 9s)	99.999999999% (11 9s)	99.999999999% (11 9s)	99.999999999% (11 9s)	99.999999999% (11 9s)	99.999999999% (11 9s)	99.999999999% (11 9s)
Designed for availability	99.99%	99.9%	99.9%	99.5%	99.9%	99.99%	99.99%
Availability SLA	99.9%	99%	99%	99%	99%	99.9%	99.9%
Availability Zones	≥3	≥3	≥3	1	≥3	≥3	≥3
Minimum capacity charge per object	N/A	N/A	128 KB	128 KB	128 KB	40 KB	40 KB
Minimum storage duration charge	N/A	N/A	30 days	30 days	90 days	90 days	180 days
Retrieval charge	N/A	N/A	per GB retrieved	per GB retrieved	per GB retrieved	per GB retrieved	per GB retrieved
First byte latency	milliseconds	milliseconds	milliseconds	milliseconds	milliseconds	select minutes or hours	select hours

Figure 5.2: Summary of storage class features

In the above summary, the cost of storage gets cheaper as we move from left to right. This means that S3 Standard has the highest cost of storage while S3 Glacier Deep Archive is the cheapest.

In this section, you have learned that AWS has a vast number of offerings for your storage use cases. Depending on how quickly the data needs to be retrieved and how durably it needs to be stored, the costs will vary and allow for savings if high durability and fast retrieval are not required. Sometimes you want to change data in runtime. For that, AWS launched a new feature called S3 Object Lambda. Let's learn more about it.

Managing data with S3 Object Lambda

Amazon S3 Object Lambda is a feature of Amazon S3 that allows users to run custom code on objects stored in S3. With S3 Object Lambda, you can define custom actions that are triggered when an object is created, updated, or deleted in S3. These actions can be used to perform a variety of tasks, such as automatically resizing images, creating thumbnails, or transcoding videos.

To use S3 Object Lambda, you first need to write custom code that defines the actions you want to perform. This code can be written in a variety of languages, such as Node.js, Python, or Java, and can be run on AWS Lambda, a serverless compute service.

Once you have written your custom code, you can create a Lambda function and attach it to an S3 bucket. When objects are created, updated, or deleted in the S3 bucket, the Lambda function will be triggered and will perform the actions defined in your code.

S3 Object Lambda is a powerful feature that can be used to automate a variety of tasks and improve the management of data stored in S3. It allows you to perform custom actions on objects in S3 and can save time and effort when working with large amounts of data.

Sometimes you want to create multiple copies of an object, in which case S3 allows versioning.

Versioning in Amazon S3

Amazon S3 can optionally store different versions of the same object. Have you ever been working on a document for hours and suddenly made a mistake where you deleted all of the content in the document, or have you made a big mistake and wanted to go back to a previous version? Many editors, such as Microsoft Word, offer the ability to undo changes and recover from some of these mistakes. However, once you save, close, and open the document again, you may not be able to undo any changes.

What if you have a document where multiple people make revisions, and you want to keep track of who made what changes?

Amazon S3 offers versioning capabilities that can assist with these use cases. So, what is versioning? Simply put, versioning is the ability to keep incremental copies. For example, if you store an important proposal document in S3, the first version of the document may have the initial architecture and statement of work, and the subsequent version may have evolved to looking at future architecture, which increases the scope of the work. Now if you want to compare these two versions, it is easy to view and recover the previous version, which has the original work statement.

As you can imagine, keeping multiple versions of the same document can get expensive if there are many changes. This is especially true if you have a high volume of documents. To reduce costs, we can implement a lifecycle policy where older versions are purged or moved to a cheaper storage option such as Amazon S3 Glacier.

The exact logic of implementing the lifecycle policy will depend on your requirements. But some possibilities are to set up your policy based on document age, the number of versions, or some other criteria. By the way, lifecycle policies are not limited to just older versions of a document. They can also be used for any document that persists in Amazon S3.

Due to S3 high availability, durability, and unlimited scalability, enterprises often use this to host critical workloads that may need backing up to other regions. Let's learn about S3 Multi-destination replication, which allows users to distribute multiple copies to different environments.

Amazon S3 Multi-Destination Replication

Amazon S3 Multi-Destination Replication is a feature of Amazon S3 that allows users to replicate objects across multiple Amazon S3 buckets or AWS accounts. With Multi-Destination Replication, you can define a replication rule that specifies which objects should be replicated and where they should be replicated to.

To use Multi-Destination Replication, you first need to create a replication rule in the Amazon S3 console. This rule defines the source bucket where objects are stored, the destination buckets where objects should be replicated, and the prefixes or tags that identify which objects should be replicated.

Once the replication rule is created, Amazon S3 will automatically replicate objects that match the specified criteria to the destination buckets. This replication is performed asynchronously, so the source and destination buckets do not have to be online at the same time.

S3 Multi-Destination Replication is a useful feature for users who need to replicate objects across multiple S3 buckets or AWS accounts. It allows you to easily replicate objects and can be used to improve the availability and durability of your data. To learn more, visit `https://docs.aws.amazon.com/AmazonS3/latest/userguide/replication-metrics.html`.

Now that we have covered Amazon Elastic Block Storage, Amazon Elastic File System, and Amazon S3, we will spend some time understanding the difference between the services and when it's appropriate to use one versus the other.

Choosing the right cloud storage type

So far, you have learned about three different kinds of cloud storage in this chapter. First, Amazon EBS stores data in blocks; you can also use this as SAN in the cloud. Second, Amazon EFS is cloud file storage that is a kind of NAS in the cloud. Finally, Amazon S3 stores data as objects. So now that we covered all these storage type services, the obvious question is which one is better to use. The following table should help you to decide what service is best for your use case:

	Performance	Cost	Availability	Storage Limit	File Size Limit
Amazon S3	By default, it supports 100 requests per second and scalable to 300	Average of $0.0235 per GB/month	99.99 % availability	No limit on the number of objects	5TB object limit
Amazon EBS	Provisioned IOPS can deliver 4000 operations per second	Anywhere from $0.025 to $0.100 per GB/month	99.99 % availability	Maximum storage size Of 16 TB	File size of up to 16 TB
Amazon EFS	Capable of up to 7000 operations per second	From $0.30 to $0.36 per GB/month	No SLA in force	No limit on system size	File size of up to 52 TB

Figure 5.3: Choosing the service based on your use case

EBS volume is always attached to a single EC2 instance so when you need high-performance, persistent storage, always use EBS volume. If you need shared file storage between multiple EC2 instances, then you want to use EFS. S3 is your choice to store any amount of data in any format that you want to use for big data analytics, backups, and even large volume content for your application.

As you are going to use S3 a lot for your day-to-day large volume (from GBs to PBs) of data storage needs, let's learn some best practices to manage S3.

Exploring Amazon S3 best practices

Amazon S3 is one of the simplest services in AWS, and at the same time, it is one of the most powerful and scalable services. We can easily scale our Amazon S3 applications to process thousands of requests per second while uploading and retrieving files. This scalability can be achieved "out of the box" without needing to provision any resources or servers.

Some customers in AWS are already leveraging Amazon S3 to host petabyte-scale data lakes and other applications storing billions of objects and performing billions of requests. These applications can upload and retrieve multiple terabytes of data per second with little optimization.

Other customers with low latency requirements have used Amazon S3 and other Amazon file storage services to achieve consistent low latency for small objects. Being able to retrieve this kind of object in 100 to 200 milliseconds is not uncommon.

For bigger objects, it is possible to achieve similar low latency responses for the *first byte* received from these objects. As you can imagine, the retrieval time to receive the complete file for bigger objects will be directly proportional to object size.

Enhancing Amazon S3 performance

One simple way to enhance performance is to know where most of your users are located and where your Amazon S3 bucket is located. Amazon S3 buckets need to be unique globally, but files will be stored in a given AWS Region. When you architect your solution, this is considered in your design. It will help reduce the time it takes to transfer files and minimize data transfer costs.

One more way to scale Amazon S3 is to scale S3 connections horizontally. Amazon S3 allows you to make many connections to any given bucket and access thousands of files per second. Highly scalable performance can be achieved by issuing multiple concurrent requests. Amazon S3 is designed to support high levels of performance and can handle a large number of requests per second. While the exact number of requests per second that the service can handle will depend on a variety of factors, it is capable of supporting at least 3,500 requests per second to add data and 5,500 requests per second to retrieve data. You can think of Amazon S3 as a highly distributed system and not just a single endpoint with only one server to support the workloads.

There are a number of ways that users can enhance the performance of Amazon S3, including the following:

- **Choose the right storage class**: S3 offers several different storage classes, each of which is optimized for different use cases. Choosing the right storage class for your data can help to improve performance and reduce latency.

- **Use caching**: S3 uses caching techniques to improve the performance of frequently accessed data. Enabling caching for your data can help to increase the number of requests per second that the service can handle and reduce the time it takes to retrieve data.
- **Use object partitioning**: S3 uses a partitioning scheme to distribute data across multiple servers and storage devices, which can help to increase the number of requests per second that the service can handle.
- **Use regional buckets**: S3 allows you to store data in regional buckets, which can help to reduce latency and improve performance by storing data closer to users.

Overall, there are many ways that users can enhance the performance of Amazon S3 and improve the speed and reliability of their data storage and retrieval. By choosing the right storage class, using caching, object partitioning, and regional buckets, users can maximize the performance of Amazon S3 for their specific use case.

We mentioned in the previous section that Amazon S3 files could be retrieved with sub-second performance. However, suppose this level of performance is not enough, and you are looking to achieve single-digit millisecond performance. In that case, you can use Amazon CloudFront to store data closer to your user base to achieve even higher performance, or Amazon ElastiCache to cache the data in memory and reduce data load time.

Amazon CloudFront

You learned about CloudFront in *Chapter 4, Networking in AWS*. Amazon CloudFront is a **Content Delivery Network** (**CDN**) that can cache content stored in Amazon S3 and distribute it across dispersed geographic regions with thousands of **Points of Presence** (**PoP**) worldwide. Amazon CloudFront enables these objects to be cached close to the people using these resources.

Amazon ElastiCache

Amazon ElastiCache is a managed AWS service that enables you to store objects in memory instead of storing them on disk. Behind the scenes and transparently, Amazon ElastiCache will provision Amazon EC2 instances that will cache objects in the instance's memory. Doing so will reduce latency when retrieving objects by orders of magnitude. Using Amazon ElastiCache does require subtly changing application logic.

First, when you want certain objects to be cached instead of stored on a disk, you need to specify that ElastiCache should be the storage medium. And when you retrieve objects, you should check the cache in ElastiCache to see whether the object you are trying to retrieve has been cached and, if they haven't, only then check the database to get the uncached object.

While CloudFront provides caching services at the edge for data distribution, ElastiCache handles data at the application level to load data faster when you request it for business logic calculations or displays it to the end user through the application web layer. Amazon ElastiCache comes in two flavors: Redis (persistent cache) and Memcached (fast indexing). You will learn about these in more detail in *Chapter 7, Selecting the Right Database Service.*

Amazon S3 Transfer Acceleration

Yet another way to achieve single-digit millisecond responses is to use Amazon S3 Transfer Acceleration. This AWS service uses CloudFront edge locations to accelerate data transport over long distances. Amazon S3 Transfer Acceleration is ideally suited to transfer a large amount of data (gigabytes or terabytes) that needs to be shared across AWS Regions.

It would help if you considered using Amazon S3 Transfer Acceleration in the following cases:

- Application requirements call for the need to upload files to a central location for many places around the globe.
- There is a need to regularly transfer hundreds of gigabytes or terabytes worth of data across AWS Regions.
- The available bandwidth is not being fully utilized and leveraged when uploading to Amazon S3.

The benefits of Amazon S3 Transfer Acceleration are as follows:

- It will allow you to transfer files faster and more consistently over long distances.
- It can reduce network variability usage.
- It can shorten the distance traveled to upload files to S3.
- It will enable you to maximize bandwidth utilization.

One critical consideration when using Amazon S3 is ensuring that the data stored is accessible only by parties that need to access the data. Everyone else should be locked out. Let's learn about AWS's capabilities to assist in data protection and data security.

Choosing the right S3 bucket/prefix naming convention

S3 bucket names must be unique, meaning that no two buckets can have the same name. Once a bucket is deleted, its name can potentially be reused, although there are some exceptions to this and it may take some time before the name becomes available again. It is therefore recommended to avoid deleting a bucket if you want to reuse its name.

To benefit from new features and operational improvements, as well as virtual host-style access to buckets, it is recommended to use bucket names that comply with DNS naming conventions, which are enforced in all regions except US East. When using the AWS Management Console, bucket names must be compliant with DNS naming conventions in all regions.

Here are some best practices for differentiating between file and bucket key names when uploading a large number of objects to S3:

- Avoid using the same key name for different objects. Each object should have a unique key name to avoid overwriting existing objects with the same name.
- Use a consistent naming convention for object key names. This will make it easier to locate and manage objects later on.
- Consider using a hierarchical naming structure for your objects. For example, you could use a directory structure in your object key names to help organize objects into logical groups.
- Use a delimiter, such as a slash (/), to separate the directory structure in your object key names. This will help you to easily navigate the structure and make it easier to organize and manage your objects.
- Avoid using special characters in your key names, as this can cause compatibility issues with different systems and applications.
- Choose key names that are descriptive and easy to understand. This will make it easier for others to navigate and understand your objects.

To ensure workload efficiency, it is recommended to avoid sequential key names (or add a random prefix) if a workload is expected to exceed 100 requests per second. This can help to evenly distribute key names across multiple index partitions, thereby improving the workload distribution and overall system performance.

All of the above best practices apply to S3 bucket naming. Amazon S3 stores bucket names as part of key names in its index.

Protecting your data in Amazon S3

Amazon makes it extremely easy to provision an Amazon S3 bucket and quickly allows you to distribute the data worldwide by simply providing a URL pointing to files in the bucket. The good news is that this is so easy to do. The bad news is that this is so easy to do.

There have been many documented cases of sensitive data lying around in publicly accessible endpoints in S3 and other people accessing this data. "Leaky" Amazon S3 buckets are a perfect example of how the shared responsibility security model works when using AWS.

AWS provides a fantastic array of security services and protocols, but data can still be exposed if not used correctly, and breaches can occur. By default, each bucket is private but you need to configure your Amazon S3 buckets and object security with the principle of least privilege when starting to provide access.

The good news is that as easy as it is to make the bucket public and leave it open to the world, it is almost as simple to lock it down and restrict access only to the required individual and services.

Some of the features that Amazon S3 provides to restrict access to the correct users are as follows.

Blocking Amazon S3 public access to buckets and objects whenever possible

Starting with the principle of least privilege, AWS blocks public access to any newly created S3 bucket by default. Amazon S3 provides a bucket policy where you can define who can access this S3 resource. **Amazon S3 Access Control Lists (ACLs)** provide granular control at the object level. You can learn more about S3 ACL by visiting the AWS user document here - `https://docs.aws.amazon.com/AmazonS3/latest/userguide/acl-overview.html`.

Further, AWS provides S3 Access Points, which are simplified management for shared bucket access by many teams. For example, a data lake bucket where you want to store all your organization data as a single source can be accessed by the finance, accounting, and sales teams, and as shown below, you can use S3 Access Points to restrict access for each team to have access to their data only based on a defined prefix.

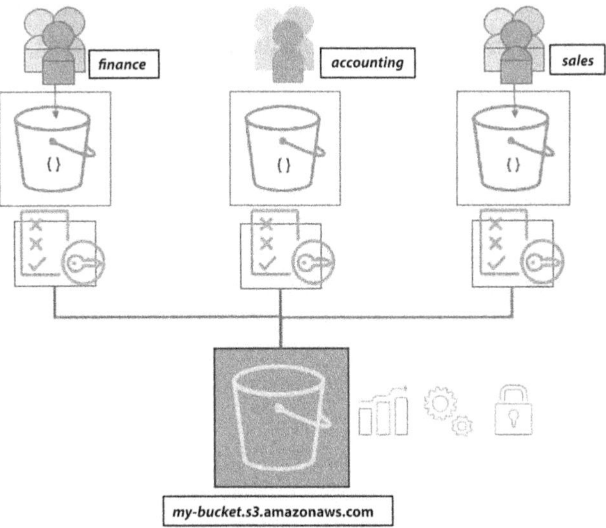

Figure 5.4: Amazon S3 Access Points

As shown in the diagram above, users are segmented into distinct groups and each group is given their own S3 access point through the specific policies applied to the group. This helps to manage access policies centrally across multiple users. The following is an example for segregation of Read and Write access in a bucket:

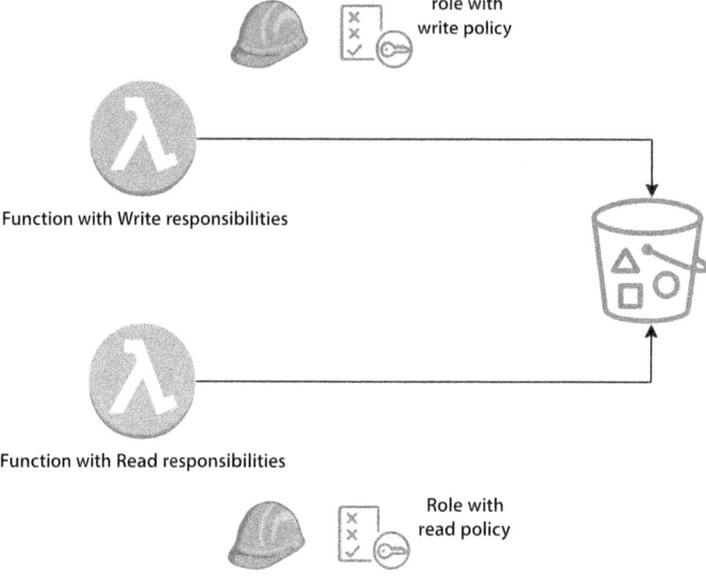

Figure 5.5: Amazon S3 access policy segregation

Leveraging Amazon S3 to block public access, Amazon S3 bucket administrators can configure a way to control access in a centralized manner and limit public access to Amazon S3 buckets and objects. This feature can deny public access regardless of how objects and buckets are created in Amazon S3.

Avoiding wildcards in policy files

Policy files allow a powerful syntax where you can use a wildcard character (*) to specify policies. Even though wildcards are permitted, they should be avoided whenever possible, and instead, names should be spelled out explicitly to name resources, principles, and others. The following is a sample policy with no wildcards:

```
{
  "Version":"2012-10-17",
  "Statement":[
    {
      "Effect":"Allow",
      "Action":[
        "s3:PutObject",
        "s3:GetObject",
        "s3:GetObjectVersion",
        "s3:DeleteObject",
        "s3:DeleteObjectVersion"
      ],
      "Resource":"arn:aws:s3:::DOC-EXAMPLE-BUCKET1/Mary/*"
    }
  ]
}
```

Figure 5.6: Sample policy with no wildcards

The same wildcard rule applies to Amazon S3 bucket **Access Control Lists** (**ACLs**). ACLs are files that can be used to deliver read, write, or full access to users, and if wildcards are used, they can potentially leave the bucket open to the world.

Leveraging the S3 API

Like other AWS services, Amazon S3 provides hundreds of APIs that you can use through the AWS **CLI** (**Command-Line Interface**) or call the API from your application code. For example, the `ListBuckets` API can be used to scan Amazon S3 buckets in a given AWS account. `GetBucketAcl` returns the ACL of a bucket and `GetBucketWebsite` returns the website configuration for a bucket, and `GetBucketPolicy` commands can monitor whether buckets are compliant and whether the access controls, policies, and configuration are properly set up to only allow access to authorized personnel. You can refer to AWS user docs to get the list of all the APIs and how to use them through the CLI or application; please find the user docs here: `https://docs.aws.amazon.com/AmazonS3/latest/API/Welcome.html`.

Leveraging IAM Access Analyzer to inspect S3

AWS **Identity and Access Management** (**IAM**) Access Analyzer for S3 can generate comprehensive findings if your resource policies grant public or cross-account access. It continuously identifies resources with overly broad permissions across your entire AWS organization. It resolves results by updating policies to protect your resources from unintended access before it occurs or archives findings for intended access.

IAM Access Analyzer continuously monitors for new or updated policies. It analyzes permissions granted using policies for your Amazon S3 buckets, AWS **Key Management Service (KMS)** keys, AWS IAM roles, and AWS Lambda functions, and generates detailed findings about who has access to what resources from outside your AWS organization or AWS account.

If the level of resource access is not intended, modify the resource policy to further restrict or expand access to the resource. If the access level is correct, you can archive the finding. IAM Access Analyzer provides comprehensive results that can be accessed through the AWS IAM, Amazon S3, and AWS Security Hub consoles and APIs. This service delivers detailed findings, allowing users to easily view and analyze access-related issues and take appropriate action to address them.

Enabling AWS Config

Another way to verify your security configuration is to deploy a continuous monitoring system using `s3-bucket-public-read-prohibited` and `s3-bucket-public-write-prohibited` and manage the configuration using AWS Config rules.

AWS Config is a service that can monitor and evaluate the way resources are configured in your AWS setup. AWS Config continuously audits the environment to comply with pre-established desired configurations. If a configuration deviates from the expected standards, alerts can be generated, and warnings can be issued. As you can imagine, it doesn't apply to just Amazon S3 but all AWS services. You will learn more about AWS Config in *Chapter 8, Best Practices for Application Security, Identity, and Compliance.*

AWS greatly simplifies the monitoring of your environment, enhances troubleshooting, and ensures that established standards are followed.

Implementing S3 Object Lock to secure resources

S3 Object Lock allows the storage of objects with **Write Once Read Many (WORM)** models. S3 Object Lock assists in preventing the accidental or nefarious deletion of important information. For example, S3 Object Lock can be used to ensure the integrity of AWS CloudTrail logs.

Implementing data at rest encryption

AWS provides multiple encryption options for S3 as explained below:

- **Server-Side Encryption with Amazon S3-Managed Keys (SSE-S3)**: To use SSE-S3, you simply need to enable the feature for your S3 bucket and Amazon S3 will automatically encrypt and decrypt your data using keys that are managed by the service.

SSE-S3 uses 256-bit Advanced Encryption Standard (AES-256) encryption, which is one of the most secure encryption algorithms available. SSE-S3 is a convenient and secure way to encrypt data at rest in Amazon S3. It automatically encrypts and decrypts your data using keys that are managed by Amazon S3, providing a simple and secure way to protect your data.

- **Server-Side Encryption with AWS Key Management Service (SSE-KMS)**: SSE-KMS is similar to SSE-S3, but with some additional benefits and charges. AWS KMS is a service that is fully managed, and enables the creation and management of **Customer Master Keys (CMKs)**, which are the keys used for encrypting your data. For using a CMK, there are different permissions available that provide extra security against unauthorized access to your Amazon S3 objects. Using the SSE-KMS option, an audit trail can be created that indicates when and by whom the CMK was used. The option also enables you to create and manage customer-managed CMKs or use AWS-managed CMKs that are exclusive to your service, your Region, and you.
- **Server-Side Encryption with Customer-Provided Keys (SSE-C)**: In the case of SSE-C, you are responsible for managing the encryption keys while Amazon S3 is responsible for encryption during the write to disk process and the decryption process when accessing your objects.
- **Client-side encryption**: You can encrypt data before sending it to Amazon S3. You have the freedom to choose your own encryption method but you are responsible for managing the encryption key.

Enabling data-in-transit encryption

Amazon S3 supports HTTPS (TLS) to prevent attacks to nefariously access or modify the traffic between your users and the Amazon S3 buckets. It is highly recommended to modify your Amazon S3 bucket policies only to permit encrypted connections that use the HTTPS (TLS) protocol.

It is also recommended to implement a rule in AWS Config that enables continuous monitoring controls using **s3-bucket-SSL-requests-only**.

Turning on Amazon S3 server access logging

By default, access is not logged. This ensures that you are not charged for the storage space these logs will take. However, it's relatively easy to turn on logging. These logs will give you a detailed record of any traffic in Amazon S3. These access logs will help determine who accessed your buckets and when they were accessed.

This will help not only from a security perspective but also to assess traffic patterns and help you to control your costs. You can also enable AWS CloudTrail to log all activity related to S3.

S3 server access logging allows users to log requests made to their S3 bucket. With server access logging, you can capture detailed information about every request made to their S3 bucket, including the requestor's IP address, the request type, the response status, and the time of the request.

To turn on server access logging for your S3 bucket, you first need to create a target bucket where the logs will be stored. This bucket can be in the same AWS account as your source bucket or in a different account.

Once you have created the target bucket, you can enable server access logging for your source bucket. As soon as server access logging is enabled, Amazon S3 will automatically log requests made to your bucket and store the logs in the target bucket. You can view the logs by accessing the target bucket in the Amazon S3 console, or by using the Amazon S3 API.

Considering the use of Amazon Macie with Amazon S3

Amazon Macie leverages the power of machine learning to automatically ensure that sensitive information is not mishandled when using Amazon S3. Amazon Macie can locate and discern sensitive data in Amazon S3 and provide data classification. Macie can recognize **Personally Identifiable Information** (PII), intellectual property, and similar sensitive information. Amazon Macie has instrumentation panels, reports, and warnings to show how data is used.

Implementing monitoring leveraging AWS monitoring services

Monitoring is a critical component of any computing solution. AWS provides a variety of services to consistently and reliably monitor Amazon S3, such as CloudWatch which offers a variety of metrics for Amazon S3 including the number of `put`, `get`, and `delete` requests.

Using VPC endpoints to access Amazon S3 whenever possible

Using **Virtual Private Cloud** (VPC) endpoints with Amazon S3 enables the use of Amazon S3 without traversing the internet and minimizing risk. A VPC endpoint for Amazon S3 is an artifact within an Amazon VPC that only allows connections from Amazon S3. To allow access from a given Amazon VPC endpoint, an Amazon S3 bucket policy can be used.

The following is the VPC endpoint policy:

```
{
  "Version": "2012-10-17",
  "Id": "Access-to-bucket-using-specific-endpoint",
  "Statement": [
    {
      "Sid": "Access-to-specific-VPCE-only",
      "Effect": "Deny",
      "Principal": "*",
      "Action": "s3:*",
      "Resource": ["arn:aws:s3:::bucket_name",
                   "arn:aws:s3:::bucket_name/*"],
      "Condition": {
        "StringNotEquals": {
          "aws:sourceVpce" : "vpce-1a2b3c4d"
        }
      }
    }
  ]
}
```

Figure 5.7: VPC endpoint policy

Below is the S3 bucket policy to accept a request from the VPC endpoint:

```
{
  "Version": "2012-10-17",
  "Id": "Access-to-bucket-using-specific-endpoint",
  "Statement": [
    {
      "Sid": "Access-to-specific-VPCE-only",
      "Effect": "Deny",
      "Principal": "*",
      "Action": "s3:*",
      "Resource": ["arn:aws:s3:::example_bucket",
                   "arn:aws:s3:::example_bucket/*"],
      "Condition": {
        "StringNotEquals": {
          "aws:sourceVpce" : "vpce-1a2b3c4d"
        }
      }
    }
  ]
}
```

Figure 5.8: S3 bucket policy

VPC endpoints for Amazon S3 use two methods to control access to your Amazon S3 data:

- Controlling the requests made to access a given VPC endpoint
- Controlling the VPCs or VPC endpoints that can make requests to a given S3 bucket by taking advantage of S3 bucket policies

Data exfiltration can be prevented by leveraging a VPC without an internet gateway.

To learn more, please check the following link: `https://docs.aws.amazon.com/AmazonS3/latest/dev/example-bucket-policies-vpc-endpoint.html`.

Leveraging Amazon S3 cross-region replication

By default, Amazon S3 persists data in more than one AZ. Still, there may be other reasons that require you to provide an even higher level of redundancy—for example, storing the data in different continents due to compliance requirements or minimizing the data access latency for the team situated in another region. **Cross-Region Replication** (**CRR**) is the storage of data across AWS Regions to satisfy those types of requirements. CRR enables asynchronous replicating objects across AWS Regions in multiple buckets.

In this section, you learned about some of the recommended best practices when implementing Amazon S3 as part of any solution, including how to achieve the best performance, minimize sticker shock at the end of the month with your monthly charges by monitoring usage, and ensure that only "need to know" users access data in your Amazon S3 buckets.

Amazon S3 cost optimization

You should configure your Amazon S3 to manage your items and keep them cost-effectively stored throughout their lifecycle. You can use an S3 Lifecycle configuration to make S3 move data from S3 Standard to S3 Glacier after it hasn't been accessed for a certain period of time. This can help you reduce your storage costs by storing data in the most cost-effective storage class. Additionally, you can use the following to reduce costs further:

- **Data transitions**: Using Amazon S3 storage classes, these define when objects transfer from one storage class to another. For example, one year later, archive it to the S3 Glacier storage class.
- **Data expirations**: Specify when objects will expire. On your behalf, Amazon S3 deletes expired objects. When you choose to expire items, the lifetime expiration costs vary. In case you transfer intermittent logs to a bucket, your application might require them for a week or a month.

After that, you might need to erase them. Some records are habitually written for a restricted period of time. After that, they are rarely accessed.

- **Archiving**: At some point you may no longer be accessing data, but your organization might require you to archive it for a particular period for administrative compliance. S3 Glacier is a proper choice for enterprises that only need to reference a group of data once or twice a year, or for backup purposes. Glacier is Amazon's most affordable storage class. When compared to other Amazon storage offerings, this allows an organization to store large amounts of data at a much lower cost. S3 Standard is suitable for frequently accessed data, while S3 Glacier is better suited for infrequently accessed data that can tolerate longer retrieval times. Choosing the right storage class can help you save money by only paying for the level of storage and retrieval performance that you need.
- **Automated cost saving**: S3 Intelligent-Tiering automatically stores objects in three access tiers:
    - A Frequent Access tier if you want access data more often.
    - An Infrequent Access tier which has 40% lower cost than the Frequent Access tier (object is not accessed for 30 consecutive days).
    - A new Archive Instant Access tier with 68% lower cost than the Infrequent Access tier (object is not accessed for 90 consecutive days).

S3 Intelligent-Tiering monitors access patterns and moves objects that have not been accessed for 30 consecutive days to the Infrequent Access tier, and now, after 90 days of no access, to the new Archive Instant Access tier.

Let's say you have an S3 bucket that contains a large number of objects, some of which are accessed frequently and some of which are accessed infrequently. If you were to use the S3 Standard storage class to store all of these objects, you would pay the same price for all of them, regardless of their access patterns.

With S3 Intelligent-Tiering, however, you can take advantage of the cost savings offered by the infrequent access tier for the less frequently accessed objects. For example, let's say you have a set of log files that are accessed frequently during the first 30 days after they are created, but then only occasionally after that. With S3 Intelligent-Tiering, these log files would be automatically moved to the infrequent access tier after 30 days of inactivity. This would result in cost savings compared to storing them in the frequent access tier for the entire time.

The movement of objects between tiers in S3 Intelligent-Tiering is fully automated and does not require any management or intervention from the user. You are charged a small monitoring and automation fee in addition to the storage and data transfer fees associated with the storage class.

Note that by opting into asynchronous, archive capabilities for objects that are rarely accessed, you can realize storage cost savings of up to 95%, with the lowest storage cost in the cloud.

You can use S3 Transfer Acceleration to reduce data transfer costs. S3 Transfer Acceleration allows you to transfer large amounts of data to S3 over long distances more quickly and cheaply than using the internet alone. This can help you save on data transfer costs, especially if you transfer a lot of data between regions or between AWS and your on-premises data centers.

Using S3 batch operations to reduce the number of requests made to the service. S3 batch operations allow you to perform multiple operations on your data in a single request, which can help you reduce the number of requests you make to the service and save on request fees.

Many application workloads on-premises today either can't be moved to the cloud or are challenging to move. Some of the more common application examples include genomic sequencing, media rendering, medical imaging, autonomous vehicle data, seismic data, manufacturing, etc. AWS provides Storage Gateway to connect those applications to the cloud.

Building hybrid storage with AWS Storage Gateway

While working on cloud migration, some applications will not be so simple to move to the cloud. Those apps might need to stay on-premises for performance reasons or compliance reasons, or they may be too complex to move into the cloud quickly. Some apps may need to remain on-premises indefinitely such as mainframe applications or legacy applications that need to meet licensing requirements. To address these use cases, you need to explore hybrid cloud storage solutions that provide ready access for on-premises apps to data stored in AWS.

AWS Storage Gateway

AWS Storage Gateway acts as a bridge to provide access to almost unlimited cloud storage by connecting applications running on-premises to Amazon storage. As shown in the diagram below, Storage Gateway allows customers to connect to and use key cloud storage services such as Amazon S3, Amazon S3 Glacier, Amazon FSx for Windows File Server, and Amazon EBS. Additionally, Storage Gateway integrates with AWS services such as AWS KMS, AWS IAM, AWS CloudTrail, and AWS CloudWatch.

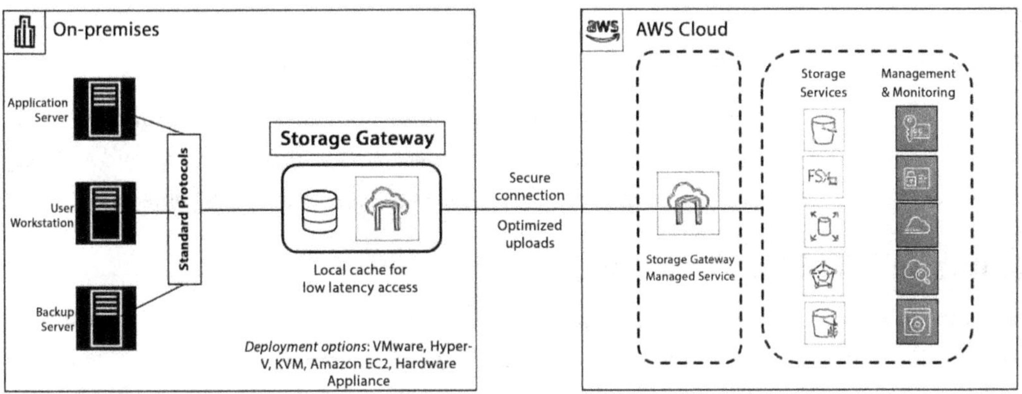

Figure 5.9: AWS Storage Gateway

Storage Gateway quickly deploys on-premises as a preconfigured hardware appliance. There is also a virtual machine option that supports all the major hypervisors. Storage Gateway provides a local cache to enable access to frequently accessed data with low-latency access. Storage Gateway supports access via standard storage protocols (NFS, SMB, and iSCSI VTL), so no changes to customers' applications are required. There are four types of Storage Gateway.

Amazon S3 File Gateway

Amazon S3 File Gateway is a service that allows you to store and retrieve files from Amazon S3 using the file protocol (i.e., **Network File System** (**NFS**) and **Server Message Block** (**SMB**)). This means that you can use S3 File Gateway as a file server, allowing you to access your S3 objects as if they were files on a local file system. This can be useful for applications that require access to files stored in S3, but don't support object storage directly. You can see the data flow in the diagram below.

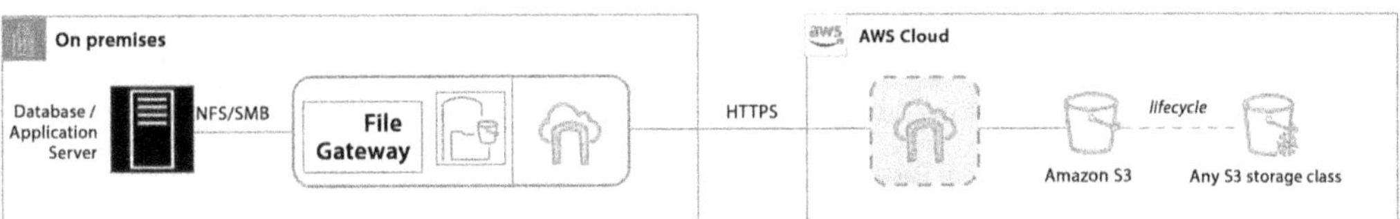

Figure 5.10: Amazon S3 File Gateway

To use S3 File Gateway, you simply create a file share and configure it to store files in your S3 bucket. You can then access the file share using the file protocol, either from within your Amazon VPC or over the internet. This allows you to easily integrate S3 File Gateway with your pre-existing applications and workflows.

Overall, S3 File Gateway is a useful service for applications that require file storage but want to take advantage of the scalability, durability, and cost-effectiveness of S3.

S3 File Gateway supports various features, such as versioning, data deduplication, and data tiering. It also integrates with other AWS services, such as AWS Backup, AWS IAM, and AWS **Key Management Service** (**KMS**), allowing you to use these services with your S3 objects.

Amazon FSx File Gateway

Amazon FSx File Gateway is a hybrid cloud storage solution that provides on-premises applications access to virtually unlimited cloud storage. It allows you to use your existing file servers and **Network-Attached Storage** (**NAS**) devices as a seamless interface to Amazon S3, Amazon FSx for Lustre, and Amazon FSx for Windows File Server. Here's an example of how Amazon FSx File Gateway works:

Suppose you have an on-premises file server that you use to store important files and data. As your storage needs grow, you begin to run out of space on your local file server. Instead of purchasing additional storage or upgrading your hardware, you can use Amazon FSx File Gateway to seamlessly extend your storage to the cloud.

First, you deploy a virtual machine on your on-premises infrastructure and install the Amazon FSx File Gateway software on it. This virtual machine serves as a gateway between your on-premises file server and Amazon S3 or Amazon FSx. Next, you create an Amazon S3 bucket or an Amazon FSx file system to store your files in the cloud. You can choose different S3 storage classes and lifecycle policies to manage the cost of your cloud storage. Then, you create a file share on the Amazon FSx File Gateway virtual machine and connect it to your on-premises file server using standard protocols such as **Server Message Block** (**SMB**) or **Network File System** (**NFS**). You can use your existing file server permissions and Active Directory to manage access to the files.

Finally, when you save a file on your on-premises file server, it is automatically backed up to the cloud using the Amazon FSx File Gateway. You can also access the files in the cloud directly from the file server without any additional steps.

Amazon FSx File Gateway also provides features such as caching, multi-protocol access, and file-level restore, making it an ideal solution for backup and disaster recovery, content distribution, and data archiving. It allows you to use your existing on-premises file servers to store and access files on the cloud, providing virtually unlimited storage capacity without the need for additional hardware or complex software configurations.

Tape Gateway

Amazon Tape Gateway is a service that allows you to store data on tapes using the tape protocol (i.e., **Linear Tape-Open** (**LTO**) and **Virtual Tape Library** (**VTL**)). This means that you can use Tape Gateway as a tape library, allowing you to access your data as if it were stored on tapes in a local tape library. This can be useful for applications that require access to data stored on tapes, but don't support tapes directly.

Tape Gateway supports various features, such as data deduplication, data tiering, and encryption. It also integrates with other AWS services, such as AWS Storage Gateway, AWS Backup, and AWS KMS, allowing you to use these services with your data on tapes.

To use Tape Gateway, you simply create a tape virtual device and configure it to store data on tapes in your tape library. You can then access the tape virtual device using the tape protocol, either from within your VPC or over the internet. This allows you to easily integrate Tape Gateway with your existing applications and workflows. Overall, Tape Gateway is a useful service for applications that require tape storage but want to take advantage of the scalability and durability of AWS.

Volume Gateway

Amazon Volume Gateway is a service that allows you to store data on cloud-backed storage volumes using the iSCSI protocol. This means that you can use Volume Gateway as a storage device, allowing you to access your data as if it were stored on a local storage volume. This can be useful for applications that require access to data stored on a storage volume, but don't support cloud storage directly.

Volume Gateway supports two storage modes: cached and stored. In cached mode, data is stored on your local storage volume and asynchronously backed up to Amazon S3, allowing you to access your most frequently accessed data quickly while still providing long-term durability. In stored mode, data is directly stored on Amazon S3, allowing you to store large amounts of data without the need for local storage.

To use Volume Gateway, you simply create a storage volume and attach it to your on-premises or Amazon EC2 instance. You can then access the storage volume using the iSCSI protocol, either from within your Amazon VPC or over the internet. This allows you to easily integrate Volume Gateway with your existing applications and workflows. Overall, Volume Gateway is a useful service for applications that require storage volumes but want to take advantage of the scalability and durability of AWS.

Storage Gateway offers customers the advantages of hybrid cloud storage by providing a seamless migration path to the cloud. Customers experience a fast deployment, which enables them to leverage the agility and scale of the cloud quickly. Storage Gateway doesn't require any application changes. It easily integrates with standard storage protocols on-prem.

Finally, Storage Gateway is managed centrally via the AWS Console. It integrates with various AWS services like CloudWatch, CloudTrail, and Identity Access Management to provide customers visibility and control over the whole solution. You often want to back up your data for various reasons, like disaster recovery. In such cases, you need an easy option to back up your data facilitated by AWS using AWS Backup.

AWS Backup

AWS Backup is a service that centralizes backup management and enables a straightforward and economical means of backing up application data across multiple AWS services to help customers comply with their business continuity and backup requirements. It automates backup scheduling and retention management, and it provides a centralized way for configuring and auditing the resources that require backup. Additionally, it keeps an eye on backup activity and alerts you in case of any issues. AWS Backup integrates with CloudTrail and AWS Organizations for governance and management, giving customers many options to help meet their recovery, restoration, and compliance needs.

AWS Backup enables centralized configuration and management of backups for various AWS resources including Amazon EC2 instances, Amazon EBS volumes, Amazon **Relational Database Service** databases, Amazon DynamoDB tables, Amazon EFS file systems, and other resources. You will learn about all of the database services we have just mentioned in *Chapter 7, Selecting the Right Database Service*. Some of the use cases where you may want to use AWS Backup are:

- Compliance and disaster recovery
- Unifying backup solutions to avoid the complexity of cloud backups being done by different groups
- Creating audit and compliance alerts, reports, and dashboards across all backups

To use AWS Backup, you simply create a backup plan and specify the AWS resources you want to back up. AWS Backup will then automatically create backups according to your specified schedule and store them in your specified storage location. You can then restore your backups as needed, either to the original location or to a new location. This allows you to easily manage your backups and recover from data loss in the event of a disaster. Overall, AWS Backup is a useful service for businesses that want to ensure the durability and availability of their critical data on AWS.

In this section, you learned about various Storage Gateway options to build a hybrid cloud by storing data into AWS cloud and AWS Backup to provide a cloud-native option for data backup.

Summary

In this chapter, you learned about **Storage Area Network** (**SAN**) in the cloud with Amazon EBS. You learned about various EBS options and how to choose the right EBS volume per your workload. You further learned about **Network Attached Storage** (**NAS**) in the cloud with Amazon EFS and file system-specific workloads with Amazon FSx.

With the ever-increasing amount of data, you need scalable storage to store petabytes of data, and AWS provides Amazon S3 to fulfill that need. You learned about various tiers of Amazon S3, including S3 Standard, Intelligent Tiering, Infrequent Access-IA, One Zone-IA, and S3 Glacier. You further learned about S3 versioning to save a copy of your file and build multi-destination replication.

Later in the chapter, you learned about Amazon S3 best practices and optimized your S3 storage for performance, cost, and security. Finally, you learned about building a hybrid cloud with AWS Storage Gateway and a cloud-native backup option with AWS Backup.

In the next chapter, you will learn how to harness the power of the cloud to create powerful applications, and we will do a deep dive into another important AWS service—Amazon EC2.

6

Harnessing the Power of Cloud Computing

Technology is transforming the world, yet according to IDC, on average enterprises only put 15% of their IT budgets toward innovation, and the other 85% is spent on maintaining existing infrastructure. In data centers, servers are at the core of any IT workload and consume most of the IT effort and budget. To run any application, you need computing. Even though the cloud brings with it the concept of serverless computing, there are still servers in the background managed by cloud vendors.

The AWS compute platform helps you to shift your budgets from maintaining existing infrastructure to driving innovation. You will learn about some of the basic compute services available in AWS and how these services came to be. In addition, you will learn about serverless compute and hybrid compute. You will also learn how AWS handles the fundamental services of computing.

In this chapter, we will discuss the following topics:

- Compute in AWS
- Learning about Amazon **Elastic Compute Cloud** (**EC2**)
- Reviewing Amazon EC2 best practices
- Amazon Elastic Load Balancing
- Learning serverless compute with AWS Lambda and Fargate
- High-performance computing
- Hybrid compute

By the end of this chapter, you will be familiar with the various compute options available in AWS, and you will be able to choose the right compute option for the right workload. Let's dive deep into the world of AWS compute.

Compute in AWS

The cloud has changed the way we see compute today. A decade ago, there was no such word as "compute," and "server" was the most used terminology. Running your application code or database was about servers with a CPU attached. These servers could be dedicated to physical bare-metal machines or VMs hosted on physical machines. The cloud started with the same concept of providing on-demand servers, which are VMs hosted in cloud providers' data centers. In AWS terminology, these servers, called Amazon **Elastic Compute Cloud** (**EC2**), are on-demand VMs available based on a per-second billing model.

With EC2, AWS takes care of the physical server, but there is still a maintenance overhead involved in patching and securing the underlying OS in these EC2 instances. Also, cloud providers such as AWS are looking to provide more optimized solutions and help you focus on the coding part to build business logic. AWS launched a serverless compute service called **AWS Lambda** to reduce OS maintenance overhead in 2014. It was the first offering where you just write a piece of code and run it using the service without worrying about servers and clusters, which generated the term **function-as-a-service** (**FaaS**). Lambda pointed the entire IT industry in the direction of building compute services without servers. However, Lambda still runs on servers behind the scenes, but that is abstracted from the end-user, resulting in the term **serverless compute**.

Initially, Lambda used to run small functions, mainly automating operations such as spin-up infrastructure and triggering CI/CD pipelines. However, AWS Lambda became more powerful over time, and organizations built complex applications such as dynamic e-commerce websites using Lambda. It's become a low-cost and scalable option for new businesses, and it helps them succeed. For example, in 2017, A Cloud Guru built an entire training content distribution website using Lambda, which scales to 300,000 students at a meagre cost. Read this SiliconANGLE article to find out more: `https://siliconangle.com/2017/08/15/a-cloud-guru-uses-lambda-and-api-gateway-to-build-serverless-company-awssummit/`.

Further down the line, customers started using serverless compute services to run their container workloads. This resulted in AWS Fargate, launched in 2017 for **Elastic Container Service** (**ECS**), which allows the customer to run their Docker containers in AWS without a server. Later, in 2019, Fargate launched **Elastic Kubernetes Service** (**EKS**) to allow customers to run Kubernetes serverless.

Now, AWS is going all-in on serverless. In 2020, they launched various serverless options for analytics services, such as Amazon Redshift Serverless for building petabyte-scale data warehouses in the cloud without a server, **Elastic MapReduce (EMR)** Serverless for transforming terabytes of data using a serverless Hadoop system in the cloud, and **Managed Streaming for Kafka (MSK)** Serverless for running Kafka workloads in the cloud without worrying about the server. You will learn about these serverless compute services throughout this book.

So now you know why the term is not called **server** but **compute**, because **server** only refers to a physical server or VM, while **compute** is much more than that, with AWS Lambda and serverless compute. AWS provides choices in how you consume compute to support existing applications and build new applications in a way that suits your business needs, whether in the form of instances, containers, or serverless compute. Let's dive into the computing world and start with AWS's core service, EC2.

Learning about Amazon EC2

As you learned in the previous section, Amazon EC2 is AWS's way of naming servers. It's nothing but virtual machines hosted on a physical server residing inside the AWS data center in a secure environment. It is all about standardizing infrastructure management, security, and growth, and building an economy of scale to quickly meet client demand for services in minutes and not months. AWS takes full advantage of virtualization technologies and can slice one computer to act like many computers. When you are using AWS, you can shut off access to resources with the same speed and agility as when you requested and started the resources, with an accompanying reduction in the billing for these resources.

EC2 was first developed to be used in Amazon's internal infrastructure. It was the idea of Chris Pinkham. He was head of Amazon's worldwide infrastructure from around 2003. Amazon released a limited beta test of EC2 to the public on August 25, 2006, providing limited trial access. In October 2007, Amazon expanded its offerings by adding two new types of instances (Large and Extra-Large), and in May 2008, two additional instance types were added to the service (High-CPU Medium and High-CPU Extra Large).

Amazon EC2 is probably the most essential and critical service on the AWS cloud computing platform. If you are trying to create something using AWS, and no other service offers the functionality you desire, you will probably be able to use EC2 as the foundation for your project. You can think of the EC2 service as a computer of almost any size and capability that you can turn on or off at any point and stop being charged when you shut it down.

We briefly mentioned that EC2 allows various computer sizes and capabilities. Let's revisit that idea and see how many choices are available. Amazon EC2 delivers a large variety of instance types. Each type addresses different needs and is optimized to fit a specific use case. Instance types are defined by a combination of their memory, CPU, GPU, storage, and networking capabilities. Each different type can provide a sweet spot for your individual use case. Each EC2 instance type that Amazon provides has a different size, allowing you to match the right instance size with your target workload.

As better CPU cores and memory chips become available, AWS continually improves its EC2 offerings to take advantage of these new components. The Amazon EC2 service is constantly improving. Staying on top of the constant changes can be quite challenging.

For example, when the T instance types were launched, AWS called them T1, but now better instances such as T4 instances types are available as AWS keeps evolving its offerings. To see the complete list of instance types offered by AWS, see the *EC2 instance families* section later in this chapter.

In general terms, the EC2 instance types and their classifications have remained unchanged, but each type's models and sizes continue to evolve. What used to be the *top-shelf* offering last year might be a medium-level offering this year due to improvements to the underlying components. Depending on budgetary constraints and workload needs, different models and sizes might offer the optimal solution for your project.

AWS supports various processors for their EC2 instances, such as Intel, AMD, NVIDIA, and their own homegrown processor Graviton. Let's take a quick peek at the Graviton processor.

AWS Graviton

From a processor perspective, for AWS, the longest-standing processor choice is Intel. Since 2006, Intel processors have been essential to powering AWS's most powerful instances. AWS recently released the latest generation of Intel instances with the second generation of Xeon Scalable for compute-intensive workloads. In 2018, AWS launched AMD processor-based instances, and at re:Invent 2018, AWS launched its own processor, an Arm-based Graviton processor. For GPU, AWS uses an NVIDIA chip to provide choice for training machine learning models.

One of the essential things that keeps AWS ahead of the game is their innovation. When AWS launched its processor in 2018, it was a masterstroke that helped them to gain a lead over other cloud providers. Graviton is an Arm chip from Annapurna Labs, a chip design company in Israel that AWS acquired in 2015.

The most important thing about having your own Graviton processor is that it is custom-built to suit your needs. To complement the Graviton processor, AWS launched a Nitro hypervisor as the backbone, and now they have an entire infrastructure system optimized for the cloud-native workload. It resulted in an added advantage for AWS as they can offer low prices and high performance for workload-focused custom instances.

EC2 A1 instances are based on the first generation of Graviton processors, with up to 16 vCPUs, 10 Gbps enhanced networking, and 3.5 Gbps EBS bandwidth. In 2019, AWS launched Graviton 2, which is their second-generation chip. These new AWS Graviton 2 processors have 4x the number of compute cores, deliver up to 7x better performance, have more support for machine learning, video, and HPC, and offer 5x faster memory compared to the Graviton 1.

The Amazon EC2 M6g, C6g, and R6g instances are powered by AWS Graviton 2 processors, which offer a significant improvement in price performance compared to current-generation x86-based instances for various workloads, such as web and application servers, media processing, and machine learning. This translates to up to 40% cost savings while maintaining high performance levels, making these instances an excellent choice for a wide range of computing requirements. These processors are designed for use in AWS's cloud computing services and are intended to provide even higher performance and lower cost than the first generation of Graviton processors. Now AWS has launched Graviton 3 processors, which have even better (25% better) compute performance than Graviton 2 processors.

Graviton processors are not available for all EC2 instances, but wherever possible it is recommended to use Graviton-backed instances for better price and performance. Let's learn more about the advantages of EC2.

Advantages of EC2

Amazon EC2 has a vast selection of instances for you to choose from. Let's look at some of them and understand the key advantages of using EC2:

- **The diverse set of instances to choose from**

  EC2 offers more than 400 instances to enable customers to run virtually every workload. You can choose from instances that offer less than a single processor (T3 instances) and up to 96 processors (C5 instances). Memory is available from hundreds of megabytes (T3 instances) to 24 terabytes (High Memory instances), the most memory of any major IaaS provider. Network performance ranges from a single gigabit (T2 instances) to 100 gigabits (Elastic Fabric Adapter).

EC2 instances can be built with extreme low-latency NVMe and massively scaled remote and block-level storage using Elastic Block Store. These instances can be built with up to eight peer-to-peer (P3 instances) connected GPUs or even a dedicated FPGA (F1 instances). EC2 also offers many instances as bare metal, with no hypervisor presence, for the most demanding performance environments or customers who intend to use their hypervisor.

EC2 even offers Apple Mac systems with macOS the highest frequency (M5 instances). AWS offers Intel Xeon Scalable processors in the cloud for high-performance computing (HPC) workloads, you can have the most local storage in the cloud with D3 and D3en instances, you can use G4 instances with the best economics for graphics processing in the cloud, and you can get extreme performance for network storage bandwidth, up to 60 Gbps, with R5 instances. AWS offers four times more EC2 instance types than it did just a couple of years ago. AWS provides Arm-based host CPUs (Graviton 2) built by AWS and customized for various workload needs, such as machine learning inference. You will learn more about these instances in the *EC2 instance families* section.

- **Scalability**

  You can scale up from a single system to thousands as your business needs grow. What if you no longer need the systems? You can scale back as quickly as you scale up. If you don't know how much capacity you will need, EC2 offers auto-scaling. Auto-scaling helps to scale out EC2 instances automatically based on defined metrics. For example, you can add two EC2 instances if your instance memory utilization reaches 60% or CPU utilization reaches 70%. You can learn more about auto-scaling in the AWS docs at `https://aws.amazon.com/autoscaling/`.

- **Performance**

  AWS Nitro gives EC2 significant and unique performance advantages. Generally, cloud server instances across the industry are given to customers as VMs because there is a hypervisor between the physical hardware and the virtual system. This abstraction layer provides flexibility and ease of use but can also negatively impact performance. In the case of EC2, virtualized instances use the Nitro hypervisor and Nitro offload cards.

  The Nitro hypervisor has been optimized for cloud instances, improving performance characteristics. Nitro takes many networks, storage, security, and system management functions.

It offloads them from the system's CPU, relieves the CPU so it can perform better on customers' workloads, and improves the actual speed of those functions because they run on dedicated ASICs rather than a general-purpose CPU, which is a significant overall differentiator for EC2. You can learn more about the Nitro hypervisor by visiting the AWS page: `https://aws.amazon.com/ec2/nitro/`.

- **Reliability**

  EC2 is built on 24 Regions and over 76 global Availability Zones and serves millions of customers ranging from large enterprises to start-ups. EC2 has an SLA commitment of 99.99% availability for each Region. Overall, this makes AWS EC2 very reliable.

- **Security**

  Every EC2 instance is built by default to be secure. Client systems that are allowed to connect to EC2 must also meet strict security standards such as PCI, SOC, and FedRAMP. If you are connecting to the AWS cloud on-premises, you can create entire networks under IPsec to define a logically isolated section of AWS using a **Virtual Private Network (VPN)**. One example of a hardware and software innovation is AWS Nitro. It gives EC2 differentiated security experiences, taking per-system security functions off the main host processor and running them on a dedicated processor, resulting in individual system protection and a minimized attack surface because security functions run on a dedicated chip rather than the system's host CPU. You can learn more about it on the Nitro Enclaves page: `https://aws.amazon.com/ec2/nitro/nitro-enclaves/`.

Let's look at EC2 instance families in more detail.

EC2 instance families

AWS provides more than 400 types of instances based on processor, storage, networking, operating system, and purchase model. As per your workload, AWS offers different capabilities, processors, platforms, instances, and more. All these options allow you to select the best instances for your business needs. As of June 2022, these are the instance types that Amazon offers:

- General Purpose (A1, M6, T4, Mac)
- Compute Optimized (C7, Hpc6a)
- Accelerated Computing (P4, G5, F1)
- Memory Optimized (R6, X2, High Memory)
- Storage Optimized (H1, D3, I4)

These are EC2 instances in a broad five-instance family, highlighting only the latest generation instances in parentheses. You can look at all older version instances in each family by visiting `https://aws.amazon.com/ec2/instance-types/`.

Instance type names combine the instance family, generation, and size. AWS provides clues about instance families through their naming convention, which indicates the key characteristics of the instance family. These are prefixes or postfixes for various instance types:

- a – AMD processors
- g – AWS Graviton processors
- i – Intel processors
- d – Instance store volumes
- n – Network optimization
- b – Block storage optimization
- e – Extra storage or memory
- z – High frequency

AWS has a standard naming convention for instance types. For example, if the instance name is c7g.8xlarge, the first position indicates the instance family, c. The second position indicates the instance generation, in this case, 7. The remaining letters before the period indicate additional capabilities, such as g for a Graviton-based instance. After the period is the instance size, which is a number followed by a size, such as 8xlarge. You can learn more about instance naming in the AWS user docs: `https://docs.aws.amazon.com/AWSEC2/latest/UserGuide/instance-types.html`.

Let's look at AWS's five instance families in more detail.

General Purpose (A1, M6, T4, Mac)

General Purpose instances balance CPU, memory, and network resources, providing a balance between cost and functionality. They are ideal for running web servers, containerized microservices, caching fleets, and development environments. Until you have identified the specific needs for your application workload in terms of compute, storage, networking, and so on, it's a good idea to start with a General Purpose instance. One of the main distinctions within this class is between instances with fixed (such as M5a) and burstable (such as T3a) performance.

T family instance types include T2/T3/T4 EC2 instances. These are AWS workhorse instances. The T family of instance types is the most popular among General Purpose compute instances. AWS provides t2.micro in their free tier, so most people starting with AWS tend to pick a T instance as their first choice.

T4g uses a Graviton 2 processor, the T2/T3 family uses Intel chips, and T3a uses AMD chips with burstable performance. Burstable performance is used when you have uneven workloads that require an occasional boost. This burst in capacity can be used to scale up compute quickly.

You need to earn CPU credits for bursts. When the CPU is not running at maximum capacity, CPU credits are earned. The credits are used when there is a need for a boost or burst. A CPU credit gives you the performance of a full CPU core for one minute.

Here's an example to explain the concept of burstable credits better. One example of a burstable instance is the t2.small instance, which is designed for workloads that do not require a consistently high level of CPU performance. The t2.small instance has a baseline performance level of 20% of a CPU core, but it can burst to higher levels of performance when needed.

When using a t2.small instance, you are allocated a certain number of burstable credits that can be used to burst to higher levels of performance. These credits are replenished at a rate of 24 credits per hour, and they are used at a rate of 1 credit per minute of bursting. For example, if your t2.small instance is idle and not using any CPU resources, it will accrue 24 credits per hour, which can be used to burst to higher levels of performance when needed. If your t2.small instance is running a workload that requires a higher level of CPU performance, it will use up its burstable credits at a rate of 1 credit per minute, and once all of the credits are used up, the instance will operate at its baseline performance level until more credits are accumulated.

If the credit allotment is exceeded, this will result in an extra charge to your bill, but it will still enable you to process requests and handle the traffic. Suppose you consistently find yourself paying for burstable traffic. In that case, it is probably an indication that it is time to add more instances to your architecture or move your application to a more powerful instance.

M family instance types include M4/M5/M6 EC2 instances, which are similar to T family instances. They are also General Purpose instances and deliver a good balance between compute, memory, and network resources. The latest M6 instances are available across all three processors: Intel Xeon (M6i instances), Graviton 2 (M6g instances), and AMD (M6a instances).

A1 instances are the first EC2 instances powered by Graviton processors. Amazon EC2 A1 instances offer good value for the amount of functionality supplied. They are often used in scale-out workloads as they are well suited for this type of job. A1 instances use an Arm chip. Therefore, this type is more suitable for application development that runs open-source languages such as Java, Ruby, and Python.

Mac instances are built on the AWS Nitro system and are powered by Apple Mac mini computers with Intel Core i7-8700 processors. This EC2 family gives you access to macOS to develop, test, and sign applications that require Apple's Xcode IDE.

Let's continue our journey through the different instance types offered by AWS.

Compute Optimized (C7, Hpc6a)

Compute Optimized instances, such as the C series instances, are designed for applications that are highly compute-intensive and require a high level of CPU performance. These instances are equipped with powerful processors, such as Intel Xeon Scalable processors, and offer a high ratio of CPU to memory to support demanding workloads.

Compute Optimized instances are well suited for a variety of workloads, including **high-performance computing** (**HPC**) applications, video encoding and transcoding, machine learning and deep learning, and other applications that require a high level of CPU performance. These instances can help users achieve high levels of performance and efficiency, making them an excellent choice for applications that are compute-intensive.

C family instance types include C4/C5/C6 and the latest C7 instances. These instance types are ideal for compute-intensive applications and deliver cost-effective high performance. C instances are a good fit for applications that require raw compute power. The latest C7g instance uses a Graviton 3 processor and C6 instances are available across all three processors: Intel Xeon (C6i instances), Graviton 2 (C6g/C6gn instances), and AMD (C6a instances) processors. Benchmarks show that Graviton-based C6 instances achieve 40% better price performance than the previous family of C5 instance types.

Hpc6a instances are optimized for high-performance computing workloads that are compute intensive. Hpc6a is available in a low-cost AMD processor and delivers network performance up to 100 Gbps with the help of an **Elastic Fabric Adapter** (**EFA**) for inter-node network bandwidth. These instances are designed for the following workloads:

- Molecular dynamics
- Weather forecasting
- Computational fluid dynamics

Let's learn about another popular instance type – the Accelerated Computing family of instances.

Accelerated Computing (P4, G5, F1)

Accelerated Computing instances include additional hardware dedicated to the instance, such as GPUs. For General Purpose, Accelerated Computing, or graphics-intensive computing, FPGAs, or inferencing chips, provide massive amounts of parallel processing for tasks such as graphics processing, machine learning (both learning and inferencing), computational storage, encryption, and compression. These instances have hardware accelerators that enable them to evaluate functions, such as floating-point number calculations, graphics, modeling, and complex pattern matching, very efficiently.

P family instance types include P2 NVIDIA K80/P3 V100/P4 NVIDIA A100 Tensor Core instances that can deliver high performance with up to 8 NVIDIA V100 Tensor Core GPUs and up to 400 Gbps of networking throughput. P4 instances can dramatically reduce machine learning training, sometimes from days to minutes.

G family instance types include G3/G4/G5 instances. G instances are cost-effective and versatile GPU instances that enable the deployment of graphics-intensive programs and machine learning modeling. G5 instances are optimized for machine learning workloads that use NVIDIA libraries. The NVIDIA A10G for G5 is often used for graphics applications and 3D modeling.

F1 instances rely on FPGAs for the delivery of custom hardware accelerations. A **Field-Programmable Gate Array (FPGA)** is an **Integrated Circuit (IC)** that is customizable in the field for a specific purpose. A regular CPU is burned at the factory and cannot be changed once it leaves the factory floor. An example of this is the Intel Pentium chip. Intel manufactures millions of these chips, all of them precisely the same. FPGAs are field-programmable, meaning the end-user can change them after they leave the factory. FPGAs can be customized for individual needs and burned by the customer.

The AWS Inferential-based Inf1 instance is a custom-designed AWS chip optimized for running deep learning inference workloads. Inf1 is ideal for customers with large amounts of image, object, speech, or text data and runs substantial machine learning on that data. Inf1 instances deliver up to 2.3x higher throughput and up to 80% lower cost per inference than Amazon EC2 G4 instances.

AWS has launched the following Accelerated Computing instances to address the specific needs of machine learning workloads:

- **DL1** – Built for training deep learning models based on an Intel Xeon processor.

- **Trn1** – Built for training deep learning models powered by AWS Trainium. They are useful for search, recommendation, ranking, machine learning training for natural language processing, computer vision, and more.
- **VT1** – Optimized for low-cost real-time video transcoding. They are useful for live event broadcasts, video conferencing, and just-in-time transcoding.

The next instance type family we will learn about is Memory Optimized instances.

Memory Optimized (R6, X2, High Memory)

Memory Optimized instances are used for anything that needs memory-intensive applications, such as real-time big data analytics, in-memory databases, enterprise-class applications that require significant memory resources, or general analytics such as Hadoop or Spark. These instances can deliver fast performance by allowing us to load large, complete datasets into memory for processing and transformation.

R family instance types include R4/R5/R6 instances. **R6i** uses the Intel chip, and R6g uses the Graviton 2 chip. These instances are best suited for memory-intensive applications. The R6 instance types use the AWS Nitro System, which reduces costs compared to its competitors.

X1 and **X2** instances deliver a high ratio of memory to compute. AWS launched a diverse set of X2 instances across processors such as Graviton 2 (X2gd) and Intel Xeon (X2idn/X2). X2 instances offer up to 50% better price-performance than X1 instances. The X1e type delivers the highest memory-to-compute ratio of all EC2 instance types.

High Memory instances deliver the most significant amount of available RAM, providing up to 24 TB of memory per server. Like X2 instances, High Memory instances are best suited for production environments of petabyte-scale databases.

In addition to that, AWS offers **z1d instances**, which provide both high compute capacity and a high memory footprint for **electronic design automation** (EDA).

Let's look at the final category of Storage Optimized instances.

Storage Optimized (H1, D3, I4)

Storage Optimized instances are ideal for tasks requiring local access to large amounts of storage, extreme storage performance, or both. Instances include both a large-capacity HDD and an extremely low-latency local NVMe. And don't forget, all EC2 instances have access to Amazon Elastic Block Store for block-level storage at any scale. These instances are best suited for workloads that need massive storage, particularly sequential read-write-like log analysis.

The **H1** and **D3** instance types form part of the dense storage family of servers that can supply sequential reads and writes with petabyte-scale datasets. These instances provide storage on HDDs. H1 instances can supply up to 16 TB, and D3 can supply up to 48 TB. Compared to EC2 D2 instances, D3 instances offer significantly faster read and write disk throughput, with an improvement of up to 45%. This enhanced disk performance enables faster data processing and storage, making D3 instances a compelling option for workloads that require high-speed access to data.

The latest **I4 instances** launched across diverse processors such as Graviton 2 (Im4gn/Is4gen). I4 instances provide SSD storage up to 30 TB while supplying lower latency than HDD-based storage. I4 instances deliver markedly improved I/O latency, with up to 60% lower latency and a reduction of up to 75% in latency variability when compared to I3 and I3en instances. Additionally, I4 instances come with always-on encryption, ensuring the security of data at rest. These performance and security enhancements make I4 instances an attractive choice for workloads that require low-latency, high-throughput I/O operations, such as data warehousing, data processing, and other demanding enterprise applications.

Amazon will likely continue to enhance its EC2 service by offering new instance types and improving the current ones. You can use AWS's new **EC2 Instance Type Explorer** to keep yourself up to date with new EC2 instance offerings. EC2 Instance Type Explorer helps you navigate and discover the right instances for your customers. Use filters to narrow down the instance family by category or hardware configuration quickly. You can access it using `https://aws.amazon.com/ec2/instance-explorer`.

You have now learned about the various EC2 types. As cost is one of the main factors when it comes to the cloud, let's learn more about the EC2 pricing model.

EC2 pricing model

While the standard cloud price model is the pay-as-you-go model, AWS provides multiple options to further optimize your costs. As servers are a significant part of any IT infrastructure, it is better to understand all the available cost options to get the most out of your dollar. The following are the four different ways to purchase compute in AWS:

- **On-Demand:** Pay for compute capacity by the second without any long-term commitment. It is best suited for fluctuating workloads, for example, stock trading or e-commerce website traffic. It is the default choice when you spin up an instance and is also suitable for quick experiments.

- **Reserved Instance (RI)**: You can commit 1 or 3 years to a specific EC2 instance family and receive a significant discount of up to 72% off On-Demand prices. This is best for a steady workload that you know will not fluctuate much, for example, an internal HR portal. An RI is like a coupon: you pay in advance, and it applies automatically when your spin-up instance belongs to the same EC2 instance family for which you pay the RI price. AWS also provides **Convertible RIs**, where you can exchange one or more Convertible RIs for another Convertible RI with a different configuration, including instance family, operating system, and tenancy. The new Convertible RI must be of an equal or higher value than the one you're exchanging. You can find details on Reserved Instance pricing in AWS at `https://aws.amazon.com/ec2/pricing/reserved-instances/pricing/`.
- **Savings Plan**: This is like an RI, but monetary commitment and compute can be used across Fargate, EC2, and AWS Lambda. In a savings plan, you don't have to make commitments to specific instance configurations but commit to a spending amount. You can get significant savings, up to 72% off On-Demand instances, with the flexibility to apply it across instance families. AWS has two types of Savings Plans: EC2 Instance Savings Plans and Compute Savings Plans.
- **Spot Instances**: Same as the pay-as-you-go pricing model of On-Demand, but at up to 90% off. EC2 can reclaim Spot Instances with a 2-minute warning. They are best for stateless or fault-tolerant workloads. You can leverage the scale of AWS at a fraction of the cost with a simplified pricing model. A Spot Instance is only interrupted when EC2 needs to reclaim it for On-Demand capacity. You don't need to worry about your bidding strategy. Spot prices gradually adjust based on long-term supply and demand trends.

All four purchasing options use the same underlying EC2 instances and AWS infrastructure across all Regions. You can combine multiple options to optimize the cost of your workload. As shown in the following diagram, you can use auto-scaling to use all four options to optimize cost and capacity.

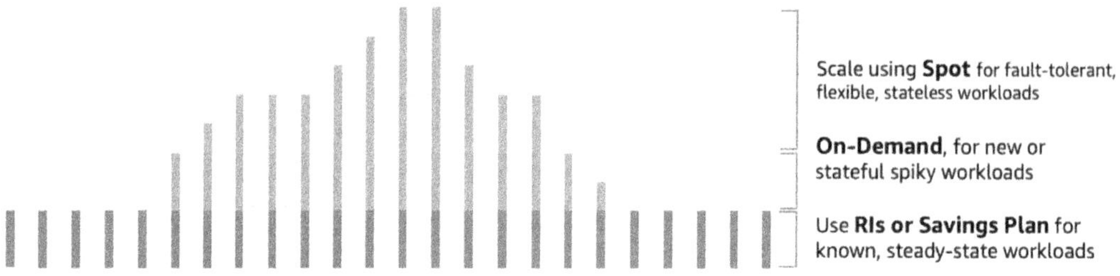

Figure 6.1: EC2 pricing model to optimize cost

Let's take an example of an e-commerce website's workload. As shown in the preceding diagram, for daily traffic patterns, you can use an RI, with which you can save up to 72% compared to On-Demand instances. But if you run a deal, such as 20% off Apple products, and get a sudden spike, then auto-scaling spins up On-Demand instances to handle the spike. At the end of the day, when you are processing orders for fulfillment, you can use a Spot Instance to expedite the order queue with 90% savings compared to an On-Demand instance.

There are so many choices in EC2 that you can get confused easily, and to address that problem, AWS provides Compute Optimizer.

AWS Compute Optimizer

AWS offers Compute Optimizer, a service that suggests the most appropriate instances from over 140 options available in the M, C, R, T, and X families for Amazon EC2 and Amazon EC2 Auto Scaling groups. By analyzing resource utilization patterns, Compute Optimizer can identify the most cost-effective and efficient instances to help optimize application performance and reduce costs. It uses machine learning models trained on millions of workloads to help customers optimize their compute resources for cost and performance across all the workloads they run. The following are the benefits of using Compute Optimizer:

- Get instance type and Auto Scaling group recommendations, making it easier for you to choose the right compute resources for specific workloads.
- Get a deep analysis of a workload's configuration, resource utilization, and performance data to identify a range of defining characteristics, such as whether the workload is CPU intensive and exhibits a daily pattern. Compute Optimizer then uses machine learning to process these characteristics to predict how the workload would perform on various hardware platforms, delivering resource recommendations.
- Get up to three recommended options for each AWS resource analyzed to choose the correct size and improve workload performance. Compute Optimizer predicts your workload's expected CPU and memory utilization on various EC2 instance types. Compute Optimizer provides the added benefit of allowing you to assess the performance of your workload on the recommended instances before you adopt them. This helps to reduce the risk of unforeseen issues arising from transitioning to new instance types and enables you to make informed decisions regarding which instances to choose for your workload. By simulating performance metrics, Compute Optimizer helps you gauge the effectiveness of recommended instance types and provides a level of confidence in the decision-making process.

When you spin up an EC2 instance, the first thing to select is an **Amazon Machine Image** (**AMI**) to decide which operating system you want to use. Let's learn more about AMIs.

Amazon Machine Images (AMIs)

Even though there are so many EC2 instance types to choose from, the number of instance types pales in comparison to the number of AMIs available. An AMI contains the information needed to start an instance. An AMI needs to be specified when launching an instance.

The chosen AMI will determine the characteristics of the EC2 instance, such as the following:

- **Operating system**: The currently supported operating systems are as follows:
    a. Ubuntu
    b. Amazon Linux
    c. CentOS
    d. Debian
    e. Red Hat Enterprise Linux
    f. FreeBSD
    g. SUSE
    h. Fedora
    i. Gentoo
    j. macOS
    k. Mint
    l. OpenSolaris
    m. Windows Server
- **Architecture**: The architecture that will be used:
    a. 64-bit (Arm)
    b. 32-bit (x86)
    c. 64-bit (x86)
    d. 64-bit (Mac)
- **Launch permissions**: The launch permissions will determine when and where the AMI can be used:
    a. Public: All AWS accounts can launch this AMI.

   b. Explicit: Only specific AWS accounts can launch the AMI.
   c. Implicit: Implicit launch permission is given to launch the AMI.

- **Root device storage**: Another option that can be specified when choosing an AMI is how the data in the root device is persisted. The options include the following:
   a. Amazon EBS: Uses an Amazon EBS volume launched using an Amazon EBS snapshot as its source
   b. Instance store: Uses an instance store volume launched from a template store in S3

Multiple instances can be launched from a single AMI. This is useful when multiple instances need to be launched with the same configuration. It does not matter if you need one instance or a thousand instances. They can be launched with the same effort by clicking a few buttons.

An AMI comprises the following:

- An EBS snapshot or a template (in the case of an instance-backed AMI) for the root volume for an EC2 instance. For example, an operating system, an application, or a server.
- Launch permissions that can be used to control the AWS accounts that will be allowed to use the AMI to generate new instances.
- A block device mapping that specifies which volumes need to be attached to the instance when it is started.

AWS enables running thousands of AMIs. Some are AMIs created by AWS, the AWS community creates some, and some are offerings from third-party vendors.

You have learned about the vast number of options available when creating and launching Amazon EC2 instances. Now let's explore the best practices to optimize the Amazon EC2 service.

Reviewing Amazon EC2 best practices

How you use and configure EC2 is going to depend on your use case. But some general EC2 best practices will ensure the security, reliability, durability, and availability of your applications and data. Let's delve into the recommended practices for handling security, storage, backup management, and so on.

Access

Like with almost any AWS service, it's possible to manage the access and security of your EC2 instances, taking advantage of identity federation, policies, and IAM. You can create credential management policies and procedures to create, rotate, distribute, and revoke AWS access credentials.

You should assign the least privilege possible to all your users and roles, like any other service. As they say in the military, your users should be given access on a *need-to-know* basis.

One advantage or disadvantage of using EC2 directly is that you are entirely in charge of managing the OS changes. For that reason, ensure that you regularly maintain and secure the OS and all the applications running on your instance.

Storage

One advantage of using EC2 instances is that you will stop getting charged when you shut down the instance. The reason that AWS can afford to do this is the fact that once you shut the instance down, AWS then reassigns the resource to someone else. But what does this mean for any data you had stored in the instance? The answer lies in understanding the difference between instance stores and EBS-backed instances.

When you launch an EC2 instance, by default, it will have an instance store. This store has high performance. However, anything that is persisted in the instance store will be lost when you shut down the instance.

IMPORTANT NOTE

If you want data to persist after you shut down the instance, you will need to ensure that you include an EBS volume when you create the instance (or add it later) or store the data in an S3 bucket. If you store the data in the instance store attached by default to the EC2 instance, it will be lost the next time it is shut down.

EBS volumes are mountable storage drives. They usually deliver lower speed and performance than instance stores but have the advantage that the data will persist when you shut down the instance.

It is also recommended to use one EBS volume for the OS and another EBS volume for data.

If you insist on using the instance store for persistence purposes, make sure there is a plan in place to store the data in a cluster of EC2 instances with a replication strategy in place to duplicate the data across the nodes (for example, using Hadoop or Spark to handle this replication).

Resource management

When launching an EC2 instance, AWS can include instance metadata and custom resource tags. These tags can be used to classify and group your AWS resources.

Instance metadata is data specified for an instance that can then be used to customize, label, and maintain the instance. Instance metadata can be classified into topics such as the following:

- The name of the host
- Events
- Security groups
- Billing tags
- Department or organizational unit tags

The following diagram illustrates the basics of tagging your EC2 instances:

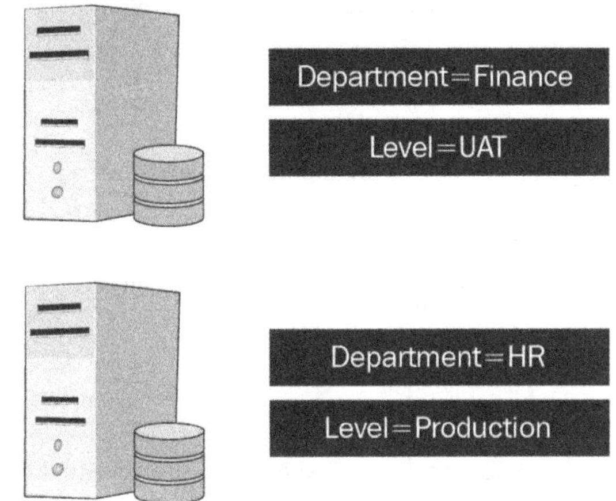

Figure 6.2: EC2 instance tags

In this example, two tags are assigned to each one of the instances—one tag is given the key **Department**, and another is given the key **Level**. In this example, you can identify and consolidate the HR and finance department workloads for billing, automation, or to apply tag-based security. You can learn more about tag strategies by referring to the AWS docs at `https://docs.aws.amazon.com/general/latest/gr/aws_tagging.html`.

Tags are a powerful yet simple way to classify EC2 instances. They can help in development, code testing, environment management, and billing. Every tag also has a corresponding value.

Limit management

By default, AWS sets limits for a variety of parameters for Amazon EC2 (as well as for other services). If you are planning to use Amazon EC2 in production environments, you should get intimately familiar with those limits.

AWS enforces service limits to safeguard against unanticipated over-provisioning and malicious actions intended to inflate your bill, and to protect service endpoints. These limits are put in place to prevent unexpected charges from excessive resource usage and to mitigate potential security risks that may result from unauthorized access to service endpoints. By implementing these limits, AWS helps to ensure the reliability, availability, and security of its services and provides customers with greater control over their usage and expenditure. AWS has the concepts of soft limit and hard limit to save you from incurring accidental costs. For example, Amazon VPC has a soft limit of 5 and a hard limit of 100 per Region, which can be increased after putting in a request to AWS.

Knowing the limits will allow you to plan when to ask for a limit increase before it becomes critical. Increasing the limits involves contacting the AWS team. It may take a few hours or a few days to get a response. These are some of the default limits for an AWS account:

- 20 instances per Region
- 5 Elastic IPs per Region (including unassigned addresses)

Keep in mind that these soft limits can be increased by contacting AWS. You can learn about AWS' service limits by referring to `https://docs.aws.amazon.com/general/latest/gr/aws_service_limits.html`.

EC2 backup, snapshots, and recovery

When it comes to backing up EC2, you have two main components: EBS volumes and AMIs. It is important to have a periodic backup schedule for all EBS volumes. These backups can be performed with EBS snapshots. You can also build your own AMI by using an existing instance and persisting the current configuration. This AMI can be used as a template to launch future instances.

To increase application and data availability and durability, it is also important to have a strategy to deploy critical application components across multiple Availability Zones and copy the application's data across these Availability Zones.

Make sure that your application's architecture can handle failovers. One of the simplest solutions is to manually attach an Elastic IP address or a network interface to a backup instance. Elastic IP provides a fixed IP address to your instance, where you can route traffic. An Elastic IP can be assigned to an **Elastic Network Interface** (**ENI**), and those ENIs can be easily attached to instances. Once you have the solution in place, it is highly recommended to test the setup by manually shutting down the primary server. This should fail the traffic over to the backup instance, and traffic should be handled with little or no disruption.

While all of these best practices will help you to get the most out of EC2, one particularly useful way to manage and distribute traffic among EC2 instances is to use AWS's load balancer service.

Amazon Elastic Load Balancing

Elastic Load Balancing (**ELB**) in AWS allows you to assemble arrays of similar EC2 instances to distribute incoming traffic among these instances. ELB can distribute this application or network traffic across EC2 instances or containers within the same AZ or across AZs.

In addition, to help with scalability, ELB also increases availability and reliability. A core feature of ELB is the ability to implement health checks on the managed instances. An ELB health check determines the *"health"* or availability of registered EC2 instances and their readiness to receive traffic. A health check is simply a message or request sent to the server and the response that may or may not be received. If the instance responds within the `200` range, everything is fine. Any other response is considered *"unhealthy"*. If an instance does not return a healthy status, it is considered unavailable, and ELB will stop sending application traffic to that instance until it returns to a healthy status. To learn more about return statuses, see `https://docs.aws.amazon.com/elasticloadbalancing/latest/classic/ts-elb-http-errors.html`.

Before we delve into the nitty-gritty of the different types of ELB services, let's understand some fundamental concepts.

ELB rules

ELB rules are typically comprised of one or more conditions and one or more actions. The conditions specify the criteria that must be met for the rule to be applied, while the actions define what should be done with the request if the rule's conditions are met.

For example, a listener rule may have a condition that requires traffic to be received on a specific port and protocol, and an action that directs that traffic to a specific target group. Similarly, a path-based routing rule may have a condition that requires a request's path to match a specific value, and an action that directs that request to a different target group.

In some cases, you may also be able to specify a priority for your rules, which determines the order in which they are evaluated. This can be important if you have multiple rules that apply to the same traffic and you need to ensure that the correct rule is applied in a specific order. Let's go into more detail about the parts that make up a rule:

- **Conditions** – A condition is a regular expression indicating the path pattern that needs to be present in the request for the traffic to be routed to a certain range of backend servers.

- **Target groups** – A target group is a set of instances. Whenever a condition is matched, traffic will be routed to a specific target group to handle requests. Any of the instances in the group will handle the request. Target groups define a protocol (HTTP, HTTPS, FTP, and others) and a target port. A health check can be configured for each target group. There can be a one-to-many relationship between ALBs and target groups. Targets define the endpoints. Targets are registered with the ALB as part of a target group configuration.
- **Priorities** – Priorities are definitions to specify in which order the ALB will evaluate the rules. A rule with a low number priority will have higher precedence than a high one. As the rules are evaluated by priority, the rules get evaluated. Whenever a pattern is matched in a rule, traffic is routed to a target group, and the evaluation stops.

Like many other AWS services, an ELB can be created and configured via the AWS console, the AWS CLI, or the Amazon API. Let's look at some specific ELB rules.

Listener rules

A listener rule is a type of rule that defines how incoming traffic is forwarded to a target group by an ELB based on the protocol and port of the incoming request. Here's an example of how a listener rule works. Suppose you have a web application running on a group of EC2 instances and you want to distribute incoming traffic across these instances using an ELB. You can create a listener rule that specifies which target group the traffic should be forwarded to based on the protocol and port of the incoming request.

For example, you could create a listener rule that forwards all HTTP traffic on port 80 to a target group named "web-servers." The listener rule would specify the protocol (HTTP), port (80), and target group ("web-servers"). Any incoming HTTP requests on port 80 would then be automatically forwarded to the EC2 instances in the "web-servers" target group. A listener rule provides a flexible way to route incoming traffic to the appropriate target group based on specific criteria. By creating multiple listener rules, you can route traffic to different target groups based on the protocol and port of the incoming request.

Target group rules

Target group rules are a type of rule in ELB that determines how traffic is distributed across the targets within a target group. Target groups are groups of resources that receive traffic from a load balancer, such as Amazon EC2 instances or containers. Target group rules help you manage how traffic is distributed across these resources. Here's an example of how target group rules work:

Suppose you have a target group named "web-servers" containing a group of EC2 instances running your web application. You can create a target group rule that specifies how incoming traffic is distributed across these instances based on specific criteria, such as response time or connection count.

For example, you could create a target group rule that distributes traffic based on the response time of each instance. The target group rule would evaluate the response time of each instance and send more traffic to the instances with the lowest response times. This helps ensure that the load is balanced evenly across the EC2 instances, and that users experience consistent performance when accessing your web application.

Target group rules provide a powerful way to manage traffic distribution across your resources. By creating multiple target group rules, you can fine-tune how traffic is distributed across your resources based on specific criteria, helping you optimize performance and ensure high availability for your applications.

Host-based routing rules

Host-based routing enables the routing of a request based on the host field, which can be set in the HTTP headers. It allows routing to multiple services or containers using a domain and path.

Host-based routing provides the ability to transfer more of the routing logic from the application level, allowing developers to focus more on business logic. It allows traffic to be routed to multiple domains on a single load balancer by redirecting each hostname to a different set of EC2 instances or containers. These rules allow you to direct incoming requests to different target groups based on the hostname in the request URL. For example, you can create a host-based routing rule that directs all requests with a certain hostname to a specific target group.

Path-based routing rules

Simply put, path-based routing is the ability to route traffic from the ELB to particular instances on the ELB cluster based on a substring in the URL path. These rules allow you to direct incoming requests to different target groups based on the path of the request URL. For example, you can create a path-based routing rule that directs all requests with a certain path to a specific target group. An example would be the following path-based routing rules:

```
/es/*

/en/*

/fr/*

*
```

We could use these rules to forward the traffic to a specific range of EC2 instances. When we deploy our servers, we could ensure that the `en` servers are using English, the `es` servers have the Spanish translation, and the `fr` servers use French strings. This way, not only will the users be able to see our content in their desired language, but the load will be distributed across the servers. In this example, it might be beneficial to monitor traffic by language constantly and deploy enough servers for each language. Even more powerfully, we could create rules that automatically launch new servers for the different language clusters based on demand by language.

Query string rules

Query string rules are a type of rule in ELB that allow you to route traffic based on the query string parameters of incoming requests. The query string is a portion of a URL that contains key-value pairs separated by an ampersand (&) symbol, and is commonly used in web applications to pass information between the client and server. Here's an example of how query string rules work. Suppose you have a web application that uses a query string parameter called "category" to identify the type of content to display. You want to route traffic to different target groups based on the value of this parameter. For example, you want traffic with the "category" parameter set to "books" to be routed to a target group containing your book servers, while traffic with the "category" parameter set to "movies" is routed to a target group containing your movie servers.

Query string rules provide a powerful way to route traffic based on the content of incoming requests. By creating multiple query string rules, you can route traffic to different target groups based on different query string parameters, allowing you to manage your resources more efficiently and provide a better experience for your users.

Now that we understand more about ELB rules, let's have a look at the different types of ELBs that AWS offers.

Elastic Load Balancer types

In August 2016, AWS launched a new service called **ALB (Application Load Balancer)**. ALB allows users of the service to direct traffic at the application level.

The old Elastic Load Balancer service offering can still be used, and it was renamed Classic Load Balancer. Also more types of ELB were later launched, named the Network Load Balancer and Gateway Load Balancer. This section will try to understand their differences and when to use one versus the other.

Classic Load Balancers

The **Classic Load Balancer (CLB)** in AWS can route traffic using the following methods:

- **Round robin**: In this method, the load balancer routes traffic to each registered instance in turn, providing an equal share of the traffic to each instance. Round Robin is the default load balancing algorithm for CLBs.
- **Least connections**: In this method, the load balancer routes traffic to the instance with the fewest active connections. This method is useful for balancing traffic across instances with varying processing capacities.
- **IP hash**: In this method, the load balancer routes traffic to a particular instance based on the source IP address of the client. This method ensures that traffic from the same source IP address is consistently routed to the same instance, which can be useful for stateful applications.

In addition to these load balancing methods, Classic Load Balancers can also route traffic based on protocols, ports, and health checks. For example, you can configure the load balancer to route traffic based on the protocol and port used by the client (such as HTTP or HTTPS on port `80` or `443`), and perform health checks on each registered instance to ensure that only healthy instances receive traffic.

It's worth noting that Classic Load Balancers are a legacy technology in AWS and are being phased out in favor of newer load balancing solutions such as Application Load Balancers and Network Load Balancers, which offer more features and better performance.

CLBs currently have a requirement where the load balancer needs a fixed relationship between the instance port of the container and the load balancer port. For example, you can map the load balancer using port `8080` to a container instance using port `3131` and to the CLB using port `4040`. However, you cannot map port `8080` of the CLB to port `3131` on a container instance and port `4040` on the other container instance. The mapping is static, requiring the cluster to have at least one container instance for each service that uses a CLB.

CLBs can operate at the request level or the connection level. CLBs don't use host-based routing or path-based routing. CLBs operate at Layer 4 of the OSI model. This means the CLB routes traffic from the client to the EC2 instances based on the IP address and TCP port.

Let's go through an example:

1. An ELB gets a client request on TCP port `80` (HTTP).

2. The request gets routed based on rules defined in the AWS console for the load balancer to direct traffic to port `4040` to an instance in the provisioned pool.
3. The backend instance processes the instructions from the request.
4. The response is sent back to the ELB.
5. The ELB forwards the payload for the response to the client.

To better understand how traffic is handled with CLBs, look at the following diagram. As you can see, all traffic gets directed to the load balancer first, which in turn directs traffic to instances that the load balancer decides are ready to handle traffic:

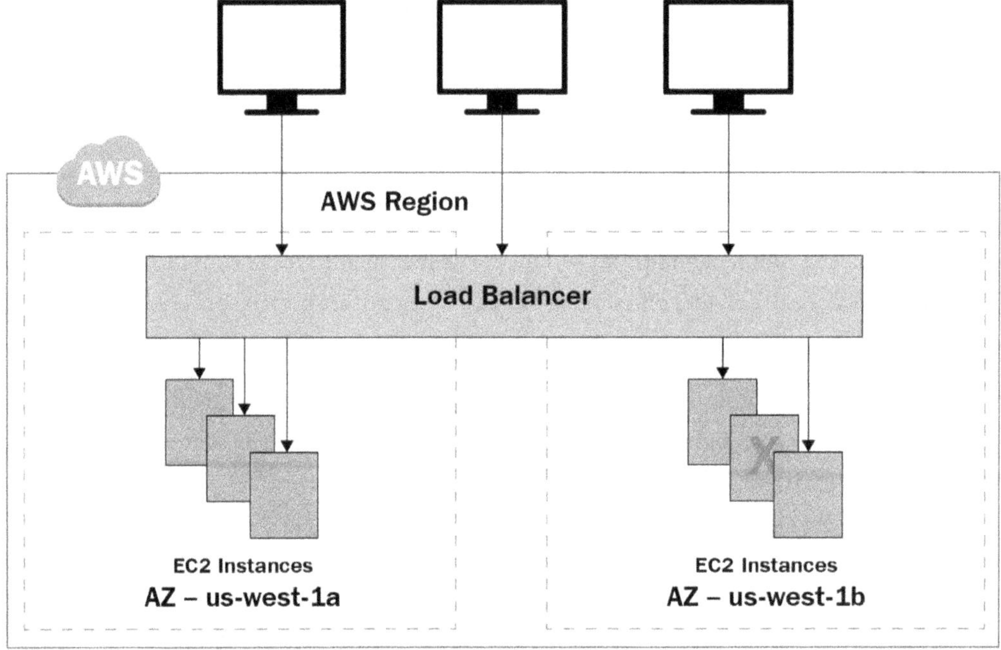

Figure 6.3: CLB architecture

From the client's perspective, the request appears to be fulfilled by the ELB. The fact that the back-end servers beyond the ELB actually handled the request will be entirely transparent for the client.

Even though it is absolutely possible to set up an ELB with only one EC2 instance supporting the load, it defeats the purpose of having an ELB. Additionally, it is best practice to set up your supporting EC2 instances across AZs in case of an AZ disruption.

Under the default configuration, the load will be distributed evenly across the enabled AZs. When using the default configuration, it is recommended to use a similar number of instances per AZ.

Application Load Balancers

The Application Load Balancer is a load balancing solution in AWS that provides advanced routing capabilities for modern web applications. It operates at the application layer (Layer 7) of the OSI model, allowing it to route traffic based on the content of the request, rather than just the source and destination IP addresses and ports. Here are some key features of the Application Load Balancer:

- **Advanced routing**: The Application Load Balancer can route traffic based on multiple criteria, including the URL path, query string parameters, HTTP headers, and source IP address. This allows you to create more sophisticated routing rules for your application.
- **Content-based routing**: The Application Load Balancer can route traffic based on the content of the request, such as the user agent, language, or MIME type. This can be useful for serving different content to different types of clients.
- **Load balancing**: The Application Load Balancer can distribute incoming traffic across multiple targets, such as EC2 instances, IP addresses, and containers. It supports both round-robin and least outstanding requests load balancing algorithms.
- **SSL/TLS termination**: The Application Load Balancer can terminate SSL/TLS connections, reducing the workload on your application servers and providing an additional layer of security.
- **Sticky sessions**: The Application Load Balancer can maintain a session affinity between a client and a target, ensuring that subsequent requests from the same client are always routed to the same target.

The Application Load Balancer is integrated with other AWS services, such as AWS Certificate Manager, AWS CloudFormation, and AWS Elastic Beanstalk, making it easier to deploy and manage your applications. The Application Load Balancer is ideal for modern web applications that use microservices and container-based architectures, as it provides advanced routing and load balancing capabilities that are optimized for these types of applications.

ALBs deliver advanced routing features that can provide host-based routing and path-based routing, and they can support containers and microservices. When you operate in the application layer (an HTTP or HTTPS request on Layer 7), the ELB can monitor and retrieve the application content, not just the IP and port. This facilitates the creation of more involved rules than with a CLB. Multiple services can be set up to share an ALB, taking advantage of path-based routing.

ALBs also easily integrate with **Elastic Container Service** (**ECS**) by enabling a Service Load Balancing configuration. Doing so enables the dynamic mapping of services to ports. This architecture can be configured in the ECS task definition. In this case, several containers point to the same EC2 instance, executing multiple services on multiple ports. The ECS task scheduler can seamlessly add tasks to the ALB.

Network Load Balancers

The **Network Load Balancer** (**NLB**) operates at the transport layer (Layer 4) of the OSI model. In this layer, there is no opportunity to analyze the request headers, so the network load balancer blindly forwards requests.

When using network load balancing, the availability of the application cannot be determined. Routing decisions are made exclusively on TCP-layer and network values without knowing anything about the application. An NLB determines *"availability"* by using an **Internet Control Message Protocol** (**ICMP**) ping and seeing if there is a response or completing a three-way TCP handshake.

The NLB is designed to handle high-throughput, low-latency workloads, such as those used by web applications, gaming, and media streaming services. The NLB can distribute traffic across multiple targets, such as EC2 instances, IP addresses, and containers, using a flow-based load balancing algorithm that ensures that each flow is consistently routed to the same target. The NLB is highly scalable and provides high availability, with the ability to automatically recover from failed targets and distribute traffic across healthy targets.

An NLB cannot distinguish whether certain traffic belongs to a certain application or another. The only way this could be possible would be if the applications were to use different ports. For this reason, if one of the applications crashes and the other doesn't, the NLB will continue sending traffic for both applications. An ALB would be able to make this distinction.

AWS has launched another load balancer called the **Gateway Load Balancer** (**GWLB**), which is a load balancing solution that provides scalable and highly available network-level load balancing for virtual network appliances, such as firewalls, intrusion detection and prevention systems, and other security appliances. The NLB is optimized for high-throughput, low-latency workloads, while the GWLB is optimized for virtual network appliances. The NLB is a Layer 4 load balancer that routes traffic based on IP protocol data, while the GWLB is a Layer 3 load balancer that routes traffic based on the content of the IP packet.

Now that we have learned about the three types of load balancers offered in AWS, let's understand what makes each type different.

CLB versus ALB versus NLB comparison

The ALB is optimized for Layer 7 traffic, such as web applications, microservices, and APIs, while the NLB is optimized for Layer 4 traffic, such as gaming, media streaming, and other TCP/UDP traffic. The CLB is a legacy load balancer that supports both Layer 4 and Layer 7 traffic, but it is less feature-rich than the ALB and NLB. The GWLB is designed for more complex network architectures and provides greater control and visibility. Here's a brief overview of each load balancer:

- **Application Load Balancer (ALB)**: The ALB operates at the application layer (Layer 7) of the OSI model, allowing it to route traffic based on the content of the HTTP or HTTPS request. It is designed for use cases such as web applications, microservices, and APIs. The ALB supports advanced features like path-based routing, host-based routing, and container-based routing. It also supports SSL/TLS offloading, content-based routing, and sticky sessions.
- **Network Load Balancer (NLB)**: The NLB operates at the transport layer (Layer 4) of the OSI model, allowing it to route traffic based on the IP protocol data, such as TCP and UDP. It is designed for use cases such as high-throughput, low-latency workloads, such as gaming, media streaming, and other TCP/UDP traffic. The NLB supports advanced routing features like source IP affinity, session stickiness, and cross-zone load balancing.
- **Classic Load Balancer (CLB)**: The CLB operates at both the application layer (Layer 7) and the transport layer (Layer 4) of the OSI model, allowing it to route traffic based on the content of the HTTP/HTTPS request as well as the IP protocol data. It is designed for use cases that require basic load balancing, such as simple web applications. The CLB supports basic features like SSL/TLS termination, cross-zone load balancing, and connection draining.
- **Gateway Load Balancer (GWLB)**: The GWLB is a load balancer that is designed for more complex and demanding network architectures. It operates at the network layer (Layer 3) of the OSI model, allowing it to route traffic based on IP addresses and ports. The GWLB is designed to handle traffic for multiple VPCs, allowing you to build more complex architectures with greater control and visibility.

The following diagram illustrates the differences between the three types of ELBs. This will help in our discussion to decide which load balancer is best for your use cases:

Feature	Application Load Balancer	Network Load Balancer	Classic Load Balancer
Protocols	HTTP, HTTPS	TCP, UDP, TLS	TCP, SSL/TLS, HTTP, HTTPS
Platforms	VPC	VPC	EC2-Classic, VPC
Layer	Layer 7		Layer 4
Generation	Newer Tech	Newer Tech	Old Tech
Performance	High	Highest	High
Health Checks	✓	✓	✓
Cloudwatch metrics	✓	✓	✓
Logging	✓	✓	✓
AZ fail-over	✓	✓	✓
Load balancing to multiple ports	✓	✓	✓
IP addresses as targets	✓	✓	
Cross-zone load balancing	✓	✓	✓
Sticky sessions	✓	✓	✓
Static and Elastic IPs		✓	
Path/Host based routing	✓		
Redirects	✓		
SSL offloading	✓	✓	✓
Server Name Indication	✓	✓	
User authentication	✓		

Figure 6.4: ELB comparison

As a general rule of thumb, it usually is better not to use a CLB on a new project and only use it in legacy applications built when CLBs were the only option.

CLB and ALB commonalities

Even though there are differences, CLBs and ALBs still have many features in common. Both support all these features:

- **Security Groups** – Leveraging a **Virtual Private Cloud** (**VPC**) architecture, a security group can be mapped with AWS services, including EC2 instances and ELBs, providing extra security to the overall architecture.

- **SSL termination** – Terminating the SSL connection at the ELB level offloads the processing of SSL traffic from the backend instances to the ELB. This removes load from the backend instances and enables them to focus on handling application traffic. It also simplifies the management of SSL certificates by centralizing the management of the certificates in one place (the ELB).
- **Idle connection timeout** – ALBs and CLBs both support the idle connection timeout period configuration. Connection timeouts enable the termination of connections that exceed a predefined threshold when the server receives no traffic from the client.
- **Connection draining** – Connection draining allows you to gracefully terminate instances and remove them from the ELB while allowing existing transactions to complete. Connections are not terminated until all pending traffic has been processed.

Now that we understand the different characteristics of the three ELB types, let's understand when it's best to use each.

The best choice of ELB by use case

One item of note when using AWS is that you don't see version numbers. There is no such thing as S3 version 1.0 and S3 version 2.0. At any given point in time, AWS offers the best version of a given service, and upgrades happen transparently. This puts a tremendous responsibility on AWS, but it makes our job easy. The fact that AWS still offers three load balancers instead of just one tells us that they see value in offering all three. And all three still exist because each could be the best for the job depending on the use case.

And that's the perfect segue. CLBs are probably the best option for legacy applications where a CLB is already in place. Many deployments were done when CLBs were the only option (at that point, they were called ELBs when that was the only option). Only later were they renamed CLBs to distinguish them from the new ALBs.

If your deployment already uses CLBs, but you are considering migrating to ALBs, these are usually some of the features that might compel you to migrate because they are not supported on a CLB:

- Support for **AWS Web Application Firewall** (**AWS WAF**)
- Support for targets for AWS Lambda
- Support for targets for IP addresses
- The ability to add several TLS/SSL certificates using **Server Name Indication** (**SNI**)

If you have a greenfield deployment and are considering which ELB to use, the best option will most likely be to use an ALB. ALBs integrate with the following:

- **Amazon Elastic Container Service** (**ECS**)
- **Amazon Elastic Kubernetes Service** (**EKS**)
- AWS Fargate
- AWS Lambda

You should have a compelling reason to choose a CLB during a brand-new deployment. A good reason to use NLBs is if performance is one of your utmost priorities and if every millisecond counts. Other reasons to choose an NLB are as follows:

- The ability to register targets using IP addresses, including a target outside the VPC that contains the load balancer.
- Support for containerized applications.
- NLBs support directing requests to multiple applications deployed on the same EC2 instance. Each instance or IP address can be registered with the same target group by assigning different ports.
- Support for traffic with high variability and high volume (millions of requests per second) for inbound TCP requests.
- Support for static or elastic IP addresses. Elastic IPs enable you to keep using the same IP address even if a physical instance goes down.

NLB supports **UDP** (**User Datagram Protocol**) traffic in addition to **TCP** (**Transmission Control Protocol**) traffic. This makes it ideal for use cases such as gaming, media streaming, IoT, and other applications that require low latency and high throughput. The NLB can load balance UDP traffic across a set of backend instances in a target group, using source IP affinity or session stickiness to ensure that each client is directed to the same backend instance for the duration of its session.

Up until this point, we have examined servers in the cloud. Let's now look at serverless compute options in AWS.

Learning about serverless computing with AWS Lambda and Fargate

AWS uses the word "serverless" to describe AWS technologies or applications that have these characteristics: no server management, automatic scaling, high availability built in, and a pay-as-you-go billing model.

AWS has serverless technologies for compute, integration, and databases, though many AWS users associate serverless with AWS's event-driven compute service, AWS Lambda.

Building serverless applications is one of the primary advantages of moving to the cloud. They reduce the admin overhead of managing infrastructure, thus increasing productivity and further reducing the **total cost of ownership** (**TCO**) in the cloud. A serverless app can be highly performant due to the ease of parallelization and concurrency. Serverless computing is the foundation of serverless apps as it manages to scale automatically, is optimized to reduce latency and cost, and increases throughput. Let's learn about the serverless compute options available in AWS.

AWS Lambda

When it comes to serverless computing, AWS Lambda comes to mind first. Lambda is a serverless compute service that allows users to run code in response to events, without having to provision or manage any underlying infrastructure. Lambda is designed to be scalable, highly available, and cost-effective, making it a popular choice for a wide range of applications.

With Lambda, users can upload their code in the form of a function and specify the events that should trigger that function. When an event occurs, Lambda automatically runs the code in response, without the user having to worry about managing any underlying infrastructure. This allows users to focus on building and running their applications, without having to worry about the details of infrastructure management.

Lambda supports a variety of languages and runtime environments, including Node.js, Java, Python, and .NET, and can be easily integrated with other AWS services, such as Amazon S3, Amazon DynamoDB, and Amazon Kinesis. This makes it an attractive option for a wide range of applications, from simple web services and microservices to complex, distributed systems.

Lambda is very economical in terms of pricing. To start with, AWS provides 1 million free requests a month with the AWS free tier. The pricing component includes the number of requests and duration metered in 1 ms increments based on the function memory setting; for example, 100 ms with 2 GB of RAM costs the same as 200 ms with 1 GB of RAM.

One example use case for AWS Lambda is building a simple web service that allows users to upload images to Amazon S3 and then automatically processes those images using machine learning. Here is how this could work:

1. The user creates a Lambda function that uses a machine learning model to process images and extract information from them.

2. The user configures an Amazon S3 bucket to trigger the Lambda function whenever a new image is uploaded to the bucket.
3. When a user uploads an image to the S3 bucket, S3 automatically triggers the Lambda function, passing the image data as input.
4. The Lambda function runs the machine learning model on the image data and extracts the desired information.
5. The Lambda function returns the results of the image processing to the caller, which could be the user's application or another AWS service.

In this use case, Lambda is used to automatically process the uploaded images using machine learning, without the user having to manage any underlying infrastructure or worry about scaling or availability. This allows the user to focus on building their application and adding new features, without having to worry about the details of infrastructure management. Serverless architecture means that the cost, size, and risk relating to change reduce, thereby increasing the rate of change.

Lambda acts as a compute service, running the user's code in response to events, providing a highly scalable, highly available, and cost-effective execution environment. The user can focus on building and running their application, without having to worry about managing any underlying infrastructure.

The purpose of this section is to introduce you to the concept of AWS Lambda. To understand it better, you need to understand how Lambda can help to achieve different architecture patterns, which you will learn about in *Chapter 14, Microservice Architectures in AWS*.

Containers are becoming famous for building microservice architectures and deploying complex code. AWS has provided the option to deploy serverless containers using Fargate. Let's learn about it in more detail.

AWS Fargate

Adopting containers requires a steep learning curve for deployment, cluster management, security, and monitoring customers. AWS serverless containers can help you focus time and resources on building applications, not managing infrastructure. Amazon **ECS** provides a simple managed control plane for containers, and AWS Fargate provides serverless container hosting. For Kubernetes, you can use Amazon **EKS** with Fargate for container hosting.

Amazon ECS and AWS Fargate give you a choice to start modernizing applications through fully managed, native container orchestration, standardized and compliant deployment paths, and automated patching and provisioning of servers. ECS Fargate's serverless model eliminates the operational complexity of managing container hosts and AMIs.

The following are the advantages of Fargate:

- **NoOps:** Yes, you read it right. You have heard about DevOps, DevSecOps, MLOps, and so on, but wouldn't life be easier if there were NoOps? AWS Fargate removes the complexity of infrastructure management and shifts primary responsibilities, such as OS hardening and patching, onto AWS. You can reduce the resources spent on these tasks and instead focus on adding value to your customers. ECS Fargate automates container orchestration with compute, networking, storage, container runtime config, auto - scaling, and self-healing and provides serverless computing without AMIs to patch, upgrade, and secure your OS.
- **Lower TCO**: In Fargate, each task runs in its dedicated host, and the resources can be tailored to the task's needs. This dramatically improves utilization, delivering significant cost savings. With fewer container hosts to manage, fewer people are needed to focus on a container infrastructure, which significantly reduces TCO. You only pay for what you provision in Fargate. You are billed for CPU and memory utilization on a per-second billing model at the container task level. You can have further savings with Spot Instances and a Savings Plan.
- **Seamless integrations**: AWS ECS Fargate integrates all the significant aspects of deployment, networking, monitoring, and security. An extensive set of third-party partners, such as Datadog, Aqua Security, Harness, and HashiCorp, provide solutions that work for the monitoring, logging, and runtime security of workloads deployed in ECS Fargate.
- **Security**: In Fargate, each task runs in its dedicated host. This security isolation, by design, eliminates multiple security concerns of sensitive containers co-existing on a host. With complete integration for IAM, security groups, key management and secret management, and encrypted, ephemeral disks, customers can deploy with peace of mind for security.

From a cost-saving perspective, Fargate Spot allows you to leverage similar savings as in your EC2 Spot. With Fargate Spot, AWS runs Fargate tasks on the same EC2 Spot instance and provides a flat discount rate of 70% compared to regular Fargate pricing.

Again, this section aims to introduce you to the concept of a serverless container. To understand it better, you need to understand how containers help to build microservice architecture patterns, which you will learn in *Chapter 13*, *Containers in AWS*.

High-Performance Computing

High-Performance Computing (HPC) is a field of computing that involves using specialized hardware and software to solve complex, compute-intensive problems. HPC systems are typically used for scientific and engineering applications that require a high level of computational power, such as weather forecasting, molecular modeling, and oil and gas exploration. HPC systems require a high level of performance and scalability, but they can help organizations achieve results faster and more efficiently, making them an essential tool for many scientific and engineering applications.

HPC workloads are characterized by a combination of multiple technologies, such as storage, compute, networking, **Artificial Intelligence** (AI), machine learning, scheduling and orchestration, and streaming visualization, combined with specialized third-party applications.

HPC workloads are classified into categories that help identify the AWS services and solutions that can best match your needs. These categories include fluid dynamics, weather Modeling, and reservoir simulation; these workloads are typically called scale-up or tightly coupled workloads. The other HPC workloads are financial risk modeling, genomics, seismic processing, and drug discovery, typically called scale-out or loosely coupled workloads. Both of these categories of workloads require a large amount of compute power using EC2 Spot instances; application orchestration using AWS Batch, AWS ParallelCluster, and scale-out computing; and high-performance storage such as FSx for Lustre and S3. Tightly coupled workloads also require high network performance using Elastic Fabric Adapter. Here are some example workloads where you should use HPC:

- Autonomous vehicle simulation and training
- Weather and climate
- Financial services, risk analysis simulation, and actuarial modeling
- **Computer-Aided Engineering** (CAE) for manufacturing and design applications
- Drug discovery
- Genomics
- Seismic processing, reservoir simulation/energy
- **Electronic Design Automation** (EDA)

AWS offers a number of services and tools that can be used to run HPC workloads on the cloud. These include:

- **EC2 P3 instances**: These instances are designed for HPC workloads and are equipped with powerful NVIDIA Tesla V100 GPUs, making them well suited for tasks such as machine learning and high-performance data analytics.
- **Amazon Elastic Fabric Adapter (EFA)**: EFA is a high-performance network interface that can be used with EC2 instances to improve the performance of HPC workloads that require low-latency communication.
- **AWS ParallelCluster**: AWS ParallelCluster is a fully managed HPC platform that allows users to easily deploy and manage HPC clusters on AWS. It includes a variety of tools and utilities that can help users run HPC workloads on AWS, such as a job scheduler and a resource manager.
- **AWS Batch**: AWS Batch is a service that allows users to run batch computing workloads on AWS. Batch workloads typically involve large numbers of independent tasks that can be run in parallel, making them well suited for HPC applications. AWS Batch can help users manage and scale their batch workloads on AWS.

Overall, AWS provides a variety of services and tools that can be used to run HPC workloads on the cloud. HPC is a vast topic; the idea of this section was to provide a basic understanding of HPC. You can learn more by visiting the AWS HPC page: `https://aws.amazon.com/hpc/`.

Hybrid compute

While you want to benefit from the advantages of using the cloud, not all your applications can be migrated to AWS due to latency or the need for local data processing. Latency-sensitive applications such as patient care flow require less than 10 ms responses, and any delays can affect critical processes, so you want your compute to be near your equipment. Similarly, there are instances when you can't afford downtime due to intermittent networking and want local data processing, for example, manufacturing execution systems, high-frequency trading, or medical diagnostics.

If you can't move to a Region because of data residency, local processing, or latency requirements, you have to build and maintain the on-premises infrastructure at your facility. In that case, you must maintain an IT infrastructure, which involves a complex procurement and provisioning process from multiple vendors with a months-long lead time. In addition, you will have the overhead to patch and update applications running on-premises and schedule maintenance downtime or arrange for on-site resources, impacting operations.

Developers need to build for different APIs and services to accommodate various other infrastructures and build different tools for automation, deployment, and security controls. That leads to separate code bases and processes for on-premises and the cloud, creating friction and operational risk. This leads to business challenges such as delayed access to new technologies and longer deployment timelines from testing to production, affecting the business' ability to deliver new features and adapt to changing dynamics.

AWS hybrid cloud services are a set of tools and services that allow you to connect on-premises infrastructure to the cloud, creating a hybrid cloud environment. This allows users to take advantage of the benefits of both on-premises and cloud computing, allowing them to run workloads in the most appropriate environment for their needs.

AWS hybrid cloud services include a range of tools and services that can help users connect their on-premises infrastructure to the cloud, such as AWS Direct Connect and AWS VPN. These services allow users to securely and reliably connect their on-premises environments to the cloud, allowing them to easily move data and workloads between on-premises and cloud environments.

AWS hybrid cloud services also include a variety of tools and services that can help users manage and operate their hybrid cloud environments, such as AWS **Identity and Access Management (IAM)** and AWS Systems Manager. These services can help users control access to resources, monitor and manage their environments, and automate common tasks, making it easier to operate and maintain their hybrid cloud environments.

From a compute perspective, let's look at AWS Outposts, which brings the cloud on-premises.

AWS Outposts

Compute and storage racks built with AWS-designed hardware, which are fully managed and scalable, are referred to as AWS Outposts. These can be used to extend AWS infrastructure, services, and tools to on-premises locations. With Outposts, users can run a consistent, native AWS experience on-premises, allowing them to use the same APIs, tools, and services that they use in the cloud.

There are two versions of Outposts: VMware Cloud on AWS Outposts, which allows users to run VMware Cloud on AWS on-premises, and AWS Outposts, which allows users to run a native AWS experience on-premises. Outposts is designed to be easily deployed and managed, and can be used to run a variety of workloads, including compute-intensive HPC workloads, latency-sensitive workloads, and applications that require access to on-premises data or resources.

Outposts' servers are 1–2 rack units high (1.75"–3.5") and fit into standard EIA-310 19" width racks. You can launch AWS Nitro-based Amazon EC2 instances with instance storage, among other services available to Outposts locally. The following services are available in Outposts.

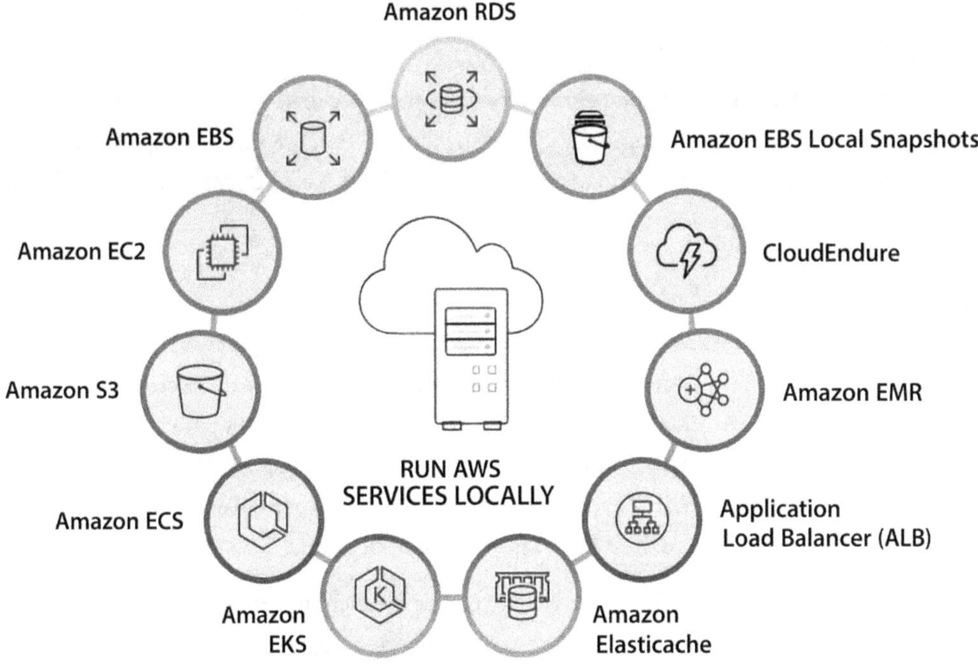

Figure 6.5: AWS Outposts locally available services

As shown in the preceding diagram, you can run virtual machines with EC2 instances in your on-premises facility using Outposts. Each instance will have instance storage that can be used for AMI launches and data volumes. You can deploy containerized workloads using Amazon ECS or EKS. You can network with Amazon VPC to introduce a logical separation between workloads and secure communication within a workload that spans the Region and your site. Outposts is a good option for IoT workloads to deploy IoT Greengrass for IoT messaging and SageMaker Neo for inference at the edge.

Outposts can help operate smaller sites such as retail stores or enterprise branch offices that run point-of-sale systems, security monitoring, smart displays, and developing next-gen facial or voice recognition to customize the customer experience. It can be helpful for healthcare providers to run the latest tech to assess patient images and process medical data quickly but benefit from cloud tools and long-term storage.

For factories, warehouses, and distribution centers, Outposts can power automation, integrate IoT data, monitor systems, and provide feedback to operators.

AWS Outposts can help users extend the benefits of AWS to on-premises locations, allowing them to run a consistent, native AWS experience on-premises and easily move workloads between on-premises and cloud environments.

In 2017, VMware launched a public cloud offering on AWS called VMware Cloud. VMware is very popular when it comes to running virtual machines. VMware Cloud simplifies migrating and extending your VMware workloads into the AWS cloud. Recently VMware Cloud became available on Outposts as well.

VMware Cloud on AWS

VMware Cloud (**VMC**) on AWS is a hybrid cloud solution built by engineers from AWS and VMware that provides a fast and efficient path to the cloud if you run VMware vSphere workloads in on-premises data centers. VMC accelerates cloud transformation with operational consistency and flexibility while scaling global business demand. VMware Cloud on AWS is a fully managed service that provides users with a consistent, native VMware experience in the cloud, allowing them to easily migrate and run their VMware-based workloads on AWS.

VMware Cloud on AWS is available in a variety of sizes and configurations, with varying levels of performance and capabilities. It can be used for a wide range of workloads, including traditional enterprise applications, cloud-native applications, and workloads that require access to on-premises data or resources.

Here are some VMC use cases:

- **Migrating VMware-based workloads to the cloud**: VMware Cloud on AWS allows users to easily migrate their VMware-based workloads to the cloud, without having to redesign their applications or learn new technologies. This can help users take advantage of the benefits of cloud computing, such as elastic scalability, high availability, and low cost, while still using the tools and technologies they are familiar with from VMware.
- **Running hybrid cloud environments**: VMware Cloud on AWS can be used to run hybrid cloud environments, allowing users to easily move workloads between on-premises and cloud environments and take advantage of the benefits of both. This can help users achieve greater flexibility, scalability, and efficiency in their environments.

- **Running disaster recovery and backup**: VMware Cloud on AWS can be used to run disaster recovery and backup environments, allowing users to quickly and easily recover from disasters and outages. This can help users ensure the availability and integrity of their applications and data, even in the face of unexpected events.
- **Running test and development environments**: VMware Cloud on AWS can be used to run test and development environments, allowing users to quickly and easily spin up new environments for testing and development purposes. This can help users speed up their development and testing processes, allowing them to release new features and applications faster.

The features of VMC allow customers to dynamically scale their environment by leveraging disaster recovery systems, highly available compute clusters, vSAN storage clusters, and NSX network virtualization.

Summary

In this chapter, you learned about compute services available in AWS, which will help you choose the right to compute per your workload requirement. You learned about why terms changed from servers to compute recently due to the broad set of options provided by the cloud.

The most popular compute service is EC2, which is the foundation for the rest of the services provided by AWS. For example, a service such as Amazon SageMaker or Amazon DynamoDB under the hood relies on core services such as EC2. You learned about various EC2 families, pricing models, and advantage.

There are so many EC2 options available, which may be confusing when it comes to optimizing your cost model. You learned about AWS compute optimization, which can help you choose the right compute option and optimize cost. You also learned about AMI, which helps you choose the operating system for your workload and spin up EC2 per your needs. Further, you learned about EC2 best practices.

For distributed computing, a load balancer is often needed to distribute the workload across multiple servers and prevent any single server from becoming overloaded. You learned about AWS-provided load balancers, which can be used for distributed computing, including CLBs, ALBs, NLBs, and GWLBs.

Compute is not limited to servers, and serverless compute is becoming more popular because it helps you to focus on your business logic and avoid the admin overhead of scaling and patching servers. You learned about the two most popular serverless compute options, AWS Lambda and AWS Fargate. You learned about HPC in AWS, which can help you to have your own mini-supercomputer to solve complex algorithmic problems.

Not every workload can be hosted on the cloud. You have learned about hybrid compute and how AWS brings its infrastructure on-premises and provides the same experience as the cloud. In the next chapter, you will get knee-deep into another set of fundamental services in AWS that are the workhorse of many successful start-ups and multinationals. That is the beautiful world of databases.

7

Selecting the Right Database Service

Building applications is all about data collection and management. If you design an e-commerce application, you want to show available inventory catalog data to customers and collect purchase data as they make a transaction. Similarly, if you are running an autonomous vehicle application, you want to analyze data on the surrounding traffic and provide the right prediction to cars based on that data. As of now, you have learned about networking, storage, and compute in previous chapters. In this chapter, you will learn the choices of database services available in AWS to complete the core architecture tech stack.

With so many choices at your disposal, it is easy to get analysis paralysis. So, in this chapter, we will first lay a foundation of how the databases and their use cases can be classified and then use these classifications to help us pick the right service for our particular use case and our circumstances. In this chapter, you will navigate the variety of options, which will give you the confidence that you are using the right tool for the job.

In this chapter, you will learn the following topics:

- A brief history of databases and data-driven innovation trends
- Database consistency model
- Database usages model
- AWS relational and non-relational database services
- Benefits of AWS database services

- Choosing the right tool for the job
- Migrating databases to AWS

By the end of this chapter, you will learn about different AWS database service offerings and how to choose a suitable database for your workload.

A brief history of databases

Relational databases have been around for over 50 years. Edgar F. Codd created the first database in 1970. The main feature of a relational database is that data is arranged in rows and columns, and rows in tables are associated with other rows in other tables by using the column values in each row as relationship keys. Another important feature of relational databases is that they normally use **Structured Query Language** (**SQL**) to access, insert, update, and delete records. SQL was created by IBM researchers Raymond Boyce and Donald Chamberlin in the 1970s. Relational databases and SQL have served us well for decades.

As the internet's popularity increased in the 1990s, we started hitting scalability limits with relational databases. Additionally, a wider variety of data types started cropping up. **Relational Database Management Systems** (**RDBMSs**) were simply not enough anymore. This led to the development of new designs, and we got the term **NoSQL databases**. As confusing as the term is, it does convey the idea that it can deal with data that is not structured, and it deals with it with more flexibility.

The term **NoSQL** is attributed to Carlo Strozzi and was first used in 1998 for a relational database that he developed but that didn't use the SQL language. The term was then again used in 2009 by Eric Evans and Johan Oskarsson to describe databases that were not relational.

The main difference between relational and non-relational databases is the way they store data and query it. Let's see an example of making a choice between a relational and non-relational database. Take an example of a banking transaction; it is critical for financial transactions in every customer's bank account to always be consistent and roll back in case of any error. In such a scenario, you want to use a relational database. For a relational database, if some information is not available, then you are forced to store null or some other value. Now take an example of a social media profile, which may have hundreds of attributes to store the user's name, address, education, jobs, personal choices, preferences, etc. However, many users do not fill in all the information; some users may add just their name, while others add more details like their address and education. In such cases, you want to use a non-relational database and store only the information provided by the user without adding null values where the user doesn't provide details (unlike in relational databases).

The following tables demonstrate the difference between relational and non-relational databases that have the same user data.

First Name	Last Name	City	Country
Maverick	Doe	Seattle	USA
Goose	Henske	NULL	NULL
John	Gayle	London	NULL

Table 7.1: Relational database

First Name	Last Name	City	Country
Maverick	Doe	Seattle	USA
Goose	Henske		
John	Gayle	London	

Table 7.2: Non-relational database

In the tables above, 3 users provided their information with their first name, last name, city, and country. You can see that only Maverick provided their full information while the other users left out either their city, country, or both. In a relational database, you need to fill in missing information with a `NULL` value across all columns, while in a non-relational database, that column doesn't exist at all.

It is nothing short of amazing what has occurred since then. Hundreds of new offerings have been developed, each trying to solve a different problem. In this environment, deciding the best service or product to solve your problem becomes complicated. And you must consider not only your current requirements and workloads, but also take into account that your choice of database will be able to cover your future requirements and new demands. With so much data getting generated, it is natural that much of innovation is driven by data. Let's look in detail at how data is driving innovation.

Data-driven innovation trends

Since high-speed internet became available in the last decade, more and more data is getting generated. Before we proceed, let's discuss three significant trends that influence your perspective on data:

- **The surge of data:** Our current era is witnessing an enormous surge in data generation. Managing the vast amount of data originating from your business applications is essential.

However, the exponential growth primarily stems from the data produced by network-connected intelligent devices, amplifying the data's diversity and quantity. These "smart" devices, including but not limited to mobile phones, connected vehicles, smart homes, wearable technologies, household appliances, security systems, industrial equipment, machinery, and electronic gadgets, constantly generate real-time data. Notably, over one-third of mobile sign-ups on cellular networks result from built-in cellular connections in most modern cars. In addition, applications generate real-time data, such as purchase data from e-commerce sites, user behavior from mobile apps, and social media posts/tweets. The data volume is expanding tenfold every five years, necessitating cloud-based solutions to manage and exploit vast data efficiently.

- **Microservices change analytics requirements**: The advent of microservices is revolutionizing organizations' data and analytics requirements. Rather than developing monolithic applications, companies are shifting towards a microservices architecture that divides complex problems into independent units. This approach enables developers to operate in smaller groups with minimal coordination, respond more efficiently, and work faster. Microservices enable developers to break down their applications into smaller parts, providing them with the flexibility to use multiple databases for various workloads, each suited for its specific purpose. The importance of analytics cannot be overstated, and it must be incorporated into every aspect of the business, rather than just being an after-the-fact activity. Monitoring the organization's operations in real time is critical to fuel innovation and quick decision-making, whether through human intervention or automated processes. Today's well-run businesses thrive on the swift utilization of data.
- **DevOps driving fast changes**: The fast-paced rate of change, driven by DevOps, is transforming how businesses approach IT. To keep up with the rapid innovation and the velocity of IT changes, organizations are adopting the DevOps model. This approach employs automated development tools to facilitate continuous software development, deployment, and enhancement. DevOps emphasizes effective communication, collaboration, and integration between software developers and IT operations. It also involves a rapid rate of change and change management, enabling businesses to adapt to evolving market needs and stay ahead of the competition.

While you see the trend that the industry is adopting, let's learn some basics of databases and learn about the database consistency model in more detail.

Database consistency model

In the context of databases, ensuring transaction data consistency involves restricting any database transaction's ability to modify data in unauthorized ways. When data is written to the database, it must adhere to a set of predefined rules and constraints. These rules are verified, and all checks must be successfully passed before the data can be accessed by other users. This stringent process ensures that data integrity is maintained and that the information stored in the database is accurate and trustworthy. Currently, there are two popular data consistency models. We'll discuss these models in the following subsections.

ACID data consistency model

When database sizes were measured in megabytes, we could have stringent requirements that enforced strict consistency. Since storage has become exponentially cheaper, databases can be much bigger, often measured in terabytes and even petabytes. For this reason, making databases ACID-compliant for storage reasons is much less prevalent. The ACID model guarantees the following:

- **Atomicity**: For an operation to be considered atomic, it should ensure that transactions within the operation either succeed or fail. If one of the transactions fails, all operations should fail and be rolled back. Could you imagine what would happen if you went to the ATM and the machine gave you money but didn't deduct it from your account?
- **Consistency**: The database is structurally sound and consistent after completing each transaction.
- **Isolation**: Transactions are isolated and don't contend with each other. Access to data from multiple users is moderated to avoid contention. Isolation guarantees that two transactions cannot coincide.
- **Durability**: After a transaction is completed, any changes a transaction makes should be durable and permanent, even in a failure such as a power failure.

The ACID model came before the BASE model, which we will describe next. If performance were not a consideration, using the ACID model would always be the right choice. BASE only came into the picture because the ACID model could not scale in many instances, especially with internet applications that serve a worldwide client base.

BASE data consistency model

ACID was taken as the law of the land for many years, but a new model emerged with the advent of bigger-scale projects and implementations. In many instances, the ACID model is more pessimistic than required, and it's *too safe* at the expense of scalability and performance.

In most NoSQL databases, the ACID model is not used. These databases have loosened some ACID requirements, such as data freshness, immediate consistency, and accuracy, to gain other benefits, such as scale, speed, and resilience. Some exceptions for a NoSQL database that uses the ACID models are the NET-based RavenDB database and Amazon DynamoDB within a single AWS account and region.

The acronym **BASE** can be broken down as follows – **Basic Availability**, **Soft-state**, and **Eventual consistency**. Let's explore what this means further:

- **Basic availability**: The data is available for the majority of the time (but not necessarily all the time). The BASE model emphasizes availability without guaranteeing the consistency of data replication when writing a record.
- **Soft-state**: The database doesn't have to be write-consistent, and different replicas don't always have to be mutually consistent. Take, for example, a system that reports sales figures in real-time to multiple destinations and uses multiple copies of the sales figures to provide fault tolerance. As sales come in and get written into the system, different readers may read a different copy of the sales figures. Some of them may be updated with the new numbers, and others may be a few milliseconds behind and not have the latest updates. In this case, the readers will have different results, but if they rerun the query soon after, they probably would get the new figures. In a system like this, not having the latest and greatest numbers may not end the world and may be good enough. The trade-off between getting the results fast versus being entirely up to date may be acceptable.
- **Eventual consistency**: The stored data exhibits consistency eventually and maybe not until the data is retrieved at a later point.

The BASE model requirements are looser than the ACID model ones, and a direct one-for-one relationship does not exist between ACID and BASE. The BASE consistency model is used mainly in aggregate databases (including wide-column databases), key-value databases, and document databases.

Let's look at the database usage model, which is a crucial differentiator when storing your data.

Database usage model

Two operations can be performed with a database: first, ingest data (or write data into the database), and second, retrieve data (or read data from the database). These two operations will always be present.

On the ingestion side, the data will be ingested in two different ways. It will either be a data update or brand-new data (such as an insert operation). To retrieve data, you will analyze the **change data capture** (CDC) set, which is changes in existing data or accessing brand new data. But what drives your choice of database is not the fact that these two operations are present but rather the following:

- How often will the data be retrieved?
- How fast should it be accessed?
- Will the data be updated often, or will it be primarily new?
- How often will the data be ingested?
- How fast does ingestion need to be?
- Will the ingested data be sent in batches or in real time?
- How many users will be consuming the data?
- How many simultaneous processes will there be for ingestion?

The answers to these questions will determine what database technology to use. Two technologies have been the standards to address these questions for many years: **online transaction processing** (OLTP) systems and **online analytics processing** (OLAP) systems. The main question that needs to be answered is - *is it more important for the database to perform during data ingestion or retrieval?* These databases can be divided into two categories depending on the use case; they need to be read-heavy or write-heavy.

Online Transaction Processing (OLTP) systems

OLTP databases' main characteristics are the fact that they process a large number of transactions (such as inserts and updates). The focus in OLTP systems is placed on fast ingestion and modification of data while maintaining data integrity, typically in a multi-user environment with less emphasis on the retrieval of the data. OLTP performance is generally measured by the number of transactions executed in a given time (usually seconds). Data is typically stored using a schema that has been normalized, usually using the **3rd normal form** (3NF). Before moving on, let's quickly discuss 3NF. 3NF is a state that a relational database schema design can possess.

A table using 3NF will reduce data duplication, minimize data anomalies, guarantee referential integrity, and increase data management. 3NF was first specified in 1971 by *Edgar F. Codd*, the inventor of the relational model for database management.

A database relation (for example, a database table) meets the 3NF standard if each table's columns only depend on the table's primary key. Let's look at an example of a table that fails to meet 3NF. Let's say you have a table that contains a list of employees. This table, in addition to other columns, contains the employee's supervisor's name as well as the supervisor's phone number. A supervisor can undoubtedly have more than one employee under supervision, so the supervisor's name and phone number will be repeated for employees working under the same supervisor. To resolve this issue, we could add a supervisor table, put the supervisor's name and phone number in the supervisor table, and remove the phone number from the employee table.

Online Analytical Processing (OLAP) systems

Conversely, OLAP databases do not process many transactions. Once data is ingested, it is usually not modified. OLTP systems are not uncommon to be the source systems for OLAP systems. Data retrieval is often performed using some query language (the **Structured Query Language** (**SQL**)). Queries in an OLAP environment are often complex and involve subqueries and aggregations. In the context of OLAP systems, the performance of queries is the relevant measure. An OLAP database typically contains historical data aggregated and stored in multi-dimensional schemas (typically using the star schema).

For example, a bank might handle millions of daily transactions, storing deposits, withdrawals, and other banking data. The initial transactions will probably be stored using an OLTP system. The data might be copied to an OLAP system to run reporting based on the daily transactions and, once aggregated, for more extended reporting periods.

The following table shows a comparison between OLTP and OLAP:

	OLTP	OLAP
Focus	Insertion and modification of data.	Retrieval and analysis of data.
Data	OLTP data is normally the source of truth and original data.	OLAP systems are fed by OLTP systems.
Transaction	OLTP has short transactions. Usually a combination of updates and inserts.	OLAP has long transactions. Usually just inserts.
Time	Low processing time of transactions.	High processing time of transactions.
Queries	Simpler queries.	Complex queries.
Normalization	Usually normalized (3NF).	Usually not normalized.
Integrity	Important. Normally ACID.	Not as important. BASE can be used.

Figure 7.1: Comparison between OLTP systems and OLAP systems

As you have learned about the database consistency model and its uses, you must be wondering which model is suitable when combining these properties; ACID is a must-have for OLTP, and BASE can be applied for OLAP.

Let's go further and learn about the various kinds of database services available in AWS and how they fit to address different workload needs.

AWS database services

AWS offers a broad range of database services that are purpose-built for every major use case. These fully managed services allow you to build applications that scale quickly. All these services are battle-tested and provide deep functionality, so you get the high availability, performance, reliability, and security required by production workloads.

The suite of AWS fully managed database services encompasses relational databases for transactional applications, such as Amazon RDS and Amazon Aurora, non-relational databases like Amazon DynamoDB for internet-scale applications, an in-memory data store called Amazon ElastiCache for caching and real-time workloads, and a graph database, Amazon Neptune, for developing applications with highly connected data. Migrating your existing databases to AWS is made simple and cost-effective with the AWS Database Migration Service. Each of these database services is so vast that going into details warrants a book for each of these services itself. This section will show you various database services overviews and resources to dive further.

Relational databases

There are many offerings in the database space, but relational databases have served us well for many years without needing any other type of database. A relational database is probably the best, cheapest, and most efficient option for any project that does not store millions of records. So, let's analyze the different relational options that AWS offers us.

Amazon Relational Database Service (Amazon RDS)

Given what we said in the previous section, it is not surprising that Amazon has a robust lineup of relational database offerings. They all fall under the umbrella of Amazon RDS. It is certainly possible to install your database into an EC2 instance and manage it yourself. Unless you have an excellent reason to do so, it may be a terrible idea; instead, you should consider using one of the many flavors of Amazon RDS. You may think running your instance might be cheaper, but if you consider all the costs, including system administration costs, you will most likely be better off and save money using Amazon RDS.

Amazon RDS was designed by AWS to simplify the management of crucial transactional applications by providing an easy-to-use platform for setting up, operating, and scaling a relational database in the cloud. With RDS, laborious administrative tasks such as hardware provisioning, database configuration, patching, and backups are automated, and a scalable capacity is provided in a cost-efficient manner. RDS is available on various database instance types, optimized for memory, performance, or I/O, and supports six well-known database engines, including Amazon Aurora (compatible with MySQL and PostgreSQL), MySQL, PostgreSQL, MariaDB, SQL Server, and Oracle.

If you want more control of your database at the OS level, AWS has now launched **Amazon RDS Custom**. It provisions all AWS resources in your account, enabling full access to the underlying Amazon EC2 resources and database environment access.

You can install third-party and packaged applications directly onto the database instance as they would have in a self-managed environment while benefiting from the automation that Amazon RDS traditionally provides.

Amazon RDS's flavors fall into three broad categories:

- **Community** (Postgres, MySQL, and MariaDB): AWS offers RDS with three different open-source offerings. This is a good option for development environments, low-usage deployments, defined workloads, and non-critical applications that can afford some downtime.
- **Amazon Aurora** (Postgres and MySQL): As you can see, Postgres and MySQL are here, as they are in the community editions. Is this a typo? No, delivering these applications within the Aurora *wrapper* can add many benefits to a community deployment. Amazon started offering the MySQL service in 2014 and added the Postgres version in 2017. Some of these are as follows:

    a. Automatic allocation of storage space in 10 GB increments up to 64 TBs
    b. Fivefold performance increase over the vanilla MySQL version
    c. Automatic six-way replication across availability zones to improve availability and fault tolerance

- **Commercial** (Oracle and SQLServer): Many organizations still run Oracle workloads, so AWS offer RDS with an Oracle flavor (and a Microsoft SQL Server flavor). Here, you will get all the benefits of a fully managed service. However, keep in mind that, bundled with the cost of this service, there will be a licensing cost associated with using this service, which otherwise might not be present if you use a community edition.

Let's look at the key benefits of Amazon RDS.

Amazon RDS Benefits

Amazon RDS offers multiple benefits as a managed database service offered by AWS. Let's look at its key attributes to make your database more resilient and performant.

Multi-AZ deployments - Multi-AZ deployments in RDS provide improved availability and durability for database instances, making them an ideal choice for production database workloads. With Multi-AZ DB instances, RDS synchronously replicates data to a standby instance in a different **Availability Zone** (AZ) for enhanced resilience. You can change your environment from Single-AZ to Multi-AZ at any time. Each AZ runs on its own distinct, independent infrastructure and is built to be highly dependable.

In the event of an infrastructure failure, RDS initiates an automatic failover to the standby instance, allowing you to resume database operations as soon as the failover is complete. Additionally, the endpoint for your DB instance remains the same after a failover, eliminating manual administrative intervention and enabling your application to resume database operations seamlessly.

Read replicas - RDS makes it easy to create read replicas of your database and automatically keeps them in sync with the primary database (for MySQL, PostgreSQL, and MariaDB engines). Read replicas are helpful for both read scaling and disaster recovery use cases. You can add read replicas to handle read workloads, so your master database doesn't become overloaded with reading requests. Depending on the database engine, you may be able to position your read replica in a different region than your master, providing you with the option of having a read location that is closer to a specific locality. Furthermore, read replicas provide an additional option for failover in case of an issue with the master, ensuring you have coverage in the event of a disaster.

While both Multi-AZ deployments and read replicas can be used independently, they can also be used together to provide even greater availability and performance for your database. In this case, you would create a Multi-AZ deployment for your primary database and then create one or more read replicas of that primary database. This would allow you to benefit from the automatic failover capabilities of Multi-AZ deployments and the performance improvements provided by read replicas.

Automated backup - With RDS, a scheduled backup is automatically performed once a day during a time window that you can specify. The backup job is monitored as a managed service to ensure its successful completion within the specified time window. The backups are comprehensive and include both your entire instance and transaction logs. You have the flexibility to choose the retention period for your backups, which can be up to 35 days. While automated backups are available for 35 days, you can retain longer backups using the manual snapshots feature provided by RDS. RDS keeps multiple copies of your backup in each AZ where you have an instance deployed to ensure their durability and availability. During the automatic backup window, storage I/O might be briefly suspended while the backup process initializes, typically for less than a few seconds. This may cause a brief period of elevated latency. However, no I/O suspension occurs for Multi-AZ DB deployments because the backup is taken from the standby instance. This can help achieve high performance if your application is time-sensitive and needs to be always on.

Database snapshots - You can manually create backups of your instance stored in Amazon S3, which are retained until you decide to remove them. You can use a database snapshot to create a new instance whenever needed. Even though database snapshots function as complete backups, you are charged only for incremental storage usage.

Data storage - Amazon RDS supports the most demanding database applications by utilizing **Amazon Elastic Block Store (Amazon EBS)** volumes for database and log storage. There are two SSD-backed storage options to choose from: a cost-effective general-purpose option and a high-performance OLTP option. Amazon RDS automatically stripes across multiple Amazon EBS volumes to improve performance based on the requested storage amount.

Scalability - You can often scale your RDS database compute and storage resources without downtime. You can choose from over 25 instance types to find the best fit for your CPU, memory, and price requirements. You may want to scale your database instance up or down, including scaling up to handle the higher load, scaling down to preserve resources when you have a lower load, and scaling up and down to control costs if you have regular periods of high and low usage.

Monitoring - RDS offers a set of 15-18 monitoring metrics that are automatically available for you. You can access these metrics through the RDS or CloudWatch APIs. These metrics enable you to monitor crucial aspects such as CPU utilization, memory usage, storage, and latency. You can view the metrics in individual or multiple graphs or integrate them into your existing monitoring tool. Additionally, RDS provides Enhanced Monitoring, which offers access to more than 50 additional metrics. By enabling Enhanced Monitoring, you can specify the granularity at which you want to view the metrics, ranging from one-second to sixty-second intervals. This feature is available for all six database engines supported by RDS.

Amazon RDS Performance Insights is a performance monitoring tool for Amazon RDS databases. It allows you to monitor the performance of your databases in real-time and provides insights and recommendations for improving the performance of your applications. With Performance Insights, you can view a graphical representation of your database's performance over time and detailed performance metrics for specific database operations. This can help you identify any potential performance bottlenecks or issues and take action to resolve them.

Performance Insights also provides recommendations for improving the performance of your database. These recommendations are based on best practices and the performance data collected by the tool and can help you optimize your database configuration and application code to improve the overall performance of your application.

Security - Controlling network access to your database is made simple with RDS. You can run your database instances in **Amazon Virtual Private Cloud (Amazon VPC)** to isolate them and establish an industry-standard encrypted IPsec VPN to connect with your existing IT infrastructure. Additionally, most RDS engine types offer encryption at rest, and all engines support encryption in transit. RDS offers a wide range of compliance readiness, including HIPAA eligibility.

You can learn more about RDS by visiting the AWS page: `https://aws.amazon.com/rds/`.

As you have learned about RDS, let's dive deeper into AWS cloud-native databases with Amazon Aurora.

Amazon Aurora

Amazon Aurora is a relational database service that blends the availability and rapidity of high-end commercial databases with the simplicity and cost-effectiveness of open-source databases. Aurora is built with full compatibility with MySQL and PostgreSQL engines, enabling applications and tools to operate without necessitating modifications. It offers a variety of developer tools to construct serverless and **machine learning** (**ML**)-driven applications. The service is completely managed and automates time-intensive administration tasks, including hardware provisioning, database setup, patching, and backups. It provides commercial-grade databases' reliability, availability, and security while costing only a fraction of the price.

Amazon Aurora has many key features that have been added to expand the service's capabilities since it launched in 2014. Let's review some of these key features:

- **Serverless configuration** - Amazon Aurora Serverless is a configuration of Aurora that offers auto-scaling features on-demand. With this configuration, your database will automatically start up, shut down, and adjust its capacity based on the needs of your application. Amazon Aurora Serverless v2 scales almost instantly to accommodate hundreds of thousands of transactions in seconds. It fine-tunes its capacity in small increments to ensure the right resources for your application. You won't have to manage the database capacity, and you'll only pay for your application's resources. Compared to peak load provisioning capacity, you could save up to 90% of your database cost with Amazon Aurora Serverless.
- **Global Database** - To support globally distributed applications, you can leverage the Global Database feature of Aurora. This enables you to span a single Aurora database across multiple AWS regions, allowing for faster local reads and rapid disaster recovery. Global Database utilizes storage-based replication to replicate your database across various regions, typically resulting in less than one-second latency. By utilizing a secondary region, you can have a backup option in case of a regional outage or degradation and can quickly recover. Additionally, it takes less than one minute to promote a database in the secondary region to full read/write capabilities.

- **Encryption** - With Amazon Aurora, you can encrypt your databases by using keys you create and manage through **AWS Key Management Service** (**AWS KMS**). When you use Amazon Aurora encryption, data stored on the underlying storage and automated backups, snapshots, and replicas within the same cluster are encrypted. Amazon Aurora secures data in transit using SSL (AES-256).
- **Automatic, continuous, incremental backups and point-in-time restore** - Amazon Aurora offers a backup feature that enables you to recover your instance to any specific second during your retention period, up to the last five minutes. This capability is known as point-in-time recovery. You can configure your automatic backup retention period for up to thirty-five days. The automated backups are stored in **Amazon Simple Storage Service** (**Amazon S3**), which is designed for 99.999999999% durability. The backups are incremental, continuous, and automatic, and they have no impact on database performance.
- **Multi-AZ Deployments with Aurora Replicas** - In the event of an instance failure, Amazon Aurora leverages Amazon RDS Multi-AZ technology to perform an automated failover to one of the up to 15 Amazon Aurora Replicas you have established across three AZs. If you have not provisioned any Amazon Aurora Replicas, in the event of a failure, Amazon RDS will automatically attempt to create a new Amazon Aurora DB instance for you.
- **Compute Scaling** - You can scale the provisioned instances powering your deployment up or down using either the Amazon RDS APIs or the AWS Management Console. The process of compute scaling typically takes only a few minutes to complete.
- **Storage auto-scaling** - Amazon Aurora automatically scales the size of your database volume to accommodate increasing storage requirements. The volume expands in 10 GB increments, up to 128 TB, as your storage needs grow. There's no need to provision extra storage to handle the future growth of your database.
- **Fault-tolerant and self-healing storage** - Each 10 GB chunk of your database volume is replicated six times across three Availability Zones, making Amazon Aurora storage fault-tolerant. It can handle the loss of up to two data copies without affecting write availability, and up to three copies without affecting read availability. Amazon Aurora storage is also self-healing, continuously scanning data blocks and disks for errors and replacing them automatically.
- **Network isolation** - Amazon Aurora operates within Amazon VPC, providing you with the ability to segregate your database within your own virtual network and connect to your existing on-premises IT infrastructure via industry-standard encrypted IPsec VPNs. Additionally, you can manage firewall configurations through Amazon RDS and govern network access to your DB instances.

- **Monitoring and metrics** - Amazon Aurora offers a range of monitoring and performance tools to help you keep your database instances running smoothly. You can use Amazon CloudWatch metrics at no additional cost to monitor over 20 key operational metrics, such as compute, memory, storage, query throughput, cache hit ratio, and active connections. If you need more detailed insights, you can use Enhanced Monitoring to gather metrics from the operating system instance that your database runs on. Additionally, you can use Amazon RDS Performance Insights, a powerful database monitoring tool that provides an easy-to-understand dashboard for visualizing database load and detecting performance problems, so you can take corrective action quickly.
- **Governance** - AWS CloudTrail keeps track of and documents account activity across your AWS infrastructure, providing you with oversight over storage, analysis, and corrective actions. You can ensure your organization remains compliant with regulations such as SOC, PCI, and HIPAA by utilizing CloudTrail logs. The platform enables you to capture and unify user activity and API usage across AWS Regions and accounts in a centralized, controlled environment, which can help you avoid penalties.
- **Amazon Aurora machine learning** - With Amazon Aurora machine learning, you can incorporate machine learning predictions into your applications through SQL programming language, eliminating the need to acquire separate tools or possess prior machine learning experience. It offers a straightforward, optimized, and secure integration between Aurora and AWS ML services, eliminating the need to create custom integrations or move data between them.

Enterprise use cases for Amazon Aurora span multiple industries. Here are examples of some of the key use cases where Amazon Aurora is an excellent fit, along with specific customer references for each:

- **Revamp corporate applications** - Ensure high availability and performance of enterprise applications, including CRM, ERP, supply chain, and billing applications.
- **Build a Software-as-a-Service (SaaS) application** - Ensure flexible instance and storage scaling to support dependable, high-performing, and multi-tenant SaaS applications. Amazon Aurora is a good choice for building a SaaS application, as it provides the scalability, performance, availability, and security features that are essential for successful SaaS applications. Amazon Aurora automatically creates and maintains multiple replicas of your data, providing high availability and failover capabilities. This ensures that your SaaS application is always available, even in the event of an outage or failure.

Amazon Aurora provides several security features, such as encryption at rest and in transit, to help protect your data and ensure compliance with industry standards and regulations.

- **Deploy globally distributed applications** - Achieve multi-region scalability and resilience for internet-scale applications, such as mobile games, social media apps, and online services, with Aurora's flexible instance and storage scaling. To meet high read or write requirements, databases are often split across multiple instances, but this can lead to over-provisioning or under-provisioning, resulting in increased costs or limited scalability. Aurora Serverless solves this problem by automatically scaling the capacity of multiple Aurora instances based on the application's needs, allowing for efficient scaling of databases and enabling the deployment of globally distributed applications. This can provide several benefits, including cost savings, flexibility, and simplicity.
- **Variable and unpredictable workloads** - If you run an infrequently-used application where you need to provision for peak, it will require you to pay for unused resources. A surge in traffic can also be mitigated through the automatic scaling of Aurora Serverless. You will not need to manage or upsize your servers manually. You need to set a min/max capacity unit setting and allow Aurora to scale to meet the load.

Amazon RDS Proxy works together with Aurora to enhance database efficiency and application scalability by enabling applications to share and pool connections established with the database. Let's learn more details about RDS Proxy.

Amazon RDS Proxy

Amazon RDS Proxy is a service that acts as a database proxy for Amazon **Relational Database Service (RDS)**. It is fully managed by AWS and helps to increase the scalability and resilience of applications in the face of database failures, while enhancing the security of database traffic. RDS Proxy sits between your application and your database and automatically routes database traffic to the appropriate RDS instances. This can provide several benefits, including:

- **Improved scalability**: RDS Proxy automatically scales to handle a large number of concurrent connections, making it easier for your application to scale.
- **Better resilience to database failures**: RDS Proxy can automatically failover to a standby replica if the primary database instance becomes unavailable, reducing downtime and improving availability.
- **Enhanced security**: RDS Proxy can authenticate and authorize incoming connections, helping to prevent unauthorized access to your database. It can also encrypt data in transit, providing an extra security measure for your data.

The following diagram shows Amazon EC2 web server provision with an Aurora database where database passwords are managed by AWS Secrets Manager. Aurora put across 2 **Availability Zones (AZs)** to achieve high availability, where AZ1 hosts Aurora's primary database while AZ2 has the Aurora read replica.

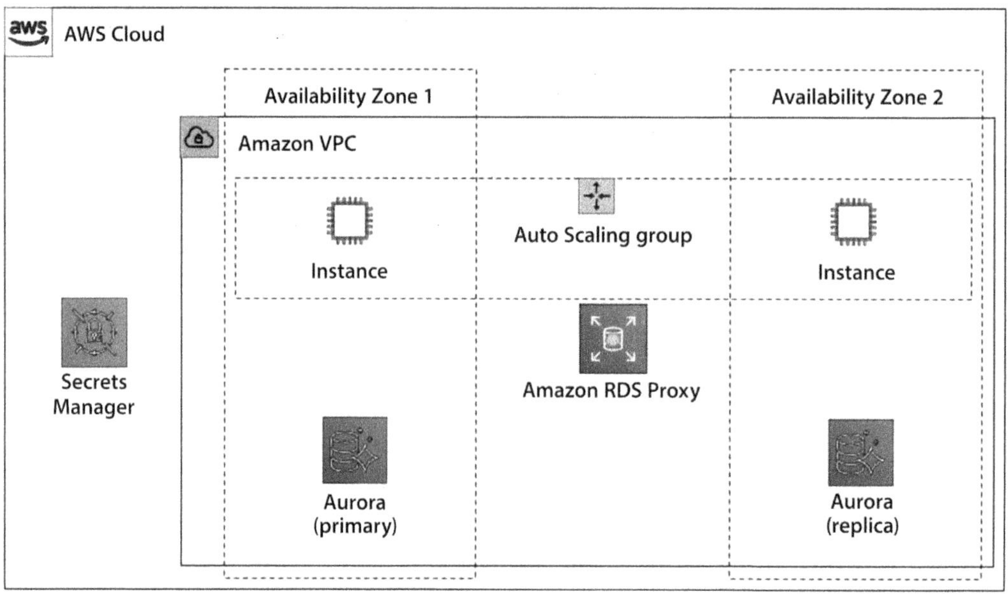

Figure 7.2: Amazon Aurora's high availability with RDS proxy

With RDS Proxy, when a failover happens, application connections are preserved. Only transactions that are actively sending or processing data will be impacted. During failover, the proxy continues to accept new connections. These connections will queue until the database connection comes online; at that point, it then gets sent over to the database.

Amazon RDS Proxy is a useful tool for improving the performance, availability, and security of your database-powered applications. It is fully managed, so you don't have to worry about the underlying infrastructure, and it can help make your applications more scalable, resilient, and secure. You can learn more about RDS Proxy by visiting the AWS page: `https://aws.amazon.com/rds/proxy/`.

High availability and performance are a database's most essential and tricky parts. But this problem can be solved in an intelligent way using machine learning. Let's look at RDS's newly launched feature, Amazon DevOps Guru, to help with database performance issues using ML.

Amazon DevOps Guru for RDS

DevOps Guru for Amazon RDS is a recently introduced capability that uses machine learning to automatically identify and troubleshoot performance and operational problems related to relational databases in an application. The tool can detect issues such as over-utilization of resources or problematic SQL queries and provide recommendations for resolution, helping developers address these issues quickly. DevOps Guru for Amazon RDS utilizes machine learning models to deliver these insights and suggestions.

DevOps Guru for RDS aids in quickly resolving operational problems related to databases by notifying developers immediately via Amazon **Simple Notification Service** (**SNS**) notifications and EventBridge when issues arise. It also provides diagnostic information, as well as intelligent remediation recommendations, and details on the extent of the issue.

AWS keeps adding innovations for Amazon RDS as a core service. Recently, they launched Amazon RDS instances available on AWS's chip Graviton2, which helps them offer lower prices with increased performance. RDS is now available in Amazon Outpost to fulfill your need to keep the database near your workload in an on-premise environment. You can learn more about RDS Proxy by visiting the AWS page: `https://aws.amazon.com/devops-guru/`.

Besides SQL databases, Amazon's well-known NoSQL databases are very popular. Let's learn about some NoSQL databases.

AWS NoSQL databases

When it comes to NoSQL databases, you need to understand two main categories, key-value and document, as those can be confusing. The key-value database needs high throughput, low latency, reads and writes, and endless scale, while the document database stores documents and quickly accesses querying on any attribute. Document and key-value databases are close cousins. Both types of databases rely heavily on keys that point to a value. The main difference between them is that in a document database, the value stored (the document) will be **transparent** to the database and, therefore, can be indexed to assist retrieval. In the case of a key-value database, the value is **opaque** and will not be scannable, indexed, or visible until the value is retrieved by specifying the key. Retrieving a value without using the key would require a full table scan. Content is stored as the value. To retrieve the content, you query using the unique key, enabling access to the value.

Key-value databases are the simpletons of the NoSQL world. They are pretty easy to use. There are three simple API operations:

- Retrieve the value for a key.
- Insert or update a value using a key reference.
- Delete a value using the key reference.

The values are generally **Binary Large Objects (BLOBs)**. Data stores keep the value without regard for the content. Data in key-value database records is accessed using the key (in rare instances, it might be accessed using other filters or a full table scan). Therefore, performance is high and scalable. The biggest strength of key-value databases is always their biggest weakness. Data access is quick because we use the key to access the data. Still, full table scans and filtering operations are neither supported nor a secondary consideration. Key-value stores often use the hash table pattern to store the keys. No column-type relationships exist, which keeps the implementation details simple. Starting in the key-value category, AWS provides Amazon DynamoDB. Let's learn more about Dynamo DB.

Amazon Dynamo DB

DynamoDB is a fully managed, multi-Region, multi-active database that delivers exceptional performance, with single-digit-millisecond latency, at any scale. It is capable of handling more than 10 trillion daily requests, with the ability to support peaks of over 20 million requests per second, making it an ideal choice for internet-scale applications. DynamoDB offers built-in security, backup and restore features, and in-memory caching. One of the unique features of DynamoDB is its elastic scaling, which allows for seamless growth as the number of users and required I/O throughput increases. You pay only for the storage and I/O throughput you provision, or on a consumption-based model if you choose on-demand. The database can be provisioned with additional capacity on the fly to maintain high performance, making it easy for an application to support millions of users making thousands of concurrent requests every second. In addition, DynamoDB offers fine-grained access control and support for end-to-end encryption to ensure data security.

Some of DynamoDB's benefits are as follows:

- Fully managed
- Supports multi-region deployment
- Multi-master deployment
- Fine-grained identity and access control

- Seamless integration with IAM security
- In-memory caching for fast retrieval
- Supports ACID transactions
- Encrypts all data by default

DynamoDB provides the option of on-demand backups for archiving data to meet regulatory requirements. This feature enables you to create full backups of your DynamoDB table's data. Additionally, you can enable continuous backups for point-in-time recovery, allowing restoration to any point in the last 35 days with per-second granularity. All backups are automatically encrypted, cataloged, and retained until explicitly deleted. This feature ensures backups are easily discoverable and helps meet regulatory requirements.

DynamoDB is built for high availability and durability. All writes are persisted on an SSD disk and replicated to 3 availability zones. Reads can be configured as "strong" or "eventual." There is no latency trade-off with either configuration; however, the read capacity is used differently. Amazon **DynamoDB Accelerator** (**DAX**) is a managed, highly available, in-memory cache for DynamoDB that offers significant performance improvements, up to 10 times faster than standard DynamoDB, even at high request rates. DAX eliminates the need for you to manage cache invalidation, data population, or cluster management, and delivers microseconds of latency by doing all the heavy lifting required to add in-memory acceleration to your DynamoDB tables.

Defining Dynamo DB Table

DynamoDB is a table-based database. While creating the table, you can specify at least three components:

1. **Keys**: There will be two parts of the key – first, a partition key to retrieve the data, and second, a sort key to sort and retrieve a batch of data in a given range. For example, transaction ID can be your primary key, and transaction date-time can be the sort key.
2. **WCU**: **Write capacity unit** (1 KB/sec) defines at what rate you want to write your data in DynamoDB.
3. **RCU**: **Read capacity unit** (4 KB/sec) defines at what rate you want to read from your given DynamoDB table.

The size of the table automatically increases as you add more items. There is a hard limit of item size at 400 KB. As size increases, the table is partitioned automatically for you. The size and provisioning capacity of the table are equally distributed for all partitions.

As shown in the below diagram, the data is stored in tables; you can think of a table as the database, and within the table, you have items.

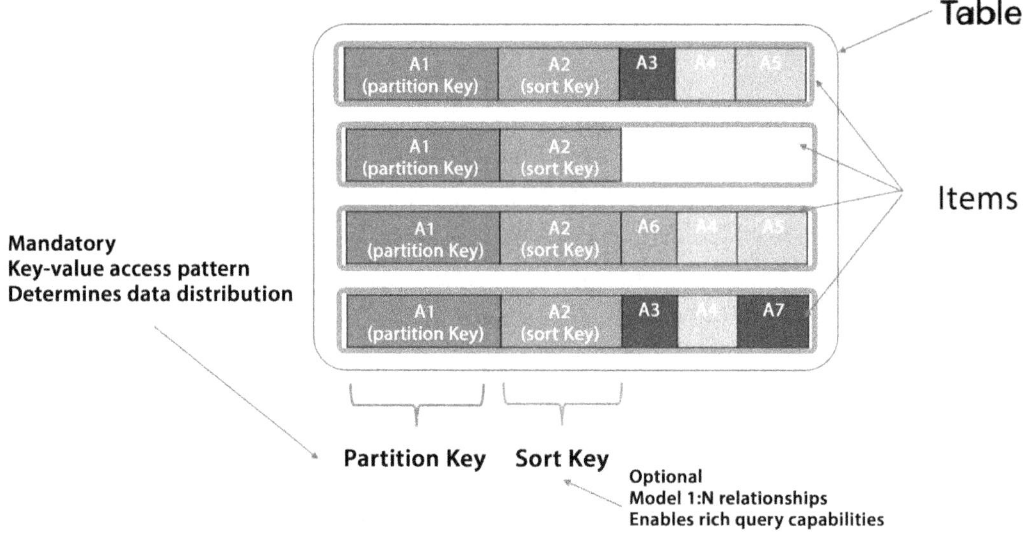

Figure 7.3: DynamoDB table with partition and sort key

As shown in the preceding diagram, the first item has five attributes, and the next item has only two. As more items are added to the table in DynamoDB, it becomes apparent that attributes can differ between items, and each item can have a unique set of attributes. Additionally, the primary key or partition key can be observed, which uniquely identifies each item and determines how the data is partitioned and stored. The partition key is required, while the sort key is optional but useful for establishing one-to-many relationships and facilitating in-range queries.

Sometimes you need to query data using the primary key, and sometimes you need to query by an attribute that is not your primary/secondary key or sort key. To tackle this issue, DynamoDB provides two kinds of indexes:

- **Local Secondary Index (LSI)** - Let's say you want to find out all fulfilled orders. You would have to query for all orders and then look for fulfilled ones in the results, which is not very efficient with large tables. But you have LSIs to help us out. You can create an LSI with the same primary key (`order_ID`) and a different secondary key (`fulfilled`). Now your query can be based on the key of the LSI. This is fast and efficient. The LSI is located on the same partition as the item in the table, ensuring consistency. Whenever an item is updated, the corresponding LSI is also updated and acknowledged.

The same primary key is used to partition both the LSI and the parent table, even though the parent table can have a different sort key. In the index, you can choose to have just the keys or other attributes projected or include all attributes – depending on what attributes you want to be returned with the query. There is a limit of 10 GB on LSI storage as it uses the partition storage of the original table.

- **Global Secondary Index (GSI)** -A GSI is an extension of the concept of indexes, allowing for more complex queries with various attributes as query criteria. In some cases, using the existing primary/sort key does not suffice. To address this, you can define a GSI as a parallel or secondary table with a partition key that is different from the original table and an alternate sort key. When creating a GSI, you must specify the expected workload for read and write capacity units. Similar to an LSI, you can choose to have just the keys or other attributes projected or include all attributes – depending on what attributes you want to be returned with the query.

The followings are the key differences between an LSI and GSI:

Local Secondary Index (LSI)	**Global Secondary Index (GSI)**
You have to define an LSI upfront, and it can be created during table creation only.	You can define a GSI at any time, even after table creation.
LSI shares WCU/RCU with the main table, so you must have enough read/write capacity to accommodate LSI need.	GSI WCU/RCU is independent of the table, so it can scale without impacting the main table.
LSI size is a maximum of 10 GB in sync with the primary table partition, which is limited to 10 GB size per partition.	As GSI is independent of the main table, so it has no size limits.
You can create a maximum of 5 LSIs.	You can create up to 20 GSIs.
As LSIs tie up to the main table, they offer "strong consistency," which means their current access to the most updated data.	GSI offer "eventual consistency," which means there may be a slight lag on data updates and lowers the chances you get stable data.

Table 7.3: DynamoDB Index – LSI vs. GSI

So, you may ask when to use an LSI vs. GSI. In a nutshell, a GSI is more flexible. An LSI is useful when you want to query data based on an alternate sort key within the same partition key as the base table.

It allows you to perform fast, efficient queries with minimal latency, and is best suited for scenarios where you know the specific queries that will be performed on your data. A GSI, on the other hand, allows you to query data based on attributes that are not part of the primary key or sort key of the base table. It's useful when you want to perform ad-hoc queries on different attributes of the data or when you need to support multiple access patterns. A GSI can be used to scale read queries beyond the capacity of the base table and can also be used to query data across partitions.

In general, if your data size is small enough, and you only need to query data based on a different sort key within the same partition key, you should use an LSI. If your data size is larger, or you need to query data based on attributes that are not part of the primary key or sort key, you should use a GSI. However, keep in mind that a GSI comes with some additional cost and complexity in terms of provisioned throughput, index maintenance, and eventual consistency.

If an item collection's data size exceeds 10 GB, the only option is to use a GSI as an LSI limits the data size in a particular partition. If eventual consistency is acceptable for your use case, a GSI can be used as it is suitable for 99% of scenarios.

DynamoDB is very useful in designing serverless event-driven architecture. You can capture the item-level data change, e.g., `putItem`, `updateItem`, and `delete`, by using DynamoDB Streams. You can learn more about Amazon DynamoDB by visiting the AWS page: `https://aws.amazon.com/dynamodb/`.

You may want a more sophisticated database when storing JSON documents for index and fast search. Let's learn about the AWS document database offering.

Amazon DocumentDB

In this section, let's talk about Amazon DocumentDB, *"a fully managed MongoDB-compatible database service designed from the ground up to be fast, scalable, and highly available"*. DocumentDB is a purpose-built document database engineered for the cloud that provides millions of requests per second with millisecond latency and can scale-out to 15 read replicas in minutes. It is compatible with MongoDB 3.6/4.0 and managed by AWS, which means no hardware provisioning, auto-patching, quick setup, good security, and automatic backups are needed.

If you look at the evolution of document databases, what was the need for document databases in this new world? At some point, JSON became the de facto standard for data interchange and data modeling within applications. Using JSON in the application and then trying to map JSON to relational databases introduced friction and complication.

Object Relational Mappers (**ORMs**) were created to help with this friction, but there were complications with performance and functionality. A crop of document databases popped up to solve the problem. The need for DocumentDB is primarily driven by the following reasons:

- Data is stored in documents that are in a JSON-like format, and these documents are considered as first-class objects within the database. Unlike traditional databases where documents are stored as values or data types, in DocumentDB, documents are the key design point of the database.
- Document databases offer flexible schemas, making it easy to represent hierarchical and semi-structured data. Additionally, powerful indexing capabilities make querying such documents much faster.
- Documents naturally map to object-oriented programming, which simplifies the flow of data between your application and the database.
- Document databases come with expressive query languages that are specifically built for handling documents. These query languages enable ad hoc queries and aggregations across documents, making it easier to extract insights from data.

Let's take user profiles, for example; let's say that Jane Doe plays a new game called ExplodingSnails, you can easily add that information to her profile, and you don't have to design a complicated schema or create any new tables – you simply add a new set of fields to your document. Similarly, you can add an array of Jane's promotions. The document model enables you to evolve applications quickly over time and build applications faster.

In the case of a document database, records contain structured or semi-structured values. This structured or semi-structured data value is called a document. It is typically stored using **Extensible Markup Language** (**XML**), **JavaScript Object Notation** (**JSON**), or **Binary JavaScript Object Notation** (**BSON**) format types.

What are document databases suitable for?

- Content management systems
- E-commerce applications
- Analytics
- Blogging applications

When are they not appropriate?

- Requirements for complex queries or table joins
- OLTP applications

Advantages of DocumentDB

Compared to traditional relational databases, Amazon DocumentDB offers several advantages, such as:

- **On-demand instance pricing**: You can pay by the hour without any upfront fees or long-term commitments, which eliminates the complexity of planning and purchasing database capacity ahead of time. This pricing model is ideal for short-lived workloads, development, and testing.
- **Compatibility with MongoDB 3.x and 4.x**: Amazon DocumentDB supports MongoDB 3.6 drivers and tools, allowing customers to use their existing applications, drivers, and tools with little or no modification. By implementing the Apache 2.0 open source MongoDB 4.x API on a distributed, fault-tolerant, self-healing storage system, Amazon DocumentDB offers the performance, scalability, and availability necessary for operating mission-critical MongoDB workloads at scale.
- **Migration support**: You can use the AWS **Database Migration Service (DMS)** to migrate MongoDB databases from on-premises, or on Amazon EC2, to Amazon DocumentDB at no additional cost (for up to six months per instance) with minimal downtime. DMS allows you to migrate from a MongoDB replica set or a sharded cluster to Amazon DocumentDB.
- **Flexible schema**: DocumentDB has a flexible schema, which means that the structure of the documents within the database can vary. This can be useful in situations where the data being stored has a complex or hierarchical structure, or when the data being stored is subject to frequent changes.
- **High performance**: DocumentDB is designed for high performance and can be well suited for applications that require fast read and write access to data.
- **Scalability**: DocumentDB is designed to be horizontally scalable, which means that it can be easily expanded to support large amounts of data and a high number of concurrent users.
- **Easy querying**: Document DB provides powerful and flexible query languages that make it easy to retrieve and manipulate data within the database.

DocumentDB has recently introduced new features that allow for ACID transactions across multiple documents, statements, collections, or databases. You can learn more about Amazon DocumentDB by visiting the AWS page: `https://aws.amazon.com/documentdb/`.

If you want sub-millisecond performance, you need your data in memory. Let's learn about in-memory databases.

In-memory database

Studies have shown that if your site is slow, even for just a few seconds, you will lose customers. A slow site results in 90% of your customers leaving the site. 57% of those customers will purchase from a similar retailer, and 25% of them will never return. These statistics are from a report by Business News Daily (`https://www.businessnewsdaily.com/15160-slow-retail-websites-lose-customers.html`). Additionally, you will lose 53% of your mobile users if a page load takes longer than 3 seconds (`https://www.business.com/articles/website-page-speed-affects-behavior/`).

We're no longer in the world of thinking our users are okay with a few seconds of wait time. These are demanding times for services, and to keep up with demand, you need to ensure that users aren't waiting to purchase your service, products, and offerings to continue growing your business and user base. There is a direct link between customers being forced to wait, and a loss of revenue.

Applications and databases have changed dramatically not only in the past 50 years but also just in the past 10. Where you might have had a few thousand users who could wait for a few seconds for an application to refresh, now you have microservices and IoT devices sending millions of requests per second across the globe that require immediate responses. These changes have caused the application and database world to rethink how data is stored and accessed. It's essential to use the right tool for the job. In-memory data stores are used when there is a need for maximum performance. This is achieved through extremely low latency per request and incredibly high throughput as you are caching data in memory, which helps to increase the performance by taking less time to read from the original database. Think of this as high-velocity data.

In-memory databases, or **IMDBs** for short, usually store the entire data in the main memory. Contrast this with databases that use a machine's RAM for optimization but do not store all the data simultaneously in primary memory and instead rely on disk storage. IMDBs generally perform better than disk-optimized databases because disk access is slower than direct memory access. In-memory operations are more straightforward and can be performed using fewer CPU cycles. In-memory data access seeks time when querying the data, which enables faster and more consistent performance than using long-term storage. To get an idea of the difference in performance, in-memory operations are usually measured in nanoseconds, whereas operations that require disk access are usually measured in milliseconds. So, in-memory operations are usually about a million times faster than operations needing disk access.

Some use cases of in-memory databases are real-time analytics, chat apps, gaming leaderboards, and caching. AWS provides Amazon ElastiCache to fulfill in-memory data caching needs.

As shown in the following diagram, based on your *data access pattern*, you can use either **lazy caching** or **write-through**. In lazy caching, the cache engine checks whether the data is in the cache and, if not, gets it from the database and keeps it in the cache to serve future requests. Lazy caching is also called the **cache aside pattern.**

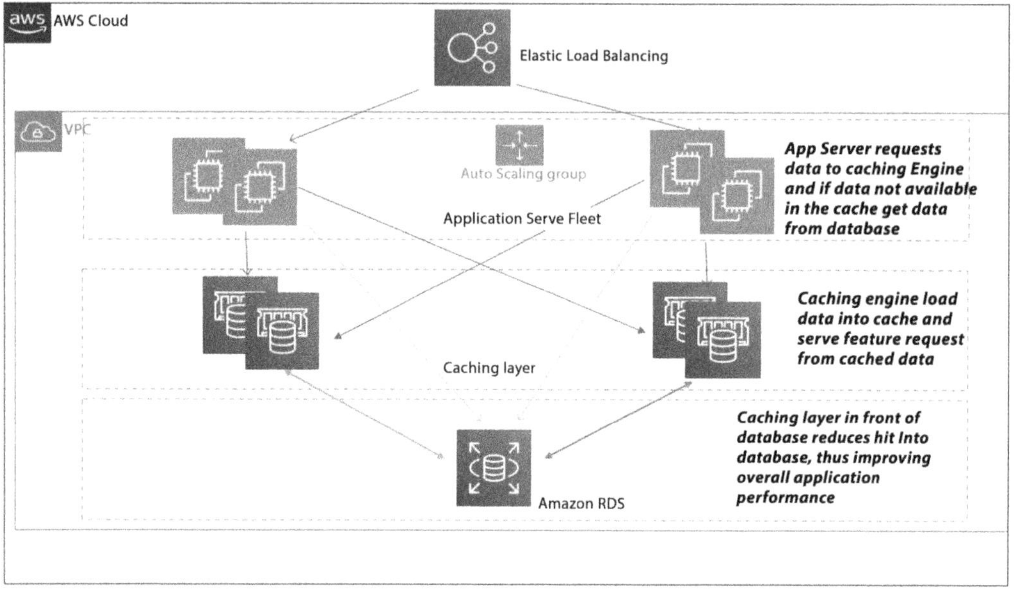

Figure 7.4: Application caching pattern architecture

You can see the caching flow in the above diagram, where the first app server sends a data request to the caching engine, which tries to load data from the cache. If data is not available in the cache, then the cache engine goes to the database and loads the required data into the cache. The Amazon ElastiCache service is an AWS-provided cache database. Let's learn more details about it.

Amazon ElastiCache

Amazon ElastiCache is a cloud-based web service that enables users to deploy and manage an in-memory cache with ease. By storing frequently accessed data in memory, in-memory caches can enhance application performance, enabling faster data access compared to retrieving data from a slower backing store such as a disk-based database. ElastiCache offers support for two popular open-source in-memory cache engines: Memcached and Redis. Both engines are well known for their reliability, scalability, and performance.

With ElastiCache, you can quickly and easily set up, manage, and scale an in-memory cache in the cloud.

ElastiCache automatically handles tasks such as provisioning cache nodes, configuring cache clusters, and monitoring the health of the cache environment, allowing you to focus on developing and deploying your application.

In addition, ElastiCache integrates seamlessly with other AWS services, making it easy to use the cache as a caching layer for other services like Amazon RDS or Amazon DynamoDB. This can help improve the performance and scalability of your overall application architecture.

Amazon ElastiCache enables users of the service to configure, run, and scale an IMDB and to build data-intensive applications. In-memory data storage boosts applications' performance by retrieving data directly from memory.

Redis versus Memcached

Since ElastiCache offers two flavors of in-memory databases, the obvious question is, which one is better? From our research, the answer now appears to be Redis, unless you are already a heavy user of Memcached. If your organization already has committed to Memcached, it is likely not worth porting it to Redis. But for new projects, the better option is Redis. This could change in the future, but as of this writing, Redis continues to gain supporters. Here is a comparison of the features and capabilities of the two:

	Memcached	Redis
Sub-millisecond latency	Yes	Yes
Developer ease of use	Yes	Yes
Data partitioning	Yes	Yes
Support for a broad set of programming languages	Yes	Yes
Advanced data structures	N/A	Yes
Multithreaded architecture	Yes	N/A
Snapshots	N/A	Yes
Replication	N/A	Yes
Transactions	N/A	Yes
Pub/Sub	N/A	Yes
Lua scripting	N/A	Yes
Geospatial support	N/A	Yes

Figure 7.5: Comparison of Redis and Memcached

The preceding table shows the key differences between Redis and Memcached. You can choose by validating your options, and you can learn more about Amazon ElastiCache by visiting the AWS page: `https://aws.amazon.com/elasticache/`.

AWS recently launched Amazon MemoryDB for Redis due to Redis's popularity. It is a durable, in-memory database service that provides ultra-fast performance and is compatible with Redis version 6.2. This service is designed explicitly for modern, microservice-based applications, and it offers Redis's flexible data structures, APIs, and commands. With Amazon MemoryDB, all data is stored in memory, allowing for microsecond read and single-digit millisecond write latency, as well as high throughput. You can learn more about Amazon MemoryDB by visiting the AWS page: `https://aws.amazon.com/memorydb/`.

Now data is getting more complicated with many-to-many relationships and several layers in social media. You need a specific database to drive the relationship, such as friends of friends and their common likes. Let's look at graph databases to solve this problem.

Graph databases

Graph databases are data stores that treat relationships between records as first-class citizens. In traditional databases, relationships are often an afterthought. In the case of relational databases, relationships are implicit and manifest themselves as foreign key relationships. In graph databases, relationships are explicit, significant, and optimized using graph database language; these relationships are called edges.

In some aspects, graph databases are similar to NoSQL databases. They are also schema-less. For certain use cases, they offer much better data retrieval performance than traditional databases. As you can imagine, graph databases are particularly suited for use cases that place heavy importance on relationships among entities.

Accessing data nodes and edges in a graph database is highly efficient. It usually can occur in constant time. With graph databases, it is not uncommon to be able to traverse millions of edges per second.

Graph databases can handle nodes with many edges regardless of the dataset's number of nodes. You only need a pattern and an initial node to traverse a graph database. Graph databases can easily navigate the adjacent edges and nodes around an initial starting node while caching and aggregating data from the visited nodes and edges. As an example of a pattern and a starting point, you might have a database that contains ancestry information. In this case, the starting point might be you, and the pattern might be a parent.

So, in this case, the query would return the names of both of your parents. The following are the components of a graph database:

- **Nodes**: Nodes are elements or entities in a graph. They contain a series of properties, attributes, or key-value pairs. Nodes can be given tags, which constitute roles in the domain. Node labels can be employed to assign metadata (such as indices or constraints) to the nodes.
- **Edges**: Edges supply directed, named, and semantically significant connections between two nodes. An edge has a direction, a type, a start node, and an end node. Like a node, an edge can also have properties. In some situations, an edge can have quantitative properties, such as weight, cost, and strength. Due to the efficient way an edge is stored, two nodes can share edges regardless of the quantity or type without a performance penalty. Edges have a direction, but edges can be traversed efficiently in both directions.

The following diagram shows the relationship between "Follower" and "Influencer" in a social media application, where the nodes depict the entity type (Follower and Influencer) and the edge (Influences) shows their relationship with their level of influence as the property weight. Here, the level of influence is 100, which means the Follower just started following the Influencer and with time, as they give more likes and views to the influencer's post, their level can increase to 200, 300, or 400.

Figure 7.6: Example of a relationship

Two primary graph models are widely used. A property graph is a common name for an attributed, multi-relational graph. The leading property graph API is the open standard Apache TinkerPop™ project. It provides an imperative traversal language, called Gremlin, that can be used to write traversals on property graphs, and many open-source and vendor implementations support it. You may opt for property graphs to represent relational models, and the Apache TinkerPop Gremlin traversal language could be a favorable option as it offers a method to navigate through property graphs. You might also like openCypher, an open-source declarative query language for graphs, as it provides a familiar SQL-like structure to compose queries for graph data.

The second is the **Resource Description Framework** (**RDF**), standardized by the W3C in a set of standards collectively known as the Semantic Web. The SPARQL query language for RDF allows users to express declarative graph queries against RDF graph models. The RDF model is also a labeled, directed multi-graph, but it uses the concept of triples, subject, predicate, and object, to encode the graph. Now let's look at Amazon Neptune, which is Amazon's graph database service.

Amazon Neptune

Amazon Neptune is a managed service for graph databases, which uses nodes, edges, and properties to represent and store data, making it a unique type of database. This data model is well suited to represent the complex relationships found in many types of data, such as the relationships between people in a social network or the interactions between different products on an e-commerce website.

Neptune supports the property graph and W3C's RDF standards, making it easy to integrate with other systems and tools that support these standards. Neptune also provides a query language called Gremlin which is powerful and easy to use, which makes it easy to perform complex graph traversals and data manipulation operations on the data stored in the database.

In addition, Neptune is highly scalable and available, with the ability to support billions of vertices and edges in a single graph. It is also fully managed, which means that Amazon takes care of the underlying infrastructure and performs tasks such as provisioning, patching, and backup and recovery, allowing you to focus on building and using your application. You can learn more about Amazon Neptune by visiting the AWS page: `https://aws.amazon.com/neptune/`.

A lot of data comes with a timestamp, and you need a specific database to store time-series data. Let's learn more about it.

Time-series databases

A **time-series database** (**TSDB**) is a database specifically designed and optimized to store events. What is an event, you ask? It is an action that happens at a specific point in time. With events, it's not only important to track *what* happened but just as important to track *when* it happened. The unit of measure to use for the time depends on the use case. For some applications, it might be enough to know on what day the event happened. But for other applications, it might be required to keep track of the time down to the millisecond. Some examples of projects that might benefit from a TSDB are as follows:

- Performance monitoring
- Networking and infrastructure applications

- Adtech and click stream processing
- Sensor data from IoT applications
- Event-driven applications
- Financial applications
- Log analysis
- Industrial telemetry data for equipment maintenance
- Other analytics projects

A TSDB is optimized to measure changes over time. Time series values can differ from other data types and require different optimization techniques.

Common operations in a TSDB are as follows:

- Millions of inserts from disparate sources potentially per second
- Summarization of data for downstream analytics
- Access to individual events

TSDBs are ideally suited for storing and processing IoT data. Time-series data has the following properties (which might not be present with other data types):

- The order in which the events occur may be necessary.
- Data is only inserted; it is not updated.
- Queries have a time interval component in their filters.

RDBMSes can store this data, but they are not optimized to process, store, and analyze this type of data. Amazon Timestream was purpose-built exclusively for this data type and, therefore, is much more efficient.

Do you feel comfortable about when you should use TSDBs? If you need to store events or track logs or trades, or the time and date when something happened to take center stage, then a TSDB is probably an excellent solution to your problem.

Amazon Timestream

Amazon Timestream is a scalable and fully managed TSDB. Amazon Timestream can persist and analyze billions of transactions per minute at about 1/10 of the cost of RDBMS equivalents. IoT devices and smart industrial machines are becoming more popular by the day. These applications generate events that need to be tracked and measured, sometimes with real-time requirements.

Amazon Timestream has an adaptive query processing engine that can make heads or tails of time-series data as it comes in by inferring data location and data format. Amazon Timestream has features that can automate query rollups, retention, tiering, and data compression. Like many other Amazon services, Timestream is serverless, so it can automatically scale up or down depending on how much data is coming into the streams. Also, because it's serverless and fully managed, tasks such as provisioning, operating system patching, configuration, backups, and tiering are not the responsibility of the DevOps team, allowing them to focus on more important tasks.

Timestream enables you to store multiple measures in a single table row with its multi-measure records feature, instead of one measure per table row, making it easier to migrate existing data from relational databases to Timestream with minimal changes. Scheduled computations are also available, allowing you to define a computation or query and its schedule. Timestream will automatically and periodically run the queries and store the results in a separate table. Additionally, Timestream automatically determines whether data should be written to the memory or magnetic store based on the data's timestamp and configured data retention window, thereby reducing costs. You can learn more about Amazon Timestream by visiting the AWS page: `https://aws.amazon.com/timestream/`.

You often want to make your database tamper-proof and keep a close record of any activity. To serve this purpose, let's learn about ledger databases.

Ledger databases

A **ledger database** (**LDB**) is a database that delivers a cryptographically verifiable, immutable, and transparent transaction log orchestrated by a central authority:

- **LDB immutability**: Imagine you deposit $1,000 in your bank. You see on your phone that the deposit was carried out, and it now shows a balance of $1,000. Then imagine you re-check it tomorrow, and this time, it says $500. You would not be too pleased, would you? The bank needs to ensure that the transaction is immutable and that no one can change it after the fact. In other words, only inserts are allowed, and updates cannot be performed. This assures that transactions cannot be changed once they are persisted.
- **LDB transparency**: In this context, transparency refers to the ability to track changes to the data over time. The LDB should be able to keep an audit log. This audit log, at a minimum, should include who changed the data, when the data was changed, and what the value of the data was before it was changed.

- **LDB cryptographic verifiability**: How can we ensure that our transaction will be immutable? Even though the database might not support update operations, what's stopping someone from using a backdoor and updating the record? If we use cryptography when the transaction is recorded, the entire transaction data is hashed. In simple terms, the string of data that forms the transaction is whittled down into a smaller string of unique characters. Whenever the transaction is hashed, it needs to match that string. In the ledger, the hash comprises the transaction data and appends the previous transaction's hash. Doing this ensures that the entire chain of transactions is valid. If someone tried to enter another transaction in between, it would invalidate the hash, and it would detect that the foreign transaction was added via an unauthorized method.

The prototypical use case for LDBs is bank account transactions. If you use an LDB for this case, the ledger records all credits and debits related to the bank account. It can then be followed from a point in history, allowing us to calculate the current account balance. With immutability and cryptographic verification, we are assured that the ledger cannot be deleted or modified. With other methods, such as RDBMSes, all transactions could be changed or erased.

Amazon Quantum Ledger Database (QLDB)

Amazon QLDB is a fully managed service that provides a centralized trusted authority to manage an immutable, transparent, and cryptographically verifiable ledger. QLDB keeps track of application value changes and manages a comprehensive and verifiable log of changes to the database.

Historically, ledgers have been used to maintain a record of financial activities. Ledgers can keep track of the history of transactions that need high availability and reliability. Some examples that need this level of reliability are as follows:

- Financial credits and debits
- Verifying the data lineage of a financial transaction
- Tracking the location history of inventory in a supply chain network

Amazon QLDB offers various blockchain services, such as anonymous data sharing and smart contracts, while still using a centrally trusted transaction log.

QLDB is designed to act as your system of record or source of truth. When you write to QLDB, your transaction is committed to the journal. The journal is what provides immutability through append-only interactions and verifiability through cryptographic hashing. QLDB treats all interactions, such as reads, inserts, updates, and deletes, like a transaction and catalogs everything sequentially in this journal.

Once the transaction is committed to the journal, it is immediately materialized into tables and indexes. QLDB provides a current state table and indexed history as a default when you create a new ledger. Leveraging these allows customers to, as the names suggest, view the current states of documents and seek out specific documents and their revisions easily. You can learn more about Amazon QLDB by visiting the AWS page: `https://aws.amazon.com/qldb/`.

Sometimes you need a database for large-scale applications that need fast read and write performance, which a wide-column store can achieve. Let's learn more about it.

Wide-column store databases

Wide-column databases can sometimes be referred to as column family databases. A wide-column database is a NoSQL database that can store petabyte-scale amounts of data. Its architecture relies on persistent, sparse matrix, multi-dimensional mapping using a tabular format. Wide-column databases are generally not relational.

When is it a good idea to use wide-column databases?

- Sensor logs and IoT information
- Geolocation data
- User preferences
- Reporting
- Time-series data
- Logging applications
- Many inserts, but not many updates
- Low latency requirements

When are wide-column databases not a good fit? They are good when the use case calls for ad hoc queries:

- Heavy requirement for joins
- High-level aggregations
- Requirements change frequently
- OLTP uses cases

Apache Cassandra is probably the most popular wide-column store implementation today. Its architecture allows deployments without single points of failure. It can be deployed across clusters and data centers.

Amazon Keyspaces (formerly Amazon Managed Apache Cassandra Service, or Amazon MCS) is a fully managed service that allows users to deploy Cassandra workloads. Let's learn more about it.

Amazon Keyspaces (for Apache Cassandra)

Amazon Keyspaces (formerly known as Amazon Cassandra) is a fully managed, scalable, and highly available NoSQL database service. NoSQL databases are a type of database that does not use the traditional table-based relational database model and is well suited for applications that require fast, scalable access to large amounts of data.

Keyspaces is based on Apache Cassandra, an open-source NoSQL database that is widely used for applications that require high performance, scalability, and availability. Keyspaces provides the same functionality as Cassandra, with the added benefits of being fully managed and integrated with other AWS services.

Keyspaces supports both table and **Cassandra Query Language** (**CQL**) APIs, making it easy to migrate existing Cassandra applications to Keyspaces. It also provides built-in security features, such as encryption at rest and network isolation, using Amazon VPC and integrates seamlessly with other AWS services, such as Amazon EMR and Amazon SageMaker.

Servers are automatically spun up or brought down, and, as such, users are only charged for the servers Cassandra is using at any one time. Since AWS manages it, users of the service never have to provision, patch, or manage servers, and they don't have to install, configure, or tune software. Cassandra in AWS can be configured to support thousands of user requests per second.

Cassandra is a NoSQL database; as expected, it doesn't support SQL. The query language for Cassandra is the CQL. The quickest method to interact with Apache Cassandra is using the CQL shell, which is called **cqlsh**. With cqlsh, you can create tables, insert data into the tables, and access the data via queries, among other operations.

Keyspaces supports the Cassandra CQL API. Because of this, the current code and drivers developed in Cassandra will work without changing the code. Using Amazon Keyspaces instead of just Apache Cassandra is as easy as modifying your database endpoint to point to an Amazon MCS service table.

In addition to Keyspaces being wide-column, the major difference from DynamoDB is that it supports composite partition keys and multiple clustering keys, which are not available in DynamoDB. However, DynamoDB has better connectivity with other AWS services, such as Athena, Kinesis, and Elasticsearch.

Keyspaces provides an SLA for 99.99% availability within an AWS Region. Encryption is enabled by default for tables, and tables are replicated three times in multiple AWS Availability Zones to ensure high availability. You can create continuous backups of tables with hundreds of terabytes of data with no effect on your application's performance, and recover data to any point in time within the last 35 days. You can learn more about Amazon Keyspaces by visiting the AWS page: `https://aws.amazon.com/keyspaces/`.

Benefits of AWS database services

In the new world of cloud-born applications, a one-size-fits-all database model no longer works. Modern organizations will not only use multiple types of databases for multiple applications, but many will use multiple types of databases in a single application. To get more value from data, you can choose the following three options available in AWS based on your workload.

Moving to fully managed database services

Managing and scaling databases in a legacy infrastructure, whether on-premises or self-managed in the cloud (on EC2), can be a tedious, time-consuming, and costly process. You have to worry about operational efficiency issues such as:

- The process of installing hardware and software, configuring settings, patching, and creating backups can be time-consuming and laborious
- Performance and availability issues
- Scalability issues, such as capacity planning and scaling clusters for computing and storage
- Security and compliance issues, such as network isolation, encryption, and compliance programs, including PCI, HIPAA, FedRAMP, ISO, and SOC

Instead of dealing with the challenges mentioned above, you would rather spend your time innovating and creating new applications instead of managing infrastructure. With AWS-managed databases, you can avoid the need to over- or under-provision infrastructure to accommodate application growth, spikes, and performance requirements, as well as the associated fixed capital costs such as software licensing, hardware refresh, and maintenance resources. AWS manages everything for you, so you can focus on innovation and application development, rather than infrastructure management. You won't need to worry about administrative tasks such as server provisioning, patching, setup, configuration, backups, or recovery. AWS continuously monitors your clusters to ensure your workloads are running with self-healing storage and automated scaling, allowing you to focus on higher-value tasks such as schema design and query optimization.

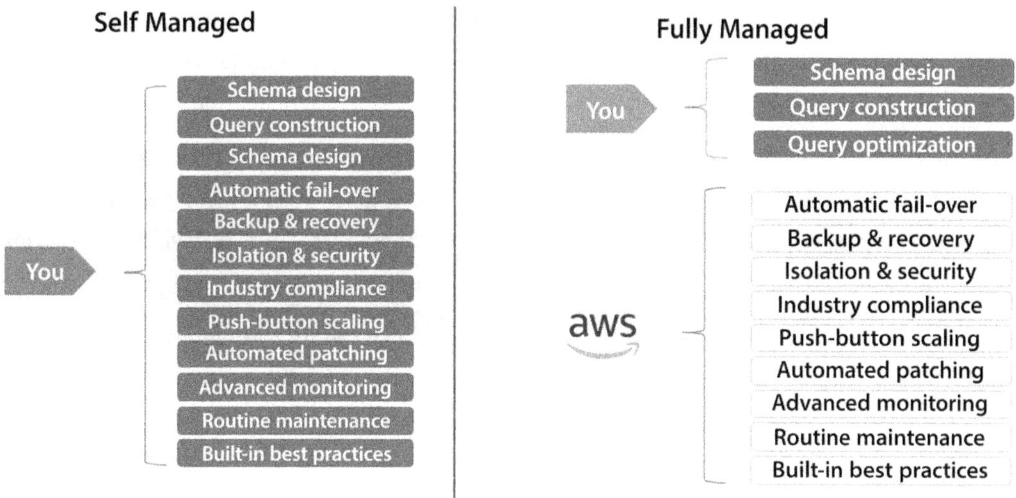

Figure 7.7: Fully managed database services on AWS

Let's look at the next benefit of using a purpose-built database. With purpose-built databases, your application doesn't need a one-fit-for-all architecture and it doesn't have to be molded to accommodate a decade-old relational database. Purpose-built databases help you to achieve maximum output and performance as per the nature of your application.

Building modern applications with purpose-built databases

In the 60s and 70s, mainframes were the primary means of building applications, but by the 80s, client-server architecture was introduced and significantly changed application development. Applications became more distributed, but the underlying data model remained mostly structured, and the database often functioned as a monolith. With the advent of the internet in the 90s, three-tier application architecture emerged. Although client and application code became more distributed, the underlying data model continued to be mainly structured, and the database remained a monolith. For nearly three decades, developers typically built applications against a single database. And that is an interesting data point because if you have been in the industry for a while, you often bump into folks whose mental model is, "Hey, I've been building apps for a long time, and it's always against this one database."

But what has changed? Fast forward to today, and microservice architectures are how applications are built in the cloud. Microservices have now extended to databases, providing developers with the ability to break down larger applications into smaller, specialized services that cater to specific tasks.

This allows developers to choose the best tool for the job instead of relying on a single, overworked database with a single storage and compute engine that struggles to handle every access pattern.

Today's developers and end-users have different expectations compared to the past. They require lower latency and the ability to handle millions of transactions per second with many concurrent users. As a result, data management systems have evolved to include specialized storage and compute layers optimized for specific use cases and workloads. This allows developers to avoid trade-offs between functionality, performance, and scale.

Plus, what we've seen over the last few years is that more and more companies are hiring technical talent in-house to take advantage of the enormous wave of technological innovation that the cloud provides. These developers are building not in the monolithic ways of the past but with microservices, where they compose the different elements together using the right tool for the right job. This has led to the highly distributed, loosely coupled application architectures we see powering the most demanding workloads in the cloud.

Many factors contribute to the performance, scale, and availability requirements of modern apps:

- **Users** – User growth is a common KPI for businesses, and the cloud's global reach enables businesses to touch millions of new customers.
- **Data volume** – Businesses are capturing more data about their customers to either increase the value of their existing products or sell them new products. This results in terabyte- or even petabyte-scale data.
- **Locality** – Businesses are often expanding their presence into new markets to reach new users, which complicates the architectures of their solutions/products.
- **Performance** – Businesses don't want to dilute the user experience to reach new markets or grow their customer base. If customers find a better alternative, they'll use it.
- **Request rate** – As businesses use the cloud's global reach to develop more interactive user experiences in more markets, they need their apps and databases to handle unprecedented levels of throughput.
- **Access/scale** – As businesses embark on their digital transformations, these scale measures are compounded by the number of devices that access their applications. There are billions of smartphones worldwide, and businesses connect smartphones, cars, manufacturing plants, devices in our homes, and more to the cloud. This means many, many billions of devices are connected to the cloud.

- **Economics** – Businesses can't invest millions of dollars in hardware and licenses up front and hope they'll succeed, that model is unrealistic in 2023. Instead, they have to hedge their success by only paying for what they use, without capping how much they can grow. These dynamics combined have changed how businesses build applications. These modern applications have wildly different database requirements, which are more advanced and nuanced than simply running everything in a relational database.

The traditional approach of using a relational database as the sole data store for an application is no longer sufficient. To address this, developers are leveraging their expertise in breaking down complex applications into smaller components and choosing the most appropriate tool for each task. This results in well-architected applications that can scale effectively. The optimal tool for a given task often varies by use case, leading developers to build highly distributed applications using multiple specialized databases.

Now you have learned about the different types of AWS databases, let's go into more detail about moving on from legacy databases.

Moving on from legacy databases

Numerous legacy applications have been developed on conventional databases, and consumers have had to grapple with database providers that are expensive, proprietary, and impose punishing licensing terms and frequent audits. Oracle, for instance, announced that they would double licensing fees if their software is run on AWS or Microsoft. As a result, customers are attempting to switch as soon as possible to open-source databases such as MySQL, PostgreSQL, and MariaDB.

Customers who are migrating to open-source databases are seeking to strike a balance between the pricing, freedom, and flexibility of open-source databases and the performance of commercial-grade databases. Achieving the same level of performance on open-source databases as on commercial-grade databases can be challenging and necessitates a lot of fine-tuning.

AWS introduced Amazon Aurora, a cloud-native relational database that is compatible with MySQL and PostgreSQL to address this need. Aurora aims to provide a balance between the performance and availability of high-end commercial databases and the simplicity and cost-effectiveness of open-source databases. It boasts 5 times better performance than standard MySQL and 3 times better performance than standard PostgreSQL, while maintaining the security, availability, and reliability of commercial-grade databases, all at a fraction of the cost. Additionally, customers can migrate their workloads to other AWS services, such as DynamoDB, to achieve application scalability.

In this section, you learned about the benefits of AWS database services. Now, there are so many database services that you have learned about, so let's put them together and learn how to choose the right database.

Choosing the right tool for the job

In the previous sections, you learned how to classify databases and the different database services that AWS provides. In a nutshell, you learned about the following database services under different categories:

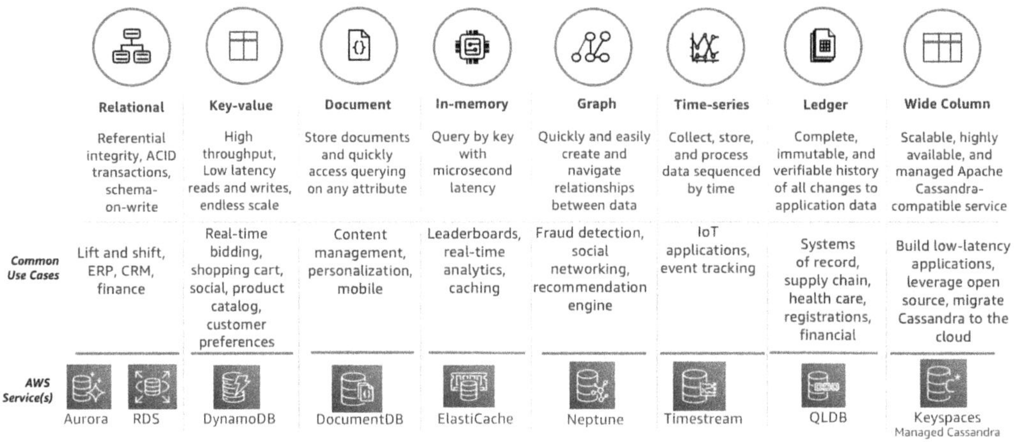

Figure 7.8: AWS database services in a nutshell

When you think about the collection of databases shown in the preceding diagram, you may think, "Oh, no. You don't need that many databases. I have a relational database, and it can take care of all this for you". Swiss Army knives are hardly the best solution for anything other than the most straightforward task. If you want the right tool for the right job that gives you the expected performance, productivity, and customer experience, you want a unified purpose-built database. So no one tool rules the world, and you should have the right tool for the right job to make you spend less money, be more productive, and change the customer experience.

Consider focusing on common database categories to choose the right database instead of browsing through hundreds of different databases. One such category is 'relational,' which many people are familiar with. Suppose you have a workload where strong consistency is crucial, where you will collaborate with the team to define schemas, and you need to figure out every single query that will be asked of the data and require consistent answers. In that case, a relational database is a good fit.

Popular options for this category include Amazon Aurora, Amazon RDS, open-source engines like PostgreSQL, MySQL, and MariaDB, as well as RDS commercial engines such as SQL Server and Oracle Database.

AWS has developed several purpose-built non-relational databases to facilitate the evolution of application development. For instance, in the key-value category, Amazon DynamoDB is a database that provides optimal performance for running key-value pairs at a single-digit millisecond latency and at a large scale. On the other hand, if you require a flexible method for storing and querying data in the same document model used in your application code, then Amazon DocumentDB is a suitable choice. This document database is designed to handle JSON documents in their natural format efficiently and can be scaled effortlessly.

Do you recall the era of XML? XML 1.0 was established in 1998. Commercial systems then added an XML data type to become an XML database. However, this approach had limitations, as many database operators needed help working with that data type. Today, document databases have replaced XML databases. Amazon DocumentDB, launched in January 2019, is an excellent example of such a database.

If your application requires faster response times than single-digit millisecond latency, consider an in-memory database and cache that can access data in microseconds. Amazon ElastiCache offers management for Redis and Memcached, making it possible to retrieve data rapidly for real-time processing use cases such as messaging, and real-time geospatial data such as drive distance.

Suppose you have large datasets with many connections between them. For instance, a sports company should link its athletes with its followers and provide personalized recommendations based on the interests of millions of users. Managing all these connections and providing fast queries can be challenging with traditional relational databases. In this case, you can use Amazon Neptune, a graph database designed to efficiently handle complex queries with interconnected data.

Time-series data is not just a timestamp or a data type that you might use in a relational database. Instead, a time-series database's core feature is that the primary axis of the data model is time. This allows for the optimization of data storage, scaling, and retrieval. Amazon Timestream is an example of a purpose-built time-series database that provides fast and scalable querying of time-series data.

Amazon QLDB is a fully managed ledger database service. A ledger is a type of database that is used to store and track transactions and is typically characterized by its immutability and the ability to append data in sequential order.

QLDB is a transactional database that uses an immutable, append-only ledger to store data. This means that once data is written to the ledger, it cannot be changed, and new data can only be added in sequential order. This makes QLDB well suited for applications that require a transparent, auditable, and verifiable record of transactions.

A wide-column database is an excellent choice for applications that require fast data processing with low latency, such as industrial equipment maintenance, trade monitoring, fleet management, and route optimization. Amazon Keyspaces for Apache Cassandra provides a wide-column database option that allows you to develop applications that can handle thousands of requests per second with practically unlimited throughput and storage.

You should spend a significant amount of time clearly articulating the business problem you are trying to solve. Some of the questions the requirements should answer are as follows:

- How many users are expected?
- How many transactions per day will occur?
- How many records need to be stored?
- Will there be more writes or reads?
- How will the data need to be accessed (only by primary key, by filtering, or some other way)?

Why are these questions important? SQL has served us well for several decades now, as it is pervasive, and has a lot of mindshare. So, why would we use anything else? The answer is performance. In instances where there is a lot of data and it needs to be accessed quickly, NoSQL databases might be a better solution. SQL vendors realize this and are constantly trying to improve their offerings to better compete with NoSQL, including adopting techniques from the NoSQL world. For example, Aurora is a SQL service, and it now offers Aurora Serverless, taking a page out of the NoSQL playbook.

As services get better, the line between NoSQL and SQL databases keeps on blurring, making the decision about what service to use more and more difficult. Depending on your project, you might want to draw up a Proof of Concept using a couple of options to determine which option performs better and fits your needs better.

Another reason to choose SQL or NoSQL might be the feature offered by NoSQL to create schema-less databases. Creating databases without a schema allows for fast prototyping and flexibility. However, tread carefully. Not having a schema might come at a high price.

Allowing users to enter records without the benefit of a schema may lead to inconsistent data, which becomes too variable and creates more problems than it solves. Just because we can create databases without a schema in a NoSQL environment, we should not forgo validation checks before creating a record. If possible, a validation scheme should be implemented, even when using a NoSQL option.

It is true that going schema-less increases implementation agility during the data ingestion phase. However, it increases complexity during the data access phase. So, make your choice by making a required trade-off between data context vs. data performance.

Migrating databases to AWS

If you find it challenging to maintain your relational databases as they scale, consider switching to a managed database service such as Amazon RDS or Amazon Aurora. With these services, you can migrate your workloads and applications without the need to redesign your application, and you can continue to utilize your current database skills.

Consider moving to a managed relational database if:

- Your database is currently hosted on-premises or in EC2.
- You want to reduce the burden of database administration and allocate DBA resources to application-centric work.
- You prefer not to rearchitect your application and wish to use the same skill sets in the cloud.
- You need a straightforward path to a managed service in the cloud for database workloads.
- You require improved performance, availability, scalability, and security.

Self-managed databases like Oracle, SQL Server, MySQL, PostgreSQL, and MariaDB can be migrated to Amazon RDS using the lift and shift approach. For better performance and availability, MySQL and PostgreSQL databases can be moved to Amazon Aurora, which offers 3-5 times better throughput. Non-relational databases like MongoDB and Redis are popularly used for document and in-memory databases in use cases like content management, personalization, mobile apps, catalogs, and real-time use cases such as caching, gaming leaderboards, and session stores. To maintain non-relational databases at scale, organizations can move to a managed database service like Amazon DocumentDB for self-managed MongoDB databases or Amazon ElastiCache for self-managed in-memory databases like Redis. These services provide a straightforward solution to manage the databases without rearchitecting the application and enable the same DB skill sets to be leveraged while migrating workloads and applications.

As you understand the different choices of databases, then the question comes of how to migrate your database to the cloud; there are five types of database migration paths available in AWS:

- **Self-service** - For many migrations, the self-service path using the DMS and **Schema Conversion Tool (SCT)** offers the tools necessary to execute with over 250,000 migrations completed through DMS, customers have successfully migrated their instances to AWS. Using the **Database Migration Service (DMS)**, you can make homogeneous migrations from your legacy database service to a managed service on AWS, such as from Oracle to RDS Oracle. Alternatively, by leveraging DMS and the SCT, heterogeneous conversions are possible, such as converting from SQL Server to Amazon Aurora. The **Schema Conversion Tool (SCT)** assesses the source compatibility and recommends the best target engine.
- **Commercially licensed to aws databases** - This type of migration is best for customers looking to move away from the licensing costs of commercial database vendors and avoid vendor lock-in. Most of these migrations have been from Oracle and SQL Server to open-source databases and Aurora, but there are use cases for migrating to NoSQL databases as well. For example, an online store may have started on a commercial or open-source database but now is growing so fast that it would need a NoSQL database like DynamoDB to scale to millions of transactions per minute. Refactoring, however, typically requires application changes and takes more time to migrate than the other migration methods. AWS provides a Database Freedom program to assist with such migration. You can learn more about the AWS Database Freedom program by visiting the AWS page: `https://aws.amazon.com/solutions/databasemigrations/database-freedom/`.
- **MySQL Database Migrations** - Standard MySQL import and export tools can be used for MySQL database migrations to Amazon Aurora. Additionally, you can create a new Amazon Aurora database from an Amazon RDS for MySQL database snapshot with ease. Migration operations based on DB snapshots typically take less than an hour, although the duration may vary depending on the amount and format of data being migrated.
- **PostgreSQL Database Migrations** - For PostgreSQL database migrations, standard PostgreSQL import and export tools such as `pg_dump` and `pg_restore` can be used with Amazon Aurora. Amazon Aurora also supports snapshot imports from Amazon RDS for PostgreSQL, and replication with AWS DMS.

- **The AWS Data Lab** is a service that helps customers choose their platform and understand the differences between self-managed and managed services. It involves a 4-day intensive engagement between the customer and AWS database service teams, supported by AWS solutions architecture resources, to create an actionable deliverable that accelerates the customer's use and success with database services. Customers work directly with Data Lab architects and each service's product managers and engineers. At the end of a Lab, the customer will have a working prototype of a solution that they can put into production at an accelerated rate.

  A Data Lab is a mutual commitment between a customer and AWS. Each party dedicates key personnel for an intensive joint engagement, where potential solutions will be evaluated, architected, documented, tested, and validated. The joint team will work for four days to create usable deliverables to enable the customer to accelerate the deployment of large AWS projects. After the Lab, the teams remain in communication until the projects are successfully implemented.

In addition to the above, AWS has an extensive Partner Network of consulting and software vendor partners who can provide expertise and tools to migrate your data to AWS.

Summary

In this chapter, you learned about many of the database options available in AWS. You started by revisiting a brief history of databases and innovation trends led by data. After that, you explored the database consistency model learning ACID vs. BASE and OLTP vs. OLAP.

You further explored different types of databases and when it's appropriate to use each one, and you learned about the benefits of AWS databases and the migration approach. There are multiple database choices available in AWS, and you learned about making a choice to use the right database service for your workload.

In the next chapter, you will learn about AWS's services for cloud security and monitoring.

8

Best Practices for Application Security, Identity, and Compliance

In the past, a common refrain from companies was that they were hesitant to move to the cloud because they believed the cloud was not secure. A big part of this pushback was that companies didn't understand the cloud or its capabilities. It is possible to have security vulnerabilities even if you use cloud infrastructure. However, as we will see in this chapter, AWS provides a comprehensive catalog of services enabling you to create highly secure sites and applications.

When creating applications and implementing workflows, it is imperative to consider security from the start of your design and not as an afterthought. First, you will understand why security is essential in any system – not just in the cloud. Next, you will learn how AWS, in general, and IAM, in particular, can help us design and build robust and secure cloud applications. Also, as you will see in this chapter, AWS provides a veritable cornucopia of other security services.

In this chapter, we will cover the following topics:

- Understanding the importance of security, identity, and compliance in AWS
- AWS's shared responsibility model
- Getting familiar with identity and access management
- Managing resources, permissions, and identities using IAM
- Applying security controls and infrastructure protection in AWS
- Building data protection

- Adhering to compliances
- Learning about other AWS security services
- AWS security best practices

By the end of this chapter, you will have learned about how to secure your AWS cloud environment and the AWS services available to make your environment secure. AWS offers a plethora of security services to assist with these requirements. In this chapter, we will review these services in detail.

Understanding the importance of security, identity, and compliance in AWS

Many organizations face challenges in maintaining and managing the security of their on-premises infrastructure. In an on-premises environment, it can be challenging to know what resources and data are out there at any given time, where they are moving, and who is utilizing/accessing them. Accurate, real-time asset inventory requires expensive and complex tooling, making it inaccessible for most organizations. This lack of visibility in their on-premises environment hinders their ability to ensure adequate security and compliance of infrastructure and data. With AWS, you can see all your infrastructure and application resources in one place and maintain servers, storage, and database inventory records and access patterns.

AWS enhances your capacity to adhere to key security and compliance standards, such as data locality, protection, and confidentiality, through its extensive services and features. Boasting the largest network of security partners and solutions, the capabilities of AWS can be further extended through familiar security technology and consulting providers. AWS is compliant with major security standards and certifications, such as PCI-DSS, HIPAA/HITECH, FedRAMP, SEC Rule 17a-4, the EU Data Protection Directive, and FISMA, thereby enabling organizations to meet compliance requirements globally.

Another common problem is the reliance on manual processes for remediation. This may involve the manual copying of access information from one tool to another or the manual application of security patches. Automating key security tasks has been challenging due to the lack of interoperability between third-party and custom-made tools. These manual processes result in inconsistent execution and longer wait times to address all systems, and often negatively impact the customer experience. Automation aims to solve these issues by programmatically managing security tasks, such as checking if access to an application server is exposed to the internet or ensuring that an S3 bucket is not left public unintentionally.

As with any computer system, ensuring that it's secure and that only authorized users access the system is paramount. Security should be incorporated at the beginning of your application design and not as an afterthought. AWS provides a broad set of security offerings that can ensure your application is secure and that your application data is safe. Notice that we used the word *assist*. Just because you are using AWS does not mean that your applications will be instantly secure.

A quick example of how easy it is to expose your data: There is nothing barring you from creating a bucket in AWS that is both unencrypted and public. You may get some warnings asking you if you are certain that you want to proceed, but AWS won't disallow it. You could then put a client file in that bucket that may contain emails, passwords, names, addresses, and so on. This combination would immediately make this data accessible to anyone in the world with an internet connection (including any threat actors).

Even though you may not have published the URL for the bucket, please don't assume it is secure. Threat actors know these mistakes happen sometimes. They constantly send requests to random AWS S3 buckets, trying to guess if they were created unsecured and exposed. And occasionally, they get lucky and hit pay dirt.

In the following section, we will learn more about what security AWS provides without involving the user and what services and tools AWS provides to its users to keep their systems secure.

Understanding the shared responsibility model

AWS uses the **shared responsibility model**, which means that AWS and its users are responsible for keeping applications secure. However, the lines of responsibility are pretty clear. AWS is solely responsible for some aspects (for example, physical data center security), and users are solely responsible for other aspects (for example, making sure that Amazon S3 buckets that will contain sensitive information are private, accessible to only authorized users, and encrypted).

This model enables AWS to reduce the burden of securing some components needed to create applications while enabling users to customize the applications to suit their clients' needs and budgets.

Depending on the service chosen, some responsibilities may fall on AWS or the user. For example, if you use Amazon RDS to stand up an instance of MySQL, the patching of the database and the underlying operating system would be performed by AWS.

Suppose you instead decide to install MySQL directly into an Amazon EC2 instance. In that case, you will still be able to use the MySQL functionality. But in this case, the responsibility to patch the operating system and the database would fall on you.

One quick note: If your use case requires you to deploy MySQL manually into an EC2 instance, there is another option rather than deploying it yourself and risking the database not being deployed properly and securely. It is better to work with an AWS Consulting Partner. AWS has a list of trusted Consulting Partners that they recommend, and that can assist AWS customers. AWS ranks these partners by the level of service that they can provide. They have changed the ranking names in the past, but as of December 2022, the rankings are as follows:

- Select Partner
- Advanced Partner
- Premier Partner

Where Premier Partner is at the highest level. The current list of Consulting Partners can be found here: `https://partners.amazonaws.com/`.

Leverage the power of AWS by incorporating security technology and consulting services from reputable and trusted providers. AWS has handpicked these providers to ensure they have extensive experience in securing every aspect of cloud adoption, from initial migration to ongoing management. The **AWS Partner Network** (**APN**) is a worldwide program of technology and Consulting Partners, many of whom specialize in delivering security solutions tailored to your specific needs and use cases. APN partner solutions promote automation, agility, and scalable growth with your workloads. You can easily access, purchase, implement, and manage these cloud-optimized software solutions, including SaaS products, within minutes on AWS Marketplace. You can find AWS security partners here: `https://aws.amazon.com/security/partner-solutions/`.

Deciding whether to use managed services versus deploying applications yourself is an important decision. Both approaches have advantages and disadvantages and the decision to use one method or another will be dictated by your business needs. For example, using Amazon RDS will require less maintenance since AWS performs the patching. Still, your organization may require you to own complete control of what changes happen to the software (perhaps because of regulatory reasons), in which case, using the approach to install MySQL on your own would make more sense. Now AWS provides Amazon RDS Custom, with which you can manage the underlying operating system and database settings as per your need while taking advantage of the scale that comes with RDS.

One common refrain heard to distinguish which components are the responsibility of AWS and which are the responsibility of the customer is as follows:

- AWS is responsible for the security **OF** the cloud.
- The AWS customer is responsible for security **IN** the cloud.

The following diagram illustrates the separation of duties:

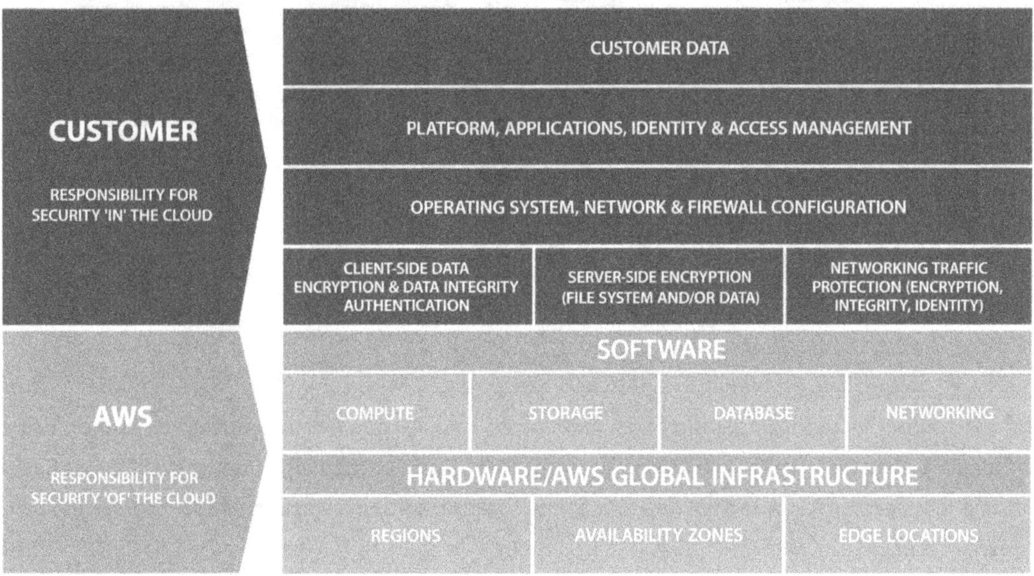

Figure 8.1: Shared responsibility model

The preceding figure shows in broad strokes how the responsibilities are broken down. For example, it clearly shows that the responsibility of AWS is for infrastructure elements such as regions, edge locations, and Availability Zones. This includes the physical security of the data centers. You may have passed an AWS data center and not noticed; AWS data centers are always unmarked buildings. On the other hand, customer data is the customer's responsibility. When it comes to customer data, the encryption of the data is also the customer's responsibility.

These areas of responsibility can be fuzzy depending on how a certain functionality is implemented. We see in the chart that databases fall under the purview of AWS, but as we saw previously, the customer can install a database, in which case they would be responsible for its management. Similarly, the chart in *Figure 8.2* shows the customer's responsibility for operating systems, the network, and firewall configuration. But the shared responsibility model varies depending on the services provided to you by AWS.

The following diagram shows various levels of security responsibilities shared by AWS:

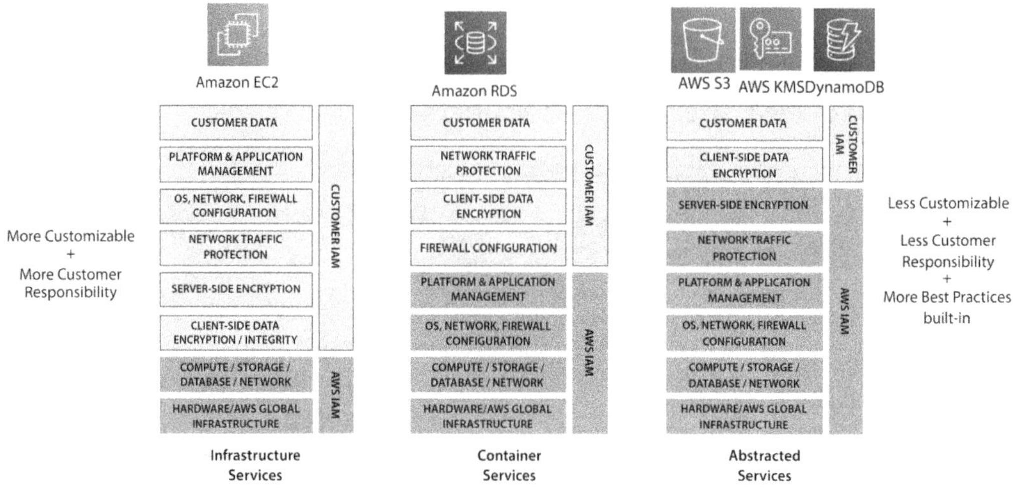

Figure 8.2: Shared responsibility model for different AWS service categories

As shown in the diagram above, in some cases, for example, when using AWS S3, the management of most items is the responsibility of AWS. For EC2, AWS only handles infrastructure security while RDS security is managed at the platform level. For DynamoDB, you just need to manage data and its access while everything else in the layer up until network traffic and server encryption is managed by AWS.

Another way to understand how security in AWS works is by using the analogy of locks and doors. AWS provides you with the doors and the locks to secure your applications and data, but you can still leave the door open and not secure the lock, leaving the contents of your home exposed to the world.

For example, Amazon RDS is a managed service. AWS does much of the heavy lifting to make a database secure. However, you can still publish the credentials to access your Amazon RDS instance on GitHub and let anyone who views these credentials access your database.

Overall, with AWS, you own your data and applications, and under the shared responsibility model, it becomes your responsibility to secure them by using various security services provided by AWS, from access management to encryption.

AWS security, identity, and compliance solutions

AWS has a broad range of security services available to fulfill every protection need of their customers. AWS is built to support the creation of secure, high-performing, resilient, and efficient infrastructure for your applications. The following AWS security services and solutions are designed to provide critical benefits that are crucial in helping you attain the best security posture for your organization:

Identity and access management	Detective controls	Infrastructure protection	Data protection	Incident response	Compliance
AWS Identity and Access Management (IAM)	AWS Security Hub	AWS Firewall Manager	Amazon Macie	Amazon Detective	AWS Artifact
AWS IAM Identity Center (successor to AWS SSO)	Amazon GuardDuty	AWS Network Firewall	AWS Key Management Service (KMS)	Amazon EventBridge	AWS Audit Manager
AWS Organizations	Amazon Inspector	AWS Shield	AWS CloudHSM	AWS Backup	
AWS Directory Service	Amazon CloudWatch	AWS WAF	AWS Certificate Manager	AWS Security Hub	
Amazon Cognito	AWS Config	Amazon VPC	AWS Secrets Manager	AWS Elastic Disaster Recovery	
AWS Resource Access Manager	AWS CloudTrail	AWS PrivateLink	AWS VPN		
	VPC Flow Logs	AWS Systems Manager	Server-Side Encryption		
	AWS IoT Device Defender				

Figure 8.3: AWS security services

As shown in the above table, AWS divides security services into the following pillars:

- **Identity and access management**: Establish, enforce, and monitor user access to AWS services, actions, and resources.
- **Detective controls**: Obtain the necessary visibility to identify potential issues before they affect your business, enhance your security posture, and minimize the risk to your environment.
- **Infrastructure protection**: Minimize the surface area to manage and enhance the privacy, control, and security of your overall infrastructure on AWS.
- **Data protection**: A collection of services that automate and simplify various data protection and security tasks, such as key management and storage, and credential management.
- **Incident response**: During a security incident, containing the event and restoring to a secure state are critical steps in a response plan. AWS offers tools to automate parts of this best practice.
- **Compliance**: Provide audit traces and artifacts in order to meet compliance requirements.

Let's look into individual services belonging to these security pillars.

Getting familiar with identity and access management

Identity and access management is the most fundamental security posture for any organization, and AWS provides the following services in this category:

- **AWS Identity and Access Management** (**IAM**) – Securely manage access to AWS services and resources
- **AWS Organizations** – Policy-based management for multiple AWS accounts
- **AWS Directory Service** – Managed Microsoft Active Directory in AWS
- **AWS IAM Identity Center** (successor to AWS SSO) – Centrally manage **single sign-on** (**SSO**) access to multiple AWS accounts and business apps
- **AWS Resource Access Manager** – A simple, secure service for sharing AWS resources
- **Amazon Cognito** – Add user sign-up, sign-in, and access control to your web and mobile apps

Let's look into each of the above services in detail.

AWS Identity and Access Management (IAM)

Perhaps the most fundamental and important service in AWS is **Identity and Access Management** (**IAM**), which can secure every single other software service offered by AWS. AWS IAM offers precise access control across all AWS services. This level of control allows you to define who can access specific services and resources and under what conditions. By creating IAM policies, you can manage access permissions for your users or applications to ensure minimal privilege access. IAM is a complimentary service provided by AWS at no extra cost. More specifically, AWS IAM can be used to do the following:

- Grant others shared access to your AWS account without sharing passwords or access keys.
- Provide granular permissions for different people and resources.
- Securely access AWS resources using IAM credentials for applications running on EC2 instances and other resources.
- Enhance security with multi-factor authentication.
- Facilitate identity federation for temporary access to your AWS account with external passwords.

- Be eventually consistent, with changes replicated globally. However, it is recommended to not include IAM changes in high-availability code paths and to verify changes have propagated before usage.

Here are a few use cases for AWS IAM:

- **Access control for AWS services**: IAM can be used to control who has access to various AWS services, such as EC2, S3, and DynamoDB, as well as what actions they can perform on those services.
- **Multi-factor authentication (MFA)**: IAM supports MFA, which can be used to add an extra layer of security to an AWS account.
- **Secure application credentials**: IAM can be used to securely provide credentials for applications running on EC2 instances and other resources so that those applications can access other AWS resources.
- **Identity federation**: IAM can be used to grant temporary access to AWS resources for users with existing passwords, for example, in a corporate network or with an internet identity provider.
- **Billing and cost allocation**: IAM can be used to manage access to billing and cost allocation information for an AWS account.

Suppose you have a company that uses AWS to host its applications. You can use IAM to create a group for your developers, granting them access to EC2 instances, S3 buckets, and DynamoDB tables, while only allowing them read-only access to your billing information. You can also use IAM to set up MFA for the root account and individual IAM users to add an extra layer of security.

Managing resources, permissions, and identities using IAM

To understand AWS IAM, we must first understand how authentication and identity management work. Users, groups, roles, permissions, and policies are fundamental concepts that need to be fully understood to grasp how resources are secured using AWS IAM. The purpose of using IAM is to regulate the authentication and authorization of individuals who wish to utilize resources. This is achieved by establishing precise permissions through IAM, thereby determining who has access to what. IAM consistently implements these permissions for every request made. By default, all requests are denied (except for the root user, which is allowed by default) unless an explicit "allow" is specified. An explicit "deny" overrides any allows.

In the following sections, you will learn AWS IAM terms.

IAM users

An IAM user is an IAM principal you create in AWS to represent the person or application that uses it to interact with AWS. An IAM principal is a user, group, or service that is authenticated and authorized to access resources in an AWS account. An IAM principal can be an AWS account root user, an IAM user, an IAM role, or a federated user.

An AWS user comprises a username and associated credentials. Take, for instance, a user named John. Upon creating an IAM user account for John, you'll need to establish a password for that user. You have the option to assign IAM user-specific permissions, such as the ability to start a particular Amazon EC2 instance.

An IAM user is an individual that needs to access, interact with, and potentially modify data and AWS resources. Users can interact through one of three ways:

- The AWS Management Console
- The AWS **Command-Line Interface** (**CLI**)
- The AWS API

Other than the root user, no implicit permissions or credentials are given when a new user is set up. That new user cannot access any resources until permission is explicitly assigned.

The IAM service in AWS enables you to securely control access to AWS resources and the actions that can be performed on those resources. You can use IAM to create and manage IAM principals, as well as to assign permissions to these principals to allow or deny access to AWS resources. For example, you can use IAM to create an IAM user for a person in your organization, and then grant that user permissions to access specific AWS resources or perform certain actions. Overall, using IAM helps you to securely and effectively manage access to your AWS resources, and helps you to enforce the principle of least privilege by granting only the necessary permissions to IAM principals.

IAM user groups

An IAM user group is an assembly of IAM users. By organizing IAM users into groups, you can efficiently manage their permissions as a collective. As an illustration, consider a user group named Dev, to which you have assigned the typical permissions required for developers. Any IAM user belonging to this group will automatically inherit the permissions assigned to the Dev user group.

When a new member joins your organization and requires developer privileges, you can grant the necessary permissions by adding them to the relevant user group.

On the other hand, if an individual changes their role within your organization, you can simply transfer them from their current user group to the appropriate new user group, rather than modifying their individual permissions. The following diagram shows IAM users assigned to different user groups:

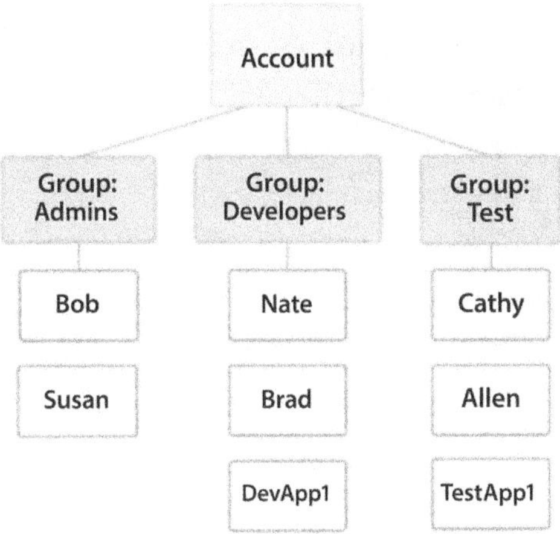

Figure 8.4: AWS IAM user groups and IAM user

The above diagram shows three user groups, Admins, Developers, and Test, and IAM users assigned to those groups with the same credentials set. Putting users into groups facilitates permission management and gives system administrators a more efficient way to administer permissions. Users that have similar profiles are grouped. They could be grouped based on similar characteristics and on having similar needs, such as the following:

- Job function or role
- Department
- Persona

Then, permissions for users that belong to one group can be managed all at once through the group. It is recommended to put all users in one group that need the same access level. Often organizations use Active Directory to group employees, and in that case, you can map IAM groups to your Active Directory groups. If you have been around technology for a while, the idea of users and groups should not be new. However, IAM roles may require a little more explanation. Let's continue discussing them in the next section.

IAM roles

An IAM role is a way to grant permission to access AWS resources to users or processes that do not have their own AWS credentials. The major difference is that, unlike users, IAM roles have no long-term credentials (i.e., passwords or access keys).

As shown in the diagram below, you can use an IAM role to allow a user to access an S3 bucket. For that, first, you need to create an IAM role that has the necessary permissions to access the S3 bucket. This can be done through the AWS Management Console or using the AWS CLI. For example, you might create a role that has the `AmazonS3FullAccess` policy attached to it. Next, create a user and associate the IAM role with the user. The user can then access the S3 bucket using the AWS Management Console or the AWS SDKs by assuming the IAM role. This will allow the user to use the permissions of the IAM role to access the S3 bucket, without the need for the user to have their own AWS credentials.

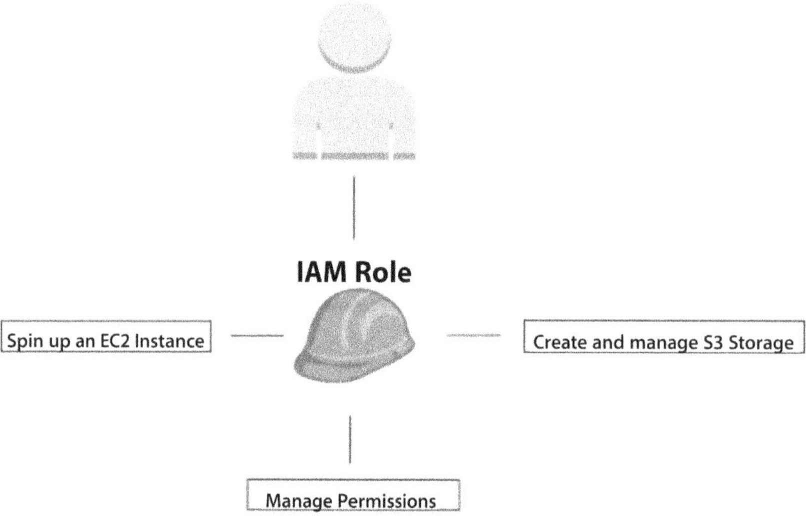

Figure 8.5: AWS IAM role

In IAM, a role is an object definition configuring a set of permissions assigned to that role. The role can be assigned to other entities, such as a user. A role is not directly connected to a person or a service. Instead, the role can be assumed by an entity that is given the role. Role credentials are always only temporary and rotated on a schedule defined by the AWS **Session Token Service (STS)**. It is best practice to use roles whenever possible instead of granting permissions directly to a user or group.

STS allows you to request short-lived, restricted credentials for both AWS IAM users and federated users. This service is frequently utilized to grant temporary access to resources for trusted users, such as by granting them an IAM role that has a more limited set of permissions compared to their standard IAM user or federated user permissions.

STS enables you to grant trusted users temporary permissions to resources without having to share long-term AWS access keys. For example, you can use STS to grant temporary access to an IAM role that allows users to perform specific tasks in your AWS account, such as creating and managing Amazon EC2 instances or uploading objects to Amazon S3. STS can also be used to provide federated users with temporary credentials to access resources in the AWS cloud.

You can use STS to grant temporary credentials in several ways:

- `AssumeRole`: This operation enables you to grant a trusted user temporary access to an IAM role.
- `GetFederationToken`: This operation enables you to grant a trusted user temporary access to AWS resources that you specify in the permissions policy associated with the token.
- `GetSessionToken`: This operation enables you to obtain temporary credentials for an IAM user or for a federated user.

Using STS helps you to secure your AWS resources and provides flexibility for granting temporary access to your resources. In Python, the user can use the `boto3` library to assume the IAM role and then access the S3 bucket like this:

```
import boto3
# Assume the IAM role
sts_client = boto3.client('sts')
assumed_role_object = sts_client.assume_role(
    RoleArn='arn:aws:iam::123456789012:role/my-iam-role',
    RoleSessionName='my_session'
)
# Use the temporary credentials provided by the assume_role method to
access S3
s3_client = boto3.client('s3', aws_access_key_id=assumed_role_
object['Credentials']['AccessKeyId',aws_secret_access_key=assumed_role_
object['Credentials']['SecretAccessKey'],
aws_session_token=assumed_role_object['Credentials']['SessionToken'])
# List the objects in the S3 bucket
```

```
objects = s3_client.list_objects(Bucket='my-s3-bucket')
print(objects)
```

Furthermore, roles enable you to grant multi-account access to users, services, and applications. Assigning a role to users not part of your organization is possible. Obviously, this has to be done judiciously and with flexibility as required.

IAM roles carry out a fundamental task in the security access landscape. By assigning permissions to a role instead of directly to a user or group, roles facilitate and simplify system administration and allow these permissions to only be given temporarily.

Policies and permissions

Access control in AWS is achieved through the creation and attachment of policies to IAM identities (such as users, groups, or roles) or AWS resources. These policies, which are objects in AWS, define the permissions of the associated identity or resource when they are attached. When an IAM principal, such as a user or role, makes a request, AWS evaluates the relevant policies to determine whether the request should be granted or denied. The majority of these policies are stored in AWS in the form of JSON documents.

A policy is a named document with a set of rules that specify what actions can be performed. Each policy laid out in the document gives a set of permissions. These policies can then be assigned to the IAM principals covered previously—users, groups, and roles. The syntax for AWS policy documents comes in two flavors:

- JSON
- YAML

The following is the syntax for defining policy and permissions:

```
Version: 2012-10-17
Statement:
  - Effect: Allow
    Action:
      - ec2:DescribeInstances
    Resource: "*"
```

The above policy allows the `ec2:DescribeInstances` action to be performed on all resources. The `Version` field specifies the version of the policy language being used. The `Statement` field is a list of individual statements that together make up the policy.

Each statement consists of an `Effect` field (either `Allow` or `Deny`), an `Action` field that lists the actions that are allowed or denied by the `Effect` field, and a `Resource` field that specifies the resources that the actions apply to. IAM policies can be attached to IAM users, groups, and roles to grant permissions to perform various actions on AWS resources.

Policies can be defined in the two following ways:

- **Managed policies**: When policies are defined as managed policies, they are created as standalone policies, and therefore they can be attached to multiple entities. Out of the box, AWS provides a set of predefined managed policies that can be used in many use cases. Managed policies can be combined to deliver additional access to roles, users, or groups. Finally, AWS users can define and customize their own managed policies.
- **Inline policies**: Inline policies are created within the definition of an IAM entity and can only be assigned to the entity to which they are attached. They do not have their own **Amazon Resource Name (ARN)**. Since inline policies are related to a specific entity, they are not reusable. An ARN is an identifier used to uniquely identify AWS resources. It is a string that consists of several different parts, including the service, region, and resource identifier. Here is an example of an AWS ARN: `arn:aws:s3:::my_bucket/example.jpg`. In this example, `arn:aws:s3` indicates that the resource is an S3 bucket, `my_bucket` is the name of the bucket, and `example.jpg` is the name of a file stored in the bucket.

It is best practice to use managed policies whenever possible and use inline policies only when there is a good reason to do so.

Permissions are lists of actions that can be taken on AWS resources. When a user or group is created, initially, they have no permissions. One or more policies can be attached to the new user or group to enable access to resources.

When creating policies, it is a good idea to abide by the principle of least privilege. In simple terms, this means that entities should be given a high enough level of access to perform assigned tasks but nothing more. For example, suppose an Amazon EC2 instance is created, and we know that only five users with five different IPs will access it. In that case, we should use `allowlist` for those IPs and only give them access instead of opening the Amazon EC2 instance to the whole world.

Here is an example IAM policy that allows an EC2 instance to perform certain actions on S3 and EC2 resources, but only from a specific IP address range:

```
{
"Version": "2012-10-17",
"Statement": [
```

```
{
"Effect": "Allow",
"Action": [
"s3:ListBucket",
"s3:GetObject"
],
"Resource": [
"arn:aws:s3:::my-s3-bucket"
],
"Condition": {
"IpAddress": {
"aws:SourceIp": "10.0.0.0/16"
}
}
},
{
"Effect": "Allow",
"Action": [
"ec2:StartInstances",
"ec2:StopInstances"
],
"Resource": "*",
"Condition": {
"IpAddress": {
"aws:SourceIp": "10.0.1.1/16"
}
        }
  }
 ]
}
```

This policy allows the EC2 instance to list the contents of the `my-s3-bucket` S3 bucket and retrieve objects from it, as well as to start and stop other EC2 instances, but only if the request originates from an IP address in the range `10.0.1.1/16`. You can attach this policy to an IAM role and then associate the role with an EC2 instance to apply the permissions to the instance.

Note: This is just one example of how IAM policies can be used to `allowlist` EC2 IP addresses. There are many other ways to write IAM policies and you should carefully consider the specific needs of your use case when writing your own policies. AWS provides a policy simulator. This policy simulator can test new policies you may create and ensure they have the correct syntax. You can learn more here: `https://docs.aws.amazon.com/IAM/latest/UserGuide/access_policies_testing-policies.html`.

Permissions can be assigned to AWS users, groups, and roles via policies. These permissions can be given with policies in one of two ways:

- **Identity-based policies**: In this case, the policies are attached to users, groups, or roles.
- **Resource-based policies**: In this case, the policies are attached to AWS resources such as Amazon S3 buckets, Amazon EC2 instances, and AWS Lambda functions.

Identity-based policies are attached to an AWS identity and grant permissions to the identity. AWS identities include IAM users, IAM roles, and AWS service accounts. Identity-based policies can be used to grant permissions to IAM users or roles in your AWS account or to grant permissions to other AWS accounts.

Resource-based policies are attached to a resource, such as an Amazon S3 bucket or an Amazon SNS topic, and grant permissions for the resource. These permissions can be used by any AWS identity that has access to the resource.

Both types of policies use the same syntax and structure, and you can use them together to fine-tune access to your resources. It is important to choose the right type of policy for your use case and to design your policies carefully to ensure that they provide the right level of access to your resources. Now, let's learn about how to manage multiple AWS accounts using AWS Organizations.

AWS Organizations

AWS Organizations is a service that can be used to manage multiple AWS accounts in a consolidated manner. It provides a centralized location where you can see all your organization's bills and manage all your AWS accounts from one place. This central location makes it much easier to establish, manage, and enforce your organization's security policies. This central control ensures that security administrators and auditors can perform their jobs more efficiently and confidently.

These are the most important and relevant concepts when working with the AWS Organizations service:

- **Organization:** The overarching owner that will control all AWS accounts.
- **Root account:** The owner account for all other AWS accounts. Only one root account can exist across the organization. The root account needs to be created when the organization is created.
- **Organizational unit:** A grouping of underlying AWS accounts and/or other organizational units. An organizational unit can be the parent of other organizational units. This enables the potential creation of a hierarchy of organizational units that resembles a family tree. See the following diagram for more clarity.
- **AWS account:** A traditional AWS account that manages AWS resources and services. AWS accounts reside under an organizational unit or the root account.
- **Service Control Policy (SCP):** An SCP specifies the services and permissions for users and roles. An SCP can be associated with an AWS account or organizational unit.

The following figure illustrates how these components interact with each other:

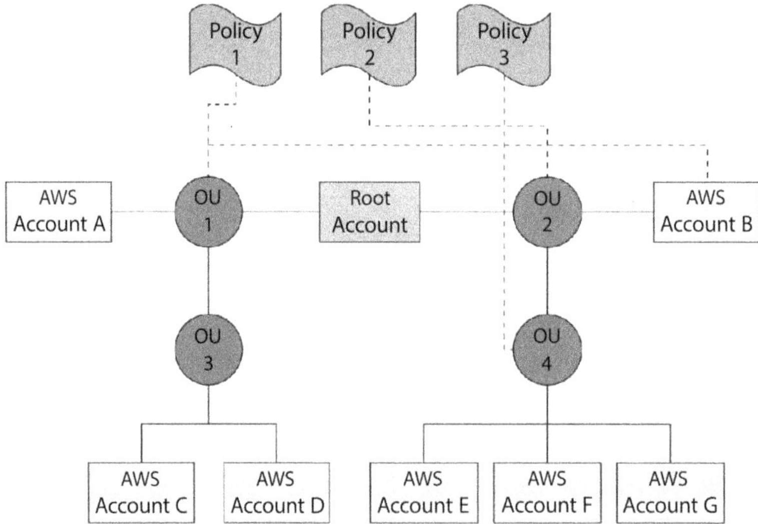

Figure 8.6: Sample organizational unit hierarchy

As you can see in the diagram above, **Policy 1** is associated with **Organizational Unit (OU) 1** and with **AWS Account B. Policy 1** is also applied to all children of **OU 1 (OU 3, AWS Account C**, and **AWS Account D)**.

Since **Policy 1** is associated with **AWS Account B** directly, it overrides **Policy 2**, which is associated with **OU 2** and all its children except for **AWS Account B**. **Policy 3** is associated with **OU 4** and all its children (**AWS Accounts E**, **F**, and **G**).

The following diagram shows an AWS organizational structure created in the AWS console:

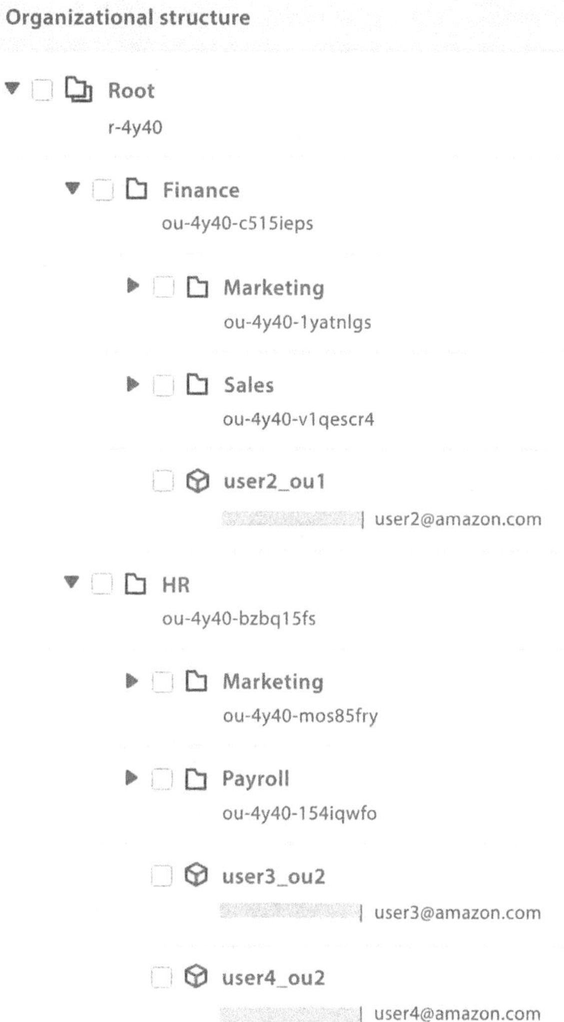

Figure 8.7: AWS organizational unit hierarchy in an AWS account

As you can see in the preceding diagram, two OUs are under the root account, and each unit has its sub-unit and AWS accounts.

The following are the key benefits of AWS Organizations:

- It provides tools to centrally govern and manage your cloud environment. You can quickly scale by creating accounts and allocating resources. You can provision common resources and permissions to new and existing accounts using AWS CloudFormation StackSets.
- You can customize your environment by applying governance policies. You can simplify access management for users by providing cross-application permissions with your identity source and AWS's SSO service.
- You can secure and audit your environment by logging all events in AWS CloudTrail.
- You can apply scheduled backups with AWS Backup for all accounts in the organization.
- You can manage costs and identify cost-saving measures. You can consolidate billing charges for your organization, and take advantage of volume discounts for qualifying services.

Without AWS Organization's SCP, all these policies would have to be repeated individually for each account. Every time there was a change to a policy, it would have to be changed individually in each account. This old approach had a high likelihood of policies that were supposed to be identical getting out of sync. You can learn more about AWS Organizations by visiting the AWS page here: `https://aws.amazon.com/organizations/`.

Managing multiple accounts could be complicated. If you'd like to start your AWS environment using a simple UI and built-in best practices it's better to use AWS Control Tower.

When you assign permission to a user or resource, you want to see the policy evaluation and how it will work. You can refer to details on IAM policy evaluation here: `https://docs.aws.amazon.com/IAM/latest/UserGuide/reference_policies_evaluation-logic.html`.

Hopefully, the concepts of users, groups, roles, permissions, and policies are clearer now. IAM is far from the only security service that AWS offers. AWS IAM is a vast topic that warrants a book in itself. You can find more detail about AWS IAM here: `https://aws.amazon.com/iam/`. Let's learn about the next service in the IAM category: AWS Directory Service.

AWS Directory Service

Microsoft Active Directory has been a popular choice for user and role management for decades, which, in computer years, is a long time. Given this popularity, AWS offers a fully managed implementation of Microsoft Active Directory. AWS Directory Service for Microsoft AD, also known as **AWS Managed Microsoft Active Directory**, allows AWS services that require directory services to integrate with Microsoft Active Directory.

AWS Managed Microsoft AD uses the actual Microsoft AD. It does not need to stay in sync because it does not copy the contents of existing ADs to the cloud. For this reason, the standard Microsoft AD administration tools can be used, and you can leverage the built-in AD capabilities, such as group policies and single sign-on. Using AWS Managed Microsoft AD, you can integrate Amazon EC2 and Amazon RDS for SQL Server instances with Microsoft AD. You can learn more about AWS Directory Service here: `https://aws.amazon.com/directoryservice/`. Let's learn about how AWS offers support for single sign-ons.

AWS IAM Identity Center (successor to AWS SSO)

Being able to sign on to multiple enterprise applications using a user's network login ID has been a pervasive way to manage application access for a while now.

AWS IAM Identity Center has replaced AWS Single Sign-On, and offers a secure way to establish and link workforce identities, as well as to centrally manage their access across AWS accounts and applications. With AWS IAM Identity Center, SSO can be implemented without too much effort, and it can also be centrally managed, even in a multi-account AWS environment. It can be used to manage user access and permissions for multiple AWS accounts in one central place by leveraging AWS Organizations. IAM Identity Center can be used to configure and maintain all account permissions automatically. It does not need additional configuration for each account. User permissions can be assigned using roles. The following are the benefits of IAM Identity Center:

- Manage users and groups where you want; connect to AWS once
- Centrally assign and manage access to AWS accounts; AWS SSO-integrated and cloud-based business applications
- Provide an SSO user portal to assigned AWS accounts; AWS and business applications
- It works with existing processes for joiners, leavers, and movers
- Increase developer productivity with the AWS CLI v2

You can use the following simple steps to set up application access through single sign-on:

1. Choose an identity resource, which could be IAM users, groups, or resources
2. Define permission sets for each role
3. Assign groups/users to permission sets in selected accounts
4. Connect cloud apps with SAML
5. Assign groups/users to apps

To manage user identities, IAM Identity Center provides an identity store or can connect with an existing identity store. Some of the supported identity stores are the following:

- Microsoft Active Directory
- Azure Active Directory
- Okta Universal Directory

Any activity that occurs when using IAM Identity Center will be recorded using AWS CloudTrail. You can find more details about configuring SSO using AWS IAM Identity Center here: `https://aws.amazon.com/iam/identity-center/`. You have now learned how to manage access for multiple users.

AWS Control Tower

If you have a simple AWS setup with a few servers and only one AWS account, then you don't need AWS Control Tower. But if you are part of an environment with hundreds or thousands of resources and multiple AWS accounts and teams, then you will want to learn about and leverage AWS Control Tower. AWS Control Tower simplifies a multi-account environment's administration, governance, and security setup.

Control Tower helps you quickly set up and govern multi-account environments securely. It automatically applies management features from existing AWS services, such as Organizations, AWS Config, and IAM Identity Center, and implements default account structure and governance policies based on AWS best practices from thousands of customers.

You can continue to use native features from Organizations, such as tag or backup policies, and integrated AWS services. AWS Control Tower enables you to set up company-wide policies and apply them across multiple AWS accounts. Without AWS Control Tower, you would have to apply the individual files to each account, opening up the possibility of having inconsistencies in your accounts. You can learn more about AWS Control Tower by visiting the AWS page here: `https://aws.amazon.com/controltower/`. Now let's learn how to manage multiple resources across organizational units using AWS Resource Access Manager.

AWS Resource Access Manager

The AWS **Resource Access Manager** (**RAM**) service allows you to share AWS resources with other AWS accounts or within your own organization. RAM allows you to share resources such as Amazon EC2 instances, Amazon RDS database instances, and **Amazon Virtual Private Clouds** (**Amazon VPCs**) with other AWS accounts or within your organization.

You can use RAM to manage resource sharing by creating resource shares, which are collections of resources that you want to share with specific AWS accounts or within your organization. You can specify the accounts or **organizational units (OUs)** that you want to share the resources with, and set permissions to control how the resources can be accessed.

RAM is useful for scenarios where you want to share resources with other teams or organizations, or when you want to centralize the management of resource sharing within your organization. It helps you to simplify resource sharing, reduce the complexity of resource management, and maintain control over the resources that you share. Here are the steps you can follow to use AWS RAM:

1. Sign in to the AWS Management Console and open the AWS RAM console at `https://console.aws.amazon.com/ram/`.
2. In the left navigation pane, choose **Resource Shares**.
3. Choose **Create resource share**.
4. On the **Create resource share** page, enter a name and optional description for your resource share.
5. Select the resources that you want to share and specify the accounts or OUs that you want to share the resources with.
6. Choose **Create resource share**.
7. To view the status of the resource share, choose the resource share in the list and then choose the **Status** tab.
8. To modify the resource share, choose the resource share in the list and then choose the **Modify** tab.

Note that you can only share resources that support sharing, and some resources have additional sharing requirements. For example, you can't share an EC2 instance unless it's in a VPC. You can learn more about AWS RAM by visiting the AWS page here: `https://aws.amazon.com/ram/`.

As of now, you have learned that managing users' security is the responsibility of your organization, but what if you are developing a web or mobile app open to the world? In those scenarios, you must manage millions of users, secure their credentials, and provide the required access. Amazon Cognito fulfills these needs. Let's learn more about it.

Amazon Cognito

Amazon Cognito enables developers to add user sign-in, sign-up, and access control to their web and mobile apps. It provides granular APIs and SDKs to manage end-user authentication, and authorization workflows that can be customized using out-of-the-box integration with AWS Lambda.

Cognito is fully managed with a built-in hosted UI and provides out-of-the-box support for open standards authentication protocols such as OAuth 2.

You can easily integrate your app to authenticate users using federation with Facebook or login with Amazon, Google, and custom OpenID Connect or SAML providers. It provides a serverless fully managed directory to store and securely manage user information using MFA authentication through SMS and email. Amazon Cognito offers authentication, authorization, and user management services for web and mobile applications. Here are some of the security features of Amazon Cognito:

- **MFA:** Amazon Cognito supports MFA to help protect against unauthorized access to user accounts. MFA can be configured to require a one-time code sent to the user's phone or email, or a hardware token.
- **Password policies**: Amazon Cognito allows you to set password policies to ensure that users choose strong passwords.
- **Encryption**: Amazon Cognito stores user data and passwords in an encrypted format, using AES-256 encryption.
- **Access control**: Amazon Cognito provides fine-grained access control to resources using IAM policies.
- **Activity tracking**: Amazon Cognito tracks user sign-in and sign-out activity, as well as changes to user attributes. This information can be used to monitor for suspicious activity and alert administrators.
- **Security tokens:** Amazon Cognito issues **JSON Web Tokens (JWTs)** to authenticated users, which can be used to access authorized resources. The JWTs have a limited lifespan and can be easily invalidated if a user's security is compromised.
- **Account recovery**: Amazon Cognito provides options for users to recover their accounts if they forget their passwords or lose access to their MFA devices.

You can learn more about Amazon Cognito by visiting the AWS page here: `https://aws.amazon.com/cognito/`.

In this section about the security services in AWS's IAM pillar you learned about managing user security in AWS. As AWS security is a vast topic that would require multiple books to cover in detail, in the upcoming section, you will learn a bit about each AWS service belonging to different security pillars with resources to learn more. Let's learn about the next security pillar, which helps you detect and control security threats.

Applying security controls

Security is more about preventive gestures than reactive as any security incident can cause significant damage to organizations, so it's better to detect and fix incidents before a security leak can cause damage. AWS provides an array of services to help you to monitor, detect, and mitigate security threats. The following is a summary of services to apply proactive security control:

- **Amazon GuardDuty**: Intelligent threat detection and continuous monitoring to protect your AWS accounts and workloads.
- **Amazon Inspector**: Automates security assessments to help improve the security and compliance of applications deployed on AWS.
- **AWS Security Hub**: Centrally view and manage security alerts and automate compliance checks.

The following are common security audit services:

- **AWS Config**: AWS Config enables you to assess, track, and evaluate the configurations of your AWS resources. With AWS Config, you can monitor the changes to your resources and assess their compliance with internal policies and regulatory standards. Additionally, you can use AWS Config to conduct security analysis and improve the visibility of your resource configurations, making it easier to identify potential security risks and respond to any incidents. Overall, AWS Config provides a centralized and automated way to manage the configuration of your AWS resources, ensuring that they remain compliant and secure over time. You can learn more about Config by visiting the AWS page here: `https://aws.amazon.com/config/`.
- **AWS CloudTrail**: AWS CloudTrail provides a record of all API calls made to your AWS account. This service enables you to monitor and audit your AWS resource activity, including changes to your resources and the actions of your users and applications. With AWS CloudTrail, you can gain greater visibility of your resource usage and security posture, as well as quickly identify and respond to any suspicious or unauthorized activity. AWS CloudTrail supports multiple platforms, including the AWS Management Console, AWS CLI, and AWS SDKs, making it easy to track and manage your AWS resource activity from a variety of sources. You can learn more about CloudTrail by visiting the AWS page here: `https://aws.amazon.com/cloudtrail/`.
- **Amazon VPC Flow Logs**: VPC Flow Logs enables you to capture information about the IP traffic going to and from network interfaces in your VPC.

This service allows you to track the traffic flow and troubleshoot network connectivity issues, as well as improve the security of your network by identifying any potential network threats or unauthorized access. You can learn more about Flow Logs by visiting the AWS page here: `https://docs.aws.amazon.com/vpc/latest/userguide/flow-logs.html`.

- **Amazon CloudWatch**: CloudWatch is a monitoring service that enables you to monitor your AWS resources and applications in real time. With CloudWatch, you can monitor metrics, logs, and events generated by your resources and applications, and set alarms to be notified of any issues. This service provides a centralized and automated way to monitor your environment, making it easier to detect and resolve issues, improve the performance of your resources, and ensure the availability of your applications. CloudWatch supports a variety of resources and services, including Amazon EC2 instances, Amazon RDS databases, AWS Lambda functions, and many more. You can also use CloudWatch to monitor custom metrics, such as the number of requests made to an application, the response time of a database, or the disk usage of an EC2 instance. You can learn more about CloudWatch by visiting the AWS page here: `https://aws.amazon.com/cloudwatch/`.

Let's learn about security control services in detail.

Amazon GuardDuty

Amazon GuardDuty is an AWS service that can detect unauthorized actors' threats, malicious behavior, and activity. It protects all other AWS resources and your enterprise's data. Getting more traffic in the application is usually good news because it typically means more business. But additional traffic requires more work to track and monitor additional logs and activity. The following screenshot shows services being monitored by GuardDuty:

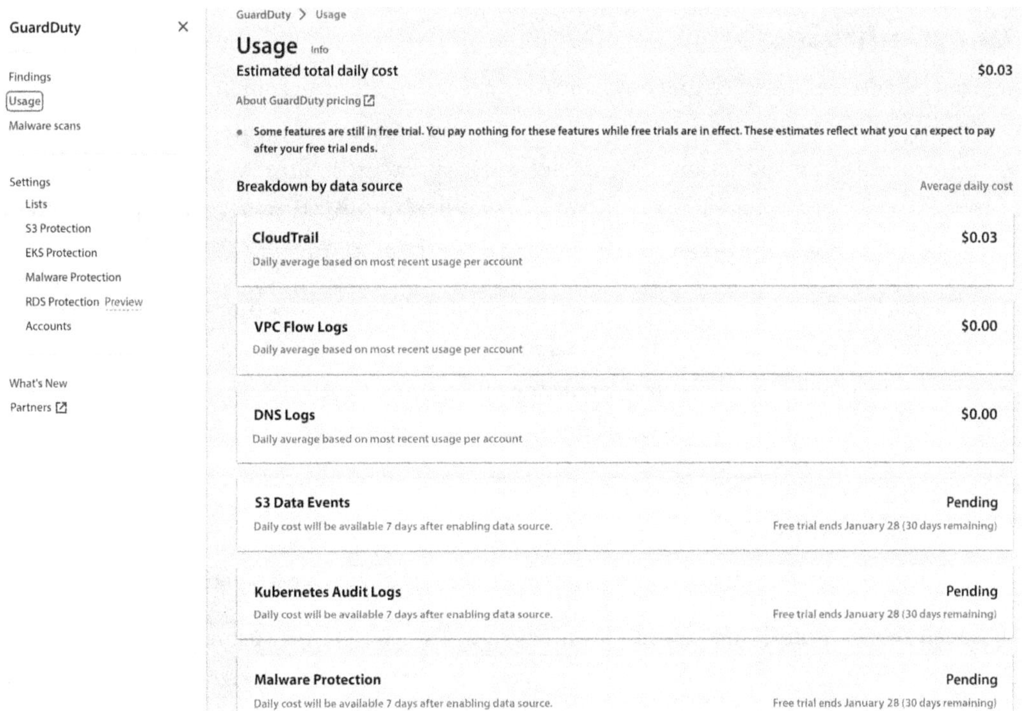

Figure 8.8: Amazon GuardDuty data source list

Amazon GuardDuty enables and simplifies the monitoring of this activity. Amazon GuardDuty leverages machine learning and advanced anomaly detection to compile, process, and prioritize potential malicious activity. GuardDuty can analyze billions of real-time events across various AWS real-time and near-real-time streams such as AWS CloudTrail logs, Amazon VPC Flow Logs, and DNS logs.

However, keep in mind that Amazon GuardDuty doesn't do anything with the analysis. It is an intrusion detection system, not an intrusion prevention system. If you need enforcement for malicious IPs, you will need a third-party solution such as Aviatrix GuardDuty Enforcement. You can learn more about GuardDuty by visiting the AWS page here: `https://aws.amazon.com/guardduty/`.

Amazon Inspector

Amazon Inspector is a service that automatically checks application compliance against certain predefined policies and is used to increase compliance. Amazon Inspector can identify vulnerabilities, exposures, and deviations from predefined best practices. Once the assessment has been completed, the service generates a comprehensive report of security flaws and issues sorted by severity level. These findings can then be used to close these security gaps.

Amazon Inspector security assessments enable users to look for unauthorized network access to Amazon EC2 instances. It can find vulnerabilities in EC2 instances and containers. Amazon Inspector assessments are available as predefined rule components that can map to security best practices and vulnerability definitions. Some samples of predefined rules are as follows:

- Someone trying to access EC2 instances from outside your network
- If someone turns on the remote root login
- Identify software and operating system versions that are due for patching

These rules are constantly monitored and enhanced by the AWS security team. You can learn more about Amazon Inspector by visiting the AWS page here: `https://aws.amazon.com/inspector/`.

Building infrastructure protection

Infrastructure protection is the first line of defense when it comes to security. AWS secures physical infrastructure with multi-layered security in its data centers. However, securing the logical infrastructure boundary and network traffic becomes your responsibility as AWS provides you with more control to manage boundaries for your logical cloud infrastructure. AWS provides the following services to protect your cloud infrastructure:

- **AWS Web Application Firewall**: Web Application Firewall is a security service that helps protect your web applications from common web exploits, such as SQL injection and **cross-site scripting (XSS)** attacks. Web Application Firewall is a firewall that allows you to monitor HTTP and HTTPS requests made to your applications and block, allow, or count requests based on conditions that you define, such as IP addresses, headers, and content.
- **AWS Firewall Manager**: Firewall Manager is a security service that makes it easier to manage the firewall rules for your Amazon VPC security groups. With Firewall Manager, you can centrally manage the firewall rules across multiple AWS accounts and VPCs, ensuring that your security policies are consistent and up to date.

- **AWS Shield:** Shield is a managed **Distributed Denial of Service (DDoS)** protection service for AWS customers. DDoS attacks are a common type of cyber attack that attempt to overwhelm a website or online service with an excessive amount of traffic, making it unavailable to users.

Let's learn about AWS infrastructure security services in detail.

AWS Web Application Firewall (WAF)

AWS **Web Application Firewall (WAF)**, as the name implies, is a firewall for your web applications. It can create a layer of protection around your web applications and RESTful APIs. It guards against the most well-known web exploits. AWS WAF can be used to control network traffic. This traffic is controlled by creating rules. These rules can target well-known exploits such as SQL injections or XSS attacks.

Furthermore, these rules can be customized to filter transactions that meet user-defined patterns. AWS WAF has Managed Rules, which simplifies management. AWS can manage these rules, and AWS Marketplace sellers also offer preconfigured rules. AWS and Marketplace rules are constantly modified as new threats are identified. AWS WAF also provides an API to assist in developing, deploying, and maintaining these security rules.

AWS WAF can be deployed on the following:

- Amazon CloudFront
- Application Load Balancer
- Origin servers running on EC2
- Amazon API Gateway
- AWS AppSync

AWS WAF pricing depends on the number of rules deployed and the number of requests that applications receive. You can learn more about WAF by visiting the AWS page here: `https://aws.amazon.com/waf/`.

AWS Firewall Manager

AWS Firewall Manager makes setting up firewalls simple. It enables users to administer firewall rules in a central dashboard. This can be achieved even across multiple AWS accounts and applications.

Cloud environments are dynamic. This can create maintenance headaches as new applications come online. AWS Firewall Manager simplifies the process of provisioning new applications and ensuring they comply with an enterprise's security policies by enabling users to manage firewall settings from one location.

If new security rules need to be created or if existing rules need to be modified, they can also be changed only once. Some of the services in AWS that can benefit from AWS Firewall Manager are the following:

- Application Load Balancer
- API Gateway
- Amazon CloudFront distributions
- Amazon EC2

AWS Firewall Manager allows adding AWS WAF rules, AWS Shield Advanced protection, security groups, and AWS Network Firewall rules to VPCs across accounts and resources using a centralized dashboard. You can learn more about Firewall Manager by visiting the AWS page here: `https://aws.amazon.com/firewall-manager/`.

AWS Shield

AWS Shield is an AWS-managed DDoS protection service used to protect systems and data. AWS Shield delivers automatic attack detection and resolution that can keep your application running, or at least reduce the amount of downtime. Since AWS Shield Standard comes with all AWS accounts, you normally have to contact AWS support to assist you if you suffer a DDoS attack. AWS Shield comes in two flavors:

- **AWS Shield Standard**: Provided at no additional charge to all AWS customers
- **AWS Shield Advanced**: Provides a higher level of protection but at an additional cost

AWS Shield Standard can protect against and handle the more common types of attacks. The more common DDoS attacks happen at the network and transport layer. AWS Shield Standard can help you protect Amazon CloudFront and Amazon Route 53 against (Layer 3 and Layer 4) attacks.

AWS Shield Advanced provides higher protection for more services. AWS Shield Advanced can be used to defend against attacks targeting the following:

- Amazon EC2 instances
- Elastic Load Balancing

- Amazon CloudFront
- AWS Global Accelerator
- Amazon Route 53

To get this level of protection, you will need to subscribe to AWS Shield Advanced and pay an additional fee. AWS Shield Advanced not only protects against network and transport layer attacks, but also delivers additional monitoring and resolution, protecting against large and sophisticated DDoS attacks and providing real-time reporting when attacks occur. It integrates with AWS WAF. AWS Shield Advanced provides 24-hour support from AWS's DDoS response team as an additional feature. Finally, with AWS Shield Advanced, AWS will cover any charges your account incurs for certain services that can be attributed to an attack. You can learn more about Shield by visiting the AWS page here: `https://aws.amazon.com/shield/`.

Data is the essential thing that any organization wants to protect. Let's learn about AWS services available for data protection.

Building data protection

Data is key for any application or organization. Most hacking attempts made to steal data, and leakage of your customer data, can be very harmful to your organization in terms of customer trust and financial damage. You need to have multi-layer security to protect your customer data. As you are the owner of the data, most of the time the responsibility for data protection lies with you. AWS provides a number of services to protect data. Let's look at them below:

- **Amazon Macie**: Amazon Macie is a security service that uses machine learning to automatically discover, classify, and protect sensitive data in AWS. Macie provides visibility of how your data is being stored and accessed, helping you to identify and secure sensitive data, such as credit card numbers, Social Security numbers, and intellectual property.
- **AWS Key Management Service (KMS)**: KMS is a managed service that makes it easy for you to create and control the encryption keys used to encrypt your data. KMS provides a central repository for your encryption keys, making it easier to manage their lifecycle, such as rotating your keys on a regular basis and enforcing security and compliance policies.
- **AWS CloudHSM**: CloudHSM is a **hardware security module** (**HSM**) service that provides secure key storage for cryptographic operations within the AWS cloud. An HSM is a dedicated, tamper-resistant hardware device that provides secure storage for encryption keys and performs encryption and decryption operations.

- **AWS Certificate Manager (ACM)**: **ACM** is a service that makes it easy for you to manage SSL/TLS certificates for your AWS-hosted websites and applications. ACM provides a simple and cost-effective way to manage SSL/TLS certificates, eliminating the need to manage and maintain your own certificate infrastructure.
- **AWS Secrets Manager**: Secrets Manager is a secure and scalable service that enables you to store, manage, and rotate your secrets, such as database credentials, API keys, and SSH keys. With Secrets Manager, you can store your secrets in a centralized and encrypted manner, making it easier for you to manage and secure access to your secrets.
- **Server-Side Encryption (SSE)**: SSE is a security feature for encrypting data stored in AWS storage services, such as Amazon S3 and Amazon EBS. SSE helps protect your data from unauthorized access by automatically encrypting your data at rest, which means that the data is encrypted when it is stored on disk. You learned about SSE in *Chapter 5, Storage in AWS – Choosing the Right Tool for the Job*. You can explore more about SSE by visiting the SSE page here: `https://docs.aws.amazon.com/AmazonS3/latest/userguide/serv-side-encryption.html`.

Let's learn about some of these services in more detail.

Amazon Macie

Amazon Macie is another fully managed security service. It can be used to protect your data and its privacy. It leverages artificial intelligence and machine learning to find and protect sensitive data in AWS environments.

In today's enterprises, data comes in at an ever-increasing speed. Handling those growing volumes of data creates scalability issues with more data and complexity, making expenses increase. Amazon Macie enables the automation of sensitive data discovery. Since it leverages machine learning, it can scale and handle petabyte-sized datasets. Macie creates a list of Amazon S3 buckets in a user's account. It can flag which ones are unencrypted, which ones can be accessed publicly, and buckets that are being shared with other AWS accounts that are not defined in AWS Organizations.

Amazon Macie uses machine learning and pattern matching on these buckets. Amazon Macie can be configured to identify sensitive data such as personally identifiable information and deliver alerts to a predefined user base. Once these alerts and issues are generated, they can be quickly sorted and filtered in the AWS Management Console. It can then be integrated with other AWS services using workflow or event management systems. It can also be used together with other AWS services.

An example is AWS Step Functions. AWS Step Functions can leverage automated remediation actions. This can assist with compliance with rules and regulations, such as the **Health Insurance Portability and Accountability Act** (**HIPAA**) and **General Data Privacy Regulation** (**GDPR**). You can learn more about Macie by visiting the AWS page here: `https://aws.amazon.com/macie/`.

AWS Key Management Service

KMS, or Key Management Service, is a service offered by AWS that simplifies the process of creating and managing encryption keys. KMS provides a central, secure location for storing and managing your encryption keys, and it integrates with other AWS services to help you easily encrypt and decrypt data in the cloud. It is a secure and fault-tolerant service. AWS KMS can be used to assist in the management of encryption of data at rest. KMS provides the ability to create and manage cryptographic keys. It can also be used to manage which users, services, and applications have access to them.

Behind the scenes KMS uses HSMs to protect your encryption keys, ensuring that they are kept secure even if an attacker gains access to your systems. It also provides auditing and logging capabilities to help you track the use of your keys and meet compliance requirements.

You can use KMS to encrypt data in a number of different ways, including:

- Encrypting data at rest, such as data stored in Amazon S3 or Amazon EBS.
- Encrypting data in transit, such as data transmitted over the network or data transmitted between AWS regions.
- Encrypting data in use, such as data stored in memory or data being processed by an application.

The HSMs that KMS uses comply with Federal Information Processing Standard 140-2. AWS KMS integrates with AWS CloudTrail so that it is simple to see who has used the keys and when. You can learn more about KMS by visiting the AWS page here: `https://aws.amazon.com/kms/`.

AWS CloudHSM

AWS makes encrypting data at rest quite simple if you use encryption keys provided by AWS through KMS. However, KMS works under the shared tenancy model, which means that behind the scenes a single HSM may be storing keys from different customers. In some instances, such as in the finance industry, you cannot use shared storage to store encryption keys in order to comply with regulations, which state you have to have your own dedicated HSM for key storage.

For that, AWS provides a service called AWS CloudHSM.

AWS CloudHSM is a **hardware security module** (**HSM**) that empowers users to generate their own encryption keys. CloudHSM provides the ability to create encryption keys using Federal Information Processing Standard 140-2 Level 3 validated HSMs. AWS CloudHSM can be integrated with other AWS services via well-defined industry-standard APIs. Some of the APIs supported are as follows:

- PKCS#11
- Microsoft **CryptoNG** (**CNG**) libraries
- **Java Cryptography Extensions** (**JCEs**)

AWS CloudHSM complies with many security standards. It is also possible to export the generated keys to various third-party HSMs. Like many of the other security services we have learned about in this section, AWS CloudHSM is fully managed by AWS, enabling you to focus on your applications and not the administration of your key management service. Some of the tasks that AWS handles when using this service are as follows:

- Provisioning the required hardware to run the service
- Applying software patching
- Making sure the service is highly available
- Performing backups

CloudHSM has a serverless architecture that allows users to seamlessly and effortlessly scale. Like other cloud services, you can use CloudHSM with an on-demand, pay-as-you-go model. You can learn more about CloudHSM by visiting the AWS page here: `https://aws.amazon.com/cloudhsm/`.

AWS Certificate Manager

AWS Certificate Manager is another security service. It can create, maintain, and deploy public and private SSL/TLS certificates that can be added to other AWS services and applications. SSL/TLS certificates can secure network communications by enabling encryption. They can also be used to authenticate a website's identity in public and private networks. AWS Certificate Manager streamlines and automates the management process for certificate management.

AWS Certificate Manager can be used to provision and renew a certificate and install it on another AWS service such as Elastic Load Balancing, Amazon CloudFront, and APIs on API Gateway. It can also be used to create private certificates for internal applications. These certificates can then be centrally managed.

There is no charge when you provision public and private certificates using AWS Certificate Manager. The cost is bundled with spinning up the underlying resources (like an EC2 instance). When you use AWS Certificate Manager Private Certificate Authority, there is a monthly charge for the use of Private Certificate Authority and for the private certificates that are issued. You can learn more about Certificate Manager by visiting the AWS page here: `https://aws.amazon.com/certificate-manager/`.

AWS Secrets Manager

AWS Secrets Manager is a security service that can be used to protect secrets. These secrets may be strings such as passwords that can be used to access services, applications, and IT resources. AWS Secrets Manager facilitates the rotation, management, and retrieval of API keys, database credentials, passwords, and other secrets. These secrets can be retrieved using the Secrets Manager APIs. The need to store passwords clearly in plain text files is obviated by using AWS Secrets Manager. Some of the services that can integrate with AWS Secrets Manager are as follows:

- Amazon RDS
- Amazon Redshift
- Amazon DynamoDB
- Amazon Neptune
- Amazon DocumentDB

AWS Secrets Manager can be customized to support additional types of secrets. Some examples of use cases are the following:

- API keys
- OAuth authentication tokens

Another feature of AWS Secrets Manager is that it allows secrets to be rotated periodically without impacting applications that use them for password management and other uses.

You can learn more about Secrets Manager by visiting the AWS page here: `https://aws.amazon.com/secrets-manager/`.

There are so many AWS services that collect data, and security needs to look across all the logs and data collected. However, collecting data across services such as VPC Flow Logs, AWS CloudTrail logs, audit logs, GuardDuty, and so on, could be very tedious. You need a unified view of logs to understand any security issues. AWS provides a way to quickly analyze the issue through a service called Amazon Detective. Let's learn about Amazon Detective in more detail.

Amazon Detective

Amazon Detective is a security solution that employs machine learning, statistical analysis, and graph theory to help customers identify and investigate security issues in their AWS accounts. This service provides a powerful tool for analyzing and understanding security-related activity in your AWS environment, making it easier for you to quickly identify the root cause of any suspicious activity or security incidents. It can be used to identify unusual activity or suspicious behavior in your account, such as resource provisioning or access patterns that deviate from normal behavior.

To use Amazon Detective, you first need to enable the service in your AWS account and then connect your AWS resources, such as Amazon EC2 instances and Amazon RDS databases, to it. Amazon Detective then analyzes log data from your AWS resources, creates a linked set of data that provides you with a comprehensive view of your security posture, and builds a graph of the interactions and relationships between them. It uses machine learning algorithms to identify patterns and anomalies in the data that may indicate security issues or suspicious activity.

Once Amazon Detective has identified a potential issue, it provides a detailed investigation summary that includes a timeline of events, relevant log data, and recommended actions for further investigation or remediation. You can use this summary to quickly understand the issue and take the appropriate action to resolve it.

With Amazon Detective, you can use advanced algorithms to analyze security-related activity in your AWS environment and gain insights into potential security risks. The service also provides visualizations and summaries that help you triage security findings and prioritize your investigations, making it easier for you to focus on the most critical issues.

By automating the collection and analysis of security data, Amazon Detective helps you streamline your security investigations and resolve security incidents more quickly. This helps you reduce the risk of security breaches and ensure that your AWS environment remains secure and compliant. You can learn more about Amazon Detective by visiting the AWS page here: `https://aws.amazon.com/detective/`.

AWS Security Hub

AWS Security Hub is a security management service that provides a central place to manage security alerts and findings from multiple AWS services, as well as from other **AWS Partner Network (APN)** security solutions. It provides a comprehensive view of your security posture across your AWS accounts, making it easier to identify and prioritize security issues.

Security Hub integrates with a number of AWS services, including Amazon GuardDuty, Amazon Inspector, and Amazon Macie, as well as third-party security solutions from APN partners. It also provides APIs that enable you to automate the process of responding to security findings. With Security Hub, you can:

- Consolidate security alerts and findings from multiple sources into a single view.
- Prioritize and triage security issues based on their severity and the likelihood of impact.
- Automate the process of responding to security findings, using AWS Config rules and AWS Lambda functions.
- Collaborate with your team to investigate and resolve security issues.

Security Hub helps you improve your organization's security posture by providing a central place to manage security alerts and findings, and by enabling you to automate the process of responding to security issues. You can learn more about Security Hub by visiting the AWS page here: `https://aws.amazon.com/security-hub/`.

While security is essential, multiple compliances are defined by the local governing body to which your application must adhere. Let's learn about AWS-provided services to fulfill your compliance needs.

Adhering to compliances

AWS offers a variety of services and tools to help organizations comply with a wide range of regulations and standards, such as the **General Data Protection Regulation** (**GDPR**), the **Health Insurance Portability and Accountability Act** (**HIPAA**), and the **Payment Card Industry Data Security Standard** (**PCI DSS**).

AWS provides broad support for security standards and compliance certifications, including HI-TECH, FedRAMP, GDPR, FIPS 140-2, and NIST 800-171, to help meet the compliance requirements of regulatory agencies around the world. This extensive coverage makes it easier for organizations to achieve and maintain compliance with a wide range of security standards and regulations, regardless of their location or the specific regulatory requirements they must adhere to.

By supporting these security standards and certifications, AWS helps organizations ensure that their data and applications are protected by rigorous security controls and processes, reducing the risk of data breaches and security incidents. This helps organizations meet their regulatory obligations and maintain the trust of their customers, employees, and stakeholders.

The following are the services provided by AWS to audit your compliance needs:

- **AWS Artifact**: No-cost, self-service portal for on-demand access to AWS compliance reports.
- **AWS Audit Manager**: Amazon Audit Manager is a security and compliance auditing service that makes it easy for customers to automate the process of auditing their AWS accounts. With Audit Manager, customers can assess their compliance with AWS security best practices, industry standards and regulations, and internal policies. You can learn more about AWS Audit Manager by visiting the AWS page here: `https://aws.amazon.com/audit-manager/`.
- **AWS IAM**: AWS IAM allows you to set up and manage users and their permissions within your AWS account. This can help you ensure that only authorized users have access to sensitive resources and data.
- **AWS Config**: Config provides visibility of resource configurations and changes in your AWS environment. It can help you track changes to resources, ensure that resources are compliant with your internal policies, and audit resource configurations for compliance with external regulations.
- **AWS Encryption SDK**: SDK is a set of libraries that you can use to build encryption into your applications. It helps you protect data in transit and at rest, and can be used to meet compliance requirements for data encryption.
- **AWS PrivateLink**: PrivateLink is a network interface that you can use to connect your on-premises data centers to AWS services, without the data traversing the public internet. This can help you comply with regulations that require the use of private networks for certain types of data.

There are many other AWS services and features that can help with compliance, depending on your specific needs. If you have specific questions about how AWS can help with compliance in your organization, you can contact AWS Support or consult with a security and compliance specialist.

Let's learn about AWS Artifact in detail.

AWS Artifact reports

AWS Artifact is a portal that provides on-demand access to AWS's security and compliance documents. It includes AWS compliance reports, Service Organization Control reports, and other documents that can be used to demonstrate compliance with various regulations and standards.

AWS Artifact Reports deliver a centralized repository to store, manage, and access a variety of compliance reports from third-party auditors who have audited and certified that a given standard or regulation is met by the AWS infrastructure or by a given service. These rules, standards, and regulations may be global, regional, or industry-specific. As these rules and regulations change, AWS is constantly engaging third parties to ensure that compliance is up to date.

The AWS Artifact Agreements service provides the ability to access, approve, terminate, and manage agreements with AWS. It can be used to manage one AWS account or leverage AWS Organizations to manage multiple AWS accounts.

Some of the types of reports that can be managed with AWS Artifact are as follows:

- Service Organization Control reports
- Payment Card Industry reports
- Certifications from accreditation agencies around the world
- Industry-specific compliance reports
- Compliance reports about AWS security controls
- Business Associate Addendums
- Nondisclosure agreements

You can learn more about AWS Artifact by visiting the AWS page here: `https://aws.amazon.com/artifact/`.

In this section, you have learned about AWS security and compliance services. Let's look at the "best of the best" tips for security in the AWS cloud.

Best practices for AWS security

While AWS provides a number of security services, it's essential to understand how to apply them to secure your application. AWS offers a wide range of security features and services, but customers are responsible for properly configuring and managing these features to meet their specific security requirements. Here are some best practices for AWS security:

1. Implement a strong IAM policy:
    - Use MFA for privileged users.
    - Grant least privilege, meaning only provide access to the resources and actions that users need to do their jobs.

- Regularly rotate AWS access keys and passwords to reduce the risk of compromise.

2. Encrypt data at rest and in transit:
    - Encrypt sensitive data, such as databases and backups, using AWS KMS or SSE.
    - Use SSL or TLS to encrypt data in transit.
3. Monitor and log activity:
    - Use Amazon CloudWatch Logs to monitor and store log data from EC2 instances, ELB, and other AWS services.
    - Use Amazon CloudTrail to track API activity and changes to your AWS resources.
    - Enable VPC Flow Logs to monitor network traffic in your VPC.
4. Implement security groups and **network access control lists (NACLs)**:
    - Use security groups to control inbound and outbound network traffic to your EC2 instances.
    - Use NACLs to control traffic to and from subnets within your VPC.
5. Use Amazon VPC to segment your network:
    - Use a VPC to create isolated networks and control access to your AWS resources.
    - Use AWS VPC peering to connect multiple VPCs for communication between resources.
6. Use AWS Shield for DDoS protection:
    - AWS Shield provides protection against DDoS attacks.
    - Consider using AWS WAF to protect against web-based attacks.
7. Implement Amazon Macie for data protection:
    - Use Macie to discover, classify, and protect sensitive data in AWS.
    - Use Macie to monitor access to your data and detect any unauthorized access or data leaks.
8. Use AWS Config to track resource configurations:
    - AWS Config is a service that enables you to assess, audit, and evaluate the configurations of your AWS resources.

- Use AWS Config to monitor changes to your resources and ensure that configurations remain compliant with your policies.

In conclusion, security is a top priority for AWS, and there are many best practices that customers can follow to secure their AWS environments. By implementing these best practices, customers can ensure that their AWS resources are secure and protected against a variety of security threats.

Overall, more automation improves security outcomes. You should minimize human intervention and always make smaller changes and do these more often to stay on top of vulnerabilities as quickly as they are discovered.

Summary

In this chapter, we laid the groundwork to enable you to understand how security is implemented in AWS. As we saw in the chapter, the shared responsibility model is a fundamental pillar. You saw how some components of security are the responsibility of AWS, and some parts are the customer's responsibility. You learned about the six security pillars into which AWS security and compliance services are divided.

You then looked at the most basic and fundamental security service in IAM. You dove deep into AWS IAM and reviewed concepts such as users, groups, permissions, roles, and policies and how they are connected to each other. Further, you briefly learned about security services in each security pillar with available resources to explore. Finally, in the last section of the chapter, you learned about security best practices and how to make your cloud environment even more secure.

Hopefully, after completing this chapter, you feel more confident about how AWS can be leveraged to write world-class applications offering the highest levels of security.

In the next chapter, you will further explore some more elements of cloud automation.

Join us on Discord!

Read this book alongside other users, cloud experts, authors, and like-minded professionals.

Ask questions, provide solutions to other readers, chat with the authors via. Ask Me Anything sessions and much more.

Scan the QR code or visit the link to join the community now.

`https://packt.link/cloudanddevops`

Driving Efficiency with CloudOps

Organizations migrating to the cloud need management and governance to ensure best practices in their cloud IT operations. Whether you manage modern applications built using microservices-based architectures, containers, serverless stacks, or legacy applications that have been re-hosted or re-architected for the cloud, you will realize that traditional application development and operations processes could be more effective.

Automation has always been vital for managing cloud operations, increasing efficiency and avoiding human error disruption. However, you will still observe many manual tasks in most organizations, especially IT workload management. With the rise of the cloud, automation has become more critical due to its pay-as-you-go model. Automation helps you improve productivity, resulting in substantial cost savings in human effort and IT resource expenditure. Automation has become key to reducing daily operational costs and cloud organizations spending more on operations than upfront capital investment.

Automation is crucial for cost and other aspects, such as enduring application security and reliability. Automation goes hand in hand with monitoring and alerts. Automation will only work if you have proper monitoring, alerting your automation script when to take a certain action, for example, if you want to run your production app server without compromising the user experience due to a capacity crunch. It's always recommended to monitor server capacity, such as if the server exhausted memory capacity to 80% or CPU capacity to 70%, and send an alert to autoscaling for server scaling as needed.

AWS provides several services and tools to automate your cloud infrastructure and application with CloudOps fully or if you want to automate security using DevSecOps. In this chapter, you will learn the following topics in detail to understand the need for cloud automation, monitoring, and alerts:

- What is CloudOps?
- AWS CloudOps pillars
- DevOps and DevSecOps in AWS
- AWS cloud management tools for automation
- Cloud automation best practice

By the end of this chapter, you will understand various automation strategies to manage cloud operations. You will learn about various AWS services available at your disposal for cloud automation, monitoring, and alerts and how to use them in your workload.

What is the cloud operation (CloudOps) model, and what role does automation play?

CloudOps, or the cloud operational model, encompasses a collection of guidelines and safeguards that are established, tracked, and adjusted as needed to manage expenses, boost productivity, and mitigate potential security risks. It can help guide your people, processes, and the technology associated with your cloud infrastructure, security, and operations. An operational model also helps you develop and implement controls to manage security, budget, and compliance across your workloads in the cloud.

Implementing cloud automation empowers organizations to construct streamlined cloud operational models through the automated creation, modification, and removal of cloud resources. Although the concept of cloud computing initially promised the ability to utilize services as required, many organizations still rely on manual processes to provision resources, conduct testing, recognize resource redundancy, and decommission resources. This approach can result in substantial labor, error-proneness, and expense.

Businesses migrating to the cloud need management and governance to ensure best practices in their cloud IT operations. AWS management and governance services provide faster innovation and firm control over cost, compliance, and security.

The following are the key benefits of the cloud operation model:

- Organizations can unlock the speed and agility that comes with the cloud and accelerate their cloud adoption and application modernization efforts as part of their digital transformation journey.
- Use the power of automation for routine tasks to reduce manual errors and interventions.
- Continue to scale your businesses with the certainty that cloud governance spans all different environments uniformly and at scale.
- Use your skilled personnel effectively to deliver business outcomes.
- Avoid unexpected cost overruns.

While implementing cloud automation can initially demand significant effort, the potential rewards are considerable. Once the initial hurdles are overcome, the ability to perform intricate tasks with just a single click can transform an organization's operations. In addition to minimizing manual labor, cloud automation offers several other advantages, including:

- **Improved security and resilience**: Automation helps you improve security as there are always chances of security lapses due to human error or changes that can be left out, which is outside of individual knowledge for setting up security credentials for newly added dev environment. Also, automation helps to improve resiliency by automated recovery of the environment; for example, if your server reaches over capacity, you can take proactive action by adding more CPU or memory to avoid downtime.
- **Improved backup processes**: Automated backup is one of the most important things for your business process continuation. Protecting your data helps minimize business loss by winning customer trust and rebuilding your environment quickly in case of a disaster recovery event. Automated backup helps you ensure all backups are secure and do not rely on one individual who can forget to take a backup.
- **Improved governance**: Automation helps you to improve governance by making sure all activity is captured across the environment. For example, you need to know what servers and database inventories are running across your company's IT workload or who is accessing those environments. All these things are possible through an automated governance model.

AWS provides a set of services and third-party tools for modern enterprises as they adopt the cloud operation model. It can help you drive more innovation, faster cloud adoption, improved application performance, and quicker response times to customer feedback while maintaining governance and compliance.

Let's look at the CloudOps pillars and the services provided to fulfill the requirements of each pillar.

CloudOps pillars

While planning your CloudOps model, you need to take a 360-degree look. You want to provision and operate your environment for business agility and governance control. Establishing a CloudOps model, regardless of your cloud migration journey, helps you attain consistent governance and efficient operations across different infrastructure environments. This helps free up critical resources to deliver business outcomes and time-to-market faster while improving safety, ease, efficiency, and cost control. The following diagram shows the key pillars of cloud operation for complete coverage of your IT workload automation.

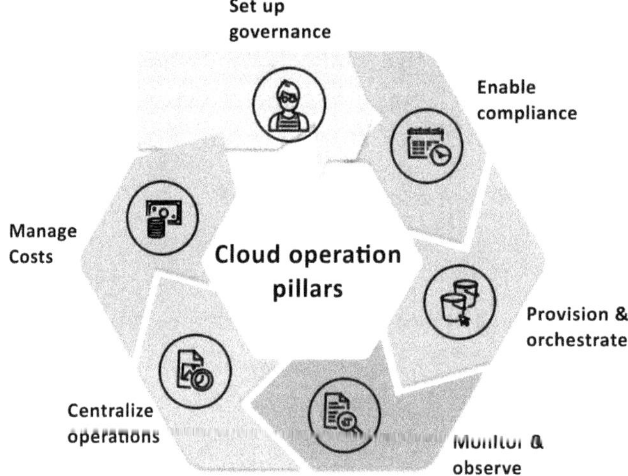

Figure 9.1: The pillars of CloudOps

As shown in the preceding diagram, the following are the key pillars of CloudOps:

1. **Set up Governance**: Set up a well-architected, multi-account AWS environment with guardrails to build the foundation for governance. AWS environments with a Well-Architected Framework checklist ensure you have covered all best practices to monitor and set alerts on your environment for security, operational excellence, cost, reliability, and performance.
2. **Enable Compliance**: Continuously monitor compliance and configurations for your resources, remediate failures in an automated fashion, and gather evidence for audits.
3. **Provision & Orchestrate**: Speed up application and resource provisioning with **infrastructure-as-code** (**IaC**) while maintaining consistency and compliance.

4. **Monitor & Observe**: Measure and manage your applications and resources to identify and resolve issues quickly.
5. **Centralize Operations**: Take seamless and automated operational actions across your entire application portfolio while maintaining safety, security, and compliance.
6. **Manage Costs**: Helps manage costs with transparency, control, regular forecasting, and optimization, thus enabling businesses to achieve greater financial efficiency and transform their operations.

Let's look at what each of these pillars helps you to achieve in your efforts to enable governance in cloud environments. You will also learn the AWS services that predominantly fulfill the requirement of each pillar.

First pillar – Set up governance

The first and the best place to start is by laying a very strong foundation for your governance. In the AWS environment, it begins by setting up a well-architected, multi-account AWS environment and setting up guardrails in each account. You learned about the Well-Architected Framework in *Chapter 2, Understanding the AWS Well-Architected Framework and Getting Certified*, where you saw that AWS has a comprehensive checklist to make sure your environment is set up properly to monitor cost, security, performance, reliability, and high availability. You can refer to AWS's well-architected labs here at `https://www.wellarchitectedlabs.com/`, which provide a very comprehensive, practical, hands-on guide to enable those guardrails against each well-architected pillar. The environment you build must be secure and extensible so that you don't halt experimentation and innovation as you grow your footprint on AWS. You need it to scale with your usage.

Your business needs to evolve continuously, so you should keep yourself from a single mode of architecting and operating in AWS. Most customers' environments don't remain static. They tend to grow with their business. You want to ensure your landing zone grows with your business without encumbrance while adhering to organizational policies. AWS Landing Zone is an offering that assists clients in swiftly configuring a secure and multi-account AWS environment, built around AWS's industry-leading practices. The solution delivers a preconfigured and secure infrastructure that encompasses key services, standardized AWS account architecture, and robust security controls. The goal of Landing Zone is to provide a secure, well-architected multi-account environment that serves as a starting point for new AWS accounts. It helps customers get started with AWS faster by providing a set of reusable blueprints for common patterns and practices, such as account VPCs, security controls, and identity and access management.

You need a well-defined AWS environment to accommodate the following needs:

- **Many Teams**: Multiple teams could be in the same account, overstepping one another.
- **Isolation**: Each team could have different security needs and want to isolate themselves from one another with a different security profile.
- **Security Controls**: Different applications might have different controls around them to address security and compliance. For example, talking to an auditor is far easier than pointing to a single account hosting the PCI solution. But even within an organization, security controls provide the ability to isolate certain things based on security isolation needs.
- **Business Process**: There are completely different **business units** (**BUs**) or products. For example, the Sales BU is different from the HR BU with an entirely different business process.
- **Billing**: An account is the primary way to divide items at a billing level. Each AWS account is billed separately and has its own set of resources and associated charges. This means that if you have multiple accounts within an organization, each account will have its own billing and cost allocation data.

To enable account control, AWS provides **AWS Organizations** that help you to establish a multi-account structure for centralized governance. You can use it to establish granular control over your AWS accounts, manage across accounts easily, and apply policies as broadly or as narrowly as you need. In the previous chapter, *Chapter 8, Best Practices for Application Security, Identity, and Compliance*, you learned about AWS Organizations.

For automated setup, AWS provides **AWS Control Tower**, a self-service solution to set up and govern a secure, compliant multi-account AWS environment. It abstracts multiple AWS services under the covers, so you can use it to set up your environment, based on best practices, without needing a lot of AWS knowledge. AWS Control Tower provides the following benefits:

- Automate the setup of your landing zone based on best-practice blueprints
- Apply guardrails for ongoing governance over your AWS workloads
- Automate your account provisioning workflow with an account factory
- Get dashboard visibility into your organizational units, accounts, and guardrails

You learned about AWS Control Tower in the previous chapter, *Chapter 8, Best Practices for Application Security, Identity, and Compliance.*

AWS professional services provide AWS **Landing Zone Accelerator** (**LZA**), which is a set of tools and resources provided by AWS to help customers accelerate the deployment of a secure, multi-account AWS environment.

LZA builds on top of the AWS Landing Zone service, which provides a pre-built, opinionated framework for setting up a secure, multi-account environment.

LZA provides a modular set of landing zone components that can be customized to meet specific requirements and leverages automation to speed up the deployment process. It also provides access to AWS experts who can provide guidance and best practices to help ensure a successful deployment. You can learn more about LZA by referring AWS user guide here: `https://aws.amazon.com/solutions/implementations/landing-zone-accelerator-on-aws/`.

LZA is designed to accelerate the process of setting up a landing zone for workloads that are migrating to AWS. LZA provides a modular set of landing zone components that can be customized to meet specific requirements and leverages automation to speed up the deployment process. This makes LZA a good fit for customers who need to set up a landing zone quickly and want more control over the individual components of their environment.

On the other hand, Control Tower is designed to help customers set up and govern a multi-account AWS environment. Control Tower provides a pre-built set of rules and policies to enforce governance and security best practices across multiple AWS accounts. CT also provides a central dashboard for managing and monitoring multiple accounts, making it easier for customers to maintain governance and compliance across their environment. This makes CT a good fit for customers who need to manage multiple AWS accounts and want a pre-built set of governance policies to enforce best practices.

It is extremely important to have the correct foundation when you are starting with your cloud journey. AWS services like Landing Zone and Control Tower, in combination with the Well-Architected Framework, help you with an automated way to establish the right environment. The teams building this out are not the bottleneck and enable you to be flexible in your approach and know that you might need new accounts, processes, or isolation solutions. That flexibility is what allows us to succeed in the long term. After setting up governance, you must ensure your applications meet compliance requirements. Let's learn more about automating compliance.

Second pillar – Managing Configuration, Compliance, and Audit

As you migrate workloads to the cloud, you need to know that you can maintain cloud compliance and get assurance for your workloads. Once compliance mechanisms and processes are in place, you can empower your development teams to build and innovate while having peace of mind that they are staying compliant.

A resource inventory helps you maintain environment configurations, track change history, depend on one another, and ensure your resources are correctly configured. Once you establish proper configurations, you want to be able to audit, manage, and remediate them quickly.

How many hours do you spend today collecting evidence in response to an audit? Whether internal or external? Wouldn't it be easier if you were able to keep a running log of all auditable events and remediation actions? And that's where AWS configuration, compliance, and auditing tools come in. You must continuously monitor configuration and compliance changes within your AWS environment and keep a running audit log to get visibility into your organization's resource configurations.

Many customers follow the **Institute of Internal Auditors (IIA)** guidance for the three lines of defense:

- **1st Line**: *How to automate compliance management and manage risk* – The implementation of AWS CloudTrail, AWS Config, AWS Control Tower, and AWS License Manager can aid in the automation of compliance management and risk mitigation within an AWS environment.
- **2nd Line**: *How to implement continuous oversight and oversee risk* – By utilizing Amazon CloudWatch and AWS Security Hub, it is possible to understand the operational health and security status of AWS accounts.
- **3rd Line**: *How to assess and independently gather assurance of risk management* – AWS Audit Manager helps assess their security, change management, and software licensing controls.

You learned about AWS Security Hub and Control Tower in the previous chapter, *Chapter 8*, *Best Practices for Application Security, Identity, and Compliance*. Let's learn about the other services, depending on mentioned above for managing cloud audits and compliance. You can use a combination of these services your IT workload needs, to automate configuration, compliance, and audit.

AWS CloudTrail

In AWS, all interactions with AWS services and resources are handled through AWS API calls, and these API calls are monitored and logged by AWS CloudTrail. AWS CloudTrail records all API calls made in your AWS account and provides a complete history of all user activity and API usage. This information can be used for security analysis, compliance auditing, and troubleshooting.

CloudTrail stores all generated log files in an Amazon S3 bucket that you define. These log files are encrypted using **Amazon S3 server-side encryption (SSE)**, which provides an additional layer of security for your logs. It's also worth noting that CloudTrail logs all API calls, regardless of whether they come directly from a user or on behalf of a user by an AWS service.

This lets you understand all API activity in your AWS environment, which can be crucial for security and compliance purposes.

AWS CloudTrail is a service that enables governance, compliance, operations, and risk auditing for AWS accounts by logging and monitoring account activity related to actions across the AWS infrastructure. By using CloudTrail, you can continuously monitor and retain logs of all account activity, providing you with a complete history of your AWS account's event history. This event history includes actions taken through the AWS Management Console, AWS SDKs, command-line tools, and other AWS services.

These logs can be used to aid in governance, compliance, and risk management, providing a clear record of activity across your AWS infrastructure. With CloudTrail, you can also create custom alerts and notifications to help you identify and respond to potential security issues and compliance risks in real time.

Once enabled, CloudTrail will automatically track all Management Events at no charge. Then, you also have several different data event sources you can opt into depending on your application and compliance needs. This event history is another source of observability data, simplifying security analysis, resource change tracking, and troubleshooting. You can learn more about AWS CloudTrail by visiting the AWS page here: `https://aws.amazon.com/cloudtrail/`.

AWS Config

You learned about AWS Config in *Chapter 5, Storage in AWS – Choosing the Right Tool for the Job*, in the context of S3. AWS Config records and evaluates your AWS resources configuration. AWS Config performs the following activities for AWS resources: record, evaluate, and visualize. Let's learn about these in more detail in the context of CloudOps:

Record

- **Configuration history of AWS resources**: AWS Config records the details of changes made to your AWS resources, providing you with a configuration history timeline. This enables you to track any changes made to a resource's configuration at any time in the past.
- **Resource relationship tracking**: AWS Config can discover, map, and track relationships between AWS resources in your account. For example, if a new **Amazon Elastic Compute Cloud (Amazon EC2)** security group is associated with an Amazon EC2 instance, AWS Config will record the updated configurations of both the Amazon EC2 security group and the Amazon EC2 instance.

- **Configuration history of software**: AWS Config can also record software configuration changes within your Amazon EC2 instances and servers running on-premises or with other cloud providers. It provides a history of both OS and system-level configuration changes and infrastructure configuration changes recorded for Amazon EC2 instances.

Evaluate

- **Configurable and customizable rules**: Assess your resource configurations and resource changes for compliance against built-in or custom rules and automate the remediation of non-compliant resources. You can customize pre-built rules provided by AWS Config or create your own custom rules with AWS Lambda to define your internal guidelines and best practices for resource configurations.
- **Conformance packs**: Simplifies organization-wide deployment and reporting of compliance. It deploys a pack of config rules and remediation actions to your AWS Organization.
- **Automatic remediation** enables you to remediate non-compliant resources using Systems Manager Automation documents.

Visualize

- **Cloud governance dashboard**: This feature provides a visual dashboard that lets you easily identify non-compliant resources and take the necessary corrective action. You can customize the dashboard to monitor resources based on cost and security.
- **Multi-account, multi-region data aggregation**: AWS Config allows you to aggregate data from multiple AWS accounts and regions, providing you with a centralized view of your resources and their compliance status with AWS Config rules. This feature is particularly useful for enterprise-scale organizations.
- **Configuration snapshots**: AWS Config can take snapshots of your resource configurations at specific points in time. This allows you to quickly identify changes to your resources and compare their configurations across different points in time.

Here is an example AWS Config rule that checks whether Amazon EC2 instances have an associated security group with inbound rules that allow traffic on port 22 (SSH):

```
{
  "Name": "ec2-security-group-has-inbound-rules-on-port-22",
  "Description": "Checks whether the security group associated with an EC2 
instance has inbound rules that allow traffic on port 22",
```

```
  "Scope": {
    "ComplianceResourceTypes": [
      "AWS::EC2::Instance"
    ]
  },
  "Source": {
    "Owner": "AWS",
    "SourceIdentifier": "EC2_INSTANCE_HAS_SECURITY_GROUP_WITH_INBOUND_
RULES_ON_PORT_22"
  },
  "InputParameters": "{\"allowedProtocols\":\"tcp\",\"portNumber\":22}"
}
```

This rule checks whether the security group associated with each Amazon EC2 instance has inbound rules that allow traffic on port 22. If any instances do not have such a security group, they will be flagged as non-compliant.

AWS Config help to keep AWS resources compliant. You can learn more about AWS Config by visiting the AWS page here: `https://aws.amazon.com/config/`. Let's look at the next service for tracking and auditing licenses.

AWS License Manager

AWS License Manager is a one-stop solution for managing licenses from various software vendors across hybrid environments. This helps you to stay compliant within your organizational structure and processes. There are no additional charges for using AWS License Manager.

AWS License Manager is targeted at IT administrators who manage licenses and software assets. This includes license administrators, procurement administrators, or asset managers who are responsible for managing license true-ups and vendor audits. In contrast, users spin up instances and use the licensed software on those instances. With AWS License Manager, the administrators can now easily manage licenses. Users in the organization are not required to do additional work to manage licenses and can focus on business as usual.

You can complete your licensing true-ups and audits using AWS License Manager. Administrators start by creating rules based on their enterprise agreements. They can do this using the AWS Management Console, CLI, or API. Furthermore, administrators can enforce licensing rules by attaching them to instance launches. Once rules are enforced, the service automatically keeps track of instances as users spin them up and down.

The organization stays compliant based on its license terms, and administrators can discover users' software after spinning up instances. Finally, administrators can keep track of usage through the AWS License Manager's built-in dashboard.

AWS License Manager automatically keeps track of instance launches, and the built-in dashboard is populated. Administrators can view usage limit alerts and take actions such as procuring more licenses as needed. When there is an upcoming license true-up or audit, administrators no longer have to determine which instances use which licenses. With AWS License Manager's built-in dashboard, figuring out how many licenses they are using and which resources are using them is no longer a challenge. You can learn more about AWS License Manager by visiting the AWS page here: `https://aws.amazon.com/license-manager/`.

Amazon CloudWatch

CloudWatch is one of the essential services for running your cloud operation. It allows you to monitor your AWS workload and take action based on alerts. In addition, CloudWatch provides observability for your AWS resources on a single platform across applications and infrastructure.

Amazon CloudWatch is a powerful monitoring service that is designed to help you optimize your AWS resources and applications. It offers a wide range of capabilities, including:

- **Data and operational insights**: CloudWatch provides valuable insights into the performance and health of your AWS resources and applications. With CloudWatch, you can collect and track metrics, monitor log files, and set alarms.
- **Resource monitoring**: CloudWatch can monitor a variety of AWS resources, including Amazon EC2 instances, Amazon S3 buckets, and Amazon RDS instances. This allows you to quickly identify and troubleshoot any issues that arise.
- **Custom metrics**: CloudWatch allows you to create custom metrics based on the data generated by your applications. This provides you with greater flexibility and control over the monitoring process.
- **Log monitoring**: CloudWatch can also monitor the log files generated by your applications. This enables you to quickly identify and troubleshoot any issues that are related to your application code.

Amazon CloudWatch is an essential tool for anyone running applications on the AWS cloud platform. Its powerful monitoring capabilities can help you optimize your resources, improve application performance, and maintain the operational health of your systems.

CloudWatch alarms are a powerful feature that enable you to receive notifications or automate actions based on the rules you define. With CloudWatch alarms, you can monitor a wide range of metrics and set up alerts that notify you when certain conditions are met. For example, you can send an email alert to the admin whenever the average network latency of an Amazon RDS database exceeds 10 seconds or when the CPU usage of an Amazon EC2 instance falls below 10%. You can also create more complex alarms that automatically trigger actions, such as launching additional instances to handle increased traffic or scaling down resources during periods of low demand.

CloudWatch alarms provide a flexible and customizable way to monitor your AWS resources and take automated actions based on your specific needs. Whether you need to monitor resource utilization, application performance, or other key metrics, CloudWatch alarms can help you stay on top of your cloud infrastructure and ensure that it is always running at peak performance.

In addition, CloudWatch provides data for the past two weeks so that you can access historical data for analysis of past events. It also integrates with other AWS services, such as Amazon EC2 Auto Scaling, Amazon SNS, and AWS Lambda, enabling you to use CloudWatch to react to changes in your resources and applications.

Some key features of CloudWatch include the following:

- **Metrics:** CloudWatch allows you to collect metrics for your resources and applications, such as CPU usage, network traffic, and the disk reads/writes. You can view these metrics in the CloudWatch console or use the CloudWatch API to retrieve them programmatically.
- **Alarms:** You can set alarms in CloudWatch to be notified when certain thresholds are breached. For example, you can schedule an alarm to send an email or SMS message to you if the CPU usage on one of your Amazon EC2 instances exceeds a certain threshold.
- **Logs:** CloudWatch allows storing and accessing your log files in a centralized location. You can use CloudWatch Logs Insights to search and analyze your log data or use CloudWatch Logs to export your log data to third-party tools for further analysis.
- **Dashboards:** You can use CloudWatch dashboards to create custom views of your metrics and log data to quickly get an overview of your system's health and performance.

Amazon CloudWatch is a powerful and flexible monitoring service that can help you ensure the availability, performance, and efficiency of your AWS resources and applications.

Amazon CloudWatch Events is a service that allows you to respond to changes in state in your AWS resources in real time. With CloudWatch Events, you can monitor for operational changes in your resources and automatically trigger actions based on those changes. For example, you can create a CloudWatch Events rule that triggers an AWS Lambda function whenever a new Amazon EC2 instance is launched in your account. This Lambda function can perform actions like tagging the instance, configuring its security groups, or starting a set of preconfigured applications on the instance.

CloudWatch Events allows you to react to operational changes in your AWS resources quickly and efficiently. Automating your response to these events can save time and reduce the risk of manual errors. With CloudWatch Events, you can easily create rules that define the conditions that trigger your actions and specify the targets for executing those actions.

CloudWatch Events rules enable you to match event patterns and take actions in response to those patterns. A rule can have one or more event patterns, and you can specify the type of action that CloudWatch Events takes when it detects a pattern. For example, you can set up a rule to send an email message when a new Amazon EC2 instance is launched or to stop an Amazon EC2 instance when the CPU utilization is too high.

CloudWatch Events can be used to schedule automated actions that self-trigger at a specific time or when a specified event occurs. For example, you can use CloudWatch Events to schedule the automatic stopping of Amazon EC2 instances so that you don't incur charges for no longer needed instances. You can learn more about AWS CloudWatch by visiting the AWS page here: `https://aws.amazon.com/cloudwatch/`.

Amazon EventBridge

Amazon EventBridge is a fully-managed, serverless event bus service that simplifies connecting your applications, integrated SaaS applications, and AWS services. By creating event-driven architectures, EventBridge allows various applications and services to communicate with each other in a flexible and scalable manner.

The following screenshot shows an EventBridge rule set up to send information to Elasticsearch using Lambda for an instance start failure during autoscaling. This Lambda function then sends information to Elasticsearch, allowing you to analyze and troubleshoot the failure.

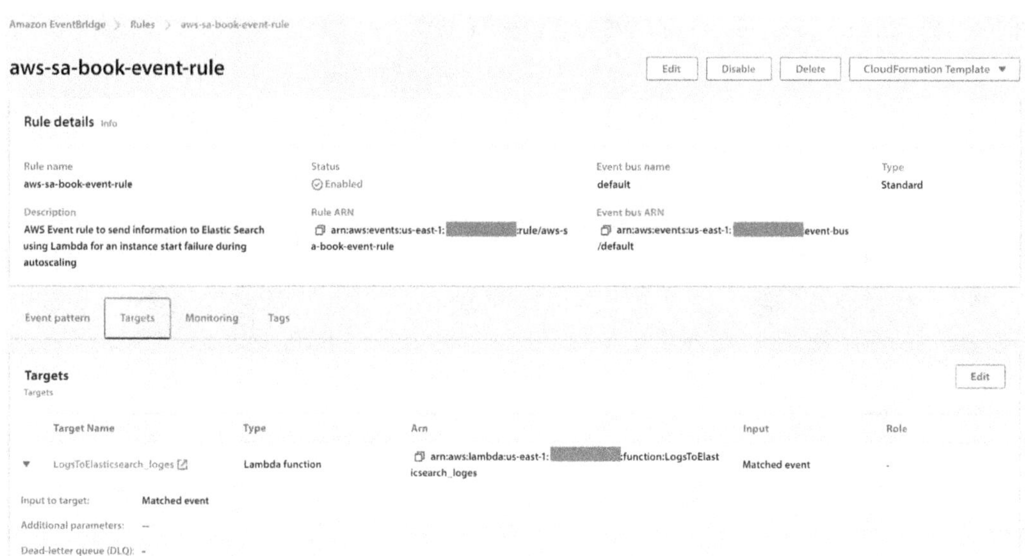

Figure 9.2: An AWS EventBridge rule for an autoscaling failure

EventBridge simplifies the setup and management of rules that dictate event routing and processing, enabling you to create complex and resilient architectures for your applications. With EventBridge, you can easily build event-driven applications and receive notifications about events from AWS DevOps services and automation application deployment pipelines. You can explore more about EventBridge by visiting the AWS page here: `https://aws.amazon.com/eventbridge/`.

AWS Audit Manager

The audit Manager continuously accesses risk and compliance controls and provides the following benefits.

- Easily map your AWS usage to controls: Use pre-built compliance frameworks or build custom frameworks to collect evidence for compliance controls.
- Save time with an automated collection of evidence across accounts: Focus on reviewing the relevant evidence to ensure your controls are working as intended.
- Be continually prepared to produce audit-ready reports: Evidence is continuously collected and organized by control so you can effortlessly search, filter, and review evidence to ensure controls are working as intended.
- Ensure assessment report and evidence integrity: When it is time for an audit, build assessment reports with evidence that has been continuously collected, securely stored, and remains unaltered.

Below you can find a screenshot of AWS Audit Manager:

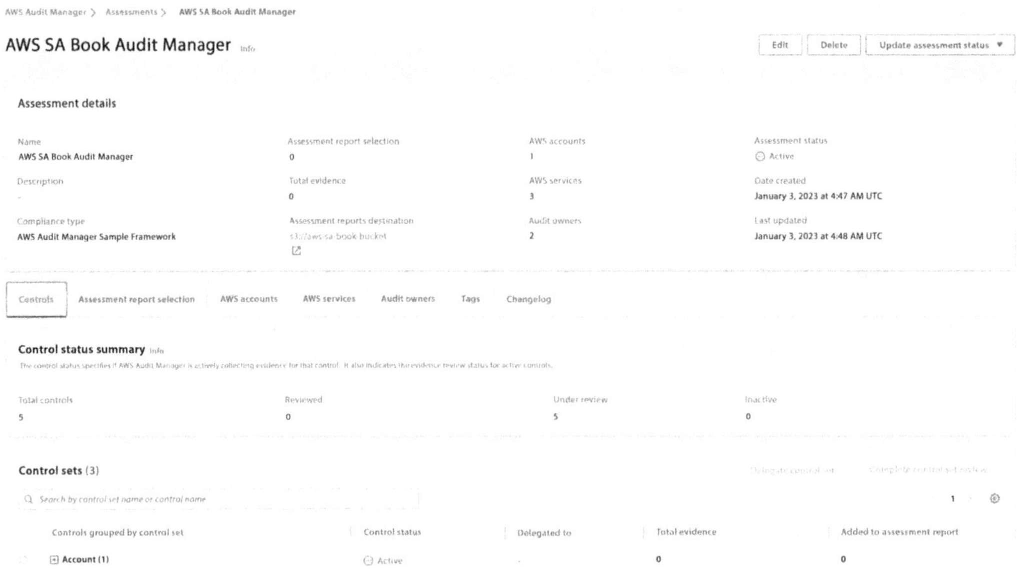

Figure 9.3: AWS Audit Manager

You can learn more about AWS Audit Manager by visiting the AWS page here: `https://aws.amazon.com/audit-manager/`.

AWS Systems Manager

AWS Systems Manager is a management service that allows you to take actions on your AWS resources as necessary. It provides you with a quick view of operational data for groups of resources, making it easy to detect any issues that could impact applications that rely on those resources. You can group resources by various criteria, such as applications, application layers, or production vs. development environments. Systems Manager displays operational data for your resource groups on a single dashboard, eliminating the need to switch between different AWS consoles. For example, you can create a resource group for an application that uses Amazon EC2, Amazon S3, and Amazon RDS. Systems Manager can check for software changes installed on your Amazon EC2 instances, changes in your S3 objects, or stopped database instances.

The following screenshot shows a configuration deployment status for servers in a given AWS account:

Figure 9.4: AWS Systems Manager host management

AWS Systems Manager provides detailed insights into the current state of your resource groups, allowing you to understand and control them quickly. The Systems Manager Explorer and Inventory dashboards offer various tools to view system configurations, such as operating system patch levels, software installations, and application configurations. Moreover, it is integrated with AWS Config, allowing you to track changes across your resources over time.

AWS Systems Manager offers several features to help maintain security and compliance in your environment. It can scan your instances against your patch, configuration, and custom policies, helping you identify and address potential security issues. With Systems Manager, you can define patch baselines, ensure that your anti-virus definitions are up-to-date, and enforce firewall policies, among other things. Systems Manager also enables you to manage your servers at scale remotely without manually logging in to each server. This feature can be especially helpful in large-scale environments, where managing resources individually can be time-consuming and error-prone.

In addition, Systems Manager provides a centralized store for managing your configuration data, including plain text items such as database strings and secrets like passwords. By separating your secrets and configuration data from your code, you can help reduce the risk of security breaches and simplify your development and deployment processes.

You can use System Manager to achieve all components of the second pillar as it provides a one-stop shop, as shown in the left-hand navigation bar in the below screenshot:

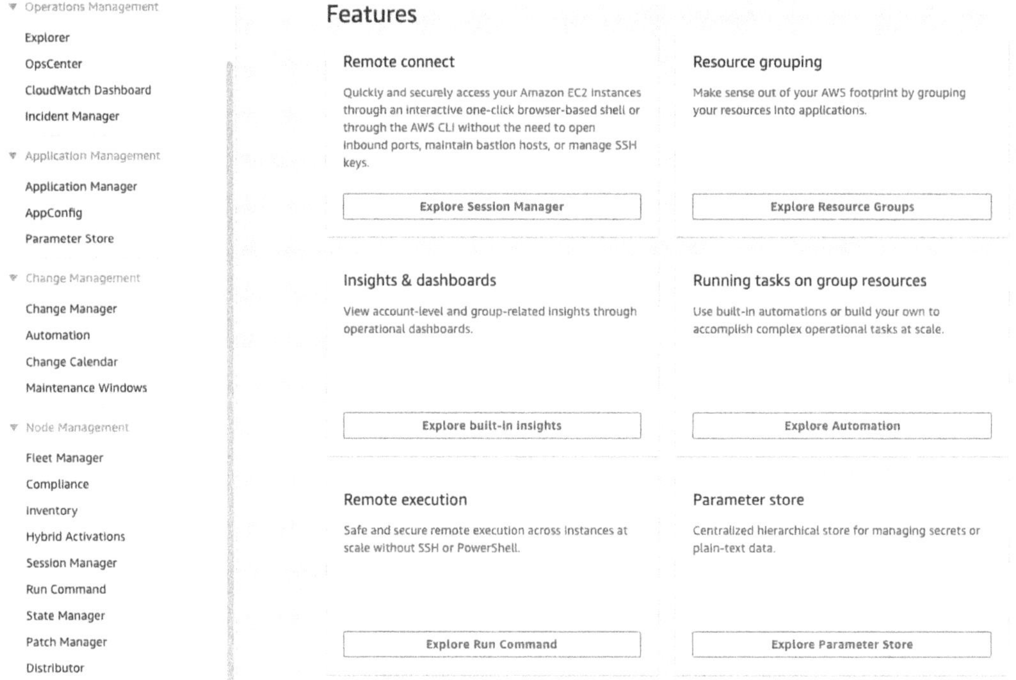

Figure 9.5: AWS Systems Manager for CloudOps monitoring and audit

AWS Systems Manager is the hub of your operation for managing all your AWS applications and resources along with your on-premise environments, keeping everything in one place for easy monitoring and auditing. AWS has done a great job explaining how Systems Manager works, which you can learn about by referring to this link: `https://docs.aws.amazon.com/systems-manager/latest/userguide/what-is-systems-manager.html`.

In this section, you learned about managing cloud configuration and compliance along with various AWS services that can help to achieve that. Now, let's learn about the following step: provision and orchestration.

Third pillar – Provisioning & orchestration

Once you have set up the environment, you need to speed up the provisioning and orchestration of your applications and any associated resources in a repeatable and immutable fashion.

Let's look at history; in the old days, infrastructure deployment started with manual deployments, where you used wikis and playbooks, which were sometimes outdated. Most of us can relate to a project where we had to use them. They were sometimes outdated, or some details needed to be mentioned, and we encountered situations during the provisioning which needed to be stated in the manual. The best way to solve the problem was to ask the person who did it the last few times in the past and hopes that this person was not on vacation and still working at the company!

The next step was scripting everything in Bash. It worked well until the complexity was too great because Bash was not designed to build complex deployment frameworks, so it was hard to maintain. The best advice was: it worked the last time, don't touch it!

As digital transformation increasingly occurs within an organization, more applications either move to or are built on the cloud. These applications themselves solve complex problems and require complex infrastructure. Teams need more tools to manage this complexity, be productive, and innovate. You need highly specialized tools to manage the applications and to be able to choose from a varied set of tools based on their use cases. Managing infrastructure is a big part of managing cloud complexity, and one of the ways to manage infrastructure is by treating infrastructure as code.

Infrastructure-as-code (**IaC**) templates help you to model and provision resources, whether AWS-native, third-party or open source, and applications on AWS and on-premises. So, you can speed up application and resource provisioning while improving consistency and compliance. For example, a developer wants to provision an S3 bucket that meets their company's security requirements. They will no longer have to dig through documentation to determine what bucket resource properties to set or how to set them. Instead, they can reuse a pre-built Secure S3 bucket module to provision a bucket quickly while automatically aligning with their company's requirements.

A cloud application typically consists of many components: networking (i.e., traffic gateways), compute (Amazon EC2, containers), databases, streams, security groups, users, roles, etc. All these servers and resources are the infrastructure components of your cloud application. Managing cloud applications involves managing the life cycle of their resources: create, update, or delete. By codifying your infrastructure, you can manage your infrastructure code in a way that is similar to your application code. This means that you can use a code editor to create it, store it in a version control system, and collaborate with your team members before deploying it to production. The advantages of using IaC are numerous, including:

- A single source of truth for deploying the entire stack.
- The ability to replicate, redeploy, and repurpose your infrastructure.

- The ability to version control both your infrastructure and your application code.
- Automatic rollback to the previous working state in case of failures.
- The ability to build and test your infrastructure as part of your CI/CD pipeline.

AWS offers multiple services that help customers manage their infrastructure. AWS CloudFormation is the provisioning engine. It helps speed up cloud provisioning with IaC.

AWS Service Catalog allows organizations to create and maintain a list of IT services authorized to be used on the AWS platform. These lists can include everything from VM images, servers, software, and databases to complete multi-tier application architectures. Users can then browse and launch these pre-approved IT services through a self-service portal, which helps ensure that they are using approved resources that meet compliance and security requirements. Additionally, administrators can set up workflows to automatically provision resources and control access and permissions to specific resources within the catalog.

You can choose to combine these services as per your workload needs. Let's learn about these services in more detail.

AWS CloudFormation

CloudFormation is a tool that supports the implementation of IaC. With CloudFormation, you can write your IaC using the CloudFormation template language, available in YAML and JSON formats. You can start from scratch or leverage any of the pre-existing sample templates to create your infrastructure. You can use the CloudFormation service through a web-based console, command-line tools, or APIs to create a stack based on your template code. Once you have defined your stack and resources in the template, CloudFormation provisions and configures them accordingly.

CloudFormation helps you model, provision, and manage AWS resources. It allows you to use a template to create and delete multiple related AWS resources in a predictable and consistent way. Here is a simple example of a CloudFormation template written in YAML syntax:

```
---
AWSTemplateFormatVersion: '2010-09-09'
Resources:
  MyEC2Instance:
    Type: AWS::EC2::Instance
    Properties:
      ImageId: ami-101013
      InstanceType: m4.xlarge
```

```
      KeyName: gen-key-pair
      SecurityGroups:
        - !Ref ServerSecurityGroup
  ServerSecurityGroup:
    Type: AWS::EC2::SecurityGroup
    Properties:
      GroupDescription: Allow ssh access
      SecurityGroupIngress:
        - IpProtocol: tcp
          FromPort: '22'
          ToPort: '22'
          CidrIp: 10.1.1.16/0
```

This template creates an Amazon EC2 instance with a security group that allows incoming SSH connections. The security group is created first and then referenced when creating the Amazon EC2 instance.

To use this template, save it to a file (e.g., `servertemplate.yml`) and then use the AWS CLI to create a stack:

```
aws cloudformation create-stack --stack-name sa-book-stack --template-body
file://servertemplate.yml
```

You can then use the AWS Management Console, the AWS CLI, or the CloudFormation API to monitor the progress of the stack creation. Once the stack is created, you will have an Amazon EC2 instance running in your AWS account. You can make changes to the stack by updating the template and using the `update-stack` command. You can learn more about AWS CloudFormation by visiting the AWS page here: `https://aws.amazon.com/cloudformation/`.

AWS Service Catalog

AWS Service Catalog provides a centralized platform to manage catalogs of IT services, ensuring adherence to corporate standards and compliance. Organizations can easily control IT service availability, configurations, and access permissions by individual, group, department, or cost center. The platform also simplifies the process of finding and deploying approved IT services for employees. Organizations can define their catalog of AWS services and AWS Marketplace software and make them available for their employees through a self-service portal.

AWS Service Management Connectors allow **IT service management** (**ITSM**) administrators to enhance the governance of provisioned AWS and third-party products.

For instance, by integrating with AWS Service Catalog, ServiceNow and Jira Service Desk can request, provision, and manage AWS and third-party services and resources for their users, streamlining the ITSM process.

AWS Service Catalog AppRegistry is a centralized repository that enables organizations to manage and govern their application resources on AWS. It provides a single place for collecting and managing application metadata, including their name, owner, purpose, and associated resources. This information can be used to improve application visibility and governance and to enable better collaboration between teams that work on different parts of the application stack. With AppRegistry, you can track and manage all your applications' resources, including AWS resources, third-party software, and external resources such as domain names or IP addresses. The following screenshot shows an app registry in the system catalog:

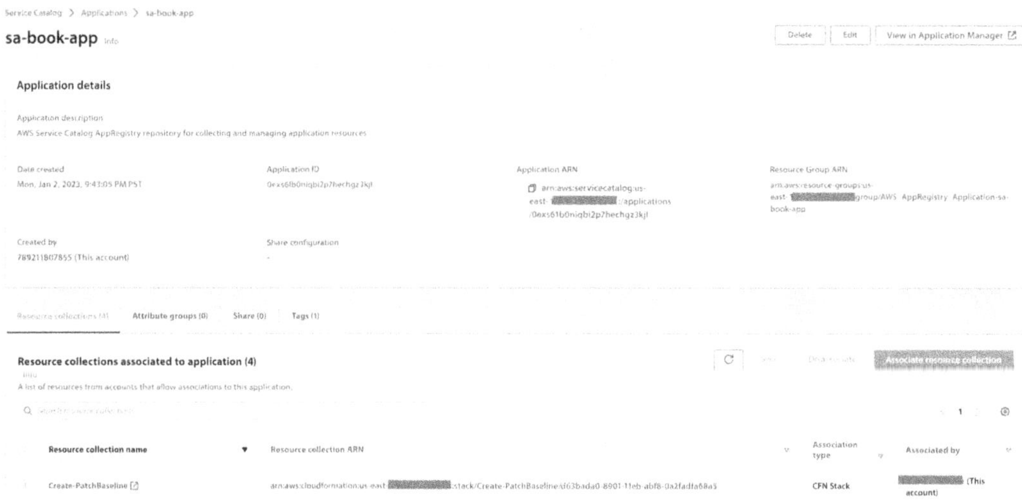

Figure 9.6: AWS System Catalog app registry

With AppRegistry, you can define your application metadata, such as ownership, data sensitivity, and cost centers, and include a reference to your application within the infrastructure code. This helps business stakeholders have up-to-date information about the application's contents and metadata. In addition, AppRegistry provides a central place to track and manage changes to your application resources, helping you maintain a comprehensive view of your applications and their dependencies. You can learn more about AWS Service Catalog by visiting the AWS page here: `https://aws.amazon.com/servicecatalog/`.

AWS Proton

AWS Proton is a managed application deployment service that allows developers to quickly and easily deploy and manage container and serverless applications on AWS. It provides a fully managed, opinionated environment for defining, deploying, and managing applications. With Proton, developers can focus on writing code and building applications while the service handles the underlying infrastructure and deployment workflows. This helps to accelerate the development process, reduce the risk of errors, and improve overall application quality.

AWS provides sample Proton templates that help you start building your application's infrastructure. You can fork those samples using AWS samples code link: (`https://github.com/aws-samples/aws-proton-cloudformation-sample-templates`) and refer to them while building the Proton environment.

AWS Proton can help you update out-of-date applications with a single click when you adopt a new feature or best practice. This helps ensure that your applications remain up-to-date and compliant with industry standards. Additionally, by providing a consistent architecture across your organization, Proton helps improve collaboration and reduces the risk of errors or misconfigurations. You can learn more about AWS Proton by visiting the AWS page here: `https://aws.amazon.com/proton/`.

AWS Cloud Development Kit (CDK)

The AWS CDK is an open-source software development framework that enables developers to define cloud infrastructure and resources using familiar programming languages such as TypeScript, JavaScript, Python, Java, and C#. It provisions and deploys the infrastructure using AWS CloudFormation, providing the benefits of IaC.

With CDK, you will work much faster because you are using your familiar language, concepts, classes, and methods without a context switch. You also have all the tool support from the programming language, such as autocomplete, inline documentation, tests, and a debugger. The most important part is that you can build your abstractions and components of the infrastructure and application. AWS provides many default values, so there is no need to read a lot of documentation; you can start quickly.

The AWS CDK consists of three main components: the core framework, the AWS-construct library, and the CLI. The core framework enables you to define and organize your AWS infrastructure using high-level programming languages. You can create and structure apps that consist of one or multiple stacks. Stacks are the fundamental deployment unit in AWS CDK. They are a logical grouping of AWS resources that are provisioned and managed as a single unit. Each stack is mapped one-to-one to a CloudFormation stack and can be independently deployed, updated, or deleted.

It is good practice to divide resources into stacks with different life cycles: i.e., you would create one stack for network infrastructure such as a VPC, another stack would have an Elastic Container Service cluster, and yet another stack would be the application that is running in this cluster.

The AWS-constructed library in CDK is a collection of pre-built components designed by AWS for creating resources for specific services. This allows for decoupling libraries and using only the necessary dependencies in your project. The library is developed with best practices and security considerations in mind to provide an excellent developer experience, ease of use, and fast iteration cycles. The CDK CLI interacts with the core framework, helping to initialize project structure, inspect deployment differences, and deploy your project quickly to AWS. Here is an example of creating an Amazon S3 bucket using CDK in TypeScript:

```
import * as cdk from 'aws-cdk-lib';
import * as s3 from 'aws-cdk-lib/aws-s3';
class MyBookStack extends cdk.Stack {
  constructor(scope: CDK.App, id: string, props?: CDK.StackProps) {
    super(scope, id, props);
    new s3.Bucket(this, 'BookBucket', {
      bucketName: 'aws-sa-book-bucket',
      publicReadAccess: true
    });
  }
}
const app = new cdk.App();
new MyBookStack(app, 'MyBookStack');
app.synth();
```

This code defines a CDK stack with a single Amazon S3 bucket and synthesizes a CloudFormation template for the stack. You can then use the `cdk deploy` command to deploy the stack to your AWS account.

AWS CDK provides a paradigm shift in how you provision multiple environments. With CloudFormation, you can use one template with parameters for multiple environments, i.e., dev and test. But with CDK, you have a shift where multiple templates are generated for each environment, ending in different stacks. This decoupling helps us to contain and maintain differences between environments by having less expensive resources in the dev environment. You can learn more about AWS CDK by visiting the AWS page here: `https://aws.amazon.com/cdk/`.

AWS Amplify

AWS Amplify is a suite of specialized tools designed to help developers quickly build feature-rich, full-stack web and mobile applications on AWS. It allows developers to utilize a wide range of AWS services as their use cases evolve. With Amplify, developers can configure a backend for their web or mobile app, visually create a web frontend UI, connect the two, and manage app content without needing to access the AWS console. At a high level, AWS Amplify provides the following features, tools, and services:

- **Amplify Libraries**: Frontend developers can use purpose-built Amplify libraries for interacting with AWS services. You can use the case-centric Amplify Libraries for connecting frontend iOS, Android, web, and React Native apps to an AWS backend and UI components for auth, data, and storage. Customers can use Amplify Libraries to build a new app backend or connect an existing backend.
- **Amplify Hosting**: Amplify Hosting is a fully managed CI/CD service for modern web apps. It offers hundreds of global points of presence for fast and reliable hosting of static and server-side rendered apps that scale with your business needs. With Amplify Hosting, you can deploy updates to your web app on every code commit to the Git repository. The app is then deployed and hosted globally using CloudFront. Amplify Hosting supports modern web frameworks such as React, Angular, Vue, Next.js, Gatsby, Hugo, Jekyll, and more.
- **Amplify Studio**: Amplify Studio is a visual development environment that provides an abstraction layer on top of the Amplify CLI. It allows you to create full-stack apps on AWS by building an app backend, creating custom UI components, and connecting a UI to the app backend with minimal coding. With Amplify Studio, you can select from dozens of popular React components, such as buttons, forms, and marketing templates, and customize them to fit your style guide. You can also import UX designs from the popular design prototyping tool, Figma, as clean React code for seamless collaboration. Amplify Studio exports all UI and infrastructure artifacts as code so you can maintain complete control over your app design and behavior.

- **The Amplify CLI**: Provides flexibility and integration with existing CI/CD tools through the new Amplify extensibility features. The Amplify CLI allows frontend developers to set up backend resources in the cloud easily. It's designed to work with the Amplify JavaScript library and the AWS Mobile SDKs for iOS and Android. The Amplify CLI provisions and manages the mobile or web backend with guided workflows for common app use cases such as authentication, data, and storage on AWS. You can reconfigure Amplify-generated backend resources to optimize for specific use cases, leveraging the entire feature set of AWS, or modify Amplify deployment operations to comply with your enterprise DevOps guidelines.

Here's a code example of how to use AWS Amplify in a web application to store and retrieve data from a cloud database:

```
import { API, graphqlOperation } from 'aws-amplify'
// Add a new item to the cloud database
async function addItem(item) {
  const AddItemMutation = `mutation AddItem($item: ItemInput!) {
    addItem(item: $item) {
      id
      name
      description
    }
  }`
  const result = await API.graphql(graphqlOperation(AddItemMutation, {
item }))
  console.log(result)
}
// Retrieve a list of items from the cloud database
async function listItems() {
  const ListItemsQuery = `query ListItems {
    listItems {
      items {
        id
        name
        description
      }
    }
  }`
```

```
  const result = await API.graphql(graphqlOperation(ListItemsQuery))
  console.log(result)
}
```

The `API` object provided by Amplify enables you to call GraphQL operations to interact with the cloud database. The `addItem` function uses the `addItem` mutation to create a new item in the database, while the `listItems` function uses the `listItems` query to retrieve a list of items.

AWS Amplify ties into a broader array of tools and services provided by AWS. You can customize your Amplify toolkit and leverage AWS services' breadth and depth to service your modern application development needs. You can choose the services that suit your application and business requirements and scale confidently on AWS. You can learn more about AWS Amplify by visiting the AWS page here: `https://aws.amazon.com/amplify/`.

In this section, you were introduced to AWS CDK, which is a provisioning and orchestration solution that facilitates the consistent and repeatable provisioning of resources. By utilizing AWS CDK, you can scale your organization's infrastructure and applications on AWS in a sustainable manner. Additionally, AWS CDK allows you to create your infrastructure as code using programming languages. You can simplify and accelerate the governance and distribution of IaC templates using the AWS Service Catalog to create repeatable infrastructure and application patterns with best practices. Now let's learn about the next step to set up monitoring and observations from your applications.

Fourth pillar – Monitor & observe your applications

As the saying goes, you manage what you measure, so after you've provisioned your application, you have to be able to start measuring its health and performance. Monitoring and observability tools help to collect metrics, logs, traces, and event data. You can quickly identify and resolve application issues for serverless, containerized, or other applications built using microservices-based architectures.

AWS provides native monitoring, logging, alarming, and dashboards with CloudWatch and tracing through X-Ray. When deployed together, they provide the three pillars of an observability solution: metrics, logs, and traces. X-Ray (tracing) is fundamental to observability and is therefore included in the motions alongside CloudWatch. Furthermore, AWS provides open-source observability for Prometheus and Grafana and support for Open Telemetry. A well-defined monitoring and observability strategy implemented with CloudWatch and X-Ray provides insights and data to monitor and respond to your application's performance issues by providing a consolidated view of the operation.

The following are the key AWS services for observability and monitoring, which you can choose to use as per your workload needs or combine them together.

AWS CloudWatch helps you collect, view, and analyze metrics and set alarms to get notified when certain thresholds are breached. Here you can see a screenshot of the billing metrics dashboard in CloudWatch:

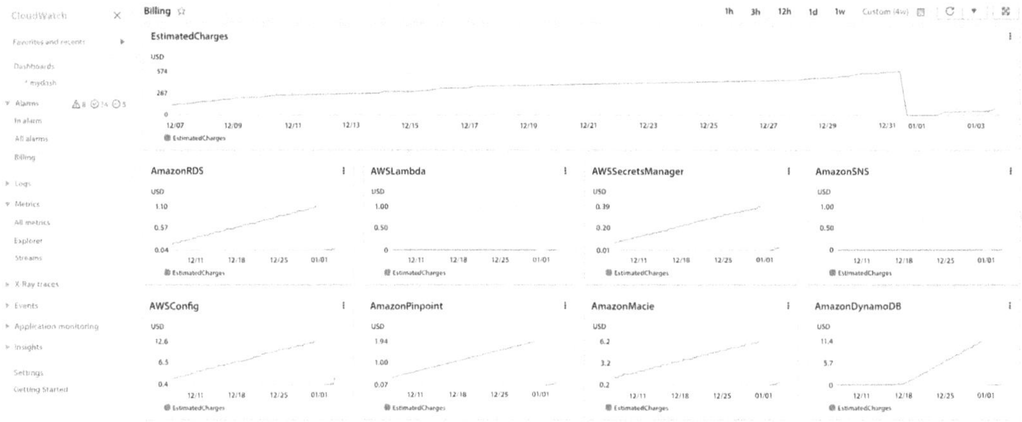

Figure 9.7: AWS CloudWatch billing metrics dashboard

You can also use CloudWatch to track log files from Amazon EC2 instances, Amazon RDS DB instances, and other resources and troubleshoot issues with your applications. You learned about AWS CloudWatch earlier in this chapter.

AWS X-Ray is a distributed tracing service that allows developers to analyze and debug their applications, especially those built using a microservices architecture. It helps identify performance bottlenecks and errors, allowing developers to optimize application performance and enhance the end-user experience.

It allows you to trace requests as they flow through your application and see the performance of each component of your application:

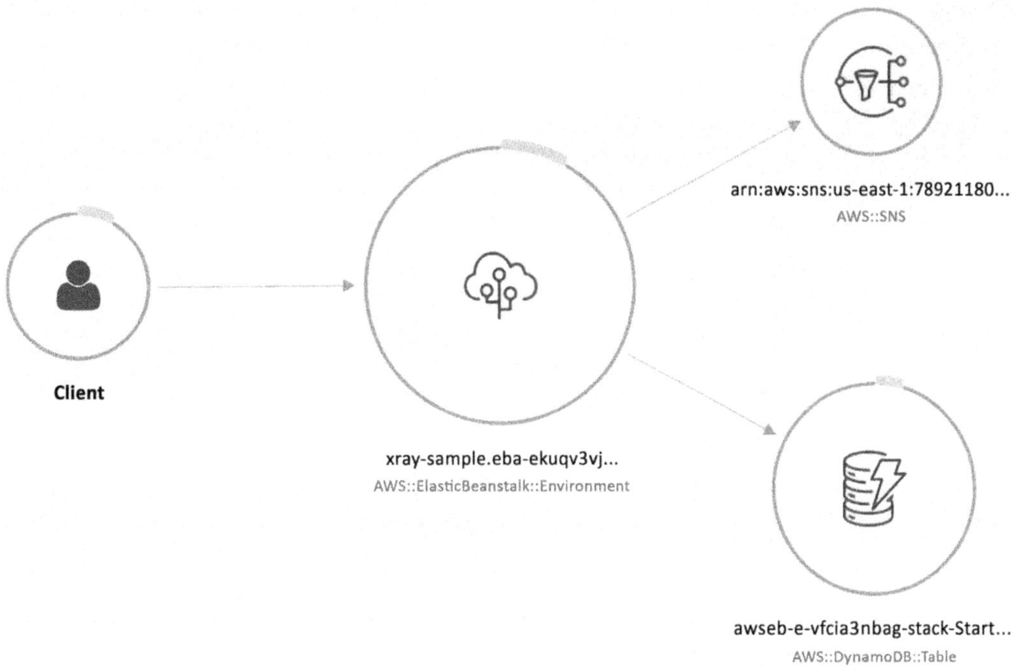

Figure 9.8: AWS X-Ray service map graph

In the AWS X-Ray console, you can view a trace of a request as it flows through your application and see the performance of each trace segment. You can also use the console to search for traces and analyze performance data for your application. To use AWS X-Ray, you first need to instrument your application code to send data to the X-Ray service. This can be done using one of the AWS SDKs or the X-Ray daemon. You can then view and analyze the data using the X-Ray console or the X-Ray API. You can learn more about AWS X-Ray by visiting the AWS page here: `https://aws.amazon.com/xray/`.

Amazon Managed Service for Prometheus (**AMSP**) is a fully managed service that makes it easy to run and scale Prometheus, an open-source monitoring and alerting system, in the cloud. AMSP automatically handles tasks such as scaling and maintenance, allowing you to focus on monitoring your applications. It also includes integration with other AWS services, such as Amazon CloudWatch and Amazon SNS, which allows you to view and analyze your monitoring data and set up alerts and notifications. The followings are the benefits of using AMSP:

- **Fully managed**: AMSP takes care of the underlying infrastructure and maintenance tasks, so you can focus on monitoring your applications.
- **Scalability**: AMSP automatically scales to handle changes in workload, so you don't have to worry about capacity planning.
- **Integration with other AWS services**: AMSP integrates with other AWS services, such as CloudWatch and SNS, which allows you to view and analyze your monitoring data and set up alerts and notifications.
- **Security**: AMSP includes built-in security measures, such as encryption at rest and network isolation, to help protect your monitoring data.
- **Cost-effective**: AMSP is a pay-as-you-go service, which means you only pay for the resources you use. This can be more cost-effective than running and maintaining your own Prometheus infrastructure.

You can learn more about AMSP by visiting the AWS page here: `https://aws.amazon.com/prometheus/`.

Amazon Managed Service for Grafana (**AMG**) is a fully managed service that simplifies the visualization and analysis of operational data at scale. It leverages the popular open-source analytics platform Grafana to query, visualize, and alert on metrics stored across AWS, third-party ISVs, databases, and other IT resources. AMG removes the need for server provisioning, software configuration, and security and scaling concerns, enabling you to analyze your metrics, logs, and traces without the heavy lifting in production. You can learn more about AMG by visiting the AWS page here: `https://aws.amazon.com/grafana/`.

In this section, you learned that an observable environment reduces risk, increases agility, and improves customer experience. Observability provides insights and context about the environment you monitor. AWS enables you to transform from monitoring to observability so that you can have full-service visibility from metrics, logs, and traces by combining AWS CloudWatch and X-Ray. Let's learn about the next step in building centralized operations.

Fifth pillar – Centralized operations management

IT teams need to take operational actions across hundreds, sometimes thousands, of applications while maintaining safety, security, and compliance simultaneously. To help make ops management as easy and efficient as possible, you must safely manage and operate your IT infrastructure at scale. To achieve that, you should have a central location and interface to view operational data from multiple AWS services. You can then automate operational tasks on applications and resources, especially common operational changes, such as rotating certificates, increasing service limits, taking backups, and resizing instances. You laid down all without compromising any safety, security, or compliance guardrails in the foundation stage.

To help enable cloud operations, you can use **AWS Systems Manager**. Systems Manager is a fully managed service that helps customers safely manage and operate their IT infrastructure at scale. It provides a central location and interfaces to view operational data from multiple AWS services. Customers can then use it to automate operational tasks on their applications and resources, especially common operational changes, such as rotating certificates, increasing service limits, taking backups, and resizing instances.

You learned about AWS Systems Manager earlier in this chapter. Here you will learn about Systems Manager's ability to view, manage, operate, and report on cloud operations. There are **four** stages of implementing CloudOps using AWS Systems Manager:

1. **Build a foundation for cloud operations**: To build a foundation for cloud operations, the Systems Manager helps you set up the management of service configurations, IT assets, infrastructure, and platforms. Systems Manager integrates with AWS Config to collect and maintain an inventory of infrastructure resources and application and OS data starting with your environment and account structure. Simple, automated setup processes allow you to quickly enable operational best practices, such as continuous vulnerability scanning and collecting insights into improving an application's performance and availability. It also helps you to automate operational best practices by codifying operations runbooks and defining execution parameters, such as freeze periods and permissions. AWS Config rules enable continuous compliance by enforcing security, risk, and compliance policies.
2. **Enable visibility into applications and infrastructure**: The second stage is to enable visibility into applications and infrastructure by continuously tracking key technical and business measures, providing visibility, and triggering automation and actions if needed.

Systems Manager provides operational visibility and actionable insights to customers through a widget-based, customizable dashboard that can be tailored for users such as IT operators, DevOps engineers, IT leaders, and executives. Operational teams can set up operational event management and reporting for their infrastructure and resources at scale using pre-defined configuration bundles that reflect operational best practices to filter out and capture specific operational events that require an operator's attention for diagnosis and action/remediation. The dashboard provides a holistic view of relevant data across multiple AWS accounts and AWS Regions, such as inventory and CMDB, patch, resource configuration and compliance, support tickets, insights from EC2 Compute Optimizer, Trusted Advisor, Personal Health Dashboard, Amazon CloudWatch, and trends on outstanding operational issues.

3. **Automate operations at scale**: To proactively automate operations at scale, Systems Manager gives teams the ability to automate patch management to keep resources secure. Systems Manager provides change management capabilities with built-in approval workflows and secures automated or manual change execution when making application and environment changes. Only approved changes can be deployed to the environment by authorized resources, and these come with detailed reporting. You can automate server administration, providing central IT teams with a consistent, integrated console to perform common administrative tasks. Additionally, you can manage and troubleshoot resources on AWS and on-premises. Operators can manage their VM fleet when manual actions are required by connecting directly from the console. You can also operationalize risk management by creating rules. Here is an example AWS Systems Manager rule that operationalizes risk management by checking for security vulnerabilities in installed software packages on Amazon EC2 instances:

```
{
  "Name": "ec2-check-for-security-vulnerabilities",
  "Description": "Scans installed software packages on EC2 instances
for security vulnerabilities",
  "ResourceId": "*",
  "ResourceType": "AWS::EC2::Instance",
  "ComplianceType": "NON_COMPLIANT",
  "RulePriority": 1,
  "Operator": "EQUALS",
  "Parameters": {
    "ExecutionFrequency": "OneTime",
```

```
    "OutputS3BucketName": "sa-book-s3-bucket",
    "OutputS3KeyPrefix": "ec2-security-scans/"
  },
  "Actions": [
    {
      "Type": "RunCommand",
      "Properties": {
        "Comment": "Scan installed software packages for security
vulnerabilities",
        "OutputS3BucketName": "sa-book-s3-bucket",
        "OutputS3KeyPrefix": "ec2-security-scans/",
        "DocumentName": "AWS-RunShellScript",
        "Parameters": {
          "commands": [
            "apt update",
            "apt-get install -y unattended-upgrades",
            "apt-get install -y --only-upgrade bash",
            "apt-get install -y --only-upgrade glibc",
            "apt-get install -y --only-upgrade libstdc++6",
            "apt-get install -y --only-upgrade libgcc1",
            "apt-get install -y --only-upgrade libc6",
            "apt-get install -y --only-upgrade libc-bin",
            "apt-get install -y --only-upgrade libpam-modules",
            "apt-get install -y --only-upgrade libpam-runtime",
            "apt-get install -y --only-upgrade libpam0g",
            "apt-get install -y --only-upgrade login",
            "apt-get install -y --only-upgrade passwd",
            "apt-get install -y --only-upgrade libssl1.0.0",
            "apt-get install -y --only-upgrade openssl",
            "apt-get install -y --only-upgrade dpkg",
            "apt-get install -y --only-upgrade apt",
            "apt-get install -y --only-upgrade libapt-pkg4.12",
            "apt-get install -y --only-upgrade apt-utils",
            "apt-get install -y --only-upgrade libdb5.3",
            "apt-get install -y --only-upgrade bzip2",
            "apt-get install -y --only-upgrade libbz2-1.0",
            "apt-get install -y --only-upgrade liblzma5",
```

```
            "apt-get install -y --only-upgrade libtinfo5",
            "apt-get install -y --only-upgrade libreadline7",
            "apt
    ]
    }
```

By running analyses to proactively detect and remediate risks across applications and infrastructure, such as expiring certificates, a lack of database backup, and the use of blocked software, identified risks are assigned to owners and can be remediated using automation runbooks with automated reporting.

4. **Remediate issues and incidents**: Finally, when unexpected issues arise, you must be able to remediate issues and incidents quickly. With the incident, event, and risk management capabilities within Systems Manager, you can employ various AWS services to trigger relevant issues or incidents. It integrates with Amazon GuardDuty for threat detection and AWS Inspector for security assessments, keeps a running check on vulnerabilities in the environment, and allows automated remediation. It provides a consolidated view of incidents, changes, operational risks and failures, operational alarms, compliance, and vulnerability management reports. It allows operations teams to take manual or automated action to resolve issues. Systems Manager speeds up issue resolution by automating common, repeatable remediation actions, such as failover to a backup system and capturing failed state for root cause analysis.

Systems Manager's incident management capability automates a response plan for application issues by notifying the appropriate people to respond, providing them with relevant troubleshooting data, and enabling chat-based collaboration. You can easily access and analyze operational data from multiple AWS services and track updates related to incidents, such as changes in alarm status and response plans. Operators can resolve incidents manually by logging into the instance or executing automation runbooks. Systems Manager integrates with AWS Chatbot to invoke commands in the appropriate channel for an incident so central IT teams can resolve issues quickly. Let's learn about the final and most important step in the cloud operation model: managing cost.

Sixth pillar – Manage your cloud's finance

Cloud adoption has enabled technology teams to innovate faster by reducing approval, procurement, and infrastructure deployment cycles. It also helps finance organizations eliminate the failure cost, as cloud resources can be terminated with just a few clicks or API calls. As a result, technology teams are no longer just builders, but they also operate and own their products.

They are responsible for most activities that were traditionally associated with finance and operations teams, such as procurement and deployment.

Cloud Financial Management (**CFM**) enables finance, product, technology, and business organizations to manage, optimize and plan costs as they grow their usage and scale on AWS. The primary goal of CFM is to enable customers to achieve their business outcomes cost-efficiently and accelerate economic and business value creation while balancing agility and control. CFM has the following four dimensions to manage and save costs:

Plan and evaluate

When planning for future cloud spending, you should first define a goal for the monthly cost of the individual project. The project team needs to make sure cloud resources related to a project are correctly tagged with cost allocation tags and/or cost categories. This way, they can calculate and track the monthly cost of the project with the cost and usage data available in their AWS Cost Explorer and AWS Cost and Usage Reports. These reports provide the data you need to understand how your AWS costs are incurred and optimize your AWS usage and cost management. These reports can be customized to include only the needed data and can be delivered to an Amazon S3 bucket or an Amazon SNS topic. You can also use the data in these reports to create custom cost and usage reports, set up cost and usage alarms, and create budgets.

You can decide on a project's budget based on the growth trend of the project as well as the available funds set aside for the project. Then, you can set the budget thresholds using AWS Budgets for cost or resource usage. You can also use AWS Budgets to set coverage and utilization targets for the project team's Reserved Instances and Savings Plans. These are two options that allow you to save money on your AWS usage costs. They both enable you to purchase a discounted rate for your AWS usage, in exchange for committing to a certain usage level over a specific period. **Reserved Instances** are a type of pricing model that allows you to save up to 75% on your Amazon EC2 and RDS usage costs by committing to a one- or three-year term. With Reserved Instances, you pay a discounted hourly rate for the usage of a specific instance type in a specific region, and you can choose between Standard and Convertible Reserved Instances.

AWS Savings Plans is a new pricing model that allows you to save up to 72% on your AWS usage costs by committing to a one-year or three-year term. With Savings Plans, you pay a discounted hourly rate for your AWS usage, and you can choose between Compute Savings Plans and Amazon EC2 Instance Savings Plans. Compute Savings Plans offer a discount on a wide range of AWS services, including Amazon EC2, Fargate, and Lambda, while Amazon EC2 Instance Savings Plans only offer a discount on Amazon EC2 usage.

The AWS Budgets Reports dashboard allows you to monitor the progress of your budget portfolio by comparing actual costs with the budgeted costs and forecasted costs with the budgeted costs. You can set up notification alerts to receive updates when the cost and usage are expected to exceed the threshold limit. These alerts can be sent via email or Amazon **Simple Notification Service** (**SNS**). You can learn more about AWS Budgets by visiting the AWS page here: `https://aws.amazon.com/aws-cost-management/aws-budgets/`. After planning your budget, let's learn about managing it.

Manage and Control

As businesses grow and scale on AWS, you need to give your team the freedom to experiment and innovate in the cloud while maintaining control over cost, governance, and security. And while fostering innovation and speed is essential, you also want to avoid getting surprised by the bill.

You can achieve this by establishing centralized ownership through a center of excellence. Cost management elements are shared responsibilities across the entire organization. A centralized team is essential to design policies and governance mechanisms, implement and monitor the effort, and help drive company-wide best practices.

You can utilize services like **Identity and Access Management** (**IAM**) to ensure secure access control to AWS resources. IAM allows you to create and manage user identities, groups, and roles and grants permissions for IAM users to access specific AWS resources. This way, you can control and restrict individual and group access to AWS resources, ensuring the security of your infrastructure and data.

Use **AWS Organizations** to enable automatic policy-based account creation, management, and billing at scale. Finally, using the **AWS Billing Console**, you can easily track overall spending and view cost breakdown by service and account by accessing Billing Dashboard. You can view the overall monthly spending from last month, the current month, and the current forecasted month.

The following screenshot is a sample billing dashboard:

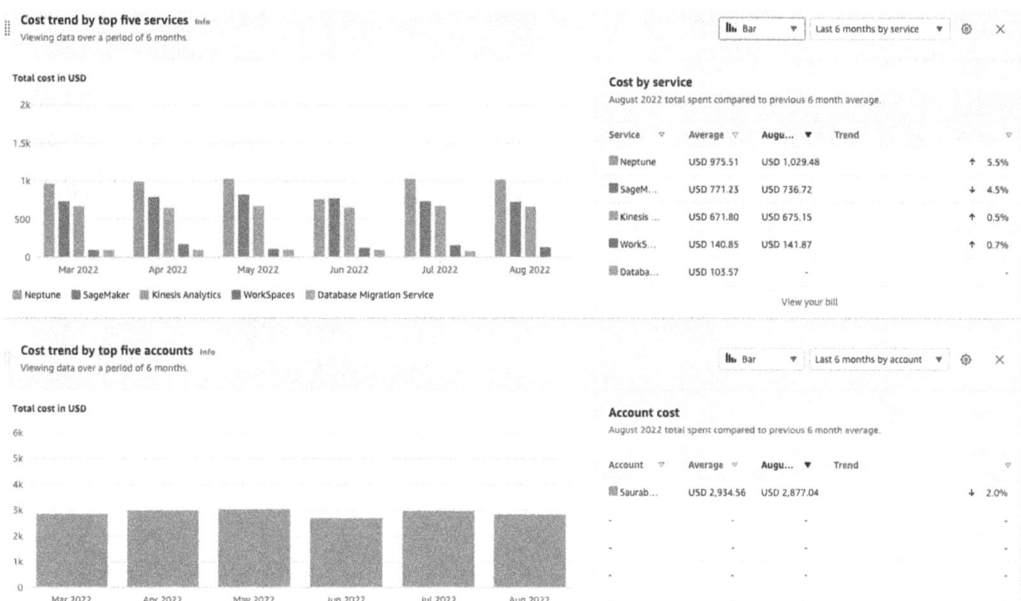

Figure 9.9: AWS Billing Dashboard

The above billing dashboard shows six months spend by service and cost trend. Using the Billing Console, you can receive a unified view of spend in a single bill and establish rules for organizing costs, sharing discount benefits associated with Reserved Instances and Savings Plans, and many other controls. You can learn more about the AWS Billing Console by visiting the AWS page here: `https://aws.amazon.com/aws-cost-management/aws-billing/`.

AWS Purchase Order Management enables you to use **purchase orders (POs)** to procure AWS services and approve invoices for payment. With this service, you can configure multiple POs, map them to your invoices, and access the invoices generated against those POs. Additionally, you can manage the status of your POs, track their balance and expiration, and set up email notifications for contacts to receive alerts when POs are running low on balance or close to their expiration date. You can learn more about AWS Purchase Order Management by visiting the AWS page here: `https://aws.amazon.com/aws-cost-management/aws-purchase-order-management/`.

AWS Cost Anomaly Detection is a machine learning service that automates cost anomaly alerts and root cause analysis. It can save time investigating spending anomalies by providing automated root cause analysis and identifying potential cost drivers, such as specific AWS services, usage types (e.g., data transfer cost), regions, and member accounts. You can learn more about AWS Cost Anomaly Detection by visiting the AWS page here: `https://aws.amazon.com/aws-cost-management/aws-cost-anomaly-detection/`. As you manage your cost, let's learn how to track it.

Track and allocate

You need to ask three questions to understand your billing uses. The **first** is, *What is causing our bill to increase?* AWS provides **AWS Cost Explorer** to help answer this question. Cost Explorer provides a quick visualization of cost and utilization with default reports and creates specific views with filters and grouping, as shown below. This tool can help show which AWS services are leading to increased spending:

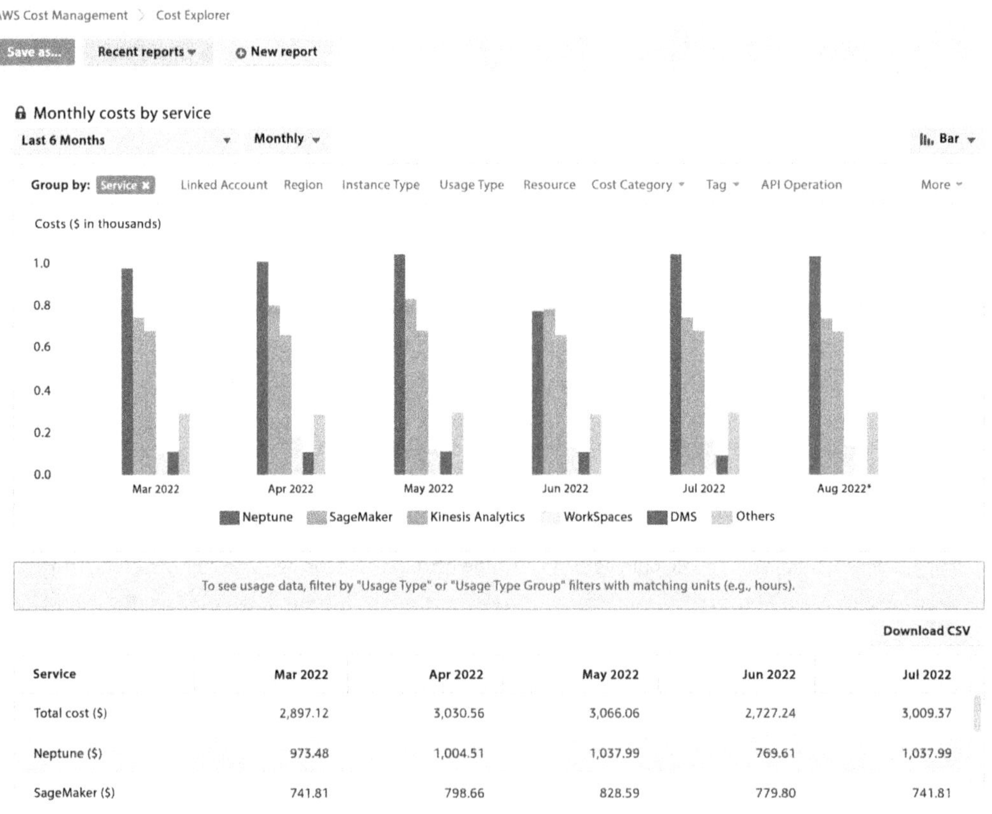

Service	Mar 2022	Apr 2022	May 2022	Jun 2022	Jul 2022
Total cost ($)	2,897.12	3,030.56	3,066.06	2,727.24	3,009.37
Neptune ($)	973.48	1,004.51	1,037.99	769.61	1,037.99
SageMaker ($)	741.81	798.66	828.59	779.80	741.81

Figure 9.10: AWS Cost Explorer

In the above Cost Explorer dashboard, you can see service expense grouping in the costs chart showing AWS Neptune has the highest cost, followed by SageMaker. It also provides the ability to download CSV files for detailed analysis. You can learn more about AWS Cost Explorer by visiting the AWS page here: `https://aws.amazon.com/aws-cost-management/aws-cost-explorer/`.

The **second** question is a common follow-up: *Which of my lines of business, teams, or organizations drove increased spending and usage?* AWS Cost Explorer's data becomes even more valuable when paired with Cost Allocation Tags. These features allow customers to categorize their resources and spending to fit their organization's needs. Categorizing spending by specific teams, sometimes referred to as show back, allows for better analysis and easier identification of savings opportunities. You can also use the AWS **Cost and Usage Report** (**CUR**) to bring in cost and usage data, including tags, into your analysis tool of choice. This approach also allows for combining the data with other business-specific data. You can learn more about CUR by visiting the AWS page here: `https://aws.amazon.com/aws-cost-management/aws-cost-and-usage-reporting/`.

Finally, the **third** question is, *How do I understand the cost impact of Reserved Instances?* AWS Cost Explorer provides multiple ways to view and dive deep into this data, such as tag service with meaningful info, e.g., owner, project, application, or you can define cost categories by group accounts, tags, services, and charge types with custom rules. You can use CUR to deliver cost data to the S3 bucket, which can be integrated with Amazon Athena and/or ingested into your ERP system.

Furthermore, **AWS Billing Conductor** is a billing and cost management tool that helps you monitor and optimize your AWS costs and usage and provides insights into how you are using your resources. AWS Billing Conductor provides recommendations for ways to optimize your costs, such as by identifying idle or underutilized resources that can be turned off or scaled down. You can learn more about AWS Billing Conductor by visiting the AWS page here: `https://aws.amazon.com/aws-cost-management/aws-billing-conductor/`.

AWS Application Cost Profiler is a service that allows you to collect and correlate usage data from your multi-tenant applications with your AWS billing information. This enables you to generate detailed, tenant-specific cost reports with hourly granularity delivered daily or monthly. This can be useful for understanding the cost breakdown of your multi-tenant application and allocating costs to individual tenants or customers. You can learn more about AWS Application Cost Profiler by visiting the AWS page here: `https://aws.amazon.com/aws-cost-management/aws-application-cost-profiler/`. Now let's learn about the final step to optimize costs and increase savings.

Optimize and save

Cost optimization is about making sure you pay only for what you need. AWS offers tools and services that make it easier for you to build cost-efficient workloads, which help you to continue saving as you scale on AWS. While there are hundreds of ways you can pull to minimize spending, at its core, two of the following most impactful levers you can pull to optimize spending are detailed next.

Using the right pricing models: AWS offers services through multiple pricing models – on-demand, pay-as-you-go, commitment-based Reserved Instances, and Spot instances for up to 90% discount compared to on-demand pricing. Amazon EC2 Spot Instances are a type of AWS computing resource that is available at a reduced price and can be used to run your applications. These instances are spare capacities in the AWS cloud that can be interrupted at any time, based on the resource demand. Spot Instances are suitable for applications with flexible start and end times and can handle interruptions without causing significant issues. You can launch a Spot Instance by specifying the maximum price you are willing to pay per hour (known as the "bid price"). If the current Spot price is less than your bid price, your Spot Instance will be launched, and you will be charged the current Spot price. However, if the current Spot price exceeds your bid price, your Spot Instance will be interrupted, and you will not be charged for the usage.

Suppose you have predictable, steady workloads on Amazon EC2, Amazon ECS, and Amazon RDS. If you use Reserved Instances, you can save up to 75% over on-demand capacity. Reserved Instances are a pricing option in AWS that allows you to pay up front for a commitment to use a certain amount of resources over a specific period in exchange for a discounted price. There are three options for purchasing Reserved Instances:

- **All up-front (AURI)**: This option requires you to pay for the entire term of the Reserved Instance up front and provides the most significant discount.
- **Partial up-front (PURI)**: This option requires a partial payment up front and provides a smaller discount than the AURI option.
- **No upfront payments (NURI)**: This option does not require any up front payment and provides the smallest discount.

By choosing the AURI option, you can receive the largest discount on your Reserved Instances. The PURI and NURI options offer lower discounts but allow you to pay less up front or avoid upfront payments altogether.

AWS offers Reserved Instances, and Savings Plans purchase recommendations via Cost Explorer based on your past usage. Cost Explorer identifies and recommends the estimated value resulting in the largest savings. It allows you to generate a recommendation specific to your purchase preference. From there, you can track your investment using cost explorer. Any usage above the commitment level will be charged at on-demand rates. You can revisit commitment levels, make incremental purchases, and track coverage and utilization using pre-built reports in cost explorer.

With AWS purchase option recommendations, you can receive tailored Reserved Instance, or Savings Plans purchase recommendations based on your historical usage. You can select parameters for recommendations, such as the type of plan, term commitment, and payment option that makes sense for your business.

Identify and eliminate idle or over-provisioned resources: AWS Cost Explorer resources can be used for top-level **key performance indicators (KPIs)**, rightsizing, and instance selection. Cost Explorer will estimate monthly savings, which is the sum of the projected monthly savings associated with each recommendation.

Cost Explorer rightsizing recommendations generate recommendations by identifying idle and underutilized instances and searching for smaller instance sizes in the same instance family. Idle instances are defined as CPU utilization of <1%, while underutilized instances are defined as those with CPU utilization between 1% and 40%.

In this section, you learned about various ways to manage your cost and make the cloud more profitable to run your workload and business.

Summary

Working in a cloud environment is different from on-premise. The out-of-the-box tools and services are available in AWS can make a huge difference when operating your workload in the cloud. To realize the full value of the cloud, it's important to understand cloud operation and how to apply automation everywhere. In this chapter, you learned about the cloud operation model and the six pillars of CloudOps, which help you to understand how to plan your cloud operation efficiently.

Under the CloudOps pillars, you learned about building cloud governance, infrastructure provisioning, monitoring, centralized operation management, and cost optimization. You learned about various AWS services that can help you to build end-to-end cloud operation pillars. These services include AWS CloudTrail, AWS Config, AWS CloudWatch, AWS Systems Manager, AWS CloudFormation, AWS Service Catalog, and AWS cost explorer.

Data is one of the important drivers of moving to the cloud. In the next chapter, you will learn about the AWS services available for extracting, transforming and loading large volumes of data in AWS.

10

Big Data and Streaming Data Processing in AWS

Traditionally, a business's most important resources are its human and financial capital. However, in the last few decades, more and more businesses have realized that another resource may be just as, if not more, vital: its data capital.

Data has taken a special place at the center of some of today's most successful enterprises. For this reason, business leaders have concluded that to survive in today's business climate, they must collect, process, transform, distill, and safeguard their data like their other traditional business capital.

In this chapter, you will dive deep into AWS's analytics services. First, you will learn about Amazon EMR, which is Hadoop in the cloud, and about AWS data cataloging offering, AWS Glue. Finally, you will look at how to handle streaming data using AWS. In this chapter, you will cover the following topics:

- Why use the cloud for big data analytics?
- Amazon **Elastic Map Reduce** (**EMR**)
- Introduction to AWS Glue
- Choosing between AWS Glue and Amazon EMR
- Handling streaming data in AWS
- Choosing between Amazon Kinesis and Amazon MSK

By the end of this chapter, you will know about the various AWS services available to build an analytics pipeline and perform **Extract, Transform, and Load** (**ETL**) operations on your significant data workload. Let's roll up our sleeves and get to it.

Why use the cloud for big data analytics?

The definition of big data has changed drastically in the last 2 decades. Now, there is a massive amount of data coming from various sources. This data can be structured, unstructured, or semi-structured. We see large technology organizations, such as Amazon, Google, Meta, and so on, flourishing as they can get insight from user data and utilize it for customer benefits, thus growing their business multifold. IDC says, *"The Global DataSphere is expected to more than double in size from 2022 to 2026,"* (Source – `https://www.idc.com/getdoc.jsp?containerId=US49018922`).

Now, it's normal for organizations to have multi-terabytes or petabytes of data, and you want to gain new insights to use the power of this collected data. You must easily access and analyze all data types, such as log files, clickstream data, voice, and video. But your team may require diverse skills and tools. You need to enable your team and applications to access the data but ensure security, privacy, and compliance regulations are met for the data. Also, it's important to clearly decide, watch, and handle who can see certain information.

It would become time-consuming, complex, and expensive if you were to collect, store, secure, and process all that data on-premises. If you were to pick up an open-source project such as a Spark, Hive, or Pig and set up the Hadoop environments, it would require a lot of expertise to ensure the open-source projects integrated well and could work with one another. Hadoop is a free software created by Apache for storing and working with big datasets. With Hadoop, you can link many computers together to simultaneously analyze huge datasets faster, rather than relying on a single large computer to store and analyze the data. You can learn more about Hadoop by visiting the AWS page – `https://aws.amazon.com/emr/details/hadoop/what-is-hadoop/`.

Big data administration skills are hard to find. Even if you have taken care of that, the infrastructure likely does not scale as needed. Innovation and development are always limited by how many resources you have. Costs add up very quickly. The tight coupling of storage and compute pushes the costs further. You are forced to buy more computing even if you just need more storage, as you will not process all the data in one go.

To address all these concerns, AWS built **Amazon Elastic Map Reduce** (**EMR**), a managed big data platform supporting the open-source project part of the Hadoop framework.

EMR is a kind of Hadoop solution for the cloud, meaning you don't need to reskill your workforce to move on to the cloud. EMR scales based on processing needs while keeping costs low by requiring you to pay only for what you use and keeping compute and storage separate. Let's learn more about EMR in detail.

Amazon Elastic Map Reduce (EMR)

Back in 2009, AWS introduced EMR, a tool that can handle extremely large amounts of data (terabytes and petabytes) using the latest open-source big data tools like Spark, Hive, Presto, HBase, Flink, and Hudi in the cloud. Amazon EMR is a managed cluster platform that makes it easier to run big data tools, such as Apache Hadoop and Apache Spark, on the AWS cloud for processing and analyzing massive datasets. It is a wrapper around distributed open-source computing frameworks. This wrapper abstracts the effort required to set up infrastructure, security, network communication, disaster recovery, and scalability. Additionally, EMR offers 100% compliance with open-source APIs. So, there is no need to change your application code when you move to EMR from the on-premises Hadoop system.

EMR runs directly against the data stored in your S3 data lake, so you don't need to move that data or transform your data. You can store data in the data lake in its raw and processed forms, as well in a variety of formats, including log files, images, and so on. S3 data lakes are scalable, secure, and cost-effective, making them a popular choice. You will learn more about AWS data lakes in *Chapter 15, Data Lake Patterns – Integrating Your Data across the Enterprise.*

EMR makes it simple to produce clusters and set up one, hundreds, or thousands of computing units to manage data of any magnitude. EMR also automatically scales cluster sizes based on usage, and you only pay for the resources you consume.

Because you're running against S3, you can have multiple clusters operating on the same data. Using Amazon S3 for storage also provides strong business continuity. Rather than depending on one cluster that will go down in the case of a DC failure, EMR clusters in multiple **Availability Zones** (**AZs**) have equal access to Amazon S3. In the event of a failure, you can quickly switch traffic to the other cluster or spin up a new cluster in another AZ.

EMR decouples compute and storage to optimize costs, allowing you to scale each independently. For storage, you can take advantage of the tiered storage of Amazon S3, and for computing, you can take advantage of **Elastic Compute Cloud** (**EC2**) Spot Instances to save up to 80% off the cost of using on-demand instances. EMR also enables data analysts' and scientists' interactive analytics by integrating with other AWS machine learning services. Let's dive deeper to learn more about EMR clusters.

Understanding EMR clusters and nodes

Amazon EMR is a service that is centered around clusters, which are groups of Amazon EC2 instances. These instances, known as nodes, each have a specific function within the cluster and are equipped with different software tools depending on their role. In an Amazon EMR cluster, each node serves a unique purpose; as you can see in the following diagrams, the node groups are Leader nodes, Core nodes, and Task nodes.

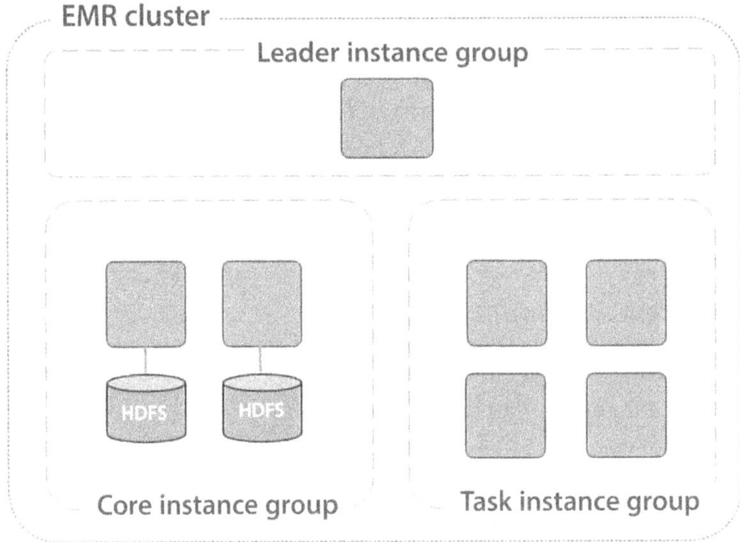

Figure 10.1: Amazon EMR node types

As shown in the preceding diagram, the following is the role of each node type:

- **Leader node:** The master node is the central point of control for the cluster. It manages the job flow and coordinates the work across the other nodes in the cluster.
- **Core nodes:** Core nodes are worker nodes that store data and process tasks. They run tasks as directed by the master node and store intermediate data in memory or on a local disk.
- **Task nodes:** Task nodes are similar to Core nodes, but they are only used to run tasks and do not store data. They are typically used when a large amount of compute resources are needed for a short period of time.

In addition to these, you have additional nodes to support EMR jobs – for example, Gateway nodes to provide a connection to external data sources and to stage data in and out of the cluster. Client nodes are used to submit jobs to the cluster and view the status of those jobs. They do not store data or run tasks, but they do have access to the data and resources of the cluster.

An Amazon EMR cluster can be configured with three Leader nodes to provide high availability. In the event that the primary Leader node fails, Amazon EMR will automatically switch to a standby Leader node to ensure that the cluster remains operational. If a Leader node does fail, Amazon EMR will also automatically replace it with a new Leader node that is configured in the same way and has the same bootstrap actions as the failed node. This helps to ensure that the cluster remains available and can continue to process data even in the event of a failure.

EMR provides a wide variety of EC2 instances to choose from. It allows you to choose the instance families suitable for your workload. The processing ability of your Core nodes and the size of your data determine how much information you can manage. While processing, the input, intermediate, and output datasets are stored on the cluster.

The cluster type could be **a persistent cluster**, where you always want to keep it on to run interactive queries, or a transient cluster, which you need for a few hours to process batch jobs for data processing. A **transient cluster** can have the same lifetime as the workload running on it. Once the application or workload completes, the results are stored inside S3, and the cluster can be terminated. This provides the benefit of cost saving while running EMR.

Amazon EMR offers a feature called **EMR Managed Scaling**, which allows you to automatically adjust the size of your cluster based on your workload. This can help you to optimize the cost and speed of your cluster by scaling it up or down as needed to meet the demands of your workload. EMR Managed Scaling continuously monitors cluster metrics to make decisions about scaling and ensures that your cluster is always sized appropriately to meet your needs. AWS manages all the configuration, with no policies for you to define except for the minimum and maximum number of instances.

AWS also provides the ability to deploy **Amazon EMR on EKS**. This is a new deployment mode that allows you to run EMR on EKS-managed Kubernetes clusters. EMR on EKS brings the power of both EMR and EKS services into a consolidated offering so you can run Spark applications on Kubernetes easily and securely. With EMR on EKS, there are no more clusters to build specifically for your analytics workload. AWS containerizes the Spark runtime, so applications can quickly run on an existing EKS cluster. You'll also be able to consolidate resources into a single cluster and improve their overall utilization, which drives cost savings. This allows you to run multiple versions of Spark on the same cluster and also allows you to build a security model that is job centric.

AWS also launched **Amazon EMR Serverless** at re:Invent 2021. EMR Serverless automatically determines and provisions the compute and memory resources to run the application and scales the resources up and down as needed based on changing requirements.

For example, Amazon EMR Serverless automatically provisions and adjusts resources required to run Spark applications as the data volumes being processed change. You can check the status of running jobs in **EMR Studio** or the AWS Console, review job history, and use familiar open-source tools to debug jobs. EMR Studio is a fully managed, web-based notebook environment that you can use to interactively explore, visualize, and analyze data using Apache Spark and other popular open-source libraries. It is integrated with Amazon EMR, so you can easily run and debug your code on a live cluster, and it includes collaboration features such as version control and the ability to share notebooks with other users.

In this section, you've learned about compute in EMR; let's look into storage in EMR with the supported file system.

Understanding the EMR File System (EMFRS)

To run a large data workload, you need scalable storage and a file system to support that storage. One major differentiation for EMR is its support for S3, for which AWS built a propriety file system called EMRFS, which continues to support other traditional file systems. Let's look into file systems supported by EMR:

- **Hadoop Distributed File System (HDFS)**: HDFS is a type of file system that is meant to operate on low-cost, commodity hardware in a distributed computing environment. EMR mainly utilizes HDFS as its primary storage system, and it is well suited for storing large amounts of data that need to be processed by `MapReduce` jobs.
- **Elastic Map Reduce File System (EMRFS)** : EMRFS is a Hadoop-compliant file system that is designed to work seamlessly with Amazon S3. It allows you to store data in S3 while still being able to access it through the HDFS interface. EMRFS provides consistent, low-latency data access while still maintaining the durability and cost-effectiveness of S3.
- **The local file system**: EMR can also use the local file system of the instances in the cluster as the file system. This can be useful for storing intermediate data that is generated by `MapReduce` jobs, or for storing small amounts of data that are used by the jobs.

Using EMRFS and utilizing the power of S3 until you need sub-millisecond latency helps you reduce cost by decoupling compute and storage.

You don't want to limit your data pipeline to just seeing historical data. The actual value for data comes when you can predict the future using machine learning and play with your data using a developed, friendly interface. AWS has launched an EMR Studio offering to make your data analysis future-looking. Let's look into more details.

Amazon EMR Studio

EMR Studio is an Integrated Development Environment that reduces the time that data scientists and engineers take to build and deploy code. The following are the key benefits of EMR Studio:

- **Use corporate identity to log into notebooks instead of the AWS Console**: You can log into Amazon EMR Studio through a secure URL to manage notebooks using corporate identities via AWS **Single Sign-On** (**SSO**). There is no need to log into the AWS Console. It is a multi-tenant studio where multiple users and groups can log into the same studio.
- **Develop, visualize, debug and optimize analytics and machine learning applications**: EMR Studio provides fully managed notebooks based on JupyterLab. It gives you the flexibility to create notebooks independent of clusters. You can attach and detach notebooks to and from clusters using a single click. You can also provision EMR clusters using cluster templates pre-configured by your administrator or create a new cluster from scratch. You can diagnose jobs on active and terminated clusters using the Spark UI, Tez UI, and **Yet Another Resource Negotiator** (**YARN**) Timeline Service. EMR Studio allows you to do this easily by browsing through all your clusters in one place and narrowing down clusters or jobs for investigation using filters.
- **Collaborate with others by sharing notebooks via GitHub:** You can collaborate with your team and analyze data from your data lakes using PySpark, Spark SQL, Spark R, and Scala. The studio integrates with AWS CodeCommit, GitHub, and Bitbucket for easy collaboration, and you can import custom Python libraries like Pandas or NumPy and install custom kernels directly from notebooks.
- **Build pipelines using orchestration services like Apache Airflow**: You can run notebooks as pipelines via Amazon's **Managed Workflows for Apache Airflow** (**MWAA**), self-managed Apache Airflow, or AWS Step functions. You can also parameterize and chain notebooks that can be run as pipelines.

Data security is an essential aspect of any analytics workload. Let's look into data security in EMR.

Securing data in Amazon EMR

Amazon EMR allows you to specify security configurations to ensure the encryption of data at rest, in transit, or both. You can use these configurations to encrypt data stored in Amazon S3 or on the local disks of your cluster instances. The security configurations are stored separately from the cluster configuration, so they can easily be reused whenever you create a new cluster. In addition, in-transit encryption can be enabled to secure data as it is transmitted between various components of the cluster.

There are several ways to secure data in Amazon EMR:

- **Encrypting data at rest:** Data at rest refers to data that is stored on disk, such as data stored in Amazon S3 or on the local disks of your EMR cluster instances. To safeguard data at rest in EMR, you can create a security configuration that establishes the necessary parameters for encrypting data stored in Amazon S3 or on the local disks of your cluster instances. This helps ensure that your data is secure and unreadable by unauthorized users.
- **Encrypting data in transit:** Data in transit refers to data that is transmitted between components of your EMR cluster, such as data transmitted between Amazon EC2 instances or between Amazon EC2 instances and Amazon S3. To encrypt data in transit in EMR, you can use **Secure Sockets Layer (SSL)**/TLS to secure data transmitted over the network.
- **Using secure access to Amazon S3:** When accessing data stored in Amazon S3 from your EMR cluster, you can use SSL to encrypt the data transmitted over the network. You can also use AWS **Identity and Access Management (IAM)** to control access to your data in Amazon S3 and to make sure that only authorized users and applications have access to your data.
- **Using security groups:** Using security groups, you can manage the flow of incoming and outgoing traffic to and from your EMR cluster instances. This helps to limit access to only authorized users and resources, and enhances the overall security of your cluster. This also allows you to restrict access to your cluster instances and to specify which IP addresses and protocols are allowed to access your cluster.
- **Using network isolation:** You can use Amazon **Virtual Private Cloud (VPC)** to create a virtual network that is isolated from the rest of the internet and to launch your EMR cluster in this virtual network. This allows you to further secure your cluster by creating a private network that is isolated from the public internet.

For authentication, use can use IAM and Kerberos. You can also use AWS SSO through the corporate active directory to verify the user's validity. Furthermore, EMR provides the ability to perform audits through logs and AWS CloudTrail.

Here is an example of using EMR to process data stored in Amazon S3 using a `MapReduce` job written in Python:

1. First, you will need to create an Amazon S3 bucket to store your input data and output data.
2. Next, you will need to upload your input data to Amazon S3. This can be done using the AWS Management Console, the AWS CLI, or the Amazon S3 API.

3. Then, you will need to create an EMR cluster using the AWS Management Console, the AWS CLI, or the Amazon EMR API. When creating the cluster, you will need to specify the number of instances you want in the cluster, the instance type, and the EC2 key pair that you want to use to access the cluster instances.
4. Once the cluster is up and running, you can submit a `MapReduce` job to the cluster using the AWS Management Console, the AWS CLI, or the Amazon EMR API. The `MapReduce` job should specify the location of the input data in Amazon S3 and the location where you want the output data to be stored.
5. The `MapReduce` job will then be executed on the EMR cluster, and the output data will be stored in the specified location in Amazon S3.

Here is an example of the AWS CLI command to submit a `MapReduce` job to an EMR cluster:

```
aws emr add-steps --cluster-id j-123456789EXAMPLE --steps Type=CUSTOM_
JAR,Name=SABookCustomJar,ActionOnFailure=CONTINUE,Jar=s3://sa-book-bucket/
book-jar.jar,Args=["s3://sa-book-bucket/input-data","s3://sa-book-bucket/
output-data"]
```

This command will submit a `MapReduce` job that runs the `book-jar.jar` JAR file on the input data located in `s3://sa-book-bucket/input-data` and stores the output data in `s3://sa-book-bucket/output-data`.

EMR is a vast topic that warrants a book in itself. You can learn more about EMR by visiting the AWS page here: `https://aws.amazon.com/emr/`.

Spark is one of the most popular big data processing frameworks due to its high performance and speed. Recently, most organizations have moved to using Spark. Another key attribute of big data analytics is data cataloging. Data catalogs help you to understand the details of your data, such as its type, volume, and structure, which help to build efficient data processing jobs. AWS provides the AWS Glue service to handle Spark workloads and data cataloging. Let's learn about it in more detail.

Introduction to AWS Glue

Data-driven businesses can increase their profitability and efficiency, reduce costs, deliver new products and services, better serve their customers, comply with regulatory requirements, and ultimately thrive. Unfortunately, as we have seen many examples of in recent years, companies that don't make this transition will not be able to survive. An important part of a data-driven enterprise is the ability to ingest, process, transform, and analyze this data.

AWS Glue is a foundational service at the heart of the AWS offering.

With the introduction of Apache Spark, enterprises can process petabytes' worth of data daily. Processing this amount of data opens the door to making data an enterprise's most valuable asset. Processing this data at this scale allows enterprises to create new industries and markets. Some examples of business activities that have significantly benefited from this massive data processing are as follows:

- Personalized marketing
- Drug discovery
- Anomaly detection (such as fraud detection)
- Real-time log and clickstream processing

AWS has created a service that leverages Apache Spark and takes it to the next level. The name of that service is AWS Glue.

What is AWS Glue? AWS Glue is a fully managed service used to extract data from data sources, ingest the data into other AWS services, such as Amazon S3, and transform this data to be used by consuming services or users. It is not meant to be used for small batches and files. Under the hood, AWS Glue uses Apache Spark, running it in a serverless environment.

Another important feature of AWS Glue is that it can handle disparate sources such as SQL and NoSQL databases – not just Amazon S3 files.

As we mentioned in the introduction, it is hard to overestimate the value of data in the current environment. Regardless of the industry, properly harnessing and leveraging data is critical to compete. AWS Glue and its underlying Apache Spark engine function as cornerstone technologies in many enterprises to process the vast amounts of data generated.

As with quite a few other AWS services, AWS Glue leverages a popular open-source technology (in this case, Apache Spark) and places wrappers around it to supercharge the technology even further.

Let's look at a simple but powerful example of this. The traditional way to set up Apache Spark is to set up a cluster of powerful machines. Depending on how much data will be ingested and how many transformations need to be performed, it is not uncommon to have Spark clusters with dozens and sometimes even hundreds of nodes. As you can imagine, a dedicated infrastructure setup like this can be costly.

Using AWS Glue, you can create a similarly powerful cluster of machines that are spun up when demand requires it, but importantly, the cluster can be spun down when demand wanes.

If no work is processed, the cluster can be completely shut down, and the compute costs go down to zero. By making costs variable and not having to pay for idle machines, the amount of use cases that can be handled by AWS Glue versus a traditional Apache Spark cluster increases exponentially. Projects that would have been prohibitively expensive before now become economically feasible.

Here is a list of common use cases that leverage AWS Glue:

- The population of data lakes, data warehouses, and lake houses
- Event-driven ETL pipelines
- The creation and cleansing of datasets for machine learning

AWS Glue has a series of components to achieve its intended purpose as an **Extract, Transform, and Load (ETL)** service. These are as follows:

- The AWS Glue console
- The AWS Glue Data Catalog
- AWS Glue classifiers
- AWS Glue crawlers
- AWS Glue code generators

Let's check out the major ones.

Operating the AWS Glue console

The AWS Glue console creates, configures, orchestrates, and develops ingestion workflows. The AWS Glue console interacts with other components in AWS Glue by calling APIs to update the AWS Glue Data Catalog and to run AWS Glue jobs. These jobs can be run to accomplish the following kind of actions:

- **Definition of AWS Glue objects such as connections, jobs, crawlers, and tables** – The console can be used to create various AWS Glue objects. We will learn more about crawlers in an upcoming section. A table in AWS Glue is simply a file after it is processed. Once processed, the file can act as a SQL table, and SQL commands can be run against it. As with any kind of SQL database, we need to create a connection to connect to the table. All these objects can be created in the AWS Glue console.
- **Crawler scheduling** – AWS Glue crawlers, which we will learn about shortly, must be scheduled. This scheduling is another action that can be performed in the AWS Console.
- **Scheduling of job triggers** – The scheduling of job triggers that will perform ETL code can also be implemented in AWS Glue.

- **Filtering of AWS Glue objects** – In the simplest AWS Glue implementations, it may be easy to locate different objects by simply browsing through the objects listed. Once things start getting a little complicated, we will need to have the ability to filter these objects by name, date created, and so on. This filtering can be performed in the AWS Glue console.
- **Transformation script editing** – Lastly, one more task that can be accomplished in the AWS Glue console is the creation and maintenance of ETL scripts.

Cataloging with the AWS Glue Data Catalog

The AWS Glue Data Catalog is a persistent metadata repository. It is another service managed by AWS that enables the storage, annotation, and publishing of metadata. Under the hood, the AWS Glue Data Catalog operates similarly to an Apache Hive metastore.

There is only one AWS Glue Data Catalog per AWS Region. Different services can persist and access the extracted metadata by having only one repository per Region. It is essential to clearly distinguish between the metadata and the data in each dataset. Often, the data is sensitive and cannot be shared unless the authority to do so is granted directly. But in many cases, sharing the metadata for a given dataset is okay. For example, if a file contains social security numbers, names, addresses, and phone numbers, only a select group of individuals may need access to the actual data. But it is okay to disseminate to a wider audience that this file contains social security numbers, names, addresses, and more.

AWS IAM policies can be created to give access permission to AWS Glue Data Catalog datasets. These policies can be used to manage access for a variety of groups. Certain groups may be allowed to publish data, others may be allowed to access the metadata, and others may be given access to the actual data. Using IAM policies, it is possible to give detailed and granular access to the appropriate parties at the required levels.

Another feature of the AWS Glue Data Catalog is its schema version history. A **schema** is the structure and format of a data record, and it is used to define the fields, types, and constraints of the data. Version history will be kept about each ingestion and each Data Catalog update so that these changes can be monitored and audited over time.

The Data Catalog also offers audit and governance functionality. It can track when schema changes are performed and when data is accessed. It allows auditors to determine when and by whom changes are performed.

The catalog can be changed using **Data Definition Language** (**DDL**) statements or the AWS Management Console. Any schemas that are created are automatically persisted until they are explicitly removed. These files can be accessed using Amazon Athena. Amazon Athena leverages a schema-on-read methodology that enables table definitions to be applied to files in Amazon S3 during query execution instead of during file ingestion. This minimizes additional file writes and data transformation. Additionally, these table definitions created by AWS Glue can be deleted, and the underlying files will persist in Amazon S3.

Crawling with AWS Glue crawlers

AWS Glue crawlers are used to discover data stored in a data store and create a table schema for the data in the AWS Glue Data Catalog. The data store can be a database, a flat file, or a collection of files stored in a directory. AWS Glue crawlers scan files, extract the file metadata, and populate the AWS Glue Data Catalog with this metadata information. An AWS Glue crawler can scan multiple file locations simultaneously. Once these files have been scanned and the tables are available, they can then be used in other jobs, and the data contained can be transformed and ingested into other downstream processes. Once the files have been crawled, users will be able to access the contents of the files while treating these files as SQL tables. The table definitions can be used to read and write data stored in the data store.

AWS Glue crawlers can be configured to access data stored in a variety of data stores, including Amazon S3, Amazon RDS, Amazon Redshift, and JDBC data stores. You can also create custom connectors to access data in other data stores. To use an AWS Glue crawler, you create a crawler definition that specifies the data store to be crawled and the classifiers to be used to identify the data. You can then schedule the crawler to run on a regular basis, or you can run it on demand.

When the crawler runs, it connects to the data store and extracts metadata about the data. It then creates table definitions for the data in the AWS Glue Data Catalog and stores the metadata in the Data Catalog. AWS Glue crawlers are a useful tool for discovering and cataloging data stored in a variety of data stores. They can save you time and effort by automating the process of creating table definitions and by providing a central location for storing and accessing metadata about your data.

AWS Glue crawlers are extremely scalable and can crawl multiple data sources simultaneously. Once the AWS Glue Data Catalog is populated, it can be fed into other processes to perform ETL tasks. In addition to discovering the schema information for new data sources, it can also discover changes in the schema that have occurred in previously ingested data sources. It will update the Data Catalog with the new metadata.

IMPORTANT NOTE

One important limitation is that while AWS Glue crawlers can discover schema information and extract metadata from individual files and tables, it does not discover relationships between the data sources.

There is one important consideration when it comes to security with this architecture. Regardless of which AWS or third-party services are used to access tables from the AWS Glue Data Catalog, any restrictions placed on the underlying S3 files will persist. If a user tries to access a resource using SQL commands from one of the tables in the AWS Data Catalog and they don't have access to the underlying table, they will not be able to view the contents of that table.

Categorizing with AWS Glue classifiers

As data is crawled from the various data sources, its metadata will be extracted, and the Data Catalog will be populated. Additionally, it can also be classified by AWS Glue classifiers. Classifiers recognize the format of the data and persist this information. Classifiers also assign a certainty score depending on how sure they are about the data format.

AWS Glue comes with a set of out-of-the-box classifiers and also provides the ability to create custom classifiers. AWS Glue classifiers are used to identify the schema of data stored in a data store. Classifiers are used by AWS Glue crawlers to determine the data format, data type, and other characteristics of the data. For example, suppose you have a collection of CSV files stored in an Amazon S3 bucket, and you want to use an AWS Glue crawler to discover the data and create table definitions for the data in the AWS Glue Data Catalog. You can use a CSV classifier to specify the format of the data and identify the delimiter used in the files.

AWS Glue will first run the custom classifiers during the classifier invocation, using the sequence specified in the crawler configuration. If the custom classifier cannot determine the format of a given data source, AWS Glue will then run the built-in classifiers to see if they can determine the format. You can then use this classifier when creating a crawler to crawl the CSV files in the Amazon S3 bucket. The crawler will use the classifier to determine the schema of the data and create table definitions in the AWS Glue Data Catalog.

Lastly, it is important to note that, in addition to providing a format, a classifier will return a certainty score with a value between 0.0 and 1.0. A score of 1.0 indicates that the classifier has 100% certainty about the data format.

As you can imagine, some of the built-in classifiers can recognize some of the most common file formats, including the following:

- Apache Avro
- Apache ORC
- Apache Parquet
- JSON
- Binary JSON
- XML
- **Comma-Separated Values** (**CSV**)
- **Tab-Separated Values** (**TSV**)

You can use these classifiers to identify the schema of the data and to create table definitions in the Data Catalog.

Generating code with AWS Glue code generators

AWS Glue automatically generates highly scalable Python or Scala ETL code to ingest and transform data. The resulting code is optimized for distributed computing. The choice of language between Python and Scala is up to you, based on your coding preferences. Once the code is generated, it can be customized and edited using AWS Glue Studio. AWS Glue Studio is an editor that allows developers to create some functionality using a drag-and-drop job editor. However, for proficient developers, editing the code directly is also possible.

If you want to customize the generated code, AWS Glue has development endpoints that enable developers to make changes to the code. It can then be tested and debugged. AWS Glue provides the ability to create custom readers, writers, and transformations. Code created with these endpoints can be incorporated into code pipelines, then versioned and managed in code repositories like any other code.

Here is a sample ETL script in Python that demonstrates how to use AWS Glue to transform data stored in S3 and write the transformed data back to S3:

```
import sys
from awsglue.transforms import *
from awsglue.utils import getResolvedOptions
from pyspark.context import SparkContext
from awsglue.context import GlueContext
from awsglue.job import Job
```

```
## @params: [JOB_NAME]
args = getResolvedOptions(sys.argv, ['JOB_NAME'])
sc = SparkContext()
glueContext = GlueContext(sc)
spark = glueContext.spark_session
job = Job(glueContext)
job.init(args['JOB_NAME'], args)
## YOUR CODE HERE
datasource0 = glueContext.create_dynamic_frame.from_catalog(database =
"mydatabase", table_name = "mytable", transformation_ctx = "datasource0")

applymapping1 = ApplyMapping.apply(frame = datasource0, mappings =
[("col1", "string", "col1", "string"), ("col2", "string", "col2",
"string"), ("col3", "string", "col3", "string")], transformation_ctx =
"applymapping1")
resolvechoice2 = ResolveChoice.apply(frame = applymapping1, choice =
"make_struct", transformation_ctx = "resolvechoice2")
dropnullfields3 = DropNullFields.apply(frame = resolvechoice2,
transformation_ctx = "dropnullfields3")
datasink4 = glueContext.write_dynamic_frame.from_options(frame =
dropnullfields3, connection_type = "s3", connection_options = {"path":
"s3://mybucket/output"}, format = "parquet", transformation_ctx =
"datasink4")
job.commit()
```

This ETL script performs the following operations:

- Reads data from a table in the Glue Data Catalog called `mytable` in a database called `mydatabase`
- Applies a mapping to the input data, specifying the data types for each column
- Resolves any data type conflicts in the input data
- Drops any `null` fields from the input data
- Writes the transformed data to an S3 bucket in the Parquet format

Once the code is developed, it can be triggered as an AWS Glue job. These jobs can be triggered in a variety of ways:

- **On a schedule** – For example, every day of the week at 9 a.m. or once a week on Tuesday at 3 p.m.
- **By manual intervention** – When the user kicks off the job via either the Console or the AWS CLI
- **Event triggers** – Based on a triggering event such as a file loading or a row in a database being inserted

Often, these jobs will have dependencies on each other. AWS Glue provides orchestration capabilities to cobble together the ETL dependencies and handles retry logic in case a job fails. The execution of all these jobs is tracked by Amazon CloudWatch, which will enable users to monitor these jobs. Alerts can be created and received for various actions, including job completion or job failure.

IMPORTANT NOTE

Integrating AWS Glue jobs with other orchestration tools such as Apache Airflow and Control-M is possible. You can learn more about **Apache Airflow** at `https://airflow.apache.org/`.

More information about **Control-M** can be found at `https://www.bmc.com/it-solutions/control-m.html`.

Now AWS provides **MWAA**, which is a fully managed service that makes it easy to create, maintain, and monitor workflows using Apache Airflow. MWAA removes the need to set up, operate, and scale infrastructure, allowing you to focus on creating, testing, and running workflows to move and transform data. With MWAA, you can define workflows as **Directed Acyclic Graphs** (**DAGs**) using Python, and then use the MWAA web console or the MWAA API to deploy and manage your workflows. MWAA provides a fully managed execution environment, with built-in support for scheduling, monitoring, and retries. It also integrates with other AWS services, such as Amazon **Simple Queue Service** (**SQS**) and Amazon **Simple Notification Service** (**SNS**), to enable you to build complex data pipelines.

AWS Glue serverless streaming ETL

You may be too young to remember, but back in the day, if you went to a store and tried paying with a credit card, they had these massive books where the checkout person had to look up your card number to determine if your card was fraudulent. Not only did this method slow down the checkout process but, as you can imagine, by the time fraudulent cards were added to the book, they could have been used many times to purchase thousands of dollars worth of merchandise.

As technology improved, this process got quicker to the point where these records became automated and were updated on a nightly basis. But fraud has always been a cat-and-mouse game. Criminals got smart and made sure to use stolen cards faster to be still able to profit from their crimes.

The ideal solution is to be able to report and disseminate the theft of the card in real time. This presents some formidable technological challenges, but technologies like AWS Glue support streaming processing.

Streaming ETL jobs can be created in AWS Glue to continuously process files from streaming services such as Amazon Kinesis and Amazon MSK. These jobs can process, clean, and transform data almost instantaneously. This data then becomes available to data analysts and data scientists so that they can run their models and analysis on the data. Other common use cases for AWS Glue streaming ETL jobs are as follows:

- Processing IoT event streams
- Consuming clickstreams and other web activities
- Analyzing application logs

AWS Glue offers streaming ETL jobs that can be integrated into data pipelines to enhance and consolidate data, merge batch and streaming data sources, and execute analytics and machine learning models. This helps to streamline the process of managing and analyzing data, and can lead to more valuable insights and predictions. All this can be done at scale, enabling the processing of hundreds of thousands of transactions per second.

AWS Glue DataBrew

AWS Glue DataBrew is a user-friendly visual data preparation tool that simplifies the task of cleaning, profiling, and converting data stored in AWS data stores. It provides an intuitive interface for users to easily perform data transformations and makes data more accessible for analysis, reporting, and machine learning.

It is fully integrated with Amazon Glue and can be accessed from the Glue console or via the Glue API. With DataBrew, you can create data transformation recipes using a visual interface, without having to write any code. You can use DataBrew to perform a wide range of data preparation tasks, including filtering and sorting data, renaming and dropping columns, pivoting and unpivoting data, and aggregating and summarizing data.

DataBrew also provides data profiling and visualization capabilities, allowing you to understand the structure and content of your data, identify data quality issues, and preview the results of your transformations. Once you have created and tested your data transformation recipes, you can use DataBrew to schedule them to run at a specific frequency or trigger them to run on demand. You can also export your recipes as Glue ETL jobs or Glue Python code, and use them as part of your larger data processing workflows.

So far, in this section, we have learned about the basics of AWS Glue. We also learned about the components that make up AWS Glue and make it a juggernaut. In the next section, we will put it together and explain how the various components work together to provide a powerful combination and deliver one of the most popular services in the AWS ecosystem.

Putting AWS Glue components together

Now that we have learned about all the major components in AWS Glue, let's look at how all the pieces fit together. The following diagram illustrates this:

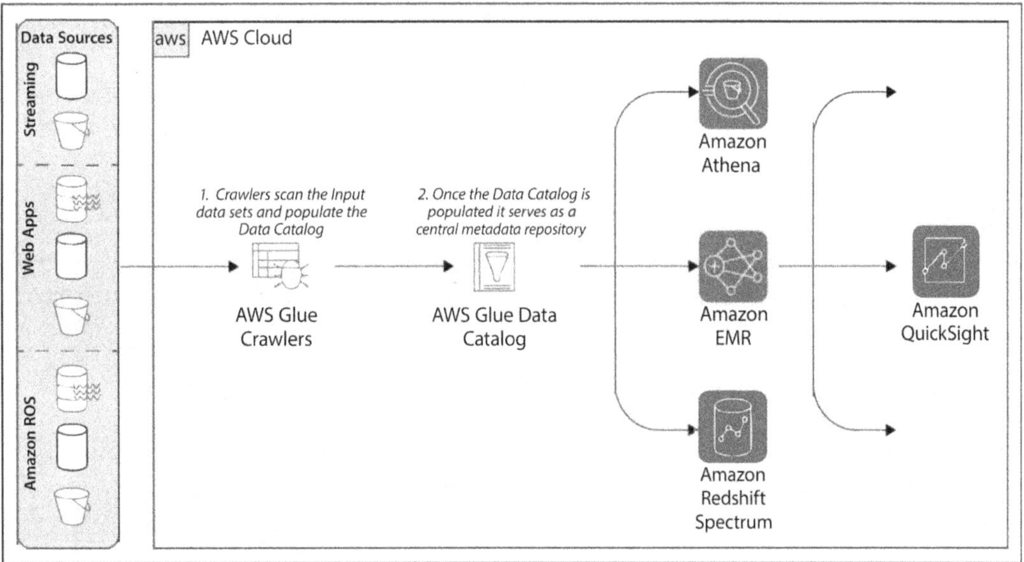

Figure 10.2: AWS Glue typical workflow steps

In the preceding diagram, we see can the various steps that can take place when AWS Glue runs. The steps are explained in the following points:

1. The first step is for the crawlers to scan sources and extract metadata from them.
2. This metadata can then be used to seed the AWS Glue Data Catalog.
3. This metadata can be used by other AWS services, such as Amazon Athena, an AWS-provided query service, Redshift Spectrum, an AWS-provided cloud data warehouse service, and Amazon EMR. These services can be used to write queries against the ingested data using the metadata from the AWS Glue Data Catalog to build these queries.
4. Finally, the results of these queries can be used for visualizations in other AWS services, including Amazon QuickSight (an AWS-provided business intelligence service).

You will learn about Amazon Redshift, Athena, and QuickSight in *Chapter 11, Data Warehouses, Data Queries, and Visualization in AWS*.

A wide variety of data sources can be ingested with AWS Glue, such as Amazon S3 objects, Amazon RDS records, or web application data via APIs.

Hopefully, the discussion in these sections has given you a good taste of the basics of AWS Glue and its importance in the AWS ecosystem. Hopefully, you are also convinced that data and the insights derived from processing and distilling it are critical for today's enterprises.

We will now spend some time learning the best ways to implement AWS Glue in your environment.

AWS Glue best practices

As we have done with many of the other services covered in the book, we will now provide some recommendations on how to best architect the configuration of your AWS Glue jobs.

Amazon Athena, under the hood, uses the open-source software Presto to process **Data Manipulation Language** (**DML**) statements and Apache Hive to process DDL statements. An example of a DML statement is a `select` statement, and an example of a DDL statement is a `create table` statement.

Similarly, under the hood, AWS Glue runs its ETL jobs using Apache Spark.

Knowing that these are the underlying technologies used by these AWS services will enable you to better leverage and optimize your use of Amazon Athena and AWS Glue.

Choosing the right worker type

AWS Glue can execute with one of three different worker types. Worker types are also known as **Data Processing Units** (**DPUs**). Each type has different advantages and disadvantages, and they should be chosen based on the use case that we have on hand.

Worker types, or DPUs, come in these configurations:

- **Standard** – This worker type has 16 GB of memory, 4 vCPUs for computing power, 50 GB of attached EBS storage, and includes two Spark executors.
- **G.1X** – G.1X worker types have 16 GB of memory, use 4 vCPUs, and come with 64 GB of attached EBS storage and only 1 Spark executor.
- **G.2X** – The G.2X worker types have 32 GB of memory, use 8 vCPUs, and come with 128 GB of attached EBS storage and only 1 Spark executor.

AWS Glue's serverless architecture takes advantage of Spark to compute parallelism and can scale horizontally regardless of the type of worker.

If a workload is more memory intensive, AWS Glue jobs that could benefit from vertical scaling should use the G1.X or G2.X worker types.

Optimizing file splitting

AWS Glue automatically splits files when processing common traditional file formats such as CSV and JSON, as well as some of the more modern formats, including AVRO and Parquet, by using something called AWS Glue DynamicFrame classes. To learn more about DynamicFrame, you can visit `https://aws.amazon.com/blogs/big-data/work-with-partitioned-data-in-aws-glue/`.

A "file split" is a section in a file that an AWS Glue worker can process independently. Out of the box, file splitting can be performed on line-delimited native formats. This enables the parallel execution of Apache Spark jobs on AWS Glue, spanning multiple nodes. AWS Glue jobs can be optimized to handle files that have a file size between hundreds of megabytes and a couple of gigabytes by leveraging horizontal scaling and attaching more AWS Glue workers.

Splitting files into smaller blocks can also improve performance when using block-based compression formats. This is because the compressed data can be processed in parallel across multiple nodes, allowing for faster data processing and analysis. Each compression block can be read on a split boundary file and processed independently and simultaneously with other files. Compression formats that don't support splitting, such as gzip, bzip2, Zstandard, LZMA, and so on, do not achieve performance gains from file splitting.

The inputs should use several medium-sized files to achieve horizontal scalability with compression formats or files that can't be split.

After files have been split, they can be stored in Amazon S3 and accessed as individual objects. These objects can then be deserialized into an AWS Glue DynamicFrame partition, which is a logical container for organizing and processing data. Once the data is in a DynamicFrame, it can be processed using Apache Spark tasks to perform various operations such as filtering, aggregating, and transforming the data. The size of a deserialized partition can be much larger than a disk block file split size of 64 MB, such as for highly compressed formats that can be split like Parquet or larger files that use compression formats such as gzip and cannot be split. When data is deserialized into an AWS Glue DynamicFrame partition, it is not loaded into memory unless required for processing. Instead, Apache Spark's lazy transformation evaluation is used, which means that transformations on the data are only performed when necessary. This approach helps to avoid memory pressure on AWS Glue tasks, as only the required data is loaded into memory at any given time.

However, when a partition is explicitly cached in memory or spills onto a disk, it can return **Out-of-Memory** (**OOM**) or out-of-disk exceptions. AWS Glue can handle these use cases with AWS Glue worker types that use DPU instances that can be vertically scaled.

Exceeding YARN's memory overhead allocation

Apache YARN is the resource manager used under the hood by Apache Spark and AWS Glue. **YARN** stands for **Yet Another Resource Negotiator**. YARN oversees allocating resources when Spark is running and handling applications workloads. On top of handling memory allocation for each executor running jobs, YARN also oversees the allocation of additional memory assigned to the JVM and metadata that needs to be loaded for the JVM to run correctly. This overhead is allocated 10% of the total executor memory by default. Operations that require a lot of memory, such as table joins or dataset processing with skewed distributions, may require additional overhead and throw an error. If you know that your application will be memory-intensive, it is recommended to allocate additional overheard memory from the start to avoid these types of errors.

Another way to avoid these OOM issues is to use AWS Glue's vertical scaling feature. Using workers that have been assigned more memory and disk space can also help to avoid this problem.

Lastly, using the dashboard provided by AWS Glue with job metrics can assist in debugging and resolving these OOM issues. For memory-intensive jobs, such as on large datasets with significant skew, use the G1.X and G2.X worker types.

For more information about how to debug these types of issues, visit `https://docs.aws.amazon.com/glue/latest/dg/monitor-profile-debug-oom-abnormalities.html`.

Leveraging the Apache Spark UI

Another helpful tool in the Spark arsenal is the Apache Spark UI. The Spark UI can inspect, monitor, and optimize AWS Glue ETL jobs. It allows you to visualize the jobs by providing **Directed Acyclic Graphs** (**DAGs**) of the job's execution. It can also be used to identify demanding stages and large shuffles and to analyze query plans. The UI will enable you to quickly identify the bottlenecks in your Spark jobs and make adjustments to increase performance and remove those bottlenecks.

More information about the Spark UI can be found at `https://docs.aws.amazon.com/glue/latest/dg/monitor-spark-ui.html`.

Processing many small files

It is not uncommon for AWS Glue to routinely handle thousands and even millions of files. This would be more the norm than the exception for use cases involving Amazon Kinesis Data Firehose. In these situations, the Apache Spark driver can run out of memory while reading these files.

Apache Spark version 2.2 can handle 600,000 files on a standard worker type. To increase the number of files that a worker can handle, AWS provides an option to process these files in larger batches. One way to do this is to use a G1.X worker to read the files instead of a standard worker.

Another way is to reduce the number of files processed at one time. This can be achieved by taking advantage of AWS Glue file groupings. Doing so reduces the chance of getting OOM exceptions. The `groupFiles` and `groupSize` parameters need to be configured to enable file grouping. Here is a sample call that sets those parameters:

```
dyf = glueContext.create_dynamic_frame_from_options("s3",
    {'paths': ["s3://path-to-files/"],
    'recurse':True,
    'groupFiles': 'inPartition',
    'groupSize': '2084236'},
    format="json")
```

The purpose of this command is to create a dynamic framework that can then be fed into other ETL jobs for processing. The `paths` parameter determines the S3 folder that contains the files used to create the frame. The `recurse` parameter indicates whether subdirectories in this folder should be included for processing.

The `groupFiles` parameter can be configured to group files in an S3 partition within a folder or across Amazon S3 partitions. In many instances, grouping in each partition is enough to bring down the number of parallel Spark tasks and reduce the amount of memory used by the Spark tasks.

In a battery of tests, ETL jobs configured using this grouping parameter proved to be about 7 times faster than other jobs without this configuration when handling over 300,000 files spanning over 100 Amazon S3 partitions. A significant portion of time is spent with Apache Spark building in-memory indices while listing Amazon S3 files and scheduling many short-running tasks to handle these files. When grouping is enabled, AWS Glue should be able to handle over one million files simultaneously using the standard AWS Glue worker type.

Tuning the `groupSize` parameter can significantly impact the number of files that can be processed at any one time, which translates into how many files can be produced. Properly tuning this parameter can achieve significant task parallelism, while not correctly configuring it can result in the cluster being underutilized and many of the workers sitting idle.

By default, when the number of files exceeds about 50,000, AWS Glue will automatically enable grouping. AWS Glue can figure out an appropriate value for the `groupSize` parameter and set it accordingly to minimize the amount of excessive parallelism.

Data partitioning and predicate pushdown

Partitioning files is an important technique to split datasets so that these files can be accessed quickly and efficiently. Picking an excellent key to split files is critical to gaining these efficiencies. For example, a dataset may be divided into folders using the ingestion date as the key. In this case, you may have a series of subfolders organized by year, month, and day.

Here is an example of what a directory using this naming scheme could look like:

```
s3://employees/year=2020/month=01/day=01/
```

You can use the `INSERT INTO` statement in HiveQL (Hive's SQL-like query language) with the `HiveOutputFormat` and the appropriate file format. For example, you can use the following HiveQL statement to write the results of a `SELECT` query to the specified S3 location as ORC files:

```
INSERT INTO TABLE employees
    PARTITION (year=2020, month=01, day=01)
    SELECT * FROM source_table
    WHERE year=2020 AND month=01 AND day=01;
```

Partitioning the data in such a way enables predicate pushdown. Predicate pushdown is a fancy way of saying that by partitioning the data, we don't need to read all the directories and files to get the results we need when we have a query with a filter.

Predicate pushdown uses filter criteria using partition columns. With predicate pushdown, the data is not read into memory first and then filtered. Instead, because the data is pre-sorted, we know what files meet the criteria being sought, and only those files are brought into memory while the rest of the files are simply skipped.

For example, imagine you have a query like this:

```
Select * from employees where year = 2019
```

Here, the `year` is the partition, and `2019` is the filter criteria. In this case, the file we had as an example previously would be skipped.

Using pruning can deliver massive performance boosts and greatly reduced response times. Performance can be improved by providing even more filters in the selection criteria, which will eliminate additional partitions.

Partitioning data while writing to Amazon S3

The last task during processing is to persist the transformed output in Amazon S3. Once this is done, other services, such as Amazon Athena, can be used for their retrieval. By default, when a `DynamicFrame` is persisted, it is not partitioned. The results are persisted in a single output path. Until recently, it was only possible to partition a `DynamicFrame` by converting it into a Spark SQL DataFrame before it persisted. However, nowadays, native partitioning using a key sequence can be used to write out `DynamicFrame`.

This can be accomplished by setting the `partition keys` parameter during sink creation. As an example, the following code can be used to output a dataset:

```
%spark
glueContext.getSinkWithFormat(
    connectionType = "s3",
    options = JsonOptions(Map("path" -> "$output_path", "partitionKeys" ->
Seq("process_year"))),
    format = "parquet").writeDynamicFrame(employees)
```

This method creates a `DataSink` that persists data to an output destination. This destination can be repositories on Amazon S3, Amazon RDS, and so on.

This method allows you to set the data format to be used when persisting the data.

In this case, `$output_path` is the output directory in Amazon S3. The `partitionKeys` parameter specifies the column used as a partition when writing the data to Amazon S3.

When data is written out, the `process_year` column is removed from the dataset and is instead used to help form the directory structure. Here is how the directory might look if we listed it out:

```
PRE year=2020
PRE year=2019
PRE year=2018
PRE year=2017
PRE year=2016
```

So, what are some good columns to use when selecting partition keys? There are two criteria that should drive this selection:

- Use columns that have a low (but not extremely low) cardinality. For example, a person's name, phone number, or email would not be a good candidate. Conversely, a column with only one or two values is also not a good candidate.
- Use columns that are expected to be used often and will be used as filters.

For example, if your dataset contains log data, using dates and partitioning them by year, month, and day is often a good strategy. The cardinality should be just right. We should have plenty of results for each day of the logs, and using predicate pushdown would result in only retrieving files for individual days.

There is another benefit to correctly partitioning files, in addition to improving query performance. A proper partition also minimizes costly Apache Spark shuffle transformations for downstream ETL jobs.

Repartitioning a dataset by frequently calling the `repartition()` or `coalesce()` functions leads workers to shuffle data. This can have a negative impact on the time it takes to run ETL jobs and will most likely require more memory. By contrast, writing data into Amazon S3 from the start using Apache Hive partitions does not require the data to be shuffled, and it can be sorted locally within a worker node. In Apache Hive, a partition is a way to divide a table into smaller and more manageable pieces, based on the values of certain columns. For example, you can partition a table by date, so that each partition corresponds to a specific day, month, or year. Partitions can improve query performance by enabling the Hive query optimizer to skip over irrelevant partitions, and by allowing data to be stored in a more efficient way.

They can also make it easier to manage and organize large datasets by allowing you to delete or exchange individual partitions as needed.

This concludes the best practices we recommend using to deploy AWS Glue. This list is by no means exhaustive and only scratches the surface. Deploying AWS Glue at scale is not trivial, and architects can build a career purely by mastering this powerful and fundamental service.

Choosing between AWS Glue and Amazon EMR

Having learned about Glue and EMR, you must be wondering, to some extent, whether these offerings do a similar job in data processing, and when to choose one over the other. Yes, AWS has a similar offering and that can be confusing sometimes, but both have a specific purpose. Amazon always works backward from the customer, so all these offerings are available because customers have asked for them.

There is a no-brainer for your data cataloging needs; you should always use AWS Glue, and these data catalogs can be utilized when you are processing a job in EMR. However, Glue only supports the Spark framework, and if you are interested in using any other open-source software such as Hive, Ping, or Presto, then you need to choose EMR.

When running data transformation using the Spark platform, you must choose between EMR and Glue. Suppose you are migrating your ETL job from an on-premises Hadoop environment. In that case, you can go with EMR, as it will require minimal code changes, but if you are starting fresh, it's better to start with Glue, as it is serverless with in-built job orchestration, which will make your work much more manageable. In addition, if you want more control over your environment at the OS level, then you can choose EMR, as Glue abstracts those details. Again, if you want to benefit from `DynamicFrame` to streamline your data at runtime, then you can choose Glue over EMR. Here are some examples of use cases where you might choose AWS Glue over Amazon EMR, or vice versa:

- **ETL and data preparation:** If you need to extract data from various sources, transform and clean it, and load it into a target data store, AWS Glue is a good choice. It provides a fully managed ETL service with a visual interface and built-in data transformation capabilities. Amazon EMR is more geared toward distributed data processing and analysis, and may not be the best choice for ETL and data preparation tasks.
- **Distributed data processing:** If you have a large dataset that needs to be processed using a distributed computing framework, such as Apache Hadoop or Apache Spark, Amazon EMR is a good choice.

It provides a managed big data platform that can run distributed applications written in various languages and can scale up or down as needed. AWS Glue also supports Apache Spark, but it is more geared towards ETL and data preparation tasks, and may not be the best choice for distributed data processing.

- **Machine learning:** If you need to build and train machine learning models on large datasets, Amazon EMR is a good choice. It integrates with Apache Spark and other machine learning libraries, and provides a range of tools and frameworks for building, training, and deploying machine learning models at scale. AWS Glue also provides some basic machine learning capabilities, such as data preparation and feature engineering, but it is not as comprehensive as the machine learning capabilities provided by Amazon EMR.
- **Data visualization and analysis:** If you need to create interactive data visualizations and perform ad hoc data analysis using SQL, Python, R, or other languages, Amazon EMR is a good choice. It provides a range of tools and frameworks for data visualization and analysis, including Apache Zeppelin, Jupyter, and RStudio. AWS Glue provides some basic data visualization capabilities, such as data profiling and previewing the results of transformations, but it is not as comprehensive as the data visualization capabilities provided by Amazon EMR.

Ultimately, whatever service you choose to run your spark workload, AWS provides multiple features and options. Before November 2021, only Glue was serverless, so if you didn't want to manage infrastructure, it was always a clear choice to go for Glue, but now after the launch of EMR serverless, you have more choices available to run any Hadoop open-source framework on the cloud, bringing the benefits of serverless capabilities and offloading all the infrastructure admin work to AWS.

Streaming data is becoming more important as customers expect real-time responses. Let's learn more about taking care of streaming data in the cloud.

Handling streaming data in AWS

In today's world, businesses aim to gain a competitive edge by providing timely tailored experiences to consumers. Consumers expect personalized experiences that meet their specific needs and reject those that don't, such as when applying for a loan, investing, shopping online, tracking health alerts, or monitoring home security systems. As a result, speed has become a critical characteristic that businesses strive to achieve. Insights from data are perishable and can lose value quickly. Streaming data processing allows analytical insights to be gathered and acted upon instantly to deliver the desired customer experience.

Batch processing data doesn't allow for real-time risk mitigation or customer authentication, and the customer experience can be ruined – and is hard to recover – if action isn't taken in real time. Acting on real-time data can help prevent fraud and increase customer loyalty. Untimely data, on the other hand, can inhibit your firm's ability to grow. The following are some use cases for streaming data:

- **Anomaly and fraud detection in real-time:** Streaming data is used to detect fraudulent activities in real time, by analyzing patterns and anomalies in financial transactions or other types of data.
- **Tailoring customer experience in real time:** Online businesses continuously push features on their websites to respond to ever-changing competition, drive higher sales, and enhance customer satisfaction. With the help of real-time streaming analytics, businesses can understand a given feature's adoption and tailor the pushed feature to drive more traffic in real time to ensure success.
- **Empowering IoT analytics:** Industrial and commercial IoT sectors have many use cases that can take advantage of real-time streaming analytics. In the IoT space, streaming data is used to track and monitor the real-time status of devices and systems, and to trigger actions based on specific events or thresholds.
- **Financial trading:** In the financial industry, streaming data is used to track market trends, analyze trading patterns, and make real-time decisions.
- **Social media:** Streaming data is used to analyze social media activity in real time and identify trends, sentiments, and patterns.
- **Supply chain management:** Streaming data is used to track and monitor the real-time status of logistics and supply chain operations, and to optimize the flow of goods and materials.
- **Telecommunications:** Streaming data is used to monitor and analyze network traffic and performance in real time, optimize network usage, and detect issues.
- **Traffic management:** Streaming data is used to track and monitor traffic patterns and conditions in real time, optimize traffic flow, and reduce congestion.

To enable real-time analytics, you need to ingest, process, and analyze large volumes of high-velocity data from various sources in real time. Devices and/or applications produce real-time data at high velocity. In the case of IoT devices, tens of thousands of data sources need to be collected and ingested in real time. After that, you store data in the order it was received for a set duration and provide the ability for it to be replayed indefinitely during this time. You need to enable real-time analytics or streaming ETL and store the final data in a data lake or data warehouse.

AWS provides a streaming data processing ability through its serverless offering, Amazon Kinesis, and Kafka offers it through Amazon **Managed Streaming for Apache Kafka** (**MSK**). Let's begin by learning about Kinesis in more detail.

Streaming data processing with Amazon Kinesis

Amazon Kinesis is a cloud-based service that provides businesses with the ability to gather, process, and analyze real-time streaming data, allowing them to gain valuable insights and respond quickly to new information. It offers powerful and cost-effective capabilities for processing large volumes of streaming data at scale, and allows you to select the best tools for your application's specific requirements. With Amazon Kinesis, you can collect different types of real-time data, including video, audio, logs, clickstreams, and IoT telemetry, and use it for analytics, machine learning, and other purposes.

Amazon Kinesis enables real-time processing of data as it arrives, providing instantaneous responses without having to wait for all the data to be collected. The service provides four fully managed options for collecting, processing, and analyzing streaming data in real time. Let's explore the different services offered by Kinesis.

Amazon Kinesis Data Streams (KDS)

KDS captures data in real time and allows you to build custom, real-time applications for data processing through popular stream processing frameworks. Amazon Kinesis stores incoming data in the order it was received, for a specified duration, and allows for indefinite replays during this time period. This provides the flexibility to process and analyze data multiple times or use it for testing and debugging. By default, KDS retain data for 24 hours, but extended retention is available up to 7 days, and data can be retained for up to 365 days.

KDS has a data shard to ingest and hold data. To simplify this, you can imagine each shard as a single water pipe and data as water stored in this pipe. If you have a large volume of water, you need multiple pipes to consume that, and in the same manner, you need to plan your shards if there is a large volume of data. Each shard can ingest 1 MB of data per second, or 1,000 records per second, and consumers can read data from the shard at the rate of 2 MB of data per second, or 5 reads per second. With the standard consumer model, the lowest latency is 200 ms, and AWS provides an **Enhanced Fan-Out** (**EFO**) data consumer, with which you can achieve 70 ms of latency.

In 2021, AWS launched long-term retention, where you can store data for up to 1 year in KDS. AWS also provides an automatically scaled capacity in response to changing data volumes, which helps to achieve built-in availability and fault tolerance by default.

Amazon Kinesis Data Firehose (KDF)

Kinesis Data Firehose (KDF) is a fully managed service that captures, transforms, and loads data streams into Amazon S3, Amazon Redshift, Amazon Elasticsearch, and Splunk for near real-time analytics through existing business intelligence tools. KDF is serverless, which means no administration and seamless elasticity. It involves direct-to-data-store integration without any coding requirements. You can ingest data in near real time and perform data format conversion to Parquet/ORC on the fly. KDF now provides data delivery to any HTTP endpoint. It supports the AWS API gateway, which helps load data directly to RDS, Amazon SNS, and other popular platforms such as Datadog, Sumo Logic, New Relic, and MongoDB.

For example, KDF can be used in a scenario where a company wants to monitor customer interactions on their e-commerce website in real-time to improve the customer experience. The website generates clickstream data, which includes user clicks, navigation, and other interactions. KDF can be used to capture this clickstream data in real-time, transform it into a structured format, and then load it into Amazon Redshift or Amazon OpenSearch Service for further analysis. The company can then use business intelligence tools such as Amazon QuickSight to visualize the data and gain insights into user behavior, enabling them to make data-driven decisions to improve the customer experience.

Another example could be in the context of IoT data. KDF can be used to capture and process sensor data generated by IoT devices and store it in Amazon S3. This data can then be analyzed to identify patterns or anomalies in device behavior, enabling predictive maintenance or other use cases that improve operational efficiency.

In both use cases, KDF allows for the processing and analysis of streaming data in near real time, enabling businesses to make quick decisions based on current data, and thus improving their operations and customer experience.

Amazon Kinesis Data Analytics (KDA)

KDA processes real-time data streams for analytics through SQL and Apache Flink applications. KDA enables advanced analytics on streaming data through built-in functions that can filter, aggregate, and transform data in real time. With sub-second latencies, it can quickly process streaming data, allowing you to analyze and respond to incoming data and events as they occur.

You can run KDA Studio in interactive mode to inspect streaming data, run ad hoc queries, and visualize data using basic charts (bar charts, pie charts, trend lines, and pivot charts) that can be used for a one-click visualization of any output data within a notebook.

Kinesis Data Analytics Studio is a web-based interface that allows you to visually build, test, and debug KDA applications. The studio provides a range of features, such as an SQL editor, a code editor, a data preview tool, and a debugger, to help you build and test your analytics applications.

KDA also has in-built support for **Apache Flink** for more sophisticated applications or if you prefer Java. The following are the key benefits of KDA for Apache Flink:

- **Simple programming** – Easy-to-use and flexible APIs make building apps fast
- **High performance** – In-memory computing provides low latency and high throughput
- **Stateful processing** – Durable application state saves strong data integrity with exactly-once processing

KDA offers native integration with Amazon KDS, Amazon KDF, and Amazon MSK, enabling you to process and analyze streaming data in real time. With KDA, you can use built-in functions to filter, aggregate, and transform data streams for advanced analytics. KDA is built on Apache Flink, which provides low-latency processing and high-throughput ingestion for real time data streams. Additionally, KDA supports other data sources that can produce data directly to Apache Flink, enabling you to bring in data from other sources and process it in real-time alongside your Kinesis data.

Amazon Kinesis Video Streams (KVS) is another offering that supports secure video streaming from connected devices to AWS for analytics, machine learning, and other processing. It can be beneficial for media streaming and processing data from video streams, such as CCTV.

Real-time data processing using Kinesis can be life-saving for healthcare and emergency services. Real-time analytics can be used in clinical healthcare to monitor patient safety, personalize patient results, assess clinical risks, and reduce patient readmission. By processing and analyzing data in real time, healthcare organizations can gain insights and take actions that can improve patient care and outcomes. For example, real-time analytics can be used to identify potential risks and intervene before they lead to adverse events, or to tailor treatment plans based on the latest data and evidence. They can also help to reduce the number of readmissions by identifying and addressing the root causes of readmission. Overall, real-time analytics can help healthcare organizations to deliver better, more personalized care to their patients. Wearable health device data, combined with geospatial data, can proactively notify relatives, caregivers, or incident commanders for a timely response. Kinesis has many use cases; you can learn more about them by referring to the AWS whitepaper *Streaming Data Solutions on AWS with Amazon Kinesis* – `https://aws.amazon.com/kinesis/whitepaper/`.

Apache Kafka is one of the most popular technologies to address streaming use cases and build an organization's **Enterprise Service Bus** (**ESB**) for communication between different applications. AWS provides a managed Kafka offering to address those use cases. Let's learn more about it.

Amazon Managed Streaming for Apache Kafka (MSK)

Apache Kafka is one of the most popular open-source platforms for building real-time streaming data pipelines and applications. Managing Apache Kafka clusters in production can be difficult, as it requires careful planning and ongoing maintenance. Setting up and configuring Apache Kafka requires provisioning servers and performing manual tasks. Additionally, you must continuously monitor and maintain the servers to ensure their reliability, security, and performance. Tasks involved in managing a cluster encompass several activities such as replacing failed servers, orchestrating patches and upgrades, designing the cluster for high availability, storing data durably, setting up monitoring and alarms, and planning scaling events to support changing workloads. Overall, managing Apache Kafka clusters in production can be a complex and time-consuming process.

Amazon MSK is a fully managed service provided by AWS that allows users to build and run production applications on Apache Kafka without requiring in-house Apache Kafka infrastructure management expertise. With Amazon MSK, AWS handles the infrastructure management tasks such as server replacement, patching and upgrades, and high availability design. This enables users to focus on building their applications and leveraging the features of Apache Kafka, such as its ability to handle real-time, high-throughput, fault-tolerant data streaming. MSK allows you to launch clusters across multiple AZs with customizable configurations to achieve high-performance and high-availability environments. You can scale out compute by adding brokers to existing clusters, and scale up storage without downtime.

Amazon MSK is a fully managed service that allows you to capture, process, and derive insights from log and event streams in real time. Amazon MSK enables users to ingest events and analyze data streams in real-time using Apache Zeppelin notebooks, providing near-instant insights. With MSK, you can build centralized data buses using the Apache Kafka log structure, enabling the creation of real time, secure, and centralized data buses. Additionally, you can create event-driven systems that can react to digital changes within your applications and business infrastructure in real time. By simplifying the process of building, running, and maintaining streaming data pipelines and event-driven systems, MSK streamlines the data processing workflow.

Amazon MSK provides native Apache Kafka APIs to enable you to work with data lakes, stream data to and from databases, and power machine learning and analytics applications. If you're already running Apache Kafka on-premises, on EC2, or with another managed service provider, you can migrate your existing Apache Kafka applications to AWS and run them without any changes to the application code. This ensures open-source compatibility, and you can continue using custom and community-built tools like MirrorMaker and Apache Flink. Apache Kafka MirrorMaker is a tool that enables you to replicate data between Apache Kafka clusters. It works by reading data from a source Kafka cluster, and then writing the data to a target Kafka cluster. MirrorMaker can be used for various purposes, such as disaster recovery, data backup, data migration, and cross-region replication.

MirrorMaker provides various configuration options, such as the ability to filter data based on topic, partition, or offset, and to customize the consumer and producer settings. It also provides features such as message transformation, error handling, and monitoring, to help you manage the data replication process.

Let's look into Amazon MSK cluster architecture in detail.

Amazon MSK cluster architecture

With MSK, you can focus on your applications and use cases, rather than worrying about the underlying infrastructure and operational tasks. MSK handles the provisioning and maintenance of the Kafka clusters and provides features such as automatic scaling, self-healing, and monitoring to ensure high availability and performance. You can see the complete list of operations available in the Amazon MSK API reference guide – `https://docs.aws.amazon.com/msk/1.0/apireference/resources.html`.

The following diagram provides insight into an Amazon MSK cluster. Amazon MSK provides the capability to create clusters that utilize Apache Kafka versions up to 3.2.0. AWS keeps on adding new versions as they become available, which allows users to take advantage of the latest features and improvements of Apache Kafka without worrying about infrastructure management. Please refer to the Amazon MSK developer guide for the latest information on the Amazon MSK-supported version of Kafka – `https://docs.aws.amazon.com/msk/latest/developerguide/supported-kafka-versions.html`:

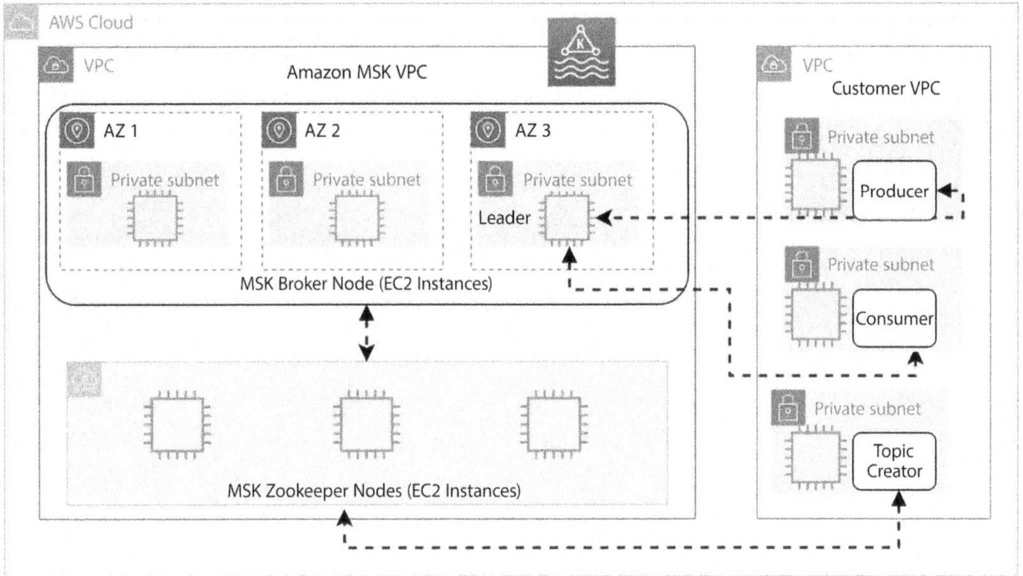

Figure 10.3: Amazon MSK architecture

The architecture of Amazon MSK consists of the following components:

- **Kafka clusters**: An MSK cluster is a group of Amazon EC2 instances that run the Apache Kafka software. An MSK cluster can have one or more Kafka brokers and can be scaled up or down as needed to support the processing and storage requirements of your applications.
- **Zookeeper**: Apache Kafka uses Apache Zookeeper to store metadata and coordinate the Kafka brokers. In an MSK cluster, Zookeeper is automatically deployed and configured as part of the cluster.
- **Producers and consumers**: Producers are applications or systems that produce data and send it to a Kafka cluster, while consumers are applications or systems that receive data from a Kafka cluster and process it. In an MSK cluster, you can use the Apache Kafka producer and consumer APIs to produce and consume data, or use higher-level libraries and tools such as Kafka Connect or KDA to simplify the process.
- **Data storage**: Apache Kafka stores data in topics, which are partitioned and replicated across the Kafka brokers in the cluster. In an MSK cluster, data is stored in Amazon EBS volumes or Amazon S3 buckets, depending on the storage type you choose.
- **Networking**: Amazon MSK uses Amazon VPC to provide a secure and isolated network environment for your Kafka clusters. You can specify the VPC, subnets, and security groups to use when you create an MSK cluster.

By default, MSK creates a new VPC and subnets for a cluster and configures the security groups to allow traffic between the Kafka brokers and the producers and consumers. However, you can also choose to use an existing VPC and subnets, or create a custom VPC and subnets using AWS CloudFormation templates. Once the MSK cluster has been created, the Kafka brokers and the Zookeeper nodes are launched in the specified subnets and are automatically registered with the security groups. The Kafka brokers and the Zookeeper nodes communicate with each other and with the producers and consumers using private IP addresses within the VPC.

You can also use VPC peering or a VPN to connect your MSK cluster to other VPCs or on-premises networks and enable communication between the Kafka brokers and the producers and consumers using public or private IP addresses. Overall, the networking configuration of an MSK cluster determines how the Kafka brokers, the Zookeeper nodes, and the producers and consumers communicate with each other and with the rest of your network. It is important to carefully plan and configure the networking for your MSK cluster to ensure the high availability and performance of your Kafka-based applications.

Amazon MSK provides a range of tools and features to help you monitor and manage your Kafka clusters and applications. This includes integration with Amazon CloudWatch for monitoring, Amazon CloudFormation for infrastructure as code, and the AWS Management Console for visual management.

At re:Invent 2021, AWS launched a new offering called MSK Serverless, which helps you to easily run Apache Kafka clusters without needing to adjust the size of the cluster capacity or worry about overprovisioning. With Amazon MSK Serverless, you can scale input and output (I/O) instantly without the need to manually manage capacity or partition reassignments. This service is designed to provide a simplified and cost-effective way to stream and retain data with pricing based on throughput. Additionally, you only pay for the data volume that you stream and retain, making it a cost-efficient option for managing streaming data workloads. If you are planning to migrate your existing Apache Kafka workload to MSK, AWS has published an MSK migration guide to help you, which you can find by visiting the link here – `https://docs.aws.amazon.com/whitepapers/latest/amazon-msk-migration-guide`.

Handling data cataloging for streaming data can be complicated. Let's learn about AWS's new offering for streaming data cataloging.

Data cataloging for streaming data using AWS Glue Schema Registry (GSR)

Data streaming technologies like Amazon MSK, Apache Kafka, and Amazon Kinesis are widely used across various industries to capture and distribute data generated by applications, websites, or machines. They serve as a highly available data transport layer, which separates the data-producing applications from the real-time routing, analytics, and machine learning data processors. This decoupling allows for greater scalability and flexibility, as well as the ability to quickly and easily respond to new information and insights in real time. Industries such as finance, healthcare, manufacturing, retail, and more use data streaming technologies to improve operational efficiency, enhance customer experiences, and gain competitive advantages through data-driven decision making.

However, it's hard to coordinate data formats and structures (schemas) across so many systems owned by different teams. Teams have difficulty using each other's data, and downstream teams have to adapt when formats change. They often build complex tools or custom code to ensure data continuity when schemas evolve.

Cataloging streaming data is challenging due to the continuous ingestion of data and various formats. AWS introduced the **Glue Schema Registry** (**GSR**) to manage data schemas for streaming data catalogs. It enables users to discover, control, and evolve data schemas easily.

AWS GSR allows you to centrally manage and store schemas for your data, and provides tools and APIs to help you create, modify, and version schemas as your data evolves. It also provides a schema discovery feature that allows you to discover and extract schemas from data sources, and a schema validation feature that allows you to validate data records against the stored schemas.

AWS GSR is designed to be used with other AWS Glue services, such as AWS Glue ETL jobs and AWS Glue DataBrew, to help you build and operate data pipelines that are based on well-defined and standardized data schemas. It can also be used with other AWS services that support data integration, such as Amazon KDS and Amazon S3, to help you ensure the integrity and quality of the data being ingested and processed.

AWS GSR prevents downstream failures caused by schema changes and boosts productivity for developers by enforcing schemas where data is produced before the data gets sent downstream. The customer can customize schema enforcement using one of eight compatibility modes (`Backward`, `Backward_All`, `Forward`, `Forward_All`, `Full`, `Full_All`, `Disabled`, or `None`). The schema registry's open source serializers allow for the efficient serialization of data into a compact binary and compressed format.

This results in reduced data transfer and storage costs for customers compared to using uncompressed JSON.

Now that you have learned about Kinesis and MSK, let's see the significant differences and when to choose one versus the other.

Choosing between Amazon Kinesis and Amazon MSK

AWS launched Kinesis in 2013, and it was the only streaming data offering until 2018 when AWS launched MSK, in response to the high demand from their customers for managed Apache Kafka clusters. Now, both are similar offerings, so you must be wondering when to choose one versus the other. If you already have an existing Kafka workload on-premises or are running Kafka in EC2, it's better to migrate to MSK, as you don't need to make any changes in the code. You can take the help of the existing MirrorMaker tool to migrate. The following diagrams show key architectural differences between MSK and Kinesis:

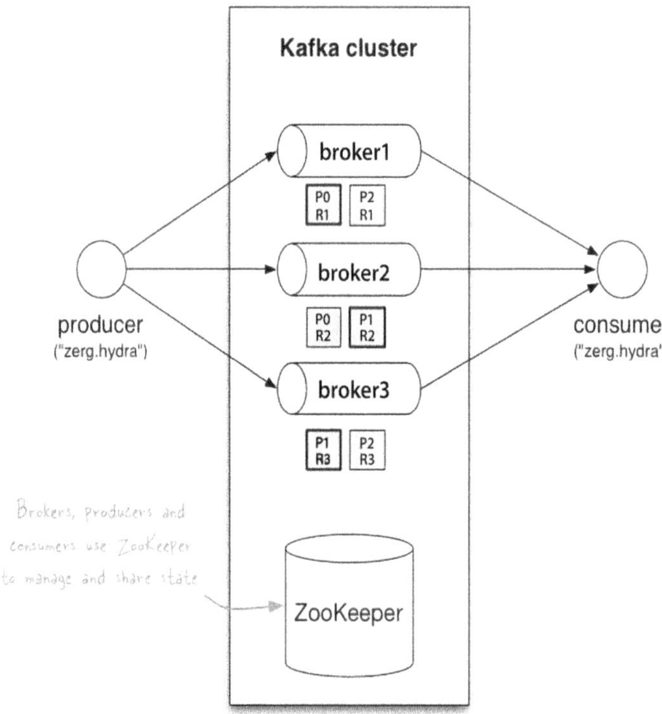

Figure 10.4: Amazon MSK architecture

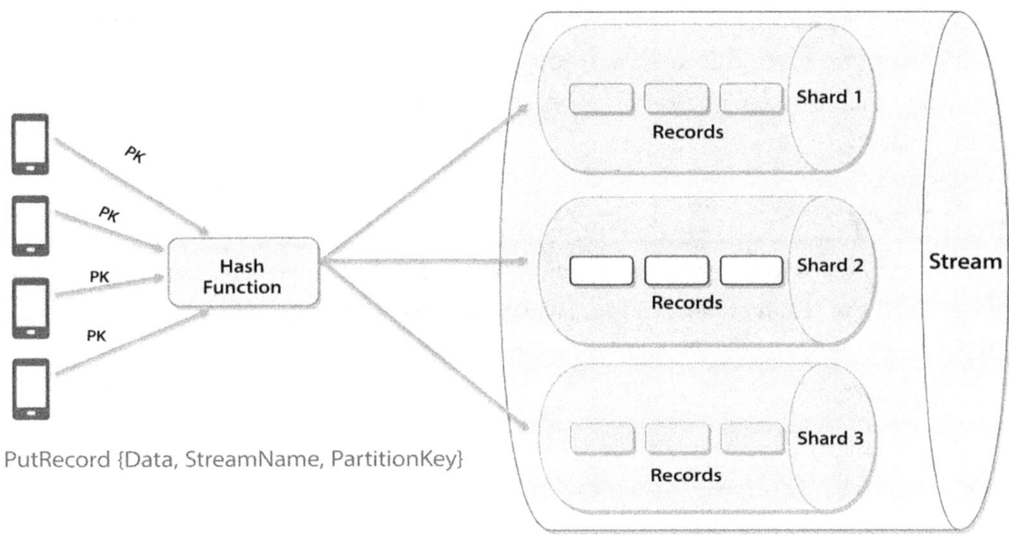

Figure 10.5: Amazon Kinesis architecture

As shown in the preceding diagrams, there are similarities between the MSK and Kinesis architectures. In the MSK cluster, you have brokers to store and ingest data, while in Kinesis, you have shards. In MSK, you need Zookeeper to manage configuration while AWS takes care of this admin overhead in Kinesis. The following table shows some more differentiating attributes:

Amazon MSK	Amazon Kinesis
You need to decide the number of clusters, brokers per cluster, topics per broker, and portions per topic to operate the MSK cluster.	You need to decide on the number of data streams and shards per stream to operate the Kinesis data stream.
MSK operates under the cluster provision model, which has a higher cost than Kinesis.	Kinesis needs a throughput provision model which has a lower cost as you only pay for the data you use.
You can only increase the number of partitions; decreasing partitions is not possible.	You can increase or decrease the number of shards.
MSK integrates with a few AWS services, such as KDA for Apache Flink.	Kinesis fully integrates with many AWS Services such as Lambda, KDA, etc.
MSK has no limit on throughput.	Kinesis throughput scales with shards support for up to 1 MB payloads.
MSK is open source.	Kinesis is not open source

Table 10.1: Comparison between MSK and Kinesis

In a nutshell, if you are starting a brand new streaming data ingestion and processing pipeline, it's better to go for Kinesis due to its ease of use and cost. Often, organizations use Kafka as an event bus to establish communication between applications, and in that case, you should continue with Kafka.

Summary

In this chapter, you started by understanding why to choose the cloud for big data analytics. You learned about the details of Amazon EMR, which is the AWS Hadoop offering on the cloud, and that in 2021, AWS also launched the server offering of EMR. You learned about EMR clusters, file systems, and security.

Later in this chapter, you were introduced to one of the most important services in the AWS stack – AWS Glue. You learned about the high-level components that comprise AWS Glue, such as the AWS Glue console, the AWS Glue Data Catalog, AWS Glue crawlers, and AWS Glue code generators. You then learned how everything is connected and how it can be used. Finally, you learned about the recommended best practices when architecting and implementing AWS Glue. You also learned when to choose Glue over EMR, and vice versa.

Real-time insights are becoming essential to the modern customer experience, and you learned about handling streaming data in the cloud. You learned about the AWS streaming data offering Amazon Kinesis and the different services in the Kinesis portfolio, including KDS for data ingestion and storage, KDA for data processing and query, and KDF for direct data loading without any code. You also learned about an AWS-managed Kafka offering called Amazon MSK, along with the MSK cluster architecture. You learned about AWS GSR for cataloging streaming data. Finally, you saw a comparison between MSK and Kinesis and discovered when to choose one versus the other.

In the next chapter, you will learn how to store and consume your data in AWS using its data warehouse, data query, and data visualization services.

11

Data Warehouses, Data Queries, and Visualization in AWS

The decreasing cost of storage in the cloud means that businesses no longer need to choose which data to keep and which to discard. Additionally, with pay-as-you-go and on-demand storage and compute options available, analyzing data to gain insights is now more accessible. Businesses can store all relevant data points, even as they grow to massive volumes, and analyze the data in various ways to extract insights. This can drive innovation within an organization and result in a competitive advantage.

In *Chapter 5, Storage in AWS – Choosing the Right Tool for the Job*, you learned about the files and object storage services offered by AWS. In *Chapter 7, Selecting the Right Database Service*, we covered many of the AWS database services. Now, the question is how to query and analyze the data available in different storage and databases. One of the most popular ways to analyze structured data is using data warehouses and AWS provides Amazon Redshift as a data warehouse service that can accommodate petabytes of data.

Say you have semi-structured data stored in an S3 bucket, and you don't want a data warehouse, as you don't need to query that data frequently. What if there was a way to combine the simplicity and cost-effectiveness of files and storage with the power of SQL? Such a way exists in AWS, and it's called Amazon Athena. When you query the data, it's essential to visualize it and complete the entire data pipeline with data visualization. For this, you can use AWS's business intelligence service, Amazon QuickSight.

Don't assume that because this service exists, we now don't need to use databases for some use cases. In this chapter, in addition to learning about the details and mechanics of Amazon Redshift and Athena, you will also learn when it makes sense to use them and when an AWS database service is more appropriate.

In this chapter, you will learn about the followings topics:

- Data warehouses in AWS with Amazon Redshift
- Introduction to Amazon Athena
- Deep-diving into Amazon Athena
- Using Amazon Athena Federated Query
- Learning about Amazon Athena workgroups
- Reviewing Amazon Athena's APIs
- Understanding when Amazon Athena is an appropriate solution
- Business intelligence in AWS with Amazon Quicksight

By the end of this chapter, you will know about different ways to query data regardless of its storage, which may be a database or object storage. You will learn about data visualization techniques in AWS to get better insight from your data.

Data warehouses in AWS with Amazon Redshift

Data is a strategic asset for organizations, not just new businesses and gaming companies. The cost and difficulty of storing data have significantly reduced in recent times, making it an essential aspect of many companies' business models. Nowadays, organizations are leveraging data to make informed decisions, such as launching new product offerings, introducing revenue streams, automating processes, and earning customer trust. These data-driven decisions can propel innovation and steer your business toward success.

You want to leverage your data to gain business insights, but this data is distributed into silos. For example, structured data resides in relational databases, semi-structured data is stored in object stores, and clickstream data that is streaming from the internet is stored in streaming storage. In addition, you also need to address emerging use cases such as **machine learning** (**ML**). Business users in your organization want to access and analyze live data themselves to get instant insights, making performance increasingly important from querying and **Extract, Transform, and Load** (**ETL**) ingestion perspectives. In fact, slower query performance can lead to missing these service-level agreements, leading to a bad end user experience. Finally, given all these challenges, you still need to solve this cost-efficiently and comply with security and compliance rules.

For a long time, organizations have used data warehouses for storing and analyzing large amounts of data. A data warehouse is designed to allow fast querying and analysis of data and is typically used in the business intelligence field. Data warehouses are often used to store historical data that is used for reporting and analysis, as well as to support decision-making processes. They are typically designed to store data from multiple sources and to support complex queries and analysis across those sources. Data warehouses are expensive to maintain, and they used to hold only the data that was necessary for gaining business insights, while the majority of data was discarded and sat in an archive. As the cloud provided cheaper options for storing data, this gave birth to the concept of a **data lake**. A data lake is different from a traditional data warehouse in that it is designed to handle a much wider variety of data types and can scale to store and process much larger volumes of data. Data warehouses are typically used to store structured data that has been transformed and cleaned, while data lakes are designed to store both structured and unstructured data in its raw form. This makes data lakes more flexible than data warehouses, as they can store data in its original format and allow you to apply different processing and analysis techniques as needed.

Transforming data and moving it into your data warehouse can be complex. Including data from your data lake in reports and dashboards makes it much easier to analyze all your data to deliver the insights your business needs. AWS provides a petabyte-scale data warehouse service called **Amazon Redshift** to address these challenges.

Redshift is a data warehouse system that automatically adjusts to optimize performance for your workloads without the need for manual tuning. It can handle large volumes of data, from gigabytes to petabytes, and is capable of supporting a large number of users concurrently. Its Concurrency Scaling feature ensures that sufficient resources are available to manage increased workloads as the number of users grows. Let's learn more about Redshift architecture and understand how Redshift achieves scale and performance.

Amazon Redshift architecture

On-premises data warehouses are data warehouses that are installed and run on hardware that is owned and operated by the organization using the data warehouse. This means that the organization is responsible for managing and maintaining the hardware, software, and infrastructure that the data warehouse runs on. Amazon Redshift is a fully managed data warehouse service that is run on AWS. This means that Amazon is responsible for managing and maintaining the hardware, software, and infrastructure that Redshift runs on.

There are a few key differences between on-premises data warehouses and Amazon Redshift:

- **Cost**: On-premises data warehouses require upfront capital expenditure on hardware and infrastructure, as well as ongoing expenses for maintenance and operation. Amazon Redshift is a pay-as-you-go service, so you only pay for the resources you use.
- **Scalability**: On-premises data warehouses may require the purchase of additional hardware and infrastructure to scale up, which can be a time-consuming and costly process. Amazon Redshift is fully managed and can scale up and down automatically and elastically, without the need to purchase additional hardware.
- **Maintenance**: With an on-premises data warehouse, you are responsible for managing and maintaining the hardware and software, including patching and upgrading. With Amazon Redshift, these tasks are handled by Amazon, so you don't have to worry about them.
- **Location**: With an on-premises data warehouse, the data and hardware are located within your organization's physical location. With Amazon Redshift, the data and hardware are located in Amazon's data centers. This can be a consideration for organizations that have data sovereignty or compliance requirements.

Amazon Redshift is a managed data warehouse where you do not have to worry about security patches, software upgrades, node deployment or configuration, node monitoring and recovery, and so on. Redshift offers several security features, including encryption and compliance with certifications such as SOC 1/2/3, HIPAA, FedRamP, and more.

Amazon Redshift started as a Postgres fork, but AWS rewrote the storage engine to be columnar and made it an OLAP relational data store by adding analytics functions. Redshift is still compatible with Postgres, and you can use a Postgres driver to connect to Redshift, but it is important to note that Redshift is an OLAP relational database – not an OLTP relational database like Postgres.

Redshift is well integrated with other AWS services such as VPC, KMS, and IAM for security, S3 for data lake integration and backups, and CloudWatch for monitoring. Redshift uses a massively parallel columnar architecture, which helps to achieve high performance. Let's take a closer look at the Redshift architecture.

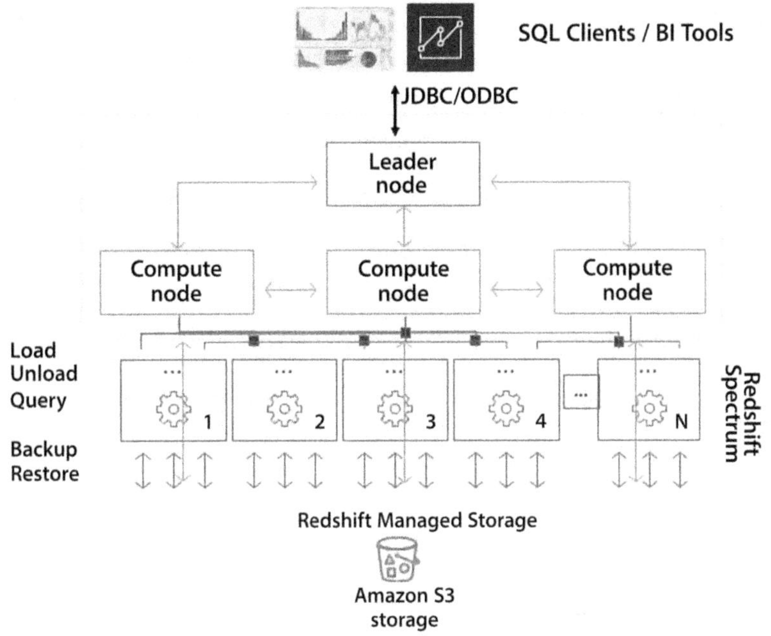

Figure 11.1: Redshift cluster architecture

As shown in the preceding diagram, Redshift has one leader node and multiple compute nodes. The leader node is required and automatically provisioned in every Redshift cluster, but customers are not charged for the leader node. The leader is responsible for being the user's JDBC/ODBC entry point to the cluster, storing metadata, compiling queries, and coordinating parallel SQL processing.

When the leader node receives your query, it converts the query into C++ code, which is compiled and sent down to all the compute nodes by the leader node. Behind the leader node are the compute nodes responsible for query execution and data manipulation. Compute nodes operate in parallel. Redshift clusters can be as small as one node that houses both the leader node and the compute node or as large as 128 compute nodes.

Next, these compute nodes also talk to other AWS services, primarily S3. You ingest data from S3 and unload data to S3. AWS continuously backs up your cluster to S3, all happening in the background and in parallel. Compute nodes also interact with Spectrum nodes, a Redshift feature that allows a Redshift cluster to query external data like that in an S3 data lake.

The following are the major responsibilities of Redshift components:

- **Leader node**:
    - SQL endpoint
    - Stores metadata
    - Coordinates parallel SQL processing and ML optimizations
    - No cost to use for clusters
- **Compute nodes**:
    - Local, columnar storage
    - Executes queries in parallel
    - Load, unload, backup, and restore from S3
- **Amazon Redshift Spectrum nodes**:
    - Redshift Spectrum nodes enable you to expand your Redshift analytics capabilities beyond the data warehouse by querying large volumes of unstructured data stored in your Amazon S3 data lake

In Redshift, compute nodes are divided into smaller units called "slices," which act like virtual compute nodes. Each slice is allocated a certain amount of memory and disk space from the physical compute node. The leader node is responsible for processing a portion of the workload assigned to the compute node and distributing data to the slices. It also assigns tasks related to queries and other database operations to the slices. The slices work in parallel and only operate on their assigned data, but they can request data from other slices if needed to complete their tasks. The number of slices per node varies depending on the instance type, with small instance types having 2 slices per node and large instance types having 16 slices per node.

In Redshift, data sharing enables you to share data with other Amazon Redshift clusters and databases, as well as with Athena and Amazon QuickSight. This is useful if you have multiple Amazon Redshift clusters that need to access the same data, or if you want to use Athena or QuickSight to analyze data stored in an Amazon Redshift cluster.

You can share data in Amazon Redshift by creating a read-only external schema that points to the data, and then grant access to that schema to other Amazon Redshift clusters or databases. This allows the other clusters or databases to query the data as if it were stored locally.

Redshift supports **materialized views** (**MVs**). MVs are pre-computed results of a `SELECT` query that are stored in a table. MVs can be used to speed up query performance by storing the results of a `SELECT` query in a table so that the `SELECT` query can be run faster the next time it is needed. MVs are especially useful when the data used in the `SELECT` query is not changing frequently because the results of the `SELECT` query can be refreshed periodically to ensure that the data in the MV is up to date. Let's learn about the Redshift instance types.

Redshift instance types

Amazon Redshift offers a variety of node types to support different workloads and performance requirements:

- **RA3 node types**: These are the latest generation of Amazon Redshift node types, and they offer the ability to scale compute and storage independently. RA3 node types are suitable for workloads that require both high-performance computing and high-capacity storage. They are available in both single-node and multi-node configurations. The RA3 node is a technology that allows independent computing and storage scaling. It utilizes **Redshift Managed Storage** (**RMS**) as its resilient storage layer, providing virtually limitless storage capacity where data is committed back to Amazon S3. This allows for new functionalities, such as data sharing, where RMS can be used as shared storage across numerous clusters.
- **Dense Compute** (**DC**) **node types**: These node types are designed for high-performance computing and are suitable for workloads that require fast query performance, such as data warehousing and business intelligence. DC node types offer a balance of CPU, memory, and storage, and are available in both single-node and multi-node configurations.

The following table shows details of the latest Redshift instance types:

Node Type	Instance type	Disk type	Size	Memory	# CPUs	# Slices
RA3	ra3.xlplus	RMS	Scales to 32 TB	32 GiB	4	2
	ra3.4xlarge	RMS	Scales to 128 TB	96 GiB	12	4
	ra3.16xlarge	RMS	Scales to 128 TB	384 GiB	48	16

Compute Optimized	dc2.large	SSD	160 GB	16 GiB	2	2
	dc2.8xlarge	SSD	2.56 TB	244 GiB	32	16

Table 11.1: Comparison between Redshift instance types

Redshift launched with **Dense Storage (DS)** nodes, but those are on the path to deprecation now. DS nodes are optimized for high-capacity storage and are suitable for workloads that require large amounts of data, such as data lakes and big data analytics.

A Redshift cluster can have up to 128 ra3.16xlarge nodes, which is 16 petabytes of managed storage. When you have a data warehouse storing such a massive amount of data, you want to make sure it can scale and provide query performance. The following are some key Redshift features:

- **Redshift Concurrency Scaling** – Redshift Concurrency Scaling is a feature that automatically adjusts cluster capacity to handle unexpected spikes in user demand, allowing thousands of users to work simultaneously without any degradation in performance.
- **Advanced Query Accelerator (AQUA)** – A hardware-level cache that takes performance to the next level, accelerating query speed up to 10x.
- **Redshift federated queries** – Allow you to combine data from multiple data sources and query it as if it were all stored in a single Amazon Redshift database. This is useful if you have data stored in different data stores, such as Amazon S3, Amazon RDS, or even other Amazon Redshift clusters, and you want to analyze the data using Amazon Redshift.
- **Automatic workload management (WLM)** – Provides fine-grained control like query monitoring rules to promote or demote query priorities at execution time based on certain runtime metrics, for example, the queue wait, execution time, CPU usage, and so on.
- **Elastic resize** – Enables the in-place addition or removal of nodes to/from existing clusters within a few minutes.
- **Auto-vacuum** – Monitors changes to your workload and automatically reclaims disk space occupied by rows affected by `UPDATE` and `DELETE` operations.
- **Redshift Advisor** – Continuously monitors and automatically provides optimization recommendations.
- **Redshift Query Editor** – Web-based query interface to run single SQL statement queries in an Amazon Redshift cluster directly from the AWS Management Console.

- **Redshift ML** – Amazon Redshift ML is a feature of Amazon Redshift that allows you to use SQL to build and train ML models on data stored in an Amazon Redshift cluster. With Redshift ML, you can use standard SQL statements to create and train ML models without having to learn a new programming language or use specialized ML libraries.

As you expand analytics throughout organizations, you need to make data easily and rapidly accessible to line of business users with little or no knowledge about data warehouse management. You do not want to consider selecting instances, sizing, scaling, and tuning the data warehouse. Instead, you want a simplified, self-service, automated data warehouse experience that allows them to focus on rapidly building business applications. To address these challenges, AWS launched **Amazon Redshift Serverless** at re:Invent 2021. You can go to the Amazon Redshift console and enable a serverless endpoint for your AWS account. You can get started with queries from the query editor tool that comes out of the box with Amazon Redshift or connect from your favorite tool via JDBC/ODBC or data API. You don't need to select node types to specify the node or do another manual configuration such as workload management, scaling configurations, and so on.

Amazon Redshift and Amazon Redshift Serverless are both fully managed data warehousing solutions. However, there are some key differences between the two offerings that you should consider when deciding which one is right for your use case. One of the main differences between Redshift and Redshift Serverless is the way they are priced. Amazon Redshift is priced based on the number and type of nodes in your cluster, as well as the amount of data you store and the amount of data you query. You pay a fixed hourly rate for each node in your cluster, and you can scale the number of nodes up or down as needed to meet changing workload demands.

In contrast, Redshift Serverless is priced based on the amount of data you store and the number of queries you run. You don't need to provision any nodes or worry about scaling the number of nodes up or down. Instead, Amazon Redshift Serverless automatically scales the number of compute resources needed to run your queries based on the workload demand. You only pay for the resources you use, and you can pause and resume your cluster as needed to save costs.

Another key difference between the two offerings is the way they handle concurrency and workload management. Amazon Redshift uses a leader node to manage the workload and distribute tasks to compute nodes, which can be scaled up or down as needed. Amazon Redshift Serverless, on the other hand, uses a shared pool of resources to run queries, and automatically allocates more resources as needed to handle increased concurrency and workload demands.

In general, Amazon Redshift is a good choice if you have a high-concurrency workload that requires fast query performance and you want to be able to scale the number of compute resources up or down as needed. Amazon Redshift Serverless is a good choice if you have a lower-concurrency workload that varies over time, and you want a more cost-effective solution that automatically scales compute resources as needed. Let's look at some tips and tricks to optimize a Redshift workload.

Optimizing Redshift workloads

There are several strategies you can use to optimize the performance of your Amazon Redshift workload:

- **Use the right node type**: Choose the right node type for your workload based on the performance and storage requirements of your queries. Amazon Redshift offers a variety of node types, including DC, DS, memory-optimized, and RA3, which are optimized for different workloads.
- **Use columnar storage**: Amazon Redshift stores data using a columnar storage layout, which is optimized for data warehousing workloads. To get the best performance from Amazon Redshift, make sure to design your tables using a columnar layout and use data types that are optimized for columnar storage.
- **Use sort keys and distribution keys**: Sort keys and distribution keys are used to optimize the way data is stored and queried in Amazon Redshift. Use sort keys to order the data in each block of data stored on a node, and use distribution keys to distribute data evenly across nodes. This can help to improve query performance by reducing the amount of data that needs to be read and processed.
- **Use Materialized Views (MVs)**: MVs are pre-computed results of a `SELECT` query that are stored in a table. MVs can be used to speed up query performance by storing the results of a `SELECT` query in a table so that the `SELECT` query can be run faster the next time it is needed.
- **Use query optimization techniques**: There are several techniques you can use to optimize the performance of your queries in Amazon Redshift, including using the `EXPLAIN` command to understand query execution plans, using the right join type, and minimizing the use of functions and expressions in your queries.
- **Use Redshift Spectrum**: Redshift Spectrum is an Amazon Redshift feature that enables you to query data stored in Amazon S3 using SQL, without having to load the data into an Amazon Redshift cluster. This can be a cost-effective way to query large amounts of data and can also help to improve query performance by offloading data processing to the scale-out architecture of Amazon S3.

In this section, you learned about the high-level architecture and key features of Redshift, which gave you a pointer to start your learning. Redshift is a very vast topic that warrants an entire book in itself. You can refer to *Amazon Redshift Cookbook* to dive deeper into Redshift – `https://www.amazon.com/dp/1800569688/`.

While Redshift is a relational engine and operates on structured data, you must be curious about getting insight from other semi-structured data coming in at a high velocity and volume. To help mine this data without hassle, AWS provides Amazon Athena. This allows you to query data directly from S3.

Querying your data lake in AWS with Amazon Athena

Water, water everywhere, and not a drop to drink... This may be the feeling you get in today's enterprise environments. We are producing data at an exponential rate, but it is sometimes difficult to find a way to analyze this data and gain insights from it. Some of the data that we are generating at a prodigious rate is of the following types:

- Application logging
- Clickstream data
- Surveillance video
- Smart and IoT devices
- Commercial transactions

Often, this data is captured without analysis or is at least not analyzed to the fullest extent. Analyzing this data properly can translate into the following:

- Increased sales
- Cross-selling opportunities
- Avoiding downtime and errors before they occur
- Serving customer bases more efficiently

Previously, one stumbling block to analyzing this data was that much of this information resided in flat files. To analyze them, we had to ingest these files into a database to be able to perform analytics. Amazon Athena allows you to analyze these files without going through an **Extract, Transform, Load** (**ETL**) process.

Amazon Athena treats any file like a database table and allows you to run `SELECT` statement queries. Amazon Athena also now supports insert and update statements. The ACID transactions in Athena enable various operations like write, delete, and update to be performed on Athena's SQL **data manipulation language** (DML).

You can greatly increase processing speeds and lower costs by running queries directly on a file without first performing ETL on them or loading them into a database. Amazon Athena enables you to run standard SQL queries to analyze and explore Amazon S3 objects. Amazon Athena is serverless. In other words, there are no servers to manage.

Amazon Athena is extremely simple to use. All you need to do is this:

1. Identify the object you want to query in Amazon S3.
2. Define the schema for the object.
3. Query the object with standard SQL.

Depending on the size and format of the file, query results can take a few seconds. As we will see later, a few optimizations can reduce query time as files get bigger.

Amazon Athena can be integrated with the AWS Glue Data Catalog. Doing so enables the creation of a unified metadata repository across services. You learned about Glue in *Chapter 10, Big Data and Streaming Data Processing in AWS*. AWS Glue crawls data sources, discovering schemas and populating the AWS Glue Data Catalog with any changes that have occurred since the last crawl, including new tables, modifications to existing tables, and new partition definitions, while maintaining schema versioning.

Let's get even deeper into the power and features of Amazon Athena and how it integrates with other AWS services.

Deep-diving into Amazon Athena

As mentioned previously, Amazon Athena is quite flexible and can handle simple and complex database queries using standard SQL. It supports joins and arrays. It can use a wide variety of file formats, including these:

- CSV
- JSON
- ORC
- Avro
- Parquet

It also supports other formats, but these are the most common. In some cases, the files you are using have already been created, and you may have little flexibility regarding the format of these files. But for the cases where you can specify the file format, it's important to understand the advantages and disadvantages of these formats. In other cases, converting the files into another format may even make sense before using Amazon Athena. Let's take a quick look at these formats and understand when to use them.

CSV files

A **Comma-Separated Value** (CSV) file is a file where a comma separator delineates each value, and a return character delineates each record or row. Remember that the separator does not necessarily have to be a comma. Other common delimiters are tabs and the pipe character (|).

JSON files

JavaScript Object Notation (JSON) is an open-standard file format. One of its advantages is that it's somewhat simple to read, mainly when it's indented and formatted. It's a replacement for the **Extensible Markup Language** (XML) file format, which, while similar, is more difficult to read. It consists of a series of potentially nested attribute-value pairs.

JSON is a language-agnostic data format. It was initially used with JavaScript, but quite a few programming languages now provide native support for it or provide libraries to create and parse JSON-formatted data.

IMPORTANT NOTE

The first two formats we mentioned are not compressed and are not optimized for use with Athena or for speeding up queries. The rest of the formats we will analyze are all optimized for fast retrieval and querying when used with Amazon Athena and other file-querying technologies.

ORC files

The **Optimized Row Columnar** (ORC) file format provides a practical method for storing files. It was initially designed under the Apache Hive and Hadoop project and was created to overcome other file formats' issues and limitations. ORC files provide better performance when compared to uncompressed formats for reading, writing, and processing data.

Apache Avro files

Apache Avro is an open-source file format used to serialize data. It was originally designed for the Apache Hadoop project.

Apache Avro uses JSON format to define data schemas, allowing users of files to read and interpret them easily. However, the data is persisted in binary format, which has efficient and compact storage. An Avro file can use markers to divide big datasets into smaller files to simplify parallel processing. Some consumer services have a code generator that processes the file schema to generate code that enables access. Apache Avro doesn't need to do this, making it suitable for scripting languages.

An essential Avro characteristic is its support for dynamic data schemas that can be modified over time. Avro can process schema changes such as empty, new, and modified fields. Because of this, old scripts can process new data, and new scripts can process old data. Avro has APIs for the following, among others:

- Python
- Go
- Ruby
- Java
- C
- C++

Avro-formatted data can flow from one program to another even if the programs are written in different languages.

Apache Parquet files

Just because we are listing Parquet files at the end, don't assume they will be ignored. Parquet is an immensely popular format to use in combination with Amazon Athena.

Apache Parquet is another quite popular open-source file format. Apache Parquet has an efficient and performant design. It stores file contents in a flat columnar storage format. Contrast this storage method with the row-based approach used by comma- and tab-delimited files such as CSV and TSV.

Parquet is powered by an elegant assembly and shredding algorithm that is more efficient than simply flattening nested namespaces. Apache Parquet is well suited to operating on complex data at scale by using efficient data compression.

This method is ideal for queries that require reading a few columns from a table with many columns. Apache Parquet can easily locate and scan only those columns, significantly reducing the traffic required to retrieve data.

In general, columnar storage and Apache Parquet deliver higher efficiency than a row-based approach such as CSV. While performing reads, a columnar storage method will skip over non-relevant columns and rows efficiently. Aggregation queries using this approach take less time than row-oriented databases. This results in lower billing and higher performance for data access.

Apache Parquet supports complex nested data structures. Parquet files are ideal for queries retrieving large amounts of data, and can handle files that contain gigabytes of data without much difficulty.

Apache Parquet is built to support a variety of encoding and compression algorithms. Parquet is well suited to situations where columns have similar data types. This can make accessing and scanning files quite efficient. Apache Parquet works with various codes, enabling the compression of files in various ways.

In addition to Amazon Athena, Apache Parquet works with serverless technologies such as Google BigQuery, Google Dataproc, and Amazon Redshift Spectrum.

Understanding how Amazon Athena works

Amazon Athena was initially intended to work with data stored in Amazon S3. As we have seen, it can now work with other source types as well.

This feature of Amazon Athena is a game-changer. You can combine disparate data sources just as easily as if they all had the same format. This enables you to join a JSON file with a CSV file or a DynamoDB table with an Amazon Redshift table.

Previously, if you wanted to combine this data, performing a combination programmatically would invariably translate into a long development cycle and more than likely not scale well when using large datasets.

Now all you have to do is write an SQL query that combines the two data sources. Due to the underlying technology, this technique will scale well, even when querying terabytes and petabytes of data.

Data scientists and data analysts will be able to work at a speed that would have been impossible just a few years ago.

Under the hood, Amazon Athena leverages Presto. Presto is an open-source SQL query engine. Queries in Amazon Athena can be quite complex and can use joins, window functions, and complex data types. Amazon Athena is an excellent way to implement a schema-on-read strategy. A schema-on-read strategy enables you to project a schema onto existing data during query execution. Doing this eliminates the need to load or transform the data before it is queried, and instead, it can be queried wherever it lives.

Presto, also called PrestoDB, is an open-source, distributed SQL query engine with a design that can support, in a scalable fashion, queries on files and other kinds of data sources. Some of the sources that are supported are listed here:

- Amazon S3
- **Hadoop Distributed File System (HDFS)**
- MongoDB
- Cassandra

It also supports traditional relational databases, such as these:

- MySQL
- Microsoft SQL Server
- Amazon Redshift
- PostgreSQL
- Teradata

It can handle petabyte-sized files. Presto can access data in place without the need to copy the data. Queries can execute in parallel in memory (without having access to secondary storage) and return results in seconds.

You might want to use Athena with SQL queries on a **Relational Database Management System (RDBMS)** database if you want to perform ad hoc queries on the data without having to load it into a data warehouse first. With Athena, you can query the data in place in S3, which can be faster and more flexible than loading the data into a data warehouse and then querying it.

Initially, Amazon Athena only leveraged Presto to access Amazon S3 files, but Amazon now offers Amazon Athena Federated Query. We will learn more about it in the next section.

Using Amazon Athena Federated Query

Unless your organization has specific requirements, it's likely that you store data in various storage types, selecting the most appropriate storage type based on its purpose. For example, you may choose graph databases when they are the best fit, relational databases for certain use cases, and S3 object storage or Hadoop HDFS when they are the most suitable. Amazon Neptune (a graph database) may be the best choice if you are building a social network application. Or, if you are building an application that requires a flexible schema, Amazon DynamoDB may be a solid choice. AWS offers many different types of persistence solutions, such as these:

- Relational database services
- Key-value database services
- Document database services
- In-memory database services
- Search database services
- Graph database services
- Time-series database services
- Ledger databases database services
- Plain object data stores (such as Amazon S3)

The reason it offers all these kinds of persistence storage systems is to accommodate the different needs that different services can have. Sometimes, corporations have mandates to only use a certain database or certain file storage, but even in such cases, there will probably be "fit-for-purpose" choices for different cases (a graph database, a NoSQL database, file storage, and more). As a design principle, this pattern is recommended and encouraged. It's about following the principle of "choosing the right tool for a particular job."

However, this plethora of choices poses a problem. As the number of different types of storage increases, running analytics and building applications across these data sources becomes more and more challenging. Overcoming this challenge is exactly what Amazon Athena Federated Query can help alleviate.

Amazon Athena Federated Query empowers data scientists, data analysts, and application engineers to run SQL queries across multiple data stores regardless of the data source type.

Before Amazon Athena Federated Query or any other way to run federated queries, we had to execute various queries across systems and merge, filter, and assemble the results once the individual queries were run.

Constructing these data pipelines to process data across data sources creates bottlenecks and requires developing customized solutions that can validate the consistency and accuracy of the data. When source systems are changed, the data pipelines must also be changed. Using query federation in Athena reduces these complexities by enabling users to run queries that retrieve data in situ no matter where it resides. Users can use standard SQL statements to merge data across disparate data sources in a performant manner. Users can also schedule SQL queries to retrieve data and store the results in Amazon S3.

This is a complicated and slow way to put together results.

Amazon Athena Federated Query allows you to execute a single SQL query across data stores, greatly simplifying your code while at the same time getting those results a lot faster, thanks to a series of optimizations provided by Amazon Athena Federated Query.

The following diagram illustrates how Amazon Athena can be leveraged against a variety of data source types (it only shows some of the data source types supported):

Figure 11.2: Illustrative example of the data source types supported by Amazon Athena

As we can see from the preceding figure, Amazon Athena Federated Query can handle a variety of disparate data sources and enables users to combine and join them with ease.

Data source connectors

Executing an SQL query against a new data source can be done simply by adding the data source to the Amazon Athena registry. The choice between the Athena registry and the Glue Catalog depends on your specific requirements and the complexity of your data and metadata management needs. If you need a simple and lightweight metadata store, the Athena registry may be sufficient. If you need a more feature-rich and powerful metadata store, the Glue Catalog may be a better choice.

Amazon Athena has open-source connectors. Additionally, AWS allows you to write your own custom connectors if there isn't a suitable one. The connector performs the following functions:

- Manages metadata information
- Determines the parts of a data source that are required to be scanned, accessed, and filtered
- Manages query optimization and query parallelism

Amazon Athena can do this for any data source type with an Amazon Athena data source connector. These connectors run on AWS Lambda. AWS provides data source connectors for the following:

- Amazon DocumentDB
- Amazon DynamoDB
- Amazon Redshift
- Any JDBC-compliant RDBMS (such as MySQL, PostgreSQL, and Oracle)
- Apache HBase
- AWS CloudWatch Metrics
- Amazon CloudWatch Logs
- And more...

These connectors can be used to run federated standard SQL queries spanning multiple data sources, all inside of the Amazon Athena console or within your code.

Amazon Athena allows you to use custom connectors to query data stored in data sources that are not natively supported by Athena. Custom connectors are implemented using the Apache Calcite framework and allow you to connect to virtually any data source that has a JDBC driver.

To use a custom connector with Athena, you first need to create a custom data source definition using the `CREATE DATA SOURCE` command. This definition specifies the JDBC driver and connection information for the data source, as well as the schema and table definitions for the data. Once the custom data source is defined, you can use SQL to query the data as if it were a regular Athena table. Athena will use the custom connector to connect to the data source and execute the SQL query and will return the results to the client.

The Amazon Athena Query Federation SDK expands on the advantage of federated querying beyond the "out-of-the-box" connectors that come with AWS. By writing a hundred lines of code or less, you can create connectors to custom data sources and enable the rest of your organization to use this custom data. Once a new connector is registered, Amazon Athena can use the new connector to access databases, schemas, tables, and columns in this data source.

Let's now learn about another powerful Athena feature – Amazon Athena workgroups.

Learning about Amazon Athena workgroups

Another new feature that comes with Amazon Athena is the concept of workgroups. Workgroups enable administrators to give different groups of users different access to databases, tables, and other Athena resources. It also enables you to establish limits on how much data a query or a whole workgroup can access, and provides the ability to track costs. Since workgroups act like any other resource in AWS, resource-level identity-based policies can be set up to control access to individual workgroups.

Workgroups can be integrated with SNS and CloudWatch as well. If query metrics are turned on, these metrics can be published to CloudWatch. Additionally, alarms can be created for certain workgroup users if their usage goes above a pre-established threshold.

By default, Amazon Athena queries run in the default primary workgroup. AWS administrators can add new workgroups and then run separate workloads in each workgroup. A common use case is to use workgroups to separate audiences, such as users who will run ad hoc queries and users who will run pre-canned reports. Each workgroup can then be associated with a specific location. Any queries associated with an individual workgroup will have their results stored in the assigned location. Following this paradigm ensures that only users that should be able to access certain data can access that data.

Another way to restrict access is by applying different encryption keys to the output files depending on the workgroup.

A task that workgroups greatly simplifies is the onboarding of new users. You can override the client-side settings and apply a predefined configuration for all the queries executed in a workgroup. Users within a workgroup do not have to configure where their queries will be stored or specify encryption keys for the S3 buckets. Instead, the values defined at the workgroup level will be used as a default.

Also, each workgroup keeps a separate history of all executed queries and any queries that have been saved, making troubleshooting easier.

Optimizing Amazon Athena

As with any SQL operation, you can take steps to optimize the performance of your queries and inserts. As with traditional databases, optimizing your data access performance usually comes at the expense of data ingestion and vice versa.

Let's look at some tips that you can use to increase and optimize performance.

Optimization of data partitions

One way to improve performance is to break up files into smaller files called partitions. A common partition scheme breaks up a file by using a divider that occurs with some regularity in data. Some examples follow:

- Country
- Region
- Date
- Product

Partitions operate as virtual columns and reduce the amount of data that needs to be read for each query. Partitions are normally defined at the time a table or file is created.

Amazon Athena can use Apache Hive partitions. Hive partitions use this name convention:

```
s3://BucketName/TablePath/<PARTITION_COLUMN_NAME>=<VALUE>/<PARTITION_
COLUMN_NAME>=<VALUE>/
```

When this format is used, the `MSCK REPAIR` command can be used to add additional partitions automatically.

Partitions are not restricted to a single column. Multiple columns can be used to partition data. Alternatively, you can divide a single field to create a hierarchy of partitions. For example, it is not uncommon to divide a date into three pieces and partition the data using the year, the month, and the day.

An example of partitions using this scheme may look like this:

```
s3://a-simple-examples/data/parquet/year=2000/month=1/day=1/
s3://a-simple-examples/data/parquet/year=2000/month=2/day=1/
s3://a-simple-examples/data/parquet/year=2000/month=3/day=1/
s3://a-simple-examples/data/parquet/year=2000/month=4/day=1/
```

So, which column would be the best to partition files and are there any best practices for partitioning? Consider the following:

- Any column normally used to filter data is probably a good partition candidate.
- Don't over-partition. Suppose the number of partitions is too high; the retrieval overhead increases. If the partitions are too small, this prevents any benefit from partitioning the data.

It is also important to partition smartly and try to choose a value that is evenly distributed as your partition key. For example, if your data involves election ballots, it may initially seem like a good idea to use them as your partition of the candidates in the election. But what if one or two candidates take most of the votes? Your partitions will be heavily skewed toward those candidates, and your performance will suffer.

Data bucketing

Another scheme to partition data is to use buckets within a single partition. When using bucketing, a column or multiple columns are used to group rows together and "bucket" or categorize them. The best columns to use for bucketing are columns that will often be used to filter the data. So, when queries use these columns as filters, not as much data will need to be scanned and read when performing these queries.

Another characteristic that makes a column a good candidate for bucketing is high cardinality. In other words, you want to use columns that have a large number of unique values. So, primary key columns are ideal bucketing columns.

Amazon Athena offers the `CLUSTERED BY` clause to simplify which columns will be bucketed during table creation. An example of a table creation statement using this clause follows:

```
CREATE EXTERNAL TABLE employee (
id string,
name string,
salary double,
address string,
timestamp bigint)
PARTITIONED BY (
timestamp string,
department string)
CLUSTERED BY (
id,
timestamp)
INTO 50 BUCKETS
```

You can learn more about data partitioning in Athena by visiting AWS document here - `https://docs.aws.amazon.com/athena/latest/ug/partitions.html`.

File compression

Intuitively, queries can be sped up by using compression. When files are compressed, not as much data needs to be read, and the decompression overhead is not high enough to negate its benefits. Also, when going across the wire, a smaller file will take less time to get through the network than a bigger file. Finally, faster reads and transmission over the network will result in less spending, which, when you multiply these by hundreds and thousands of queries, will result in real savings over time.

Compression offers the highest benefits when files are of a certain size. The optimal file size is around 200 megabytes to 1 gigabyte. Smaller files translate into multiple files being able to be processed simultaneously, taking advantage of the parallelism available with Amazon Athena. If there is only one file, only one reader can be used on the file while other readers sit idle.

One simple way to achieve compression is to utilize Apache Parquet or Apache ORC format. Files in these formats can be easily split, and these formats are compressed by default. Two compression formats are often combined with Parquet and ORC to improve performance further. These compression formats are Gzip and Bzip2. The following chart shows how these compression formats compare with other popular compression algorithms:

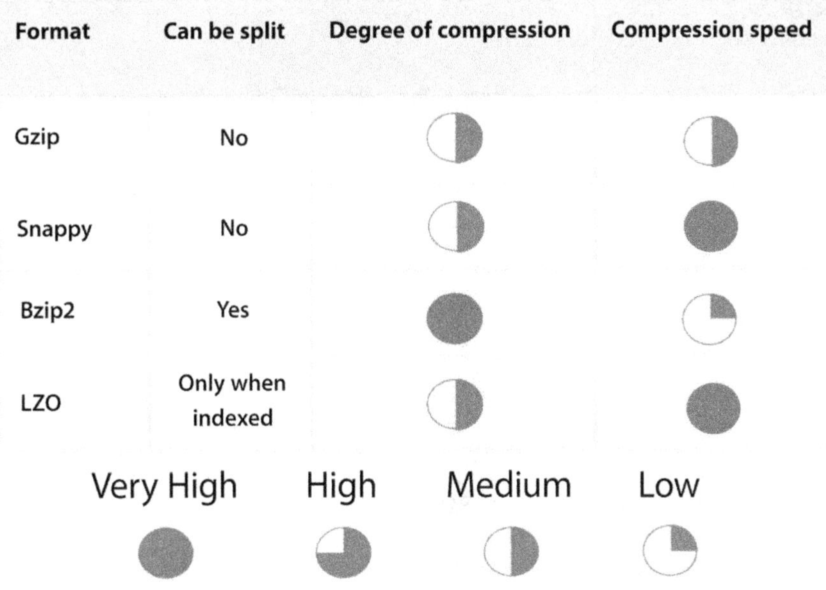

Format	Can be split	Degree of compression	Compression speed
Gzip	No	Medium	Medium
Snappy	No	Medium	Very High
Bzip2	Yes	Very High	Low
LZO	Only when indexed	Medium	Very High

Figure 11.3: Compression formats

Each format offers different advantages. As shown in the figure, **Gzip** and **Snappy** files cannot be split. **Bzip2** can be split. **LZO** can only be split in special cases. Bzip2 provides the highest compression level, and LZO and Snappy provide the fastest compression speed.

Let's continue learning about other ways to optimize Amazon Athena. Another thing to do is to ensure the optimal file size.

File size optimization

As we have seen in quite a few examples in this book, one of the game-changing characteristics of the cloud is its elasticity. This elasticity enables us to run queries in parallel easily and efficiently. File formats that allow file splitting assist in this parallelization process. If files are too big or are not split, too many readers will be idle, and parallelization will not occur. On the flip side, files that are too small (generally in the range of 128 megabytes or less) will incur additional overhead with the following operations, to name a few:

- Opening files
- Listing directories
- Reading file object metadata
- Reading file headers
- Reading compression dictionaries

So, just as it's a good idea to split bigger files to increase parallelism, it is recommended to consolidate smaller files. Amazon EMR has a utility called S3DistCP that can be used to merge smaller files into larger ones. S3DistCP can also be used to transfer large files efficiently from HDFS to Amazon S3 and vice versa, as well as from one S3 bucket to another. Here is an example of how to use S3DistCP to copy data from an S3 bucket to an EMR cluster:

```
aws s3-dist-cp --src s3://sa-book-source-bucket/path/to/data/ \
              --dest hdfs:///path/to/destination/sa-book/ \
              --s3-client-region us-east-2 \
              --s3-client-endpoint s3.us-east-2.amazonaws.com \
              --src-pattern '*.csv' \
              --group-by '.*(part|PARTS)\..*'
```

The example above copies all `.csv` files from the `sa-book-source-bucket` S3 bucket to the `/path/to/destination/sa-book/` directory on the EMR cluster. The `--src-pattern` option specifies a regular expression to match the files that should be copied, and the `--group-by` option specifies a regular expression to group the files into larger blocks for more efficient transfer.

The `--s3-client-region` and `--s3-client-endpoint` options specify the region and endpoint of the S3 bucket.

S3DistCP has many other options that you can use to customize the data transfer process, such as options to specify the number of mappers to use, the maximum number of retries, and the maximum number of concurrent connections. You can find more information about these options in the S3DistCP documentation – `https://aws.amazon.com/fr/blogs/big-data/seven-tips-for-using-s3distcp-on-amazon-emr-to-move-data-efficiently-between-hdfs-and-amazon-s3/`.

Columnar data store generation optimization

As mentioned earlier, Apache Parquet and Apache ORC are popular columnar data store formats. The formats efficiently compress data by leveraging the following:

- Columnar-wise compression scheme
- Datatype-based compression
- Predicate pushdown
- File splitting

A way to further optimize compression is to fine-tune the file's block size or stripe size. Having bigger block and stripe sizes enables us to store more rows per block. The default Apache Parquet block size is 120 megabytes, and the default Apache ORC stripe size is 64 megabytes. A larger block size is recommended for tables with a high number of columns. This ensures that each column has a reasonable size that enables efficient sequential I/O.

When datasets are 10 gigabytes or less, using the default compression algorithm that comes with Parquet and ORC is enough to have decent performance, but for datasets bigger than that, it's not a bad idea to use other compression algorithms with Parquet and ORC, such as Gzip.

Yet another parameter that can be customized is the type of compression algorithm used on the storage data blocks. The Parquet format, by default, uses Snappy, but it also supports these other formats:

- Gzip
- LZO
- No compression

The ORC format uses Zlib compression by default, but it also supports the following:

- Snappy
- No compression

The recommended way to choose a compression algorithm is to use the default algorithm. No further optimization is needed if the performance is good enough for your use case. If it's not, try the other supported formats to see if they deliver better results.

Column selection

An obvious way to reduce network traffic is to ensure that only the required columns are included in each query. Therefore, it is not recommended to use the following syntax unless your application requires that every single column in a table be used. And even if that's true today, it may not be true tomorrow. If additional columns are later added to the table schema, they may not be required for existing queries. Take this, for instance:

```
Select * from the table
```

Instead of that, use this:

```
select column1, column2, column3 from table
```

By explicitly naming columns instead of using the star operator, we reduce the number of columns that get passed back and lower the number of bytes that need to be pushed across the wire.

Let's now learn about yet another way to optimize our use of Amazon Athena and explore the concept of predicate pushdown.

Predicate pushdown

The core concept behind predicate pushdown (also referred to as predicate filtering) is that specific sections of an SQL query (a predicate) can be "pushed down" to the location where the data exists. Performing this optimization can help reduce (often drastically) the time it takes a query to respond by filtering out results earlier in the process. Sometimes, predicate pushdown is achieved by filtering data in situ before transferring it over the network or loading it into memory.

The ORC and the Parquet formats support predicate pushdown. These formats have data blocks representing column values. In each block, statistics are stored for the data held in the block. Two examples of the statistics stored are the minimum and the maximum value. When a query is run, these statistics are read before the rest of the block and, depending on the statistics, it is determined whether the complete block should be read.

To take maximum advantage of predicate pushdown, it is recommended to identify the column that will be used the most when executing queries before writing to disk and to sort by that column. Let's look at a quick example to drive the point home.

File 1	File 2	File 3
Stats: Min=1; Max 3	Stats: Min=4; Max 6	Stats: Min=7; Max 9
Value	Value	Value
1	4	7
2	5	8
3	6	9

Figure 11.4: Predicate pushdown example

In the preceding example, there are three files. As you can tell, the data is already sorted using the value stored in the column labeled **Value**. Let's say we want to run the following query:

```
select * from Table where Value = 5
```

As mentioned before, we can look at the statistics first and observe that the first file's maximum value is **3**, so we can skip that file. In the second file, we see that our key (`Value = 5`) falls within the range of values in the file. We would then read this file. Since the maximum value of the second file is greater than the value of our key, we don't need to read any more files after reading the second file.

Predicate pushdown is used to reduce the amount of data that needs to be scanned when executing a query in Amazon Athena. Predicate pushdown works by pushing down filtering conditions (predicates) to the data sources being queried, so that the data sources can filter the data before returning it to Athena. This can significantly reduce the amount of data that needs to be scanned and processed by Athena, which can improve query performance and reduce costs. You should use it whenever you have a query that has predicates that can be applied to the data sources being queried.

ORDER BY clause optimization

Due to how sorting works, when we invoke a query containing an `ORDER BY` clause, it needs to be handled by a single worker thread. This can cause query slowdown and even failure. There are several strategies you can use to optimize the performance of the `ORDER BY` clause in Athena:

- **Use a sort key**: If you have a large table that you frequently need to sort, you can improve query performance by using a sort key. A sort key is a column or set of columns that is used to order the data in the table. When you use a sort key, Athena stores the data in the table in a sorted order, which can significantly reduce the time it takes to sort the data when you run a query.

- **Use a LIMIT clause**: If you only need the top **N** rows of a query, you can use the `LIMIT` clause to limit the number of rows returned. This can reduce the amount of data that needs to be sorted and returned, which can improve query performance.
- **Use a computed column**: If you frequently need to sort a table based on a derived value, you can create a computed column that contains the derived value and use the computed column in the `ORDER BY` clause.

Join optimization

Table joins can be an expensive operation. Whenever possible, they should be avoided. In some cases, it makes sense to "pre-join" tables and merge two tables into a single table to improve performance when queries are executed later.

That is not always possible or efficient. Another way to optimize joins is to ensure that larger tables are always on the left side of the join, and the smaller tables are on the right-hand side. When Amazon Athena runs a query with a `join` clause, the right-hand side tables are delegated to worker nodes, bringing these tables into memory, and the table on the left is then streamed to perform the join. This approach will use a smaller amount of memory, and the query performs better.

And now, yet another optimization will be explored by optimizing `GROUP BY` clauses.

Group by clause optimization

When a `GROUP BY` clause is present, the best practice is arranging the columns according to the highest cardinality. For example, if you have a dataset that contains data on ZIP codes and gender, it is recommended to write the query like this:

```
SELECT zip_code, gender, COUNT(*)FROM dataset GROUP BY zip_code, gender
```

This way is not recommended:

```
Select zip code, gender, count(*) from the dataset group by gender
```

This is because it is more likely that the ZIP code will have a higher cardinality (there will be more unique values) in that column.

Additionally, this is not always possible, but minimizing the number of columns in the select clause is recommended when a `GROUP BY` clause is present.

Approximate function use

Amazon Athena has a series of approximation functions. For example, there is an approximation function for the `DISTINCT()` function. If you don't need an exact count, you can instead use `APPROX_DISTINCT()`, which may not return the exact number of distinct values for a column in a given table, but it will give a good approximation for many use cases.

For example, to get an approximation, you should *not* use this query:

```
Select DISTINCT(last_name) from employee
```

Instead, you should use this query:

```
Select APPROX_DISTINCT(last_name) from employee
```

This may be suitable for a given use case if an exact count is not required.

This concludes the optimization section for Amazon Athena. It is by no means a comprehensive list, but rather it is a list of the most common and practical optimization techniques that can be used to gain efficiency and increase query performance quickly.

You have now learned about Amazon Redshift and Amazon Athena. Let's see some examples of when to use Athena and when to use Redshift Spectrum for querying data.

Using Amazon Athena versus Redshift Spectrum

Amazon Athena and Redshift Spectrum are two data querying services offered by AWS that allow users to analyze data stored in Amazon S3 using standard SQL.

Amazon Athena is a serverless interactive query service that quickly analyzes data in Amazon S3 using standard SQL. It allows users to analyze data directly from Amazon S3 without creating or managing any infrastructure. Athena is best suited for ad hoc querying and interactive analysis of large amounts of unstructured data that is stored in Amazon S3.

For example, imagine a marketing team needs to analyze customer behavior data stored in Amazon S3 to make informed decisions about their marketing campaigns. They can use Athena to query the data in S3, extract insights, and make informed decisions about how to improve their campaigns.

On the other hand, Amazon Redshift Spectrum (an extension of Amazon Redshift) allows users to analyze data stored in Amazon S3 with the same SQL interface used to analyze data in their Redshift cluster. It extends the querying capabilities of Redshift beyond the data stored in its own nodes to include data stored in S3.

Redshift Spectrum allows users to store data in S3 and query it as if it were in their Redshift cluster without loading or transforming the data. Redshift Spectrum is best suited for users who want to query large amounts of structured data stored in S3 and join it with data already stored in their Redshift cluster.

For example, a retail company might store its transactional data in Redshift and its historical data in S3. The company can use Redshift Spectrum to join its Redshift transactional data with its historical data in S3 to gain deeper insights into customer behavior.

In summary, Amazon Athena and Amazon Redshift Spectrum are both powerful data querying services that allow users to analyze data stored in Amazon S3 using standard SQL. The choice between the two largely depends on the type of data being analyzed and the specific use case. Athena is best suited for ad hoc querying and interactive analysis of large amounts of unstructured data, while Redshift Spectrum is best suited for querying large amounts of structured data stored in S3 and joining it with data already stored in a Redshift cluster.

As someone said, one picture is worth a thousand words, so it is always preferable to show data insight in a visual format using a business intelligence tool. AWS provides a cloud-based business intelligence tool called Amazon QuickSight, which visualizes your data and gets ML-based insights. Let's learn more details about business intelligence in AWS.

Visualizing data with Amazon QuickSight

Data is an organizational asset that needs to be available easily and securely to anyone who needs access. Data is no longer solely the property of analysts and scientists. Presenting data simply and visually enables teams to make better and more informed decisions, improve efficiency, uncover new opportunities, and drive innovation.

Most traditional on-premises business intelligence solutions come with a client-server architecture and have minimum licensing requirements. To start with business intelligence tools, you must sign up for annual commitments around users or servers, requiring upfront investments. You will need to build extensive monitoring and management, infrastructure growth, patches for software, and periodic data backups to keep your systems in compliance. On top of that, if you want to deliver data and insights to your customers and other third parties, this usually requires separate systems and tools for each audience.

Amazon QuickSight is an AWS-provided cloud-native business intelligence SaaS solution, which means no servers or software to manage, and it can scale from single users to thousands of users under a pay-as-you-go model. With Amazon QuickSight, you can address a number of use cases to deliver insights for internal or external users. You can equip different lines of business with interactive dashboards and visualization and the ability to do ad hoc analysis. QuickSight gives you the ability to distribute highly formatted static reports to internal and external audiences by email. Further, you can enhance your end-user-facing products by embedding QuickSight visuals and dashboards into a website or application. There are several ways you can use QuickSight to analyze your data:

- **Visualize and explore data**: QuickSight allows you to create interactive visualizations and dashboards using your data. You can use a variety of chart types, including line graphs, bar charts, scatter plots, and heat maps, to explore and visualize your data. You can also use QuickSight's built-in filters and drill-down capabilities to drill down into specific data points and get more detailed insights.
- **Perform ad hoc analysis**: QuickSight includes a powerful SQL-based analysis tool, **Super-fast, Parallel, In-memory, Calculation Engine** (**SPICE**), that allows you to perform ad hoc analysis on your data. You can use SPICE to write custom SQL queries and perform calculations on your data, and then visualize the results using QuickSight's visualization tools. SPICE provides consistently fast performance for concurrent users automatically. You can import quite a bit of data into your SPICE datasets – up to 500 million rows each – and have as many SPICE datasets as you need. You can refresh each SPICE dataset up to 100 times daily without affecting performance or downtime.
- **Use ML**: QuickSight includes built-in ML capabilities that allow you to use predictive analytics to forecast future trends and patterns in your data. You can use QuickSight's ML algorithms to create predictive models and generate forecasts, and then visualize the results using QuickSight's visualization tools. QuickSight leverages ML to help users extract more value from their data with less effort. For instance, QuickSight Q is a **natural language query** (**NLQ**) engine that empowers users to ask questions about their data in plain English. QuickSight also generates insights using **natural language processing** (**NLP**) to make it easy for any user, no matter their data savviness, to understand the key highlights hidden in their data. QuickSight also provides 1-click forecasting and anomaly detection using an ML model.

Below is an example of a QuickSight dashboard that provides an analysis of home prices in the USA:

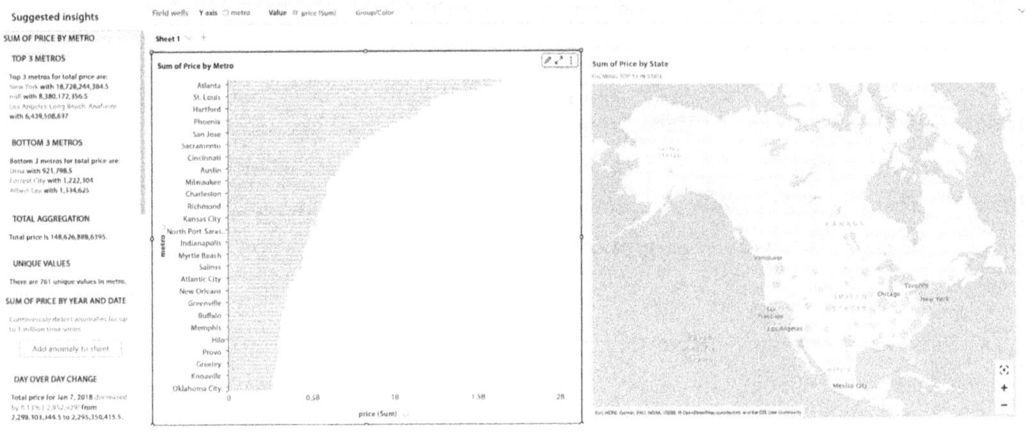

Figure 11.5: AWS QuickSight dashboard

In the dashboard above, you can see that QuickSight is able to show a bar chart for median home prices in the US by city in the first chart, and a geolocation graph with bubbles in the second chart. Also, you can see ML-based insights on the left-hand side, which makes it easy to understand the graph in simple language.

Up until now, you have been learning about various AWS analytic services. Let's use an example to put them together.

Putting AWS analytic services together

In the previous chapter, *Chapter 10, Big Data and Streaming Data Processing in AWS*, you learned about AWS ETL services such as EMR and Glue. In this chapter, let's combine that with learning how to build a data processing pipeline. The following diagram shows a data processing and analytics architecture in AWS that applies various analytics services to build an end-to-end solution:

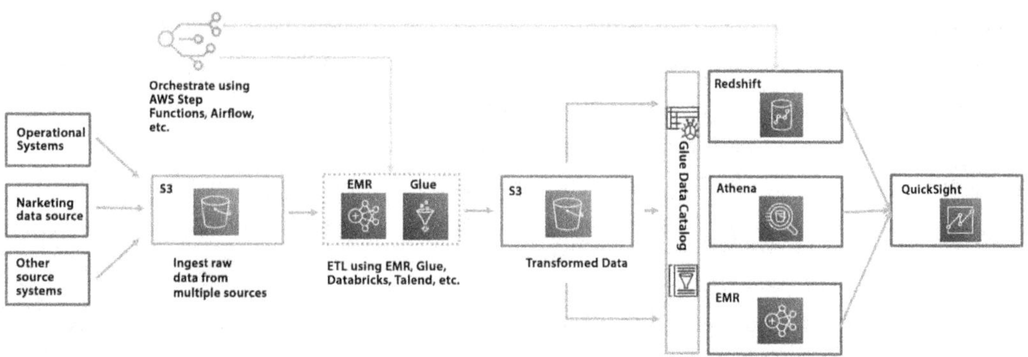

Figure 11.6: Data analytic architecture in AWS

As shown in the preceding diagram, data is ingested from various sources such as operational systems, marketing, and other systems in S3. You want to ingest data fast without losing it, so this data is collected in a raw format first. You can clean, process, and transform this data using an ETL platform such as EMR or Glue. Using the Apache Spark framework and writing data processing code from scratch is recommended when using Glue; otherwise, you can use EMR if you have Hadoop skill sets in your team. Transformed data is stored in another S3 bucket, which is further consumed by the data warehouse system in Redshift, the data processing system in EMR, and direct queries with Athena. Now, to visualize this data, you can connect QuickSight to any consumer.

The above is just one way to build a data pipeline; however, multiple ways are available to build data analytics architecture, such as data lakes, lake houses, data meshes, etc. You will learn about these architectures in *Chapter 15, Data Lake Patterns – Integrating Your Data Across the Enterprise.*

Summary

In this chapter, you learned how to query and visualize data in AWS. You started with learning about Amazon Redshift, your data warehouse in the cloud, before diving deeper into the Redshift architecture and learning about its key capabilities. Further, you learned about Amazon Athena, a powerful service that can "convert" any file into a database by allowing us to query and update the contents of that file by using the ubiquitous SQL syntax.

You then learned how we could add some governance to the process using Amazon Athena workgroups and how they can help us to control access to files by adding a level of security to the process. As you have learned throughout the book, there is not a single AWS service (or any other tool or product, for that matter) that is a silver bullet for solving all problems. Amazon Athena is no different, so you learned about some scenarios where Amazon Athena is an appropriate solution and other use cases where other AWS services, such as Amazon RDS, may be more appropriate for the job.

Further, you learned about the AWS-provided, cloud-native business intelligence service Amazon QuickSight, a powerful data visualization solution available under the SaaS model. You can achieve high performance in QuickSight using SPICE, its built-in caching engine. Finally, you combined multiple AWS analytics services and saw an example of an end-to-end data processing pipeline architecture in AWS.

In the next chapter, you will learn about making your data future-proof by applying AWS services to more advanced use cases in the areas of ML, IoT, blockchain, and even quantum computing.

12

Machine Learning, IoT, and Blockchain in AWS

Emerging technology such as **Machine Learning** (**ML**), **Artificial Intelligence** (**AI**), blockchain, and the **Internet of Things** (**IoT**) started as experiments by a handful of technology companies. Over the years, major technology companies, including Amazon, Google, Facebook, and Apple, have driven exponential growth by utilizing the latest emerging technology and staying ahead of the competition. With the cloud, emerging technologies have become accessible to everyone. That is another reason why organizations are rushing to adopt the cloud as it opens the door for innovation with tested technology by industry leaders like Amazon, Microsoft, and Google through their cloud platforms.

Today, the most prominent emerging technologies becoming mainstream are ML and AI. IoT is fueling industry revolutions with smart factories, and autonomous cars and spaces. Blockchain has seen tremendous growth recently, with a boom in cryptocurrencies and temper-proof record tracking. Even now, all major cloud providers are investing in quantum computing (which could bring the next revolution in the coming decade) and making it accessible to everyone through their platforms.

In this chapter, you will learn about the following emerging technology platforms available in AWS:

- ML in AWS with Amazon SageMaker
- Using AI in AWS using the readily available trained model
- Building an IoT solution in AWS

- Using **Amazon Managed Blockchain** (**AMB**) to build a centralized blockchain application
- Quantum computing with Amazon Braket
- Generative AI

Let's start diving deep and learn about these innovative technologies in detail.

What is AI/ML?

ML is a type of computer technology that allows software to improve its performance automatically by learning from data without being explicitly programmed. It is a way of teaching computers to recognize patterns and make predictions based on examples. In simple terms, ML is a way for computers to learn from data and make predictions or decisions. There are several types of ML, each with its unique characteristics and use cases. The main types of ML include:

- **Supervised Learning**: Supervised learning is the most widespread form of ML, involving training a model on a labeled dataset to predict the output for new, unseen data. Linear regression, logistic regression, and decision trees are some examples of supervised learning algorithms.
- **Unsupervised Learning**: Unsupervised learning, on the other hand, does not use labeled data and instead discovers patterns and structures in the input data. Examples of unsupervised learning algorithms include clustering, dimensionality reduction, and anomaly detection.
- **Semi-Supervised Learning**: This type of ML is a combination of supervised and unsupervised learning, where the model is given some labeled data and some unlabeled data and must find patterns and structure in the input data while also making predictions.
- **Reinforcement Learning**: Reinforcement learning is used in decision-making and control systems, where an agent interacts with an environment and learns to perform actions that maximize a reward signal. This type of learning is used in decision-making and control systems.
- **Deep Learning**: Deep learning is a subset of ML that employs deep neural networks with multiple layers to learn from data and make predictions or decisions. This method is particularly useful for tasks such as image and speech recognition, **Natural Language Processing** (**NLP**), and decision-making.
- **Transfer Learning**: This type of ML is used when the data or task of interest is different from the data or task on which the model was originally trained. This technique leverages the knowledge learned from a pre-trained model to improve the new model's performance.

"Artificial intelligence" is a more comprehensive term that encompasses not only ML but also other technologies that empower machines to undertake activities that conventionally necessitate human intelligence, including comprehending natural language, identifying objects, and making decisions. In basic terms, AI is a means for computers to accomplish tasks that ordinarily demand human intelligence, such as understanding spoken language, recognizing facial features, and playing strategic games like chess. AI can be implemented in many ways, from simple rule-based systems to more advanced techniques like ML and deep learning, which allow computers to learn from data and make predictions or decisions. There are several types of AI, each with its characteristics and use cases. The main types of AI include:

- **Reactive Machines**: These types of AI can only react to their environment; they can't form memories or learn from past experiences. Reactive machines are typically used in applications such as self-driving cars and video game AI.
- **Limited Memory**: These types of AI can take into account past experiences and use that information to make decisions. Examples of limited memory AI include robots that can navigate a room or a self-driving car that can change its driving behavior based on recent experiences.
- **Narrow AI**: These are AI systems designed to perform a specific task, such as image recognition or speech recognition. These systems are not general purpose and can only perform the task they were designed for.
- **Theory of Mind**: This type of AI is designed to understand mental states such as beliefs, intentions, and desires. This type of AI is still in the research phase and has not been fully implemented.
- **Self-Aware**: This is the most advanced type of AI, where the AI has the ability to be aware of its own existence and consciousness. This type of AI is still in the realm of science fiction and has not yet been achieved.
- **General AI**: AI systems that can perform any intellectual task that a human can, also known as artificial general intelligence. These systems do not yet exist but are the ultimate goal of AI research.

In this section, you saw a quick overview of AI/ML. This is a very broad topic, and there are multiple books that explain these concepts in detail. Within the context of this book, let's focus on AI/ML in AWS.

AI/ML in AWS

In recent years, ML has rapidly transitioned from a cutting-edge technology to a mainstream one; however, there is still a long way to go before ML is embedded everywhere in our lives. In the past, ML was primarily accessible to a select group of large tech companies and academic researchers. But with the advent of cloud computing, the resources required to work with ML, such as computing power and data, have become more widely available, enabling a wider range of organizations to utilize and benefit from ML technology.

ML has become an essential technology for many industries, and AWS is at the forefront of providing ML services to its customers. Some of the key trends in ML using AWS include:

- **Serverless ML**: AWS is making it easier to build, train, and deploy ML models without the need to manage servers. With services like Amazon SageMaker, customers can build and train models using managed Jupyter Notebook and then deploy them to a serverless endpoint with just a few clicks.
- **Automated ML**: Automating the model-building process is becoming increasingly popular, allowing customers to achieve good results with minimal expertise. AWS offers services like Amazon SageMaker Autopilot, which automatically builds and tunes ML models and selects the best algorithm with hyperparameters for a given dataset.
- **Transfer Learning**: With the amount of data available today, it is becoming increasingly difficult to train models from scratch. Transfer learning allows customers to use a pre-trained model as a starting point and fine-tune it for their specific use case.
- **Reinforcement Learning**: Reinforcement learning is a type of ML that is well suited for problems where the feedback is delayed or non-deterministic. AWS offers services like Amazon SageMaker RL, which allows customers to easily build, train, and deploy reinforcement learning models.
- **Federated Learning**: Federated learning is a distributed ML technique that allows customers to train models on multiple devices while keeping the data private.

AWS provides a wide range of services that make it easy for you to build, train, and deploy ML models. With the growing adoption of ML, AWS is well positioned to continue to lead the way in providing ML services to its customers. The following figure represents the services stack for AI/ML in AWS, divided into three parts: **AI services**, **ML services**, and **ML frameworks and infrastructure**.

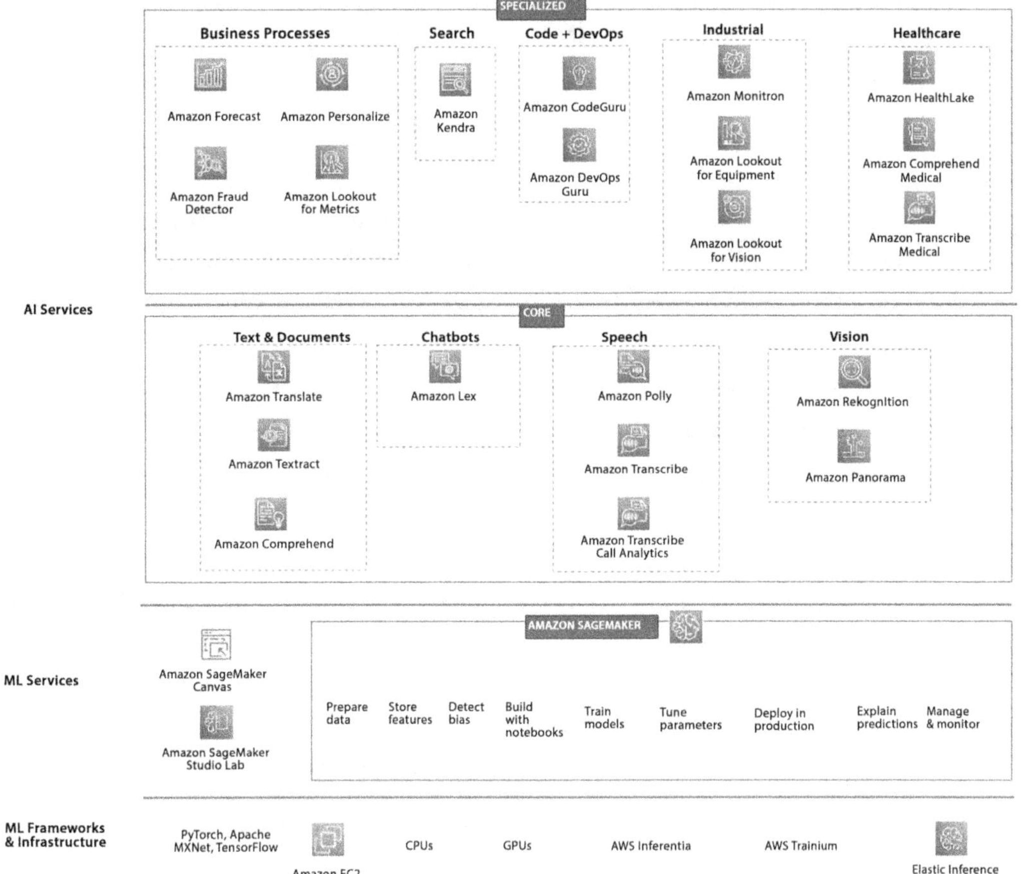

Figure 12.1: AWS ML Services Stack

The diagram illustrates a stack of options for working with ML; starting with the lowest level, ML frameworks and infrastructures require detailed programming and are best suited for field data scientists. This option offers the most flexibility and control, allowing you to work on an ML model from scratch using open-source libraries and languages.

At the top, purpose-built AI services are pre-built and ready to be invoked, such as Amazon Rekognition, which can perform facial analysis on an image without requiring any ML code to be written.

In the middle is Amazon SageMaker, the most feature-rich option, which offers a complete suite of subservices for preparing data, working on notebooks, performing experiments, monitoring performance, and more, including no-code visual ML.

Let's look into each layer of the above service stack in detail, starting with ML frameworks and infrastructure and moving upwards.

AWS ML frameworks and infrastructure

AWS provides a variety of infrastructure services for building and deploying ML models. Some of the key services include:

- **Amazon EC2 for ML workloads**: AWS provides a variety of EC2 instance types that can be used for ML workloads. Depending on the workload's needs, these instances can be configured with different amounts of CPU, memory, and GPU resources. For example, the P3 and G5 instances are designed explicitly for ML workloads and provide high-performance GPU resources.
- **Amazon Elastic Inference**: This is a service that enables you to attach GPU resources to Amazon EC2 or Amazon SageMaker instances to accelerate ML inference workloads.
- **AWS Inferentia**: AWS provides a custom-built chip called Inferentia, which can be used to perform low-latency, high-throughput inferences on deep learning workloads. It is designed to provide high performance at a low cost and can be used with Amazon SageMaker.
- **AWS Trainium**: AWS Trainium is a chip designed specifically to address the budget constraints development teams face while training their deep learning models and applications. AWS Trainium-based EC2 Trn1 instances provide a solution to this challenge by delivering faster training times and cost savings of up to 50% compared to similar GPU-based instances, allowing teams to train their models more frequently and at a lower cost.

AWS provides a variety of frameworks and libraries for ML development, allowing customers to easily build, train, and deploy ML models. Some of the main ML frameworks and libraries available on AWS include:

- **TensorFlow**: TensorFlow is an open-source ML framework developed by Google, which can be used for a wide variety of tasks, such as NLP, image classification, and time series analysis.
- **Apache MXNet**: MXNet is an open-source ML framework developed by Amazon, which can be used for tasks such as image classification, object detection, and time series analysis.
- **PyTorch**: PyTorch is an open-source ML framework developed by Facebook, which can be used for tasks such as image classification, NLP, and time series analysis.
- **Keras**: Keras is a high-level open-source ML library that can be used as a wrapper for other ML frameworks such as TensorFlow and MXNet, making it easier to build, train, and deploy ML models.

In this section, you learned about the ML frameworks and infrastructure provided by AWS. Let's learn about the middle layer of the service stack, Amazon SageMaker, which is the key ML service and the backbone of AWS ML. We will also see how to use this infrastructure to train, build, and deploy an ML model.

AWS ML services: Amazon SageMaker

Amazon SageMaker is a fully managed service for building, deploying, and managing ML models on the AWS platform. It provides a variety of tools and features for data preparation, model training, and deployment, as well as pre-built algorithms and models. One of the main features of SageMaker is its ability to train ML models in a distributed manner, using multiple machines in parallel, allowing customers to train large models quickly and at scale. SageMaker also provides a variety of pre-built algorithms and models, such as image classification, object detection, and NLP, which can be easily integrated into a customer's application.

You can use SageMaker to train a model to predict product prices based on historical sales data. A retail company could use SageMaker to train a model on a dataset containing information about past sales, such as the date, product, and price. The model could then be deployed and integrated into the company's e-commerce platform, allowing it to predict prices for new products and adjust prices in real time based on demand. If you want to improve the accuracy of detecting and classifying objects in images, you can use SageMaker to train object detection models using a dataset of labeled images.

Amazon SageMaker offers SageMaker Studio, an integrated development environment accessible through a web browser, to create, train, and deploy ML models on AWS. The studio provides a single, web-based interface that simplifies the process of building, training, deploying, and monitoring ML models.

The end-to-end ML pipeline is a process that takes a business use case and turns it into a working ML model. The pipeline typically consists of several stages, including data engineering, data preparation, model training, model evaluation, and deployment. AWS SageMaker enables this process by providing a suite of services that support each stage of the ML pipeline. The ML pipeline typically includes the following stages:

1. **Business use case**: Identifying a business problem that can be solved using ML.
2. **Data engineering**: Collecting and integrating the required data, which is often stored in Amazon S3 due to its ability to store large amounts of data with durability and reliability. Other AWS services, such as AWS Data Migration Service, AWS DataSync, and Amazon Kinesis, can also help with data integration.

3. **Data preparation**: Cleansing, transforming, and pre-processing the data to prepare it for model training.
4. **Model training**: Training the ML model using an assortment of algorithms, such as supervised and unsupervised learning, on the prepared data.
5. **Model evaluation**: Evaluating the performance of the trained model using metrics such as accuracy, precision, and recall.
6. **Model deployment**: Deploying the trained model to a production environment, where it can be used to make predictions or decisions.

As shown in the diagram below, SageMaker provides a suite of services for each stage in the ML. SageMaker provides a Jupyter-based notebook environment that allows data scientists and developers to interactively work on their ML models and quickly iterate on their experiments. SageMaker provides various monitoring and debugging tools, such as real-time metrics and logging, allowing customers to easily monitor and troubleshoot their models. SageMaker also provides a variety of pre-built algorithms and models, such as image classification, object detection, and NLP, which can be easily integrated into a customer's application.

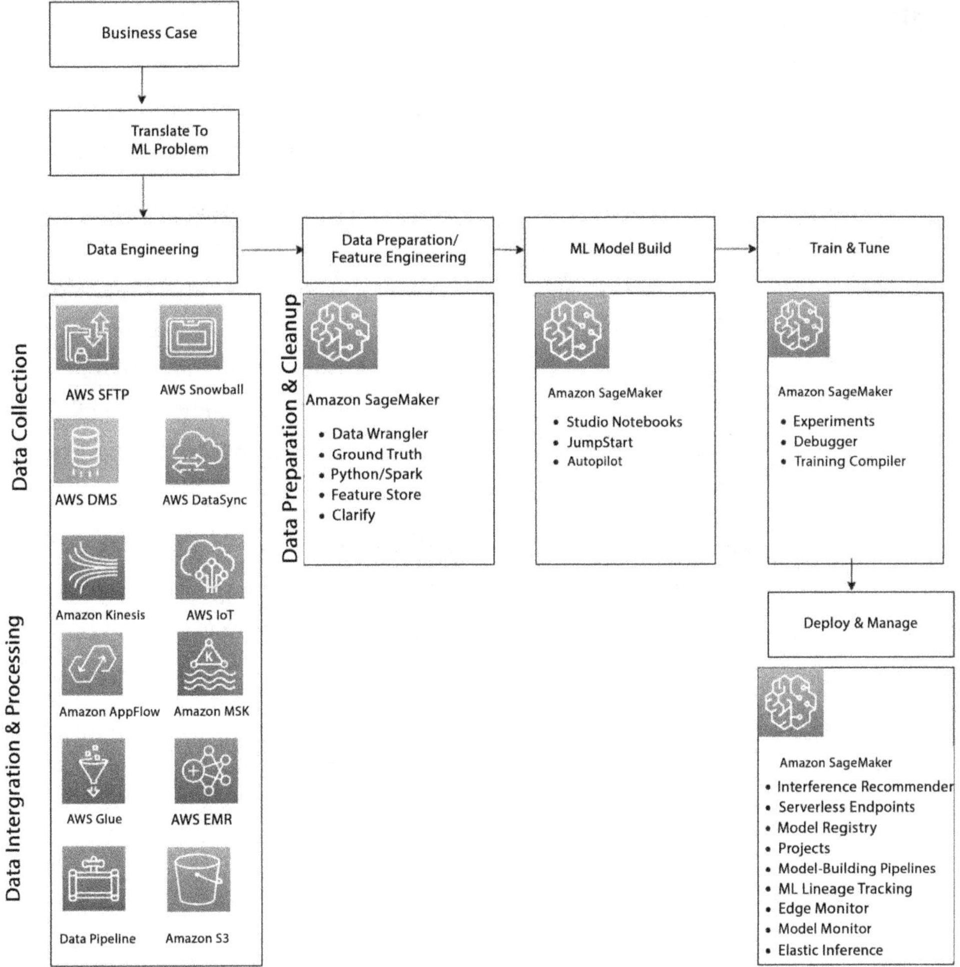

Figure 12.2: AI/ML Pipeline and Amazon SageMaker

As shown in the diagram above, Amazon SageMaker's capabilities can be understood by diving into four main categories: data preparation; model building; training and tuning; and deployment and management.

ML data preparation

Data preparation, also known as data pre-processing or feature engineering, is a crucial step in the ML pipeline. It involves cleaning, transforming, and preparing the data for model training. It is essential to understand the data first and figure out what kind of preparation is needed.

One common feature engineering case is dealing with missing data. Ignoring missing data can introduce bias into the model or impact the model's quality. There are several techniques that can be used to handle missing data, such as imputing the missing values with the mean or median of the data or using ML algorithms that can handle missing data. Another important case is when dealing with imbalanced data, where one class has significantly more samples than others. This can impact the model's performance and can be addressed by oversampling the small dataset, undersampling the large dataset, or using techniques such as cost-sensitive learning or synthetic data generation.

Outliers can also have a negative impact on the model's performance and can be handled by techniques such as data transformation, removing the outliers, or using robust models. Text-based data can also be transformed into numerical columns through techniques such as one-hot encoding or word embedding.

Data preparation is a critical step in the ML pipeline, and feature engineering techniques can be used to improve the quality and effectiveness of the model. SageMaker provides a Jupyter-based notebook environment and data preparation tools, such as Data Wrangler, to make it easy to prepare data for ML.

Data Wrangler is a tool within SageMaker Studio that allows data scientists and developers to easily prepare and pre-process their data for ML visually and interactively. With Data Wrangler, you can import, analyze, prepare, and add features to your data with no or minimal coding. Data Wrangler provides a simple and intuitive user interface that allows you to perform common data preparation tasks such as filtering, renaming, and pivoting columns, as well as more advanced tasks such as feature engineering, data visualization, and data transformations. Data Wrangler also integrates with other AWS services, such as Amazon S3 and Amazon Redshift, making it easy to import and export data from various data sources. Additionally, Data Wrangler allows you to add custom scripts and data transformations, providing flexibility and extensibility for your data preparation needs. After data preparation, the next step is model building.

ML model building

Amazon SageMaker Studio notebooks are a popular service within SageMaker that allow data scientists and ML engineers to build ML models without worrying about managing the underlying infrastructure. With Studio notebooks, data scientists and developers can effectively collaborate on their ML models and promptly refine their experiments by using a Jupyter-based notebook environment that facilitates interactive work.

One of the key features of Studio notebooks is single-click sharing, which makes collaboration between builders very easy. Studio notebooks also support a variety of popular ML frameworks, such as PyTorch, TensorFlow, and MXNet, and allow users to install additional libraries and frameworks as needed. In addition to Studio notebooks, SageMaker also provides other "no-code" or "low-code" options for building models. **SageMaker JumpStart**, for example, provides pre-built solutions, example notebooks, and pre-trained models for common use cases, making it easy for customers to get started with ML.

SageMaker Autopilot is another offering that allows customers to automatically create ML models to build classification and regression models quickly. It automatically pre-processes the data, chooses the best algorithm, and tunes the model, making it easy for customers to get started with ML even if they have no experience. These tools make it easy for customers to quickly build, train, and deploy ML models on the AWS platform. Amazon SageMaker provides a variety of built-in algorithms that can be used for various ML tasks such as classification, regression, and clustering. Some of the popular built-in algorithms provided by SageMaker are:

- **Linear Learner**: A supervised learning algorithm that can be used for classification and regression tasks.
- **XGBoost**: A gradient-boosting algorithm that can be used for classification and regression tasks.
- **Random Cut Forest**: An unsupervised learning algorithm that can be used for anomaly detection.
- **K-Means**: A clustering algorithm that can be used to group similar data points.
- **Factorization Machines**: A supervised learning algorithm that can be used for classification and regression tasks.
- **Neural Topic Model**: An unsupervised learning algorithm that can be used for topic modeling.

The algorithms above are designed to work well with large datasets and can handle sparse and dense data. These built-in algorithms can quickly train and deploy models on SageMaker and can be easily integrated into a customer's application. Additionally, SageMaker allows customers to use custom algorithms or bring their pre-trained models.

After building the model, the next step is to train and tune it.

ML model training and tuning

After building an ML model, it needs to be trained by feeding it with training data as input. This process may involve multiple iterations of training and tuning the model until the desired model quality is achieved.

Automated ML training workflows establish a consistent process for managing model development steps to accelerate experimentation and model retraining. With **Amazon SageMaker Pipelines**, you can automate the complete workflow for building models, starting from data preparation and feature engineering, to model training, tuning, and validation. You can schedule SageMaker Pipelines to run automatically, triggered by specific events or on a predetermined schedule. Additionally, you can launch them manually when required.

SageMaker Automatic Model Tuning uses thousands of algorithm parameter combinations that are automatically tested to arrive at the most precise predictions, ultimately saving weeks of time and effort.

Amazon SageMaker Experiments is a service that helps to capture, organize, and compare every step of the experiment, which makes it easy to manage and track the progress of the model-training process. It allows data scientists and developers to keep track of different versions of the model, compare their performance, and select the best version to deploy.

Amazon SageMaker Debugger is another service that helps to debug and profile the training data throughout the training process. It allows data scientists and developers to detect and diagnose issues during training, such as overfitting or underfitting, by providing real-time metrics and alerts on commonly occurring error scenarios, such as too large or small parameter values.

SageMaker Experiments and SageMaker Debugger work together to provide an end-to-end solution for managing and tracking the ML pipeline. You can learn more about model training using SageMaker by visiting the AWS user docs here – `https://aws.amazon.com/sagemaker/train/?`.

Now your ML model is ready and it is time to deploy it in production.

ML model deployment and monitoring

Once you are satisfied with the quality of the ML model that you have built, it is time to deploy it in a production environment to realize its business benefits. Amazon SageMaker provides several options for deploying models, including:

- **SageMaker Endpoints:** A serverless option to host your ML model with automatic scaling capability. This means that the number of instances used to host the model will automatically adjust based on the number of requests it receives.
- **SageMaker Projects:** A service that helps to create end-to-end ML solutions with **continuous integration and continuous deployment** (**CI/CD**) capabilities. This allows for easy collaboration and version control of the models and code.
- **SageMaker Model Monitor:** A service that allows you to maintain the accuracy of deployed models by monitoring the model quality, data quality, and bias in production. It also allows you to detect and diagnose issues with the deployed model, such as drift or bias, and take corrective actions.

Amazon SageMaker provides a comprehensive and easy-to-use platform for deploying ML models in production, with built-in support for serverless hosting, CI/CD, and monitoring and debugging capabilities to ensure the accuracy of the deployed models over time.

The following reference architecture example explains an end-to-end ML pipeline implemented using AWS SageMaker services:

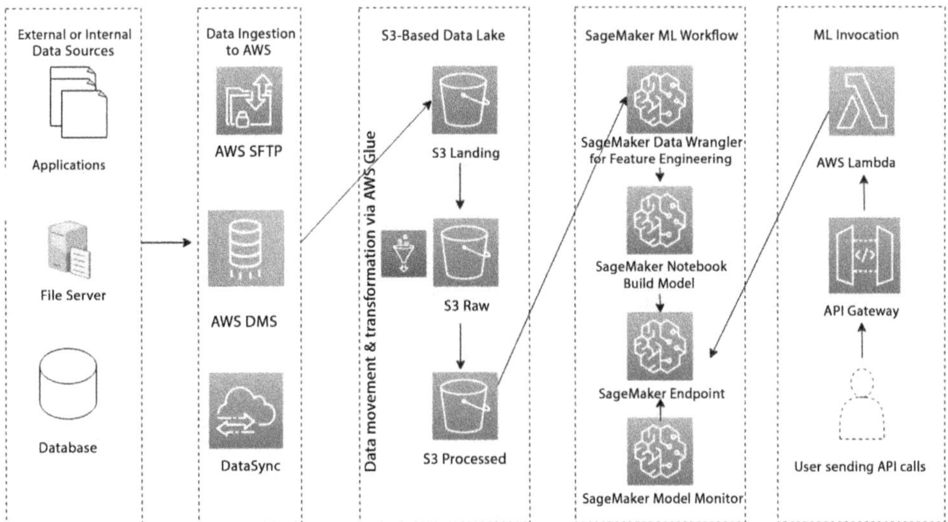

Figure 12.3: End-to-end ML Pipeline in AWS

This reference architecture is an example of how an end-to-end ML pipeline can be implemented using AWS SageMaker services:

1. **Data ingestion**: Various types of data are ingested into an Amazon S3-based data lake. This source data can originate internally in an organization or come from external source systems. The data is typically stored in three S3 buckets, and AWS Glue is used to integrate and transform the data in the lake.
2. **Data preparation**: Amazon SageMaker then feature engineers the data in the lake using Data Wrangler. This step involves cleaning and pre-processing the data and adding any necessary features to the dataset.
3. **Model building**: Using SageMaker notebooks, data scientists and ML engineers can create and train models using the prepared data. This step involves selecting an appropriate algorithm and instances, adjusting parameters to optimize performance, and training the model.
4. **Model deployment**: Once the model is trained, it is deployed as an endpoint in production using SageMaker Endpoints. The endpoint is then ready to be invoked in real time.
5. **Real-time invocation**: To invoke the SageMaker endpoint, an API layer is created using AWS API Gateway and AWS Lambda functions. This allows the endpoint to be accessed by various applications and systems in real time. You can also use Amazon SageMaker Batch Transform to perform batch inference on large datasets. With Batch Transform, you can easily process large volumes of data and get inference results in a timely and cost-effective manner.

This reference architecture demonstrates how AWS SageMaker services can be used to create an end-to-end ML pipeline, from data ingestion and preparation to model building, deployment, and real-time invocation. Let's look at AWS AI services and where to use them; you only need a little ML knowledge.

AWS AI services

In *Figure 12.1*, AI services are at the top of the stack, representing pre-trained AI services that can be easily integrated into your applications or workflows with just a few API calls without the need for ML, specialized skills, or training. These services are divided into several categories as you will learn in the subsections below.

Vision

Services such as Amazon Rekognition and Amazon Textract provide image and video analysis, object and scene recognition, and text extraction capabilities.

Amazon Rekognition is a deep learning-based computer vision service that allows you to analyze images and videos and extract information from them, such as objects, people, text, scenes, and activities. This service can be used for a range of use cases, such as object recognition, image search, facial recognition, and video analysis.

With Rekognition, you can upload an image or video to the API, which will analyze it and return information about the content. The service can detect and identify objects, people, text, and scenes in the image or video. It can also detect and recognize activities, such as a person riding a bike or a dog playing fetch. It can detect inappropriate content in an image or video, making it suitable for use in sensitive applications such as child safety.

One of the most powerful features of Rekognition is its facial recognition capabilities. The service can perform highly accurate facial analysis, face comparison, and face searching. It can detect, analyze, and compare faces in both images and videos, making it well suited for various applications, such as user verification, cataloging, people counting, and public safety.

You can use it to build applications for facial recognition-based security systems, photo tagging, and tracking people in a video.

Amazon Textract extracts text and data from nearly any type of document. It can process documents in various formats, including PDFs, images, and Microsoft Office documents. The service can automatically detect and extract text, tables, forms, and even handwriting and symbols, which can greatly reduce the manual tasks of reading, understanding, and processing thousands of documents.

The service can extract text and data from various documents such as invoices, contracts, and forms. The extracted data can be used to automate document-based workflows, such as invoice processing and data entry. It can also be used to extract structured data from unstructured documents to improve business processes and decision-making.

Textract can be integrated with other AWS services, such as Amazon SageMaker, to build ML models that can automatically classify and extract data from documents. It can also be integrated with Amazon Comprehend to extract insights from text, such as sentiment analysis and entity recognition. Additionally, it can be integrated with Amazon Translate to translate text automatically.

Textract can greatly improve the efficiency and accuracy of document-based workflows by automating the process of extracting text and data from documents. This can help organizations to save time, reduce costs, and improve the accuracy of their business processes.

Speech

Services such as Amazon Transcribe and Amazon Polly provide automatic speech recognition capabilities, including transcription and translation of audio files in multiple languages and formats.

Amazon Polly is a text-to-speech service that uses deep learning-based technologies to convert text into lifelike speech. Polly enables you to develop applications with speech capabilities, which allows you to create novel speech-enabled products and services.

The service supports a wide range of natural-sounding voices in multiple languages and dialects, including English, Spanish, Italian, French, German, and many more. You can also customize the pronunciation of words and use **Speech Synthesis Markup Language** (**SSML**) to control the generated speech's pitch, speed, and volume.

Amazon Polly is particularly useful for creating applications that are accessible to visually impaired users or for situations where reading is not possible, such as while driving or working out. It can be used to create voice-enabled applications such as audiobooks, language learning applications, and voice assistants.

Polly can be integrated with other AWS services to create more advanced applications. Polly is a powerful service that allows you to add natural-sounding speech to your applications, making them more accessible and user-friendly.

Amazon Transcribe employs automatic speech recognition technology to transcribe speech into text. It can transcribe audio files in various languages and formats, including MP3, WAV, and OGG. Additionally, the service can automatically detect the primary language in an audio file and produce transcriptions in that language. You can also add custom vocabulary to support generating more accurate transcriptions for your use case.

Transcribe can be used to transcribe audio files in a wide range of applications, such as media and entertainment, education, and business. For example, it can be used to transcribe audio from podcasts, videos, and webinars to make them more accessible to a wider audience. It can also be used to transcribe speech in customer service calls, focus groups, and interviews to gain insights into customer needs and preferences.

One of the notable capabilities of Transcribe is the capacity to construct and train your own custom language model tailored to your specific use case and domain. Custom language models allow you to fine-tune the transcription engine to your specific use case by providing additional context about the vocabulary, grammar, and pronunciation specific to your domain. It allows you to improve transcription accuracy, even in noisy or low-quality audio environments.

Amazon Transcribe is a powerful service that allows you to transcribe audio files into text quickly and accurately. It can help you to make audio content more accessible, improve customer service, and gain insights into customer needs and preferences. For example, you can use Amazon Transcribe to transcribe speech to text and then use Amazon Comprehend to analyze the text to gain insights, such as sentiment analysis or key phrase extraction.

Language

Services such as Amazon Comprehend and Amazon Translate provide NLP capabilities, including sentiment analysis, entity recognition, topic modeling, and language translation.

Amazon Translate is an NLP service that uses deep learning-based neural machine translation to translate text from one language in to another. The service supports a wide range of languages, including English, Spanish, Chinese, French, Italian, German, and many more. One of the key features of Translate is its ability to support various content formats, including unstructured text, PowerPoint presentations, Word documents, Excel spreadsheets, and more. This makes it easy to integrate into a wide range of applications and workflows.

Amazon Translate can be used in a variety of applications, such as e-commerce, customer service, and content management. For example, it can be used to automatically translate product descriptions on a website to make them more accessible to a global audience. It can also be used to translate customer service emails and chat transcripts to improve communication with customers who speak different languages.

Translate can be integrated with other AWS services, such as Amazon Transcribe, Amazon Comprehend, and Amazon Transcribe Medical, to create more advanced applications. It can help you to expand your reach to a global audience, improve customer service, and streamline content management.

Amazon Comprehend is an NLP service that allows you to extract insights from unstructured text data. It uses ML algorithms to automatically identify key phrases, entities, sentiments, language, syntax, topics, and document classifications.

This service can be used in a wide range of applications, such as social media monitoring, sentiment analysis, content classification, and language detection. For example, you can use Amazon Comprehend to analyze customer feedback in social media posts to understand customer sentiment and identify common themes. It can also be used to process financial documents, such as contracts and invoices, to extract key information and classify them into different categories.

One of the key advantages of Comprehend is its ability to process text in multiple languages. The service supports many languages, including English, Spanish, Chinese, French, Italian, German, and many more. This allows you to analyze text data in its original language without requiring manual translation. Comprehend can help you to understand customer sentiment, identify common themes, classify content, and process text data in multiple languages. With this service, you can gain a deeper understanding of your text data to make data-driven decisions.

Chatbots

Services such as Amazon Lex provide NLP and automatic speech recognition capabilities for building chatbots and voice-enabled applications.

Amazon Lex allows you to build conversational chatbots for your business using natural language understanding and automatic speech recognition technologies. With Amazon Lex, you can create chatbots that understand the intent of the conversation and its context, allowing them to respond to customer inquiries and automate simple tasks. One of the key benefits of Lex is that it makes it easy to build chatbots without requiring specialized skills in ML or NLP. The service has a visual drag-and-drop interface, pre-built templates, and pre-trained models to help you quickly create and deploy chatbots.

Lex chatbots can be integrated with a variety of platforms, including mobile and web applications, messaging platforms, and voice assistants. They can also be integrated with other AWS services, such as Amazon Lambda and Amazon Connect, to perform tasks like data lookups, booking appointments, and more. Some common use cases for Lex include customer service, e-commerce, and lead generation. For example, you can use Lex to create a chatbot that can answer customer questions, help customers find products, and even place orders.

Amazon Lex makes it easy to create chatbots that understand the intent of the conversation and automate simple tasks. With Amazon Lex, you can improve customer service, increase sales, and streamline business processes.

Forecasting

Services such as Amazon Forecast provide time series forecasting capabilities, allowing you to predict future events or trends based on historical data.

Amazon Forecast is a fully managed service that uses ML to make accurate predictions based on time-series data. The service allows you to quickly create, train, and deploy forecasts without any prior ML experience. Amazon Forecast can be used to predict a wide range of business outcomes, such as demand forecasting, inventory management, and sales forecasting. For example, a retail company could use Amazon Forecast to predict demand for its products, allowing it to optimize inventory levels, reduce stockouts, and improve customer satisfaction.

One of the key benefits of Forecast is its ability to handle large amounts of data and make predictions at scale. The service can automatically process data from different sources, such as Amazon S3, Redshift, and Glue. It can handle data in various formats, such as CSV, JSON, and Parquet. Forecast also provides an easy-to-use web interface and APIs, which allow you to create, train, and deploy forecasts with just a few clicks. Additionally, it also provides pre-built models for everyday use cases such as demand forecasting, which eliminates the need for data scientists to build models from scratch.

Amazon Forecast is a powerful service that helps you make accurate predictions based on time-series data. With Forecast, you can improve demand forecasting and planning, optimize inventory management, and make data-driven decisions to drive business growth.

Recommendations

Services such as Amazon Personalize provide personalized recommendations based on user behavior and interactions.

Amazon Personalize is a fully managed service that makes it easy to create and deliver real-time personalized recommendations for your customers. This service utilizes ML to understand your customers' behavior and predict the items they are most likely interested in.

With Personalize, you can easily build personalized experiences for your customers across a wide range of use cases, such as personalized product re-ranking, product recommendations, and customized direct marketing. For example, an e-commerce company can use Amazon Personalize to provide personalized product recommendations to its customers, increasing their likelihood of purchasing.

The service has a simple and intuitive interface, making it easy to use even for those without ML experience. It also includes pre-built models easily customizable to fit your business use cases. Personalize can process data from a variety of sources, including Amazon S3, Amazon DynamoDB, and Amazon Redshift. It also integrates seamlessly with Amazon Personalize campaigns, to deliver personalized recommendations in real time to your customers.

With its easy-to-use interface, customizable pre-built models, and the ability to process data from various sources, Personalize makes it easy to deliver a personalized experience to your customers, increasing engagement and driving sales.

You've now learned about various AWS AI/ML stacks and their use cases. It is essential to launch your model in production seamlessly and take action when there is any model drift. Let's learn about **Machine Learning Operations** (**MLOps**) to understand how to put an ML model in production using AWS offerings.

Building ML best practices with MLOps

MLOps are the practices and tools used to manage the full lifecycle of ML models, from development to deployment and maintenance. The goal of MLOps is to make deploying ML models to production as seamless and efficient as possible.

Managing an ML application in production requires a robust MLOps pipeline to ensure that the model is continuously updated and relevant as new data becomes available. MLOps helps automate the building, testing, and deploying of ML models. It manages the data and resources used to train and evaluate models, apply mechanisms to monitor and maintain deployed models to detect and address drift, data quality issues, and bias, and finally enables communication and collaboration between data scientists, engineers, and other stakeholders.

The first step in implementing MLOps in AWS is clearly defining the ML workflow, including the data ingestion, pre-processing, model training, and deployment stages. The following are the key MLOps steps for managing an ML application in production using AWS:

1. **Set up a data pipeline**: AWS offers a wide range of services for data pipeline management, such as AWS Glue, Amazon Kinesis, and Amazon S3, which can be used to automate data ingestion, pre-processing, and storage. Use Amazon SageMaker Data Wrangler for data engineering.

2. **Use SageMaker for model training**: Use SageMaker for ML model training and deployment. As you learned, it provides a variety of built-in algorithms and tools for feature engineering, model training, and hyperparameter tuning. Use Amazon SageMaker Pipelines to build a training pipeline.
3. **Automate model testing and validation:** Use SageMaker Ground Truth, SageMaker Debugger, and SageMaker Experiments to automate the testing and validation of your models.
4. **Implement CI/CD**: Use AWS CodePipeline and CodeBuild to automate the continuous integration and deployment of your ML models so that you can quickly and easily update your models as new data becomes available. Use source control management tools like Git to store and manage your ML code and version control.
5. **Monitor and maintain your models:** Use Amazon CloudWatch and Amazon SageMaker Model Monitor to monitor the performance of your models in production and take action when there is any model drift.
6. **Deploy models in real time**: Use Amazon SageMaker endpoints to deploy your models and make real-time predictions.
7. **Use auto-scaling**: Use auto-scaling to adjust the number of instances based on the traffic automatically.
8. **Security and Compliance**: Use SageMaker's built-in security features to ensure that your data and models are protected, and comply with relevant industry and regulatory standards.

By following the above best practices, you can ensure that your ML models are built, trained, and deployed as efficiently and effectively as possible and perform well in production. You can learn more about how to build MLOps using Amazon SageMaker by referring to the AWS page here – `https://aws.amazon.com/sagemaker/mlops/`.

As you learned about AI/ML in this section, now let's learn about the next technology trend, IoT, which is becoming mainstream and driving the modern-day industrial revolution.

What is IoT?

IoT stands for "Internet of Things," and it refers to the idea of connecting everyday devices to the internet so that they can share data and be controlled remotely. A simple example of this would be a smart thermostat in your home. A smart thermostat is a device you can control from your phone; it learns your temperature preferences and can even detect when you're away and adjust the temperature accordingly to save energy.

So, instead of manually adjusting the temperature, you can control it remotely using your phone or voice commands. This is just one example of the many ways that IoT can make our lives more convenient and efficient. Another example is a smart fridge, which can keep track of your groceries and alert you when you're running low on certain items or even order them for you automatically.

IoT refers to the interconnectedness of everyday physical objects, such as devices, vehicles, and buildings, to the internet through sensors and other technologies. These connected devices are able to collect and share data with each other and with other systems, such as cloud-based servers and analytics platforms. This allows for the creation of smart systems and applications that can be used for a wide range of use-cases, such as monitoring, control, automation, and prediction.

Another real-life example is fleet management; you can connect your fleet of trucks to the internet. This allows you to track and monitor them remotely, giving you insights and control over them. You can put IoT sensors on the rented trucks, which send information such as location back to the company. This allows the company to easily track the location of their trucks in near real time without having to check on them physically. This can help with logistics, maintenance, and security.

IoT can also be used in many industries, such as manufacturing, healthcare, transportation, and retail. For example, IoT can monitor and control machines and equipment in manufacturing, predict when maintenance is needed, and improve overall efficiency. In healthcare, IoT can monitor patients remotely and improve patient outcomes. In transportation, IoT can be used to optimize routes and improve fleet management. And in retail, IoT can be used to track inventory and optimize supply chain logistics. Overall, IoT has the potential to revolutionize many industries by providing valuable insights and automating processes. Let's learn how AWS can help to implement IoT workloads.

Building IoT applications in AWS

AWS IoT is a platform that allows you to connect, monitor, and control millions of IoT devices. It provides services that allow you to easily and securely collect, store, and analyze data from IoT devices. Let's understand AWS IoT services by looking at the following architecture diagram.

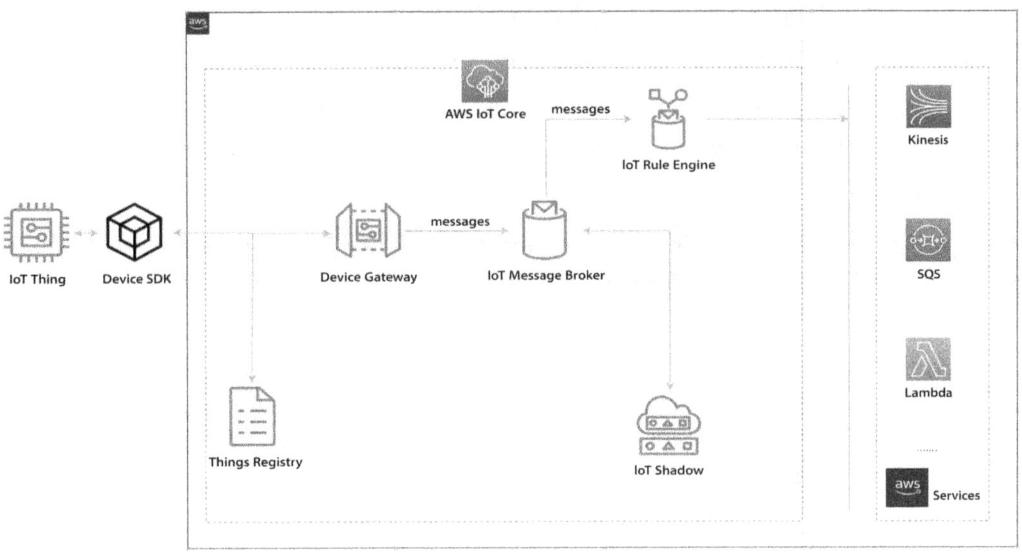

Figure 12.4: AWS IoT Services

As shown above, the process of connecting IoT devices to AWS typically starts with connecting the devices to AWS IoT Core. This can be done using different protocols such as MQTT, HTTP, and WebSocket. Once connected, the devices send data to the IoT Core service, which then securely transmits it to the IoT Message Broker using the Device Gateway. The IoT Rules Engine filters and processes the data, which can then be sent to other AWS services for storage, analysis, and visualization. Even when the devices are offline, the IoT Shadow service can be used to track their status. This architecture allows for real-time data processing and analysis, as well as the secure communication and management of IoT devices in the cloud.

AWS provides several IoT services to help developers and businesses connect, manage, and analyze IoT devices and data. Let's learn about some of the main AWS IoT services here.

AWS IoT Core

IoT Core is the foundation of the AWS IoT platform and allows you to securely connect, manage, and interact with your IoT devices. The various components of AWS IoT Core are:

- **Things Registry**: A database to store metadata about the devices, such as the device type, serial number, location, and owner.
- **Device Gateway**: A gateway to manage bidirectional connections and communications to and from IoT devices using protocols such as MQTT, WebSocket, and HTTP.

- **IoT Message Broker**: A component used to understand and control the status of devices at any time, providing two-way message streaming between devices and applications.
- **IoT Rules Engine**: A rules engine to connect IoT devices to other AWS services such as Kinesis, SQS, SNS, Lambda, and more, with data pre-processing capabilities such as transform, filter, and enrich.
- **IoT Shadow**: A virtual representation of a device at any given time, used to report the last known status of a device, change the state of a device, and communicate with devices using REST APIs.

AWS IoT Device Management

IoT Device Management is a service that helps to manage, organize, and monitor your IoT devices at scale. The service allows you to onboard and register your devices, organize them into groups, and perform actions on those groups. The first step in using the service is to onboard your devices. This process involves creating and registering device identities with the service, such as certificates and policies. You can also add metadata to each device, such as location, owner, and device type. This makes it easy to find and manage your devices later on.

Once your devices are registered, you can use the service to organize them into groups. These groups can be based on any combination of device attributes, such as location, hardware version, or device type. This makes it easy to perform actions on a specific subset of devices, such as sending a firmware update to all devices in a particular location. You can also use the service to monitor your fleet of devices. You can use Amazon CloudWatch to view the aggregate state of your devices periodically. This can help you identify and troubleshoot issues with your devices, such as low battery levels or connectivity issues.

In addition to these features, the service also allows you to create jobs that can be used to perform actions on a group of devices. For example, you can create a job to send a firmware update to all devices in a specific group or to reboot a group of devices. This can help to automate common device management tasks, making it easier to manage your fleet of devices at scale.

IoT Device Management allows you to easily onboard, organize, and manage your IoT devices at scale. It provides a range of tools and features that can help you to automate common device management tasks, such as device registration, grouping, monitoring, and job management. This service helps you to keep your IoT devices up to date, healthy, and responsive while keeping track of them.

AWS IoT Analytics

AWS IoT Analytics is managed entirely by AWS, which means that you don't have to worry about the cost and complexity of building your own analytics infrastructure. With IoT Analytics, you can collect, pre-process, enrich, store, and analyze massive amounts of IoT data, which enables you to identify insights and improve your business. This service is designed to handle sophisticated analytics on IoT data, making it easier for you to act on the insights you gain. The service includes several key features that make it easy to work with IoT data, including:

- **Data collection:** IoT Analytics allows you to collect data from IoT devices and other sources, such as AWS IoT Core, Amazon Kinesis Data Streams, and Amazon S3. It also supports the ability to filter, transform, and enrich the data before storing it.
- **Data storage:** IoT Analytics automatically stores your data in a highly secure, scalable, and low-cost data store that is optimized for IoT data. It also provides a SQL-like query language for easy data access and exploration.
- **Data analysis:** IoT Analytics provides a set of pre-built IoT analytics models and tools, such as anomaly detection and forecasting, that you can use to gain insights from your data. It also supports the ability to run custom SQL queries, and R and Python code to analyze your data.
- **Data visualization:** IoT Analytics provides a built-in visualization tool that allows you to easily create visualizations of your data and share them with others.
- **Data pipeline automation:** IoT Analytics allows you to automate the entire data pipeline, from data collection to analysis and visualization, using AWS Step Functions and AWS Lambda.

AWS IoT Analytics also integrates with other AWS services, such as AWS IoT Core, Amazon Kinesis Data Streams, Amazon S3, Amazon QuickSight, and Amazon Machine Learning, to make it easy to build complete IoT solutions. IoT Analytics makes it easy to process and analyze IoT data at scale, so you can gain insights and make better decisions for your business.

AWS IoT Greengrass

IoT Greengrass is a service that allows you to run AWS Lambda functions and access other AWS services on connected devices securely and reliably. This enables you to perform edge computing, where you can perform local data processing and respond quickly to local events, even when disconnected from the cloud.

With IoT Greengrass, you can easily create and deploy Lambda functions to your connected devices and have them securely communicate with other devices and the cloud. The service also provides a local data store for your device data, allowing you to perform local analytics and ML on the data without needing to send it to the cloud constantly.

IoT Greengrass also provides a feature called Greengrass Discovery, which makes it easy for devices to discover and communicate with each other securely, regardless of their location. This is particularly useful for large-scale IoT deployments where devices are distributed across multiple locations.

In addition, IoT Greengrass provides a feature called Greengrass Core, which is a software component that runs on the connected device and provides the runtime environment for your Lambda functions and other AWS services. Greengrass Core provides a secure communication channel between the device and the cloud using mutual authentication and encryption.

IoT Greengrass allows you to build IoT solutions that can perform local data processing and respond quickly to local events while still being able to communicate with the cloud and other devices securely. This enables you to build IoT solutions that are highly responsive, secure, and reliable.

AWS IoT Device Defender

IoT Device Defender is a fully managed service that makes it easy to secure your IoT devices. It helps you to detect and mitigate security threats by continuously monitoring your IoT devices and alerting you to potential security issues. The service includes a set of security checks that are performed on your devices to ensure they meet best practices for security. These checks include ensuring that devices use the latest security protocols, have strong authentication and access controls, and are free from malware and other threats.

IoT Device Defender also allows you to set-up custom security policies that can be used to detect and mitigate security threats. These policies can be configured to check for specific security issues, such as devices communicating with known malicious IP addresses or sending sensitive data to unauthorized recipients. When a security threat is detected, AWS IoT Device Defender can take a variety of actions to mitigate the threat. This can include things like blocking traffic from a device, shutting down a device, or sending an alert to the device administrator.

In addition to these security features, AWS IoT Device Defender also provides a range of reporting and analytics capabilities that allow you to track the security status of your devices over time.

This can help you to identify trends and patterns in security threats and to take proactive steps to improve the security of your IoT devices.

IoT Device Defender helps to secure your IoT devices and protect your business from security threats. It is easy to use and can be integrated with other AWS services to provide a comprehensive security solution for your IoT devices.

AWS IoT Things Graph

AWS IoT Things Graph is a service that makes it easy to visually connect devices, web services, and cloud-based systems using a drag-and-drop interface. The service allows you to quickly create and deploy IoT applications without writing any code, making it easy to connect devices, cloud services, and web services to create IoT workflows. One of the key features of IoT Things Graph is its ability to connect different devices and services easily. This is achieved through Things, which are pre-built connectors for various devices and services. These Things can be dragged and dropped onto a graph and wired together to create a workflow.

IoT Things Graph also provides a set of pre-built flow templates that can quickly create common IoT workflows such as device provisioning, data collection, and alerting. These templates can be customized to suit the specific needs of your application. In addition to its visual interface, IoT Things Graph also provides a set of APIs that can be used to create and manage IoT workflows programmatically. This allows developers to integrate IoT Things Graph into their existing applications and systems.

IoT Things Graph also provides a set of security and compliance features to help ensure the security of your IoT deployments. These include role-based access controls, encryption of data in transit and at rest, and the ability to meet compliance requirements such as SOC 2 and PCI DSS. IoT Things Graph makes it easy to connect devices and services to create IoT workflows without coding. Its visual interface and pre-built templates make it easy for developers of all skill levels to create IoT applications. At the same time, its security and compliance features help ensure the safety of your data and systems.

AWS IoT SiteWise

AWS IoT SiteWise is managed by AWS and designed to simplify the process of collecting, storing, processing, and analyzing large amounts of data from industrial equipment. With IoT SiteWise, businesses can easily manage and analyze data from their industrial equipment at scale.

It allows you to create a centralized industrial data model to organize and analyze data from multiple industrial gateways and devices and provides pre-built connectors for standard industrial protocols such as OPC-UA and Modbus.

One of the key features of IoT SiteWise is its ability to create a standardized data model for industrial equipment. This allows users to easily access and analyze data from multiple devices and gateways, regardless of their individual data formats or protocols. It also allows users to create custom data models that align with their industrial use case.

SiteWise can also be used alongside other AWS services to collect, store, and process data in near real time using AWS IoT Core and AWS Lambda and easily visualize and analyze the data using Amazon QuickSight. Additionally, it also enables you to perform asset modeling and create hierarchical structures of industrial equipment, so you can easily navigate and understand the relationships between different assets. AWS IoT SiteWise also provides a set of pre-built connectors for common industrial protocols such as OPC-UA and Modbus, which allow you to connect industrial gateways and devices to the service easily.

AWS IoT SiteWise can also be integrated with other AWS services like Amazon S3, Amazon Kinesis, and Amazon SageMaker to build more advanced analytics and ML models and to perform more complex data processing and analysis.

AWS IoT SiteWise is a highly capable and adaptable service that simplifies the collection, storage, processing, and analysis of data from industrial equipment at scale. This is made possible through the use of a centralized industrial data model, pre-built connectors, and integration with other AWS services. With these tools, businesses can easily handle the complexities of industrial data, and quickly gain insights that can help them optimize their operations and improve their bottom line.

AWS IoT TwinMaker

IoT TwinMaker is a service that allows customers to create digital twins of their physical equipment and facilities. A digital twin is a digital replica of a physical asset that can be used to monitor, control, and optimize the performance of the physical asset. AWS IoT TwinMaker allows you to develop digital replicas of your equipment and facilities, which can be utilized to visualize forecasts and insights derived from data collected by connected sensors and cameras.

Moreover, the service incorporates pre-built connectors that make it effortless to access and use data from various sources, including equipment sensors, video feeds, and business applications.

You can also import existing 3D visual models to produce digital twins that update instantly with data from connected sensors and cameras. This service can be used across various industries, such as manufacturing, energy, power and utilities, and smart buildings.

AWS Industrial IoT (IIoT)

The **Industrial Internet of Things** (IIoT) refers to the use of IoT technology in industrial settings, such as manufacturing, energy, and transportation. It involves connecting industrial equipment, machines, and devices to the internet to collect and analyze data, automate processes, and improve efficiency and productivity.

AWS provides a variety of services for building and deploying IIoT solutions, such as AWS IoT Core for securely connecting and managing devices, AWS IoT Device Defender for securing device connections, AWS IoT Greengrass for running local compute, messaging, and data caching on IoT devices, and AWS IoT Things Graph for building IoT applications with pre-built connectors to AWS and third-party services. AWS provides industry-specific services for IIoT, such as Amazon Monitron for monitoring industrial equipment.

One use case of IIoT is in the manufacturing industry. A manufacturing company can use IoT sensors on their production line machines to collect data on machine performance, such as temperature, vibration, and power consumption. This data can be analyzed to identify patterns and anomalies, which can indicate potential maintenance issues. The company can proactively reduce downtime and increase productivity by proactively addressing these issues. The data can also be used to optimize the production process, resulting in improved efficiency and reduced costs.

Another use case of IIoT is in the energy industry. An energy company can use IoT sensors on their power generators to collect data on generator performance and energy usage. This data can be analyzed to identify patterns and anomalies, which can indicate potential maintenance issues. The company can reduce downtime and increase power generation efficiency by proactively addressing these issues. The data can also be used to optimize the energy distribution process, resulting in improved efficiency and reduced costs.

AWS provides a comprehensive and flexible set of services for building and deploying IIoT solutions, allowing customers to easily collect, analyze, and act on data from industrial equipment and devices, improving their operations' efficiency and performance.

Let's learn about best practices when building AWS IoT applications.

Best practices to build AWS IoT applications

When building an IoT application on AWS, you should keep the following best practices in mind:

- **Secure your devices**: Ensure that all your devices are correctly configured and have the latest security updates. Use AWS IoT Device Defender to monitor and secure your devices against potential security threats.
- **Use MQTT or HTTPS for communication**: These protocols are designed for low-bandwidth, low-power devices and are well suited for IoT applications.
- **Use AWS IoT Analytics to process and analyze your data**: This service provides tools for cleaning, filtering, and transforming IoT data before it is analyzed.
- **Store your data in the right place**: Depending on your use case, you may want to store your data in a time-series database like Amazon Timestream or a data lake like Amazon S3.
- **Use AWS IoT Greengrass for edge computing**: With Greengrass, you can run AWS Lambda functions on your devices, allowing you to process and analyze data locally before sending it to the cloud.
- **Use AWS IoT Things Graph to create visual, drag-and-drop IoT workflows**: This service allows you to quickly connect devices and AWS services to create IoT applications without writing any code.
- **Use AWS IoT Device Management to manage your fleet of devices**: This service allows you to easily onboard and organize your devices and trigger actions on groups of devices.
- **Use AWS IoT SiteWise to handle data from industrial equipment**: This service allows you to collect and organize data from industrial equipment and create a digital twin of your physical assets, helping you to improve your operations.
- **Use AWS IoT Device Defender to secure your IoT devices and data**: This service allows you to monitor and secure your devices against potential security threats.
- **Use AWS IoT EventBridge to route and process IoT data**: This service allows you to route and process IoT data efficiently and integrates with other AWS services like AWS Lambda, Amazon Kinesis, and Amazon SNS.

You learned about various IoT services and their use cases in this section. Now let's learn about the next technology evolution in progress with blockchain and how AWS facilitates that with their platform.

Blockchain in AWS

Blockchain is a digital ledger that is used to record transactions across a network of computers. It is a decentralized system, which means that it is not controlled by any single entity, and it is highly secure because it uses cryptography to secure and validate transactions and keep them private. Each block in the chain contains a record of multiple transactions, and after a block has been added to the chain, it cannot be altered or deleted. This makes blockchain technology useful for a variety of applications, including financial transactions, supply chain management, and secure record-keeping.

Blockchain allows multiple parties to securely and transparently record and share information without a central authority. The most well-known use of blockchain technology is in creating digital currencies like Bitcoin, but it can be used for a wide range of applications, such as supply chain management, smart contracts, and voting systems. Blockchain technology is based on a network of computers that all have copies of the same data, which makes it difficult for any single party to manipulate or corrupt the information.

AWS offers AMB, which enables customers to easily create and manage blockchain networks, regardless of their chosen framework.

AMB: AMB is a service that is fully managed by AWS, which means that it simplifies the process of creating and managing scalable blockchain networks using popular open-source frameworks such as Hyperledger Fabric and Ethereum. This service enables customers to easily set up and manage a blockchain network using just a few clicks in the AWS Management Console, without requiring specialized expertise in blockchain technology. In short, AMB takes the complexity out of blockchain network management, allowing customers to focus on their core business activities.

The service also provides built-in security, scalability, and performance optimizations, enabling customers to easily create secure and reliable blockchain networks that can scale to meet the needs of their applications.

One of the key features of AMB is its ability to easily add new members to the network, enabling customers to easily collaborate with other organizations and share data securely and transparently. This can be done through a self-service portal, and customers can also use the service to set fine-grained permissions for different network members.

AMB also integrates with other AWS services such as **Amazon Elastic Container Service** (**ECS**) for data storage and container management, respectively.

This allows you to easily store and manage the data on your blockchain network and also perform analytics on the data using other AWS services such as Amazon QuickSight. It allows you to store and track data changes without the need for a central authority.

AMB also provides a set of APIs and SDKs that allow customers to interact easily with their blockchain network and integrate it with their applications and workflows. Some potential use cases for AMB include:

- **Supply chain traceability**: By using blockchain to record and track the movement of goods throughout the supply chain, companies can increase transparency and reduce the risk of fraud and errors.
- **Digital identity management**: Blockchain can create a decentralized system for managing digital identities, making it more secure and private than traditional centralized systems.
- **Tokenization**: Blockchain can create tokens representing assets such as company shares or a certificate of authenticity for a piece of art.
- **Smart contracts**: Blockchain can create "smart contracts" that execute automatically when certain conditions are met. This can automate processes such as insurance claims or real estate transactions.
- **Payment and financial services**: Blockchain can be used to create secure and efficient payment networks and facilitate cross-border transactions and remittances.

AMB makes it easy for customers to create and manage scalable blockchain networks without needing specialized expertise in blockchain technology. It enables you to collaborate with other organizations easily, share data securely and transparently, and also integrate your blockchain network with other AWS services for data storage and analytics.

In this section, you had a brief introduction to blockchain and AMB, which provides a platform to address blockchain-based use cases.

Quantum computing is another emerging technology waiting to revolutionize the world, but it may take the next 5 to 10 years to make it stable enough to solve daily use cases in production. AWS makes quantum computing accessible through AWS Braket. Let's see an overview of it.

Quantum computing with AWS Braket

Quantum computing is a computing method that employs quantum-mechanical phenomena to execute data operations. In quantum computing, data is expressed as qubits, or quantum bits, which can simultaneously exist in multiple states.

This unique attribute empowers quantum computers to perform specific calculations much more rapidly than classical computers. Despite its potential, this technology is still in its infancy and necessitates specialized hardware and expertise to operate. Some of the key use cases where quantum computing can be very efficient are:

- **Drug discovery and materials science**: Quantum computing can be used to simulate complex chemical and biological systems, which can help in the discovery of new drugs and materials.
- **Financial modeling**: Quantum computing can solve complex financial problems such as portfolio optimization, option pricing, and risk analysis.
- **ML**: Quantum computing can be used to develop new algorithms for ML and AI, which can help solve complex tasks such as image recognition and NLP.
- **Supply chain optimization**: Quantum computing can optimize logistics and supply chain management by predicting demand, optimizing routes, and scheduling deliveries.
- **Cybersecurity**: Quantum computing can be used to develop new encryption methods that are resistant to hacking and to break existing encryption methods.

AWS Braket is a fully managed service from AWS that allows developers and scientists to experiment with quantum computing. It provides a development environment that allows users to explore and test quantum algorithms, circuits, and workflows using different quantum hardware technologies.

Braket supports quantum hardware from leading quantum hardware providers such as D-Wave, IonQ, and Rigetti Computing and allows users to access these devices through a unified interface. This enables users to test their quantum algorithms and workflows on different quantum hardware technologies and compare the results.

AWS Braket also includes a quantum development kit that allows users to write, simulate, and debug quantum algorithms using Python or Q#, a domain-specific quantum programming language developed by Microsoft. This allows users to test their algorithms on a simulator before running them on quantum hardware.

AWS Braket also has a built-in Jupyter notebook interface for running and visualizing quantum algorithms. It also integrates with other AWS services, such as Amazon S3, Amazon SageMaker, and Amazon ECS, to provide a complete development environment for quantum computing. Braket makes it easy for developers and scientists to experiment and explore the possibilities of quantum computing without significant investments in hardware and infrastructure.

Quantum computing is a complex topic and requires lots of details to understand the basics. To learn about quantum computing in simple language, please refer to *Solutions Architect's Handbook* available on Amazon – `https://www.amazon.com/Solutions-Architects-Handbook-Kick-start-architecture/dp/1801816611/`.

The final emerging technology we will discuss in this chapter has gained massive momentum over recent months; let's take a quick look at generative AI and AWS's offerings in this domain.

Generative AI

With the launch of ChatGPT (**Generative Pre-trained Transformer**), generative AI has become the talk of the town. It has opened endless possibilities for revolutionizing the way we work today. This revolution is comparable to the innovation brought about by computers, and how the world moved from typewriters to shiny new computers, which made things more efficient. ChatGPT is just one dimension that shows the world the art of possibility and brings much-needed innovation that the world has been waiting for for a long time. Over the last two decades, you might have wondered who can challenge the position of Google in the AI market, especially Google Search. But, as you know, there is always a disrupter; if you don't innovate fast enough, someone else will do it. ChatGPT has brought that innovation to the hands of everyone.

Let's first understand what generative AI is. Generative AI uses AI algorithms to create new content that resembles content from a particular domain. This type of AI differs from other types of AI designed to recognize patterns or make predictions based on existing data. Generative AI is focused on creating new data that did not exist before. Generative AI can be used in various applications, from creating realistic images and videos to generating text and audio. For example, generative AI can be used to create realistic images of people, animals, or landscapes and generate new pieces of music or poetry that are similar to existing works. One of the advantages of generative AI is its ability to create new content that is personalized and unique. With generative AI, it is possible to create custom content tailored to a specific audience or user based on their preferences or other data.

Generative AIs using **LLMs** (**Large Language Models**) use these language models to generate new text that is similar in style and content to an existing text. These models are trained on large amounts of text data and can generate coherent, natural-sounding text in various contexts. It has many applications, from creating chatbots and virtual assistants, to understanding and responding to natural language queries, to generating text for marketing campaigns, and other content-creation tasks. With generative AIs that use LLMs, it is possible to create personalized, engaging content that resonates with users and drives engagement.

In recent years, everyone has been jumping onto the bandwagon of generative AI: whether it is Google with their LLM called **BERT** (**Bidirectional Encoder Representations from Transformers**), or Microsoft putting their weight behind OpenAI's ChatGPT and embedding it in their Office 365 products and Bing search engine. While big tech companies are rolling out their offerings and launching hundreds of AI tools every day, Amazon has not been left behind; Amazon recently launched its own offering in this space with **Amazon Bedrock**.

Amazon Bedrock is an AWS service that helps you choose from different pre-built AI models that other companies make. These models can help you with tasks like making predictions or recognizing patterns. With Bedrock, you can easily customize these models with your data and put them into your applications without worrying about managing any technical stuff, such as model training using SageMaker or figuring out how to use IT infrastructure to train the model at scale. It's easy to use, and you can integrate it with other AWS services you are already familiar with. You can learn more about Amazon Bedrock by referring to the AWS page here: `https://aws.amazon.com/bedrock/`.

The other generative code tool launched by AWS is **Amazon Codewhisperer**. It is an AI service trained on billions of lines of code. Based on your comments and existing code, it can quickly suggest code snippets or even entire functions in real time. This means you can save time on coding tasks and speed up your work, especially when working with unfamiliar APIs. You can learn more about Codewhisperer by visiting the AWS page here: `https://aws.amazon.com/codewhisperer/`.

However, generative AI also presents challenges, particularly when ensuring the generated content is high-quality and free from biases or other errors. As with all AI algorithms, it is crucial to carefully evaluate and test generative AI models to ensure they produce accurate and reliable results. In particular, generative AI models may sometimes produce biased or inappropriate content. It is essential to carefully review and edit the generated text to ensure it meets ethical and legal standards.

Summary

Organizations must drive innovation and stay agile by using emerging technologies to stay ahead of the competition. With cloud providers like AWS, these technologies are easily accessible for you to experiment with and add to your use case.

In this chapter, you began by learning about ML and AI. You learned how AWS services help build an end-to-end ML pipeline, taking an ML workload from ideation to production. You learned about three layers of AWS AI/ML services, starting with the ML infrastructure provided by AWS to train your model.

After that, you learned about Amazon SageMaker, which is at the center of the AWS ML tech stack to build, train, deploy, tune, and monitor ML models. Next, you learned about the top stack where AWS AI services reside, providing pre-trained models that can be used with simple API calls without any knowledge of ML. This AI service is available to address multiple use cases involving vision, speech, chatbots, forecasting, and recommendations. Finally, you learned about applying ML best practices using MLOps to productionize the ML workload.

You then dove deep into the next emerging technology, IoT, and how AWS helps to build IoT applications with services like IoT Core, IoT Analytics, IoT Device Management, IoT SiteWise, and so on. You learned about the 10 best practices for building IoT applications in AWS.

Next, you learned about AMB and how it helps build blockchain applications. You then learned about the next technology revolution in the making, quantum computing, and how AWS Braket makes it accessible for everyone to experiment with quantum computing. Finally, you had a brief look at generative AI, and the AWS tools on offer in this domain.

Containers are becoming key to optimizing cost and increasing efficiency. In the next chapter, you will learn about container patterns and AWS services for container workloads.

13

Containers in AWS

In this chapter, you will learn about various patterns commonly used by many top technology companies worldwide, including Netflix, Microsoft, Amazon, Uber, eBay, and PayPal. These companies have survived and thrived by adopting cloud technologies and the design patterns that are popular on the cloud. It is hard to imagine how these companies could exist in their present form if the capabilities delivered by the cloud did not exist. In addition, the patterns, services, and tools presented in this chapter make the cloud much more powerful.

Containers are an evolution of virtualization technology – virtualized hardware and virtualized machines are what you have been used to for many years. Many vendors provide this kind of virtualization, including AWS.

In this chapter, you will first learn about the concept of containerization with the most popular container platforms, Docker, Kubernetes, OpenShift, and the related offerings in AWS.

In this chapter, we will cover the following topics:

- Understanding containerization
- **Virtual machines** (**VMs**) and virtualization
- Containers versus VMs
- Learning about Docker
- Learning about Kubernetes
- Learning about AWS Fargate

- **Red Hat OpenShift Service on AWS (ROSA)**
- Choosing between container services

Let's get started.

Understanding containerization

It's almost 6 o'clock, and dinner time is getting close. You are getting hungry. And you feel like cooking some roasted vegetables. Time to fire up the grill. But think about everything that's going to be required:

- Vegetables
- A grill
- Matches
- Charcoal or gas
- Condiments
- Tongs

So, it's more than just roasted vegetables.

Some companies specialize in bundling all the necessary elements to facilitate this process and you can buy everything in a package. A similar analogy would be if you went to a restaurant. The cook handles all of the elements listed here for you; all you have to do is eat.

It's the same with software. Installing something like a website is much more than just installing your code. It might require the following:

- An **Operating System** (**OS**)
- A database
- A web server
- An app server
- Configuration files
- Seeding data for the database
- The underlying hardware

In the same way, the restaurant chef handles everything for you, and container technology can help create a standalone bundle that can take care of everything related to deployment and simplify your life. Containers enable you to wrap all the necessary components into one convenient little package and deploy them all in one step.

Containers are standardized packages of software that include all dependencies, enabling applications to run smoothly, uniformly, and reliably regardless of how many times they are deployed. Container images are lightweight, independent, standalone, and executable software bundles that include all that is needed to run an application:

- Source code
- The runtime executable
- System tools
- System libraries and JAR files
- Configuration settings

Containerization is bundling your application into containers and running them in isolation, even if other similar containers are running on the same machine. Containers enable you to innovate faster and innovate better. Containers are portable – all app dependencies are packaged in the container and are consistent – they run the same way on all Linux OSes. This portability and consistency enable you to build end-to-end automation, which speeds up the delivery of software and delivers efficiency such as cost and less resource overhead. Containers are used to make it easier to develop, deploy, and run applications. They are popular because they allow developers to create and deploy applications quickly, and they make it easy to run those applications in a variety of different environments, including on-premises, in the cloud, and in hybrid environments.

Let's now look at the advantages of containers.

Advantages of containers

There is a reason that containers are so popular. They have many advantages over non-containerized software deployed on bare metal. Let's analyze the most relevant advantages.

Containers enable you to build modern applications

Containers allow us to deploy applications more efficiently for a variety of reasons. Many applications today require a loosely coupled and stateless architecture. A **stateless** architecture doesn't store any state within its boundaries. They simply pass requests forward. If the state is stored, it is stored outside of the container, such as in a separate database. Architectures like this can be designed to easily scale and handle failures transparently because different requests can be handled independently by different servers. A **loosely coupled** architecture is one where the individual components in the architecture have little or no knowledge of other components in the system. Containers are ideally suited for this type of application.

Using containers to build modern applications can help developers create and deploy applications more efficiently, while also making it easier to run those applications in a variety of different environments. Some reasons why containers are ideal for building modern applications are:

- **Improved efficiency and enhanced portability**: Containers allow developers to build an application once and run it on any other Linux machine, regardless of any customized settings that the machine might have. This makes it easy to deploy applications in a variety of environments, including on-premises, in the cloud, and in hybrid environments.
- **Simplified deployment**: Containers can be used to package and run existing applications without the need for modification, which makes it easier to migrate these applications to the cloud and integrate them into newer development processes and pipelines. While using containers in this way can be beneficial, it is often more effective to refactor the application in order to take full advantage of the benefits that containers offer. This may involve reworking certain aspects of the application or building new features on top of the existing application. By containerizing and refactoring the application, it becomes more portable and can be more easily integrated into modern development workflows.

Fewer infrastructure wastes

With the low cost and speed associated with bringing instances up and down, resources such as memory can be allocated more aggressively. If we can spin up a server quickly if traffic spikes, we can run our servers at a higher CPU utilization rate without the risk of overloading our systems. Think of web applications having fluctuating user traffic, this traffic depends on many factors (such as the time of day, day of the week, and so on). If we use containers, we can spin up new instances whenever traffic increases. For example, think about Amazon.com. It would be surprising if their web traffic were not considerably higher during the holidays and weekends than on weekdays as most people shop more over holiday periods. Containers allow you to isolate applications and run multiple applications on a single host, which can lead to better resource utilization. They also make it easier to scale applications up or down, as needed, by allowing you to deploy additional containers as needed to meet demand.

Containers are simple

Containers enable isolated, autonomous, and independent platforms without the overhead of an OS. Developers can redeploy a configuration without managing the application state across multiple virtual machines. Some containers are cross-platform and can be deployed on Mac, Windows, or Linux environments. Containers can be deployed and managed using a container orchestration tool, such as Kubernetes, which simplifies the process of deploying and managing applications at scale.

Containers can increase productivity by accelerating software development

The fast and interactive nature of the deployment of containers can offer fast feedback to accelerate the development cycle. The deployment of containers can be automated, further enhancing productivity. Containers can be started in a repeatable and consistent manner in one instance or multiple instances, regardless of the instance type or size. Containers allow developers to package an application with all its dependencies and ship it as a single package, making it easier to develop, deploy, and run the application.

As more and more applications are designed with cloud-native and microservices architectures, containers have become a popular way to package and deploy these components. In order to support agile development practices, such as DevOps and **continuous integration/continuous deployment** (CI/CD), it is important to have tools that can automate the process of deploying and managing distributed cloud-native applications. Container orchestration and management systems are designed to do just that, and they are essential for managing applications at scale. By using containers to package code and leveraging container orchestration and management systems, it is possible to build and deploy modern, cloud-native applications efficiently and effectively.

Using containers to deploy applications can enable you to deploy your application across an array of servers. It doesn't matter if that server array has ten servers, 100 servers, or 1,000 servers.

Disadvantages of containers

There is always a downside to every technology. There is no silver bullet. In the case of containers, these are some of the disadvantages.

Container speeds are slightly slower compared to bare-metal servers

A **bare-metal** server is a server that one user can utilize. Before the age of virtualization, there was no other kind of server. There was no way to slice a server and have multiple users on each slice. Multiple users could use a server but without any real separation. **Virtualization** enables us to slice up a server and provide dedicated slices to individual users.

In this case, the user will think they have complete and exclusive use of the server when, in actuality, they are only using a portion of the server. In this case, a performance penalty is paid compared to the bare-metal approach.

The performance of containers has higher overhead constraints compared to bare metal due to the following:

- **Overlay networking**: To provide virtualization, an extra network layer must be overlaid on top of the OS. This overlay creates overhead.
- **Interfacing with other containers**: The connections between containers will not be as fast if they exist within the same container engine as opposed to connecting containers that are running on separate hosts. This is because communication between containers within the same engine typically involves some level of virtualization, which can add latency and reduce throughput.
- **Connections to the host system**: There are also connections between the containers and the underlying host system. There will also be some latency with these connections compared to intra-process connections.

The overhead is small, but if your application requires you to squeeze performance to gain the edge no matter how small, you will want to use bare metal instead of containers. An example of this use case is high-frequency trading platforms, where performance is measured in microseconds.

Ecosystem inconsistencies

Although the popular Docker platform is open-source and pervasive, it is not fully compatible with other offerings such as Kubernetes and Red Hat's OpenShift. This is due to the normal push/pull forces between competitors and their desire to grow the market together (by offering compatible and uniform features) while at the same time growing their market share (by offering proprietary features and extensions).

For example, Docker and Kubernetes are not fully compatible. Docker uses its own container runtime, while Kubernetes supports multiple container runtime options, including Docker. This means that certain features and functionality that are available in the Docker runtime may not be available when using Kubernetes. Both platforms have different approaches to volume management, which can make it difficult to use persistent storage with containers in certain environments. They also have different approaches to security, which can make it difficult to secure containers in certain environments.

While it is possible to use Docker and Kubernetes together, there may be some limitations and challenges to consider. It is important to carefully evaluate the specific needs and requirements of your application when deciding which platform to use.

In summary, containers can be great for certain use cases, but they are not a magic bullet for all scenarios. Containers are well suited to running microservices that don't require microsecond performance. Containers can simplify microservice delivery by enabling a packaging mechanism around them.

Virtualization has been a popular method for optimizing the use of IT infrastructure for several years, with virtual machines being widely used to run multiple applications on a single physical server. In recent years, containers have gained popularity as a way to further optimize idle resources within VMs by allowing multiple applications to be run in isolated environments on a single OS. Before discussing containers in more detail, it is important to understand the basics of virtual machines and virtualization.

Virtual machines (VMs) and virtualization

In order to understand VMs and virtualization, let's first look at an analogy. For many of us, one of our goals is to own a house. Can you picture it? Three bedrooms, a beautiful lawn, and a white picket fence, maybe? For some of us, at least for now, that dream may not be achievable, so we must settle on renting an apartment in a big building.

You can think of the beautiful house as a normal standalone server that serves only one client or application. The apartment, in this case, is the VM. The apartment serves its purpose by providing housing with some shared services. It might not be as beautiful and convenient as the house, but it does the job. With the house, you are wasting resources if you live alone because you can only use one room at a time. Similarly, with a standalone server, especially if you have an application with variable traffic, you will have lulls in your traffic where a lot of the capacity of the machine is wasted.

As you can see from the example, both approaches have advantages and drawbacks, and your choice will depend on your use case. However (unlike in the houses versus apartments metaphor), from the perspective of VM users, they would be hard-pressed to know whether they are using a dedicated machine or a VM.

To create virtualization and isolation on top of a bare-metal physical server, VMs use a hypervisor. A VM manager, also called a hypervisor, is a software application that enables several OSes to utilize a single hardware host concurrently. It creates a layer of abstraction between the hardware and the OSes, allowing multiple VMs to run on a single physical machine. Hypervisors allow you to share and manage hardware resources and provide you with multiple isolated environments all within the same server. Many of today's hypervisors use hardware-enabled virtualization and hardware designed explicitly for VM usage.

The two primary categories of hypervisors are Type 1, also referred to as bare-metal or native hypervisors, which operate directly on the hardware of the host, and Type 2, also known as hosted hypervisors, which operate on top of a host OS.

Hypervisors are used for a variety of purposes, including server consolidation, testing and development, and enabling legacy applications to run on modern hardware. They are an important tool for maximizing the utilization of hardware resources and enabling organizations to run multiple applications on a single physical machine. You can have two VMs running alongside each other on the same physical machine and have each one running a different OS. For example, one could be running Amazon Linux, and the other VM could be running Ubuntu.

Now that we have learned about these concepts, let's compare containers and VMs.

Containers versus VMs

There is a definite line of distinction between VMs and containers. Containers allow you to isolate applications within an OS environment. VMs allow you to isolate what appears to the users and represent it as a completely different machine to the user, even with its own OS.

The following diagram illustrates the difference:

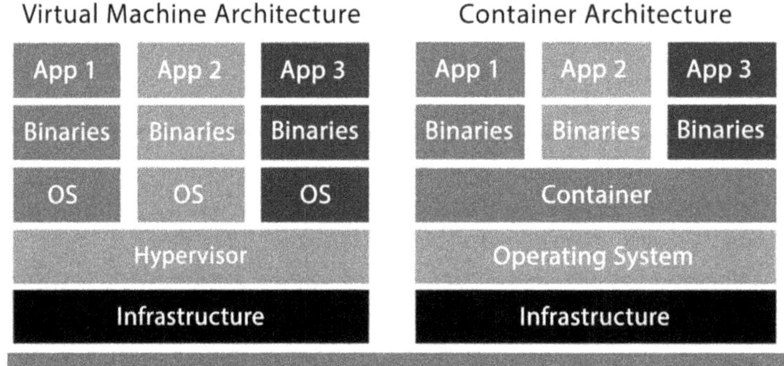

Figure 13.1: VMs versus containers

As we can see in *Figure 13.1*, in the case of VM architecture, each virtual slice has its own OS and all the slices sit on top of the hypervisor. In the case of container architecture, there is only one OS installed for all the instances. There is only one container engine, but multiple binaries and applications can be installed for each slice.

Containers share a kernel at the OS level; all components are built into the OS kernel, which makes containers fast to start and, when compared to VMs, they generally have lower overhead.

VMs have a more defined isolation boundary; you must run a full OS (and kernel) to use a VM. Each VM handles boot processes, including device initialization, which requires more overhead than containers.

It's also useful to highlight that, in most cases, when you run containers in AWS (and in most cloud environments, for that matter), you will run these containers on a VM. Therefore, there will be multiple containers running in a VM. In turn, that VM will be running alongside a set of other VMs in the same hypervisor on top of a physical machine. The only exception to this rule might be if you pay extra to get a dedicated instance.

You can see in the following diagram the foundation layer of the infrastructure. You can have a bare-metal physical server sitting in the data center. On top of that, you have a hypervisor that creates VMs with OSes installed. In this case, you can see three VMs on top of a single physical server. Now, here comes the beauty of containers; you can see that each VM has two containers, so that's a total of 6 in one physical server. Now without containers, you can only deploy three applications, one in each VM, but the container provides environment-level isolation, so now you can utilize your VMs fully by deploying two applications in each VM even though the underlying OS is the same.

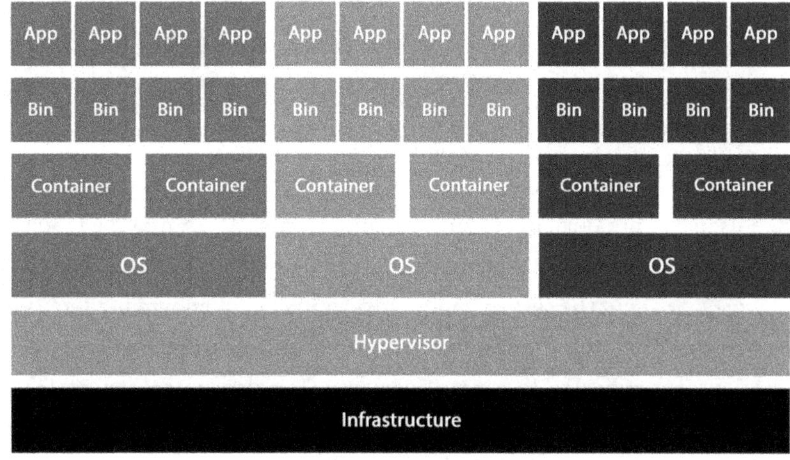

Figure 13.2: Architecture for container virtualization

VMs and hypervisors are transparent to you when using AWS. Whenever you launch an **Elastic Compute Cloud** (**EC2**) instance at the hypervisor layer, AWS does a lot of work for you behind the scenes. The EC2 instance appears to you as your own dedicated instance, but in truth, the new instance is just another VM in an army of VMs that AWS has launched for other AWS users.

When utilizing a VM, you run an application within a virtualized OS, along with the necessary binaries and libraries, all of which are encapsulated within a virtual environment. In contrast, containers operate at a higher level in the stack, where OS-level components are virtualized instead of the entire OS and hardware. The OS makes processes believe they are running in their own dedicated environment. They cannot see the other processes running on that OS and have access to their own virtualized resources, including the file system tree.

So far, we have learned about the general concepts of containerization and virtualization. In the next sections, we will drill down into more specific topics and learn about actual implementations of these concepts, starting with the popular open-source software Docker, and then moving onto Kubernetes and OpenShift.

Learning about Docker

It would be a disservice to you, reader, for us to talk about containers and not mention Docker. **Docker** is not the only way to implement containers, but it is a popular container software; perhaps the most popular one. Docker has almost become synonymous with the term container. Docker, Inc., the product maker, follows a freemium model, offering both a free and a premium version. Docker was released to the public in 2013 at the PyCon Conference.

As container software, Docker can package an application with its libraries, configuration files, and dependencies. Docker can be installed in Linux environments as well as on Windows. The virtual containers that Docker enables allow applications to run in isolation without affecting any other processes running on the same physical machine.

Docker is often used by both developers and system administrators, making it an essential tool for many DevOps teams. Developers like using it because it allows them to focus on writing code without worrying about the system's implementation and deployment details where it will eventually be deployed. They can be assured that the characteristics of the environment will be identical regardless of the physical machine. Developers can also leverage many of the programs and extensions that come bundled with Docker. System administrators use Docker frequently because it gives them flexibility and its light footprint allows them to reduce the number of servers needed to deploy applications at scale.

The complete Docker documentation, installation instructions, and a download link for the Community edition of Docker can be found here: `https://docs.docker.com/`.

Docker components

Docker does not have a monolithic architecture. It has a set of well-defined components, each in charge of an individual function and fully dedicated to performing only that function.

The following architecture shows the major Docker components.

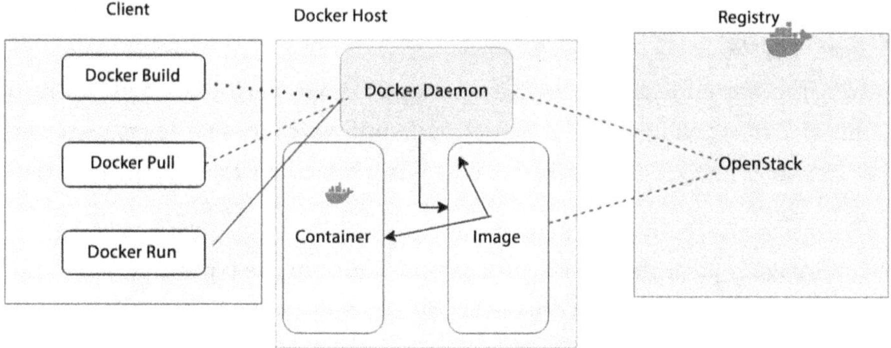

Figure 13.3: Docker architecture

As shown in the preceding diagram, the Docker system operates on a client-server model where the Docker client communicates with the Docker daemon. The Docker daemon handles the complex tasks associated with building, running, and administering Docker containers. The daemon has the flexibility to run on the same host as the client or establish a connection with a remote host. The Docker client and daemon can run on a variety of OSes, including Windows and Linux. Let's go through the Docker components in detail to increase our understanding of Docker.

Dockerfile

Every Docker container needs to have a **Dockerfile**. A Dockerfile is a plain old text file containing instructions showing how the Docker image will be built. Don't worry; we'll cover Docker images in a second.

Some of the instructions that a Dockerfile will contain are the following:

- **The OS supporting the container**: What is the OS associated with the container? For example, Windows, Linux, and so on.
- **Environmental variables used**: For example, most deployments require a list of variables. Also, is this a production or test deployment? What department is this deployment for? What department should be billed?

- **Locations of files used**: For example, where are the data files located? Where are the executable files?
- **Network ports used**: For example, what ports are open? Which port is used for HTTP traffic?

Let's now move on to the Docker image component.

Docker images

After creating the Dockerfile, the next step is creating an image. The Docker build utility can take a Dockerfile and create an image. The Docker build utility's purpose is to create ready-for-deployment container images. The Dockerfile contains instructions that specify how the Docker image will be built.

The **Docker image** is portable across environments and instance types, and that's one of the reasons for Docker's popularity. You can deploy the same image in a Linux or Windows environment, and Docker will handle the details to ensure that the deployment functions correctly in both environments. One recommended best practice is to ensure that any external dependencies specified in the Dockerfile have the version of the dependency explicitly declared. If this is not done, inconsistencies may result from the same Dockerfile because a different library version may be picked up.

Docker run

Docker run is a utility where commands can be issued to launch containers. In this context, a container is an image instance. Containers are designed to be transient and temporary. The Docker run utility can restart, stop, or start containers. The utility can launch several instances of the same image, and those instances can run simultaneously to support additional traffic. For example, if you have ten similar instances taking traffic and the traffic increases, you can use the Docker run utility to launch an additional instance.

Docker Hub

When you build a container, you can configure it from scratch, creating your own Dockerfile and configuring it yourself. However, many times, it is not necessary to reinvent the wheel. If you want to leverage the work that others have done already, you can use Docker Hub. **Docker Hub** is a collection of previously created containers shared by Docker users. In Docker Hub, you will find Docker images created by Docker and by other vendors who sometimes support those containers. Also, other Docker users publish versions of the containers they have created that they have found useful.

You can also share your containers with the public if you choose to do so. However, if you choose, you can also upload containers into a local Docker registry, keep them private, and only share them with select groups and individuals.

Docker Engine

Docker Engine is the heart of Docker. When someone says they are using Docker, it is shorthand for saying "Docker Engine." Docker Engine instantiates and runs containers. The company offers two versions of Docker Engine: the open-source version, dubbed Docker Engine Community Edition, and Docker Engine Enterprise Edition.

Docker launched Docker Engine Enterprise Edition in 2017. However, as with many companies that use the freemium model, the original open-source version is still available and maintained. It is now called Docker Engine Community Edition. The Enterprise Edition has added advanced features, such as vulnerability monitoring, cluster management, and image management.

Docker Compose

Docker Compose is another Docker tool that can be used to configure and instantiate multi-container Docker applications. In order to configure it, a YAML file is used. Once the YAML configuration is defined, the service can be started with one command. Some of the advantages of using Docker Compose are as follows:

- More than one isolated environment can be deployed per instance
- Volume data can be preserved as new containers are instantiated
- Only containers that have been modified need to be instantiated
- Variables can be passed in via the configuration file

A common use case for Docker Compose is setting up development, testing, and UAT environments on one host.

Docker Swarm

Docker Swarm groups VMs or physical machines that are running Docker Engine and are configured to run as a cluster. Once the machines have been clustered, you can run regular Docker commands, and those commands will be executed on the cluster rather than on individual services. The controller for a swarm is called the swarm manager. The individual instances in the cluster are referred to as nodes.

The process of managing nodes in a cluster in unison is called **orchestration**.

Operating instances as a cluster or a swarm increases application availability and reliability. Docker swarms consist of multiple worker nodes and at least one manager node. The worker nodes perform the application logic and handle the application traffic, and the manager oversees the management of the worker nodes, thus managing resources efficiently.

Let's look into the AWS-managed container service for hosting Docker in the cloud.

Amazon Elastic Container Service (ECS)

The core of container management is automation, which includes container build/deploy pipelines, observability for ensuring health, **Service Level Agreements** (**SLAs**), and security at all steps. Container orchestration is an important piece that manages computers, networking, and storage and handles critical aspects such as scheduling and auto-scaling. This is where ECS comes in, providing an end-to-end orchestration service for containers.

Amazon **Elastic Container Service** (**ECS**) is a container orchestration service. It enables users to launch EC2 containers in the form of tasks. In this case, a task is one or more EC2 instances with a Docker container. These EC2 instances can send traffic to other AWS services, such as AWS RDS. A cluster of EC2 instances may run within an ECS Auto Scaling group with predefined scaling rules. For this to happen, the ECS container agent will constantly poll the ECS API, checking whether new containers need to be launched and whether old containers need to be made idle depending on traffic. All of this may seem fine and dandy, but a degree of EC2 instance management still needs to happen, which increases complexity.

ECS is a fully managed orchestration platform and control plane where you don't have to manage, patch, or upgrade anything. It is fully integrated with all the core services that are needed for end-to-end orchestration. It operationalizes your container workload at an immense scale without having you install any software. It's a multi-tenant service that can spin up many clusters, services, and tasks.

Scheduling and orchestration are key components of ECS, and the cluster manager and placement engine play specific roles in helping with this. Let's learn about the working of ECS.

Amazon ECS architecture

The cluster manager manages the health of the instances within your cluster. You set up an Auto Scaling group and register your instances with your cluster. ECS is then aware of the capacity you desire for your containers.

Placement engines, on the other hand, enable much more advanced techniques for how you want to place your tasks onto the EC2 instance. For example, if you have certain tasks that you want to land on certain instance types or if you desire super-efficient bin-packing for better economics, the placement engine enables you to do that. The following diagram shows ECS constructs:

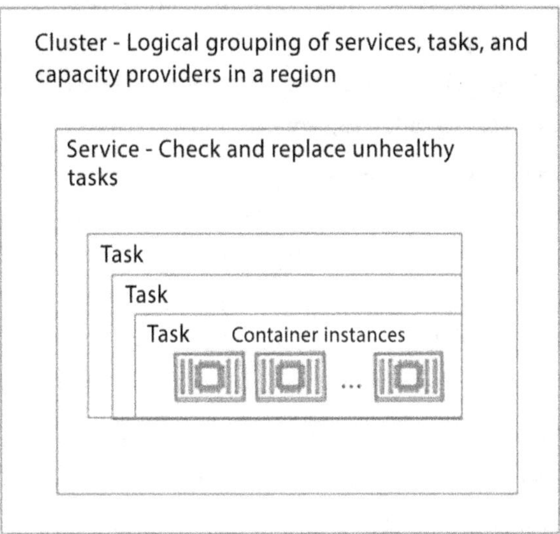

Figure 13.4: Amazon ECS architecture

As shown in the diagram above, the following are the components of ECS:

- An ECS **container instance** refers to an EC2 instance that runs the ECS container agent and is registered with an ECS cluster. When tasks are launched using the EC2 launch type or an Auto Scaling group capacity provider, they are deployed on active container instances. These instances are responsible for executing the containers specified in the task definition and communicating with the ECS service to receive updates and report their status. The EC2 launch type provides the flexibility to configure and scale instances according to the application's needs.
- A **task** represents an instantiation of a task definition that runs on a container instance. A task definition serves as a blueprint for a task and includes details such as the task's name, revisions, container definitions, and volume information.
- An Amazon ECS **service** allows for the simultaneous operation and maintenance of a specified number of instances of a task definition within an ECS cluster. The service scheduler automatically launches, terminates, and maintains the desired number of tasks for the service.

This guarantees that the application runs the intended number of tasks continuously and automatically recovers from failures. To create a service, you specify the number of tasks to run and the task definition to use. The service scheduler then launches the necessary number of tasks and maintains that count. If a task stops or fails, the service scheduler deploys another instance of the task definition to replace it and keep the desired count. Moreover, if you scale your service, the service scheduler adjusts the number of running tasks correspondingly. This relieves you of the responsibility of managing the underlying infrastructure and scaling, allowing you to concentrate on your application code.

- An Amazon ECS **cluster** represents a logical grouping of tasks or services that help to manage and organize containerized applications. When running tasks or services that use the EC2 launch type, a cluster groups container instances together. When you start using Amazon ECS, a default cluster is created automatically for you. However, you can also create additional clusters within your account to segregate your resources. These clusters are secured by IAM permissions that regulate access to the resources within the cluster.

Let's look at a scenario where you had 20 container instances. To start, you'll request to run some tasks or create a service. You'll specify the CPU, memory, or port requirements as part of that request. In addition, you'll also provide other constraints, such as a specific **Availability Zone** (**AZ**), **Amazon Machine Image** (**AMI**), or instance type. Finally, you will define a strategy when starting the tasks, which could range from the spread for availability, optimization, placing them together or placing them apart, and so on. At the end of that process, ECS identifies a set of instances that satisfies the task you want to run and places those tasks across your cluster based on the specified requirements.

Now, AWS has launched **ECS Anywhere** (**ECS-A**), using which you can run a container anywhere regardless of the environment, whether it is cloud or on-premises. ECS-A is managed, cloud-delivered ECS control plane that is infrastructure-agnostic and works with both VMs and on-premises bare metal. You can use the same control plane to run, update, and maintain container orchestrators on-premises.

You only need to send information for managing tasks to the ECS-A control plane. Even in disconnected scenarios, ECS-A tasks will continue to run. ECS-A offers uniform APIs and tools for all applications, irrespective of the operating environment. It also simplifies the management of your hybrid footprint by enabling the deployment of applications in on-premises environments.

For a serverless option, AWS Fargate provides a serverless compute engine for containers that are a part of ECS. It allows customers to run containerized applications without having to manage the underlying infrastructure.

With Fargate, customers can simply specify the resources that their application requires, such as CPU and memory, and Fargate will take care of provisioning the necessary resources, scaling them as needed, and managing the underlying infrastructure. You will learn about Fargate in much more detail later in this chapter, but first, let's learn about the components of ECS.

ECS components

Multiple factors come into play when running containers in ECS, like networking, storage, and security. Let's learn about them in detail.

Networking

There are four primary modes of networking available for containers running on ECS (on EC2, AWS Fargate, and ECS-A):

1. **Bridge** – The bridge mode in an Amazon ECS task uses Docker's built-in virtual network, which runs inside each container instance. In this mode, containers connect to the Docker virtual bridge, which allows multiple containers on the same host to use the same ports without conflict. This is because a range of dynamic ports maps the container ports to the host ports. However, this mode does not offer the best performance compared to other networking modes like `awsvpc` mode. In bridge mode, containers on the same host share the same network namespace, which can lead to increased network latency and reduced network throughput. Additionally, because the containers share the host's IP address, it can be more difficult to secure communication between containers and external networks.
2. **Host** – In host mode, container ports are mapped directly to the EC2 instance's network interface. This bypasses Docker's built-in virtual network, which can result in better performance, as the containers have direct access to the host's network resources. However, this mode has some limitations compared to other networking modes. If port mappings are being used, running multiple instances of the same task on a single container instance is not possible in host mode. This is because the ports are mapped directly to the host's network interface, so multiple tasks cannot use the same ports on the same host. Additionally, because the containers share the host's IP address, it can be more difficult to secure communication between containers and external networks. It's also important to note that host mode is not compatible with many of the features of Amazon ECS, like service discovery and load balancing. Because of this, it's generally recommended to use other networking modes like `awsvpc` for most use cases. Containers configured to run in host mode share the EC2 instances network namespace.

Containers can share the same IP as your host; this also means that you cannot have multiple containers on the same host using the same port. In other words, a port used by one container cannot be used by another container on the same host if host networking mode is configured.

3. **Task networking or awsvpc** – When using the `awsvpc` networking mode, every task launched from the corresponding task definition is assigned its own **Elastic Network Interface** (**ENI**) and a primary private IP address. This grants tasks running on Amazon ECS, on either EC2 or Fargate, networking properties similar to those of Amazon EC2 instances. By using the `awsvpc` network mode in task definitions, container networking is simplified, and more control is offered over how containerized applications interact with each other and other services within your **Virtual Private Cloud** (**VPC**). This mode also provides enhanced security for your containers by enabling the use of security groups and network monitoring tools at a more granular level within your tasks. With the `awsvpc` mode, you can assign a specific IP address and security group to each task, and also control the ingress and egress traffic of each task through security groups and **Network Access Control Lists** (**NACLs**).
4. **None** – In none mode, the task has no external network connectivity.

Let's look at storage, a critical component of hosting containers.

Storage

The following are the storage modes for ECS.

- **Ephemeral storage** – For Amazon ECS on Fargate, tasks running platform version 1.4.0 or later are allocated 20 GiB of ephemeral storage, which can be configured as needed. This temporary storage is free for up to 20 GiB, with any additional storage incurring charges. By increasing the ephemeral storage for tasks on AWS Fargate, various workloads, such as machine learning inference, ETL, and data processing, can be run. This feature also allows you to run tasks on Fargate with container images larger than 20 GiB, as these must be downloaded locally before starting the task.
- **Amazon Elastic File System (EFS) storage** – Containers running on either ECS or AWS Fargate can use EFS as a shared storage option. This enables the deployment and execution of containerized applications that require shared storage, including content management systems, internal DevOps tools, and machine learning frameworks, among others.

Enabling ECS and Fargate to use EFS allows a wide range of workloads to take advantage of the benefits of containers, including faster deployment, better use of infrastructure, and more resilient systems. This can help customers to improve their application's performance and reduce their operational costs.

Security

You learned about the cloud shared responsibility security model in *Chapter 8, Best Practices for Application Security, Identity, and Compliance.* Let's look at it in the context of Amazon ECS with EC2 instances.

With IAM roles for Amazon ECS tasks, you can specify an IAM role that the containers in a task can use. The IAM role allows the containers to access AWS resources that are specified in the permissions of the role. This functionality enables you to handle credentials for your applications in a similar way to how Amazon EC2 instance profiles grant credentials to EC2 instances. Rather than generating and distributing your AWS credentials to the containers or relying on the EC2 instance's role, you can assign an IAM role to an ECS task definition or `RunTask` API operation. This allows you to grant your containerized applications permission to access AWS services and resources without having to hardcode the credentials in the application.

IAM roles for tasks also enable you to manage and rotate the credentials used by the containerized applications, keeping them secure and ensuring that access is granted only to the resources that are required by the task. This improves the security of your applications and makes it easier to manage the access control of your AWS resources. With IAM roles for tasks, permissions can be applied at the task level, ensuring containers only have privileges to do the things they need to do.

With Fargate, AWS takes care of the underlying infrastructure, including the EC2 instances and the OS, so that you can focus on running your containerized applications. Fargate isolates each task within its cluster, providing a secure and managed environment for running containers. AWS Fargate does not allow privileged mode for containers, which gives them more access to the Docker daemon and host, improving security. Instead, it uses the `awsvpc` network mode, which provides an isolated network interface for each task. This allows you to leverage security group ingress and egress rules to control the network traffic for each task. This improves security and allows you to define more granular network access controls for your containerized applications.

Amazon Elastic Container Registry (**ECR**) is a container registry service provided by AWS that simplifies the sharing and deployment of container images and artifacts via public or private repositories.

ECR stores your images in a scalable and highly available architecture, ensuring reliable container deployment for your applications. By integrating with **AWS Identity and Access Management** (**AWS IAM**), ECR provides resource-level control over each repository, enabling image sharing within your organization or with individuals worldwide. You can use the CLI to push, pull, and manage Docker images, **Open Container Initiative** (**OCI**) images, and OCI-compatible artifacts.

In the next section, we will learn about Kubernetes, an alternative to Docker Swarm and another way to handle node orchestration.

Learning about Kubernetes

Kubernetes is an open-source container orchestration platform that is popular for managing and deploying containerized applications. It automates many of the manual tasks involved in deploying, scaling, and maintaining containerized applications. Kubernetes can be thought of as a train conductor; it orchestrates and manages all the rail cars (containers), making sure that they reach their destination reliably and efficiently. Kubernetes provides features such as automatic scaling, self-healing, and rolling updates, which can help to improve the availability and performance of your containerized applications.

Kubernetes also provides a rich set of APIs that can be used to automate the deployment and management of containerized applications. This makes it easy to integrate Kubernetes with other tools and platforms, such as CI/CD pipelines and monitoring systems.

Kubernetes, often abbreviated as K8s, was invented by Google. Kubernetes was developed by engineers at Google, led by Joe Beda and Craig McLuckie, based on the experience of running containers at scale in production. The project was originally called "Borg" and was used internally at Google to orchestrate the deployment of containerized applications. In 2014, Google open-sourced the Kubernetes project, which is now maintained by the Cloud Native Computing Foundation and has become one of the most popular open-source projects for container orchestration.

AWS also has its own Kubernetes service called Amazon **Elastic Kubernetes Service** (**EKS**), which allows you to run and manage Kubernetes clusters on AWS. EKS provides many of the same features and benefits as Kubernetes, but with the added benefit of being fully integrated with other AWS services, making it easy to build and run highly available and scalable applications on AWS.

In addition to Google and AWS, Kubernetes has the backing and support of a cadre of big players:

- Google
- Microsoft

- IBM
- Intel
- Cisco
- Red Hat

Kubernetes enables the deployment of a container-based infrastructure in production environments. Some of the functionality that Kubernetes enables includes the following:

- The orchestration of containers across multiple hosts and data centers
- The optimization of hardware utilization and enablement
- The control and automation of application deployments
- The scaling of containerized applications
- Declarative language for service management
- Enhanced application reliability and availability by minimizing single points of failure
- Health checks and self-healing mechanisms, including auto-restart, auto-replication, auto-placement, and auto-scaling

Kubernetes leverages a whole ecosystem of ancillary applications and extensions to enhance its orchestrated services. Some examples include:

- **Registration services**: Atomic Registry, Docker Registry
- **Security**: LDAP, SELinux, **Role-Based Access Control** (**RBAC**), and OAuth
- **Networking services**: Open vSwitch and intelligent edge routing
- **Telemetry**: Kibana, Hawkular, and Elastic
- **Automation**: Ansible playbooks

Some benefits of Kubernetes are as follows:

- Give teams control over their resource consumption.
- Enable the spread of the workload evenly across the infrastructure.
- Automate load balancing over various instances and AZs.
- Facilitate the monitoring of resource consumption and resource limits.
- Automate the stopping and starting of instances to keep resource usage at a healthy level.
- Automate deployments in new instances if additional resources are needed to handle the load.
- Effortlessly perform deployments and rollbacks and implement high availability.

You will learn more benefits of Kubernetes later in this chapter. Let's first look at the components of Kubernetes in more detail.

Components of Kubernetes

The fundamental principle that Kubernetes follows is that it always works to make an object's "current state" equal to its "desired state." Let's learn about the key components of Kubernetes.

- **Pod** – In Kubernetes, a Pod is the smallest deployable unit that can be created, scheduled, and managed. It is a logical collection of one or more containers that belong to the same application, and these containers share the same network namespace. This allows the containers in the Pod to communicate with each other using localhost. A Pod is also created in a namespace, which is a virtual cluster within a physical cluster. Namespaces provide a way to divide the resources in a cluster and control access to them. Pods within the same namespace can communicate with each other without any network address translation, and Pods in different namespaces can communicate through network address translation. Pods have their storage resources, which are shared among all containers inside the Pod; these resources are called Volumes, which can provide shared storage for all containers inside the Pod, such as configuration files, logs, and data.
- **DaemonSet** – In Kubernetes, a DaemonSet is a controller that ensures that all (or some) of the nodes in a cluster run a copy of a specified Pod. A DaemonSet is useful for running Pods that need to run on every node, such as system daemons, log collectors, and monitoring agents. When you create a DaemonSet, Kubernetes automatically creates a Pod on every node that meets the specified label selector criteria and makes sure that a specified number of replicas are running at all times. If a node is added to the cluster, Kubernetes automatically creates a Pod on the new node, and if a node is removed from the cluster, Kubernetes automatically deletes the corresponding Pod. DaemonSet also ensures that the Pods are running on the nodes that match the given nodeSelector field. This allows us to have the Pod running only on specific nodes.
- **Deployment** – A Deployment is a declarative way to manage a desired state for a group of Pods, such as the number of replicas, updates, and rollbacks. The Deployment controller in a Kubernetes cluster ensures that the desired state, as defined in the Deployment configuration, matches the actual state of the Pods. When you create a Deployment, it creates a ReplicaSet, which is a controller that ensures that a specified number of Pod replicas are running at all times. The deployment controller periodically checks the status of the replicas and makes necessary adjustments to match the desired state.

If a Pod dies or a worker node fails, the deployment controller automatically creates a new replica to replace it. A Deployment also provides a way to perform rolling updates and rollbacks to your application. This allows you to update your application with zero downtime and roll back to a previous version if needed.

- **ReplicaSet** – A ReplicaSet is a controller that ensures that a specified number of replicas of a Pod are running at all times. It is used to ensure the high availability and scalability of applications. A ReplicaSet can be created by a Deployment or can be created independently. It watches for the Pods that match its label selector and makes sure that the desired number of replicas are running. If a Pod dies or is deleted, the ReplicaSet automatically creates a new replica to replace it. If there are extra replicas, the ReplicaSet automatically deletes them. ReplicaSet also provides a way to perform rolling updates and rollbacks to your application. This allows you to update your application with zero downtime and roll back to a previous version if needed.
- **Job** – A Job is a Kubernetes controller that manages the creation and completion of one or more Pods. Its primary function is to ensure that a specified number of Pods are successfully created and terminated. Jobs are used to run batch workloads, long-running tasks, or one-off tasks that don't need to run continuously. Upon creation, a Job controller initiates the creation of one or more Pods and ensures that the specified number of Pods complete successfully. Once the specified number of Pods has been completed successfully, the Job is marked as completed. If a Pod fails, the Job automatically creates a new replica to replace it. Jobs are complementary to ReplicaSet. ReplicaSet is used to manage Pods that are expected to run continuously, such as web servers, and a Job controller is designed to manage Pods that are expected to complete or terminate after running, such as batch jobs.
- **Service** – A Service in Kubernetes is an abstraction that defines a logical set of Pods and a policy for accessing them. It provides a stable endpoint for a group of Pods, independent of their individual IP addresses or network locations. Services abstract the underlying Pods and enable load balancing across the Pods. They can also route traffic to specific subsets of Pods based on labels. Kubernetes simplifies Service discovery by giving Pods their IP addresses and a single DNS name for a group of Pods without requiring modifications to your application. This simplifies access to an application running on a set of Pods and improves the availability and scalability of your application.
- **Labels** – Labels in Kubernetes are utilized to attach key-value pairs to various objects like Services, Pods, and Deployments. They allow users to assign identifying attributes to objects that hold significance for them, but do not affect the core system's semantics directly.

These labels can be utilized for organizing and grouping objects within a Kubernetes cluster. They can be used to specify attributes such as the environment (production, staging, development), version, and component type. Labels can also be used to select a subset of objects. This is done by using label selectors, which are used to filter sets of objects based on their labels. For example, you can use a label selector to select all Pods with the label `env=production` and expose them as a Service.

- **kubectl (Kubernetes command-line tool)** – It is a CLI for running commands against Kubernetes clusters. It is the primary way to interact with a Kubernetes cluster, and it allows you to manage and troubleshoot your applications running on a cluster. With `kubectl`, you can perform a wide range of operations on a Kubernetes cluster, such as creating and managing resources, scaling your application, and troubleshooting issues. `kubectl` can be used to deploy and manage resources, inspect and troubleshoot the cluster, and gather detailed information about the state of the cluster and its components. It can also be used to view and update the configuration of resources and to access the logs and metrics of your applications.

Let's now look at the advantages of Kubernetes.

Kubernetes advantages

As more enterprises move their workloads to the cloud and leverage containers, Kubernetes keeps getting more and more popular. Some of the reasons for Kubernetes' popularity are as follows.

Faster development and deployment

Kubernetes facilitates the enablement of self-service **Platform-as-a-Service** (**PaaS**) applications. Kubernetes provides a level of abstraction between the bare-metal servers and your users. Developers can quickly request only the resources they require for specific purposes. If more resources are needed to deal with additional traffic, these resources can be added automatically based on the Kubernetes configuration. Instances can easily be added or removed, and these instances can leverage a host of third-party tools in the Kubernetes ecosystem to automate deployment, packaging, delivery, and testing.

Cost efficiency

Container technology, in general, and Kubernetes in particular, enables better resource utilization than that provided just by hypervisors and VMs. Containers are more lightweight and don't need as many computing and memory resources.

Cloud-agnostic deployments

Kubernetes can run on other environments and cloud providers, not just on AWS. It can also run on the following:

- Microsoft Azure
- **Google Cloud Platform** (GCP)
- On-premises

Kubernetes enables you to migrate workloads from one environment to another without modifying your applications, and it avoids vendor lock-in. This means that you can easily move your workloads between different environments, such as between different cloud providers or between a cloud and on-premises environment, without having to make any changes to your application code or configuration. It also provides you with the flexibility to choose the best infrastructure that suits your needs without being locked into a specific vendor.

In that case, if the whole cloud provider stops delivering functionality, your application still won't go down.

Management by the cloud provider

It is hard to argue that Kubernetes is not the clear leader and standard bearer regarding container orchestration when it comes to the open-source community. For this reason, all the major cloud providers, not just AWS, offer managed Kubernetes services. Some examples are these:

- Amazon EKS
- Red Hat OpenShift
- Azure Kubernetes Service
- Google Cloud Kubernetes Engine
- IBM Cloud Kubernetes Service

These managed services allow you to focus on your customers and the business logic required to serve them, as shown in the following figure:

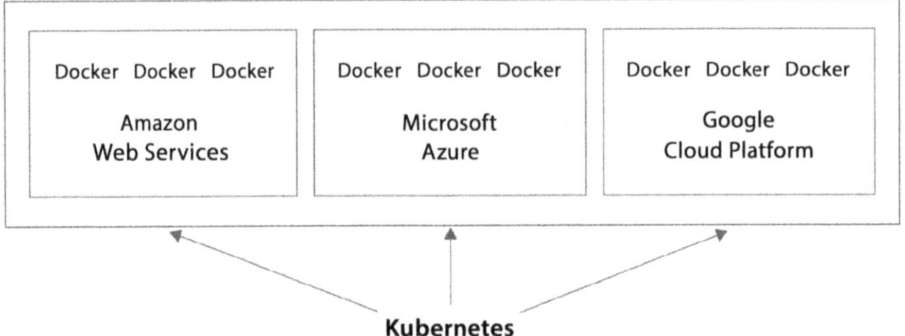

Figure 13.5: Sample architecture for a multi-cloud Kubernetes deployment

As shown in the figure, as long as there is connectivity, Kubernetes can sit on one cloud provider and orchestrate, manage, and synchronize Docker containers across multiple cloud provider environments. Some of those Docker containers could even sit in an on-premises environment.

Kubernetes works with multiple container runtimes like Docker, containerd, and CRI-O. Kubernetes is designed to work with any container runtime that implements the Kubernetes **Container Runtime Interface** (**CRI**). Kubernetes provides a set of abstractions for containerized applications, such as Pods, Services, and Deployments, and it does not provide a container runtime of its own. Instead, it uses the container runtime that is installed and configured on the nodes in the cluster. This allows Kubernetes to work with any container runtime that implements the CRI, giving users the flexibility to choose the runtime that best suits their needs.

Docker is the most commonly used container runtime, and it is the default runtime in Kubernetes. Docker is a platform that simplifies the process of creating, deploying, and running applications in containers. Containers in Docker are portable and lightweight, enabling developers to package their application and its dependencies together into a single container. containerd is an industry-standard container runtime that provides an API for building and running containerized applications. It is designed to be a lightweight, high-performance container runtime that is easy to integrate with other systems. It is an alternative runtime to Docker that is gaining popularity among Kubernetes users. CRI-O is a lightweight container runtime for Kubernetes that is designed to be an alternative to using Docker as the container runtime. CRI-O only implements the Kubernetes CRI and focuses on providing a stable and secure runtime for Kubernetes.

Let's look at a comparison between Kubernetes and Docker Swarm as both are popular orchestration platforms.

Kubernetes versus Docker Swarm

So, at this point, you may be wondering when to use Kubernetes and when it's a good idea to use Docker Swarm. Both can be used in many of the same situations. In general, Kubernetes can usually handle bigger workloads at the expense of higher complexity, whereas Docker Swarm has a smaller learning curve but may not be able to handle highly complex scenarios as well as Kubernetes. Docker Swarm is recommended for speed and when the requirements are simple. Kubernetes is best used when more complex scenarios and bigger production deployments arise.

Amazon Elastic Kubernetes Service (Amazon EKS)

AWS provides a managed service called Amazon **Elastic Kubernetes Service** (**EKS**) that simplifies the deployment, scaling, and management of containerized applications using Kubernetes on AWS. EKS eliminates the need to provision and manage your own Kubernetes clusters, which simplifies the process of running Kubernetes workloads on AWS. It automatically scales and updates the Kubernetes control plane and worker nodes, and it integrates with other AWS services, such as ELB, RDS, and S3.

Amazon EKS is simply a managed wrapper around the Kubernetes kernel, which ensures that existing Kubernetes applications are fully compatible with Amazon EKS. This allows you to use the same Kubernetes APIs, tooling, and ecosystem that you use for on-premises or other cloud-based deployments, with the added benefits of the AWS infrastructure and services.

Amazon EKS facilitates running Kubernetes with effortless availability and scalability. It greatly simplifies restarting containers, setting up containers on VMs, and persisting data. Amazon EKS can detect unhealthy masters and replace them automatically. You never have to worry about Kubernetes version management and upgrades; Amazon EKS handles it transparently. It is extremely simple to control when and if certain clusters are automatically upgraded. If you enable EKS to handle these upgrades, Amazon EKS updates both the masters and nodes.

The combination of AWS with Kubernetes allows you to leverage the performance, scalability, availability, and reliability of the AWS platform. EKS also offers seamless integration with other AWS services, such as **Application Load Balancers** (**ALBs**) for load balancing, AWS IAM for fine-grained security, AWS CloudWatch for monitoring, AWS CloudTrail for logging, and AWS PrivateLink for private network access.

In the following sections, we will explore the various features of EKS.

EKS-managed Kubernetes control plane

Amazon EKS provides a system that offers high scalability and availability that can run over multiple AWS AZs. It is referred to as the managed Kubernetes control plane. Amazon EKS can handle the availability and scalability of the Kubernetes masters and individual clusters. Amazon EKS automatically instantiates three Kubernetes masters using multiple AZs for fault tolerance. It can also detect if a master is down or corrupted and automatically replace it.

The following diagram shows the architecture of the EKS control plane:

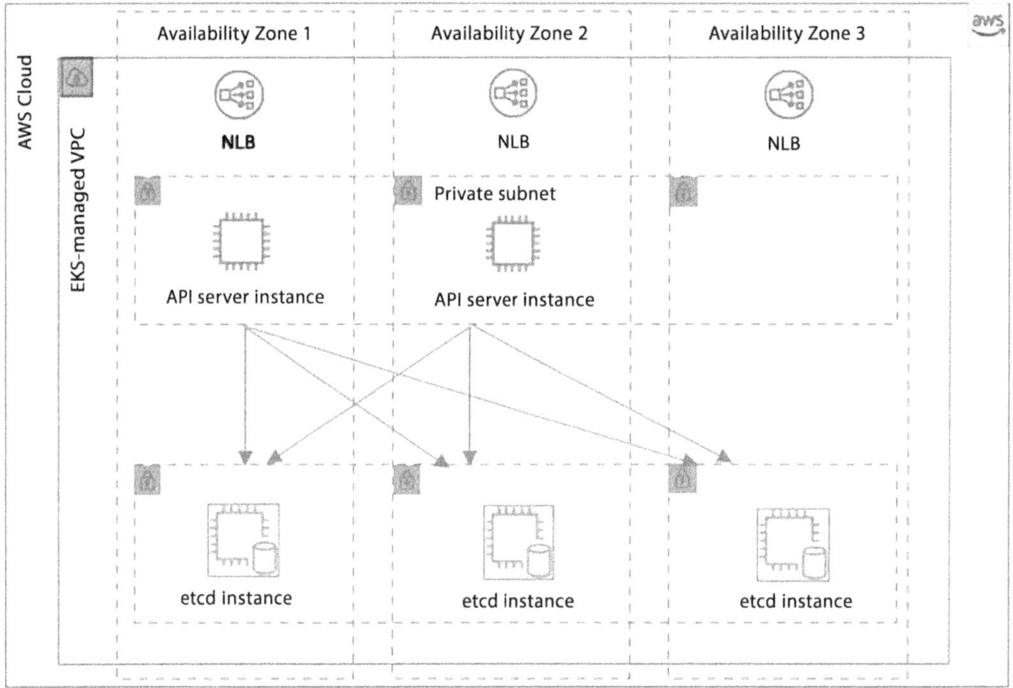

Figure 13.6: Amazon EKS control plane architecture

As shown in the preceding diagram, EKS operates a dedicated Kubernetes control plane for each cluster, ensuring that the cluster is secure and isolated. The control plane infrastructure is not shared across clusters or AWS accounts, meaning that each cluster has its own control plane. This control plane is composed of at least two API server instances and three etcd instances, which are distributed across three AZs within an AWS Region. This provides high availability for the control plane and allows for automatic failover in the event of a failure.

Amazon EKS continuously monitors the load on control plane instances and automatically scales them up or down to ensure optimal performance. It also detects and replaces any unhealthy control plane instances, restarting them across the AZs within the AWS Region if necessary. This ensures that the control plane is always available and running optimally.

Amazon EKS is designed to be highly secure and reliable for running production workloads. To ensure security, EKS uses Amazon VPC network policies to restrict communication between control plane components within a single cluster. This means that components of a cluster cannot communicate with other clusters or AWS accounts without proper authorization through Kubernetes RBAC policies. This helps provide an additional layer of security to your clusters.

Additionally, EKS uses a highly available configuration that includes at least two API server instances and three etcd instances running across three AZs within an AWS Region. EKS actively monitors the load on the control plane instances and automatically scales them to ensure high performance. It also automatically replaces unhealthy control plane instances, ensuring that your clusters remain healthy and reliable. With its automatic monitoring and scaling capabilities, and the ability to run across multiple AZs, it ensures the high availability of your Kubernetes clusters, and it also provides an additional layer of security for your application by using VPC network policies and Kubernetes RBAC policies.

EKS EC2 runtime options

If you use EC2 as a runtime option, you can choose one of two options for your node groups:

- **Self-managed node groups** – One of the options for managing the worker nodes in an EKS cluster is to use self-managed node groups. With this option, EKS nodes are launched in your AWS account and communicate with your cluster's control plane via the API server endpoint. A node group refers to a collection of one or more Amazon EC2 instances that are deployed within an Amazon EC2 Auto Scaling group. The instances in the node group run the Kubernetes worker node software and connect to the EKS control plane. The instances are managed by an Auto Scaling group, which ensures that the desired number of instances is running at all times and automatically scales the number of instances based on demand. Self-managed node groups give you more control over the instances, such as the ability to choose the instance types and sizes, configure the security groups, and customize the user data. It also allows you to connect to existing resources such as VPCs, subnets, and security groups.

- **Managed node groups** – Another option for managing the worker nodes in an EKS cluster is to use managed node groups. With this option, Amazon EKS handles the automatic creation and management of the EC2 instances that serve as nodes for the Kubernetes clusters running on the Service. Managed node groups automate the process of creating, scaling, and updating the EC2 instances that make up the worker nodes in your EKS cluster. This eliminates the need to manually create and manage the Auto Scaling groups and EC2 instances that make up the worker nodes. With managed node groups, you can specify the desired number of nodes, the instance type, and the AMI to use for the instances, and Amazon EKS takes care of the rest. It automatically provisions the instances, updates them when needed, and scales the number of instances based on demand.

You can choose the compute options/instance types that suit your workload characteristics. If you want more control over the instances and have specific requirements, such as using specific instance types, configuring security groups, or connecting to existing resources such as VPCs, subnets, and security groups, self-managed node groups would be a better option. On the other hand, if you want to minimize the management overhead of your worker nodes and have a more simplified experience, managed node groups would be a better option.

Bring Your Operating System (BYOS)

BYOS is a feature that allows you to run your own custom OS on top of a cloud provider's infrastructure. This feature is typically used when you want to run an application on an OS that is not supported by the cloud provider, or when you want to use a specific version of an OS that is not available as a pre-built image.

In the case of EKS, AWS provides open-source scripts on GitHub for building an AMI that is optimized for use as a node in EKS clusters. The AMI is based on Amazon Linux 2 and includes configurations for components such as kubelet, Docker, and the AWS IAM authenticator for Kubernetes. Users can view and use these scripts to build their own custom AMIs for use with EKS. These build scripts are available on GitHub – `https://github.com/awslabs/amazon-eks-ami`.

The optimized Bottlerocket AMI for Amazon EKS is developed based on Bottlerocket, an open-source Linux-based OS tailored by AWS for running containers. Bottlerocket prioritizes security by including only essential packages for container operations, thereby minimizing its attack surface and the impact of potential vulnerabilities. As it requires fewer components, it is also easier to meet node compliance requirements.

Kubernetes application scaling

There are three main types of auto-scaling in EKS.

1. **Horizontal Pod Autoscaler (HPA)** – An HPA is a built-in Kubernetes feature that automatically scales the number of Pods in a Deployment based on resource utilization. The HPA constantly monitors the CPU and memory usage of the Pods in a Deployment, and when the usage exceeds a user-defined threshold, the HPA will automatically create more Pods to handle the increased load. Conversely, when resource utilization falls below a certain threshold, the HPA will automatically remove Pods to reduce the number of running instances. This allows for better utilization of resources and helps to ensure that the Pods in a Deployment can handle the current load. The HPA can be configured to scale based on other metrics as well, such as custom metrics, in addition to the standard metrics like CPU utilization and memory usage.
2. **Vertical Pod Autoscaler (VPA)** – A VPA is a Kubernetes add-on that automatically adjusts the resources (such as CPU and memory) allocated to individual Pods based on their observed usage. A VPA works by analyzing the resource usage of Pods over time and making recommendations for the target resource usage. The Kubernetes controller manager will then apply these recommendations to the Pods by adjusting their resource requests and limits. This allows for more efficient resource usage, as Pods are only allocated the resources they actually need at any given time. A VPA can also be integrated with other Kubernetes add-ons such as an HPA to provide a more complete autoscaling solution.
3. **Cluster Autoscaler** – This is a Kubernetes tool that automatically increases or decreases the size of a cluster based on the number of pending Pods and the utilization of nodes. It is designed to ensure that all Pods in a cluster have a place to run and to make the best use of the available resources. When there are Pods that are pending, due to a lack of resources, the Cluster Autoscaler will increase the size of the cluster by adding new nodes. Conversely, when there are nodes in the cluster that are underutilized, the Cluster Autoscaler will decrease the size of the cluster by removing unnecessary nodes. The Cluster Autoscaler can be configured to work with specific cloud providers such as AWS, GCP, and Azure.

It's important to note that a Cluster Autoscaler is different from an HPA or VPA; a Cluster Autoscaler focuses on scaling the cluster, while HPA and VPA focus on scaling the number of Pods and resources allocated to them respectively.

AWS created an open-source offering for cluster auto-scaling called Karpenter. Karpenter is a cluster auto-scaler for Kubernetes that is built with AWS and is available as open-source software. It is designed to enhance the availability of applications and the efficiency of clusters by quickly deploying compute resources that are correctly sized for changing application loads. Karpenter works by monitoring the combined resource requests of unscheduled Pods and making decisions about launching new nodes or terminating them, in order to reduce scheduling delays and infrastructure expenses. It is designed to work with AWS and it's built on top of the AWS Auto Scaling Groups and the Kubernetes API. It aims to provide an alternative to the built-in Kubernetes Cluster Autoscaler and other cloud-provider-specific solutions. When deciding whether to use Karpenter or the built-in Kubernetes Cluster Autoscaler, there are a few factors to consider:

- **Cloud Provider**: Karpenter is built specifically for use with AWS, while the built-in Cluster Autoscaler can be configured to work with various cloud providers. If you are running your Kubernetes cluster on AWS, Karpenter may be a better choice.
- **Features**: Karpenter provides additional features such as just-in-time compute resources, automatic optimization of cluster's resource footprint, and more flexibility on scaling decisions.
- **Scalability**: Karpenter is built to scale with large, complex clusters and can handle a high number of nodes and Pods.
- **Customization**: Karpenter allows for more customization in terms of scaling decisions and can be integrated with other Kubernetes add-ons.

In general, if you are running your Kubernetes cluster on AWS and need more control over your scaling decisions and want to optimize costs, Karpenter might be a good choice. On the other hand, if you are running your cluster on other cloud providers, or don't need those extra features, the built-in Cluster Autoscaler may be sufficient. In the end, it's good to test both options and see which one works best for your specific use case.

Security

EKS provides a number of security features to help secure your Kubernetes clusters and the applications running on them. Some of the key security features include:

- **Network isolation**: EKS creates a dedicated VPC for each cluster, which isolates the cluster from other resources in your AWS account. This helps to prevent unauthorized access to the cluster and its resources.
- **IAM authentication**: EKS integrates with AWS IAM to provide fine-grained access control to the cluster's resources.

This allows you to grant or deny access to specific users, groups, or roles.

- **Encryption**: EKS encrypts data in transit and at rest, using industry-standard AES-256 encryption. This helps to protect sensitive data from unauthorized access.
- **Kubernetes RBAC**: EKS supports Kubernetes RBAC to define fine-grained access controls for Kubernetes resources. This allows you to grant or deny access to specific users, groups, or roles based on their role within the organization.
- **Cluster security groups**: EKS allows you to create and manage security groups for your cluster to control inbound and outbound traffic to the cluster.
- **Pod security policies**: EKS supports Pod Security policies that specify the security settings for Pods and containers. This can be used to enforce security best practices, such as running containers as non-root users, and to restrict access to the host's network and devices.
- **Kubernetes audit**: EKS provides an integration with the Kubernetes audit system. This allows you to log and examine all API requests made to the cluster, including who made the request, when, and what resources were affected.
- **Amazon EKS Distro (EKS-D)**: Amazon EKS-D is a Kubernetes distribution that provides a secure and stable version of Kubernetes optimized for running on AWS, which makes the cluster more secure and stable.

By using these security features, EKS helps to protect your clusters and applications from unauthorized access and data breaches and helps to ensure that your clusters are running securely and compliantly. You can learn more about EKS security best practices by referring to the AWS GitHub repo – `https://aws.github.io/aws-eks-best-practices/security/docs/`.

PrivateLink support

Amazon EKS supports **PrivateLink** as a method to provide access to Kubernetes masters and the Amazon EKS service. With PrivateLink, the Kubernetes masters and Amazon EKS service API endpoint display as an ENI, including a private IP address in the Amazon VPC. This provides access to the Kubernetes masters and the Amazon EKS service from inside the Amazon VPC without needing public IP addresses or traffic through the internet.

Automatic version upgrades

Amazon EKS manages patches and version updates for your Kubernetes clusters. Amazon EKS automatically applies Kubernetes patches to your cluster, and you can also granularly control things when and if certain clusters are automatically upgraded to the latest Kubernetes minor version.

Community tools support

Amazon EKS can integrate with many Kubernetes community tools and supports a variety of Kubernetes add-ons. One of these tools is KubeDNS, which allows users to provision a DNS service for a cluster. Like AWS offers console access and a CLI, Kubernetes also has a web-based UI, and a CLI tool called `kubectl`. Both of these tools offer the ability to interface with Kubernetes and provide cluster management. EKS provides a number of add-ons that can be used to enhance the functionality of your Kubernetes clusters. Some of the key add-ons include:

- **ExternalDNS**: ExternalDNS is an add-on that allows you to automatically create and manage DNS entries for services in your cluster.
- **Kubernetes Dashboard**: Kubernetes Dashboard is a web-based UI for managing and monitoring your Kubernetes clusters.
- **Prometheus**: Prometheus is an open-source monitoring system that allows you to collect and query metrics from your Kubernetes clusters.
- **Fluentd**: Fluentd is an open-source log collector that allows you to collect, parse, and forward logs from your Kubernetes clusters.
- **Istio**: Istio is an open-source service mesh that allows you to manage the traffic and security of your microservices-based applications.
- **Helm**: Helm is an open-source package manager for Kubernetes that allows you to easily install and manage Kubernetes applications.
- **Linkerd**: Linkerd is an open-source service mesh that allows you to manage the traffic, security, and reliability of your microservices-based applications.
- **Kured**: Kured is a Kubernetes reboot daemon that allows you to automatically reboot worker nodes during maintenance windows.

By using these add-ons, EKS allows you to enhance the functionality of your clusters and to better manage and monitor your applications running on them.

This section completes our coverage of Kubernetes. We now move on to a service offered by AWS that can also be used to manage massive workloads. When using ECS or EKS to manage complex containerized applications, you still need to manage more than just containers; there are additional layers of management. To overcome this challenge, AWS launched the serverless offering AWS Fargate.

Learning about AWS Fargate

AWS Fargate is a serverless way to run containers. ECS and EKS support running containerized workloads using AWS Fargate.

Let's look at an example to better understand how Fargate helps you run serverless containers. Without Fargate, you have an EC2 instance with multiple tasks running on it. So here, to support the tasks, you have to manage the underlying instance, such as the instance OS, the container runtime, and the ECS agent, in the case of Amazon ECS. This is still quite a bit of operational overhead. You have to patch and update the OS, ECS/EKS agent, and so on, while also scaling the instance fleet for optimal utilization. All of these tasks are still required, adding management layers to your application.

AWS Fargate simplifies the management of ECS/EKS services and enables users to focus on application development rather than infrastructure management. With AWS Fargate, the provisioning of infrastructure and the management of servers is handled by AWS.

The benefits of using AWS Fargate are as follows:

- Obviate the provisioning and management of servers
- Reduce costs by matching resources with workloads
- Enhance security with an application isolation architecture

Why isn't Amazon ECS or Amazon EKS enough by itself, and why would we use AWS Fargate to manage these workloads?

AWS Fargate is not a container management service in itself; it is a method to launch container services. It simplifies the management of Kubernetes and Docker deployments. Without AWS Fargate, setting up these two services would require a good understanding of how to provision, schedule, and manage Pods, services, containers, masters, and minions, as well as how to administer server orchestration. Typically, you would need a skilled DevOps engineer to set this up. AWS Fargate takes the burden away from your engineers and greatly simplifies these deployments. Importantly, you don't have to commit to using AWS Fargate from the start.

You can start by using Amazon ECS or Amazon EKS, test it out, and once the process is working, your containers can then be migrated to Amazon Fargate. This can simplify your operations and reduce the cost of running your application. Migrating to Fargate can be done by creating a new task definition, and then updating your service to use that task definition. Once that is done, you can then monitor your application to make sure it's running correctly and make any necessary adjustments.

If AWS EC2 offers **Infrastructure as a Service (IaaS)**, then AWS Fargate offers **Containers as a Service (CaaS)**. This means that we do not need to worry about setting up containers. All the details involved in their launching are handled by AWS Fargate, including networking, security, and, most importantly, scaling. The details of how this happens are abstracted away. AWS Fargate further simplifies the management of containers in the cloud while leveraging Amazon ECS and Amazon EKS.

Choosing between Fargate and EC2

When deciding whether to use Fargate or EC2 for running your containerized applications on ECS/EKS, there are a few factors to consider:

- **Control**: If you want more control over the underlying infrastructure and the ability to customize it to meet your specific needs, EC2 might be the better choice. With EC2, you can choose the instance type and configure the OS and other software to meet your requirements. With Fargate, you don't have direct access to the underlying infrastructure, and the resources are managed by AWS.
- **Ease of use**: Fargate is a serverless compute engine for containers, which eliminates the need to manage the underlying infrastructure, making it easier to use. With Fargate, you don't need to worry about provisioning and scaling resources, as this is handled automatically by the service. With EC2, you are responsible for managing the underlying infrastructure.
- **Cost**: Fargate can be more cost-effective than EC2 when you have a varying workload. With Fargate, you only pay for the resources that you actually use, whereas with EC2, you pay for the resources whether you are using them or not. However, if your workload is consistent and always on then Fargate can be costly.
- **Flexibility**: EC2 instances can be used for more than just running containers and can be more flexible. Fargate is designed specifically for running containers, therefore it may not be a good fit for workloads that are not containerized.

In general, if you have specific requirements that aren't met by Fargate or you want more control over the underlying infrastructure, EC2 is the way to go. If you want to minimize the operational overhead and focus on running your application, Fargate is the best option.

Red Hat OpenShift Service on AWS (ROSA)

OpenShift is another container platform developed and supported by Red Hat. It's built on top of Red Hat Enterprise Linux and Kubernetes, two of the world's largest and fastest-growing open-source projects, and adds several services to offer a well-rounded platform experience out of the box. These include cluster services such as monitoring, managing, and updating the cluster; cluster services such as built-in CI/CD pipelines and logging; application services such as databases, language runtimes, and many others through what's known in Kubernetes as Operators; and developer services such as a rich console, CLI, and tools for code editors, IDEs and more.

Red Hat OpenShift Service on AWS (**ROSA**) is a fully managed service provided by Red Hat and jointly supported by AWS. ROSA offers pay-as-you-go billing options (hourly and annual) on a single invoice through AWS and provides the option to contact either Red Hat or AWS for support. With ROSA, users can enjoy the benefits of a fully managed Red Hat OpenShift environment without having to worry about infrastructure management. It provides a simple and easy way to deploy, manage, and scale containerized applications using Kubernetes and Red Hat OpenShift.

ROSA provides the full functionality of Red Hat OpenShift, including built-in support for Kubernetes, as well as additional features such as automated scaling, self-healing, and automatic updates. It also provides integration with other AWS services such as Amazon **Elastic Block Store** (**EBS**) for storage and Amazon VPC for networking. ROSA is fully compatible with other Red Hat OpenShift services, such as OpenShift Container Platform and OpenShift Dedicated, and allows you to use the same tools and APIs for deploying and managing your applications. Additionally, it provides a full set of monitoring and logging tools to help you troubleshoot and debug issues with your applications.

ROSA is built on top of AWS, meaning that it benefits from the security, compliance, and global infrastructure of AWS; this allows you to take advantage of the security features and compliance certifications of AWS and also the scalability and reliability of the AWS infrastructure. ROSA can run Docker containers as it is built on top of Kubernetes, which is a container orchestration system that supports Docker. In ROSA, you can use the standard Kubernetes tooling, such as `kubectl` and `oc` (the OpenShift CLI) to deploy and manage your Docker containers as part of a Kubernetes cluster. This means that you can use standard Docker images and container registries to deploy your applications, and use the Kubernetes API to manage and scale your containers.

ROSA provides a set of custom resources and controllers for deploying and managing Red Hat OpenShift and Kubernetes clusters on AWS, but it does not provide any additional functionality for running and managing Docker containers. Instead, it utilizes Kubernetes as the underlying container orchestration system to run and manage Docker containers as part of a Kubernetes cluster. The following diagram shows a ROSA cluster in AWS.

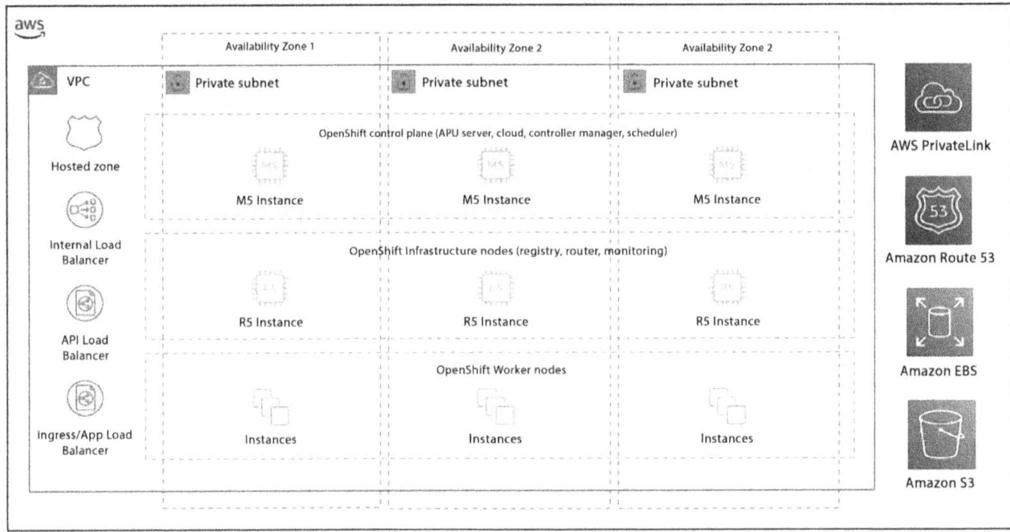

Figure 13.7: ROSA private cluster architecture

The preceding diagram shows the simplified architecture of a private, multi-AZ ROSA cluster deployed in an AWS account, which is the most common configuration. ROSA clusters can also be deployed in single-AZ mode and with a public subnet to expose application ingress and the API endpoint directly to the internet.

ROSA is a fully managed service that allows you to deploy and manage containerized applications using Red Hat OpenShift and Kubernetes on the AWS cloud; it provides the full functionality of Red Hat OpenShift and benefits from the security, compliance, and global infrastructure of AWS.

Choosing between AWS container services

So, at this point, you are probably asking yourself when you should choose Amazon ECS, EKS, or ROSA as the right solution. When choosing between ECS, EKS, and ROSA, it's important to consider the specific requirements of your application and use case:

- EKS is a managed Kubernetes service that allows you to easily deploy, manage, and scale containerized applications on the AWS cloud. It provides a fully managed Kubernetes control plane and integrates with other AWS services such as Elastic Load Balancing and Amazon RDS. If you are already familiar with Kubernetes and want to leverage its flexibility and scalability, EKS is a good choice.
- ECS is a container orchestration service that allows you to deploy, manage, and scale containerized applications on the AWS cloud. It provides a simple and easy-to-use interface for deploying and managing containerized applications and integrates with other AWS services such as Elastic Load Balancing and Amazon RDS. If you are looking for a simpler and more integrated service that is tightly integrated with the AWS ecosystem, ECS is a good choice.
- ROSA is a fully managed service that allows you to run Red Hat OpenShift clusters on the AWS cloud. It provides a simple and easy way to deploy, manage, and scale containerized applications using Kubernetes and Red Hat OpenShift. It also provides integration with other AWS services such as Amazon EBS for storage and Amazon VPC for networking. If you are looking for a fully managed service that provides the full functionality of Red Hat OpenShift and benefits from the security, compliance, and global infrastructure of AWS, ROSA is a good choice.

Ultimately, it's important to evaluate the features and capabilities of each service, and how well they align with your specific use case and requirements. The following table shows a comparison between these three container services in AWS.

ECS	EKS	ROSA
An AWS-native platform to provide simplicity when running containers	Provides open flexibility for running Kubernetes clusters	Provides a turnkey platform to run the container with Open Redshift

The AWS way to run containers at scale	AWS-optimized managed Kubernetes clusters	An integrated Kubernetes-based application platform with built-in CI/CD, monitoring, and developer tools
Reduces decision-making without sacrificing scale or features	Builds your custom platform for compliance and security with AWS services and community solutions	Activate ROSA and continue with existing OpenShift skills and processes, from on-prem environments to the cloud
Reduces the time to build, deploy, and migrate applications	Accelerates your containerization and modernization with canonical patterns using AWS Blueprints	Accelerates application migration and modernization by re-hosting, re-platforming, or re-factoring workloads

Table 13.1: Comparison between AWS container services

The total costs of building and operating container platforms start with the choice of container orchestrators and add-on tools for end-to-end application development, deployment, and operations. EKS and ECS provide flexibility to mix and match with both AWS and best-in-class solutions from the community. ROSA offers an out-of-the-box integrated platform ready for developers and DevOps engineers.

Amazon ECS is usually a good option for simple use cases. Amazon ECS provides a quick solution that can host containers at scale. For simple workloads, you can be up and running quickly with Amazon ECS. Amazon EKS is a favorable choice due to its active ecosystem and community, uniform open-source APIs, and extensive adaptability. It is capable of managing more intricate use cases and demands, but it may require more effort to learn and utilize effectively.

If you are currently running OpenShift applications on-premises and intend to migrate your application to the cloud, ROSA provides fully managed Red Hat OpenShift. You can take advantage of an integrated approach for creating and scaling clusters, along with a unified billing system that supports on-demand pricing. It may also be beneficial to test and deploy a proof of concept with each service before making a final decision.

AWS also offers the **App2Container (A2C)** service, which is a command-line tool that helps migrate and modernize Java and .NET web applications into container format. A2C analyzes and inventories all applications running on physical machines, Amazon EC2 instances, or in the cloud; packages application artifacts and dependencies into container images; configures network ports; and generates the necessary deployment artifacts for Amazon ECS and Amazon EKS. With A2C, you can efficiently manage the container and benefit from a unified and streamlined deployment process.

You can learn more about A2C service by visiting the AWS page – `https://aws.amazon.com/app2container/`.

Summary

In this chapter, you explored in depth what containers are. You also learned about the different types of container tools that are available. In particular, you investigated Docker. Docker is quite a popular container tool today, and it is a foundational piece of software for many successful companies. You learned about Amazon ECS, AWS's way of managing containers at scale. You learned about how it helps to run Docker containers.

You also learned about the orchestration tool Kubernetes, which is quite popular and helps many companies simplify their DevOps processes. You looked at how Kubernetes and Docker can work together, as well as with other AWS services. These tools were specifically created to host and maintain containers. You also spent some time reviewing Amazon EKS and how it works with Kubernetes.

You learned about running the serverless container option Fargate and when to choose running containers with EC2 or Fargate. Furthermore, you learned about ROSA and finally learned when to use EKS, ECS, or ROSA.

The software and services covered in this chapter will be instrumental in ensuring the success of your next project. The more complex the project, the more important it is to use the tools covered in this chapter.

In the next chapter, we will learn about the microservices architecture pattern, which builds upon the concepts we learned about in this chapter.

14

Microservice Architectures in AWS

This chapter builds upon the concepts and AWS services you learned about earlier in the areas of serverless architecture and containers in *Chapter 6, Harnessing the Power of Cloud Computing,* under the *Learning serverless compute with AWS Lambda and Fargate* section, and in *Chapter 13, Containers in AWS*. Now that you know the basics of containers and have discovered what some of the most popular container implementations are today, you can continue to learn about higher-level concepts that use containers to create modern, modular, and nimble applications. If your company operates in the cloud, it is very likely that it is taking advantage of the capabilities of the cloud. One architectural pattern that is extremely popular nowadays is microservice architecture.

In this chapter, you will do a deep dive into the ins and outs of microservice patterns. Specifically, you will learn about the following topics:

- Understanding microservices
- Microservice architecture patterns
- Building layered architecture
- Benefits of **event-driven architecture** (EDA)
- Disadvantages of EDA
- Reviewing microservices best practices
- Implementing **Domain-Driven Design** (DDD)

By the end of this chapter, you will have learned about microservice architecture design and popular pattern-like architectures, such as event-driven architecture and Domain-Driven Design, and their pros and cons. Let's get started.

Understanding microservices

Like many ideas that become popular in technology, it is hard to pin down an exact definition of microservices. Different groups co-opt the term and provide their own unique twist on the definition, but the popularity of microservices is hard to ignore. It might be the most common pattern used in new software development today. However, the definition has not stayed static and has evolved over time.

Given these caveats, let's try to define what a microservice is.

A **microservice** is a software application that follows an architectural style that structures the application as a service that is loosely coupled, easily deployable, testable, and organized in a well-defined business domain. A **loosely coupled system** is one where components have little or no knowledge about other components and there are few or no dependencies between these components.

In addition, a certain consensus has been reached, to some degree, around the concept of microservices. Some of the defining features that are commonly associated with microservices are the following:

- In the context of a **microservice architecture**, services communicate with each other over a network with the purpose of accomplishing a goal using a technology-agnostic protocol (most often HTTP).
- Services can be deployed independently of each other. The deployment of a new version of one of the services, in theory, should not impact any of the associated services.
- Services are assembled and built around business domains and capabilities.
- Services should be able to be developed using different operating systems, programming languages, data stores, and hardware infrastructure and still be able to communicate with each other because of their common protocol and agreed-upon **APIs (Application Programming Interfaces)**.
- Services are modular, small, message-based, context-bound, independently assembled and deployed, and decentralized.
- Services are built and released using an automated process – most often a **continuous integration** (CI) and **continuous delivery** (CD) methodology.

- Services have a well-defined interface and operations. Both consumers and producers of services know exactly what the interfaces are.
- Service interfaces normally stay the same or at least have background compatibility when code is changed. Therefore, clients of these services do not need to make changes when the code in the service is changed.
- Services are maintainable and testable. Often, these tests can be fully automated via a CI/CD process.
- Services allow for the fast, continuous, and reliable delivery and deployment of large and complex projects. They also facilitate organizations to evolve their technology stack.

Microservices are the answer to monolithic architectures that were common in mainframe development. Applications that follow a monolithic architecture are notoriously hard to maintain, tightly coupled, and difficult to understand. Also, microservices aren't simply a layer in a modularized application like was common in early web applications that leveraged the **Model/View/Controller (MVC)** pattern. Instead, they are self-contained, fully independent components with business functionality and clearly delineated interfaces. This doesn't mean that a microservice might not leverage other architectural patterns and have its own individual internal components.

Doug McIlroy is credited with describing the philosophy surrounding Unix; microservices implement the Unix philosophy of *"Do one thing and do it well."*

Martin Fowler describes microservices as those services that possess the following features:

- Software that can leverage a CI/CD development process. A small modification in one part of the application does not require the wholesale rebuild and deployment of the system; it only requires rebuilding, deploying, and distributing a small number of components or services.
- Software that follows certain development principles such as fine-grained interfaces.

Microservices fit hand in glove with the cloud and serverless computing. They are ideally suited to be deployed using container and serverless technology. In a monolithic deployment, if you need to scale up to handle more traffic, you will have to scale the full application. When using a microservice architecture, only the services that are receiving additional calls need to be scaled. Depending on how the services are deployed and assuming they are deployed in an effective manner, you will only need to scale up or scale out the services that are taking additional traffic and you can leave the servers that have the services that are not in demand untouched.

Microservices have grown in popularity in recent years as organizations are becoming nimbler. In parallel, more and more organizations have moved to adopt a DevOps and CI/CD culture. Microservices are well suited for this. Microservice architectures, in some ways, are the answer to monolithic applications. A high-level comparison between the two is shown in the following diagram:

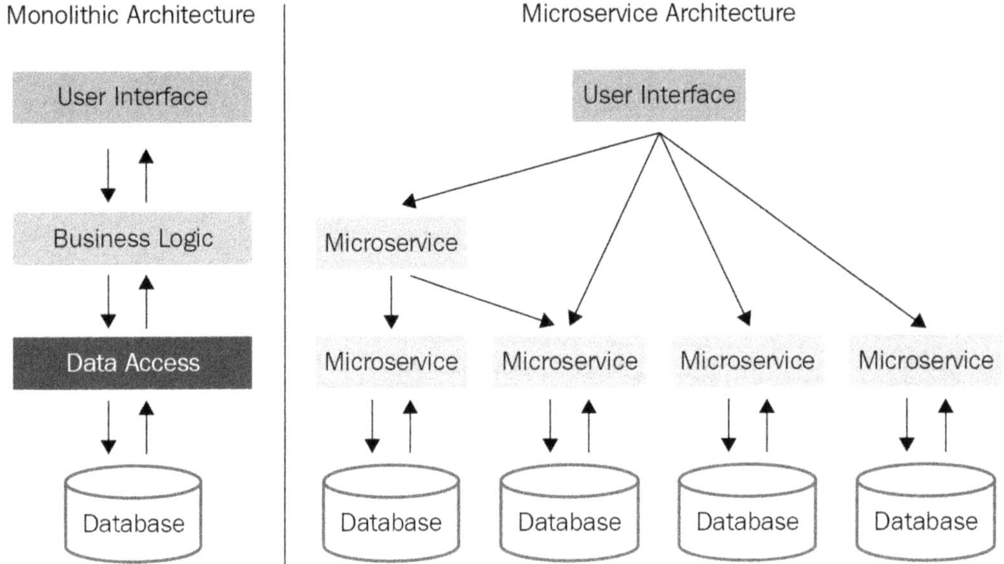

Figure 14.1: Monolithic versus microservice architectures

In a monolithic architecture, communication occurs across the whole application independent of business boundaries. Initially, and for simple applications, this architecture may be appropriate, but complexity increases quickly as the number of business domains that the application handles increases.

In a microservice architecture, each service is typically responsible for a specific business capability and is built and deployed independently of other services. As part of this separation, each service typically has its own database and API. Having a separate database for each service allows for better scalability, as the data storage and retrieval needs of each service can be optimized independently. It also allows for more flexibility in terms of the technology choices for each service, as different services can use different types of databases depending on their needs.

Having a separate API for each service allows for a clear separation of concerns and promotes loose coupling between services. It also allows for easier evolution of the services, as changes to one service's API will not affect other services.

This can also facilitate the versioning of the service. However, it's important to note that there are also some trade-offs with this approach. One of the main trade-offs is the increased complexity of managing and integrating multiple services.

The following diagram shows a microservice architecture in AWS at a high level. In this architecture a request goes through API Gateway and is routed to a different microservice based on the container manager Amazon ECS and the serverless microservices built on AWS Lambda. All microservices have their own Amazon Aurora database instances.

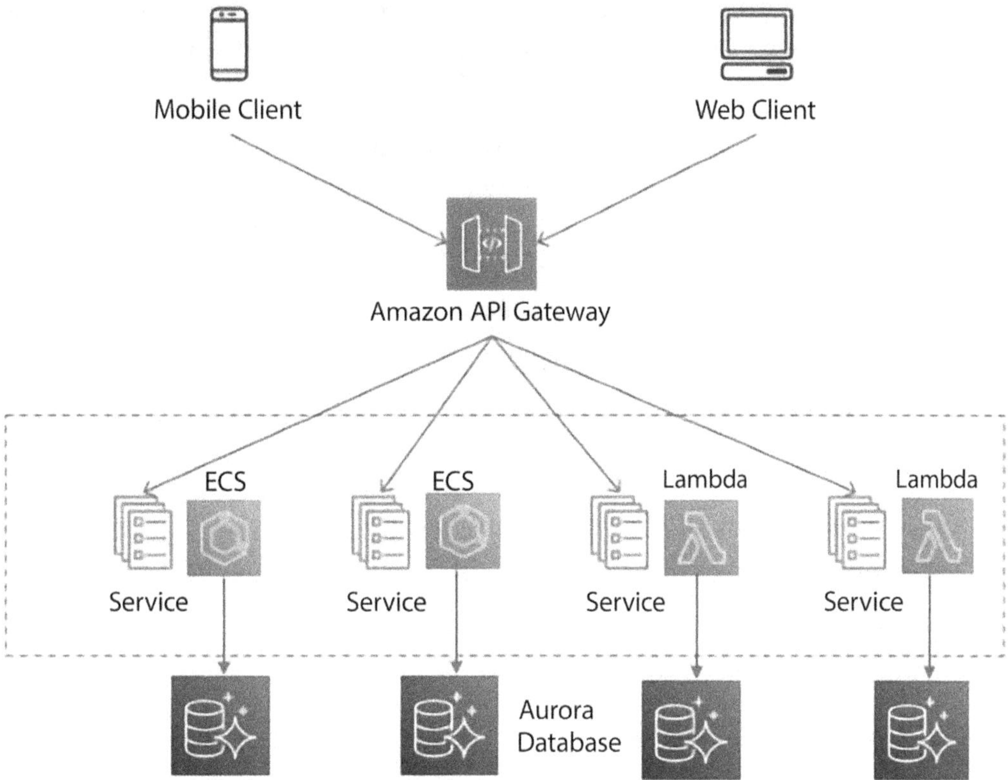

Figure 14.2: Microservice architectures in AWS

With this architecture, requests to the microservices would go through API Gateway, which would then route the requests to the appropriate microservice running in a container on ECS. The microservice would then interact with its own Aurora database to retrieve or store data:

- **API Gateway**: This service can be used to create and manage APIs for microservices. It allows for the creation of RESTful and WebSocket APIs, as well as the ability to handle authentication and authorization, traffic management, and caching.

- **ECS:** This service can be used to deploy and manage the containers that run the microservices. ECS allows you to easily scale and update the services, and it also provides service discovery and load balancing.
- **Aurora:** This service can be used as a managed relational database for microservices. Aurora can be used to create, configure, and manage relational databases that can be used by the microservices; it also provides automatic backups, software patching, and replication for high availability. You can also use Aurora Serverless to further reduce operational overhead.

This is just one example of how to build a microservice architecture using AWS services, and there are many other services and configurations that can be used depending on the specific requirements of the application.

There are other components that go into microservice architecture, like security, networking, caching, etc., which are not mentioned in the diagram to keep it simple. However, you will learn about these in more detail in upcoming sections. In a microservice architecture, the boundaries between services are well defined according to business domains. This enables applications to scale more smoothly and increases maintainability.

In this section, you saw the fundamentals of microservices. Next, we will learn about two popular architecture patterns that are often used when creating microservices.

These patterns are as follows:

- Layered architecture
- Event-driven architecture

In the following sections, you will learn about these common architectures in detail and go through the advantages and disadvantages of each of them.

Layered architecture

This pattern is quite common in software development. As indicated by the name, in this pattern, the code is implemented in layers. Having this layering enables the implementation of *"separation of concerns."* This is a fancy way of saying that each layer focuses on doing a few things well and nothing else, which makes it easier to understand, develop, and maintain the software.

The topmost layer communicates with users or other systems. The middle layer handles the business logic and routing of requests, and the bottom layer's responsibility is to ensure that data is permanently stored, usually in a database.

Having this separation of concerns or individual duties for each layer allows us to focus on the most important properties for each layer. For example, in the presentation layer, accessibility and usability are going to be important considerations, whereas, in the persistence layer, data integrity, performance, and privacy may be more important. Some factors will be important regardless of the layer. An example of a ubiquitous concern is security. But, by having these concerns separate, it enables teams to not require personnel that are experts in too many technologies. With this pattern, we can hire UI experts for the presentation layer and database administrators for the persistence layer. It also provides a clear delineation of responsibilities. If something breaks, it can often be isolated to a layer, and once it is, you can reach out to the owner of the layer.

From a security standpoint, a layered architecture offers certain advantages over more monolithic architectures. In a layered architecture, you normally only place the presentation layer services in a public subnet and place the rest of the layers in a private subnet. This ensures that only the presentation layer is exposed to the internet, minimizing the attack surface. As a best practice, you should only put the load balancer in the public domain with the protection of a web application firewall.

If a hacker wanted to use the database in an unauthorized manner, they would have to find a way to penetrate through the presentation layer and the business logic layer to access the persistence layer. This by no means implies that your system is impenetrable. You still want to use all security best practices and maybe even hire a white hat group to attempt to penetrate your system. An example of an attack that could still happen in this architecture is a SQL injection attack. That said, the layered architecture will limit the attack surface to the presentation layer only, so this architecture is still more secure than a monolithic architecture.

Another advantage of having a layered architecture is gaining the ability to swap out a layer without having to make modifications to any of the other layers. For example, you may decide that AngularJS is no longer a good option for the presentation layer and instead you want to start using React. Or you may want to start using Amazon Aurora PostgreSQL instead of Oracle. If your layers were truly independent and decoupled, you would be able to convert the layers to the new technology without having to make modifications to the other layers.

In a microservice-based architecture, the layers are typically broken down as follows:

- **Presentation layer:** This layer is responsible for handling the user interface and presenting the data to the user. This layer can be further divided into the client-side and server-side parts.

- **Business layer**: This layer is responsible for implementing the business logic of the system. It communicates with the presentation layer to receive requests and with the data access layer to retrieve and update data.
- **Data access layer**: This layer is responsible for communicating with the database and other data storage systems. It provides an abstraction layer between the business layer and the data storage, allowing the business layer to focus on the logic and not worry about the details of data access.

You can keep an additional layer that hosts services for security, logging, monitoring, and service discovery. Each layer is a separate microservice, which can be developed, deployed, and scaled independently. This promotes the flexibility, scalability, and maintainability of the system. In microservice architectures, it is also possible to add more layers in between as per the requirements, such as a security layer, API Gateway layer, service discovery layer, etc.

The following diagram shows a three-layer architecture in AWS, where the user experience frontend is deployed in the presentation layer, all business logic is handled by the business layer, and data is stored in the data access layer:

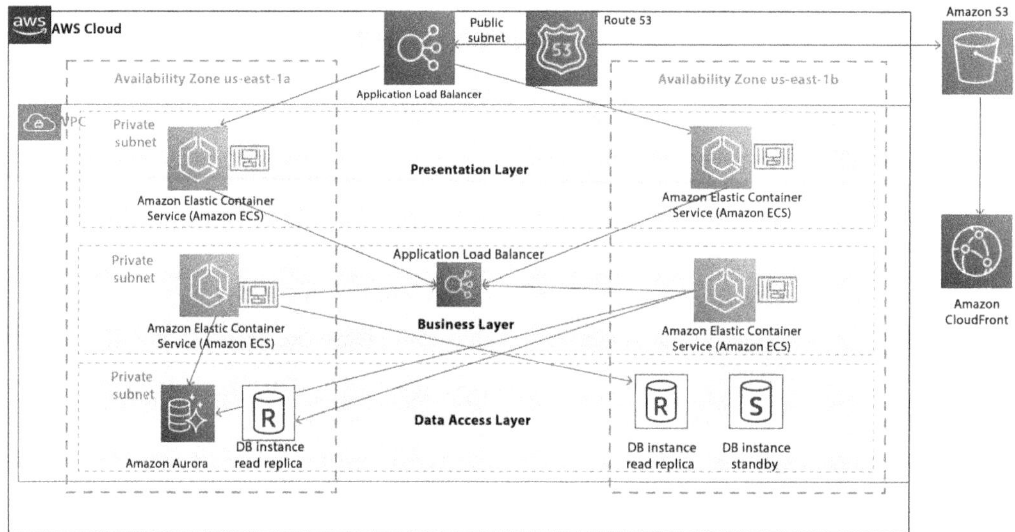

Figure 14.3: Three-layer microservice architecture in AWS

As shown in the preceding diagram, all web and application servers are deployed in containers managed by Amazon ECS, where requests are routed through an elastic load balancer and the entire environment is protected by a VPC. You can also choose Lambda or Fargate to have a completely serverless implementation, along with Aurora Serverless for your database.

Just because you are using a layered approach, it does not mean that your application will be bug-free or easy to maintain. It is not uncommon to create interdependencies among the layers. When something goes wrong in a layered architecture, the first step in troubleshooting the issue is to identify which layer the problem is occurring in. Each layer has a specific role and responsibility, and the problem will typically be related to that layer's functionality. Once the layer has been identified, you can focus on the specific components within that layer that are causing the problem.

Here are some examples of how troubleshooting might proceed for different layers:

- **Presentation layer**: If the problem is related to the user interface, you might investigate issues with the client-side code, such as JavaScript errors or browser compatibility issues. On the server side, you might investigate issues with the routing, rendering, or handling of user input.
- **Business layer**: If the problem is related to the business logic, you might investigate issues with the implementation of the logic itself, such as incorrect calculations or validation rules. You might also investigate issues with communication between the business layer and other layers, such as the presentation layer or data access layer.
- **Data access layer**: If the problem is related to data access, you might investigate issues with the database connections, queries, or transactions. You might also investigate issues with the mapping between the data model and the database schema, such as incorrect column names or data types.

Finally, if the problem is related to the underlying infrastructure, you might investigate issues with the network connections, security configurations, or service discovery mechanisms. Once you have identified the specific component causing the problem, you can use various debugging and monitoring tools to gather more information and diagnose the issue.

It's worth noting that having a clear and well-defined layered architecture can make troubleshooting more straightforward and efficient, as it allows you to focus on a specific layer and its related components instead of having to consider the entire system as a whole.

Event-driven architecture (EDA)

Event-driven architecture (EDA) is another pattern commonly used when implementing microservices. When the event-driven pattern is used, creating, messaging, processing, and storing events are critical functions of the service. Contrast this with the layered pattern we just looked at, which is more of a request/response model and where the user interface takes a more prominent role in the service.

Another difference is that layered architecture applications are normally synchronous whereas an EDA relies on the asynchronous nature of queues and events.

More and more applications are being designed using EDA from the ground up. Applications using EDA can be developed using a variety of development stacks and languages. EDA is a programming philosophy, not a technology and language. EDA facilitates code decoupling, making applications more robust and flexible. At the center of EDA is the concept of events. Let's spend some time understanding what they are.

Understanding events

To better understand the event-driven pattern, let's first define what an event is. Events are messages or notifications that are generated by one component of the system and consumed by other components. These events represent something significant or important that has occurred within the system and that other components need to know about in order to take appropriate action. Essentially, an event is a change in state in a system. Examples of changes that could be events are the following:

- A modification of a database
- A runtime error in an application
- A request submitted by a user
- An EC2 instance fails
- A threshold is exceeded
- A code change that has been checked into a CI/CD pipeline
- A new customer is registered in the system
- A payment is processed
- A stock price changes
- A sensor reports a temperature reading
- A user interacts with a mobile app

Not all changes or actions within a system are considered events in an EDA. For example, a change to a configuration setting or a log message might not be considered an event because it does not represent something significant that other components of the system need to know about.

It's also worth noting that the distinction between an event and a non-event can be context-dependent and may vary depending on the specific implementation of the EDA.

In some cases, certain changes or actions that would not typically be considered events might be treated as such if they are deemed important or relevant to certain components or use cases within the system.

In the next section, we'll discuss two other critical elements in EDA: the concepts of producers and consumers.

Producers and consumers

Events by themselves are useless. If a tree falls in the forest and no one is around to hear it or see it fall, did it really fall? The same question is appropriate for events. Events are worthless if someone is not consuming them, and in order to have events, producers of the events are needed as well. These two actors are essential components of EDA. Let's explore them at a deeper level:

- **Producers:** An event producer first detects a change of state and if it's an important change that is being monitored, it generates an event and sends a message out to notify others of the change.
- **Consumers:** Once an event has been detected, the message is transmitted to a queue. Importantly, once the event has been placed in the queue and the producer forgets about the message, consumers fetch messages from the queue in an asynchronous manner. Once a consumer fetches a message, they may or may not perform an action based on that message. Examples of these actions are as follows:
    - Triggering an alarm
    - Sending out an email
    - Updating a database record
    - Opening a door
    - Performing a calculation

  In essence, almost any process can be a consumer action.

As you can imagine, due to the asynchronous nature of EDA, it is highly scalable and efficient.

EDA is a loosely coupled architecture. Producers of events are not aware of who is going to consume their output and consumers of events are not aware of who generated the events. Let's now learn about two popular types of models designed around EDA.

EDA models

There are a couple of ways to design an event-driven model. One of the main design decisions that needs to be made is whether events need to be processed by only one consumer or by multiple consumers. The first instance is known as the event streaming pattern. The second pattern is most commonly known as the publish and subscribe pattern. EDA can be implemented using either of these two main patterns. Depending on the use case, one pattern may be a better fit than the other. Let's learn more about these two models.

Event streaming (a message queuing model)

In the event streaming model, events are *"popped off"* the queue as soon as one of the consumers processes the message. In this model, the queue receives a message from the producer and the system ensures that the message is processed by one and only one consumer.

Event streaming is well suited for workloads that need to be highly scalable and can be highly variable. Adding capacity is simply a matter of adding more consumers to the queue, and we can reduce capacity just as easily by removing some of the consumers (and reducing our bill). In this architecture, it is extremely important that messages are processed by only one consumer. In order to achieve this, as soon as a message is allotted to a consumer, it is removed from the queue. The only time that it will be placed back in the queue is if the consumer of the message fails to process the message and it needs to be reprocessed.

Use cases that are well suited for this model are those that require that each message is processed only once but the order in which the messages are processed is not necessarily important.

Let's look at a diagram of how an event streaming architecture would be implemented:

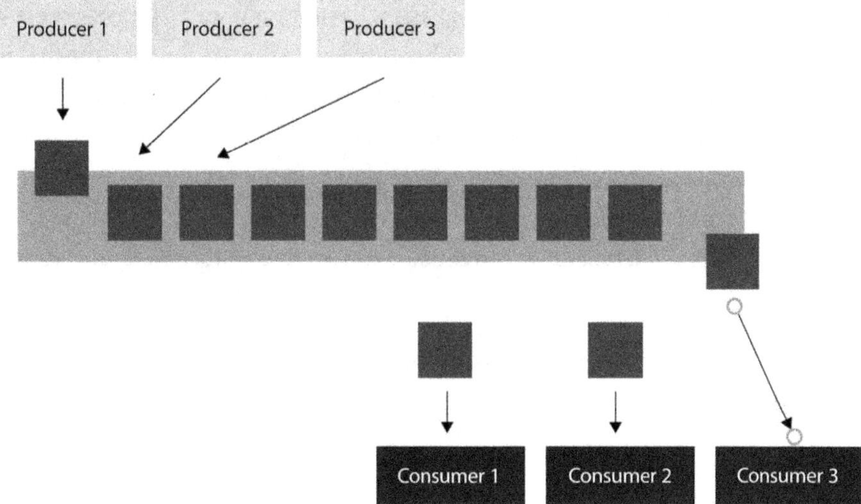

Figure 14.4: Event streaming model

In the preceding diagram, we have multiple producers generating events and placing them into a single queue (on the left-hand side). We also have multiple consumers consuming events off the queue (on the right-hand side). Once a consumer takes an event from the queue, it gets removed and no other consumer will be able to consume it. The only exception is if there is an error and the consumer is unable to complete the consumption of the event. In this case, we should put some logic in our process to put the unconsumed event back in the queue so that another consumer can process the event.

Let's make this more concrete with a real-life example.

Example scenario

In order to visualize this model, think of the queues that are common in banks, where you have a single queue that feeds into all the tellers. When a teller becomes available, the first person in the queue goes to that teller for processing and so forth. The customer needs to visit only one teller to handle their transaction. As tellers go on a break or new tellers come in to handle the increased demand, the model can gracefully and transparently handle these changes. In this case, the bank customers are the producers – they are generating events (for example, making a check deposit), and the bank tellers are the consumers – they are processing the events that the customers are creating.

You can use Amazon **Simple Queue Service** (**SQS**) to implement a queue model as shown in the following diagram.

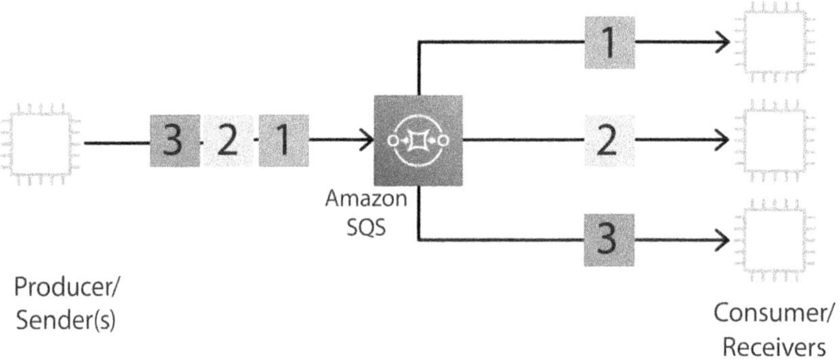

Figure 14.5: Event-driven message queuing model in AWS

As shown in the preceding diagram, here, messages are coming from the producer and going into SQS. Amazon SQS is a serverless, scalable queue service. It allows consumers to take messages from the queue and process them as per their needs. If your application is using an industry-standard queue service like JMS or RabbitMQ, you can use Amazon MQ, which provides managed support for RabbitMQ and Apache ActiveMQ.

Now let's move on and learn about another type of event-driven model – the pub/sub model.

Publish and subscribe model (pub/sub model)

As happens with event streaming, the **publish and subscribe** model (also known as the **pub/sub** model) assists in communicating events from producers to consumers. However, unlike event streaming, this model allows several consumers to process the same message. Furthermore, the pub/sub model may guarantee the order in which the messages are received.

As the publishing part of the name indicates, message producers broadcast messages to anyone that is interested in them. You express interest in the message by subscribing to a topic.

The pub/sub messaging model is suited for use cases in which more than one consumer needs to receive messages. In this model, many publishers push events into a **pub/sub cache** (or queue). The events can be classified by topic. As shown in the following diagram, subscribers listen to the queue and check for events being placed in it. Whenever events make it to the queue, the consumers notice them and process them accordingly. Unlike the model in the previous section, when a subscriber sees a new event in the queue, it does not pop it off the queue; it leaves it there and other subscribers can also consume it, and perhaps take a completely different action for the same event.

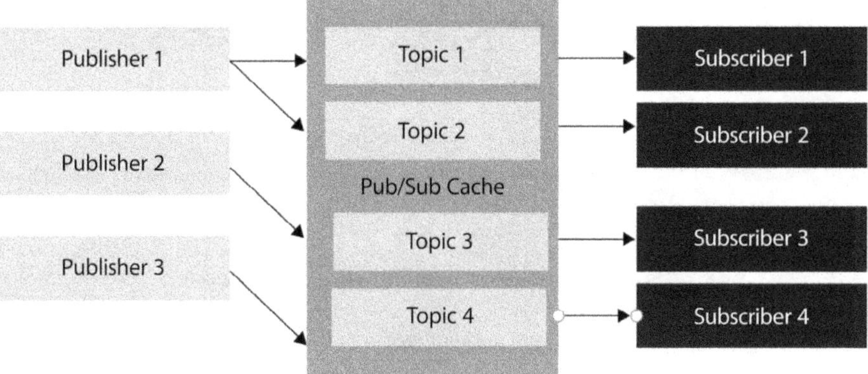

Figure 14.6: The pub/sub model

Optionally, the events in the cache can be classified by topic, and subscribers can subscribe only to the topics they are interested in and ignore the rest. The following diagram shows the pub/sub model as achieved by Amazon **Simple Notification Service** (**SNS**).

A managed service provided by AWS for a pub/sub model is EventBridge. AWS EventBridge is a serverless event bus service that allows you to connect different applications and services together using a pub/sub model. With EventBridge, you can create rules that automatically trigger specific actions in response to events from various sources, such as changes in an S3 bucket or the creation of a new item in a DynamoDB table. This allows you to easily integrate different parts of your application and automate tasks without having to write custom code. EventBridge supports both custom events and events from AWS services, making it a powerful tool for building event-driven architectures.

Example scenario

An example of this is a stock price service. In this case, typically, many market participants are interested in receiving prices in real time on a topic of their choosing (in this case, the topics are the individual tickers). In this case, the order in which the order tickers are received is incredibly important. If two traders put in a purchase to buy stock for the same price, it is critical that the system processes the order that was received first. If it doesn't, the market maker might get in trouble with accusations of front-running trades.

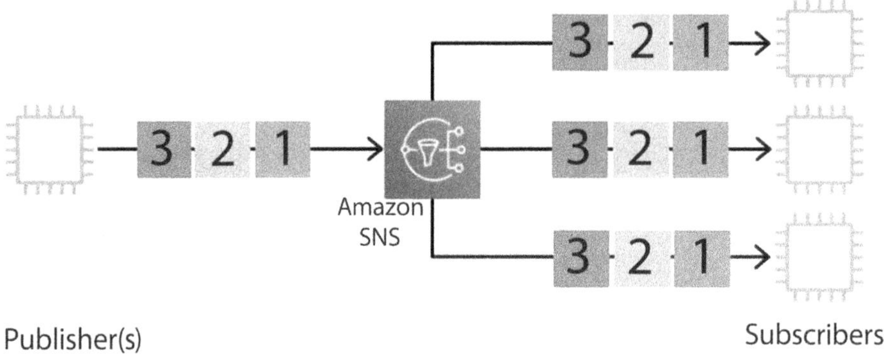

Figure 14.7: Event-driven pub/sub model in AWS

As shown in the preceding diagram, all messages from different publishers go to SNS, where multiple consumers are subscribed to receive them. SNS fans out messages to all the subscribers for further processing, as per the application's requirements.

The pub/sub model is frequently used with stateful applications. In a stateful application, the order in which the messages are received is important, as the order can impact the application state.

Benefits of EDA

EDA can assist an organization to obtain an edge over its competitors. This edge stems from the benefits that the pub/sub model can provide. Some of the benefits are explained in the following sub-sections.

No more polling

The pub/sub model delivers the benefit of real-time events through a *"push"* delivery mechanism. It eliminates the need to constantly be fetching sources to see whether data has changed. If you use a polling mechanism, you will either waste resources by checking for changes when no changes have occurred, or you will delay actions if changes occur when you haven't polled.

Using a push mechanism minimizes the latency of message delivery. Depending on your application, delays in message delivery could translate into a loss of millions of dollars.

Example: Let's say you have a trading application. You want to buy stock only when a certain price is reached. If you were using polling, you would have to constantly ping every so often to see if the price had changed. This has two problems:

- Computing resources will have to be used with every ping. This is wasteful.
- If the price changes in between pings, and then changes again, the trade may not execute even though the target price was reached.

With events, the ping will be generated only once when the target price is reached, greatly increasing the likelihood that the trade will happen.

Dynamic targeting

EDA simplifies the discovery of services and does so in an effortless and natural way, minimizing the number of potential errors. In EDA, there is no need to keep track of data consumers and, instead, interested parties simply subscribe to the topics that are of interest. If there are parties interested in the messages, the messages get consumed by all of them. In the pub/sub model, if there aren't any interested consumers, the message simply gets broadcast without anyone taking any action.

Example: Continuing with our trading application example, let's assume that each stock represents a topic. Letting users of the application select what topic/stock interests them will greatly reduce the number of events generated and therefore will reduce resource consumption.

Communication simplicity

EDA minimizes code complexity by eliminating direct point-to-point communication between producers and consumers. The number of connections is greatly reduced by having a central queue where producers place their messages and consumers collect messages.

Example: Let's assume that our trading application has 10 stock shares and 10 users. If we didn't have an intermediate queue to hold the events, every stock share would have to be connected to every user, for a total of 100 connections. But having a queue in the middle would mean that we only have 10 connections from the stock to the queue and 10 connections from the users to the queue, giving us a total of 20 connections, greatly simplifying the system.

Decoupling and scalability

The pub/sub model increases software flexibility. There is no explicit coupling between publishers and subscribers. They all are decoupled and work independently of each other. Having this decoupling promotes the individual development of services, which, in turn, allows us to deploy and scale these services independently. Functionality changes in one part of the application should not affect the rest of the application so long as design patterns are followed, and the code is truly modularized. So long as the agreed-upon APIs stay stable, making a change in the publisher code should not affect the consumer code.

Example: In our trading application, if a new stock ticker is added, users don't need a new connection to the new stock. We simply create a connection from the new stock to the queue and now anybody can listen for events in that new topic. Something similar happens when new users get added. The user just needs to specify which stocks they are interested in. Nothing else needs to be changed in the system. This makes the overall architecture quite scalable.

As we have seen, the advantages of EDA are many. However, no software solution is perfect, and EDA is no exception. Let's now investigate the disadvantages that come with it.

Disadvantages of EDA

As with other technologies, EDA also has drawbacks. Some of the drawbacks are explained in the following sub-sections.

EDA is not a silver bullet

It is worth noting that, like any other technology, the EDA pattern should not be viewed as a solution that can solve all problems. A problem may not require the added complexity of setting up a message queue. We might only require a "point-to-point" communication channel because we don't foresee having additional producers or consumers. The EDA pattern is quite popular with new IoT applications, but it is not suitable for other use cases. If your application is synchronous in nature and it only requires accessing and updating a database, using EDA may not be necessary and might be overcomplicated. It is important to determine how much interactivity and inter-process communication will be required in our application before recommending EDA as a pattern for a given problem. EDA applications require some effort to maintain and troubleshoot when problems arise (by having to check consumers, producers, and queues) and an individual problem might not warrant their use.

Example: What if our trading application only focused on one stock share? In that particular example, we might want to avoid the complexity of creating queues, topics, and so on and keep it simple without using a queue.

When things go wrong

Like any other technology that depends on an underlying infrastructure, it is possible in an EDA implementation for messages to get lost for various reasons, including the failure of hardware components. Dealing with such failures can be difficult to troubleshoot and even more difficult to find a solution to recover from. These issues stem from the asynchronous nature of the architecture. This property makes the resulting applications massively scalable but with the downside of potentially losing messages. Overcoming this shortcoming can be challenging.

Example: Due to the asynchronous nature of EDA applications, it is not easy to troubleshoot them. In our trading application, we might lose a message due to hard failure. We obviously want to minimize or even eliminate these occurrences. However, trying to replicate the behavior to debug them may be difficult, if not impossible. You can use managed, serverless, AWS-native services such as EventBridge to reduce the risk.

Microservices best practices

As with any technology, the devil is in the details. It is certainly possible to create bad microservices. Let's delve into how some common pitfalls can be avoided and some recommended best practices.

Best practice #1 – decide whether microservices are the right tool

The world's leading technology companies, such as eBay, Facebook, Amazon, Microsoft, Twitter, and PayPal, are all heavy users of microservice architecture and rely on it for much of their development. However, it's not a panacea. As technologists, once we get a hammer, everything looks like a nail. Make sure that your particular use case is best suited for this architecture. If it's hard to break down your application into functional domains, a microservice architecture might not be the best choice.

Best practice #2 – clearly define the requirements and design of the microservice

Creating microservices, like other software projects, requires preparation and focus. A sure way for a software project to fail is to start coding without having a clear goal in mind for the function of the software.

Requirements should be written down in detail and approved by all stakeholders. Once the requirements are completed, a design should be created using a language and artifacts that are understood by all parties involved, including domain experts.

A clear distinction should be made between business requirements and functions, the services that will be provided, and the microservices that will be implemented to provide the services. Without this delineation, it is likely the microservices will be too big and not fragmented enough and no benefit will be delivered from using a microservice architecture. On the other hand, it is also possible for your design to have too many microservices and for you to over-engineer the solution. If there are too many microservices, the solution will be difficult to maintain, understand, and troubleshoot.

Best practice #3 – leverage Domain-Driven Design to create microservices

Later in this chapter, we will learn about the Domain-Driven Design methodology. We will learn more about it in a moment, but Domain-Driven Design is ideally suited for the development of microservices. Domain-Driven Design is a set of design principles that allow us to define an object-oriented model using concepts and nomenclature that all stakeholders can understand using a unified model language. It allows all participants in the software definition process to fully understand the relevant business domains and deliver better microservices because you can get buy-in and understanding from everyone more quickly.

Best practice #4 – ensure buy-in from all stakeholders

Software development involves many parties in an organization: developers, architects, testers, domain experts, managers, and decision-makers, among others. In order to ensure the success of your project, you need to make sure to get buy-ins from all of them. It is highly recommended that you get approval from all stakeholders at every major milestone – particularly during the business requirement and design phase. In today's Agile culture, the initial requirements and design can often change, and in those instances, it is also important to keep stakeholders updated and in agreement.

Deploying a microservice entails much more than just technology. Getting approval and mindshare from the status quo is key. This cultural transformation can be arduous and expensive. Depending on the team's exposure to this new paradigm, it might take a significant effort, especially if they are accustomed to building their applications in a monolithic manner.

Once you start delivering results and business value, it might be possible to start getting into a cadence and a harmonious state with all team members. And for that reason, it is important to make sure that you start delivering value as soon as possible. A common approach to achieve this is to deliver a minimum viable product that delivers the core functionality in order to start deriving value, and to then continue building and enhancing the service once the minimum viable product is deployed to production and starts being used.

Best practice #5 – leverage logging and tracing tools

One of the disadvantages of using a microservice architecture is the added burden of logging and tracing many components. In a monolithic application, there is one software component to monitor. In a microservice architecture, each microservice generates its own logging and error messages. With a microservice architecture, software development is simplified but operations become a little more complicated. For this reason, it is important that your services leverage the logging and tracing services that AWS offers, such as AWS CloudWatch, AWS X-Ray, and AWS CloudTrail, where the logging and error messages generated are as uniform as possible. Ideally, all the microservice teams will agree on the logging libraries and standards to increase uniformity. Two products that are quite popular to implement logging are the **ELK** stack (consisting of **Elasticsearch, Logstash, and Kibana**) and Splunk.

Best practice #6 – think microservices first

Software development can be a fine art more than a hard science. There are always conflicting forces at play. You want to deliver functionality in production as quickly as possible but, at the same time, you want to ensure that your solution endures for many years and is easily maintainable and easily expandable. For this reason, some developers like using a monolithic architecture at the beginning of projects and then try to convert it to a microservice architecture.

If possible, it is best to fight this temptation. The tight coupling that will exist because of the architecture choice will be difficult to untangle once it is embedded. Additionally, once your application is in production, expectations rise because any changes you make need to be thoroughly tested. You want to make sure that any new changes don't break existing functionality. You might think that code refactoring to ease maintenance is a perfectly valid reason to change code in production. However, explaining to your boss why the production code broke when you were introducing a change that did not add any new functionality will not be an easy conversation. You may be able to deliver the initial functionality faster using a monolithic architecture, but it will be cumbersome to later convert it into a more modular architecture.

It is recommended to spend some time on correctly designing your microservices' boundaries from the start. If you are using an Agile methodology, there will no doubt be some refactoring of microservices as your architecture evolves and that's okay. But do your best to properly design your boundaries at the beginning.

Best practice #7 – minimize the number of languages and technologies

One of the advantages of the microservice architecture is the ability to create different services using different technology stacks. For example, you could create Service A using Java, the Spring MVC framework, and MariaDB and you could create Service B using Python with a Postgres backend. This is doable because when Service A communicates with Service B, they will communicate through the HTTP protocol and via the RESTful API, without either one caring about the details of the other's implementation.

Now, just because you can do something, doesn't mean you should do it. It still behooves you to minimize the number of languages used to create microservices. Having a small number of languages, or maybe even using just one, will enable you to swap people from one group to another, act more nimbly, and be more flexible.

There is a case to be made that one stack might be superior to the other and more suited to implement a particular service, but any time you have to deviate from your company's standard stack you should make sure that you have a compelling business case to deviate from the standards and increase your technological footprint.

Best practice #8 – leverage RESTful APIs

A key feature of the microservice pattern is to deliver its functionality via a RESTful API. **RESTful APIs** are powerful for various reasons, among them the fact that no client code needs to be deployed in order to start using them, as well as the fact that they can be self-documenting if implemented properly.

Best practice #9 – implement microservice communication asynchronously

Whenever possible, communication between microservices should be asynchronous. One of the tricky parts about designing microservices is deciding the boundaries between the services. Do you offer granular microservices or do you only offer a few services? If you offer many services that perform a few tasks well, there will undoubtedly be more inter-service communication.

In order to perform a task, it may be necessary for Service A to call Service B, which, in turn, needs to call Service C. If the services are called synchronously, this interdependency can make the application brittle. For example, what happens if Service C is down? Service A won't work and will hopefully return an error. The alternative is for the services to communicate asynchronously. In this case, if Service C is down, Service A will put a request in a queue and Service C will handle the request when it comes back online. Implementing asynchronous communication between services creates more overhead and is more difficult than synchronous communication, but the upfront development cost will be offset by increasing the reliability and scalability of the final solution.

There are many ways to implement asynchronous communication between microservices. Some of them are as follows:

- **Amazon SNS**: SNS is a distributed pub/sub service. Messages are pushed to any subscribers when messages are received from the publishers.
- **Amazon SQS**: SQS is a distributed queuing system. With SQS, messages are NOT pushed to the receivers. Receivers pull messages from the queue and once they pull a message, no one else can receive that message. The receiver processes it, and the message is removed from the queue.
- **Amazon Kinesis**: Amazon SNS and Amazon SQS are good options with simple use cases. Amazon Kinesis is more appropriate for real-time use cases that need to process terabytes of data per minute.
- **Amazon Managed Streaming for Kafka (MSK)**: Amazon MSK is a fully managed service for Apache Kafka. As well as the rest of the options listed below, it is an open source solution. With Amazon MSK, you can create and manage Kafka clusters in minutes, without the need to provision or manage servers, storage, or networking. The service automatically handles tasks such as software patching, backups, and monitoring, enabling you to focus on your application logic. Apache Kafka supports both a queue and a pub/sub architecture.
- **Amazon MQ**: Amazon MQ is a managed message broker service for Apache ActiveMQ, which is another popular open source messaging tool. With Amazon MQ, you can set up a message broker using ActiveMQ in minutes, without the need to provision or manage the underlying infrastructure. The service automatically handles tasks such as software patching, backups, and monitoring, enabling you to focus on your application logic. Amazon MQ supports multiple messaging protocols, including JMS, NMS, AMQP, STOMP, MQTT, and WebSocket. This allows you to easily connect to your existing applications and devices and use the messaging protocol that best suits your needs.

- **AWS EventBridge**: EventBridge allows you to publish events to a centralized event bus, which can then be consumed by other microservices in a decoupled manner. This decoupling allows microservices to communicate with each other without requiring a direct connection or knowledge of each other's implementation details.

Best practice #10 – implement a clear separation between microservice frontends and backends

Even today, many backend developers have an outdated perspective about what it takes to develop UIs and tend to oversimplify the complexities involved in constructing user-friendly frontends. The UI can often be neglected in design sessions. A microservice architecture with fine-grained backend services that has a monolithic frontend can run into trouble in the long run. There are great options out there that can help create sharp-looking frontends. Some of the most popular frontend web development frameworks currently are the following:

- Vue
- React
- Angular

However, picking the hottest SPA tool to develop your frontend is not enough. Having a clear separation between backend and frontend development is imperative. The interaction and dependencies between the two should be absolutely minimal, if they are not completely independent.

As new UIs become more popular or easier to use, we should be able to swap out the frontend with minimal interruptions and changes to the backend.

Another reason for having this independence comes about when multiple UIs are required. For example, our application may need a web UI, an Android application, and an Apple iOS application.

Best practice #11 – organize your team around microservices

On a related note to the previous best practice, there might be different teams for individual microservices and it's important to assign ownership of each of these services to individuals in your team. However, hopefully, your team is as cross-functional as possible and team members can jump from one microservice to another if the need arises. In general, there should be a good reason to pull one team member from the development of one service to another, but when this does happen, hopefully, they are able to make the leap and fill the gap.

In addition, the team should have a decent understanding of the overall objectives of the projects, as well as knowledge of the project plan for all services. Having a narrow view of only one service could prove fatal to the success of the business if they don't fully understand the business impact that a change in their service could have on other services.

Best practice #12 – provision individual data stores for each individual microservice

Separating your garbage into recyclables and non-recyclables and then watching the garbage collector co-mingle them can be frustrating. The same is true of microservices that have well-defined and architected boundaries and then share the same database. If you use the same database, you create strong coupling between the microservices, which we want to avoid whenever possible. Having a common database will require constant synchronization between the various microservice developers. Transactions will also get more complicated if there is a common database.

Having a separate data store makes services more modular and more reusable. Having one database per microservice does require that any data that needs to be shared between services needs to be passed along with the RESTful calls, but this drawback is not enough to not separate service databases whenever possible.

Ideally, every microservice will have an individual allocation for its data store. Every microservice should be responsible for its own persistence. Data can be reused across services, but it should only be stored once and shared via APIs across the services. However, whenever possible, you should avoid data sharing across microservices as data sharing leads to service coupling. This coupling negates some of the advantages of the separation of concerns of a microservice architecture, so it should be avoided as much as possible.

Best practice #13 – self-documentation and full documentation

A well-designed RESTful API should be intuitive to use if you choose your domain name and operation names correctly.

Take special care to use labels for your APIs that closely match your business domains. If you do this, you won't need to create endless documents to support your application. However, your documentation should be able to fill the gaps and take over where the intuitiveness of your API ends. One of the most popular tools to create this documentation is a tool called **Swagger**. You can learn more about the Swagger tool here: `https://swagger.io/`.

Best practice #14 – use a DevOps toolset

Another methodology that goes hand in hand with microservice development (in addition to Domain-Driven Design) is the popular **DevOps paradigm**. Having a robust DevOps program in place along with a mature CI/CD pipeline will allow you to develop, test, and maintain your microservices quickly and effortlessly.

A popular combination is to use Jenkins for deployment and Docker as a container service with GitHub. AWS CodePipeline can be used to automate an end-to-end DevOps pipeline.

Best practice #15 – invest in monitoring

As we learned in the preceding section regarding the disadvantages of microservices, they can be more difficult to monitor and troubleshoot than legacy monolithic architectures. This increased complexity must be accounted for, and new monitoring tools that can be adapted to the new microservice architecture need to be used.

Ideally, the monitoring solution offers a central repository for messages and logs regardless of what component of the architecture generated the event.

The monitoring tools should be able to be used for each microservice, and the monitoring system should facilitate root cause analysis. Fortunately, AWS offers a nice selection of monitoring services, including the following:

- Amazon CloudWatch
- Amazon CloudTrail
- Amazon X-Ray

To learn more about these and other monitoring services in AWS, you can visit:

`https://docs.aws.amazon.com/AWSEC2/latest/UserGuide/monitoring_ec2.html`

Best practice #16 – two pizzas should be enough to feed your team

This is a rule popularized by Jeff Bezos. He famously only invites enough people to meetings so that two large pizzas can feed the attendees. Bezos popularized the *two-pizza* rule for meetings and project teams to encourage a decentralized, creative working environment and to keep the start-up spirit alive and well.

This rule's goal is to avoid groupthink. *Groupthink* is a phenomenon that occurs when you have large groups and people start going with the consensus instead of feeling comfortable pushing back against what they think are bad ideas. In some ways, it is human nature to be more hesitant to disagree in large groups.

It is not uncommon for members of the group that are lower in the corporate hierarchy to be intimidated by authority figures such as their boss and people with bigger titles. By keeping groups small and encouraging dialogue, some of this hesitancy may be overcome and better ideas may be generated.

Bezos' idea to keep meetings and teams small to foster collaboration and productivity can be backed up by science. During his 50 years of studies and research of teams, J. Richard Hackman concluded that 4 to 6 is the optimal number of team members for many projects and that teams should never be larger than 10.

According to Hackman, communication issues "*grow exponentially as team size increases.*" Perhaps counterintuitively, the larger a team is, the more time will be used to communicate, reducing the time that can be used productively to achieve goals.

In the context of microservice development, the two-pizza rule is also applicable. You don't want your microservice development and deployment teams to be much bigger than a dozen people or so. If you need more staff, you are probably better off splitting the microservice domains so that you can have two teams creating two microservices rather than one huge team creating an incredibly big and complex microservice.

Obviously, there is no hard rule about exactly how many people is too many people, but at some point, the number becomes too big and unmanageable. For example, having a 100-person monolithic team with no hierarchy or natural division in it most likely would be too unmanageable.

Best practice #17 – twelve-factor design

A popular methodology that is out there to enhance microservice development is one dubbed *the twelve-factor design*. This methodology accelerates and simplifies software development by making suggestions such as ensuring that you are using a version control tool to keep track of your code.

The twelve-factor design is a methodology for building **software-as-a-service (SaaS)** applications that are easy to scale and maintain. It was first introduced in a 2011 article by Adam Wiggins, co-founder of Heroku, a cloud platform for building and deploying web applications.

The twelve factors are:

1. **Code base**: One code base is tracked in revision control for many deployments
2. **Dependencies**: Explicitly declare and isolate dependencies
3. **Config**: Store config in the environment
4. **Backing services**: Treat backing services as attached resources
5. **Build, release, run**: Strictly separate build and run stages
6. **Processes**: Execute the app as one or more stateless processes
7. **Port binding**: Export services via port binding
8. **Concurrency**: Scale out via the process model
9. **Disposability**: Maximize robustness with fast startup and graceful shutdown
10. **Dev/prod parity**: Keep development, staging, and production as similar as possible
11. **Logs**: Treat logs as event streams
12. **Admin processes**: Run admin/management tasks as one-off processes

By following these principles, the twelve-factor methodology aims to make it easy to scale and maintain SaaS applications by breaking them down into small, loosely coupled services that can be run in different environments and easily deployed on cloud-based platforms. You can learn more about this methodology here: `https://12factor.net/`.

Many of the best practices mentioned in this section don't just apply to microservice development but are also useful in software development in general. Following these practices from the beginning of your project will greatly increase the chances of a successful implementation that is on time and on budget, as well as making sure that these microservices are useful, adaptable, flexible, and easily maintainable.

In today's world, software is used to solve many complicated problems. From meeting worldwide demand for your e-commerce site to enabling a real-time stock trading platform, many companies, big and small, are leveraging Domain-Driven Design to bring their products and services to market on time. Let's take a look into the Domain-Driven Design pattern.

Domain-Driven Design (DDD)

Domain-Driven Design (**DDD**) might fall into the shiny new object category, as many people see it as the latest trendy pattern. However, DDD builds upon decades of evolutionary software design and engineering wisdom. To better understand it, let's briefly look at how the ideas behind DDD came about with a brief overview of **Object-Oriented Programming** (**OOP**).

DDD has its roots in the OOP concepts pioneered by Alan Key and Ivan Sutherland. The term OOP was coined by Alan Key around 1966 or 1967 while in grad school. OOP is a powerful programming paradigm that allows for the creation of well-structured, maintainable, and reusable code, and is widely used in the development of modern software applications.

OOP is a way of thinking about programming that is based on the concept of "objects." Objects can be thought of as instances of a class, and are used to represent and manipulate real-world entities. OOP uses objects and their interactions to design and write programs. It's a bit like building a house, where you use different blocks (objects) to build different rooms (programs), and you can use the same blocks (objects) in different ways to build different rooms (programs).

Imagine you're making a video game where you control a character, like Mario in Super Mario Bros. In OOP, you would create an "object" that represents Mario, and give it properties like its position on the screen, how fast it can move, and how many lives it has. You would also give it "methods" that tell it what to do, like moving left or right, jumping, and so on. The whole game would be made up of many different objects, each with its own properties and methods. For example, there would be objects for the Goombas (enemies), pipes, coins, and so on. All these objects would interact with each other in a way that makes sense for the game.

OOP also has some other concepts, like inheritance, polymorphism, encapsulation, and abstraction, which help to make the code more organized and easier to maintain.

OOP languages like Java, C++, Python, C#, etc. are widely used in the industry. These languages provide features like classes, objects, inheritance, polymorphism, encapsulation, and so on to build OOP-based applications.

Ivan Sutherland created an application called Sketchpad, an early inspiration for OOP. Sutherland started working on this application in 1963. In this early version of an OOP application, objects were primitive data structures displayed as images on the screen. They started using the concept of inheritance even in those early days. Sketchpad has some similarities with JavaScript's prototypal inheritance.

OOP came about because developers and designers were increasingly ambitious in tackling more complex problems, and procedural languages were insufficient. Another seminal development was the creation of a language called **Simula**. Simula is considered the first fully OOP language. It was developed by two Norwegian computer scientists—Ole-Johan Dahl and Kristen Nygaard.

A lot of development and many projects relied heavily on OOP for a long time. Building upon the advances of OOP, Eric Evans wrote the book *Domain-Driven Design: Tackling Complexity in the Heart of Software* in 2003. In his book, Evans introduced us to DDD and posited that DDD represents a new, better, and more mature way to develop software building on the evolution of **Object-Oriented Analysis and Design (OOAD)**.

DDD builds upon OOP by providing a set of principles and practices for designing software that models complex business domains. While OOP focuses on the implementation of objects and their interactions, DDD focuses on the modeling of the business domain and the creation of a rich, domain-specific language that accurately captures its complexities. DDD uses this language to drive the design and implementation of the software. DDD and OOP have a lot of similarities, and many of the concepts of OOP are present in DDD. Some of the key OOP concepts that are present in DDD include:

- **Encapsulation**: DDD encourages the use of encapsulation to hide the internal details of domain objects and expose their behavior through a public interface. This allows the domain objects to be treated as black boxes that can be interacted with through a set of predefined methods, without the need to understand their internal workings.
- **Inheritance**: DDD uses inheritance to model "is-a" relationships between domain objects. For example, a specific type of product might inherit from a more general product class.
- **Polymorphism**: DDD uses polymorphism to model "like" relationships between domain objects. For example, different types of products might share some common behavior, but also have unique behaviors specific to their type.
- **Abstraction**: DDD encourages the use of abstraction to break down complex problems into smaller, more manageable parts.

In addition to the above OOP concepts, DDD also introduces several other concepts, such as bounded contexts, aggregates, domain services, value objects, entities, repositories, and so on, which help to model the business domain in a more accurate and efficient way.

Definition of a domain

Now that we have taken a drive down memory lane regarding the history of DDD, let's first nail down what a domain is before we delve into the definition of DDD. According to the Oxford English Dictionary, one of the definitions of a domain is *"a sphere of knowledge or activity."*

Applying this definition to the software realm, domain refers to the subject or topic area that an application will operate in. In application development terms, the domain is the *sphere of knowledge and activity used during application development* and the activity that is specific to a particular business or application. It includes the concepts, rules, and relationships that make up the problem space that the application is trying to solve. The domain is the core of the application, and it is where the business logic resides.

For example, if you are building an e-commerce application, the domain would include concepts such as products, customers, orders, and payments. It would also include rules and relationships such as how products are categorized, how customers can place orders, and how payments are processed. The domain is the starting point for DDD, and it is the source of the domain-specific language that is used throughout the development process. By creating a rich, domain-specific language, the development team can communicate more effectively and create a more accurate and efficient design. The domain model is the representation of the domain in the software application; it is the core of the application and it contains the business logic, rules, and relationships. The model should be created from the domain experts' knowledge; it should be accurate and should be able to capture the complexity of the domain.

Another common way this word is used is to refer to the domain layer or the domain logic. Many developers also refer to this as the business layer or the business logic. In software development, the business layer refers to the layer of the application that contains the business logic and implements the business rules of the application. The business logic is the set of rules and processes that govern how an application behaves and interacts with the domain. Business objects are the objects that represent the business entities and implement the business logic.

A business rule is a specific rule or constraint that governs the behavior of the business objects and the application as a whole. These rules can be specific to a business or industry, and they dictate how the business operates and interacts with the outside world.

For example, in an e-commerce application, a business rule might be that customers must be at least 18 years old to make a purchase. This rule would be implemented in the business logic and would be enforced by the application when a customer attempts to make a purchase. The business layer also contains the business object, a representation of a business entity, such as a customer, product, or order. These objects encapsulate the data and behavior of the corresponding business entity, and they provide a way for the application to interact with the domain. The business objects are responsible for implementing the business logic, including enforcing the business rules.

Suppose a bank account holder tries to retrieve a certain amount of money from their bank, and their account does not have enough balance to honor the request. In that case, the bank should not allow the account holder to retrieve any funds (and charge them an *insufficient funds fee*).

Can you spot the potential business objects in this example? Pause for a second before we give you the answer to see if you can figure it out. Two candidates are these:

- Bank account holder
- Bank account

Depending on the application, you might not want to model the holder as a separate object and rely on the account, but it will depend on the operations that need to be performed on the objects. If you decide to merge the account with the holder, this might generate data duplication (for example, you might store the same address twice when a holder has two accounts and only one address). This issue might not be an issue at all in your implementation.

Principles of DDD

As we mentioned earlier, Eric Evans coined the term DDD, so who better to ask for a definition than Evans? As it turns out, even for him, the definition has been a moving target, and the definition he initially gave in his book is no longer his preferred definition. Moreover, defining DDD is not a simple exercise, and Evans defines DDD in multiple ways. This is not necessarily a bad thing—by having multiple definitions, we can cover the term using different lenses.

DDD focuses on understanding and modeling the complex business domains that software systems support. The goal of DDD is to align software systems with the underlying business domains they support, resulting in systems that are flexible, scalable, and maintainable. Here are the core principles of DDD in detail:

- **Ubiquitous language**: This principle states that a common language should be established between domain experts and software developers. This language should be used consistently throughout the development process, including modeling, coding, testing, and documentation. This helps to ensure that everyone involved in the development process has a shared understanding of the domain and reduces the risk of misunderstandings and miscommunication. For example, a financial institution's domain experts and software developers establish a common language to describe financial instruments such as bonds, stocks, and mutual funds. They use this language consistently throughout the development process, which helps to ensure that everyone involved has a shared understanding of these concepts and reduces the risk of misunderstandings and miscommunication.

- **Bounded contexts**: This principle states that different parts of a complex business domain should be divided into separate contexts. Each context should have a clear boundary and its own ubiquitous language. This helps to ensure that each context can be understood, modeled, and developed in isolation, which can reduce complexity and improve maintainability. For example, a retail company's business domain is divided into separate contexts for customer management, order management, inventory management, and shipping management.
- **Strategic design**: This principle states that the overall architecture and design of the software system should align with the long-term goals and vision of the business domain. This helps to ensure that the system is flexible and scalable, and can support the changing needs of the business over time. For example, a manufacturing company's software system is designed with a strategic focus on supporting the company's long-term goals and vision. The system is designed to be flexible and scalable, and to support the changing needs of the company over time, such as changes to the product line or manufacturing processes.

By following the above principles, DDD helps to ensure that software systems are aligned with the core business domains they are intended to support. Let's look into the components of DDD.

Components of DDD

While you have learned about the principles of DDD, to build your architecture, it is important to understand various components of it. The following are the key components that make up DDD:

- **Context mapping**: Context mapping is a technique for defining and organizing the different contexts within a business domain. Each context represents a distinct part of the business and has its own set of business rules and processes. The goal of context mapping is to identify the boundaries of each context and to define a common language that is used within each context. For example, a retail company may have a context for its online store, a context for its brick-and-mortar store, and a context for its fulfillment center. Each of these contexts would have a different set of business rules and processes, and a common language that is used within each context would help to ensure clear communication between the different parts of the business.
- **Domain model**: The domain model is the heart of DDD and represents the business domain in the form of entities, value objects, services, and aggregates. The domain model provides a way to understand and describe the business domain and to align the software system with the business domain.

For example, in a retail company, the domain model might include entities for products, customers, and orders, and value objects for prices and addresses.

- **Entity**: An entity is an object that represents a core business concept and has an identity that distinguishes it from other objects. An entity should encapsulate business logic and represent a meaningful, persistent part of the business domain. For example, in a retail company, the customer entity might include information about the customer, such as their name, address, and order history, as well as methods for performing actions, such as placing an order or updating their information.
- **Value object**: A value object is an object that represents a value or attribute and lacks an identity of its own. A value object should be freely used and shared, and should not change once created. For example, in a retail company, the price value object might represent the cost of a product, while the address value object might represent the shipping address for an order.
- **Aggregate**: An aggregate is a cluster of objects that should be treated as a single unit with regard to data changes. An aggregate should have a root object and a clear boundary that defines what objects belong to the aggregate. The goal of aggregates is to ensure consistency and maintain data integrity when making changes to the data. For example, in a retail company, the order aggregate might include the order entity, the customer entity, and the products that are part of the order.
- **Service**: A service is an object that encapsulates business logic that doesn't fit neatly into entities or value objects. A service should represent a business capability or process. For example, in a retail company, the order service might handle the process of creating and submitting an order, including checking inventory levels and calculating shipping costs.
- **Repository**: A repository is a pattern that defines a data access layer that abstracts the persistence of entities and aggregates. The goal of a repository is to provide a way to retrieve and store data in persistent storage, such as a database, while abstracting the underlying storage mechanism. For example, the order repository might provide a way to retrieve an order by its order number or to store a new order in the database.
- **Factory**: A factory is a pattern that defines a way to create objects, typically entities or aggregates, in a consistent and maintainable way. The goal of a factory is to provide a way to create objects in a standardized way, with any necessary dependencies, without having to write repetitive code. For example, the order factory might provide a way to create a new order object, complete with the customer and product entities that are part of the order.

- **Modules**: Modules are a way of organizing the code and defining boundaries within a system. A module is a collection of related entities, value objects, services, and repositories that work together to provide a specific business capability. Modules are used to separate the concerns of the system and to reduce complexity. Modules should be autonomous and self-contained and maintain their own integrity and consistency. An example of a module could be a module for handling customer orders in an e-commerce system. This module could include entities such as `Order`, `OrderItem`, `Customer`, and `Payment`, as well as services such as `OrderService`, `PaymentService`, and `ShippingService`.

Now you have learned about the principles and components of DDD, let's understand how you can implement it in the AWS platform.

Implementing DDD in AWS

Every application you build is associated with solving a specific business problem, especially when solving real-life problems belonging to an industry domain. An industry use case can be very complex, as seen in the previous section, where we used a retail industry use case to help understand various components of DDD. Now let's understand how to design this complex architecture using services provided by AWS. Implementing an Amazon.com-like e-commerce application using DDD in AWS would be a complex and multi-step process, but here is a general outline of the steps involved:

1. **Define the business domain**: Start by defining the different contexts within the business domain, such as the shopping context, the product context, and the fulfillment context. Create a domain model that represents the core business concepts, such as products, customers, and orders, and define their relationships with each other.
2. **Choose the right AWS services**: Based on the domain model, choose the right AWS services to implement the different components of DDD. For example, Amazon DynamoDB can be used to store entities and aggregate roots, Amazon SQS can be used to implement services, and Amazon S3 can be used for file storage.
3. **Implement the entities and value objects**: Implement the entities and value objects as DynamoDB tables, each with its own set of attributes and methods. Ensure that the data model is consistent with the domain model and that the entities and value objects are properly encapsulated.
4. **Implement the aggregates**: Implement the aggregates as a set of DynamoDB tables, with the root aggregate as the main table. Ensure that the aggregate boundaries are well defined and that the data is consistent within the aggregate.

Implement the aggregates as classes that represent a set of related entities and that enforce consistency within the aggregate.

5. **Implement the services**: Implement the services as classes using AWS Lambda functions, which use SQS to handle messages. Ensure that the services are aligned with the business processes and that they have access to the necessary data and entities.
6. **Implement the repositories**: Implement the repositories as DynamoDB Data Access Objects, which provide a way to store and retrieve data in persistent storage. Ensure that the repositories are aligned with the domain model and that they provide a consistent way to access data.
7. **Implement the factories**: Implement the factories as AWS Lambda functions, which use DynamoDB tables to store and retrieve data. Ensure that the factories are aligned with the domain model and that they provide a consistent way to create objects.
8. **Implement the user interface**: Implement the user interface as a web application that is hosted in AWS and that communicates with the backend services and repositories. Ensure that the user interface is aligned with the domain model and that it provides a consistent and intuitive experience for customers.
9. **Deploy and test the system**: Deploy the system in AWS using the appropriate AWS services and tools, such as AWS CloudFormation or AWS Elastic Beanstalk. Test the system to ensure that it is working as expected and that the data is consistent and accurate.
10. **Monitor and optimize**: Monitor the system using AWS CloudWatch and other AWS tools to ensure that it is running efficiently and that any issues are quickly addressed. Optimize the system as needed to improve performance and reduce costs.

You can choose an OOP language such as Java or Python to implement the entities, value objects, aggregates, services, repositories, and factories. In this case, objects and classes are used to represent the core business concepts and their attributes and behaviors. Here is an example of how objects and classes might be used in an e-commerce website:

- **Product**: A product is a core business concept in an e-commerce website and represents a physical or digital item that can be sold. A product object might have attributes such as name, description, price, and image. A product class might have methods such as `addToCart()`, `removeFromCart()`, and `getDetails()`.
- **Customer**: A customer is another core business concept in an e-commerce website and represents a person who can purchase products. A customer object might have attributes such as name, address, email, and phone number. A customer class might have methods such as `signUp()`, `login()`, and `updateProfile()`.

- **Order**: An order is a key business concept in an e-commerce website and represents a request by a customer to purchase one or more products. An order object might have attributes such as order number, customer, products, and total cost. An order class might have methods such as `placeOrder()`, `cancelOrder()`, and `getOrderHistory()`.
- **Cart**: A cart is a useful business concept in an e-commerce website and represents temporary storage for products that a customer has selected for purchase. A cart object might have attributes such as products and total cost. A cart class might have methods such as `addProduct()`, `removeProduct()`, and `checkout()`.

These objects and classes can be used in combination to implement the business processes and workflows of an e-commerce website, such as adding products to a cart, placing an order, and updating the customer's profile. By using OOP techniques, such as inheritance, encapsulation, and polymorphism, it is possible to build a scalable, maintainable, and reusable system that meets the needs of the business.

The above steps are just a general outline and the implementation details will vary depending on the specific requirements of your e-commerce business use case. However, by following the principles of DDD and using the right AWS services, you can build a scalable, reliable, and efficient system that meets the needs of your business.

Reasons to use DDD

In this section, we will learn about the most compelling benefits of DDD and what makes DDD so powerful. These benefits are described in the following list:

- **Better alignment with business goals**: DDD emphasizes the importance of a deep understanding of the business domain and its needs, leading to better alignment between the software system and the business goals.
- **Increased developer productivity**: By using clear and ubiquitous language and concepts, DDD helps to reduce misunderstandings and improve communication between developers, stakeholders, and domain experts. This leads to faster development and fewer mistakes.
- **Improved maintainability**: DDD encourages the use of a rich and expressive domain model, which can help to make the software system more understandable and maintainable over time.
- **Improved scalability**: DDD promotes the use of modular, scalable, and flexible architecture patterns, which can help to ensure that the software system can be easily adapted to meet changing business needs.

- **Improved domain knowledge**: By working closely with domain experts, developers can gain a deeper understanding of the business domain, which can help to inform future development efforts and lead to better software solutions.
- **Better testing and validation**: DDD encourages the use of **test-driven development** (**TDD**) and **behavior-driven development** (**BDD**) techniques, which can help to ensure that the software system meets the needs of the business and can be easily validated and tested.

The use of DDD can lead to improved software development outcomes and better alignment with business goals, resulting in increased productivity; improved maintainability, scalability, and domain knowledge; and better testing and validation.

Challenges with DDD

As is the case with any technology and any design philosophy, DDD is not a magic bullet. Now we will examine the challenges that you might encounter when implementing the DDD methodology in your projects in your organization:

- **Domain expertise**: Your project might have experienced developers and architects who are well versed in the tools being used, but if at least some of your team members don't have domain expertise in the domain being modeled, then the project is destined to fail. If you don't have this domain expertise, it's probably best not to use DDD and perhaps not even start your project until someone on your team acquires this skill set, regardless of the methodology used.
- **Iterative development**: Agile development has become a popular methodology. A well-implemented Agile program allows companies to deliver value quicker and for less cost. DDD heavily relies on iterative practices such as Agile. One of the key benefits of combining DDD and Agile is the ability to quickly and iteratively refine the software system as the needs of the business change over time. This can help to ensure that the software system remains aligned with business goals and is capable of adapting to changing business requirements. However, enterprises often struggle to transition from the traditional and less flexible waterfall models to the new methodologies.
- **Technical projects**: There is no magic hammer in software development, and DDD is no exception. DDD shines with projects that have a great deal of domain complexity. The more complicated the business logic of your application, the more relevant DDD is. DDD is not well suited for applications with low domain complexity but a lot of technical complexity.

An example of low domain complexity with high technical complexity could be a system for tracking weather data. The domain itself is relatively simple, with a limited number of concepts, such as temperature, humidity, and wind speed. However, the technical complexity of the system could be high, due to the need to process large amounts of data in real time, handle multiple data sources, and display the data in a user-friendly way. An example of high domain complexity with low technical complexity could be a banking system. The domain itself is complex, with many concepts, such as accounts, transactions, loans, and investments. However, the technical complexity of the system may be low, as the implementation could be based on established and well-understood banking software systems. DDD is well suited for projects with high domain complexity and low technical complexity, where a deep understanding of the business domain is essential to the success of the project. This is because DDD focuses on building a rich and expressive domain model, which is used as the foundation for the software system, and to ensure that the software system accurately reflects the business domain.

Although these disadvantages exist, using DDD for microservice architectures can still be an excellent way of improving software development outcomes in many scenarios.

Summary

In this chapter, you explored microservice architecture and learned about popular patterns such as layered architecture, EDA, and DDD. You learned about the advantages and disadvantages of EDA, when to use it, and how to troubleshoot if things go wrong.

Next, you went through the recommended best practices in the development of microservices. You can leverage the list of tried-and-true best practices in your next project and benefit from them.

Not using architectures such as EDA in a modern-day enterprise is no longer an option. If you continue to use legacy patterns, it is a surefire way for your project and your company to stay stuck in the past and lag behind your competition. A microservice architecture will make your application more scalable, more maintainable, and relevant.

Finally, you further explored how DDD has evolved and can address complex industry use cases to solve business problems. You learned about the principles and components of DDD and used them to design a domain-heavy e-commerce app using AWS services.

Once you build your business app, getting data insight for continuous growth is essential. In the next chapter, you will learn about data lake patterns to get insight from your enterprise data.

15

Data Lake Patterns – Integrating Your Data across the Enterprise

Today, technology companies like Amazon, Google, Netflix, and Facebook drive immense success as they can get insight from their data and understand what customers want. They personalize the experience in front of you, for example, movie suggestions from Netflix, shopping suggestions from Amazon, and search selections from Google. All of their success is credited to being able to dig into data and utilize that for customer engagement. That's why data is now considered the new oil.

Picture this – you are getting ready to watch television, excited to see your favorite show. You sit down and try to change the channel, only to find that the remote control is not working. You try to find batteries. You know you have some in the house but you don't remember where you put them. Panic sets in, and you finally give up looking and go to the store to get more batteries.

A similar pattern repeats over and over in today's enterprises. Many companies have the data they need to survive and thrive but need help accessing the data effectively, turning it into actionable and valuable information, and getting that information to the right people on a timely basis.

The data lake pattern is handy in today's enterprise to overcome this challenge. In this chapter, you will learn about data lakes through the following main topics:

- The definition of a data lake
- The purpose of a data lake
- Data lake components

- AWS Lake Formation
- Data lake best practices
- Key metrics of a data lake
- Lakehouse and data mesh architecture
- Choosing between a data lake, lakehouse, and data mesh architecture

Let's dive deep into the world of data and ways to get meaningful data insight.

Definition of a data lake

Data is everywhere today. It was always there, but it was too expensive to keep it. With the massive drops in storage costs, enterprises keep much of what they were throwing away before. And this is the problem. Many enterprises are collecting, ingesting, and purchasing vast amounts of data but need help to gain insights from it. Many Fortune 500 companies are generating data faster than they can process it. The maxim *data is the new gold* has a lot of truth, but just like gold, data needs to be mined, distributed, polished, and seen.

The data that companies are generating is richer than ever before, and the amount they are generating is growing at an exponential rate. Fortunately, the processing power needed to harness this data deluge is increasing and becoming cheaper. Cloud technologies such as AWS allow us to process data almost instantaneously and in a massive fashion.

A **data lake** is an architectural approach that helps you manage multiple data types from a wide variety of structured and unstructured sources through a unified set of tools. A data lake is a centralized data repository containing structured, semi-structured, and unstructured data at any scale. Data can be stored in its raw form without any transformations, or some preprocessing can be done before it is consumed. From this repository, data can be extracted and consumed to populate dashboards, perform analytics, and drive machine learning pipelines to derive insights and enhance decision-making. Hence, the data stored in a data lake is readily available to be categorized, processed, analyzed, and consumed by diverse organizational groups.

Data lakes allow you to break down data silos and bring data into a single central repository, such as Amazon S3. You can store various data formats at any scale and at a low cost. Data lakes provide you with a single source of truth and allow you to access the same data using a variety of analytics and machine learning tools.

The following diagram shows the key components of modern data architecture:

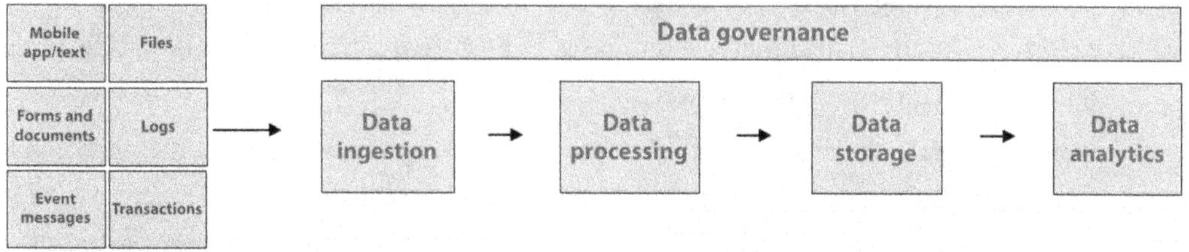

Figure 15.1: Key components of a modern data lake

The above diagram shows modern data architecture where data is ingested in different formats such as logs, files, messages, documents, and so on. After that, this data is processed as per business needs, and processed data get stored and consumed by various businesses for data analytics.

The key considerations of modern data lakes include the ability to handle the increasing volume, velocity, and variety of data where each component, such as data storage and processing, should be independently scalable and data should be easily accessible by various stack holders.

The purpose of a data lake

You might not need a data lake if your company is a bootstrap start-up with a small client base. However, even the smaller entities that adopt the data lake pattern in their data ingestion and consumption will be nimbler than their competitors. Especially if you already have other systems in place, adopting a data lake will come at a high cost. The benefits must outweigh these costs, but this might be the difference between crushing your competitors and being thrust into the pile of failed companies in the long run.

The purpose of a data lake is to provide a single store for all data types, structures, and volumes, to support multiple use cases such as big data analytics, data warehousing, machine learning, and more. It enables organizations to store data in its raw form and perform transformations as needed, making it easier to extract value from data. When you are building a data lake, consider the following five V's of big data:

1. **Volume:** Refers to the sheer amount of data generated and stored by various sources, such as social media, IoT devices, and transactional systems. For example, a large retailer may generate and store petabytes of data from online and in-store sales transactions, customer behavior data, and product information.

2. **Velocity**: Refers to the speed at which data is generated and processed. Data can be generated in real time, such as stock market prices or weather readings from IoT devices. For example, a financial firm may need to process high-frequency stock market data in real time to make informed trading decisions.
3. **Variety**: Refers to the different types of data generated by various sources, including structured data (for example, relational databases), semi-structured data (for example, XML, JSON), and unstructured data (for example, text, images, and audio). For example, a healthcare organization may need to process and analyze a variety of data types, including electronic medical records, imaging data, and patient feedback.
4. **Veracity**: Refers to the uncertainty, ambiguity, and incompleteness of data. Big data often comes from sources that could be controlled better, such as social media, and may contain errors, inconsistencies, and biases. For example, a political campaign may use social media data to gain insights into public opinion but must be aware of the potential for false or misleading information.
5. **Value**: Refers to the potential of data to provide insights and drive business decisions. The value of big data lies in its ability to reveal patterns, trends, and relationships that can inform strategy and decision-making. For example, a retail company may use big data analytics to identify purchasing patterns and make personalized product recommendations to customers.

Some of the benefits of having a data lake are as follows:

- **Increasing operational efficiency**: Finding your data and deriving insights from it becomes more accessible with a data lake.
- **Making data more available across the organizations and busting silos**: Having a centralized location will enable everyone in the organization to access the same data if they are authorized to access it.
- **Lowering transactional costs**: Having the correct data at the right time and with minimal effort will invariably result in lower costs.
- **Removing load from operational systems such as mainframes and data warehouses**: Having a dedicated data lake will enable you to optimize it for analytical processing and enable you to optimize your operational systems to focus on their primary mission of supporting day-to-day transactions and operations.

C-Suite executives are no longer asking, *"Do we need a data lake?"* but rather, *"How do we implement a data lake?"* They realize that many of their competitors are doing the same, and studies have shown that organizations derive real value from data lakes. An Aberdeen survey saw that enterprises that deploy a data lake in their organization could outperform competitors by 9% in incremental revenue growth. You can find more information on the Aberdeen survey here: `https://tinyurl.com/r26c2lg`.

Components of a data lake

The concept of a data lake can vary in meaning to different individuals. As previously mentioned, a data lake can consist of various components, including both structured and unstructured data, raw and transformed data, and a mix of different data types and sources. As a result, there is no one-size-fits-all approach to creating a data lake. The process of constructing a clean and secure data lake can be time-consuming and may take several months to complete, as there are numerous steps involved in the process. Let's take a look at the components that need to be used when building a data lake:

- **Data ingestion**: The process of collecting and importing data into the data lake from various sources such as databases, logs, APIs, and IoT devices. For example, a data lake may ingest data from a relational database, log files from web servers, and real-time data from IoT devices.
- **Data storage**: The component that stores the raw data in its original format without any transformations or schema enforcement. Typically, data is stored in a distributed file system such as Hadoop HDFS or Amazon S3. For example, a data lake may store petabytes of data in its raw form, including structured, semi-structured, and unstructured data.
- **Data catalog**: A metadata management system that keeps track of the data stored in the data lake, including data lineage, definitions, and relationships between data elements. For example, a data catalog may provide information about the structure of data in the data lake, who created it, when it was created, and how it can be used.
- **Data processing**: The component that performs transformations on the data to prepare it for analysis. This can include data cleansing, enrichment, and aggregation. For example, a data processing layer may perform data cleansing to remove errors and inconsistencies from the data or perform data enrichment to add additional information to the data.

- **Data analytics**: The component that provides tools and technologies for data analysis and visualization. This can include SQL engines, machine learning libraries, and visualization tools. For example, a data analytics layer may provide an SQL engine for running ad-hoc queries or a machine learning library for building predictive models.
- **Data access**: The component that provides access to the data in the data lake, including data APIs, data virtualization, and data integration. For example, a data access layer may provide APIs for accessing data in the data lake, or data virtualization to provide a unified view of data from multiple sources.

It is common to divide a data lake into different zones based on data access patterns, privacy and security requirements, and data retention policies. Let's look at various data lake zones.

Data lake zones

Creating a data lake can be a lengthy and demanding undertaking that involves substantial effort to set up workflows for data access and transformation, configure security and policy settings, and deploy various tools and services for data movement, storage, cataloging, security, analytics, and machine learning. In general, many data lakes are implemented using the following logical zones:

- **Raw zone**: This is the initial storage area for incoming data in its original format without any modification or transformation. The data is stored as-is, allowing for easy access and preservation of its original state. An example use case for this zone could be storing social media data as raw JSON files for later analysis.
- **Landing zone**: The landing zone is a temporary storage area for incoming data that undergoes basic validation, quality checks, and initial processing. Data is moved from the raw zone to the landing zone before being moved to the next stage. An example use case for the landing zone could be performing data quality checks such as duplicate removal and data type validation on incoming sales data before it is moved to the next stage.
- **Staging zone**: The staging zone is where data is transformed and integrated with other data sources before being stored in the final storage area. The data is processed in this zone to prepare it for analysis and to help ensure consistency and accuracy. An example use case for the staging zone could be transforming incoming sales data into a common format and integrating it with other data sources to create a single view of the data.
- **Analytics zone**: The analytics zone is optimized for data analysis and exploration. Data stored in this zone is made available to data scientists, business analysts, and other users for reporting and analysis. An example use case for this zone could be storing sales data in a columnar format for faster querying and analysis.

- **Data mart zone:** The data mart zone is used to create isolated and curated data subsets for specific business or operational use cases. This zone is optimized for specific business requirements and can be used to support reporting, analysis, and decision-making. An example use case for the data mart zone could be creating a data subset of sales data for a specific product line for analysis.
- **Archive zone:** The archive zone is the final storage area for data that is no longer needed for active use but needs to be retained for compliance or historical purposes. Data stored in this zone is typically rarely accessed and is optimized for long-term storage. An example use case for this zone could be storing customer data that is no longer needed for active use but needs to be retained for compliance reasons.

Each zone in a data lake has specific security and access controls, data retention policies, and data management processes, depending on the specific use case and data requirements.

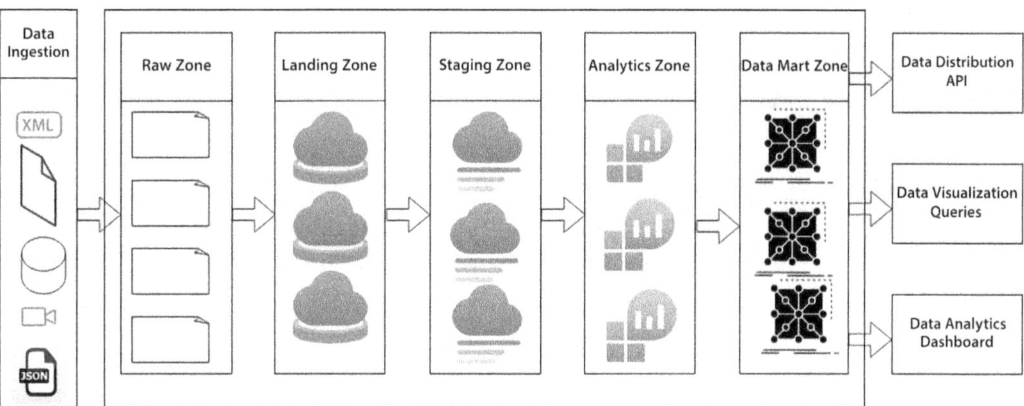

Figure 15.2: The different zones of a data lake

As shown in the diagram above, the flow of data among the different zones in a data lake is a key aspect of the architecture. It typically follows the steps below:

1. Raw data is collected and stored in the raw zone in its original format.
2. The data is then moved to the landing zone, where it undergoes initial processing such as basic validation, quality checks, and removal of duplicates.
3. After the initial processing, the data is moved to the staging zone, where it undergoes transformation and integration with other data sources to prepare it for analysis.
4. The processed data is then moved to the analytics zone, where it is optimized for analysis and made available to data scientists, business analysts, and other users for exploration and reporting.

5. Based on specific business or operational requirements, subsets of the data may be created and stored in the data mart zone for specific analysis and reporting needs.

This flow ensures that the data is processed and stored to support its intended use and meets the required security, privacy, and compliance requirements. The flow also helps ensure data consistency and accuracy as the data moves through the different processing stages. If data is no longer needed for active use but needs to be retained for compliance or historical purposes, you can also create an archive zone for long-term storage.

These zones and their names should not be taken as dogma. Many folks use other labels for these zones and might use more or fewer zones. But these zones capture the general idea of what is required for a well-architected data lake.

An analogy that can help to understand how the various zones in a data lake work is how gold is mined, distributed, and sold. Gold is a scarce resource and is often found in small quantities combined with many other materials that have no value to the people mining it.

When it's mined in industrial quantities, excavators dump dirt into a truck or a conveyor belt (this is the ingestion step in the landing zone and raw zone). This dirt goes through a cleansing process (analogous to the data quality step in the curated or staging zone). The gold is set aside, turned into ingots or bars, and transported for further processing (like the curation in the analytics zone). Finally, these gold bars may be melted down and turned into jewelry or industrial parts so individuals can use them for different purposes, which can relate to the data mart zone.

Data lakes in AWS with Lake Formation

Lake Formation is a fully managed data lake service provided by AWS that enables data engineers and analysts to build a secure data lake. Lake Formation provides an orchestration layer combining AWS services such as S3, RDS, EMR, and Glue to ingest and clean data with centralized fine-grain data security management.

Lake Formation lets you establish your data lake on Amazon S3 and begin incorporating readily accessible data. As you incorporate additional data sources, Lake Formation will scan those sources and transfer the data into your Amazon S3 data lake. Utilizing machine learning, Lake Formation will automatically structure the data into Amazon S3 partitions, convert it into more efficient formats for analytics, such as Apache Parquet and ORC, and eliminate duplicates and identify matching records to enhance the quality of your data.

It enables you to establish all necessary permissions for your data lake, which will be enforced across all services that access the data, such as Amazon Redshift, Amazon Athena, and Amazon EMR. This eliminates the need to reapply policies across multiple services and ensures consistent enforcement and adherence to those policies, streamlining compliance.

Lake Formation relies on AWS Glue behind the scenes, where Glue crawlers and connections aid in connecting to and identifying the raw data that requires ingestion. Glue jobs then generate the necessary code to transfer the data into the data lake. The Glue data catalog organizes the metadata, and Glue workflows link together crawlers and jobs, enabling the monitoring of individual work processes. The following diagram shows a comprehensive view of the AWS data lake:

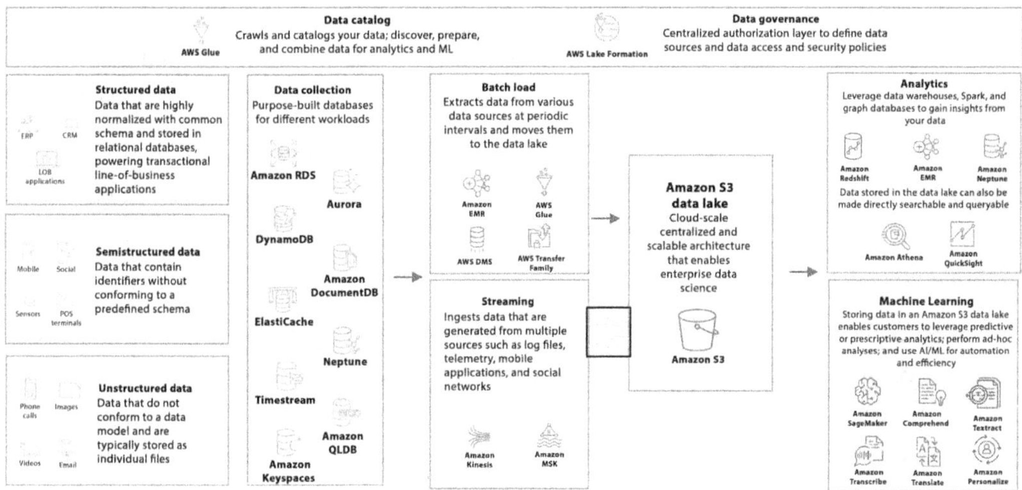

Figure 15.3: AWS data lake components

As shown in the preceding diagram, below are the steps to create a data lake in AWS using Lake Formation:

1. Set up an AWS account and create an **Identity and Access Management** (**IAM**) role with the necessary permissions to access Lake Formation and other AWS services.
2. Launch the Lake Formation console and create a new data lake.
3. Ingest data into the data lake from a variety of sources such as Amazon S3, Amazon Redshift, Amazon RDS, and others.
4. Define the data catalog by creating tables, columns, and partitions and registering them with the Lake Formation data catalog.

5. Set up data access and security policies using IAM and Lake Formation to control who can access the data and what actions they can perform.
6. Perform transformations on the data in the data lake using AWS Glue or other tools.
7. Analyze the data using Amazon QuickSight, Amazon Athena, or other analytics tools.

Let's say you want to create a data lake to store customer data from an e-commerce website. For that, you need to ingest customer data into the data lake from your e-commerce website's database, which is stored in Amazon RDS. Then you can define the data catalog by creating tables for customer information, purchase history, and product information and registering them with the Lake Formation data catalog. You can perform transformations on the customer data in the data lake using AWS Glue to convert the data into a common format, remove duplicates, and perform data validation. Finally, you can analyze the customer data using Amazon QuickSight or Amazon Athena to create visualizations and reports on customer behavior and purchase patterns.

The steps and tools used may vary depending on the requirements and data sources. These steps are provided as a general guide and may need to be adapted based on the specific needs of your use case. You can refer AWS Lake formation guide for more details – `https://docs.aws.amazon.com/lake-formation/latest/dg/getting-started.html`.

From a data security perspective, the Lake Formation admin set up permission on the database, table, and column and granted granular row and column level permission to data lake users for data access. Lake Formation works in conjunction with AWS IAM to build security controls. Lake Formation enhances the search functionality by enabling text-based and faceted search across all metadata. It also adds attributes such as data owners and stewards as table properties, along with column properties and definitions such as data sensitivity level. Additionally, it offers audit logs for data lake auditing during data ingestion and cataloging while notifications are published to Amazon CloudWatch events and the console.

Data lake best practices

In this section, we will analyze best practices to improve the usability of your data lake implementation that will empower users to get their work done more efficiently and allow them to find what they need more quickly.

Centralized data management

Depending on your company culture, and regardless of how good your technology stack is, you might have a mindset roadblock among your ranks, where departments within the enterprise still have a tribal mentality and refuse to disseminate information outside of their domain.

For this reason, when implementing your data lake, it is critical to ensure that this mentality does not persist in the new environment. Establishing a well-architected enterprise data lake can go a long way toward breaking down these silos.

Centralized data management refers to the practice of storing all data in a single, centralized repository rather than in disparate locations or silos. This makes managing, accessing, and analyzing the data easier and eliminates the risk of data duplication and inconsistency.

A use case for centralized data management could be for a large e-commerce company that has customer data stored in multiple systems, such as an online store, a call center database, and a mobile app. The company could centralize this data in a data lake to improve data accuracy, ensure consistency, and provide a single source of truth for customer data.

The process of centralized data management in this scenario would involve extracting data from the various systems, cleaning and transforming the data to ensure consistency, and then storing it in a data lake. This centralized repository could be accessed by various departments within the company, such as marketing, sales, and customer service, to support their decision-making and improve customer experience.

By centralizing data, the company can improve data governance, minimize the risk of data duplication and inconsistency, and reduce the time and effort required to access and analyze the data. This ultimately leads to improved business outcomes and competitive advantage.

Data governance

One of the biggest challenges when implementing a data lake is the ability to fully trust the current data's integrity, source, and lineage.

For the data in a lake to provide value, more is needed than just dumping the data into the lake. Raw data will not be valuable if it does not have structure and a connection to the business and is not cleansed and deduplicated. If data governance were built for the lake, users would be able to trust the data in the lake. Ungoverned data that does not possess data lineage is much less valuable and trustworthy than data with these qualities. Data lineage refers to the complete history of a data element, including its origin, transformations, movements, and dependencies. Ungoverned data increases regulatory and privacy compliance risks. Analysis and transformation of initially incorrect and incomplete data will result in incorrect and incomplete data, and most likely, any insights derived from this data will be inaccurate.

To fully trust and track the data in the lake, we need to provide context to the data by instituting policy-driven processes to enable the classification and identification of the ingested data. We need to put a data governance program in place for the data lake and leverage any existing data governance programs. Wherever possible, we should use existing data governance frameworks and councils to govern the data lake.

The enormous volume and variability of data in today's organizations complicate the tagging and enrichment of data with the data's origin, format, lineage, organization, classification, and ownership information. Most data is fluid and dynamic, and performing exploratory data analysis to understand it is often essential to determine its quality and significance. Data governance provides a systematic structure to gain an understanding of and confidence in your data assets. To set a foundation, let's agree on a definition of data governance.

Data governance refers to the set of policies, processes, and roles that organizations establish to ensure their data's quality, security, and availability. Data governance aims to improve data management and decision making by ensuring that data is accurate, consistent, secure, and accessible to those who need it.

A use case for data governance could be for a healthcare organization that collects patient data from various sources, such as electronic medical records, clinical trials, and wearable devices. The organization needs to ensure that this data is protected and used in a manner that complies with privacy regulations and patient consent.

The process of implementing data governance in this scenario would involve defining policies and processes for data collection, storage, use, and protection. This could include processes for data classification, data access controls, data quality control, and data auditing. The organization would also establish roles and responsibilities for data governance, such as data stewards, administrators, and security personnel.

By implementing data governance, the healthcare organization can ensure that patient data is protected and used responsibly, improve the quality and consistency of its data, and reduce the risk of data breaches and regulatory violations. This ultimately leads to improved patient trust and better decision-making based on accurate and secure data.

If the data's integrity can be trusted, it can guide decisions and gain insights. Data governance is imperative, yet many enterprises need to value it more. The only thing worse than data that you know is inaccurate is data that you think is accurate, even though it's inaccurate.

Here are a few business benefits of data lake governance:

- Data governance enables the identification of data ownership, which aids in understanding who has the answers if you have questions about the data. For example, were these numbers produced by the CFO or an external agency? Did the CFO approve them?
- Data governance facilitates the adoption of data definitions and standards that help to relate technical metadata to business terms. For example, we may have these technical metadata terms: `f_name`, `first_name`, and `fn`, but they all refer to the standardized business term "*First Name*." They have been associated via a data governance process.
- Data governance aids in the remediation processes that need to be done for data by providing workflows and escalation procedures to report inaccuracies in data. For example, a data governance tool with workflows, such as Informatica MDM, Talent Data Stewardship, or Collibra, may be implemented to provide this escalation process. Has this quarter's inventory been performed, validated, and approved by the appropriate parties?
- Data governance allows us to make assessments of the data's usability for a given business domain, which minimizes the likelihood of errors and inconsistencies when creating reports and deriving insights. For example, how clean is the list of email addresses we received? If the quality is low, we can still use them, knowing we will get many bouncebacks. You can use tools like ZeroBounce or NeverBounce to validate emails.
- Data governance enables the lockdown of sensitive data and helps you implement controls on the authorized users of the data. This minimizes the possibility of data theft and the theft of trade secrets. For example, for any sensitive data, we should consistently implement a "need to know" policy and lock down access as much as possible. A "need to know" policy is a principle that restricts access to information only to those individuals who need it in order to perform their job responsibilities effectively.

Data cataloging

Data cataloging refers to the process of organizing, documenting, and storing metadata about data assets within an organization. The purpose of data cataloging is to provide a central repository of information about data assets, making it easier for organizations to discover, understand, and manage their data. For example, a company maintains a customer information database, including customer name, address, phone number, and order history. The data catalog for this database might include metadata about the database itself, such as its purpose, data sources, update frequency, data owners and stewards, and any known data quality issues. It would also include information about each data element, such as its definition, data type, and any transformations or calculations performed.

It would be best if you used metadata and data catalogs to improve discovery and facilitate reusability. Let's list some of the metadata that is tracked by many successful implementations and that we might want to track in our implementation:

- **Access Control List (ACL)**: Access list for the resource (allow or, in rare cases, deny). For example, Joe, Mary, and Bill can access the inventory data. Bill can also modify the data. No one else has access.
- **Owner**: The responsible party for this resource. For example, Bill is the owner of the inventory data.
- **Date created**: The date the resource was created. For example, the inventory data was last updated on 12/20/2022.
- **Data source and lineage**: The origin and lineage path for the resource. In most cases, the lineage metadata should be included as part of the ingestion process in an automated manner. In rare cases where metadata is not included during ingestion, the lineage metadata information may be added manually. An example of this would be when files are brought into the data lake outside of the normal ingestion process. Users should be able to quickly determine where data came from and how it got to its current state. The provenance of a certain data point should be recorded to track its lineage.
- **Job name**: The name of the job that ingested and/or transformed the file.
- **Data quality**: For some of the data in the lake, data quality metrics will be applied to the data after the data is loaded, and the data quality score will be recorded in the metadata. The data in the lake is only sometimes perfectly clean, but there should be a mechanism to determine the data quality. This context will add transparency and confidence to the data in the lake. Users will confidently derive insights and create reports from the data lake with the assurance that the underlying data is trustworthy. For example, the metadata may be that a list of emails had a 7% bounce rate the last time it was used.
- **Format type**: With some file formats, it is not immediately apparent what the file format is. Having this information in the metadata can be helpful in some instances. For example, types may include JSON, XML, Parquet, Avro, and so on.
- **File structure**: In the case of JSON, XML, and similar semi-structured formats, a reference to a metadata definition can be helpful.
- **Approval and certification**: Once either automated or manual processes have validated a file, the associated metadata indicating this approval and certification will be appended to the metadata. Has the data been approved and/or certified by the appropriate parties?

Datasets should only be moved to the trusted data zone once this certification has been achieved. For example, inventory numbers may be approved by the finance department.

- **Business term mappings**: Any technical metadata items, such as tables and columns, always have a corresponding business term. For example, a table cryptically called `SFDC_ACCTS` could have an associated corresponding business term, such as `Authorized Accounts`. This business term data doesn't necessarily have to be embedded in the metadata. We could reference the location of the definition for the business term in the enterprise business glossary.
- **Personally Identifiable Information (PII), General Data Protection Regulation (GDPR), confidential, restricted, and other flags and labels**: Sometimes, we can determine whether data contains PII depending on where the data landed, but to increase compliance further, data should be tagged with the appropriate sensitivity labels.
- **Physical structure, redundancy checks, and job validation**: Data associated with data validation. For example, this could be the number of columns, rows, and so on.
- **Business purpose and reason**: A requirement to add data to a lake is that the data should be at least potentially useful. Minimum requirements should be laid out to ingest data into the lake, and the purpose of the data or a reference to the purpose can be added to the metadata.
- **Data domain and meaning**: It is only sometimes apparent what business terms and domains are associated with data. It is helpful to have this available.

There are a variety of ways that data governance metadata can be tracked. The recommended approaches are as follows:

- S3 metadata
- S3 tags
- An enhanced data catalog using AWS Glue

Data cataloging plays a crucial role in modern data management, enabling organizations to understand their data assets better, improve data quality, and support data-driven decision-making.

Data quality control

You need to validate and clean data before it is stored in the data lake to ensure data accuracy and completeness. Data quality control refers to the set of processes, techniques, and tools used to ensure that data is accurate, complete, consistent, and reliable. Data quality control aims to improve the quality of data used in decision-making, reducing the risk of errors and increasing trust in data.

For example, a retail company wants to ensure that the data it collects about its customers is accurate and up to date. The company might implement data quality control processes such as data profiling, data cleansing, and data standardization to achieve this. Data profiling involves analyzing the data to identify patterns and anomalies, while data cleansing involves correcting or removing inaccuracies and duplicates. Data standardization involves ensuring that data is consistently formatted and entered in a standardized manner. The following are some use cases for data quality control:

- **Decision-making**: By ensuring that data is accurate, complete, and consistent, data quality control enables organizations to make informed decisions based on reliable data.
- **Data integration**: Data quality control is critical for successful data integration, as it helps to ensure that data from different sources can be seamlessly combined without errors.
- **Customer relationship management**: High-quality data is critical for effective customer relationship management, as it allows enterprises to understand their customers better and provide them with personalized experiences.
- **Fraud detection**: Data quality control helps organizations to detect and prevent fraud by identifying and correcting errors and inconsistencies in data.
- **Compliance**: By ensuring that data is accurate and consistent, data quality control helps organizations to meet regulatory compliance requirements and avoid penalties.

Data quality control is a crucial aspect of modern data management for helping organizations ensure their data is reliable, and supporting informed decision making.

Data security

You should implement security measures to ensure your data's confidentiality, integrity, and availability. Data security best practices for data lakes can be divided into several categories, including:

- **Access control**: Control access to the data lake and its contents through **role-based access management** (**RBAC**) and multi-factor authentication. Use access control policies that specify who can access what data and what actions they can perform. For example, an online retailer can use access control to restrict access to its customer data to only those employees who need it to perform their job functions.
- **Data encryption**: Encrypt sensitive data at rest, in transit, and while being processed. The data lake can use encryption keys managed by **Key Management Service** (**KMS**) to encrypt data. For example, a healthcare organization can use data encryption to secure patient health information stored in the data lake.

- **Data masking**: Mask sensitive data elements within the data lake to prevent unauthorized access. Masking can be applied to columns, rows, or entire tables. For example, a financial organization can use data masking to protect sensitive customer information like account numbers and personal details within the data lake.
- **Data auditing**: Monitor and log all access to data in the data lake, including who accessed it, when, and what actions were performed. This helps to detect and respond to security incidents. For example, an energy company can use data auditing to monitor and log access to its data in the data lake to help detect and respond to security incidents.

Security is always a critical consideration when implementing search projects across the enterprise. AWS realized this early on. Like many other services in the AWS stack, many AWS offerings in the search space integrate seamlessly and easily with the **AWS Identity and Access Management (AWS IAM)** service. Having this integration does not mean we can push a button, and our search solution will be guaranteed secure. Similar to other integrations with IAM, we still have to ensure that our IAM policies match our business security policies. We have robust security to ensure that authorized users can only access sensitive data and that our company's system administrators can only change these security settings.

As mentioned previously in this chapter, AWS Lake Formation is a service that makes it easier to build, secure, and manage data lakes. It also provides several security features to ensure that the data stored in the data lake is secure:

- **Access control**: Lake Formation provides fine-grained access control to data in the lake using AWS IAM policies. You can grant or revoke permissions to access the data lake and its contents, such as data tables and columns, based on user identities, such as AWS accounts or AWS **Single Sign-On (SSO)** identities.
- **Data encryption**: Lake Formation integrates with AWS KMS to provide encryption of data at rest and in transit. You can encrypt data in the lake using encryption keys managed by KMS to secure sensitive data.
- **VPC protection**: Lake Formation integrates with Amazon VPC to provide network-level security for data in the lake. You can secure access to the data lake by limiting access to specific VPC or IP addresses.
- **Audit logging**: Lake Formation provides audit logging for data access, modification, and deletion. You can use audit logs to monitor and track activities performed on the data lake and its contents.

- **Data masking**: Lake Formation provides data masking to protect sensitive data in the lake. You can mask sensitive data elements within the data lake to prevent unauthorized access, including columns, rows, or entire tables.
- **Data governance**: Lake Formation provides data governance features to manage and enforce data usage and protection policies. This includes classifying data based on its sensitivity, implementing retention policies, and enforcing data retention schedules.

These security features in Lake Formation help you secure data in the data lake and meet regulatory requirements for protecting sensitive data. They allow you to control access to the data lake and its contents, encrypt sensitive data, and monitor and log all activities performed on the data lake.

Data ingestion

You should automate data ingestion from various sources to ensure timely and consistent data loading. To ensure efficient, secure, and high-quality data ingestion, it's important to follow best practices, including:

- **Data validation**: Validate the data before ingestion to ensure it's complete, accurate, and consistent. This includes checking for missing values, incorrect data types, and out-of-range values. For example, an e-commerce company can use data validation to ensure that customer data is complete, accurate, and consistent before storing it in the data lake.
- **Data transformation**: Transform the data into a consistent format suitable for storage in the data lake. This includes standardizing data types, converting data into a common format, and removing duplicates. For example, a telecommunications company can use data transformation to convert customer call records into a common format suitable for storage in the data lake.
- **Data normalization**: Normalize the data to ensure it's structured in a way that makes it easier to analyze. This includes defining common data definitions, data relationships, and data hierarchies. For example, a financial organization can use data normalization to ensure that financial data is structured in a way that makes it easier to analyze.
- **Data indexing**: Index the data to make it easier to search and retrieve. This includes creating metadata indices, full-text indices, and columnar indices. For example, an online retailer can use data indexing to make it easier to search and retrieve customer data stored in the data lake.
- **Data compression**: Compress the data to reduce its size and improve ingestion performance. This includes using compression algorithms like Gzip, Snappy, and LZ4.

For example, a media company can use data compression to reduce the size of video files stored in the data lake, improving ingestion performance.

- **Data partitioning**: Partition of the data to improve performance and scalability. This includes partitioning the data by date, time, location, or other relevant criteria. For example, a logistics company can use data partitioning to improve the performance and scalability of delivery data stored in the data lake, partitioning the data by delivery location.

Your data lake may store terabytes to petabytes of data. Let's see data lake scalability best practices.

Data lake scalability

You should design your data lake to be scalable to accommodate future data volume, velocity, and variety growth. Data lake scalability refers to the ability of a data lake to handle increasing amounts of data and processing requirements over time. The scalability of a data lake is critical to ensure that it can support growing business needs and meet evolving data processing requirements.

Data partitioning divides data into smaller chunks, allows for parallel processing, and reduces the amount of data that needs to be processed at any given time, improving scalability. You can use distributed storage to store the data across multiple nodes in a distributed manner, allowing for more storage capacity and improved processing power, increasing scalability. Compressing data can reduce its size, improve scalability by reducing the amount of storage required, and improve processing time.

From an AWS perspective, you can use Amazon S3 as your storage, which helps you with a serverless computing model for data processing and allows for the automatic scaling of resources based on demand, improving scalability. You can use EMR and Glue to process data from S3 and store it back whenever needed. In that way, you will be decoupling storage and compute, which will help achieve scalability and reduce cost. Let's look at best practices to reduce costs.

Data lake cost optimization

Using cost-effective solutions and optimizing data processing jobs, you should minimize storage and processing costs. Data lake costs can quickly add up, especially as the amount of data stored in the lake grows over time. To reduce and optimize the cost of a data lake, it's important to follow best practices such as: compressing data to reduce its size, reducing storage costs and improving processing time; partitioning data into smaller chunks to allow for parallel processing; and reducing the amount of data that needs to be processed at any given time, improving processing performance and reducing costs.

Further, you can optimize the use of compute and storage resources, reduce costs by reducing resource waste, and maximize resource utilization and cost-effective storage options, such as Amazon S3 object storage or tiered storage, which can reduce storage costs while still providing adequate storage capacity. Implementing a serverless computing model with AWS Glue for data processing can reduce costs by allowing for the automatic scaling of resources based on demand, reducing the need for expensive dedicated resources.

Monitoring a data lake for performance optimization

You should monitor the performance of your data lake and optimize it to ensure that it meets your performance requirements. Data lake monitoring and performance optimization are critical components of a well-designed data lake architecture. These practices help to ensure that the data lake is functioning optimally and that any performance issues are quickly identified and resolved.

Continuously monitoring the performance of the data lake, including storage and compute utilization, can help identify and resolve performance issues before they become critical. You should define and track performance metrics, such as query response time and data processing time, which can help identify performance bottlenecks and inform optimization efforts.

Further, analyzing log data can provide insight into the performance of the data lake and help identify performance issues by regularly loading and testing the data lake can help identify performance bottlenecks and inform optimization efforts. Automatically scaling resources, such as compute and storage, based on usage patterns can improve performance and prevent performance issues.

Flexible data processing in the data lake

You should choose a data processing solution that can handle batch, real-time, and streaming data processing to accommodate a variety of use cases. Flexible data processing is an important aspect of data lake design, allowing for processing different types of data using various tools and techniques. Data lake should support a variety of data formats, including structured, semi-structured, and unstructured data, to allow for flexible data processing and flexible use of open-source tools such as Apache Spark and Apache Hive, which can allow for flexible data processing and minimize the cost of proprietary tools.

A data lake should support multiple processing engines, such as batch processing, stream processing, and real-time processing, to allow for flexible data processing. A data lake with a decoupled architecture, where the data lake is separated from the processing layer, can allow for flexible data processing and minimize the impact of changes to the processing layer on the data lake.

The data lake should be integrated with data analytics tools, such as business intelligence and machine learning tools, to allow for flexible data processing and analysis.

Now that we have gone over some of the best practices to implement a data lake, let's now review some ways to measure the success of your data lake implementation.

Key metrics in a data lake

Now more than ever, digital transformation projects have tight deadlines and are forced to continue doing more with fewer resources. It is vital to demonstrate added value and results quickly.

Ensuring the success and longevity of a data lake implementation is crucial for a corporation, and effective communication of its value is essential. However, determining whether the implementation is adding value or not is often not a binary metric and requires a more granular analysis than a simple "green" or "red" project status.

The following list of metrics is provided as a starting point to help gauge the success of your data lake implementation. It is not intended to be an exhaustive list but rather a guide to generate metrics that are relevant to your specific implementation:

- **Size**: It's important to monitor two metrics when evaluating a lake: the overall size of the lake and the size of its trusted zone. While the total size of the lake alone may not be significant or informative, the contents of the lake can range from valuable data to meaningless information. Regardless, this volume has a significant impact on your billing expenses. Implementing an archival or purging policy is an effective method for controlling the volume and minimizing costs. Your documents can either be transferred to a long-term storage location like Amazon S3 Glacier or eliminated altogether. Amazon S3 offers an easy approach to erasing files using life cycle policies. A larger size of the trusted zone indicates a better scenario. It represents the extent of clean data within the lake. Although you can store massive amounts of data in the raw data zone, it only serves its purpose when it undergoes transformation, cleaning, and governance.
- **Governability**: Measuring governability can be challenging, but it is crucial. It's important to identify the critical data that requires governance and add a governance layer accordingly, as not all data needs to be governed. There are many opportunities to track governability. The criticality of data is key to establishing an efficient data governance program. Data on the annual financial report for the company is more critical than data on the times the ping pong club meets every week. Data deemed critical to track is dubbed a **Critical Data Element** (**CDE**).

To ensure efficient governability, you can assign CDEs and associate them with the lake's data at the dataset level. Then, you can monitor the proportion of CDEs matched and resolved at the column level. Another approach is to keep track of the number of authorized CDEs against the total number of CDEs. Lastly, you can track the count of CDE modifications made after their approval.

- **Quality**: Data quality is not always perfect, but it should meet the standards for its intended domain. For instance, when using a dataset to generate financial reports for the current quarter, the accuracy of the numbers used is crucial. On the other hand, if the use case is to determine recipients for marketing emails, the data still needs to be reasonably clean, but a few invalid emails may not significantly impact the results.
- **Usage**: Usage tracking is crucial for maintaining an effective data lake. It is important to keep track of data ingestion rate, processing rate, error and failure rate, as well as individual components of the lake. These metrics can provide valuable insights into where to focus your efforts. If a particular section of the data lake needs more traffic, you may want to consider phasing it out. AWS offers an easy way to track usage metrics through SQL queries against AWS CloudTrail using Amazon Athena.
- **Variety**: It is useful to assess the variety aspect of the data lake and evaluate the capability of the system to handle various types of data sources. It should be able to accommodate different input types such as relational database management systems and NoSQL databases like DynamoDB, CRM application data, JSON, XML, emails, logs, and more. While the data ingested into the lake can be of diverse types, it is recommended to standardize the data format and storage type as much as possible. For example, you may decide to standardize on the Apache Parquet format or ORC format for all data stored in your Amazon S3 buckets. This allows users of the data lake to access it standardly. Achieving complete uniformity in the data lake might not always be practical or necessary. It is important to consider the context and purpose of the data before deciding on the level of homogenization required. For instance, it may not make sense to convert unstructured data into Parquet. Therefore, it is best to use this metric as a general guideline rather than a rigid rule.
- **Speed**: When it comes to speed, two measurements are valuable. Firstly, track the time it takes to update the trusted data zone from the start of the ingestion process. Secondly, track the time it takes for users to access the data. It's not necessary to squeeze every millisecond out of the process, but it should be good enough. For example, if the nightly window to populate the data lake is four hours, and the process takes two hours, it might be acceptable. However, if you expect the input data to double, you may need to find ways to speed up the process to avoid hitting the limit.

Similarly, if user queries take a few seconds to populate reports, the performance might be acceptable, and optimizing the queries further might not be a priority.

- **Customer satisfaction**: Continuous tracking of customer satisfaction is crucial, as it is one of the most important metrics after security. The success of your data lake initiative depends on your users' satisfaction, and a lack of users or unhappy users can lead to its failure. There are several ways to measure customer satisfaction, ranging from informal to formal approaches. The informal method involves periodically asking the project sponsor for feedback. However, a formal survey of the data lake users is recommended to obtain a more accurate metric. You can multiply the opinions of each survey participant by their usage level. For instance, if the lake receives low ratings from a few sporadic users but excellent ratings from hardcore users, it could imply that your data lake implementation has a steep learning curve, but users can become hyper-productive once they become familiar with it.
- **Security**: Security is a crucial aspect of data lake management, and compromising it is not an option. It is vital to ensure that the data lake is secure and that users only have access to their data to prevent any unauthorized access or data breaches. Even a single breach can lead to a significant loss of critical data, which can be used by competitors or other malicious entities. Another essential factor related to security is the storage of sensitive and **personally identifiable information** (**PII**). Mishandling PII data can result in severe penalties, including reputation damage, fines, and lost business opportunities. To mitigate this risk, AWS provides Amazon Macie, which can automatically scan your data lake and identify any PII data in your repositories, allowing you to take necessary actions to safeguard it. However, even with security metrics, there might be instances where good enough is acceptable. For example, banks and credit card issuers have a certain level of credit card fraud that they find acceptable. Eliminating credit card fraud might be a laudable goal, but it might not be achievable.

AWS provides a range of services for building and operating data lakes, making it an attractive platform for data lake implementations. Amazon S3 can be used as the primary data lake storage, providing unlimited, scalable, and durable storage for large amounts of data. AWS Glue can be used for data cataloging and ETL, providing a fully managed and scalable solution for these tasks. Amazon Athena can be used for interactive querying, providing a serverless and scalable solution for querying data in S3. You can use Amazon EMR for big data processing: Amazon EMR can be used for big data processing, providing a fully managed and scalable solution for processing large amounts of data.

The data lake can be integrated with other AWS services, such as Amazon Redshift for data warehousing and Amazon SageMaker for machine learning, to provide a complete and scalable data processing solution.

Now that you have learned about the various components of a data lake, and some best practices for managing and assessing data lakes, let's take a look at some other evolved modern data architecture patterns.

Lakehouse in AWS

A lakehouse architecture is a modern data architecture that combines the best features of data lakes and data warehouses, while a data lake is a large, centralized repository that stores structured and unstructured data in its raw form. To have a structured view of data, you need to load data into the data warehouse. The lakehouse architecture combines a data lake with a data warehouse to provide a consolidated view of data.

The key difference between a lakehouse and a data lake is that a lakehouse architecture provides a structured view of the data in addition to the raw data stored in the data lake, while a data lake only provides the raw data. In a lakehouse architecture, the data lake acts as the primary source of raw data, and the data warehouse acts as a secondary source of structured data. This allows organizations to make better use of their data by providing a unified view of data while also preserving the scalability and flexibility of the data lake.

In comparison, a data lake provides a central repository for all types of data but does not provide a structured view of the data for analysis and reporting. Data must be prepared for analysis by cleaning, transforming, and enriching it, which can be time-consuming and require specialized skills.

Let's take an example to understand the difference between a data lake and a lakehouse. A media company stores all of its raw video and audio content in a data lake. The data lake provides a central repository for the content, but the media company must perform additional processing and preparation to make the content usable for analysis and reporting. The same media company implements a lakehouse architecture in addition to the data lake. The data warehouse provides a structured view of the video and audio content, making it easier to analyze and report on the content. The company can use this structured data to gain insights into audience engagement and improve the quality of its content.

Here are the steps to implement a lakehouse architecture in AWS:

1. **Set up a data lake**: Start by setting up a data lake using Amazon S3 as the storage layer. This will provide a central repository for all types of data, including structured, semi-structured, and unstructured data.
2. **Define data ingestion pipelines**: Use tools like Amazon Kinesis, Amazon Glue, or AWS Data Pipeline to define data ingestion pipelines for your data sources. This will allow you to automatically collect and store data in the data lake as it becomes available.
3. **Create a data warehouse**: Use Amazon Redshift as your data warehouse. Amazon Redshift provides fast, managed data warehousing that can handle large amounts of data.
4. **Load data into the data warehouse**: Use Amazon Glue or AWS Data Pipeline to load the data from the data lake into the data warehouse. This will provide a structured view of the data for analysis and reporting.
5. **Perform data transformations**: Use Amazon Glue or AWS Data Pipeline to perform data transformations on the data in the data lake, if necessary. This will ensure that the data is clean, consistent, and ready for analysis.
6. **Analyze data**: Use Amazon Redshift to perform data analysis and reporting. Amazon Redshift provides fast and flexible data analysis capabilities, making it easy to perform complex data analysis. You can use Redshift Spectrum to join data residing in a data lake with Redshift data in a single query and get the desired result. You don't need to load all data in the data warehouse for a query.
7. **Monitor and manage the lakehouse architecture**: Use Amazon CloudWatch and AWS Glue metrics to monitor and manage your lakehouse architecture. This will help ensure that the architecture performs optimally and that any issues are quickly identified and resolved.

These are the general steps to implement a lakehouse architecture in AWS. The exact implementation details will vary depending on the specific requirements of your organization and the data sources you are using.

Data mesh in AWS

While data lakes are a popular concept, they have their issues. While putting data in one place creates a single source of truth, you are also creating a single source of failure, violating standard architecture principles to build high availability.

The other problem is that the data lake is maintained by a centralized team of data engineers who may need more domain knowledge to clean data. This results in back-and-forth communication with business users. Over time your data lake can become a data swamp.

The ultimate target of collecting data is to get business insight and retain business domain context while processing that data. What is the solution? That's where data mesh comes into the picture. With data mesh, you can treat data as a product where the business team owns the data, and they expose it as a product that can be consumed by various other teams who need it in their account. It solves the problem of maintaining domain knowledge while providing the required isolation and scale for business. As data is accessed across accounts, you need centralized security governance.

Data mesh is an architectural pattern for managing data that emphasizes data ownership, consistency, and accessibility. The goal of data mesh is to provide a scalable and flexible data architecture that can support multiple domains, organizations, and products. In a data mesh architecture, data is treated as a first-class citizen and managed independently from applications and services. Data products are created to manage and govern data, providing a single source of truth for the data and its metadata. This makes it easier to manage data, reduces data silos, and promotes data reuse.

Data mesh also emphasizes the importance of data governance, providing clear ownership of data and clear processes for data management. This makes managing and maintaining data quality, security, and privacy easier. Organizations typically use a combination of data products, pipelines, APIs, and catalogs to implement a data mesh architecture. These tools and services are used to collect, store, and manage data, making it easier to access and use data across the organization. For example, an e-commerce company can use data mesh to manage customer, product, and sales data. This can include creating data products for customer profiles, product catalogs, and sales data, making it easier to manage and use this data across the organization.

The following diagram shows the data mesh architecture in AWS for a banking customer:

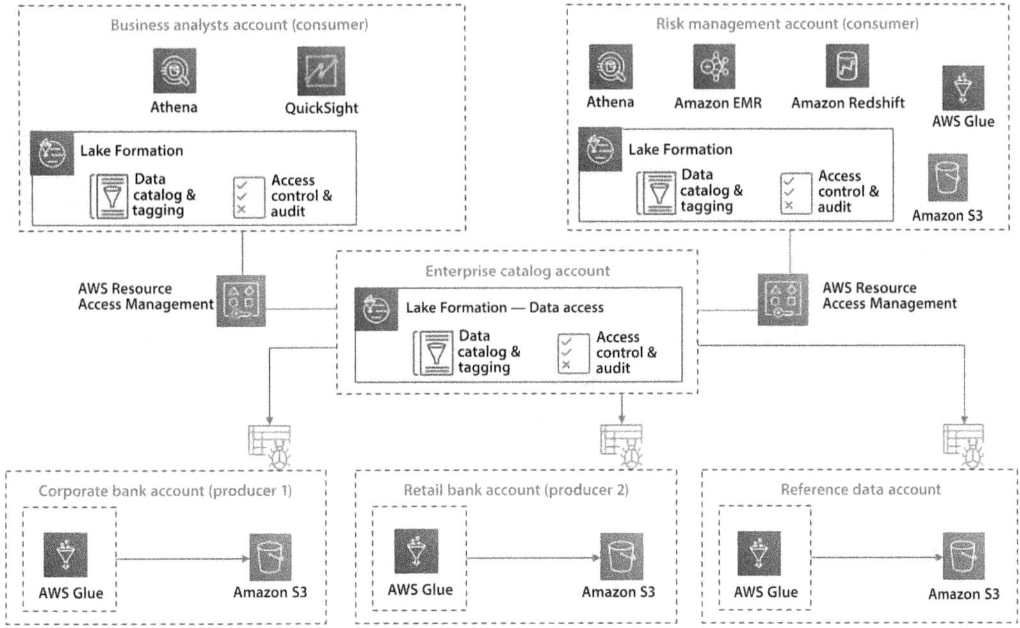

Figure 15.4: Data mesh architecture in AWS

As shown in the preceding diagram, the consumer account and consumer risk departments manage their data and expose it as a product consumed by the corporate account and retail account departments. Each of these departments operates in its account, and cross-account access is managed by a centralized enterprise account. The centralized account also manages the data catalog and tagging, and handles resource access management, which facilitates the producer and consumer of the data to talk to each other and consume data as per their need.

Here are the steps to implement data mesh in AWS:

1. **Define data domains:** The first step in implementing data mesh is to define the data domains in your organization. This involves identifying the different areas of the business that produce and use data and determining the relationships between these data domains.

2. **Create data products**: Once you have defined your data domains, the next step is to create data products. A data product is a self-contained unit of data that can be managed and governed independently from the rest of the organization. In AWS, you can create data products using AWS Glue, Amazon S3, and Amazon Redshift.
3. **Implement data pipelines**: To ensure that data is consistent and accurate, you need to implement data pipelines. A data pipeline is a series of steps that are used to extract, transform, and load data from various sources into a data lake or data warehouse. In AWS, you can implement data pipelines using AWS Glue, Amazon S3, and Amazon Redshift.
4. **Use data catalogs**: To make it easier to manage and access data, you need to use data catalogs. A data catalog is a metadata repository that provides a centralized location for storing and managing metadata about your data products. In AWS, you can use AWS Glue or Amazon Athena as your data catalog.
5. **Implement data APIs**: To make it easier to access data, you need to implement data APIs. A data API is a set of APIs that provides a programmatic interface for accessing data products. In AWS, you can implement data APIs using AWS Lambda and Amazon API Gateway.
6. **Ensure data security**: To ensure that data is secure, you need to implement data security measures. In AWS, you can use Amazon S3 bucket policies, IAM policies, and encryption to secure your data.

To implement data mesh in AWS, you need to define data domains, create data products, implement data pipelines, use data catalogs, implement data APIs, and ensure data security. These steps can help you build a scalable and flexible data architecture that can support multiple domains, organizations, and products.

Choosing between a data lake, lakehouse, and data mesh architecture

In a nutshell, data lake, lakehouse, and data mesh architectures are three different approaches to organizing and managing data in an organization.

A data lake is a centralized repository that allows you to store all your structured and unstructured data at any scale. A data lake provides the raw data and is often used for data warehousing, big data processing, and analytics. A lakehouse is a modern data architecture that combines the scale and flexibility of a data lake with the governance and security of a traditional data warehouse. A lakehouse provides raw and curated data, making it easier for data warehousing and analytics.

A data mesh organizes and manages data that prioritizes decentralized data ownership and encourages cross-functional collaboration. In a data mesh architecture, each business unit is responsible for its own data and shares data with others as needed, creating a network of data products. Here are some factors to consider when deciding between a data lake, data mesh, and lakehouse architecture:

- **Data governance**: Data lakes are great for storing raw data, but they can be challenging to manage, especially when it comes to data governance. Data mesh focuses on data governance and provides a way to manage and govern data across the organization. On the other hand, lakehouse combines the benefits of data lakes and data warehouses, providing a centralized repository for storing and managing data with a focus on data governance and performance.
- **Data processing**: Data lakes are ideal for big data processing, such as batch processing and real-time data processing. Data mesh focuses on enabling flexible data processing and creating data products that different parts of the organization can easily consume. On the other hand, lakehouse provides a unified platform for storing and processing data, making it easier to run ad-hoc and real-time queries.
- **Data access**: Data lakes can be difficult to access, especially for users who need to become more familiar with the underlying technologies. Data mesh focuses on providing easy access to data through data products and APIs. Lakehouse, on the other hand, provides a unified platform for accessing and querying data, making it easier for users to get the data they need.
- **Cost**: Data lakes can be more cost-effective than data warehouses, especially for large data sets. Data mesh can be more expensive due to the additional layer of management and governance. Lakehouse can also be more expensive, especially if you need to store and process large amounts of data.

Consider using a data lake if you need to store large amounts of raw data and process it using big data technologies. Consider using a data mesh if you need to manage and govern data across the organization. Consider using a lakehouse if you need a centralized repository for storing and managing data with a focus on data governance and performance.

Summary

In this chapter, you explored what a data lake is and how a data lake can help a large-scale organization. You learned about various data lake zones and looked at the components and characteristics of a successful data lake.

Further, you learned about building a data lake in AWS with AWS Lake Formation. You also learned about data mesh architecture, which connects multiple data lakes built across accounts. You also explored what can be done to optimize the architecture of a data lake. You then delved into the different metrics that can be tracked to keep control of your data lake. Finally, you learned about lakehouse architecture, and how to choose between data lake, lakehouse, and data mesh architectures.

In the next chapter, we will put together everything that we have learnt so far and see how to build an app in AWS.

16

Hands-On Guide to Building an App in AWS

In this chapter, you will combine many concepts you learned about in previous chapters to build a practical, e-commerce serverless architecture for a fictional online store called *AWSome Store*. After reading this chapter, you should be able to build your application using some or all of the components that you will review in this chapter.

For many of the services, you can plug and play and pick and choose the services that will be used in the application you develop. For example, your application may be more user-centric and may not require any asynchronous services. In this case, you can pull the asynchronous component out of your architecture. However, including some of the services in your architecture is highly advisable. For example, suppose your application is going to have a front end. In that case, you will want to ensure that you have an authentication component so that every user is authenticated before using any other application services.

In this chapter, you will first review the use case and build architecture upon your previous learning of *Domain Driven Architecture* in *Chapter 14*. You will build an architecture using AWS services and implement them using the AWS command line interface. You will cover the following topics:

- Understanding the use case
- Building the architecture for a fictional e-commerce website called *AWSome Store*
- Deciding on your programming language
- Implementing *AWSome Store* in AWS
- Optimizing with the Well-Architected Framework

Let's start building in AWS now.

An introduction to the use case

This chapter will allow you to combine and practice many concepts we have covered throughout this book. You'll need to design the architecture of your system to scale without impacting application performance. You can use a serverless architecture, which involves building small, independent functions triggered by events, such as changes in a database or the arrival of a new message. This allows you to scale your system as needed, paying only for the resources you use.

To build upon your existing knowledge, let's go into more detail about implementing domain-driven design for a retail e-commence application use case that you learned about in *Chapter 14, Microservice Architectures in AWS,* under the section *Domain-Driven Design*. Let's take a trip down memory lane to understand the use case.

To make it a fun learning experience, we'll give a name to the retail store we will use to learn AWS, let's name it *AWSome Store*. Our imaginary online store provides AWS merchandise, such as stickers, books, water bottles, etc. You first need to identify the core business concepts, or entities, that make up the *AWSome Store* system to build **domain-driven design** (**DDD**). In the context of a retail e-commerce app, these entities include products, orders, customers, and payments. Next, you'll need to identify the different contexts in which these entities exist. For example, the product context might include product details, availability, and pricing, while the order context might include information about order status, shipping, and billing.

Once you've identified the bounded contexts, you'll need to define the relationships between the entities within each context. For example, an ordered aggregate might include an order, the customer who placed the order, and the purchased products. You may also identify services within each context that perform specific operations, such as calculating the total price of an order or processing a payment. Finally, you'll need to identify domain events that trigger actions within the system, such as a new order being placed or a product becoming unavailable.

Figure 16.1 shows a context map diagram for the *AWSome Store* for identified bounded contexts in the different business areas or contexts that make up the *AWSome Store* system, such as order management, payment processing, order fulfillment, shipping and customer management, etc.

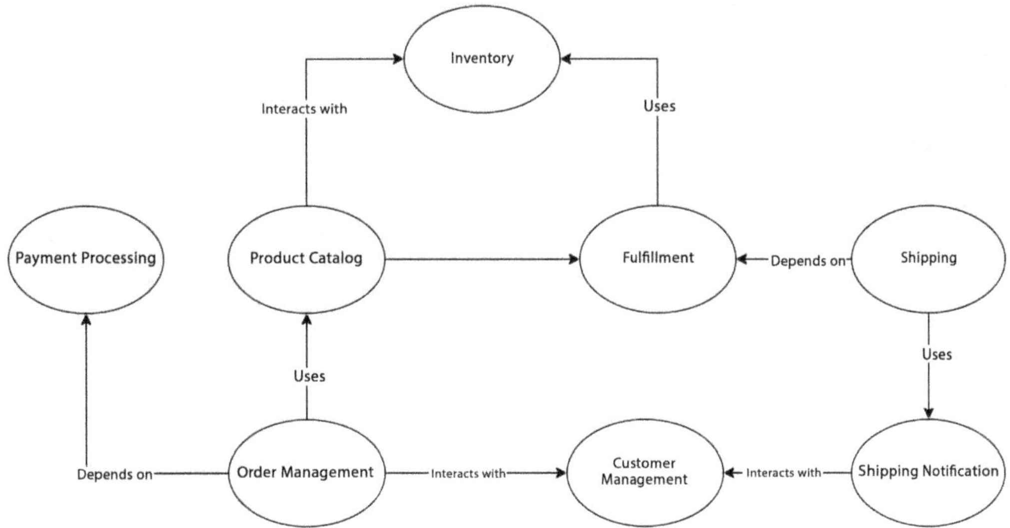

Figure 16.1: Domain-driven design context map diagram for AWSome Store

Figure 16.1 defines the relationships between the different bounded contexts. For example, the payment processing context might be related to the order management context because products are ordered and sold. We have represented each bounded context as a separate oval on the diagram and we labeled each oval with the name of the context and the main entities within that context. The lines between the ovals represent the relationships between the bounded contexts and the type of relationship, such as *uses, depends on*, or *interacts with*. You can further refine the diagram as needed and review it with stakeholders to ensure that it accurately represents the relationships and dependencies between the bounded contexts.

By creating a context map diagram, you can understand the relationships between the different business areas of the *AWSome Store* e-commerce retail app, helping you make informed decisions about architecture, design, and implementation.

Let's start looking at the design for our serverless microservice application. First, we'll present the high-level architecture, and afterward, we'll analyze each component or *domain* independently in detail:

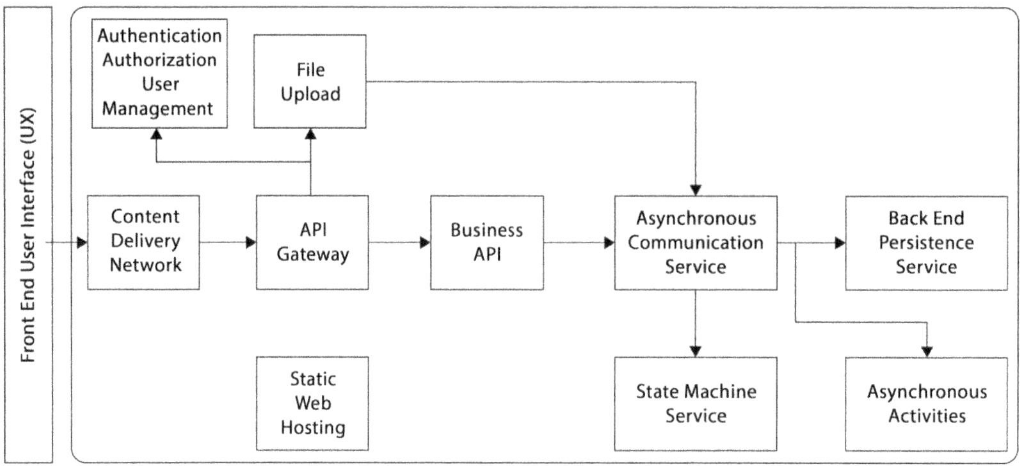

Figure 16.2: Serverless web-application architecture

As you can see, the architecture provides services for static web hosting, business services, an asynchronous service, a state-machine service, and file uploads, among other components. In the following sections, we will look in detail into each of these components.

In *Figure 16.2*, each block represents delimited domains and technical functionality in many serverless implementations. Depending on the methodology used and whether you decide to use a microservice architecture, each of these blocks will represent one or more microservices. For example, the business API should be broken down into a series of microservices and not just one. You might have a microservice to handle *accounts* and another microservices to manage *companies*.

Building architecture in AWS

Now that you understand different domains and relationships, lets take a shot at building an architecture diagram using AWS services. AWS offers several services that you can use to build a robust, scalable, and resilient system. For example, you can use Amazon Lambda to build serverless functions, Amazon DynamoDB to store data, Amazon S3 to store files, and Amazon API Gateway to create APIs. Also, implementing proper error handling and retry logic is crucial for building a resilient and robust system with AWS Lambda.

To allow for the quick implementation of new features, you'll need to implement a CI/CD pipeline that automatically builds, tests, and deploys new code to production. Let's look at *AWSome Store*'s proposed architecture using AWS cloud-native services:

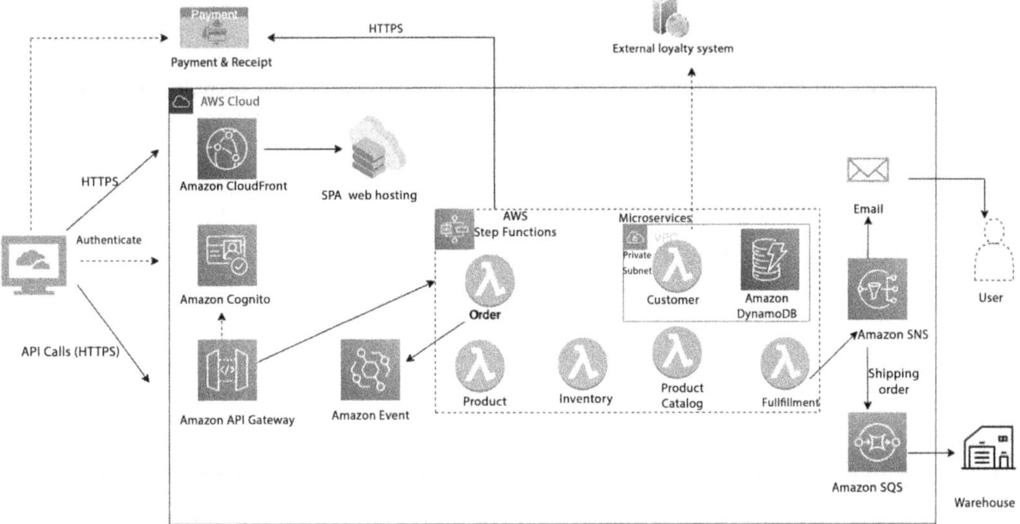

Figure 16.3: AWS cloud-native architecture to build AWSome Store

As shown in *Figure 16.3*, AWS provides various cloud-native serverless technologies to implement a scalable and resilient e-commerce retail app, such as AWS Lambda, Amazon API Gateway, Amazon DynamoDB, Amazon S3, and Amazon EventBridge. These services could be used to implement a cloud-native serverless architecture for the following key components of the *AWSome Store*:

- **Front end**: The front end of the *AWSome Store* could be built using a JavaScript framework such as React and hosted on Amazon S3. Amazon CloudFront is used as a **Content Delivery Network (CDN)** to make sure website content is available to global users close to their location.
- **Authentication and Authorization**: Amazon Cognito is used to authenticate end customers and authorize them to use the application for profile creation and placing orders.
- **API Gateway**: Amazon API Gateway is used to create RESTful APIs for the front end to access the back-end services and to securely call them. API Gateway provides several features to help protect your API calls, including authentication and authorization mechanisms such as OAuth 2.0, API keys, and Amazon Cognito user pools. You can also use API Gateway to implement throttling, rate limiting, and caching to help prevent abuse and improve performance.

- **Lambda functions**: AWS Lambda is used to build the back-end functionality of the *AW-Some Store*. The application logic could be broken down into multiple Lambda functions, each handling a specific aspect of the app, such as product catalog management, order management, and payment processing.
- **DynamoDB**: Amazon DynamoDB is the primary data store for the *AWSome Store*, providing a scalable and managed NoSQL database for storing customer information, the product catalog, and order information.
- **EventBridge**: Amazon EventBridge is used to build event-driven architectures, enabling the application to respond to events such as new orders and payment transactions.
- **S3**: Amazon S3 could store and retrieve product images and other static assets such as a PDF file for a product manual.

Other AWS services can be used in conjunction with the above key services to ensure security, build deployment pipelines, carry out log monitoring, raise system alerts, etc. For example, AWS IAM helps you control access to AWS resources. You can use IAM to create and manage user accounts, roles, and permissions, which can help you ensure that only authorized users have access to your serverless app services. You can use CloudFormation to define and manage your infrastructure as code. AWS CloudTrail records API calls and events for your AWS account. You can use CloudTrail to monitor activity in your serverless app services and to troubleshoot issues by reviewing the history of API calls and events. You can also use CloudWatch to collect and track metrics, collect and monitor log files, and set alarms. You can use AWS Config to provide a detailed inventory of your AWS resources, including configurations and relationships between resources.

You will learn about them as we move forward with the implementation details.

Deciding which is the best language

An important question is what language is best for you, your project, and your company. As a general rule of thumb, if you have a greenfield project where you have a wide choice of languages to pick from, it may be best to go with one of the newer languages, and it also makes sense to pick a popular language such as Golang.

This choice is not always straightforward and clear cut. A language's popularity is not static. As an example, Perl was one of the most popular languages in the 1990s, but its popularity has severely waned. So, it's not enough to consider the popularity of a language, but also how fast it's growing or fading away. Similarly, JavaScript was the most popular, but it was overtaken by Python in 2022. You can refer to this article published by GitHub to see the current trends in programming language popularity – `https://octoverse.github.com/2022/top-programming-languages`.

If a language is popular, you will easily find resources for your project. Some other considerations to keep in mind are shown in the following list:

- **Compiled versus interpreted**: If you don't expect your project to become the next Airbnb and know that the number of users or the workload will be capped, you might be better off using an interpreted language rather than a compiled language. Interpreted languages allow you to prototype and ramp up your application quickly. Being able to fail fast is key to succeeding fast eventually. Fast development cycles allow us to test our ideas quickly and discard the ones that don't perform as expected. Usually, the development life cycle is quicker with an interpreted language because the code doesn't need to be compiled every time there is a code change. A compiled language may be better if your application has strict security requirements.
- **Problem domain**: If you have a small project and you are not working in the context of a company, the better choice may hinge on what other people have already done. You may be a highly experienced Java developer, but perhaps someone has already solved 90% of the requirements you are trying to cover. In this case, you may be better off teaching yourself Python to save replicating a lot of work.
- **Staff availability**: After researching, you may conclude that Ruby is the best language and has everything you need. But if you expect the application to require a sizable team to take it to completion and Ruby developers are in short supply (and therefore command high rates), it may be best to settle for second best and not be a language purist.

Regardless of your language selection, if you design your application correctly and leverage the advantages of a microservice architecture, you will be well on your way to a successful implementation. The combined microservice architecture with serverless deployment in AWS or a similar environment has been the recipe for many recent hits, some so successful that billion-dollar companies have been created around these products and services.

It is time to start putting some components together using the microservice architecture we learned about in *Chapter 14, Microservice Architectures in AWS.*

Setting up services

To initiate the development of an application, the initial step involves establishing the essential infrastructure services. As you have chosen to utilize AWS services extensively, these services can be configured via various means, such as the AWS Console, AWS **Cloud Development Kit (CDK)**, AWS CloudFormation, the **Command Line Interface (CLI)**, or through third-party tools like Chef, Puppet, Ansible, Terraform, etc.

In this section, the main emphasis is on how to use these services while building cloud-native applications rather than constructing the infrastructure itself. Therefore, this chapter will focus on the process of setting up services utilizing CLI. You will go through the following steps to implement *AWSome Store* in AWS:

1. Set up an AWS account
2. Install the AWS CLI
3. Set up IAM users, roles, and groups
4. Create the AWS infrastructure
5. Implement authentication and authorization for end customers
6. Define database attributes
7. Write the code for *AWSome Store* using Lambda functions
8. Deploy and test your code
9. Logging and monitoring

Set up an AWS account with a billing alert

The first step is to set up an AWS account. By now, you have likely already set up an account, but here are the steps to set up an AWS account in case you haven't:

1. Open a web browser and navigate to the AWS home page at `https://aws.amazon.com/`.
2. Click on the **Create an AWS Account** button located in the top-right corner of the page.
3. Fill in your account information, including your email address, password, and account name.
4. Provide your contact information, such as your name, company name, and phone number.
5. Enter your payment information, including your credit card details.
6. Choose a support plan that meets your needs, whether it's Basic, Developer, Business, or Enterprise.
7. Read and accept the AWS Customer Agreement and the AWS Service Terms.
8. Click the **Create Account and Continue** button.
9. AWS will send a verification code to your email address or phone number. Enter the code to verify your account.
10. Once your account is verified, you can start using AWS services.

11. To find your AWS account number, click on your name or account ID in the navigation bar at the top-right corner of the console. On the **My Account** page, you will see your 12-digit AWS account number displayed in the **Account Identifiers** section under **Account Number**.

After completing the verification process, you will have access to the AWS Management Console and can start using AWS services. It's important to note that you may need to provide additional information or documentation to fully activate your AWS account, especially if you plan to use AWS services that involve payment or access to sensitive data.

Additionally, it's a good idea to set up billing alerts to ensure that you are aware of the costs incurred while using AWS services. The costs can add up fast if you are not careful.

Here are the steps to set up billing alerts in AWS:

1. In the AWS console, navigate to **AWS Budget** by clicking on the **Services** drop-down menu and selecting **AWS Cost Management.**
2. On the **Budgets** screen, click on the **Create budget** button.
3. You can use a template to create a budget, for example, **Monthly cost budget**.
4. Provide a name for your budget, the budgeted amount, and the email recipients and select the **Create Budget** button to create the budget and complete the setup process.

Your final billing alert will look like *Figure 16.4*.

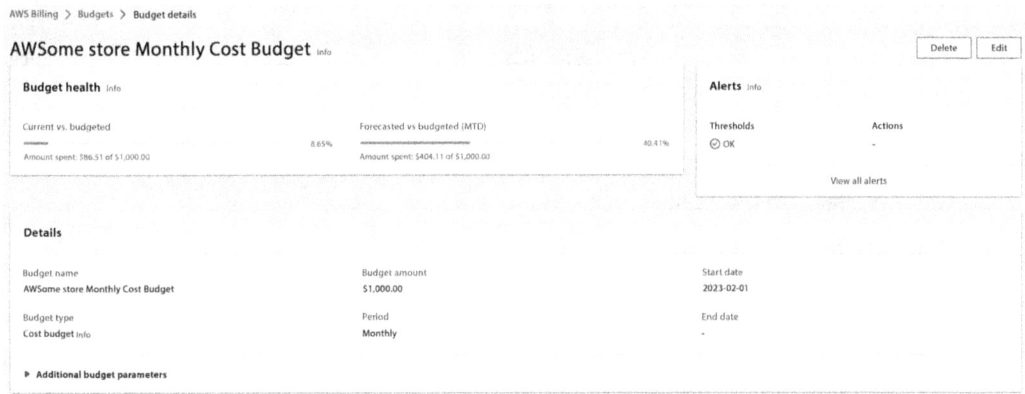

Figure 16.4: AWS billing alert dashboard

After setting up a budget, you will receive alerts via email when the budget threshold is exceeded. It's a good idea to regularly review your budgets and make adjustments as needed to ensure that you are always aware of your AWS spending.

As you have created an AWS account and set up your billing alert, now install CLI to create the rest of the services in AWS.

Install the AWS Command Line Interface (CLI)

The AWS CLI is available for Windows, macOS, and Linux. You can install the AWS CLI using the bundled installer, pip, or Homebrew. You can download the CLI installer and get started with AWS CLI by visiting the AWS user docs here – `https://aws.amazon.com/cli/`.

The root account has unrestricted access to all AWS services and resources in the account, which makes it a valuable target for attackers. If the root account is compromised, an attacker could gain complete control of your AWS resources and data, potentially causing significant harm to your business.

Creating an admin account in AWS is a best practice. It is important to have separate accounts with appropriate permissions to help ensure the security of your AWS resources and data. Creating an admin account with limited permissions reduces the risk of unauthorized access and reduces the impact of a potential security breach. Admin accounts can be given permissions to manage specific AWS services and resources, without granting them the full access of the root account.

By creating an admin account, you can better control and monitor the use of AWS services and resources and reduce the risk of security breaches or accidental changes that can impact the availability, integrity, and confidentiality of your data.

To configure the CLI, you need an IAM user with an access key ID and secret access key, so let's create an admin user by following the below steps:

1. Log in to the AWS Management Console and go to the IAM dashboard.
2. Click on **Users** in the navigation menu.
3. Click on the **Add user** button.
4. Enter a username for the new user; in this case you can give the name *store admin*, and click the **Next** button to land on the **Set Permissions** screen.
5. Select the option **Attach policies directly** and tick the **AdministratorAccess** checkbox as shown below. To keep things simple, we have defined an admin user. As a best practice, always follow least-privilege permissions; when you set permissions with IAM policies, only grant the permissions required to perform a task. You can learn more here: `https://docs.aws.amazon.com/IAM/latest/UserGuide/best-practices.html`.

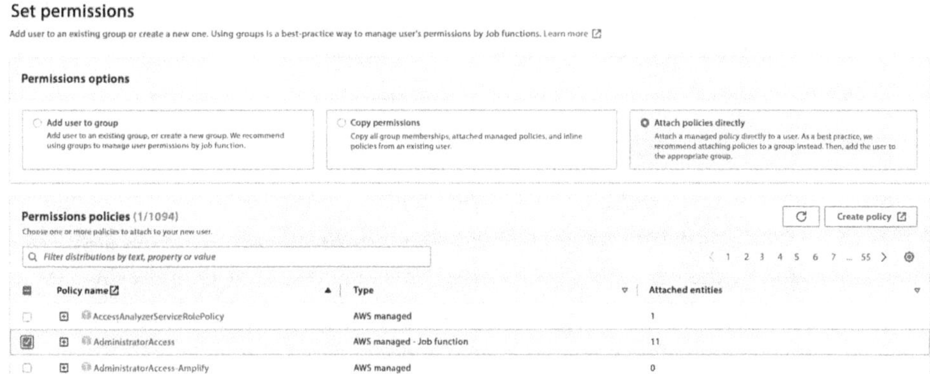

Figure 16.5: AWS IAM policy attachment

6. Review the user details and click on the **Create user** button.
7. Now go to the newly created *store admin* user by navigating to **Users**.
8. Select the **Security credentials** tab and click on **Create access key** in the **Access Key** section.
9. Retrieve the CSV file containing the access key ID and secret access key and ensure that it is stored securely, as it will only be accessible once and cannot be retrieved again later.

Now the new user has been created and has administrative permissions. You can now use the access key ID and secret access key to access AWS services using the CLI programmatically.

To configure the CLI, you need to run the `aws configure` command and provide your AWS access key ID, secret access key, default region name, and output format.

Here is an example of the configuration process:

```
$ aws configure
AWS Access Key ID [None]: AKIAIOSFODNN7EXAMPLE
AWS Secret Access Key [None]: wialrXUtnFEMI/K7MDENG/bPxRfiCYEXAMPLEKEY
Default region name [None]: us-west-2
Default output format [None]: json
```

Figure 16.6: Sample configuration code

The AWS CLI will prompt you for the following information:

- **AWS Access Key ID**: Your AWS access key ID allows you to access AWS services.
- **AWS Secret Access Key**: Your secret access key provides secure access to your AWS account.

- **Default region name**: The region where your AWS resources will be created. For example, us-west-2 for Oregon or us-east-1 for North Virginia.
- **Default output format**: The output from the AWS CLI commands. For example, JSON or text.

It's important to note that you will need to have an AWS account and the necessary permissions to perform actions using the AWS CLI. When creating an IAM user, role, or group in AWS, it's important to follow the principle of **zero trust**. This means that by default, you should assume that any user or entity is untrusted until proven otherwise. You don't want anyone to have admin access so let's create some IAM credentials using the CLI.

Set up IAM users, roles, and groups

Following the principle of **zero trust**, let's create a dev user with read/write access to S3, Lambda, and API Gateway using the AWS CLI. You can follow these steps:

Open the command line or terminal on your system and run the following command to create a dev user:

```
aws iam create-user --user-name dev-user
```

Next, create an IAM policy for read/write access to S3:

```
aws iam create-policy \
--policy-name S3-ReadWriteAccess \
--policy-document file://s3-readwrite-policy.json
```

Where the `s3-readwrite-policy.json` file contains the following policy:

Note: The placeholder text `<bucket-name>` should be replaced with a unique name of your choice for the S3 bucket. For instance, you could use a name like `aws-for-sa-book-s3-app`. It's important to ensure that the S3 bucket name is available and not already in use by another AWS account. Additionally, it's recommended to follow AWS naming conventions for S3 bucket names, which include using lowercase letters, numbers, and hyphens, and not using underscores or uppercase letters.

```
{
    "Version": "2012-10-17",
    "Statement": [
```

```
        {
            "Effect": "Allow",
            "Action": [
                "s3:ListBucket",
                "s3:GetObject",
                "s3:PutObject"
            ],
            "Resource": [
                "arn:aws:s3:::<bucket-name>/*"
            ]
        }
    ]
}
```

Similarly, create a policy for read/write access to Lambda:

```
aws iam create-policy \
--policy-name Lambda-ReadWriteAccess \
--policy-document file://lambda-readwrite-policy.json
```

Where the `lambda-readwrite-policy.json` file contains the following policy:

```
{
    "Version": "2012-10-17",
    "Statement": [
        {
            "Effect": "Allow",
            "Action": [
                "lambda:ListFunctions",
                "lambda:GetFunction",
                "lambda:CreateFunction",
                "lambda:UpdateFunctionCode",
                "lambda:DeleteFunction"
            ],
            "Resource": "*"
        }
    ]
}
```

And similarly, create a policy for read/write access to the API Gateway:

```
aws iam create-policy \
--policy-name API-Gateway-ReadWriteAccess \
--policy-document file://apigateway-readwrite-policy.json
```

Where the `apigateway-readwrite-policy.json` file contains the following policy:

Note: When creating an API gateway in AWS, you need to replace the placeholders `<region-id>` and `<api-id>` with the actual values for your environment. The `<region-id>` should be replaced with the AWS region identifier where you want to create the API gateway. For example, `us-east-1` for the US East (N. Virginia) region.

The `<api-id>` should be replaced with a unique identifier for your API Gateway. This identifier is used to generate the API Gateway endpoint URL, so it's important to choose a unique name that reflects the purpose of your API. For example, `my-api-gateway` or `ecommerce-api`. Make sure to choose appropriate values for both placeholders, as they will affect the configuration and functionality of your API Gateway.

```
{
    "Version": "2012-10-17",
    "Statement": [
        {
            "Effect": "Allow",
            "Action": [
                "apigateway:GET",
                "apigateway:POST",
                "apigateway:PUT",
                "apigateway:DELETE",
                "apigateway:PATCH"
            ],
            "Resource": "arn:aws:apigateway:<region-id>:<api-id>/*"
        }
]
}
```

Attach the policies to the dev user:

Note: When you create a new AWS account, it is assigned a unique 12-digit account number. When executing commands in AWS that require specifying the account number, you will need to replace the placeholder text with the actual account number for your account. For example, if a command requires specifying the account number as `<account-number>`, you should replace this placeholder with your actual 12-digit account number, like `123456789012`. Using the correct account number is important to ensure that the command is executed in the correct AWS account, especially if you have multiple AWS accounts.

```
aws iam attach-user-policy --user-name dev-user --policy-arn
arn:aws:iam::<account-id>:policy/S3-ReadWriteAccess
aws iam attach-user-policy --user-name dev-user --policy-arn
arn:aws:iam::<account-id>:policy/lambda-ReadWriteAccess
aws iam attach-user-policy --user-name dev-user --policy-arn
arn:aws:iam::<account-id>:policy/apigateway-ReadWriteAccess
```

Finally, verify the policies have been attached to the dev user:

```
aws iam list-attached-user-policies --user-name dev-user
```

Similarly, you should create policies for other users as needed. You can use a policy generator to build the right policy for each user by referring to this link – `https://awspolicygen.s3.amazonaws.com/policygen.html`.

Security is most important for your application, so make sure to use the below best practices when creating IAM entities with zero-trust principles in mind:

- **Least privilege:** Assign the minimum permissions necessary to accomplish a task. For example, if a user only needs to access a specific S3 bucket, only grant them access.
- **Role-based access control**: Use IAM roles instead of long-term access keys. Roles are more secure because they are limited to a specific set of permissions and can be revoked at any time.
- **Multi-factor authentication**: Require **multi-factor authentication** (**MFA**) for all IAM entities, including root, users, roles, and groups. MFA provides an extra layer of security and helps to prevent unauthorized access.

- **Use policies and conditions**: Define policies and conditions that limit access to AWS resources based on factors such as the time of day, IP address, and user agent.
- **Monitor and audit**: Regularly monitor and audit your AWS environment to detect potential security issues and ensure that users are only accessing resources as intended.
- **Use managed policies**: Use managed policies instead of custom policies whenever possible. Managed policies are pre-built policies reviewed and approved by AWS security experts.
- **Regularly rotate credentials**: Regularly rotate access keys, passwords, and other credentials to ensure that only authorized users can access your AWS resources.

By following these best practices, you can ensure that your AWS environment is secure and that only authorized users can access your resources.

Let's move on to the next step of creating cloud infrastructure for architecture.

Create the AWS infrastructure

After creating IAM credentials, let's create the app infrastructure. For simplicity and to explain the concept, you will use the CLI to bring-up various AWS services; however, as a best practice you should choose the route of writing a CloudFormation template and using that to bring up your AWS infrastructure. Here is an example of how to create an API Gateway, S3, DynamoDB, CloudFront, and Lambda instance using the AWS CLI:

Create an S3 bucket:

```
aws s3 mb s3://<bucket-name>
```

Note: The placeholder text `<bucket-name>` should be replaced with a unique name of your choice for the S3 bucket.

Create a DynamoDB table:

```
aws dynamodb create-table --table-name awesome-store-table
--attribute-definitions AttributeName=id,AttributeType=S --key-
schema AttributeName=id,KeyType=HASH --provisioned-throughput
ReadCapacityUnits=1,WriteCapacityUnits=1
```

Create a CloudFront distribution:

```
aws cloudfront create-distribution --distribution-config file://
cloudfront-config.json
```

Here is some example code for a CloudFront configuration file in the JSON format. The file `cloudfront-config.json` should contain the CloudFront distribution configuration:

```
{
  "Comment": "My CloudFront Distribution Configuration",
  "Logging": {
    "Bucket": "<my-logs-bucket>",
    "IncludeCookies": true,
    "Prefix": "my-cloudfront-logs/"
  },
  "Origins": {
    "Quantity": 1,
    "Items": [
      {
        "Id": "my-origin",
        "DomainName": "<my-origin-domain>",
        "CustomOriginConfig": {
          "HTTPPort": 80,
          "HTTPSPort": 443,
          "OriginProtocolPolicy": "https-only",
          "OriginSslProtocols": {
            "Quantity": 1,
            "Items": ["TLSv1.2"]
          }
        }
      }
    ]
  },
  "DefaultCacheBehavior": {
    "TargetOriginId": "my-origin",
    "ForwardedValues": {
      "QueryString": false,
      "Cookies": {
        "Forward": "none"
      }
    },
    "TrustedSigners": {
      "Enabled": false,
```

```
        "Quantity": 0
      },
      "ViewerProtocolPolicy": "redirect-to-https",
      "MinTTL": 0,
      "MaxTTL": 86400,
      "DefaultTTL": 3600
    },
    "Enabled": true,
    "PriceClass": "PriceClass_All",
    "DefaultRootObject": "index.html",
    "Aliases": {
      "Quantity": 2,
      "Items": [
        "<www.mydomain.com>",
        "<mydomain.com>"
      ]
    },
    "ViewerCertificate": {
      "ACMCertificateArn": "<my-acm-certificate-arn>",
      "SSLSupportMethod": "sni-only"
    }
  }
```

This configuration file defines a CloudFront distribution that uses one origin, enables logging to an S3 bucket, and specifies cache behavior settings. Note that some values, such as `<my-logs-bucket>` and `<my-origin-domain>`, need to be replaced with actual values specific to your environment. For example, `<my-logs-bucket>` should be replaced with the name of an existing S3 bucket where CloudFront can store log files, such as `my-cloudfront-logs-bucket`. In the same line, `<my-origin-domain>` should be replaced with the domain name of an existing origin server for your CloudFront distribution, such as `www.example.com`.

When creating an API Gateway API and a Lambda function in AWS, you can use any valid name of your choice for these resources, as long as the name is unique within your AWS account and follows the naming rules and restrictions for AWS resource names. In the examples below, `awesome-store-api` and `awesome-store-lambda` are just example names that could be replaced with other names of your choosing. Just make sure to use the same names consistently throughout your code and configurations when referring to these resources.

Create an API Gateway REST API:

```
aws apigateway create-rest-api --name awesome-store-api --description
"Awesome Store API"
```

Create a Lambda function:

```
aws lambda create-function --function-name awesome-store-lambda --runtime
nodejs12.x --handler index.handler --zip-file fileb://lambda.zip
```

Note: The `lambda.zip` file typically contains the code for the AWS Lambda function that you want to deploy. In the example command you provided, the code in `lambda.zip` is for a Node.js 12.x runtime environment. However, AWS Lambda supports a variety of other programming languages and runtime environments, including Python, Java, C#, Go, and Ruby, among others. To deploy code for a different runtime environment, you would need to make sure that the code is compatible with that specific runtime environment, and then package it into a new ZIP file with the appropriate file extension for that language (such as `.py` for Python or `.jar` for Java). Once you have the new ZIP file with your code for the desired runtime environment, you can use a similar command to the one you provided, but specify the appropriate runtime flag and other parameters as needed for the specific language and environment.

Create the AWS infrastructure using CloudFormation

Above was a basic example of creating these AWS resources using the CLI. Here's an example CloudFormation template to deploy the resources needed for an *AWSome Store* e-commerce website:

```
---
AWSTemplateFormatVersion: '2010-09-09'
Description: CloudFormation template to deploy resources needed for an
AWSome Store e-commerce website
Resources:
  S3Bucket:
    Type: AWS::S3::Bucket
    Properties:
      BucketName: awesome-store-bucket
      WebsiteConfiguration:
        IndexDocument: index.html
  DynamoDBTable:
    Type: AWS::DynamoDB::Table
```

```
    Properties:
      TableName: awesome-store-table
      AttributeDefinitions:
        - AttributeName: id
          AttributeType: S
      KeySchema:
        - AttributeName: id
          KeyType: HASH
      ProvisionedThroughput:
        ReadCapacityUnits: 1
        WriteCapacityUnits: 1
  CloudFrontDistribution:
    Type: AWS::CloudFront::Distribution
    Properties:
      DistributionConfig:
        Origins:
          - Id: awesome-store-origin
            DomainName: !Join ['.', [!Ref S3Bucket, 's3.amazonaws.com']]
            S3OriginConfig:
              OriginAccessIdentity: !Join ['/', ['origin-access-identity/cloudfront', !Ref AWS::AccountId]]
        DefaultCacheBehavior:
          TargetOriginId: awesome-store-origin
          ViewerProtocolPolicy: redirect-to-https
        Enabled: true
  APIGateway:
    Type: AWS::ApiGateway::RestApi
    Properties:
      Name: awesome-store-api
      Description: Awesome Store API

  LambdaFunction:
    Type: AWS::Lambda::Function
    Properties:
      FunctionName: awesome-store-lambda
      Runtime: nodejs12.x
      Handler: index.handler
```

```
    Code:
      S3Bucket: !Ref S3Bucket
      S3Key: lambda.zip
```

The above is just an example; you may need to modify it to meet your specific requirements. Additionally, you may need to add additional resources, such as IAM roles and policies, to implement the *AWSome Store* e-commerce website fully. You will learn more about writing Lambda code and putting it in `lambda.zip` later in this chapter. For the time being, you can copy the above code in `awsome-store-app.yaml` and run the following command to deploy the CloudFormation template:

```
aws cloudformation create-stack --stack-name <stack-name> --template-body
file://<template-file>
```

Replace `<stack-name>` with the desired name of your CloudFormation stack and `<template-file>` with the name of your CloudFormation template file, for example:

```
aws cloudformation create-stack --stack-name awsome-store --template-body
file://awsome-store-app.yaml
```

To monitor the progress of the CloudFormation stack creation, you can use the following command:

```
aws cloudformation describe-stacks --stack-name <stack-name>
```

Once the CloudFormation stack is created successfully, it will return a status of `CREATE_COMPLETE`.

Creating an EventBridge instance and a queue

You can use AWS EventBridge and SQS to build loosely coupled architecture and send asynchronous messages like emails for customer notifications. Here are the high-level steps to set up AWS EventBridge and SQS for the *AWSome Store* using the AWS CLI:

1. **Create an SQS queue**:

   You can use the following AWS CLI command to create a new SQS queue:

   ```
   aws sqs create-queue --queue-name awsome-store-queue
   ```

2. **Get the ARN of the SQS queue**:

   You can use the following AWS CLI command to get the ARN of the SQS queue:

   ```
   aws sqs get-queue-attributes --queue-url <queue-url> --attribute-
   names QueueArn
   ```

Note: To use the command above, you need to replace <queue-url> with the actual URL of the SQS queue for which you want to retrieve the attribute. For example, if the URL of your SQS queue is https://sqs.us-west-2.amazonaws.com/123456789012/my-queue, you would replace <queue-url> with that URL, like this:

```
aws sqs get-queue-attributes --queue-url https://
sqs.us-west-2.amazonaws.com/123456789012/my-queue
--attribute-names QueueArn
```

This command would retrieve the QueueArn attribute for the my-queue SQS queue in the us-west-2 region.

3. **Create a new AWS EventBridge rule**:

   You can use the following AWS CLI command to create a new AWS EventBridge rule using QueueArn retrieved from the previous command:

   ```
   aws events put-rule --name awsome-store-rule --event-pattern
   '{"source":["aws.sqs"],"detail-type":["SQS Message Received"],"detai
   l":{"queue":["<queue-arn>"]}}'
   ```

4. **Add a target to the EventBridge rule**:

   You can use the following AWS CLI command to add a target to the EventBridge rule:

   ```
   aws events put-targets --rule awsome-store-rule --targets
   Id=1,Arn=<lambda-function-arn>
   ```

The aws events put-targets command adds one or more targets to an Amazon EventBridge rule, specified by the --rule parameter. In this case, the target being added is an AWS Lambda function, specified by its ARN using the --targets parameter. To use this command, you need to replace awsome-store-rule with the name of the EventBridge rule to which you want to add the target. You also need to replace <lambda-function-arn> with the ARN of the AWS Lambda function that you want to use as the target.

For example, if you have an EventBridge rule called my-event-rule and an AWS Lambda function with an ARN of arn:aws:lambda:us-west-2:123456789012:function:my-lambda-function, you would replace awsome-store-rule with my-event-rule, and replace <lambda-function-arn> with arn:aws:lambda:us-west-2:123456789012:function:my-lambda-function, like this:

```
aws events put-targets --rule my-event-rule --targets
Id=1,Arn=arn:aws:lambda:us-west-2:123456789012:function:my-lambda-function
```

This command would add the `my-lambda-function` AWS Lambda function as a target to the `my-event-rule` EventBridge rule in the `us-west-2` region.

Next, send a message to the SQS queue. You can use the following AWS CLI command to send a message to the SQS queue by using the queue URL you captured earlier:

```
aws sqs send-message --queue-url <queue-url> --message-body "Hello, this
is a test message."
```

Once these steps are completed, you have successfully set up AWS EventBridge and SQS for the *AWSome Store* using the AWS CLI. You will learn about best practices to set up AWS infrastructure later, in the Optimization with Well-Architected Review section of this chapter.

Implement authentication and authorization for end users

Earlier you set up IAM credentials for the internal development team, but what about end users who will access your *AWSome Store* and build their profile? You need to give them a way to create their account securely and give them the required access. You can use Amazon Cognito, to simplify user authentication and authorization for cloud-based applications. It can help you with the following scenarios:

- **User sign-up and sign-in**: Cognito provides secure user authentication, with features such as multi-factor authentication, forgot password, and social identity sign-up.
- **Mobile and web app authentication**: Cognito supports users' authentication in mobile and web applications and integrates with the AWS Mobile SDK.
- **Unauthenticated and authenticated access to APIs**: Cognito integrates with Amazon API Gateway and AWS AppSync to provide authorization for API access.
- **User data storage**: Cognito provides user profile storage, which can be used to store user information such as preferences, custom data, and more.

Here is an example of how you can use the AWS CLI to implement authentication and authorization for end users for the *AWSome Store* website using Amazon Cognito:

1. Create a Cognito user pool:

   ```
   aws cognito-idp create-user-pool --pool-name awsomestore-pool
   ```

The `aws cognito-idp create-user-pool` command creates a new Amazon Cognito user pool with the specified pool name, using the default settings. To use this command, you need to replace `awsomestore-pool` with the name that you want to give to your user pool. For example, if you want to create a user pool called `my-user-pool`, you would replace `awsomestore-pool` with `my-user-pool`, like this:

```
aws cognito-idp create-user-pool --pool-name my-user-pool
```

This command would create a new Amazon Cognito user pool with the name `my-user-pool`. You can customize the settings of your user pool using additional parameters and options with this command.

2. Next, create a group for the user pool:

```
aws cognito-idp create-group --user-pool-id awsomestore-pool-id
--group-name awsomestore-group
```

The `aws cognito-idp create-group` command creates a new group in the specified Amazon Cognito user pool with the specified group name. To use this command, you need to replace `awsomestore-pool-id` with the ID of the Amazon Cognito user pool in which you want to create the group. You also need to replace `awsomestore-group` with the name of the group that you want to create.

For example, if you have an Amazon Cognito user pool with an ID of `us-west-2_abc123xyz`, and you want to create a new group called `my-group`, you would replace `awsomestore-pool-id` with `us-west-2_abc123xyz`, and replace `awsomestore-group` with `my-group`, like this:

```
aws cognito-idp create-group --user-pool-id us-west-2_abc123xyz
--group-name my-group
```

This command would create a new group called `my-group` in the `us-west-2_abc123xyz` Amazon Cognito user pool.

3. Next, attach policies to the group:

```
aws cognito-idp add-user-to-group --user-pool-id awsomestore-pool-id
--username <username> --group-name awsomestore-group
```

The `aws cognito-idp add-user-to-group` command adds a user to a specified group in an Amazon Cognito user pool. To use this command, you need to replace `awsomestore-pool-id` with the ID of the Amazon Cognito user pool in which the group exists.

You also need to replace `<username>` with the username of the user you want to add to the group. Finally, you need to replace `awsomestore-group` with the name of the group to which you want to add the user.

For example, if you have an Amazon Cognito user pool with an ID of `us-west-2_abc123xyz`, and you want to add a user with the username `myuser` to a group called `my-group`, you would replace `awsomestore-pool-id` with `us-west-2_abc123xyz`, replace `<username>` with `myuser`, and replace `awsomestore-group` with `my-group`, like this:

```
aws cognito-idp add-user-to-group --user-pool-id us-west-2_abc123xyz
--username myuser --group-name my-group
```

This command would add the user with the username `myuser` to the `my-group` group in the `us-west-2_abc123xyz` Amazon Cognito user pool.

4. Next, create a Cognito user pool client:

```
aws cognito-idp create-user-pool-client --user-pool-id awsomestore-
pool-id --client-name awsomestore-client
```

The `aws cognito-idp create-user-pool-client` command creates a new app client in an Amazon Cognito user pool. To use this command, you need to replace `awsomestore-pool-id` with the ID of the Amazon Cognito user pool in which you want to create the app client. You also need to replace `awsomestore-client` with a name of your choice for the app client. For example, if you have an Amazon Cognito user pool with an ID of `us-west-2_abc123xyz`, and you want to create a new app client called `my-app-client`, you would run the following command:

```
aws cognito-idp create-user-pool-client --user-pool-id us-west-2_
abc123xyz --client-name my-app-client
```

This command would create a new app client called `my-app-client` in the `us-west-2_abc123xyz` Amazon Cognito user pool. The command will return the newly created app client's `ClientId` value, which will be required to authenticate the users.

5. Next, create a Cognito identity pool:

```
aws cognito-identity create-identity-pool --identity-pool-name
awsomestore-identity-pool --allow-unauthenticated-identities
--cognito-identity-providers ProviderName=cognito-idp.us-east-1.
amazonaws.com/awsomestore-pool-id,ClientId=awsomestore-client-id
```

The `aws cognito-identity create-identity-pool` command creates a new Amazon Cognito identity pool. To use this command, you need to replace `awsomestore-identity-pool` with a name of your choice for the identity pool. You also need to replace `awsomestore-pool-id` with the ID of the Amazon Cognito user pool that you created earlier. Additionally, you need to replace `awsomestore-client-id` with the `ClientId` value of the Amazon Cognito user pool client that you created earlier. For example, if you want to create a new Amazon Cognito identity pool called `my-identity-pool`, and you have an Amazon Cognito user pool with an ID of `us-west-2_abc123xyz` and a client ID of `1234567890abcdef`, you would use these.

6. Finally, grant permissions to the identity pool:

```
aws cognito-identity set-identity-pool-roles --identity-
pool-id awsomestore-identity-pool-id --roles
authenticated=arn:aws:iam::<aws_account_id>:role/awsomestore-auth-ro
le,unauthenticated=arn:aws:iam::<aws_account_id>:role/awsomestore-
unauth-role
```

The `aws cognito-identity set-identity-pool-roles` command sets the roles for the authenticated and unauthenticated identities in an Amazon Cognito identity pool.

To use this command, you need to replace `awsomestore-identity-pool-id` with the ID of the Amazon Cognito identity pool that you created earlier. You also need to replace `<aws_account_id>` with your actual AWS account ID and replace `awsomestore-auth-role` and `awsomestore-unauth-role` with the names of the IAM roles that you want to use for authenticated and unauthenticated identities, respectively.

For example, if you want to set the roles for an Amazon Cognito identity pool with an ID of `us-west-2_abc123xyz`, and you have two IAM roles named `my-auth-role` and `my-unauth-role` that you want to use for authenticated and unauthenticated identities, you would replace the relevant fields with these labels..

With the above steps, you can implement authentication and authorization for end customers for the *AWSome Store* website using Amazon Cognito. When using Amazon Cognito for authentication and authorization, it is best to follow these best practices:

- Use MFA to enhance the security of your user pool.
- Implement a password policy requiring strong passwords with letters, numbers, and special characters.
- Regularly monitor the security of your Cognito user pool, such as tracking sign-in attempts and detecting any suspicious activity.

- Use Amazon Cognito's built-in user sign-up and sign-in process for a smooth and secure experience for your users.
- Use the appropriate user pool attributes to store user data, such as email addresses and phone numbers.
- Use Amazon Cognito's built-in features for storing user data, such as custom attributes and user pools, to reduce the risk of data breaches.
- Store encrypted sensitive information, such as passwords, in the Amazon Cognito user pool.
- Enable logging and monitoring for Amazon Cognito to help detect security issues and respond to them quickly.
- Consider using Amazon Cognito federated identities for secure **single sign-on (SSO)** across multiple AWS services and applications.

Finally, regularly review and update your Amazon Cognito user pool's security policies to ensure they are up to date with the latest security standards. You can refer to AWS's user documentation to explore more best practices – `https://docs.aws.amazon.com/cognito/latest/developerguide/multi-tenant-application-best-practices.html`.

Now let's jump into building your app, starting with the database.

Define database attributes

To define database tables and attributes for your *AWSome Store* e-commerce website, you can start by considering the data you need to store in your e-commerce website.

- **Products**: This table can store information about each product available in the store, such as product name, product ID, description, price, image URL, and so on.
- **Customers**: This table can store information about each customer, such as customer name, email address, password, billing address, etc.
- **Orders**: This table can store information about each order placed by a customer, such as order ID, customer ID, product ID, order date, shipping address, and so on.
- **Categories**: This table can store information about product categories, such as category name, category ID, and so on.
- **Inventory**: This table can store information about the inventory of each product, such as product ID, quantity available, and so on.
- **Promotions**: This table can store information about promotions and discounts available for products, such as promotion ID, product ID, discount amount, etc.

When creating these tables, you can set the primary key as the unique identifier for each table, such as product ID, customer ID, and order ID. You can also define secondary indexes to support querying data in your application.

Amazon DynamoDB is a good choice for the *AWSome Store* as you require fast and flexible data storage. DynamoDB is optimized for low latency and high throughput, making it ideal for storing large amounts of data that need to be retrieved quickly. It automatically scales with the growth of your data, allowing you to store and retrieve any amount of data without having to worry about capacity planning. DynamoDB is a cost-effective solution, as you only pay for the read and write capacity that you use, and there are no upfront costs and minimum fees. It integrates seamlessly with other AWS services, making building complex, scalable, and highly available applications easy.

Here is a sample CLI command to create DynamoDB tables and their attributes for the *AWSome Store*:

```
aws dynamodb create-table \
--table-name awsome_store_products \
--attribute-definitions \
AttributeName=product_id,AttributeType=S \
AttributeName=product_name,AttributeType=S \
--key-schema \
AttributeName=product_id,KeyType=HASH \
AttributeName=product_name,KeyType=RANGE \
--provisioned-throughput \
ReadCapacityUnits=5,WriteCapacityUnits=5

aws dynamodb create-table \
--table-name awsome_store_orders \
--attribute-definitions \
AttributeName=order_id,AttributeType=S \
AttributeName=order_date,AttributeType=S \
--key-schema \
AttributeName=order_id,KeyType=HASH \
AttributeName=order_date,KeyType=RANGE \
--provisioned-throughput \
ReadCapacityUnits=5,WriteCapacityUnits=5
```

You can create more tables and customize the table names, attributes, and provisioned throughput as per your requirements. The following are some best practices to follow when using DynamoDB:

- **Use partition keys wisely**: Selecting a good partition key that distributes your data evenly is crucial for performance.
- **Consider provisioned throughput**: Ensure you set the right amount of throughput to ensure the required performance.
- **Use secondary indexes**: Secondary indexes can optimize queries based on different attributes.
- **Batch operations**: Use batch operations like `BatchGetItem` and `BatchWriteItem` for efficient data retrieval and modification.
- **Use the Time to Live (TTL) attribute**: Use the TTL attribute to delete old or expired items from your table automatically.
- **Store data in a denormalized form**: Storing data in a denormalized form in DynamoDB can simplify and speed up queries.
- **Use automated backups**: Take advantage of DynamoDB's automatic backups to ensure data durability and reduce the risk of data loss.
- **Monitor and troubleshoot**: Monitor your DynamoDB usage and performance regularly to identify any potential issues and optimize accordingly.
- **Use DynamoDB Streams**: DynamoDB Streams allow you to capture changes made to your DynamoDB tables and process them in real time.

You should use a serverless architecture and AWS Lambda functions to integrate with DynamoDB and offload compute-intensive tasks. You can explore more best practices here – `https://docs.aws.amazon.com/amazondynamodb/latest/developerguide/best-practices.html`. After putting your database together, let's define Lambda functions to know how to use it.

Define order context and write AWS Lambda functions

In the previous section on use cases, we defined the order bounded context in an e-commerce retail application as follows:

- **Order class**: Start by defining the `Order` class, which represents a customer's request to purchase one or more products. The Order class could have attributes such as order number, date, customer information, and a list of order items.

- **Order Item class**: Next, define the `Order Item` class, which represents a single product in an order. The Order Item class could have attributes such as product ID, name, quantity, and price.
- **Customer class**: Also define the `Customer` class, which represents the person placing the order. The Customer class could have attributes such as customer ID, name, address, and email.
- **Payment class**: Define the `Payment` class, which represents the payment information for an order. The Payment class could have attributes such as payment method, card number, and expiration date.

Add methods to the classes to represent the actions that can be performed on them. For example, an Order class could have a method for calculating the total cost of the order. Also, an Order class could have a one-to-many relationship with the Order Item class, indicating that an order can have multiple order items as shown below:

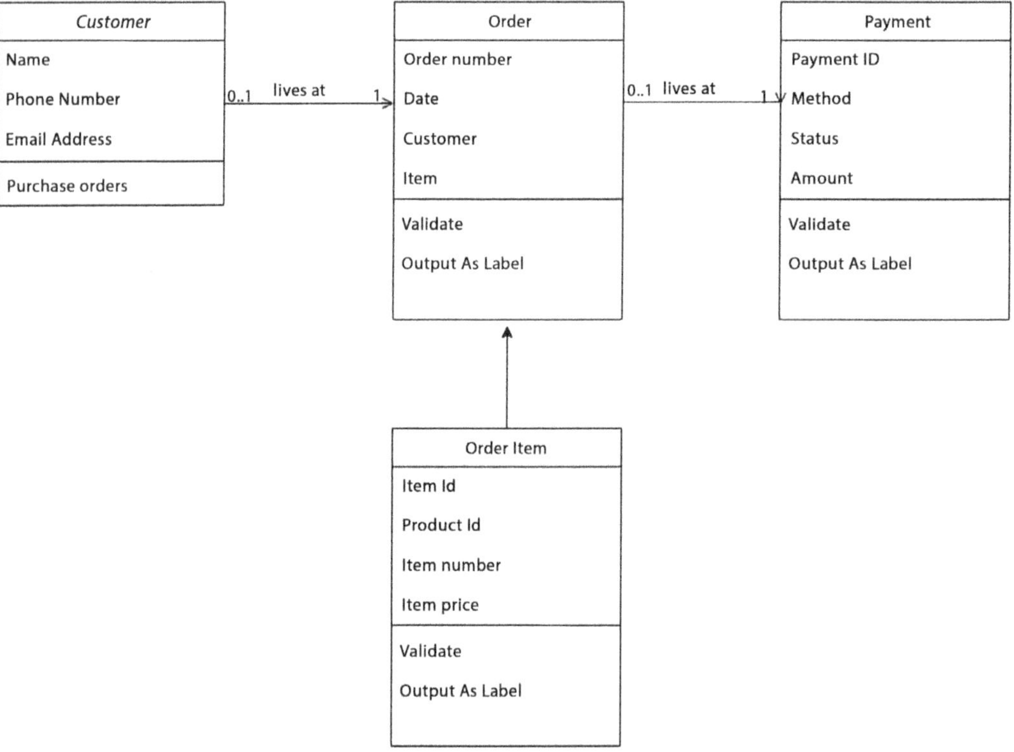

Figure 16.7: Order context class diagram

Here is an example of how you could implement the `Order`, `OrderItem`, `Payment`, and `Customer` classes in Node.js using AWS Lambda functions:

```
const AWS = require('aws-sdk');
class Order {
  constructor(orderId, customerId, orderDate, items, payment) {
    this.orderId = orderId;
    this.customerId = customerId;
    this.orderDate = orderDate;
    this.items = items;
    this.payment = payment;
  }
  save() {
    const dynamoDB = new AWS.DynamoDB.DocumentClient();
    const params = {
      TableName: 'AwesomeStoreOrders',
      Item: {
        orderId: this.orderId,
        customerId: this.customerId,
        orderDate: this.orderDate,
        items: this.items,
        payment: this.payment
      }
    };
    return dynamoDB.put(params).promise();
  }
}
class OrderItem {
  constructor(productId, quantity) {
    this.productId = productId;
    this.quantity = quantity;
  }
}
class Payment {
  constructor(paymentId, amount, paymentDate, paymentMethod) {
    this.paymentId = paymentId;
    this.amount = amount;
    this.paymentDate = paymentDate;
```

```
      this.paymentMethod = paymentMethod;
    }
  }
  class Customer {
    constructor(customerId, firstName, lastName, email) {
      this.customerId = customerId;
      this.firstName = firstName;
      this.lastName = lastName;
      this.email = email;
    }
    save() {
      const dynamoDB = new AWS.DynamoDB.DocumentClient();
      const params = {
        TableName: 'AwesomeStoreCustomers',
        Item: {
          customerId: this.customerId,
          firstName: this.firstName,
          lastName: this.lastName,
          email: this.email
        }
      };
      return dynamoDB.put(params).promise();
    }
  }
```

This code defines the classes `Order`, `OrderItem`, `Payment`, and `Customer` with their respective properties. The save method in each class uses the AWS SDK for JavaScript to interact with Amazon DynamoDB and store instances of the class as items in a DynamoDB table. Each save method defines the table's name in the `TableName` parameter. You can modify this code to fit your specific needs and add more functionality. Here are some best practices for AWS Lambda:

- **Keep functions small and focused**: Minimize the code in each function and make it perform a single, specific task.
- **Use environment variables for configuration**: Store configuration values as environment variables to avoid hardcoding values in code. Parameter Store is better suited for managing application configuration data that needs to be shared across multiple hosts or environments, requires encryption, and needs versioning and auditing capabilities.

Environment variables, on the other hand, are simpler to use and can be useful for storing smaller amounts of configuration data that only need to be available to a single process or host.

- **Design for statelessness**: Lambda functions should be stateless, meaning they do not persist data between invocations.
- **Optimize cold start time**: Reduce the time it takes for your function to start by minimizing the amount of initialization code and reducing the size of the deployment package.
- **Use VPC for network isolation**: If your function needs to access resources in a VPC, use VPC connectivity to provide network isolation.
- **Use versioning and aliases**: Use versioning and aliases to manage multiple versions of your functions and deploy changes incrementally.
- **Secure secrets and sensitive data**: Store encryption keys and sensitive data in AWS **Key Management Service** (**KMS**) or **AWS Secrets Manager**, rather than in the function code.
- **Monitor function performance**: Use CloudWatch metrics and X-Ray to monitor function performance, and track requests and errors.
- **Automate deployment**: Use AWS CloudFormation, AWS CodeDeploy, or other tools to automate deployment and reduce manual error.

Finally, you should regularly test and validate functions in development and production to validate that they are functioning as intended. You can refer to more Lambda best practices here – `https://docs.aws.amazon.com/lambda/latest/dg/best-practices.html`. Now that you've written your code and built your table, let's deploy and test your code.

Deploy and test

Here are the steps to deploy a Lambda function for the *AWSome Store* and connect it with API Gateway:

1. Compress your Lambda function code and any required dependencies into a `.zip` file.
2. Use the AWS CLI `aws lambda create-function` command to create a new Lambda function in your AWS account. In this command, you need to specify the name of the function, the runtime environment (Node.js), the path to the `.zip` file, the name of the handler function, and the IAM role that your function will use to execute. Here is some example code:

```
aws lambda create-function \
    --function-name my-nodejs-function \
    --runtime nodejs14.x \
```

```
    --handler index.handler \
    --memory-size 128 \
    --zip-file fileb://lambda.zip \
    --role arn:aws:iam::<aws_account_id>:role/my-lambda-role
```

This command creates a new Lambda function named `my-nodejs-function` using the Node.js 14.x runtime. The `index.handler` specifies the entry point to the function code within the `lambda.zip` file, which is uploaded as the function's code. The `memory-size` specifies the amount of memory in megabytes allocated to the function. The `role` parameter specifies the IAM role that the function uses to access other AWS resources.

3. Use the `aws apigateway create-rest-api` command to create a new REST API in API Gateway. In this command, you need to specify the name of the API, the description, and the endpoint type (REGIONAL). Here is an example code:

```
aws apigateway create-rest-api --name MyRestApi --description "My
new REST API"
```

In this example, the command creates a new REST API with the name `MyRestApi` and the description *My new REST API*. You can then use other API Gateway commands to add resources, methods, and integrations to this API.

4. Use the `aws apigateway create-resource` command to create a new resource in the REST API. In this command, you need to specify the parent resource, the path, and the REST API ID. Here is syntax:

```
aws apigateway create-resource --rest-api-id <rest-api-id> --parent-
id <parent-resource-id> --path-part <path-part>
```

In this command, you need to replace `<rest-api-id>` with the ID of the REST API that the resource belongs to. You also need to replace `<parent-resource-id>` with the ID of the parent resource of the new resource you're creating. The `<path-part>` parameter specifies the last part of the resource's path. For example, if you wanted to create a new resource with the path `/products`, and its parent resource had an ID of `abc123`, the command would look like this:

```
aws apigateway create-resource \
    --rest-api-id abcd1234 \
    --parent-id abc123 \
    --path-part products
```

This would create a new resource with the path `/products` under the parent resource with ID `abc123`.

5. Use the `aws apigateway put-method` command to create a new method (such as `GET` or `POST`) for the resource. In this command, you need to specify the REST API ID, the resource ID, and the HTTP method. Here is example code:

```
aws apigateway put-method \
    --rest-api-id <rest-api-id> \
    --resource-id <resource-id> \
    --http-method <http-method> \
    --authorization-type <authorization-type> \
    --request-parameters <request-parameters>
```

   In this command, you need to replace `<rest-api-id>` with the ID of the REST API that the resource belongs to. You also need to replace `<resource-id>` with the ID of the resource that the method belongs to. The `<http-method>` parameter specifies the HTTP method (e.g., `GET`, `POST`, `PUT`, `DELETE`) for the method. The `<authorization-type>` parameter specifies the type of authorization used for the method (e.g., `NONE`, `AWS_IAM`, `CUSTOM`). The `<request-parameters>` parameter is a JSON object that specifies the request parameters accepted by the method.

   For example, if you wanted to create a new method for a resource with the ID `abc123` that responds to HTTP `GET` requests and uses AWS IAM authorization, the command would look like this:

```
aws apigateway put-method \
    --rest-api-id abcd1234 \
    --resource-id abc123 \
    --http-method GET \
    --authorization-type AWS_IAM \
    --request-parameters '{"method.request.querystring.foo": true,
"method.request.querystring.bar": true}'
```

   This would create a new method for the `GET` HTTP method that accepts two query string parameters (`foo` and `bar`) and uses AWS IAM authorization.

6. Use the `aws apigateway put-integration` command to integrate the API method with your Lambda function. In this command, you need to specify the REST API ID, the resource ID, the HTTP method, the type of integration, and the ARN of the Lambda function.

```
aws apigateway put-integration \
--rest-api-id <rest-api-id> \
--resource-id <resource-id> \
--http-method <http-method> \
--type <type> \
--integration-http-method <integration-http-method> \
--uri <uri> \
--credentials <arn-of-iam-role>
```

Here's a brief description of the parameters used:

- `rest-api-id`: The ID of the REST API in API Gateway to which you want to add the integration.
- `resource-id`: The ID of the resource to which you want to add the integration.
- `http-method`: The HTTP method for which you want to create an integration.
- `type`: The type of the integration. This can be `HTTP` for integrating with an HTTP backend or `AWS` for integrating with an AWS service.
- `integration-http-method`: The HTTP method used to call the backend. This is typically `POST`, `GET`, `PUT`, `DELETE`, or `PATCH`.
- `uri`: The **Uniform Resource Identifier** (**URI**) of the backend service or resource. For example, if you're integrating with an HTTP backend, this would be the URL of the HTTP endpoint.
- `credentials`: The ARN of an IAM role that API Gateway assumes when calling the backend service or resource.

Here is a sample code:

```
aws apigateway put-integration \
--rest-api-id abcdef1234 \
--resource-id abc123 \
--http-method POST \
--type AWS_PROXY \
--integration-http-method POST \
```

```
--uri arn:aws:apigateway:us-east-1:lambda:path/2015-03-31/functions/
arn:aws:lambda:us-east-1:123456789012:function:myLambdaFunction/
invocations \
--passthrough-behavior WHEN_NO_MATCH \
--content-handling CONVERT_TO_TEXT
```

This command creates an AWS Lambda proxy integration for a `POST` method on a specific API Gateway resource. The `--rest-api-id` parameter specifies the ID of the API Gateway REST API, while the `--resource-id` parameter specifies the ID of the resource to which the method is attached. The `--http-method` parameter specifies the `HTTP` method for the method.

The `--type` parameter specifies the type of integration. In this case, it is set to `AWS_PROXY`, which means that the Lambda function is invoked directly from the API Gateway. The `--integration-http-method` parameter specifies the HTTP method used to invoke the Lambda function. In this case, it is set to `POST`.

The `--uri` parameter specifies the ARN of the Lambda function to integrate with.

The `--passthrough-behavior` parameter specifies the passthrough behavior for unmapped requests. In this case, it is set to `WHEN_NO_MATCH`. The `--content-handling` parameter specifies how to handle the request payload. In this case, it is set to `CONVERT_TO_TEXT`.

7. Use the `aws apigateway create-deployment` command to deploy the API to a stage, such as *prod* or *test*. In this command, you need to specify the REST API ID and the stage's name:

```
aws apigateway create-deployment --rest-api-id <rest-api-id>
--stage-name <stage-name>
```

Replace <rest-api-id> with the ID of the REST API you want to deploy, and <stage-name> with the name of the deployment stage you want to create.

You can also include additional parameters to customize the deployment, such as the description of the deployment, stage variables, and tags. For more information on the available parameters, you can refer to the AWS CLI documentation for this command.

Here's an example:

```
aws apigateway create-deployment --rest-api-id abc123 --stage-name
prod --description "Production deployment"
```

This command creates a new deployment of the API with ID `abc123` to the prod stage with the description *Production deployment.*

8. Finally, use the CLI `aws apigateway get-invoke-url` CLI command to get the URL of the deployed API. You can then test the API using this URL. Here is the syntax:

```
aws apigateway get-invoke-url --region <region> --rest-api-id <rest-api-id> --stage-name <stage-name>
```

Where:

- `<region>` is the AWS region where the API is deployed.
- `<rest-api-id>` is the ID of the REST API for which to retrieve the endpoint URL.
- `<stage-name>` is the name of the API deployment stage for which to retrieve the endpoint URL.

The command returns the public URL of the API endpoint that can be used to make HTTP requests to the API. This URL can be used by clients to access the API.

DevOps is an important step toward automating the entire software delivery pipeline and improving efficiency. Let's learn about DevOps in detail.

DevOps in AWS

DevOps is a methodology that integrates cultural philosophies, practices, and tools to enhance an organization's capacity to deliver applications and services at a rapid pace. It helps the organization to evolve and improve products faster than traditional software development and infrastructure management processes. This speed allows organizations to serve their customers better and compete in the market more effectively.

To build a **CI/CD** (**Continuous Integration/Continuous Deployment**) pipeline for the *AWSome Store* app, follow these steps:

1. **Code repository**: Store the source code of the *AWSome Store* app in a version control system such as AWS CodeCommit or GitHub/GitLab. Ensure your code is stored in a branch suitable for production deployment.
2. **Build and test**: Use a build tool such as AWS CodeBuild to compile the source code and run tests. This step ensures that the code is stable and working as expected.

3. **Continuous integration**: Integrate the build and test process with the code repository so that the pipeline is triggered automatically when code changes are pushed to the repository. AWS provides several tools to support continuous integration and delivery, including AWS CodePipeline, AWS CodeBuild, and AWS CodeDeploy. These tools enable teams to automate their applications' building, testing, and deployment.
4. **Monitoring**: Use AWS CloudWatch to monitor the app's health and detect and alert on any issues. AWS provides various monitoring and logging services, including Amazon CloudWatch, AWS X-Ray, and AWS CloudTrail. These services enable teams to monitor the performance and health of their applications, diagnose issues, and troubleshoot problems.
5. **Continuous deployment**: Automate the deployment of new releases to the production environment whenever the code is integrated and tested successfully.
6. **Roll back**: Plan to roll back to the previous version of the app in case of any issues with the new release.

By implementing a CI/CD pipeline, you can ensure that the *AWSome Store* app is continuously integrated, tested, deployed, and monitored, which helps improve the reliability and speed of software delivery.

After setting up your code repository, the following are the steps to build a CI/CD pipeline using AWS CodePipeline:

1. **Create a build stage**: The build stage will compile your code and create the artifacts that will be deployed. You can use AWS CodeBuild to create the build stage. You will need to define a `buildspec.yml` file that specifies the commands to build your code. The artifacts should be stored in an S3 bucket.
2. **Create a deployment stage**: The deployment stage will deploy your code to your production environment. You can use AWS CodeDeploy to create the deployment stage. You will need to define an AppSpec file that specifies how the deployment will be done.
3. **Create a pipeline**: Create a new pipeline in AWS CodePipeline and specify the source code repository, build, and deployment stages. You can configure triggers to start the pipeline automatically when code changes are committed to the repository.
4. **Test the pipeline**: Test your pipeline by committing code changes to the repository and verifying that the pipeline is triggered, builds your code, and deploys it to your production environment.

5. **Configure pipeline notifications:** Configure pipeline notifications to receive notifications when pipeline stages succeed or fail. This will help you monitor your pipeline and respond quickly to any issues.
6. **Fine-tune the pipeline:** As you use the pipeline, you may find areas for improvement. You can fine-tune the pipeline by adjusting the pipeline settings or by adding new stages to the pipeline.

As you can see, building a CI/CD pipeline using AWS CodePipeline requires some initial setup and configuration. However, once the pipeline is set up, it can automate the process of building, testing, and deploying your code, which can save you time and help you deliver software more quickly and reliably.

Rollback planning is an essential aspect of any deployment process, as it allows you to revert changes if something goes wrong. Here are some steps you can follow to plan a rollback:

1. **Define the criteria for a rollback:** Identify the conditions that warrant a rollback, such as a critical error that affects the functionality of your application or a significant decrease in performance. Make sure the criteria are well defined and communicated to all stakeholders.
2. **Identify the rollback process:** Determine the steps needed to perform a rollback. This should include taking backups of your data, rolling back to a previous version of your application or code, and ensuring that all changes made during the deployment are appropriately rolled back.
3. **Prepare the rollback plan:** Document the rollback plan, including all the steps you need to take, the timeline for each step, and the roles and responsibilities of everyone involved. Make sure the plan is easily accessible to all stakeholders and that everyone is aware of their responsibilities.
4. **Test the rollback plan:** Before deploying your application, test it to ensure it works as expected. This will help you identify any issues or gaps in the plan before using it in a real-world scenario.
5. **Communicate the rollback plan:** Communicate the rollback plan to all stakeholders, including developers, QA, operations, and management. Ensure everyone knows the plan and what to do in case a rollback is required.
6. **Monitor the deployment:** During the deployment, monitor the performance of your application and keep an eye out for any signs that a rollback may be necessary. This will help you identify issues early and take action before they become critical.

By following these steps, you can ensure that you have a well-defined and tested rollback plan in place, which will help you minimize downtime and avoid potential losses in case something goes wrong during the deployment.

AWS offers a range of adaptable services specifically created to help businesses develop and distribute products more quickly and consistently by utilizing AWS and DevOps methodologies. These services streamline the processes of setting up and maintaining infrastructure, releasing application code, automating software updates, and overseeing the performance of both applications and infrastructure.

Logging and monitoring

Setting up logging and monitoring helps organizations better understand their systems, improve their performance and reliability, meet compliance requirements, and enhance the security of their systems. It provides insights into the system's behavior and performance. This information can be used to identify and troubleshoot issues more quickly. Monitoring the system for potential issues and triggering alerts makes it easier to identify and resolve problems before they become critical.

Logging and monitoring provide detailed performance data that can be used to identify and resolve bottlenecks, leading to improved system performance. They help ensure that the system is meeting compliance requirements and provide evidence in the event of an audit. Monitoring also helps detect and respond to security incidents, protecting sensitive data and maintaining the system's integrity. Here are the high-level steps to set up logging and monitoring for the *AWSome Store* app in AWS using the CLI:

1. Create a CloudWatch Logs group for your Lambda function.

   ```
   aws logs create-log-group --log-group-name awsomestore-log-group
   ```

2. Enable AWS X-Ray for your Lambda function:

   To enable AWS X-Ray for a Lambda function, you can use the following command:

   ```
   aws lambda update-function-configuration --function-name <function-
   name> --tracing-config Mode=Active
   ```

   Replace `<function-name>` with the name of your Lambda function. This command enables active tracing for the Lambda function using AWS X-Ray.

3. Create a CloudWatch alarm to monitor the error rate of your Lambda function:

   ```
   aws cloudwatch put-metric-alarm
   ```

```
    --alarm-name awsomestore-error-rate    # The name of the alarm
    --comparison-operator GreaterThanThreshold    # The comparison
operator
    --evaluation-periods 1    # The number of periods to evaluate the
alarm
    --metric-name Errors    # The metric to evaluate
    --namespace AWS/Lambda    # The namespace of the metric
    --period 300    # The period of the metric in seconds
    --statistic SampleCount    # The statistic to apply to the metric
    --threshold 1    # The threshold for the alarm
    --alarm-actions arn:aws:sns:us-east-1:123456789012:awsomestore-
alerts    # The ARN of the SNS topic to send notifications
    --dimensions FunctionName=awsomestore    # The dimensions to
apply to the metric
    --treat-missing-data breaching    # The action to take if data is
missing
```

In this command, you need to replace `awsomestore` with the name of your Lambda function and `123456789012` with your AWS account ID. You also need to replace `arn:aws:sns:us-east-1:123456789012:awsomestore-alerts` with the ARN of the SNS topic to which you want to send notifications.

4. View and analyze your logs and metrics in the CloudWatch console.

   Configure your Lambda function to send logs and metrics to CloudWatch. You can use the following AWS CLI command:

```
aws lambda update-function-configuration --function-name <function-
name> --handler <handler> --role <role-arn> --environment
Variables={LOG_GROUP_NAME=/aws/lambda/<function-name>,METRICS_
NAMESPACE=<namespace>}
```

   Here, you need to replace `<function-name>` with the name of your Lambda function, `<handler>` with the name of your function's handler, `<role-arn>` with the ARN of the execution role for your Lambda function, and `<namespace>` with the namespace for your CloudWatch metrics.

   You can also replace the `LOG_GROUP_NAME` environment variable with the name of the CloudWatch Logs group where you want to send your function's logs.

To view logs and metrics in the CloudWatch console, here are the steps:

5. Open the AWS Management Console and navigate to the CloudWatch service.
6. In the left sidebar, click on **Logs** to view logs or **Metrics** to view metrics.
7. To view logs, click on the log group associated with your Lambda function, then select a log stream to view the logs.
8. To view metrics, select **Lambda** as the namespace, then select your function name and the metric you want to view (such as **Errors**).
9. You can adjust the time range using the drop-down menu at the top-right corner of the page.

Here are some best practices for logging and monitoring in AWS:

- **Centralized logging**: Centralize logs from multiple services and resources in a single location such as Amazon CloudWatch Logs.
- **Automated alerting**: Set up automated alerts to notify you of potential issues and failures in real time.
- **Real-time monitoring**: Use real-time monitoring tools like Amazon CloudWatch metrics, Amazon CloudWatch alarms, and Amazon CloudWatch dashboards to track key performance indicators.
- **Log retention policy**: Define a log retention policy to ensure that logs are stored for sufficient time to meet compliance and business requirements.
- **Security logging**: Enable security logging for all critical resources to detect and respond to security incidents. You can enable AWS CloudTrail to log API calls made to the resource, enable Amazon S3 server access logging to log requests made to an S3 bucket, and enable VPC Flow Logs to log network traffic to and from an EC2 instance.
- **Monitoring of third-party services**: Monitor the performance and health of third-party services and dependencies to ensure a smooth end-to-end experience.
- **Error logging and debugging**: Ensure detailed error logs are captured and stored for debugging purposes.
- **Log analysis tools**: Use log analysis tools like CloudWatch Log Insights, Amazon Athena, and Amazon QuickSight to analyze log data and identify trends and patterns.
- **Monitoring of resource utilization**: Monitor resource utilization of critical services to ensure they are running optimally and within budget.

You can explore more logging and monitoring best practices here – `https://docs.aws.amazon.com/prescriptive-guidance/latest/logging-monitoring-for-application-owners/logging-best-practices.html`.

This section took you through the high-level steps to build an app. You can extend the provided AWS infrastructure and code based upon your needs. You can refer to the AWS Builder library to learn about implementing a different pattern – `https://aws.amazon.com/builders-library`. Also, there are multiple cloud solutions available to explore from AWS as per your industry use case here – `https://aws.amazon.com/industries/`.

Optimization with Well-Architected Review

You learned about the well-architected review in *Chapter 2, Understanding the AWS Well-Architected Framework and Getting Certified.* A well-architected review report is a comprehensive review of your AWS infrastructure and applications, designed to help you improve the robustness, security, and performance of your solutions.

A typical well-architected review report would include a summary of your current architecture and recommendations for improvement in each of the six pillars. The report would also include a list of best practices and guidelines for ensuring that your solutions are well-architected. Here are some best practices to consider when setting up the AWS infrastructure for your use case:

- Use AWS Organizations to manage multiple AWS accounts for production, testing, and development purposes. In this chapter, you deployed your app in a single dev account, but for production and test environments, you may want to have separate accounts and manage them using AWS Organizations.
- Use IAM policies and roles to control access to AWS resources and limit the permissions of users and services.
- Use **Virtual Private Clouds** (**VPCs**) to create a virtual network with a logically isolated section of the AWS cloud where you can launch AWS resources. You learned about AWS networking in *Chapter 4, Networking in AWS*. In this chapter, to keep things simple, we have not covered networking, but you can build VPCs and put Lambda inside them for security, especially for customer management functions.
- Use Amazon S3 to store user data, application backups, and website hosting.
- Use Amazon DynamoDB for NoSQL data storage to store information such as customer profiles, orders, and products.
- Use Amazon API Gateway to create, deploy, and manage APIs for your application.

- Use Amazon Lambda to run your application code and to execute business logic.
- Use Amazon CloudWatch to monitor, troubleshoot, and alert on the performance of your AWS resources.
- Use Amazon CloudFront for content delivery and to distribute your application to multiple locations for low latency and high performance.
- Use AWS Certificate Manager to secure your website using SSL/TLS certificates.
- Use Amazon Route 53 for domain name registration and for routing users to your application.
- Implement disaster recovery strategies, such as backups and multiple availability zones.
- Monitor and manage costs with the AWS Cost Explorer and monitor security with AWS Security Hub.

Finally, adhere to the AWS Well-Architected Framework and perform regular reviews to ensure your infrastructure is secure, reliable, and cost-effective.

Summary

In this chapter, you have put together many of the technologies, best practices, and AWS services we have covered in this book. You weaved it together into an e-commerce website architecture that you should be able to leverage and use for your own future projects.

You built architecture using AWS services following domain driven-design. You learned about implementing various AWS services, including IAM, S3, DynamoDB, Lambda, and API Gateway, and using the AWS CLI. You learned several best practices, along with a well-architected framework to optimize your architecture.

As fully featured as AWS has become, it will continue providing more services to help large and small enterprises simplify their information technology infrastructure. You can rest assured that AWS is creating new services and improving the existing services by making them better, faster, easier, more flexible, and more powerful, as well as by adding more features.

As of 2023, AWS offers 200+ services. That's a big jump from the two services it offered in 2004. AWS's progress in the last 18 years has been monumental. I cannot wait to see what the next 18 years will bring for AWS and what kind of solutions we can deliver with their new offerings.

I hope you are as excited as I am about the possibilities that these new services will bring.

Join us on Discord!

Read this book alongside other users, cloud experts, authors, and like-minded professionals.

Ask questions, provide solutions to other readers, chat with the authors via. Ask Me Anything sessions and much more.

Scan the QR code or visit the link to join the community now.

`https://packt.link/cloudanddevops`

Other Books You May Enjoy

If you enjoyed this book, you may be interested in these other books by Packt:

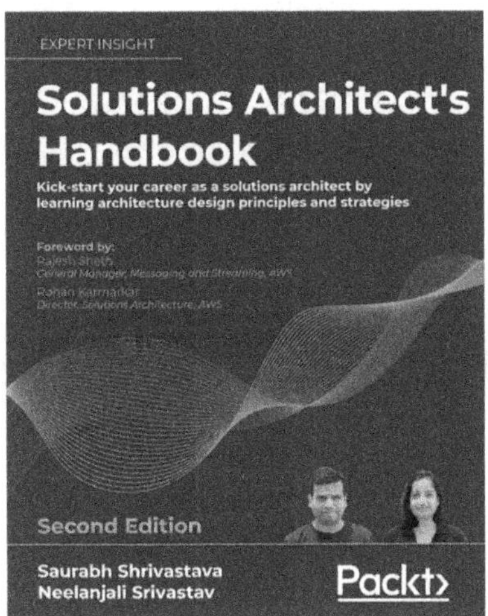

Solutions Architect's Handbook, Second Edition

Saurabh Shrivastava, Neelanjali Srivastav

ISBN: 9781801816618

- Explore the various roles of a solutions architect in the enterprise landscape
- Implement key design principles and patterns to build high-performance cost-effective solutions
- Choose the best strategies to secure your architectures and increase their availability
- Modernize legacy applications with the help of cloud integration

- Understand how big data processing, machine learning, and IoT fit into modern architecture
- Integrate a DevOps mindset to promote collaboration, increase operational efficiency, and streamline production

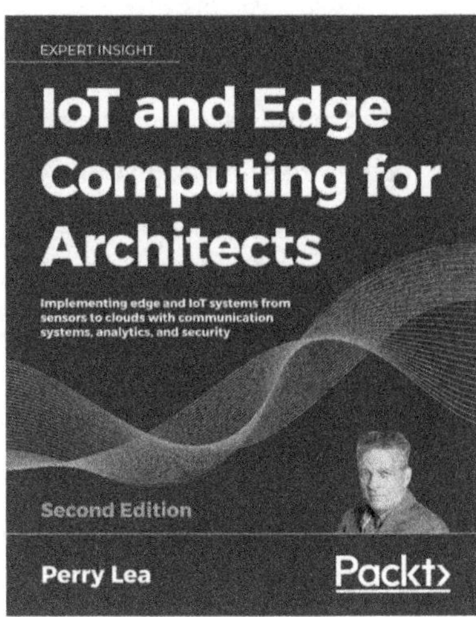

IoT and Edge Computing for Architects, Second Edition

Perry Lea

ISBN: 9781839214806

- Understand the role and scope of architecting a successful IoT deployment
- Scan the landscape of IoT technologies, from sensors to the cloud and more
- See the trade-offs in choices of protocols and communications in IoT deployments
- Become familiar with the terminology needed to work in the IoT space
- Broaden your skills in the multiple engineering domains necessary for the IoT architect
- Implement best practices to ensure reliability, scalability, and security in your IoT infrastructure

Packt is searching for authors like you

If you're interested in becoming an author for Packt, please visit `authors.packtpub.com` and apply today. We have worked with thousands of developers and tech professionals, just like you, to help them share their insight with the global tech community. You can make a general application, apply for a specific hot topic that we are recruiting an author for, or submit your own idea.

Share your thoughts

Now you've finished *AWS for Solutions Architects, Second Edition*, we'd love to hear your thoughts! Scan the QR code below to go straight to the Amazon review page for this book and share your feedback or leave a review on the site that you purchased it from.

`https://packt.link/r/180323895X`

Your review is important to us and the tech community and will help us make sure we're delivering excellent quality content.

Index

Symbols

A

B

C

D

E

F

G

H

I

J

K

N

Q

R

S

X

Y

Z

Download a free PDF copy of this book

Thanks for purchasing this book!

Do you like to read on the go but are unable to carry your print books everywhere? Is your eBook purchase not compatible with the device of your choice?

Don't worry, now with every Packt book you get a DRM-free PDF version of that book at no cost.

Read anywhere, any place, on any device. Search, copy, and paste code from your favorite technical books directly into your application.

The perks don't stop there, you can get exclusive access to discounts, newsletters, and great free content in your inbox daily

Follow these simple steps to get the benefits:

1. Scan the QR code or visit the link below

https://packt.link/free-ebook/9781803238951

2. Submit your proof of purchase
3. That's it! We'll send your free PDF and other benefits to your email directly

CPSIA information can be obtained
at www.ICGtesting.com
Printed in the USA
JSHW050827130723
44661JS00009B/192